THIRD EDITION

Transition Education and Services for Adolescents with Disabilities

Patricia L. Sitlington

The University of Northern Iowa

Gary M. Clark

University of Kansas

Oliver P. Kolstoe

Professor Emeritus,
University of Northern Colorado

Allyn and Bacon

Boston ▪ London ▪ Toronto ▪ Sydney ▪ Tokyo ▪ Singapore

Vice President, Editor in Chief, Education:
Paul A. Smith
Senior Editor: *Virginia C. Lanigan*
Editorial Assistant: *Karin Huang*
Marketing Manager: *Brad Parkins*
Editorial-Production Administrator: *Annette Joseph*

Editorial-Production Service: *Lynda Griffiths*
Editorial-Production Coordinator: *Holly Crawford*
Composition Buyer: *Linda Cox*
Electronic Composition: *TKM Productions*
Manufacturing Buyer: *Suzanne Lareau*
Cover Administrator: *Linda Knowles*

Copyright © 2000 by Allyn & Bacon
A Pearson Education Company
160 Gould Street
Needham Heights, MA 02494

Internet: www.abacon.com

Between the time website information is gathered and then published, it is not unusual for some sites to have closed. Also, the transcription of URLs can result in unintended typographical errors. The publisher would appreciate being notified of any problems with URLs so that they may be corrected in subsequent editions. Thank you.

Library of Congress Cataloging-in-Publication Data

Sitlington, Patricia L.
   Transition education and services for adolescents with
disabilities / Patricia L. Sitlington, Gary M. Clark, Oliver P.
Kolstoe. -- 3rd ed.
     p.   cm.
   Rev. ed. of: Career development and transition education for
adolescents with disabilities / Gary M. Clark. 2nd ed. © 1995.
   Includes bibliographical references (p. 384) and index.
   ISBN 0-205-30901-1
   1. Handicapped teenagers--Education (Secondary)--United States.
2. Handicapped teenagers--Vocational education--United States.
3. Vocational guidance for the handicapped--United States.
I. Clark, Gary M. II. Kolstoe, Oliver P. III. Clark, Gary M.
Career development and transition education for adolescents with
disabilities. IV. Title.
LC4031.S58 1999
371.9'0473--dc21   99-36235
                                      CIP

Printed in the United States of America

10 9 8 7 6 5 4 3 2   04 03 02 01 00

CONTENTS

PREFACE

The changes in secondary special education and transition education and services have been dramatic since the second edition of this book was prepared in 1993–94. In 1993, the Individuals with Disabilities Act (IDEA) regulations had been out only a little more than a year and schools were adjusting not only to the changes in the IDEA of 1990 and the new regulations but also to the reform activities of the time. Flurries of activity directed at inclusive education models and practices, effective education and charter schools, performance-based assessment, and state- and districtwide assessments for accountability absorbed a lot of professional time and energy. Transition education and services in the mid-1990s were just getting started nationally and the literature of the field was just beginning to expand with research results and recommended practices from early and innovative programs.

From 1993–94 to the present, there has been a tremendous surge in activity and achievement in transition education and services. Some of this is due to state and local efforts to implement the transition requirements of the IDEA. Some is due to the activities of the federally funded statewide transition systems change grants and the activities of the National Transition Network and National Transition Alliance. Some is attributed to outstanding preservice and in-service training programs across the nation. Some is due to the activities and leadership of the Division on Career Development and Transition of the Council for Exceptional Children and the 1997 IDEA Amendments and their regulations.

Overview of Changes

This third edition of *Transition Education and Services for Adolescents with Disabilities* captures many of the ideas that have been generated by professionals in the field and families of students in transition programs, as well as students and former students who are more openly sharing their views about the transition process. We three authors and the two guest authors of Chapters 3 and 10 represent four generations of professionals in secondary special education spanning about 35 years. We are not only observers but also participants in the development of educational programs concerned with the transition of youths from school to adult living, and can reflect on current directions and practices. At the same time, we believe it is important to communicate to you who are new to the field (and those who have been involved for a number of years) about your professional roots and a sense of where you are in time in this exciting professional field. To achieve that, we share some historical perspectives with you.

One of the major changes in this edition is the introduction of a new model of comprehensive transition education and services. The model presented in the first two editions served a purpose, but we believe that it is important to take a fresh look at the areas of transition education and transition services and be more specific about the elements that are critical to successful transition planning and service delivery. Our thinking led us to see two mutually important ways to view transition from school to adult living. We hope that the separation and equal emphasis of each of our two model components will help you see your own role more clearly.

The content of each chapter and appendix has also been modified extensively with updated information and references as well as more emphasis on working with general education and on involving individuals with disabilities in their own education. Other changes include the addition of a chapter on postsecondary education and an extensive listing of commercially available assessment instruments.

Acknowledgments

We wish to acknowledge those individuals and groups who contributed to our thinking and efforts for this edition of the book. First, we thank our support systems for their help while we were employed but significantly engaged in work on this revision. These support systems include the University of Northern Iowa; California State University, Los Angeles; and the Utah State Office of Education. In particular, we thank the administrators at these institutions, including Sandra Alper, Diane Klein, and Donna Suter.

We particularly owe our gratitude to the graduate students who have worked tirelessly with us through the different stages of preparing this edition. These individuals include Rhonda Reichardt and Christine Folkerts, who helped us with early research, and Michael Cavin, who updated the appendix on resource agencies and the glossary of terms. In particular, we acknowledge Jennifer McGlashing, who assisted with final research activities, proofreading, and tying up the many loose ends during the final stages of preparing this edition. We could not have done it without each of these individuals. In addition, we thank Charlotte Mull, whose extensive collection of research on postsecondary education provided much of the content included in Chapter 8.

We also acknowledge undergraduate and graduate students in the vocational and transition programming classes at the University of Northern Iowa who provided reviews of the previous edition and suggestions for improvement. In addition, we thank the following reviewers of this book for their comments and suggestions: Jane A. Razeghi, George Mason University; Patricia R. Renick, Wright State University; and Janice J. Seabrooks, University of North Florida.

Furthermore, we acknowledge Karen Gray, who produced all of the original graphics submitted with the manuscript. In addition, we extend our thanks to the various publishers who gave permission to use the copyrighted materials that we have included. We also thank Karin Huang and Lynda Griffiths for their editorial assistance in getting this third edition into its final form.

Our appreciation goes to the thousands of teachers, administrators, family members, support staff, adult providers, and individuals with disabilities with whom we have worked and continue to work. They provided us with the questions that needed to be addressed and many of the proposed answers to these questions. Finally, we thank our families and friends. They have supported us not only as we wrote this book but also in all our experiences that provided us with the information included here.

We are excited about the content of the pages that follow. We hope that this book will help you as you assist individuals with disabilities and their families in their transition to all aspects of adult life.

P. L. S.
G. M. C.
O. P. K.

Secondary Special Education in Perspective

Progress, for the most part, only substitutes one partial and incomplete truth for another; the new fragment of truth being more wanted, more adapted to the needs of the time, than that which it displaces.

—John Stuart Mill

To regard people with disabilities as a potentially valuable resource requires a belief in human potential and a recognition that potential must be discovered, nurtured, and developed. It requires a willingness to invest time, effort, patience, and support until a satisfactory level of work and personal living skills can be achieved. To be certain that each student with a disability has a chance to discover his or her potential, belief must be backed up by educational programs that are realistically crafted to allow students to pursue options to reach their goals.

For the students, their families, the teachers, and others in the training program, the investments of time and energy are substantial. Yet, the returns are more than worth it. To convert dependents on tax dollars into taxpayers, and to provide anxious parents with emotional strength, employers with able workers, and people who have disabilities with unparalleled feelings of self-worth is a labor of considerable value.

Each local school district has the continuing tasks of charting the educational course for its own locality and of ensuring the availability of education from one generation to the next while balancing pressures from all sectors of the public. Local and state education agencies receive considerable pressure to bring about reforms in public education. Increasingly, they are pressured to use a back to basics approach.

Whether schools should provide any kind of school-to-work programs, or even vocational education, is far from being an agreed-upon issue. Some circles vigorously resist any departure from teaching the basics. Other circles just as vigorously defend school-to-work and transition education. Those who are of the second view believe that education should prepare young people to assume their rightful places in the adult world—socially, economically, and politically—but that there may be alternative ways of reaching those outcomes.

Recognizing the value of people with some or several disabilities has neither universal acceptance nor wholehearted support. Yet within this large group of people with disabilities, heroes exist: Tom Sullivan, a businessman who, despite his blindness, has become one of the top motivational speakers in the world; Marlee Matlin, the actress who plays a variety of roles, not as a person who is deaf but as a person whose deafness is just one of her personal traits; Stephen W. Hawking, the brilliant physicist who, despite his lack of natural speech and body movement, continues to enlighten us on the origins of the universe; and James Earl Jones, whose acting career is unhampered by a severe stutter, are but a few examples. Not only do these people serve as role models for others who have yet to develop their personal skills and abilities to satisfactory levels but they also provide living proof to the world in general of the value of people with pronounced, significant disabilities.

Despite these demonstrations of outstanding contributions to society and the more modest contributions of thousands of other people with disabilities who work, pay taxes, contribute to the nation's gross national product, and otherwise enrich society, there remains a substantial segment of the population that is ignorant of or unable or unwilling to acknowledge the value of people with disabilities. In defense of this segment, it should be pointed out that many of the handicaps imposed by disabilities can only be overcome in the course of training. Thus, the potential value of a person with a disability may not be apparent until considerable effort and time have been invested. For example, without mentors, teachers, parents, and supportive adults and peers, it is unlikely that the talents of these famous persons with disabilities would ever have emerged. Of course, the same is true for most of us.

This chapter sets the stage for the remainder of the book. First, it discusses some major historical attempts to train adolescents and young adults with various disabilities. Next, it examines the guiding principles of secondary education programs. The chapter then highlights the development of special education programs as these efforts have been focused to provide training (within the limits of the U.S. high school) to prepare people with disabilities for the adult world of working and living.

Historical Overview

Importance of a Historical Perspective

People who have some characteristic in common can be studied in any society and in any historical period relative to their place in society and the esteem accorded them. People who have some disability, although they may exhibit great individual variability, can be studied as a group because of the common thread of disability that unites them. Their welfare may then become a mirror of the value accorded them by the societies that record their experiences.

A historical record of persons with disabilities participating as workers in a society is a concrete example that reflects their value to that society and contributes to the characterization of that period of history. Chronologically, historical records reveal changes in values that societies have held toward people who have disabilities. From those changes, one should be able to see patterns on which future directions for action can be built. The best of the past becomes the basis for blueprints for the future, whereas the failures are the warning signs of pitfalls to be avoided.

Development of Programs in the United States

As the United States matured, prevailing social climates had their effects on the treatment of persons with disabilities. From the first development of asylums in New England for people with severe disabilities who were blind or who were classified as mentally deficient until the mid-1800s, there was little change in early U.S. values or practice in care and treatment. The period of the Civil War was a time of great concern for human rights. The mechanism for assuring these rights came from federal laws and private efforts, both probably unevenly administered. Concern for the welfare of slaves was extended to others who were afforded limited human rights, among them people with disabilities. Educators recognized that many people with mild mental retardation had been previously denied successful learning because of standards too demanding for them to achieve, and so special schools were started to provide them with opportunities for success.

The Victorian era brought marked change to the social climate. Attitudes toward crime and degeneracy became more sharply focused, and new concerns about morality arose. Coincidentally, the emergence of information on the heritability of traits led to the identification of a disability as not only the punishment for presumed behavior transgressions but also as a heritable trait (Goddard, 1912; Dugdale, 1910). Whether by sterilization or segregation, the prevention of procreation among people with mental disabilities and, by extension, any other person with disabilities whose morals were suspect, quickly put the brakes on any societal movement toward liberal social policies.

In the early 1900s, public education for children with disabilities began to develop according to two principles that seemed to have universal applicability: (1) the principle of opportunity and (2) the principle of proof. The *principle of opportunity* simply meant that any child should be allowed to enroll in any class open to other children, with no prior restrictions placed on participation. The *principle of proof*, however, provided that continuance in a class, school experience, or school activities would be contingent on meeting the standards used to determine satisfactory performance. Unlike the principle of opportunity, the principle of proof imposed a qualitative expectation on the behavior of the student. Thus, each child had to prove his or her ability and willingness to meet the standards set for each class.

The application of these two principles in governing programs for people with disabilities has a curious history. Earliest records of secondary programs for people with disabilities, as described by Descoeudres (1928) and Duncan (1943) in Europe and Ingram (1960) and Hungerford (1943) in the United States, implied that all persons had to demonstrate progress to stay in their programs. Although no qualitative standards were mentioned, the progression of activities from simple to complex and from concrete to abstract made it easy to implement a hierarchy of performance objectives. The principle of proof seemed to be operating. However, this practice should not be construed to imply that special education programs were really much different from regular programs. Both have a long history of using tests and other methods of evaluation to assign grades (A, B, C, D, and F) as an index of a person's level of achievement. Those students who get Fs are presumed to be demonstrating that they have no right to continue in the program. Clearly, the principle of proof has been used for some time with children who have no disabilities for determining who can continue and who cannot, although inter- and intraschool standards vary considerably in their subjective views as to what constitutes failure. It seems possible that the principle of proof played a role in programs for students with disabilities also but probably was tempered considerably in application.

Another manifestation of the principle of proof is the accumulation of units of credit. In 1899, a Subcommittee on History as a College Entrance Requirement made a report to the National Education Association. In that report, the subcommittee used the term *unit* and defined it arithmetically and precisely (Savage, 1953). However, it was not until 1906 that the Carnegie Foundation for the Advancement of Teaching (1909) described how a unit of credit could be established. The foundation described a unit (which became known as the *Carnegie unit*) as the satisfactory completion of a class dealing with some subject that met five days per week for a minimum of 40 minutes each day or a minimum of 120 hours per year. It is clear from several historical accounts (Carnegie Foundation for the Advancement of Teaching, 1909; *Encyclopedia of Education,* 1971; Savage, 1953) that the Carnegie unit was designed solely to provide a quantitative device for appraising school instruction for college admission. Schools began to recognize 14 Carnegie units of credit as the requirement for graduation as of 1906. The number has increased over the years to the 20 to 22 units required today. It seems reasonable to assume that these units made it easier for college officials to determine eligibility for admission. By embracing the unit concept, colleges and advocates of reform in higher education contributed to the movement to recognize the Carnegie unit as the standard of credit for high school coursework and significantly affected the nature of high school requirements.

Although the agreed-upon measurement of accomplishment in secondary education is a Carnegie unit or some variation of it, the mere accumulation of units is not enough to ensure graduation. Nearly all states have their respective core academic requirements. Even though the requirements are minimal, they include classes in English, science, mathematics, and history—the basic blocks of knowledge required to make an industrial society function. Beyond bare literacy, however, most students are afforded the chance to develop to the broadest possible extent by taking classes in a variety of other subjects that also grant units of credit.

Such is not the case for the principle of opportunity. Education has practiced exclusivity from its beginning. Although this point is not within the scope of this book, you can find documentation in Jordan (1973). Suffice it to say that equal educational opportunity has never been universally practiced in the United States, and the possession of a disability imposes even further limitations on educational opportunities.

Early on, few, if any, special educational provisions were made in public schools for persons with disabilities, but educational opportunities were, theoretically, fairly unrestricted. Furthermore, they continued to be unrestricted so long as the standards of expected achievement continued to be met. Obviously, the principles that controlled participation in programs included both the principle of opportunity and the principle of proof.

With the outbreak of World War I, another swing in the attitude toward people with disabilities occurred. First, the development and widespread use of IQ tests (the Army Alpha and Beta tests) revealed that the number of persons with scores below what was thought to be "normal" was much larger than originally expected (Anastasi, 1976). For the first time, a national picture of subnormality appeared, and it was found to be a large problem. Second, the sudden appearance of many war veterans whose combat wounds left them with permanent disabilities prompted people to recognize the problem as universal. The sudden visibility of people with disabilities acquired in combat may also have had the effect of attacking the myth of the heritability of a disability. Certainly, the time was one of compassion, and the result was a scramble to provide services of all kinds.

The Special Class Movement.   Often billed as "opportunity" classes or programs, the educational model prevailing after World War II was an exclusive one. Self-contained classes and even schools composed of children sharing the same or similar disabilities proliferated for those children and youth whose disabilities or family situations did not warrant placement in special schools or institutions. *Equal opportunity* was interpreted to mean "modified to compensate for the disability." Blind children, for example, were taught in groups with other blind children. As time went on, two major problems were found to be a consequence of blindness: (1) difficulty in traveling independently and (2) cognitive problems related to perceptual-spatial closure. Since these issues are largely due to the lack of training for blind children, the self-contained class model was found to be ideally suited to instruction in these skills. Thus, equal educational opportunity required instruction to be modified to deal with the difficulties imposed by a disability. At the same time, standards of achievement uniquely appropriate to the goals of the instruction were used. This service-delivery model was dominant until well into the 1970s.

Opportunity for participation in segregated programs increased almost exponentially beginning in the 1950s (U.S. Department of Education, 1983). Over the next 25 years, most youngsters with a mild disability living anywhere in the United States had a class or a program available. It scarcely made sense to advocate for more services, because they were nearly universally available to those with mild to moderate disabilities.

From the earliest efforts, it was recognized that educational curricula used with students without disabilities did not provide the kind of content that would help some persons with disabilities learn to become independent adults. This led to placement in special classes where the emphasis was on self-development and work skills. Special education teachers in these programs rejected the general education academic criterion and concentrated their efforts on preparing students for work. Looking at some of the data on vocational performance during this period, one can get a picture of rather remarkable success.

Findley (1967) followed up performance of adolescents and young adults in Texas and Colorado and found that

1. IQ was an influencing factor in employment when comparing persons with IQs above 60 with persons with IQs below 60.
2. The above-60 group needed less help and got better jobs, but an equal percentage from both groups got jobs. Most importantly, both groups returned the cost of training in income tax alone in less than 10 years.

In Altoona, Pennsylvania, Dinger (1961) found that

1. Eighty-five percent were employed four years after leaving school.
2. Forty-two percent earned more than a beginning teacher's salary.

Chaffin, Spellman, Regan, and Davison (1971) found that

1. Sixty-eight percent of a non-work-study group were employed versus 94 percent of work-study groups.
2. Two years later, 75 percent versus 83 percent of persons in these respective groups had jobs. This was not a significant difference in employment rate, although the work-study group had significantly higher wage rates than the non-work-study group.

In Kent County, Michigan, Warren (1976) found that

1. More than 95 percent of the students from the program were employed.
2. Average starting wage was $2.65 (when minimum wage was $1.65), and the highest wage was $4.85.

These and other landmark studies of work experience and work-training programs during the 1960s and 1970s were basically optimistic, and the lack of sophistication in the research methodology was largely overlooked. One important exception to this neglect was a critique by Butler and Browning (1974) of the studies most often quoted. However, the studies did nothing to raise questions about the work-study model. This was not the case with special education program research, however, particularly research that focused on special classes.

Evolving Program Philosophies

The major outcome of the proliferation of special education program research was confusion over what the programs were actually accomplishing for people with disabilities. Although many studies were done to try to assess the effectiveness of special education programs (thus named *efficacy studies*), most of the findings were equivocal. One obvious reason for this is that if there is no agreement on what is supposed to be accomplished, effectiveness cannot be demonstrated. Confining the criterion of success to academic achievement provided the chance for a host of people to criticize the programs (Johnson, 1962; Dunn, 1968; Kolstoe, 1972; MacMillan, 1977). Unfortunately, no amount of in-depth analysis can help programs that really have no agreed-upon goals or directions in the first place, particularly if the analyses examine only the means and ignore the ends or vice versa.

The 1960s and the Normalization Concept.   A goal did emerge as a by-product of the civil rights movement that began in the 1960s. The 1960s were years of idealism in which the major thrust was one of assuring every segment of society the right to participate in the American way of life. Out of this movement came the principle of normalization, the goal of which was to ensure a normal existence for people with disabilities. Although much controversy surrounded the meaning of the normalization principle (Roos, 1970; Throne, 1975), there is little doubt as to its effect. The normalization principle established the goal for all people with disabilities to have the right to as normal an existence as possible using the most normal means possible. Essentially, the principle of normalization reestablished the principle of opportunity and the principle of proof as rights for people with disabilities to achieve as normal an existence as possible using means that are as normative as possible. For many people, however, the traditional academic program is viewed as the most "normalizing" environment available, and academic achievement has again become the school criterion for success.

Historical Development of Work-Training Programs

It fell to John Duncan in England to develop a systematic program of training that would help people with disabilities become prepared for jobs in society. Duncan's school at Lankhills, Hampshire, England, was a residential school for youngsters sent by the social services agencies of Hampshire. Although many may have had disabilities, many others were children of the streets who had few assets to help them merge into society. In today's terms, they would probably be categorized as *disadvantaged* or *dropouts*.

Duncan (1943) discovered that, although the verbal IQs of his young charges averaged about 66, their performance IQ scores were about 30 points higher, averaging 96. He interpreted that discrepancy to mean the youngsters had greater concrete than abstract intelligence, and he designed a program to capitalize on that fact. Duncan analyzed the jobs in the community that demanded concrete intelligence. Jobs such as beekeeping, carpentry, baking, cooking, and other rural domestic jobs were arranged in a hierarchy of steps from using a model for copying schematics, to following written or oral directions, and, finally, designing a new way of performing the task. Duncan kept very careful records of the physical health of the youngsters. For instance, he related the youngsters' rates of growth and general health with the quantity and quality of food they consumed. He was particularly concerned with the relationship of animal protein intake and growth, and his records made him a firm believer in the importance of a well-balanced diet, not only for health but also to facilitate learning and working effectively. He was concerned with both the intellectual and the physical health of his students.

The analysis of community jobs into their component skills and then the incorporation of those skills into the curriculum as practiced by Duncan was also the hallmark of the program developed by Richard Hungerford in New York City in the early 1940s. As the director of the Bureau for Children with Retarded Mental Development, Hungerford (1941, 1943) published a series of tradelike journals called *Occupational Education* between 1941 and 1944. They provided teachers with step-by-step instructions for teaching skills in the needle trades, service occupations, light industry, and various unskilled and semiskilled jobs in which Hungerford had observed youngsters with mental retardation working.

In 1958, Kolstoe and Frey initiated a series of studies that yielded data on successfully and unsuccessfully employed young men with mental retardation. The extensive records kept on the young men made it possible to compare them on personal, academic, social, and occupational skills. The analyses enabled the investigators to go considerably beyond job skills to include the behaviors, knowledge, and attitudes that were displayed by the successfully employed young men. These attributes (Kolstoe, 1961) were incorporated into their work-preparation curriculum and subsequently into similar programs across the nation. Thus, in addition to the job performance skills, those academic, personal, and social skills so important to satisfying life-styles were also recognized. These were presented in the book *A High School Work Study Program for Mentally Subnormal Students* (Kolstoe & Frey, 1965). Even though the needs of students with mental retardation were specifically addressed, the curriculum and techniques were presented as being applicable to a much broader range of persons with disabilities. Because many of the young men studied had associated physical and sensory disabilities, those with visual, auditory, motor, perceptual, sensory, and linguistic problems were also included. Thus, the basic work skill development approach became much more widely applicable and acceptable, with the inclusion of the academic, personal, and social skill training that had been found to differentiate between the successful and unsuccessful young men.

Most of the emphasis during the decades before 1970 was on persons with mild mental retardation. Today, many of those persons would be diagnosed and classified as having learning disabilities or behavior disorders. The group classified as moderately to severely mentally retarded was rarely singled out for attention in occupational or job training. It was this group that Gold targeted in the late 1960s to demonstrate that even the lowest functioning among them could perform complex assembly tasks with training (Gold, 1972, 1973). His "Try Another Way" theme caught the imagination of many professionals in secondary special education and rehabilitation and began a trend toward an ideology and technology that culminated in the major movement now associated with the term *supported employment*.

Beginnings of Vocational Education

Another movement to identify curricula appropriate for youths with disabilities had its roots in the 1960s, but it did not become widely accepted until the 1970s. Criticisms of special education services were generally directed at elementary-level programs, partly because there were not many secondary programs of which to be critical. Nonetheless, some criticisms of secondary work-training and vocational rehabilitation programs did surface. Nearly all the criticisms alleged that the training efforts were restricted to only a few jobs in each area of exceptionality and that the levels of training were so low that they precluded people with disabilities from all but the most menial jobs. People who were blind were often restricted to learning how to tune pianos, cane chairs, or become street musicians. Individuals who were deaf were trained to be linotype operators, dry cleaners, or bakers. Persons with mental retardation were trained for food service or janitorial tasks, and those with physical disabilities were relegated to watch repair or office work (Brolin & Kolstoe, 1978).

Whether the allegations were justifiable was largely irrelevant. The charges that training programs limited students with disabilities to few career options and jobs that underutilized their skills were forcefully presented to lawmakers at state and national levels. This caused them to turn their attention to the need for legislation that would free people with disabilities from these restrictive practices.

One other source of major concern was that self-contained special education teachers taught not only the academics but also the vocational skills and the skills of independent living. They also did the job placement and follow-up supervision. Although it could be readily acknowledged that the teachers were reasonably well trained to teach academic skills, it was more difficult to justify their teaching of work skills and skills of independent living while doing work placement and follow-up. Few, if any, college training programs provided opportunities in those years for would-be teachers to learn those skills, and those programs that did address those skills did so minimally (Clark & Oliverson, 1973). Vocational educators were trained to teach work skills, but they often were reluctant to work with students with disabilities. Some feared that if people with disabilities were admitted and successful in vocational education programs, those programs might be thought to have low requirements or standards compared with other, more academic programs. Student safety and their assumed inability to read were further sources of concern.

Despite these concerns, Congress passed the Vocational Education Act of 1963, which specified that persons with disabilities could be included in ongoing vocational education along with their peers without disabilities. The intent of the law was to ensure that students who have disabilities should have opportunities to learn their work skills from people who were experts at teaching work skills (vocational educators) and their academics and daily living skills from experts in those areas (special and general educators).

Unfortunately, no funds were appropriated in the 1963 act that would make it financially attractive for vocational educators to serve students with disabilities. As a result, these students were not served in any great number. That began to change, however, when Congress passed the Vocational Education Act Amendments (1968) to the Vocational Education Act. Among the many provisions, two were significant. First, 10 percent of the funds for vocational education were set aside to serve youths with disabilities. Second, each state was required to file a plan with the Bureau of Adult and Vocational Education that described how the funds that were set aside were to be used to serve students with disabilities. The penalty for not providing vocational education programs for this population was the loss of all those set-aside funds.

Many states made no more than a token response to the financial incentives of the set-aside funds and did not use all available funds. It was not until the passage of PL 94-142, the Education for All Handicapped Children Act (1975), that some leverage could be applied to this situation. PL 94-142 stipulated a free and appropriate education for all youths with disabilities. The penalty for noncompliance was more stringent—loss of *all* federal funds to any state that failed to comply. The combination of money to provide services and the threat of the loss of all federal funds for not serving students with disabilities in regular vocational education programs had its desired effect: From 1973 to 1978, enrollment figures increased by 66 percent (U.S. Department of Education, 1983). Chapter 3 gives an update on vocational education and its evolving role with students with disabilities since the mid-1970s.

The Career Education Movement

As dramatic as these figures are, they tell only a story of quantity. The even more unexpected outcome was the emergence of a concept encompassing but parallel to vocational special needs education—career education. This was a qualitative flavor added to the rapid increase of services that affected students with or without disabilities.

Definitions.   Career education was considered an alternative to the narrow job-preparation approach of vocational education and was also a response to the problems associated with the general education course of study in the nation's high schools. (General education is basically the course of study leading to minimal graduation requirements and includes anything that is not college preparatory or vocational education.) The career education concept, first presented by Sidney Marland in a speech to school administrators in Houston, Texas, in 1971, was conceived by members of the National Advisory Council on Vocational Education. Marland (1974) described the concept in these words:

I do not speak of career education solely in the sense of job training, as important as it is. I prefer to use career in a much broader connotation—as a stream of continued growth and progress. Career in that sense strongly implies that education can be made to serve *all* the needs of an American—teaching, to begin with, the skills and refinements of the workaday world, for if we cannot at the minimum prepare a man or woman to earn a living, our efforts are without worth. But career education must go beyond occupational skills—the interpersonal and organizational understanding without which one simply cannot exist in a modern nation-state, addressing effectively the matter of living itself, touching on all its pragmatic, theoretical, and moral aspects. That is what I mean in the broadest sense by career education—and that is the way in which I envision the learning process being carried forward in the schools of this Nation, in its homes and businesses, and government offices, and perhaps its streets, since for some, much of what is really educational occurs there. (p. 1)

When Marland introduced the concept of *career education*, he defined it broadly—that is, not only as preparation to earn a living but also as a way to learn about living itself. Hoyt (1975) defined *career education* as "the totality of experiences through which one learns about and prepares to engage in work as part of her or his way of living" (p. 4). He defined *work* (paid or unpaid) as a "conscious effort (other than that involved in activities whose primary purpose are either coping or relaxing) aimed at producing benefits for oneself and/or for oneself and others" (p. 3). In this context, career education was conceptualized as considerably less than all of life or one's reason for living, as Marland had visualized it, but clearly more than paid employment.

In a later elaboration, Hoyt (1977) defined *career education* as "an effort at refocusing American education and the actions of the broader community in ways that will help individuals acquire and utilize the knowledge, skills, and attitudes necessary for each to make *work* a meaningful, productive, and satisfying part of his or her way of living" (p. 5). He clarified his use of the term *work* by indicating that it "is individualistically decided by the person, not the nature of the task. What is *work* to one person may well be play to another and drudgery to another. The human need to work will, hopefully, be met by others in productive use of leisure-time, in volunteerism, or in duties performed as a full-time homemaker who is not employed for wages" (p. 7). Thus, Hoyt clarified his position on what constitutes productive work—something many conceptualizers have failed to do.

These and various other interpretations have led to confusion about the exact nature of career education. Some people think of it as vocational education and have said that career education is just an old concept dressed in new verbiage. Some have restricted career education to students in the lower track of school programs, while others have included elements for students in all of the educational tracks. Some have felt that career education is not respectable enough to be offered to college-bound students, while others have gone to the other extreme and excluded students with disabilities from their career education offerings.

Many conceptualizers of career education define *career education* as education that focuses on the roles a person is likely to play in his or her lifetime. These include student, paid worker, recreator, family member, citizen, and pensioner. Career education is what people do to learn how to engage in these roles. This is exemplified by the definition approved in December 1977 by the Board of Governors of the Council for Exceptional Children (Brolin & D'Alonzo, 1979).

Development of Career Education Models

So many program variations have been developed that it is impossible to describe all of them. Even when the names of the programs are the same, details differ from school to school and even within the same school from year to year. Rather than this being a cause for concern, it may well be a tribute to the sincerity of the professionals who continuously evaluate their efforts, changing, adding, and discarding elements, materials, and practices as they seek better ways to help young people who have disabilities become better prepared to work and live in a complex and changing society. Two models characteristic of most program development during the 1970s and 1980s are described next.

Life-Centered Career Education Model. Brolin and Kokaska presented a model (Brolin & Kokaska, 1979; Kokaska & Brolin, 1985) that captured many features of special education work-study programs with their variations and modifications, but broadened them to encompass the concept of career education for all ages. They defined *career education* as a purposeful and sequential planning approach to help students in their career development. A three-dimensional model of competencies was proposed by the authors: (1) stages of career development; (2) school, family, and community experiences; and (3) a set of 22 basic life-centered competencies that collectively contribute to the maturity of youngsters with disabilities.

The 22 major competencies students need to master to become successful as adults were identified from research in the field (Brolin & Thomas, 1971). These have been grouped into three major areas: daily living skills, personal-social skills, and occupational guidance and preparation. The groups are broken down as follows:

Daily Living Skills
1. Managing family finances
2. Selecting, managing, and maintaining a home
3. Caring for personal needs
4. Raising children and living as a family
5. Buying and preparing food
6. Buying and caring for clothes
7. Engaging in civic activities
8. Using recreation and leisure
9. Getting around the community (mobility)

Personal-Social Skills

10. Achieving self-awareness
11. Acquiring self-confidence
12. Achieving socially responsible behavior
13. Maintaining good interpersonal skills
14. Achieving independence
15. Achieving problem-solving skills
16. Communicating adequately with others

Occupational Guidance and Preparation

17. Knowing and exploring occupational possibilities
18. Selecting and planning occupational choices
19. Exhibiting appropriate work habits and behaviors
20. Exhibiting sufficient physical-manual skills
21. Gaining a specific occupational skill
22. Seeking, securing, and maintaining employment

Rather than being presented at that time as a specific curriculum, the Life-Centered Career Education (LCCE) curriculum was designed for the concepts embodied in the 22 competencies to be *infused* into the general education curriculum, beginning with the kindergarten level and extending well into adulthood. Experience with the infusion approach for the past decade led Brolin (1988) to a modified view, however, when he proposed that for some students an alternative curriculum, such as the Life-Centered Career Education curriculum, must be provided instead of primarily academic programs, the goals of which are unattainable for them. The LCCE curriculum (Brolin, 1992a; 1993) was developed to be used through infusion or through separate instruction.

All life experiences—whether at home, at school, or in the community—are geared to allow each person to learn the behaviors appropriate to his or her life roles at each stage of development. Dependent-children roles interact with the roles of student life until individuals become able to secure jobs and assume the roles of the work world. These work roles may then be superimposed on their adult roles of parent and citizen. Finally, there are expected behaviors that define the role of pensioner or retiree. The behavior requirements of each stage of development differ from those of every other stage. Each stage requires the developing person to learn new skills of living, personal-social relations, and occupational knowledge or behaviors for a variety of life roles. Clearly, career education is forever changing. It has been described as "lifetime learning," seemingly an apt description.

Career Education for Exceptional Children and Youth. Gillet (1981) presented a developmental model specifically for exceptional youngsters that builds around a core program modified to fit the type and degree of disability. It suggests a continuum of services beginning at the elementary level. Learning the meaning of the world of work and developing social competencies form the bases upon which students learn about the requirements of many jobs from which occupational choices are made. Personal adequacy, work habits, skill development, decision-making ability, and the opportunity to participate in a job with constructive supervision are systematically developed.

The program requires the cooperation of pupils, teachers, service staff, parents, administrators, and community leaders to successfully relate special education to career development. The development proceeds through the following stages of career conceptual understanding:

1. Self-understanding in terms of daily activities.
2. Awareness of individual characteristics.
3. Developing proper social relations.
4. Conserving and caring for materials.
5. School as a job.
6. Responsibilities of various family members.
7. Responsibility for one's own actions.
8. Relating of things done in the present to future jobs/roles.
9. Relating work in school and jobs in the future.
10. Work as a productive way of life.
11. Importance of performing a job to the best of one's ability.
12. Both men and women can work in any occupation.
13. The existence of different work values.
14. Likes and dislikes in selected tasks.
15. Each person is a unique individual.
16. What is "interest"?
17. Jobs are dependent on each other.
18. Study of specific jobs.
19. Meaning of leisure time and examples of leisure activities.
20. Concept of a career cluster.
21. Familiarity with career clusters.
22. Different levels of jobs are found within each cluster.
23. A wide range of jobs exist in each cluster.
24. Identification as a "worker."
25. All people do not have the same abilities and interests.
26. All work and all jobs are important.
27. It takes many jobs to make a functioning business.
28. Reasons for working.
29. Each job has different responsibilities.
30. Locations and times of work.
31. Work can be part time or seasonal.
32. Awareness of the nature of individual role and group roles in a work setting.
33. People work for different reasons.
34. Role of work in meeting needs.
35. Concept of volunteerism.
36. Concept of self-employment.

37. Meaning of division of labor, goods, and services.
38. Structure and interrelatedness of the economic system.
39. Determination of likes/dislikes.
40. Relationship between interests, jobs, and leisure-time activities.
41. Exploring specific jobs.
42. Some jobs depend on geographic location and seasons of the year.
43. Decision-making process.
44. Jobs require different kinds and levels of training.
45. The world of work is always changing.
46. Awareness of specific strengths and limitations in relation to work.
47. Some jobs I can do; others I can't.
48. Reasons why people change jobs.
49. Using community resources for leisure activities/jobs.
50. Career advancement.
51. Formulating a general career preference.

The scope and sequence of the program certainly make it a very attractive proposal, but it clearly focuses on work and occupational roles, ignoring personal and social skills and independence in daily living tasks outside of employment.

School-Based Career Development and Transition Education Model

The School-Based Career Development and Transition Education Model was originally a career education model developed for students with disabilities, adapting the Marland Career Education Model described by Goldhammer and Taylor (1972). The initial versions of the model appeared in Clark (1979, 1980). In the late 1980s, the model was revised to incorporate the concept of *transition* and appeared in earlier editions of this book (Clark & Kolstoe, 1990, 1995) and other sources (cf. Gajar, Goodman, & McAfee, 1993; Brolin, 1995; Wehman, 1992, 1996). A new version of this model will be presented in Chapter 2 as the conceptual basis for our current thinking about career development, transition education, and transition service delivery.

Development of Career Education Programs

National acceptance of the concept of *career education* was facilitated by the appointment of Kenneth Hoyt in 1972 to coordinate program efforts in the U.S. Office of Education. However, without the aid of persons such as Melville Appell in the Bureau of Education for the Handicapped (BEH) and the endorsement of the American Vocational Association and the Council for Exceptional Children, especially the Division on Career Development, career education might not have made quite the impact it has made on students with disabilities. Fortunately, its acceptance was not confined to the national level. It permeated practices at the local level in every corner of the nation. The effect was to significantly increase opportunities in secondary programs for students with disabilities.

However, career education programs never were fully implemented nationally. At the crest of the career education movement, Reichard (1979) analyzed programs in a five-state area; each state reported having a career education curriculum for students with disabilities. He found that nearly 70 percent of the programs stated they did not schedule field trips to business and industrial settings, even though 60 percent reported they had cooperative work programs through local businesses. Also, 55 percent said they did not provide any job placement help for their students. Most disappointing was that only 25 percent of the students with disabilities at the junior high school level participated in a career education program; at the high school level, only 42 percent of the students with disabilities were involved.

Reichard's (1979) findings were essentially the following:

1. Career education is too frequently viewed synonymously with vocational education or rehabilitation.
2. Of those existing efforts, there appear to be no agreed-upon competencies, philosophies, guidelines, or functional intraagency communications.
3. Knowledge of—or the provision and/or development of—career education materials is nearly nonexistent.
4. Definitions of career education appear to vary significantly among vocational programs.
5. Philosophical differences between administrators and teachers of regular and special classes are evident.
6. Noneducational personnel apparently are not being included in the process.
7. For those programs in existence, accountability—that is, competencies and programmatic evaluations and publications of results—is taking a low profile.
8. Agreement with the career education concept appears to be widely accepted, but implementation is varied.

There is no reason to believe that the problems discovered by Reichard were locally unique or that they were characteristic of a specific period of the late 1970s. On the contrary, the need for more and better programs is greater than ever. This is basically what led to a new conceptualization of career education programs through the School-to-Work Opportunities Act.

Independent Living for Persons with Disabilities

Special educators once thought that the state vocational rehabilitation agency was the natural and appropriate bridge to employment and "happily-ever-after" community living for their graduates. This expectation developed during the 1960s, when schools saw state vocational rehabilitation agencies taking a new look at special education populations, particularly those classified with mild mental retardation. The number of cases closed successfully by vocational rehabilitation increased dramatically from 1960 to 1975. This served only to heighten special educators' expectations that there was someone to assume responsibility for students after they left or completed school. School personnel welcomed the commitment that divisions of vocational rehabilitation were making to the rehabilitation closures (defined as "closed in employment status") of special education graduates and assumed that it was a permanent policy commitment.

At the heart of this optimism was the rather spectacular success of many state departments of education and state vocational rehabilitation agencies in working together through local school districts in programming and funding. Interestingly, even the term *transition* was used in the late 1960s to describe an orderly passage from school or institutional programming to adult services and full community participation (Chaffin, 1968; Younie, 1966). Unfortunately, the momentum waned in the late 1970s as state education agencies and schools became immersed in implementing PL 94-142. During that time, state vocational rehabilitation agencies began quietly withdrawing from school cooperative programs and turning their attention to the demands for services for persons with more severe disabilities.

Two separate yet parallel movements set the stage for the field to move to the current concept of *transition*. These movements rekindled hopes for an organized, effective process for students and their families. Both occurred in the context of ending school programming and beginning adult living. The first of these was the career education movement as described in the previous section. The second was the independent living movement. While the career education movement was reaching its zenith in the U.S. public education system, the independent living movement was unfolding in the field of rehabilitation with adults. Both have contributed to a return to the goal of interagency cooperation but through a new and improved delivery system—transition programs and services.

Like the word *transition*, the term *independent living* has both a generic meaning and a symbolic meaning. The generic connotation of independent living may be thought of as the choice, opportunity, and ability to participate actively in the community through home and family life, work, and civic and recreational involvement (Nosek, 1992). Symbolically, however, independent living implies much more than this. One of the early and definitive statements of the meaning of independent living was provided by the Independent Living Research Utilization Project–Texas Institute for Rehabilitation Research (1978). *Independent living* was defined as

> control over one's life based on the choice of acceptable options that minimize reliance on others in making decisions and in performing everyday activities. This includes managing one's own affairs; participating in day-to-day life in the community; fulfilling a range of social roles; and making decisions that lead to self-determination and the minimization of psychological or physical dependence upon others. Independence is a relative concept, which may be defined personally by each individual. (p. 1)

Independent living rehabilitation (ILR) started as a disability-rights movement in the early 1970s by persons with severe physical disabilities in reaction to years of legislation and rehabilitation policies that stopped short of *vocational* rehabilitation. From the beginning, vocational rehabilitation services were restricted by federal policy to the provision of services only to those for whom there was a "reasonable expectation" that the services would result in remunerative employment. It was the view of many vocational rehabilitation professionals, that independent living services were developed for those for whom a vocational goal was thought to be impossible or unfeasible (DeJong, 1980), rather than a means of making vocational goals feasible.

During the period from 1959 to 1972, Congress made several attempts to pass legislation for special comprehensive rehabilitation services to improve the independent living of persons with disabilities without regard to their ultimate employability. Consumers of rehabilitation services, especially those considered the most severely disabled physically, challenged this concept with the notion that gainful employment is one of several ways an individual can become truly independent. They argued that both comprehensive independent living rehabilitation services *and* vocational rehabilitation services not only were needed but were a basic right. The Rehabilitation Act of 1973 was the first legislation to pass that clearly made a commitment to the provision of vocational rehabilitation services to persons with disabilities who needed more than assistance in gaining employment. Although it did not mandate independent living rehabilitation or vocational rehabilitation services, it did provide a legal base in the Act for prohibiting denial of services and discrimination through Sections 501, 502, 503, and 504. It also directed the secretary of the Department of Health, Education, and Welfare to conduct a comprehensive needs study, including research and demonstration projects of various methods of providing rehabilitation and related services to the most severely handicapped individuals (Arkansas Rehabilitation Research and Training Center, 1978).

Because it was a logical extension of the civil rights movement of the 1960s, the independent living movement was receptive to and influenced by other social movements of the 1970s. Among these were consumerism, or self-advocacy, demedicalization and self-care, deinstitutionalization and normalization, and mainstreaming (DeJong, 1983). At the heart of all of these movements was the theme of rejection by the prevailing social system. Their impact on both educators and rehabilitation personnel alike set the stage for a readiness for the concept of *transition*.

Transition Programs and Services

Just as the career education movement of the 1970s was an expansion of the work-study movement of the 1960s, in 1984, Madeline Will, director of the Office of Special Education and Rehabilitative Services, championed the transition movement that extended the career education issue into the realm of transition programs and services in schools and linkages with adult community services.

Like its predecessors, work-study and career education, the early stages of the transition movement owed much of its acceptance to the fact that it was introduced as a federal initiative. As such, the initiative carried the weight of legislative legitimacy and substantial funding to support innovative and imaginative programs. It emphasized the preparation of people with disabilities for work, and made possible such innovations as supported employment and job coaching. However, it paid little attention to preparation for independent living and the notions of self-determination.

Fortunately, there has been a broadening of the view of the transition concept beyond merely a transition from school to work. The current perspective of transition held by the Division on Career Development and Transition, framed by Halpern (1994), presents the idea that the transition concept should include concerns for employment, postsecondary education, independent living, community participation, and social and interpersonal relationships. This shift of thinking about transition from the narrow concern about employment to all quality-of-life areas was influenced by the state and national follow-up and follow-along studies of the period from 1985 through 1995. Seminal studies from among the 20 or more that appeared during this 10-year period began with the landmark studies of Mithaug, Horiuchi, and Fanning (1985), Hasazi, Gordon, and Roe (1985), Wehman, Kregel, and Seyfarth (1985), and Kranstover, Thurlow, and Bruininks (1989). Studies in the early to mid-1990s were characterized by their impressive sample sizes and systematic inquiry techniques (Affleck, Edgar, Levine, & Kortering, 1990; Frank & Sitlington, 1993; Frank, Sitlington, & Carson, 1991; Sitlington & Frank, 1990, 1993, 1994; and Sitlington, Frank, & Carson, 1993) and the SRI National Longitudinal Transition Study and its numerous analysis reports (cf. Valdes, Williamson, & Wagner, 1990; Marder & D'Amico, 1992; Wagner, Blackorby, Cameto, Hebbeler, & Newman, 1993). Most of these studies focused on high-incidence populations (learning disabilities, mild mental retardation, or behavior disorders) who were in high school special education programs or received special education services while in school. These findings have direct bearing on the issues of transition from school to adult living.

The early unidimensional view of transition from school to working life is attributed to Madeline Will by many people as a result of her initiatives and influence of federal priorities as head of the Office of Special Education and Rehabilitative Services of the Department of Education (Will, 1984). Actually, this single-focus view goes back to the influence of Gold (1980) and others, who stake early claim in vocational training of persons with severe disabilities and the supported employment concept (Bellamy, Peterson, & Close, 1975; Rusch, 1986; Wehman, 1981). In any case, it is clear that Will's priority for federal support in transition efforts was targeted on employment and influenced the general perceptions many people have about transition. Politically, there are any number of reasons for focusing transition as a concept on employment outcomes, but it caused some debate early on over the interpretation of the concept of transition (Rusch & Menchetti, 1988; Clark & Knowlton, 1988).

We affirm the position of Halpern (1994) and numerous others (cf. Brolin, 1995a, 1995b; Browning, 1997; Kortering & Elrod, 1991; Wehman, 1996) that transition from school to adult living is a life-career focus that families, school personnel, and adult service agencies should have in developing transition programs.

In the Individuals with Disabilities Education Act of 1990 (IDEA; PL 101-476), Congress institutionalized the life-centered outcome focus of transition services when it defined transition services as a service-delivery system in the following way:

> Transition services means a coordinated set of activities for a student, designed within an outcome oriented process, which promotes movement from school to post-school activities, including post-secondary education, vocational training, integrated employment (including supported employment), continuing and adult education, adult services, independent living or community participation. (Section 300.18)

The definition of *transition* by the Division on Career Development and Transition of the Council for Exceptional Children (DCDT-CEC), framed by Halpern (1994), is the definition we prefer because it does not limit the concept of transition to a service-delivery notion. It emphasizes transition from school to adult life as a *process*. Halpern's definition states:

> Transition refers to a change in status from behaving primarily as a student to assuming emergent adult roles in the community. These roles include employment, participating in post-secondary education, maintaining a home, becoming appropriately involved in the community, and experiencing satisfactory personal and social relationships. The process of enhancing transition involves the participation and coordination of school programs, adult agency services, and natural supports within the community. The foundations for transition should be laid during the elementary and middle school years, guided by the broad concept of career development. Transition planning should begin no later than age 14, and students should be encouraged, to the full extent of their capabilities, to assume a maximum amount of responsibility for such planning. (p. 117)

Transition and the Individuals with Disabilities Education Act

The IDEA (PL 101-476) made some significant additions and changes to PL 94-142, Education of the Handicapped Act. Social work services in schools as *related services* were expanded to any social work services rather than just those in school. Other changes in IDEA related to the addition of rehabilitation counseling as a related service, the definition of *assistive technology device* and *assistive technology service*, and some new revisions to the process of planning and documenting the Individualized Educational Program (IEP).

In the context of this book, the most significant provision of IDEA in 1990 was the mandate for transition planning. It placed the initial responsibility for transition planning on state and local education agencies. IDEA used the term *transition services* in the language of the law and the regulations for the first time.

The Individuals with Disabilities Education Act Amendments of 1997 (IDEA Amendments; PL 105-17) introduced several important changes that relate to the school mandate to provide transition services. These will be elaborated in more detail in Chapter 3, but it is important in this section on historical context to note the primary changes. In the IDEA of 1990, Congress established age 16 as the beginning point for requiring transition services, but allowed for the possibility of transition planning to begin at an earlier age (i.e., ages 14 to 15, or earlier when appropriate). Subsequent to 1992, some states, on their own initiatives, took positions in their transition guidelines or state regulations to include students who were age 14 or 15. The DCDT definition (Halpern, 1994) (cited previously) took the strong position that age 14 was a minimum age for beginning transition planning and services. In response to these actions, concerns about dropout rates for students with disabilities (U.S. Department of Education, 1995), and lobbying efforts by advocacy groups, Congress amended the IDEA of 1990 in the 1997 reauthorization amendments to include students ages 14 and 15 in a transition planning process. It also made explicit what had previously been implicit—that is, related services are included among the transition services that should be considered in developing a statement of needed transition services.

IDEA legislation makes it clear that programs and services needed by a student should be highly individualized, based on individual needs, preferences, and interests. Programs and instructional arrangements are not to be based on currently available programs and services. The individualized educational program required under PL 94-142 is expanded under IDEA and its amendments to ensure better individual planning for transition outcomes. The regulations specify that all goals, objectives, instruction, and related services must be planned and delivered within an outcome-oriented process. This process begins with a set of expectations or long-range goals and moves backward to the developing of appropriate current goals to progress toward or reach the desired outcomes.

Conclusion

Little historical evidence exists before the 1970s that people with disabilities were considered capable of traditional schooling, competitive employment, or valued citizens of the community. Even so, pioneering efforts for education and training through the years kept hope alive for some individuals and their families. Taking advantage of the principle of opportunity, families were able to get minimal educational programs for their children by forcing schools to be aware of them and their needs. In certain cases, a handful of accommodations were made and the students were able to continue in general education programs because they were able to prove their abilities through performance. Although the principle of proof worked in favor of some students, it led to the denial of general education opportunities for many others. Fortunately, educational goals were broadened to include vocational education and career education. This gave students with disabilities and their families different ways to access educational opportunities to be included and to prove their competence.

The validity of career and vocational education for persons with disabilities has been well established. There is no question that life career-development outcomes represent a healthy evolution from the narrowly defined outcomes of academic programs, occupational programs, crafts programs, and so-called therapeutic environment programs of the past. Now that the concept of transition services has embraced the best of life career-development and vocational approaches, there is reason to be optimistic about moving closer to meeting the needs of all adolescents with disabilities.

CHAPTER

2 Transition Education and Services Models

The discovery of what is true and the practice of that which is good are the two most important objects of philosophy.

—Voltaire

A model for programming for the needs of all secondary special education students must be one with multiple options. To that end, the model proposed in this chapter is based on a commitment to individualized program *content* (academics, functional academics, life-centered competencies, or vocational), across *learning environment options* (general education with specialized environments as needed or preferred), and in *instructional approaches* (remedial-tutorial, learning strategies, and community-referenced or didactic instruction) within each content option. The underlying assumption here is that individualization of environment, content, and instructional approaches will lead to the best approximation of what constitutes appropriate education.

Philosophical Foundations

Sound programming for secondary special education students without a consistent, clearly stated philosophy is a problem, but it is not the only one. There is the basic dilemma of curriculum options. High school curriculum alternatives typically provide students with choices limited to the following:

1. Preparation for college
2. General education
3. Some type of vocational education
4. Various alternative programs (alternative high schools, programs within residential facilities, fine arts high schools, performing arts high schools, community-based programs, etc.)

None of these alternatives currently provides an educational philosophy that is based on a commitment to comprehensive life-career preparation outcomes for students with mild to moderate disabilities and their transition to adult life. Thus, the primary philosophical position presented here addresses the need for adolescents receiving special education services to have access to a comprehensive educational program. This should be designed to prepare them for their lifelong career demands. Further, this program should not be viewed as a segregated track with a different diploma or exit document, but rather as a legitimate, approved curriculum option. This option should be open to *any* student in *any* high school and it should be available to students with disabilities if they and their families choose it.

Lifelong career demands are those tasks of living that exist in all areas of careers. The first relevant definition of the word *career* in the *Oxford English Dictionary* (Clarendon Press, 1961, p. 10) is: "a person's course or progress through life." Career preparation, then, is that formal and informal effort to make one ready for the course of one's life. This course involves various roles (e.g., family member, neighbor, citizen, and worker), various environments (e.g., home, neighborhood, school, and community), and countless events (e.g., home living, mobility, consumer activities, interpersonal relations, leisure activities, and work activities). It also involves many transition periods throughout life, with age-appropriate independent living skills expected in each period. This approach to preparation for life careers—career development and transition education—for individuals with disabilities has been advocated for over two decades by many authors, including Brolin (1974, 1983, 1989), Brolin and Kokaska (1979), Clark (1974, 1979, 1981), Clark and Knowlton (1988), Edgar (1987), Goldhammer (1972), Gordon (1973), Gysbers and Moore (1974), Halpern (1985), Hoyt (1979), Wehman, Moon, and McCarthy (1986), and many others.

Assumptions for a Comprehensive Transition Education Services Approach

A proposal for a secondary special education program model that is philosophically centered on the goal of preparation for life-career demands is not new. Brolin (1976, 1982), DeProspo and Hungerford (1946), Hungerford (1941), Kirk and Johnson (1951), Kolstoe (1970), and Martens (1937), among others, have taken similar positions over the past 60 or more years. They have focused their positions, for the most part, on the student classified as having mental retardation. More recently, Halpern (1994) and Clark, Field, Patton, Brolin, and Sitlington (1994) have called for a comprehensive career development and transition approach for *all* students with disabilities. We agree with the appropriateness of this philosophy and submit the following assumptions, which provide a foundation for the model that follows later in the chapter:

1. Career development and transition services are needed for *all* persons—young and old, with and without disabilities, male and female, poor and affluent, and of all races and ethnic groups.

2. One's career is one's progress, or transition, through life as a family member, citizen, and worker. A career is a developmental process and is subject to planning, programming, choices, and changes.

3. Programming in life-career development and transition is concerned with age-appropriate independent living. As such, it promotes protecting each developing person's freedom to make choices and decisions, while assisting him or her to learn what alternatives there are and how to make decisions about them.

4. Significant neglect or adversity in any aspect of human growth can affect one's life-career development. Significant neglect or adversity during any of life's basic transition periods or during a person's unique transition periods can affect his or her adjustment in independent living.

5. Society still imposes limits on the life-career development and transitions of persons with disabilities. These factors restrict their independent living.

6. Any person choosing to participate as a producer or consumer in today's complex and changing world must possess a variety of life skills in adaptability.

7. Life-career development and transitions for persons with physical or mental disabilities differ significantly enough in nature or degree from those of persons without disabilities that some special attention to training and services is required.

8. Just as there is a need for different programming between people who are disabled and nondisabled, there is also a need for some differentiated programming among the various disability groups and levels of functioning within each population.

9. Life-career development and transition planning and training for any person should begin during infancy and continue throughout adulthood. Early training is especially critical for individuals with disabilities.

10. A democratic philosophy of education and a realistic philosophy of normalization dictate that all students have the same educational opportunities. These philosophies do not dictate, however, that all students have the same specific educational experiences, be in the same instructional programs, or achieve the same educational outcomes.

When an instructional program focused on life-career development and transition demands begins with the question of what educators want students to know, do, or be when they leave high school, the issue of appropriate education inevitably begins with placement. Unfortunately, whether students should be placed in a special class, a resource room, or some other administrative arrangement has become the focus of "appropriateness." The decision process frequently becomes distorted when normalization philosophy and advocacy for full inclusion override individual preferences and needs. One might wonder whether the decision makers have truly considered the question, Appropriate for what?

Proposed Comprehensive Transition Education and Services Models

The Career Development and Transition Education Model used in the first two editions of this book targeted some basic program content elements and possible school and community delivery alternatives at a time when the field needed that kind of focus. Our current understanding of life transitions and the process of planning and delivering transition education programs and services leads us to move to another level of thinking. The proposed models presented in Figures 2.1 and 2.2 are a reflection of our current perspective of critical student outcomes across age/developmental levels, transition exit points for students as they move from one educational level to the next, and the educational and service systems needed to deliver transition education and transition services.

Our first major shift in conceptualizing the transition education and service-delivery process in a new way was to move away from a focus on educational content for preparing individuals with disabilities for graduation or exit from public schools. The previous model presented four curricular content areas—Values, Attitudes, and Habits; Human Relationships; Occupational Information; and Job and Daily Living Skills—as the undergirding educational content that schools should provide during the K–12 years and that needed to be addressed even in postsecondary and adult continuing education. The present models reflect an outcome-oriented set of performance areas or domains that must be addressed as transition planning areas for students rather than as specifically designated curriculum and instruction areas that schools must provide. We believe there is a major difference in what happens when a model is used to organize and implement programs and services if the model focuses on knowledge and skill outcomes rather than knowledge and skill curriculum content. Figure 2.1, Comprehensive Transition Education Model, features this idea in the list of Knowledge and Skill Domains. Nine domains are proposed as the framework for responding to the Individualized Education Program (IEP) requirement under the IDEA for determining what a student needs to meet his or her transition services needs in the areas of *instruction, community experiences, employment,* and *other postschool adult living objectives.*

Another major shift in this model from the career development and transition education model of earlier editions of the book is the recognition that there is not just one transition in life, but many. Our focus as secondary school educators is definitely on the transition period from school to adult living in the community, but that is only one major transition. A comprehensive model of transition education and services must take into account the idea that success in one transition increases the likelihood of success in later transitions. We believe strongly in that part of the Division on Career Development and Transition (DCDT) definition (Halpern, 1994), expanded in other DCDT position statements (Clark, Carlson, Fisher, Cook, & D'Alonzo, 1991; Clark, Field, Patton, Brolin, & Sitlington, 1994), that states that education for life transitions and support in making life transitions needs to begin as early as possible. Figure 2.1 reflects this view in the Exit Points

Exit Points and Outcomes

Developmental / Life Phases	Exit Points
Infant/toddler and home training	Exit to preschool programs and integrated community participation
Preschool and home training	Exit to elementary school programs and integrated community participation
Elementary school	Exit to middle school/junior high school programs, age-appropriate self-determination, and integrated community participation
Middle school/junior high school	Exit to high school programs, entry-level employment, age-appropriate self-determination, and integrated community participation
High school	Exit to postsecondary education or entry-level employment, adult and continuing education, full-time homemaker, self-determined quality of life, and integrated community participation
Postsecondary education	Exit to specialized, technical, professional, or managerial employment, graduate or professional school programs, adult and continuing education, full-time homemaker, self-determined quality of life, and integrated community participation

Knowledge and Skills Domains

Communication and Academic Performance

Self-Determination

Interpersonal Relationships

Integrated Community Participation

Health and Fitness

Independent/Interdependent Daily Living

Leisure and Recreation

Employment

Further Education and Training

FIGURE 2.1   Comprehensive Transition Education Model

27

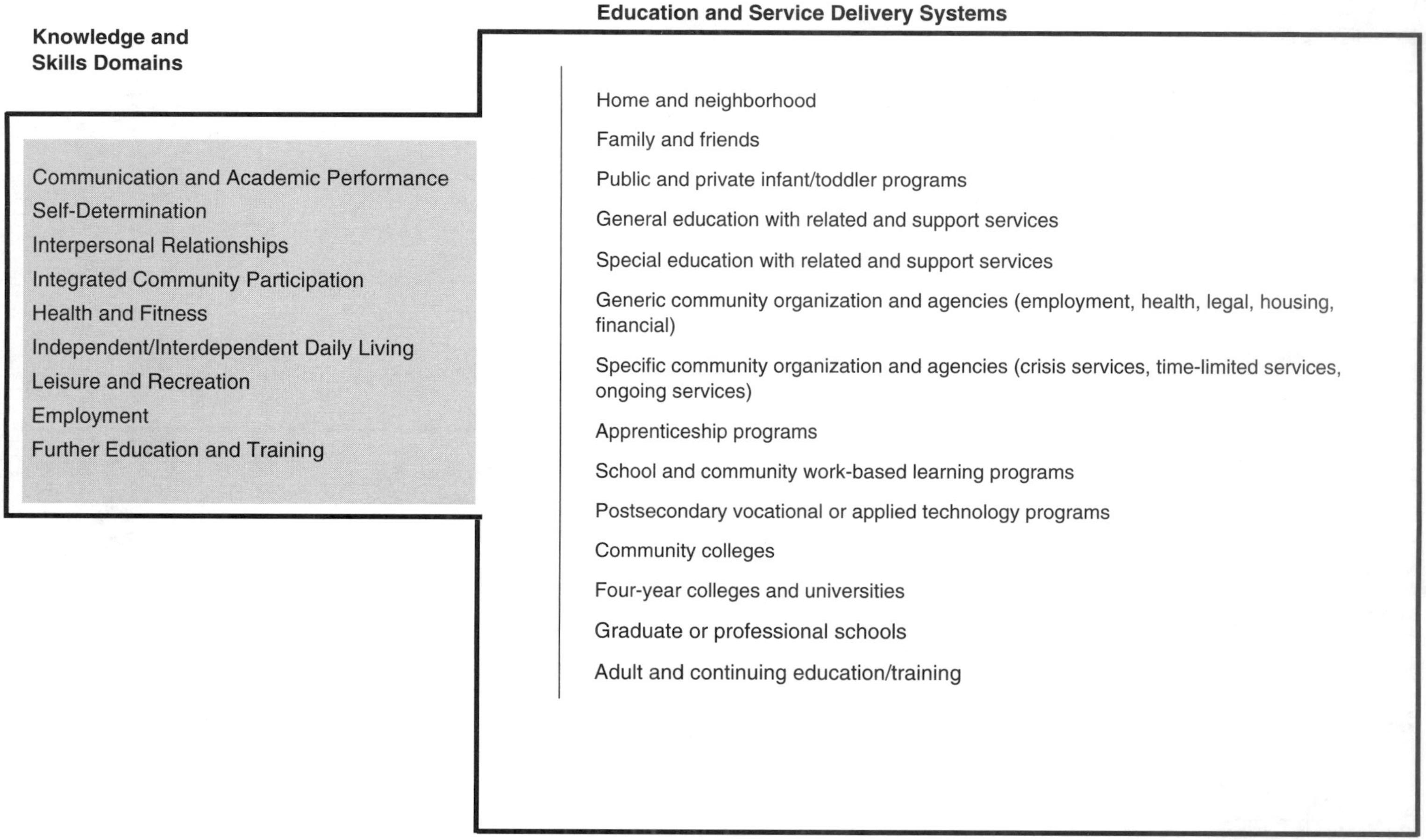

Education and Service Delivery Systems

**Knowledge and
Skills Domains**

Communication and Academic Performance

Self-Determination

Interpersonal Relationships

Integrated Community Participation

Health and Fitness

Independent/Interdependent Daily Living

Leisure and Recreation

Employment

Further Education and Training

Home and neighborhood

Family and friends

Public and private infant/toddler programs

General education with related and support services

Special education with related and support services

Generic community organization and agencies (employment, health, legal, housing, financial)

Specific community organization and agencies (crisis services, time-limited services, ongoing services)

Apprenticeship programs

School and community work-based learning programs

Postsecondary vocational or applied technology programs

Community colleges

Four-year colleges and universities

Graduate or professional schools

Adult and continuing education/training

FIGURE 2.2   Comprehensive Transition Services Model

and Outcomes component. Developmental or life phases include all phases of life and a life span continuum, beginning with infants and toddlers. Each phase has its own set of benchmark outcomes and/or exit points so that families and teachers can see their targeted outcomes for short-term planning. Too often, transition advocates emphasize the long-term adult outcomes of transition when communicating about the concept of transition and the nature of transition services. Long-term outcomes are too far removed for families and teachers of young children, and so there is a tendency to assume that those outcomes will be addressed adequately at a later age.

The third and final major shift in the present models from the previous model used is the notion that educational systems are not the only desirable or responsible educational or service-delivery systems in transition considerations. Stakeholders in transition decision making and problem solving have become increasingly aware that collaborative, interdependent efforts are much more effective than independent, isolated efforts. Public schools are required to be responsible for transition planning for children with disabilities moving from infant/toddler programs to early childhood programs at age 3 and for students 14 years of age and older preparing to leave school between the ages of 17 and 22. In neither case, however, can they assume responsibility for planning or supporting the transition process alone. The students, their families, and appropriate community service agencies must be involved, as well. To that end, the model reflects a comprehensive range of educational and support service systems as part of the process. Figure 2.2, Comprehensive Transition Services Model, reflects the connection between knowledge and skill domains and the multiple service delivery alternatives that can be considered in any individual's transition planning.

The language used in describing the various components of the models should be clear to whose who are familiar with current transition literature. Some of the terms, though, may need clarification for our particular use of them in the context of transition education and services. For that reason, we will discuss briefly each of the three components of the models and the language used within them.

Knowledge and Skill Domains

Knowledge and skill domains refer to those skills or performance areas that we believe are important for successfully coping with life demands across developmental levels. That is, at every stage of life, from birth to death, there are demands or expectations of people that require certain kinds and amounts of knowledge or skill to adjust successfully to that stage of life. For example, young children normally develop a functional use of their family's language system by the age of 5. They have enough vocabulary to express their needs and understand most of the language that is directed specifically toward them. This is a communication skills outcome that is expected and reached by most children. No one would say, however, that that level of communication was adequate for success in upper elementary school, middle school, high school, or adulthood. In a comprehensive model for transition education that takes into account early intervention, knowledge and skills in critical areas need to be thought of relative to children at different ages, from different environments, and with different cultural expectations and demands.

Each of the nine knowledge and skill areas presented in both Figures 2.1 and 2.2 are briefly defined and explained here. Hopefully, it will be clear how there is a direct relationship between knowledge and skills in each domain and content areas for curriculum and instruction in educational settings.

Communication and Academic Performance Skills.   *Communication skills* refer to expressive skills (e.g., speaking, signing, and augmentative communication skills) and listening skills (e.g., oral comprehension, sign reading, and speech reading). *Academic skills* range from basic reading skills for acquiring information or pleasure to advanced reading speed and comprehension of difficult materials, as well as written language (grammar, syntax, and spelling), math comprehension, and math computation skills. Communication and academic skill outcome goals should be age or grade-level appropriate for current and next anticipated performance settings.

Self-Determination Skills.   Field and Hoffman (1994) stated in their model that self-determination begins with an awareness of one's self and valuing one's self. From that stage, an individual has the basic information to make decisions and set personal goals, plan actions to meet those goals, and anticipate some specific results. Self-determined action follows planning and sets the stage for experiencing outcomes and learning from the entire process. *Self-determination skills* obviously vary in relation to the complexity of the outcome goals and the environments within which they occur. Still, as a developmental skill that one hopes will gain in power over time in life, it is important to view it as a teachable skill. Educational and support-service systems must be attentive to the self-determination skill-development process over time and not wait until the last stages of the school experience to address it. Field, Hoffman, and Spezia (1998) expanded and clarified the concept of self-determination and strategies for developing self-determination knowledge and skills in adolescents. Field, Martin, Miller, Ward, and Wehmeyer (1997) presented the current major models of self-determination and existing curricula and materials. Their publication is a superb practical source for teachers in curriculum and instructional planning for knowledge and skills in self-determination.

Interpersonal Relationship Skills.   *Interpersonal relationship skills,* or *socialization skills,* vary across age levels but comprise the basic interpersonal skills used in family, school, and community relationships. Skills include positive social behaviors, such as sharing, cooperating and collaborating, respecting others' privacy and property, being sensitive to other's feelings and preferences, being sensitive to cultural differences and values, and exhibiting specific environment social behavior expectations. Knowledge includes knowing socially appropriate and inappropriate behaviors and understanding how cultural, moral, ethical, legal, and religious influences guide one's individual social behavior as well as one's community and government public policies.

When skills and knowledge of interpersonal relationships are described in this way, it is difficult to omit the role that values, attitudes, and habits play in social interactions. People's values and attitudes are the basis for what they find worthy in themselves and in others. Values and attitudes undergird codes of conduct, preferences, beliefs, ideas, habits, and even decision making. On the other hand, the mention of values worries some people who believe that this is an area that schools cannot afford to address because of the controversial issues inherent in values education. We are persuaded by the eloquence of Noddings (1992) in *The Challenge to Care in Schools: An Alternative Approach to Education* and Brendtro, Brokenleg, and Van Bockern (1990) in *Reclaiming Youth at Risk: Our Hope for the Future* that the school can and should model and teach caring and moral responsibility.

Historically, public schools in the United States have concentrated their efforts in educating the nation's students in academic skills. Classroom discipline, behavior management, and meeting students social and emotional needs have, for the most part, been integral parts of the instructional process. But these areas have been handled almost exclusively with classroom "rules" and incidental or crisis management rather than through clear-cut, purposeful instruction. Specific, purposeful instruction in the area of personal-social behavior is rejected by some people who see it as the responsibility of the family, religious teachers, or, even broader, "everyone's" responsibility. Others take the attitude that personal-social behaviors develop naturally over time (e.g., "These things work out—just let kids grow up and they will learn").

Two studies in the early 1990s explored the perceived importance of social skills training from the perspectives of parents, teachers, and other professionals, respectively. Results from both investigations indicated that teachers and related professionals believe that the teaching of social skills is important (Baumgart, Filler, & Askvig, 1991; Sacks, Tierney-Russell, Hirsch, & Braden, 1992). Baumgart and colleagues found also that although a majority of the teachers viewed social skills training as important, certain barriers prevented teachers from teaching such skills. These barriers included teachers' inadequacies in writing appropriate social goals and objectives for IEPs, as well as knowing how to implement specific social skills instructional strategies or methods. Sacks and colleagues validated the results of the study by Baumgart and associates and expanded the notion that teachers and other professionals need further training in teaching social and interpersonal skills.

Integrated Community Participation Skills.   Recently, in a meeting of a small group of twelfth-grade students in a Los Angeles high school with their teacher and new rehabilitation counselors, John was asked by his counselor what he was interested in. He shrugged, "I don't know." His counselor then asked if he had any hobbies. John replied that he had none. The counselor probed further and asked John how he spent his spare time. He responded, "I stay at home and watch TV." Without knowing any more about this student or his situation, most people in educational and professional roles who are strong advocates of community participation and self-determination would be concerned about this student's isolation and lack of community involvement. Obviously, Los Angeles is a city with almost unlimited community participation opportunities, so lack of opportunity is ruled out as a barrier. Knowing that this student has some academic learning difficulties could lead one to conclude that what he needs is instruction and experience in accessing his community. This might be the wrong conclusion to draw in John's case. He could be sitting at home watching television because he does not know what his interests really are, how to verbalize them, or how to see the connection between interests and opportunities in the community.

Integrated community participation for adolescents with disabilities sometimes depends more on personal choice and parental approval or permission than whether they have the skills for participation. For example, in the case just described, perhaps John could be someone who truly enjoys television and could fire off answers to television trivia questions about actors, talk shows, situation comedies, sports events, and even consumer products at a level that makes him an interesting person to talk to at school or on his part-time job. Perhaps he chooses to watch TV because of his interest in all that goes on in that medium. Or, as another possibility in this student's case, perhaps John lives in an area or community within Los Angeles that is considered dangerous and there are few appropriate recreation or leisure activity opportunities. Furthermore, maybe he and his family cannot afford to get out of the neighborhood to take advantage of the many exciting opportunities of Los Angeles. What if John, concerned about his dangerous neighborhood, is making the personal choice of avoiding those dangers or refusing to engage in gang or "hanging out" behavior after school or at night? Watching TV at home then may be a reasonable alternative at this time. Another possibility is that his parents are so concerned about John's safety or social learning in the dangerous environment that they exert parental control over John's leaving the house.

The school's responsibility to assess a student's preferences and interests should go beyond occupational or postsecondary education preferences and interests. The nature of a student's preferences and interests in relation to participating in his or her neighborhood or community should guide the school on that student's instructional needs. Integrated community participation skills range from knowledge about how to access community interest settings to actual knowledge or skills in participating in those settings. Examples of community participation activities are unique to specific communities and neighborhoods, but common interest and preference areas include accessing and participating in shopping alternatives, community special events (e.g., festivals, parades, fairs, etc.), parks and recreation centers, religious organization or community activities, volunteering, voting, advocacy for disability rights, public libraries (free loan of books, compact discs, videos, and audiocassettes), and the like.

Health and Fitness Skills.   The area of *physical health and fitness* covers the expected areas of general health concerns (health status, nutrition, weight, chronic symptoms, and medications) and physical fitness (physical condition related to wellness and prevention of health problems and physical condition related to strength, stamina, endurance, range of motion, and mobility). Knowledge of one's health status and fitness is important for preventing health problems or self-injury as well as the need for medications, consistency in following treatment procedures, periodic examinations or medical procedures, and the possible need for physical therapy, prosthetics, orthotics, or assistive technology. Skills in self-care and fitness are important for wellness.

Students and families who are not informed or educated about the relationship between nutrition and general health, exercise and fitness, diet and weight control, and mental or emotional stress and physical symptoms may not show a high level of interest in health and fitness as a transition education planning issue. Schools that have good health education programs and use health services personnel to observe and evaluate student needs can take the initiative in assessing health and fitness concerns and reporting these to students and their families. Schools that do not necessarily have good health education or health services can still address health and fitness concerns in careful and creative curriculum decisions and/or linkages to appropriate health services.

Independent/Interdependent Daily Living Skills.   Independent living skills are highly valued in U.S. society. With appropriate training or support, most persons with disabilities achieve satisfactory levels of independence. Indicators of independent living vary across age levels. For children, independent behaviors are essentially what is referred to as *adaptive behaviors*—dressing, eating, bathing, taking care of personal belongings, performing simple chores, and the like. In adolescence, adaptive behaviors begin to take on the form of daily living skills and independent living skills—advanced dressing skills and decision making on clothing, personal hygiene skills, basic food preparation, care and maintenance of clothing, driving or use of public transportation, managing one's own money, taking responsibility for one's own medications or support requests, and complying with the rules of authority at home, school, and in the community. Adult adaptive behavior skills are much the same as independent living skills, including all areas of daily living at home, community participation, employment, personal decision making, and taking responsibility for one's own financial, legal, and personal-social life.

The concept of *interdependence* is also important because few individuals are totally independent in life. Most people, with or without disabilities, do not live truly independently, but rather conduct their individual affairs through mutual reliance with other people (Klein, 1992). Interdependent living skills across all ages may refer to (1) being able to know one's self and understand when one needs support or assistance, (2) knowing that different people in families and living groups play different types of interdependent roles, and (3) understanding the roles of personal attendants or professional support people in interdependent relationships.

Leisure and Recreation Skills.   The importance of satisfying use of *leisure time* for rest, recreation, and renewal is often neglected in transition programs that focus exclusively (or predominantly) on transition from school to work or school to careers. Brannan (1999) made the case that leisure, recreation, and play are inherent aspects of the human experience and are essential to health and well-being. Certainly, persons with disabilities that limit their participation in home, school, and community activities have the same needs for and right to leisure, recreation, and play. Access to leisure, recreation, or play events or facilities is critical for this, but from the school's perspective, access is not enough. Students with disabilities must develop and expand their awareness and knowledge of leisure alternatives, and understand the value of asserting their needs and rights for leisure opportunities as well as skills relating to activities, social expectations, and self-determination.

Employment Skills.   Within the model presented here, *employability skills* for adolescents with disabilities making the transition from school to adult living refers to general employability skills, occupational skills, and vocational skills. *General employability skills* are general work skills such as following directions, on-task behavior, concern for quality work, concern for work rate, recognizing and correcting errors or problems, attendance and punctuality, and ability to take instruction and criticism. *Occupational skills* include skills in seeking and obtaining a job; marketable entry-level skills in reading, math, communication, and interpersonal relationships; speed, accuracy, and precision in job tasks assigned; adjustment to work environment changes; adjustment to repetition and monotony of job performance; and skills in job maintenance. *Vocational skills* are specific skills learned through training or experience in job performance, such as industrial skills (welding, machine operation, etc.), business and office occupations (bookkeeping, secretarial, computer operation, etc.), construction trade skills (carpentry, plumbing, electrical, masonry, etc.), health occupations, and the like.

Further Education and Training Skills.   *Further education and training* as a knowledge and skill or instructional content area refers to readiness for any formal education or training experiences after leaving the public education system. The most common of these options include preparation in high school for postsecondary vocational and technical schools, community colleges, four-year colleges and universities, graduate and professional education, education and training provided in the military or business and industry, adult education, and personal or vocational continuing education. Preparation of students for taking advantage of postsecondary education and training options includes awareness of application procedures and admission requirements, and successfully completing all the secondary school courses or programs possible that will help ensure successful postsecondary education or training.

Increasingly, the need for assuming the role of a lifelong learner is being accepted in society. Too many changes occur in work and societal demands to depend solely on any one level of educational attainment. Individuals with disabilities have enough difficulties in accessing and maintaining satisfying roles in the workplace and in the community without getting farther behind others because they discontinue their education and training. This model also emphasizes the importance of continuing education and training, regardless of the basic choice after high school of going to college or some type of vocational training school versus going directly to work or being a full-time homemaker. Continuing education highlights the importance of knowing how to learn about and access information related to family and community living and all aspects of integrated community participation.

Exit Points and Outcomes

The exit points and outcomes shown in Figure 2.1 reflect the lifelong process of vertical transitions of life, using developmental or life phases as a continuum. On the other hand, developmental or life phases connected with educational benchmarks or life outcomes also involve lifelong horizontal transitions. *Transition education*, a term used in the title of this book, implies that although vertical and horizontal transitions in life are natural and inevitable, people can be more prepared for those transitions if they learn what they need to know about life demands and expectations in transition periods. Since the late 1980s, the term *transition* has been used so frequently and in so many contexts that it seems important to anchor an understanding of life transitions here not only by domains of concern (knowledge and skills) but also by transition exit points.

A comprehensive model of transition education and services that takes a lifelong transitions approach must take into account all the major exit points in transition education and services from infancy through adulthood. Professionals and families need to be reminded that at each major educational level, there is a transition process with age-appropriate and environment-specific expectations. For example, elementary schoolchildren receiving special education and/or related services will, at a certain grade level or socially determined decision point, move on to middle school or junior high school in a public or private school program. The decision to exit is not always based on mastery of all elementary school standards; rather, it usually is based on age appropriateness and readiness for a more advanced level of education. Good transition education and services, however, would extend its academic preparation of a student not only to be ready for middle or junior high school but to ensure that the student is also ready for more advanced levels of integration in community participation.

The emphasis in this book is on transition education and services for adolescents with disabilities. The comprehensive models presented here reflect that at the high school level, transition education and services efforts should be to prepare students for exit and transition into postsecondary education or entry-level employment, adult and continuing education, full-time homemaker roles, and a self-determined quality of life and integrated community participation. This may sound lofty and ideal, but the two models are meant to focus on the ideal so as not to settle for something much less. It is better to have models with high standards spelling out some specific exit-point accomplishments rather than have no model and viewing the high school's responsibility as merely getting students through a high school diploma core curriculum. The difference in vision between these two views is at the heart of the discouragement the general public feels about today's schools.

Education and Service Delivery Systems

The education and comprehensive delivery systems presented in Figure 2.2 are meant to emphasize the collaborative nature of transition education. Too many secondary special education teachers feel alone in the effort to provide transition education and services in multiple knowledge and skill domains. One reason teachers feel this way is a result of an administrative delegation of responsibility for transition services without adequate support or training. Another reason teachers might feel alone is that they have an awareness of the responsibility of the need and the federal requirement to provide transition services, but feel neglected and abandoned by administrators. Congress requires local education agencies (not just teachers or designated transition specialists) to provide transition services through instruction (general or special education) and related services. No one who understands the challenges of providing transition education and services believes that teachers, or even schools, can successfully accomplish the goals of outcome-oriented transitions alone. Even from the outset, the 1990 federal mandate for transition services under the IDEA (PL 101-476) called for linkages with appropriate nonschool agencies and service-delivery systems. In the 1997 IDEA Amendments, Congress added related services, which are school-based service-delivery systems, as additional linkage alternatives. To address the issue of doing the job of transition education and services, our models present an array of formal and informal systems that should be involved in developing knowledge and skills for one or more of the many transitions that individuals with disabilities will face in their lifetimes.

Home, family, neighborhood, and friends vary in availability and potential power as educational and support systems for students in secondary special education programs. We know that many home situations, involving parents and families, are excellent environments for learning about and reinforcing skills in the outcome areas of our comprehensive models. Other times, parents or family members are actual barriers to learning and development. The same is true for neighborhoods and friends and all the other programs, agencies, and systems cited in the transition services model. Some sources will be available, accessible, and highly supportive, and others will be difficult to access and limited in what they will offer. All of the systems cited need to be included, though, because each has potential. If one of the system options is not functioning well as a source for learning, encouraging learning, or support for learning at any one point in time, there are ways to make systems change. When change does not occur, or does not occur quickly enough for an individual student's benefit, other educational and support delivery system alternatives must be selected.

Conclusion

The model or approach used by a high school special education program to provide the best transition services possible will depend on the vision and task commitment of its staff and administrators. This book is intended to provide new visions or to provide support for existing visions. It is also intended to supply, through the comprehensive model and the chapters that follow, some specific strategies for how to implement the model or a school's own variation of it. The content of instruction for students is the key to effective knowledge and skills outcomes. Targeted goals and objectives that are tied directly to a student's age-appropriate preferences, interests, and needs and that are supported by multiple education and support system-delivery options lead to satisfying outcomes for each student's next exit point.

It is our intent in revising the career development and transition education model of the first two editions of the book to (1) emphasize the major knowledge and skill domains that are evolving in transition services, (2) highlight the lifelong aspects of transitions and the different expectations for various transition exit points, and (3) stress the shared responsibility and potential of a variety of transition education and service-delivery systems. We realize that a dual model such as this (Figures 2.1 and 2.2) does not cut to the heart of a plan of action, since the model used by most high schools is not a transition education model. Rather, most high schools are structured around a predetermined academic core curriculum, specified electives, and some established criteria for satisfactory completion of the high school diploma program.

A wide range of flexibility exists both within and across states on how local schools provide a "free and appropriate education" for students with disabilities under a high school diploma track. Students with disabilities who are able to meet the expectations of a traditional academic general education curriculum, with or without support, are encouraged to do that, but often with the assumption that if they can do that, they do not need any transition education or special considerations for transition planning. Others are placed in programs that play the academic rules game but with variations that allow students to take core courses with appropriate titles, but which, in fact, are distinctly different in content and/or level of rigor while yielding the needed course credits for graduation. Finally, there are programs that deviate significantly from the general education core curriculum in titles and content, yet still qualify the students for graduation under the justification that the program was agreed to by the IEP team. The good news is that these students are able to receive diplomas and be acknowledged similarly to any student without disabilities who gets a diploma by attending school, staying out of major trouble, and showing some effort to complete school. The bad news is that many students in both general and special education are not receiving the adult outcome-oriented transition education they need.

Schools in some states do not allow much flexibility in educational programming that leads to a diploma. Students with disabilities are caught in the school's requirements for meeting either (or both) graduation credits or minimum competency exams. The students with disabilities who cannot, even with support, earn the required number of credits or score high enough to pass the minimum competency exams have no diploma options and have to settle for a certificate of attendance or certificate of completion. Under this system, the academic focus usually prevents much in the way of transition education content except for those who are able to succeed in the system and who plan to go to college under an academic degree program. For those who are interested in vocational training or employment after high school, the system is a lose-lose situation, in both inadequacy of curriculum content and inability to earn a diploma.

Can the comprehensive transition education and services models presented here work in today's high schools? We believe they can work in those states and local school districts that allow flexibility in diploma options. That is especially true in modified curriculum options (self-contained or resource rooms where at least some curriculum content is determined and taught by special education teachers) and alternative curriculum options (self-contained or community-based instruction programs). The models definitely fit any school that has adopted the Life-Centered Career Education Curriculum Program (Brolin, 1992). They also can fit the general framework being described and developed under new school-to-work or school-to-careers programs. More difficult, but not impossible, is the task of making the models work for students in general education diploma tracks under strict compliance with prescribed curriculum content and minimum competency testing standards. It may be more feasible in these programs to try to apply the models to the individual needs of students through electives, extracurricular activities, innovative summer programs, and home and community learning opportunities.

The ultimate accountability criterion for a school system is that its educational program proves useful to its students in all aspects of their lives. As a thematic goal around which curriculum content and instructional approaches are woven, a functional, life-centered, lifelong learning competencies approach speaks to the ultimate issue of *usefulness*. The theme presented in this chapter is such that it may alienate educators or critics of education who are concerned only about academic excellence, academic accountability, and achievement standards. For those individuals, we would defer to Marland (1974, p. 13), who quoted Alfred North Whitehead as saying, "Pedants sneer at an education that is useful, but if it is not useful, what is it?" Without apology, that view is supported in presenting our ideas on transition education and services in this book.

CHAPTER

3

Transition Education and Services Guidelines

DEBRA A. NEUBERT

What the best and wisest parent wants for his own child, that must the community want for all its children. Any other ideal for our schools is narrow and unlovely; acted upon, it destroys our democracy.

—John Dewey

Career, vocational, and school-to-adult life transition programs for students with disabilities have evolved over the years in response to legislation, research, and educational reform movements. Federal laws in the fields of special education, rehabilitation, vocational-technical education, and workforce training have provided legal mandates for the provision of various vocational and transition services to individuals with disabilities. If you work with students with disabilities, you must be familiar with these mandates to ensure that your students have access to a range of educational and vocational options and receive appropriate transition planning services. Research findings, especially studies documenting postsecondary outcomes for students with disabilities, have also influenced the development of career, vocational, and transition programs. More recently, researchers have sought to identify recommended practices in secondary special education, including the delivery of transition services. These findings have also served as benchmarks for practitioners and policy makers to develop guidelines for secondary programs.

Educators and policy makers have also had to respond to a number of educational reform movements that have had an impact on all students in secondary settings for the past two decades. Educational reform efforts in the 1980s resulted in an increased emphasis on academic achievement, which means students have to earn more credits in English, math, science, and social studies courses. Many students have also been required to pass minimum competency tests that serve as documentation of their mastery of academic content and, in many instances, determine the type of diploma they receive. Secondary educators who provide career, vocational, or transition services have had to mesh their practices and programs with the requirements of these educational reform movements. Students with disabilities and their families are increasingly asked to make difficult choices regarding not only curricular content but also diploma options during the middle and high school years.

Educational reform efforts in the 1990s focused on the need for diverse outcomes through school-to-work programs for *all* students. At the same time, schools were and are under pressure to raise academic standards for all students and are held accountable when they fail to do so. These social, political, and educational influences have had an impact on the high school curriculum. Often, the mandates for transition programs and better postsecondary outcomes have had to compete with the mandates to raise academic standards.

This chapter provides a review of legislation in the fields of special education, rehabilitation, vocational-technical education, and workforce training that have affected the development of programs and policies found in secondary settings. A discussion of recent legislation that targets educational reform is also included. This is followed by a discussion of educational reform movements and their effect on curricula and diploma options for secondary students. Finally, a review of recommended practices for secondary special education and transition programs is provided.

Legislation

Educational, vocational, and transitional services for individuals with disabilities are mandated in legislation that spans the fields of special education, vocational-technical education, rehabilitation, and workforce development. Current laws in these fields call for interdisciplinary efforts to serve individuals with disabilities in educational, vocational, and employment settings. The following sections provide a historical review of legislation to provide you with a framework for understanding patterns of federal initiatives and how the nation has progressed to this point. The current laws will help you understand the differences in the funding and the structure of various programs available to students with disabilities (see Figure 3.1). A good understanding of the law will ultimately enhance transition planning for students with disabilities during the middle and high school years.

Special Education

The Education for All Handicapped Children Act of 1975, PL 94-142.   Signed into law in 1975, PL 94-142 was the landmark legislation that provided all children with disabilities the right to a free and appropriate public education in the least restrictive environment. The Education for All Handicapped Children Act (EHA) mandated that each child have a written Individualized Education Program (IEP) that addressed the present levels of functioning, long- and short-term goals, ser-

FIGURE 3.1   **Selected Legislation Related to Transition Services**

Special Education Legislation
- The Education for All Handicapped Children Act of 1975, PL 94-142
- The Education of the Handicapped Act Amendments of 1983, PL 98-199
- The Education of the Handicapped Act Amendments of 1986, PL 99-457
- The Individuals with Disabilities Education Act of 1990, PL 101-476
- The Individuals with Disabilities Education Act Amendments of 1997, PL 105-17

Rehabilitation and Civil Rights Legislation
- Vocational Rehabilitation Act of 1973, PL 93-112
- Rehabilitation Act Amendments of 1983, PL 98-221
- Rehabilitation Act Amendments of 1986, PL 99-506
- Rehabilitation Act Amendments of 1992, PL 102-569
- Rehabilitation Act Amendments of 1998, PL 105-220 (Title IV of the Workforce Investment Act of 1998)
- Americans with Disabilities Act of 1990, PL 101-336

Vocational-Technical Education Legislation
- The Smith-Hughes Act of 1917, PL 347
- The Vocational Education Act of 1963, PL 88-210
- The Vocational Education Act Amendments of 1968, PL 90-210
- Education Amendments of 1976, Title II, PL 94-482
- The Carl D. Perkins Vocational Education Act of 1984, PL 98-524
- The Carl D. Perkins Vocational and Applied Technology Education Act Amendments of 1990, PL 101-392
- The Carl D. Perkins Vocational and Applied Technology Educational Act Amendments of 1998, PL 105-332

Work Force Training Legislation
- Comprehensive Employment and Training Act of 1973, PL 93-203
- Comprehensive Employment and Training Act Amendments of 1978, PL 95-524
- Job Training Partnership Act of 1982, PL 97-300
- Job Training Partnership Act Amendments of 1986, PL 99-496
- Job Training Reform Amendments of 1992, PL 102-367
- Workforce Investment Act of 1998, PL 105-220

Recent Educational Reform Legislation
- Goals 2000: Educate America Act of 1994, PL 103-227
- The School-to-Work Opportunities Act of 1994, 103-239
- Improving America's Schools Act of 1994, PL 103-382

vices to be provided, and plans for initiating and evaluating services. The evaluation process for each student was to be nondiscriminatory and made by a multidisciplinary team. Parents had to be notified when their children were to be evaluated for and placed in special education services.

Much of the literature and research concerning EHA was initially focused on younger students with disabilities. During the late 1970s, there was a growing awareness that secondary special education students needed increased vocational training and independent living skills. Phelps and Frasier (1988) pointed out that the least restrictive environment provision clearly suggested that for secondary students, the least restrictive and most responsive environment included placements where students could work on vocationally related goals and objectives. In fact, the Final Rules for PL 94-142 specifically stated that both state and local education agencies had to take steps to ensure that students with disabilities were able to access the same types of programs and services available to students without disabilities. At the time, these programs generally included industrial arts, home economics, and vocational education (*Federal Register,* August 23, 1977). Researchers also began to document the poor postsecondary outcomes of students with disabilities in terms of employment and independent living. This, in turn, provided an increased focus on the needs of secondary students with disabilities and provided some of the basis for the school-to-work transition movement that became prominent in the 1980s.

The Education of the Handicapped Act Amendments of 1983 and 1986.   Section 626 of the Education of the Handicapped Act Amendments of 1983, PL 98-199, was the first act that authorized $6.6 million in funding to develop and support school-to-work transition services for youths with disabilities in the form of model demonstration programs, research projects, and personnel preparation projects (Rusch & Phelps, 1987). These projects served as starting points for others to develop transition programs and to shape future policy regarding school-to-work programming. The federal Office of Special Education and Rehabilitative Services also spotlighted school-to-work transition as a national priority and provided a model for secondary special educators to bridge the gap between school and work (Will, 1984). However, there were no specific mandates for transition planning in this Act and state and local education agencies were allowed to develop and fund transition services at their own discretion. During this time, it was also suggested that the school-to-work concept be broadened to include school-to-adult life components, such as personal/social adjustment and community participation (Halpern, 1985). This followed the same pattern of the 1970s' federal initiatives for career education, emphasizing occupational aspects of life-career development and subsequent calls for emphasis on personal/social adjustment and daily living skills (Brolin, 1978; Clark, 1974).

The Education of the Handicapped Act Amendments of 1986, PL 99-457, reauthorized the funding for discretionary programs (model demonstration, research, and personnel preparation projects) under Section 626 and authorized funding for research projects to investigate postsecondary outcomes for students with disabilities who had dropped out of school. Most importantly, PL 99-457, Part H, mandated the provision of services to infants and toddlers with disabilities. This increased the spectrum of services offered to individuals with disabilities from birth to age 21 (or 22) and focused on the need for interdisciplinary efforts during the early years of life. Parallels between the transition process at the early childhood and secondary levels have been discussed (Repetto & Correa, 1996), along with the need to provide seamless and interdisciplinary services for all students with disabilities.

Public Laws 98-199 and PL 99-457 did not actually mandate transition services for students with disabilities, but the foundation was intact for the sweeping changes that took place with the Individuals with Disabilities Education Act of 1990.

The Individuals with Disabilities Education Act of 1990, PL 101-476. The Individuals with Disabilities Education Act of 1990 (IDEA) was the first federal legislation mandating that a statement of needed transition services be included in students' IEPs by age 16 (or at a younger age when appropriate). This Act clearly designated that special educators were responsible for initiating the transition planning process. The IEP was also to include (when appropriate) a statement of each public agency's responsibilities or linkages before the student exited the school system. This mandate clearly stated that transition planning was to include individuals and organizations who provided postsecondary services to individuals with disabilities.

Defining Transition Services. The definition of *transition services* that was included in IDEA clearly broadened the concept to include multiple postsecondary outcomes (DeStefano & Wermuth, 1992). Transition services included the following:

> A coordinated set of activities for a student, designed within an outcome-oriented process, that promotes movement from school to post-school activities, including postsecondary education, vocational training, integrated employment (including supported employment), continuing and adult education, adult services, independent living, or community participation. (Department of Education, 1992, p. 44804)

The *transition services* definition also stated that students were to be involved in the transition planning process and that assessment data were to be used in formulating transition goals:

> The coordinated set of activities must be based on the individual student's needs, taking into account the student's preferences and interests; and include instruction, community experiences, the development of employment and other post-school adult living objectives; and acquisition of daily living skills and functional vocational evaluation (if appropriate). (Department of Education, 1992, p. 44804)

Student Involvement. The IDEA of 1990 highlighted and mandated the need for students to be involved in planning their transition services and goals at IEP meetings. This mandate coincided with the self-determination movement that called for students to become actively involved in expressing their needs and goals, and in planning for the future (Ward, 1992). PL 101-476 stated the following:

> If a purpose of the meeting is the consideration of transition services for a student, the public agency shall invite the student; and a representative of any other agency that is likely to be responsible for providing or paying for transition services. If the student does not attend, the public agency shall take other steps to ensure that the student's preferences and interests are considered; and if an agency invited to send a representative to a meeting does not do so, the public agency shall take other steps to obtain the participation of the other agency in the planning of any transition services. (Department of Education, 1992, p. 44814)

Interagency Planning.   The IDEA stated that transition services and planning be considered by a team of individuals, which could include personnel from community and adult service agencies (e.g., rehabilitation counselors). Interagency planning was to be initiated by special educators, and personnel from outside agencies were to be invited to students' IEP meetings when appropriate. The IDEA also addressed the need for secondary special educators to reconsider a student's needs and goals if an outside agency could not provide the agreed-upon services:

> If a participating agency fails to provide agreed-upon transition services contained in the IEP of a student with a disability, the public agency responsible for the student's education shall, as soon as possible, initiate a meeting for the purpose of identifying alternative strategies to meet the transition objectives, and if necessary, revising the student's IEP. Nothing in this part relieves any participating agency, including a State vocational rehabilitation agency, of the responsibility to provide or pay for any transition service that the agency would otherwise provide to students with disabilities who meet the eligibility criteria of that agency. (Department of Education, 1992, p. 44815)

The Individuals with Disabilities Education Act Amendments of 1997, PL 105-17.   Whereas the IDEA of 1990 provided the first federal mandate for transition planning in special education, the Individuals with Disabilities Education Act Amendments of 1997 (IDEA Amendments of 1997) and the Final Regulations for this Act (Department of Education, 1999) broadened the scope of transition planning in a number of ways.

Defining Transition Services.   The definition for *transition services* remained the same as in the IDEA of 1990 (Section 602), with the exception that the coordinated set of activities could include related services such as transportation and support services such as speech and language pathology and audiology services, psychological services, physical and occupational therapy, recreation, social work services, counseling services (including rehabilitation counseling), orientation and mobility services, and medical services (for diagnostic and evaluation purposes). Providing related services may be especially significant to students with more significant disabilities who participate in community-based transition programs until the age of 21 (or 22).

Earlier Transition Planning. A significant change in the IDEA Amendments of 1997 related to when transition planning must begin for students. PL 105-17, Section 614 states, "Beginning at age 14, and updated annually, a statement of the transition service needs of the child under the applicable components of the child's IEP that focuses on the child's courses of study (such as participation in advanced-placement courses or a vocational education program)" (IDEA 1997, p. 84). This mandate requires special educators, students, and families to be aware of curricula and diploma options, prerequisites for vocational-technical programs, and college entrance requirements as early as the middle school years. For example, if a student is college bound, the IEP team should determine what courses are needed throughout middle school and high school that will enable the student to enter a postsecondary institution. The IDEA Amendments of 1997 also continued to mandate that a statement of needed transition services for the child, including, when appropriate, a statement of the interagency responsibilities or any needed linkages, be included in the IEP by age 16.

The final regulations for IDEA Amendments of 1997 (Department of Education, 1999) also specify that if an IEP team determines that a student does not need transition services in one or more of the areas included in the definition of *transition*, there is no need to justify why this decision was made with a statement in the IEP. This is a change from the IDEA of 1990 and its subsequent regulations.

Transferring Rights at Age of Majority. A final point relevant to transition planning is the option states have concerning the transfer of rights at the age of majority. "In a state that transfers rights at the age [of] majority, beginning at least one year before a student reaches the age of majority under state law, the student's IEP must include a statement that the student has been informed of his or her rights" (Department of Education, 1999, p. 12442). If students are determined not to have the ability to provide informed consent with respect to their educational and transition programs, the state has to establish procedures to appoint the parent of the student or another appropriate individual as a legal guardian (IDEA, 1997).

Evaluation of Students. PL 105-17 contained significant changes regarding how students are evaluated, how IEPs are written, and how educational placements are determined. The IEP must be oriented toward a student's participation in the *regular education curriculum*. If it is not, educators must justify why the student is not capable of participating in regular education activities.

The IDEA Amendments of 1997 (Section 614, p. 84) stated the students' IEPs must include the following:

- A statement of measurable annual goals, including benchmarks or short-term objectives, related to meeting the child's needs that result from the child's disability to enable the child to be involved in and progress in the general curriculum, and meeting each of the child's other educational needs that result from the child's disability

- A statement of the special education and related services and supplementary aids and services to be provided to the child, or on behalf of the child, and any program modifications or support for school personnel necessary for the child to advance toward attaining the annual goals, to be involved and progress in the general education curriculum, and to participate in extracurricular and other nonacademic activities, and to be educated and participate with other children with and without disabilities in activities
- An explanation of the extent, if any, to which the child will not participate with children without disabilities in the regular class and in activities (Section 614, p. 84)

The makeup of the IEP team meeting must include the parents, a *general education teacher* (if the student is or may be participating in general education); a representative of the local education agency (LEA) who is knowledgeable about general curriculum and availability of resources in the LEA; the student, if he or she chooses to participate; an individual who can interpret the instructional implications of evaluation results; and other individuals at the discretion of parents or the agency. The mandate to include general education teachers in IEP meetings reinforces the need for students with disabilities to be included in classes available to the entire student population in secondary settings.

The IDEA Amendments of 1997 have far-reaching implications for including students with disabilities in regular education settings, for earlier transition planning, and for including students with disabilities in educational reform efforts that emphasize accountability and outcomes for all students. In addition, interagency planning is required during the IEP process. Vocational rehabilitation personnel are often involved in interagency planning as students make the transition from high school to work or adult service programs. The next section highlights the legislation, funding, and structure of rehabilitation programs.

Rehabilitation

The legislative history of vocational rehabilitation services for people with disabilities dates back to 1918 when the federal government sponsored rehabilitative services for veterans of World War I. Rehabilitation services initially served persons with physical disabilities with a goal of returning adults with disabilities to employment. Over the years, the scope of rehabilitation services has expanded to serve a diverse group of individuals with disabilities. Many students with disabilities will need time-limited services (e.g., counseling, vocational training, work adjustment services) through vocational rehabilitation after they exit the school system. Therefore, secondary educators need to understand the eligibility requirements for rehabilitation services and the types of available services. Secondary educators must also be familiar with the legal mandates in rehabilitation that provide the basis for reasonable accommodations in education and employment settings today.

The Vocational Rehabilitation Act of 1983 and 1973, PL 93-112. The Vocational Rehabilitation Act of 1973 was landmark legislation, for it included mandates calling for equal opportunity and nondiscrimination in workplace and education settings for individuals with disabilities. This Act required an Individualized Written Rehabilitation Plan (IWRP) to be developed for each person, which documented the long-range rehabilitation goals, the types of services to be provided, the dates for services, and the evaluation procedures (Shafer, 1988). It is interesting to note that this element of the mandate closely resembles its counterpart found in the EHA of 1975, the IEP.

Section 503. Section 503 of the Vocational Rehabilitation Act established not only federal policy but also federal leadership in the practices of hiring, training, advancing, and retaining qualified workers with disabilities. The provisions of Section 503 covered all governmental employment as well as any employer under contract to the federal government for more than $2,500. Every business or agency covered under this Act needed an affirmative action plan for all employment openings. Also, any government contractor holding a contract for $50,000 or greater, or who had at least 50 employees, needed an affirmative action plan.

Section 504. Section 504 of this Act had an impact on education and training opportunities for persons with disabilities. It included a statement that "no otherwise qualified handicapped individual in the United States, as defined by Section 7(6) shall, solely by the reason of his handicap, be excluded from the participation in, be denied the benefits of, or be subjected to discrimination under any program or activity receiving Federal financial assistance." This excerpt shows the intent of the law was to provide nondiscriminatory access to programs, services, and employment. As a result, secondary and postsecondary schools initiated and continue to offer an array of services that provide reasonable accommodations to students with disabilities. For example, Section 504 provides the legal basis for individuals with disabilities to access and receive accommodations or support services in secondary and postsecondary institutions (Brinckerhoff, Shaw, & McGuire, 1993). Although individuals with disabilities are not entitled to receive special education services in postsecondary settings, they are able to receive reasonable accommodations. For the past 20 years, many community colleges and universities have offered support services (reasonable accommodations) for students with disabilities to comply with Section 504.

In secondary settings, students with disabilities who are not eligible for special education but who have a disability pursuant to Section 504 of the Rehabilitation Act of 1973 also may receive services or accommodations. In some cases, these students have a Section 504 plan and are provided with accommodations as specified in the plan. The students most likely to receive services under Section 504 are those with attention deficit disorder, with visual or hearing impairments, or with physical disabilities. Examples of reasonable accommodations include untimed tests, enlarged print in books and assignments, note-takers, and interpreters.

The Rehabilitation Act Amendments of 1983 and 1986.   The Rehabilitation Act was amended in 1983 (PL 98-221) and in 1986 (PL 99-506). The Rehabilitation Act Amendments of 1986 were important in terms of providing funds for supported employment services to individuals with more severe disabilities. Supported employment was an opportunity for adults with disabilities to work in integrated settings, earn wages, and receive ongoing support in the employment community. This Act provided funds for personnel training, model demonstration programs, and systems change grants for states to convert sheltered workshops and day activity programs to supported employment programs. The implementation of supported employment programs in rehabilitation programs, along with a growing awareness that individuals with significant disabilities could work in the community, provided the foundation for many of the community-based secondary programs that serve students with more significant disabilities (ages 16 to 22) in high schools today.

The Rehabilitation Act Amendments of 1992, PL 102-569.   The Rehabilitation Act Amendments of 1992 have been hailed as a consumer empowerment bill. The purpose of this Act was "to empower individuals with disabilities to achieve economic self-sufficiency, independence, and inclusion and integration into society" (NISH, 1996, p. 5). In addition, the Rehabilitation Act mirrored the self-determination and inclusion movements in special education to actively involve individuals with disabilities in planning and implementing their educational, vocational, and transitional services in integrated environments. This Act also (1) created Consumer-majority Rehabilitation Advisory Councils, (2) mandated that IWRPs be jointly developed and signed by the rehabilitation counselor and the consumer, (3) strengthened the priority to serve individuals with severe disabilities, and (4) substituted the term *community rehabilitation program* (CRP) for *community-based rehabilitation facility* to reflect the movement to provide services to individuals with disabilities in the community.

The Rehabilitation Act Amendments of 1992 were significant for secondary students with disabilities for a number of other reasons. First, the definition of *transition services* duplicates the definition included in the IDEA of 1990 and mandated that "the State plan must assure that the IWRP for a student with a disability who is receiving special education services is coordinated with the individualized education programs (IEP) for that individual in terms of the goals, objectives, and services identified in the IEP" (Department of Education, 1997, pp. 6354–6355). This encourages greater collaboration between secondary special educators, rehabilitation personnel, and students with disabilities.

Second, there was a significant change in determining eligibility for rehabilitation services. Up to this point, most individuals were determined eligible for services when rehabilitation counselors examined psychological reports, vocational evaluation reports, and/or medical reports. This Act stated that existing assessment data—provided by the individual with a disability, the family, an advocate, or an educational agency—could be used for determining a person's eligibility for rehabilitation services. This meant that assessment data collected on a secondary student in work and community settings should be passed on to rehabilitation personnel if that student is referred to vocational rehabilitation. Therefore, it is important that secondary educators collect and compile assessment data that can be used to support a student's needs and goals for employment outcomes. The Final Regulations for PL 102-569 stated that assessment data may include counselor observations, education records, information provided by the individual or the individual's family, and information used by the Social Security Administration.

Many states have developed cooperative agreements between the departments of special education, rehabilitation, and vocational-technical education to facilitate a smooth transition of eligible students from school to rehabilitation programs. In fact, there has been evidence of collaborative partnerships between special education and rehabilitation programs since the 1960s (Kolstoe & Frey, 1965; Neubert, 1997). However, it is important for educators to understand that rehabilitation services are based on eligibility criteria. These criteria include a documented disability; the fact that the disability requires rehabilitation service to prepare for, enter into, or retain employment; and the presumption that the individual can benefit in terms of an employment or independent living outcome from rehabilitation services. It is also important for educators to understand that rehabilitation services are based on the availability of federal and state funds and must follow established "order of selection" policies. All educators need to be aware of their states' policies and procedures for order of selection. It is estimated that rehabilitation services are provided to only 7 percent of the 13.4 million potentially eligible people (NISH, 1996).

The Rehabilitation Act Amendments of 1998, Title IV of PL 105-220 (Workforce Investment Act of 1998). The Rehabilitation Act Amendments of 1998 are now included under legislation that links the state vocational rehabilitation system to the state work force investment system. The Rehabilitation Act Amendments, Title IV of the Workforce Investment Act of 1998, were signed into law on August 7, 1998. Although the final regulations on PL 105-220 have yet to be published (as of this writing), this law makes clear that employment and training programs for all individuals should be coordinated and administered through a state work force investment system. This is significant for individuals with disabilities who do not meet state order of selection criteria for rehabilitation services, since they will also be able to access other services and programs through their work force investment system.

Although the intended outcome of vocational rehabilitation services in the Rehabilitation Amendments of 1998 remains employment, the definition of *employment* is broad, including (1) full or part-time employment in the integrated labor market, (2) satisfying the vocational outcome of supported employment, and (3) satisfying any other vocational outcomes such as self-employment, telecommuting, or business ownership. Teachers who work with individuals with significant disabilities should also be aware of the term *presumption of benefit*. This term implies that all individuals can benefit from vocational rehabilitation services unless the state unit can demonstrate by clear and convincing evidence that an individual is incapable of benefiting in terms of an employment outcome due to the severity of the disability of the individual (Section 102).

The Rehabilitation Act Amendments of 1998 have a number of themes that are carried over from the Rehabilitation Act Amendments of 1992. First, the concept of *empowering* individuals with disabilities is strengthened and emphasizes the need for informed choice. Individuals with disabilities are to be involved in choosing assessment strategies, in determining training options, in designing individualized employment plans, and in determining independent living options. It should be noted that the term *Individualized Written Rehabilitation Plan (IWRP)* was changed to *Individualized Plan for Employment (IPE)* in the 1998 Rehabilitation Amendments. Second, the definition of *transition services* remains the same as the definition found in the Individuals with Disabilities Education Act of 1997. Finally, the need to use existing assessment data for determining eligibility and in planning the Individualized Plan for Employment is emphasized and expanded from the 1992 Rehabilitation Amendments. The term *assessment for determining eligibility and vocational rehabilitation needs* (Section 6: Definitions) means a review of existing data should be made to determine whether an individual is eligible for vocational rehabilitation services and to assign priority for an order of selection. This definition also highlights the need to collect information from the individual, family, and other programs. If additional assessment data are needed to determine eligibility, this law is specific in describing the types of assessment activities that can take place, including:

- An assessment of personality, interests, interpersonal skills, intelligence and related functional capacities, educational achievements, work experience, vocational aptitudes, personal and social adjustments, and employment opportunities of the individual.
- An assessment of the medical, psychiatric, psychological, and other vocational, educational, cultural, social, recreational, and environmental factors that affect the employment and rehabilitation needs of the individual.
- An appraisal of the patterns of work behavior of the individual and services needed to acquire occupational skills and to develop work attitudes, work habits, work tolerance, and social and behavior patterns for successful job performance. This can include work in real job situations.
- Referral for rehabilitation technology services to assess and develop the capacities of the individual to perform in a work environment.
- An exploration of the individual's abilities, capabilities, and capacity to perform in work situations, which are assessed periodically during trial work experiences (which can include training and support).

The Americans with Disabilities Act of 1990

The Americans with Disabilities Act (ADA), PL 101-336, provides broad civil rights protection to individuals with disabilities across education, employment, public services, public accommodations, transportation, and telecommunications.

The ADA extends Section 504 of the Rehabilitation Act of 1973 to the private sector in terms of access to and reasonable accommodations in employment, schools, and community facilities. Educators should be able to acquaint students and their parents with the ADA so they can access employment opportunities and community services. This responsibility can be met by altering curriculum content (e.g., teaching about the ADA and Section 504 in the social studies curriculum) and by providing parents with pertinent information at transition planning meetings. For example, Title I of ADA, Employment, extends the provisions of Section 504 by requiring both private (over 15 employees) and public employers to provide *reasonable accommodations* to qualified individuals with disabilities. Title I mandates that employers must only make reasonable accommodations if they are informed of the person's disability. For some students, this means that they must decide when to disclose a disability and how to describe their needs in terms of reasonable accommodations. For other students, teachers, parents, or advocates will have to assume the responsibility of informing employers about the need for reasonable accommodations. In addition, secondary teachers must work with students to identify their strengths, abilities, and needs in order to determine if they can perform the *essential functions of the job*. Essential functions of the job relate to the actual tasks that are required in specific jobs.

Title II of the ADA, Public Services, "provides for extension of Section 504 prohibitions against discrimination to all programs, activities, and services of state and local governments regardless of whether they receive federal financing" (Linthicum, Cole, & D'Alonzo, 1991, p. 2). Title II also includes provisions for making public transportation systems accessible. Title III, Public Accommodations, expands the scope of Section 504 to include businesses and community services that are used every day by most people (e.g., department stores, grocery stores, laundromats, parks, movie theaters, schools, public community agencies, theaters, hotels, and recreational facilities). Title IV includes telecommunications (voice and nonvoice systems), and Title V, Miscellaneous, contains provisions that individuals with disabilities do not have to accept offered accommodations, services, or benefits that they choose not to accept (Linthicum, Cole, & D'Alonzo, 1991). The ADA has far-reaching implications for employment and community living opportunities for people with disabilities. However, students with disabilities and their families need to be educated about how to advocate for their rights under ADA; otherwise, those rights will remain unfulfilled or denied.

Vocational-Technical Education

Federal support for vocational education has long recognized the need to prepare students to participate in the work force. The Smith-Hughes Act of 1917, PL 347, provided funding for public schools to develop secondary vocational education programs. Vocational education during this period focused on skill training in the areas of agriculture, trade and industry, and home economics (Scott & Sarkees-Wircenski, 1995). Since that time, vocational education legislation has targeted the need for diverse vocational programs and the need to include special populations in vocational programs. Students with disabilities have gained access to many vocational programs in the past two decades. The inclusion of vocational-technical education programming as an option in the transition planning process can ensure students with disabilities opportunities to prepare themselves to enter the work force in many areas.

The Vocational Education Act of 1963 and the 1968 Amendments.   Congress passed the Vocational Education Act, PL 88-210, in 1963, broadening the definition of *vocational education* to provide funding for business education and cooperative work-study programs. In addition, this Act provided support for students with special needs (which included students with disabilities and disadvantages) to participate in vocational education programs and related services (Cobb & Neubert, 1998).

The Vocational Education Amendments of 1968, PL 90-576, continued to broaden the range of vocational programs offered to students in secondary and postsecondary settings and to emphasize the need for improved access for all students to vocational opportunities. PL 90-576 was important because it introduced the practice of providing set-aside funding for special populations in vocational education. This funding included 10 percent of all the state grant vocational education funds designated for supporting programs for youths with disabilities and 15 percent to support programs for youths with disadvantages. The 1968 Amendments required each state to have an advisory committee made up of parents, business personnel, special educators, teachers, higher education leaders, and vocational educators to monitor state plans and practices for compliance with the provisions of the Act. This practice contributed to the development of vocational programs and services to serve individuals with disabilities. Although it took some states as many as five years to develop programs within their states, others used the full set-aside allotments immediately for vocational evaluation services and, in some cases, separate vocational programs for individuals with disabilities.

The Education Amendments of 1976, PL 94-482.   Students with disabilities were generally underrepresented in vocational education programs during the 1970s. For example, in 1971, only 2.1 percent of students enrolled in vocational education had disabilities and 70 percent of these students were placed in separate classes (Hagerty, Halloran, & Taymans, 1981). The Education Amendments of 1976, PL 94-482 (which included amendments to the Vocational Education Act), increased the funding for these students in vocational programs. These amendments required the 10 percent set-aside funds for students with disabilities to be matched with state and local funds. In addition, the set-aside funding for students with disadvantages was increased to 20 percent.

The purpose of this Act was to improve and expand vocational education programs, to overcome sex discrimination and sex stereotyping, and to improve the accountability of vocational education with the development of the Vocational Education Data System (Nystrom & Bayne, 1979). PL 94-482 mandated that vocational education programs be coordinated with other federal vocational and education programs. These amendments, together with the EHA of 1975 and the Rehabilitation Act of 1973, served as cornerstone legislation for providing interdisciplinary services such as assessment, training, and employment activities to students with disabilities in vocational education programs (Neubert, 1997).

The Carl D. Perkins Vocational Education Act of 1984, PL 98-524. Conway (1984) reported that the number of students with disabilities in vocational education programs increased 95 percent between 1976 and 1982. The Perkins Act of 1984 continued to focus on the need to serve students who had traditionally been underrepresented in vocational programs. Dominant themes in this Act related to equal access of all programs and to services that would assist individuals with special needs in entering and/or succeeding in vocational programs. The following provisions applied to students with special needs under Title II of this Act:

1. Of the funds allocated to states for vocational education, 57 percent had to be spent on supplemental programs and services for special groups. These groups included individuals with disabilities (10 percent), individuals with disadvantages (22 percent), adults in need of training or retraining (12 percent), single parents and displaced homemakers (8.5 percent), individuals in training for nontraditional occupations based on their sex (3.5 percent), and persons in correctional institutions (1 percent).
2. Annual federal appropriations to states for students with special needs had to be matched equally by state and local funding. These appropriations were designated to support the costs of special supplemental services or modified programs for such students (e.g., vocational support services to assist students in succeeding in vocational programs). Other changes in the funding formula of the 1984 Perkins Act helped eliminate many of the separate vocational education programs and facilities for students with disabilities, resulting in increased mainstreaming.
3. Section 204 of Title II contained assurances that individuals with disabilities be offered equal access to a full range of vocational education programs, including recruitment, enrollment, and placement activities. Local schools had to provide students with special needs supplemental services, which included (a) an assessment of interests, abilities, and special needs with respect to successfully completing the program; (b) special instructional services such as adaptations of curricula, instruction, equipment, and facilities; (c) guidance, counseling, and career development activities; and (d) counseling services to facilitate the transition from school to postschool employment and career opportunities. In addition, parents and guardians were to be informed of available options in vocational education programs prior to students entering the ninth grade. Finally, programs and services had to be coordinated for students with IEPs in the spirit of the least restrictive environment provisions in PL 94-142.

The Perkins Act of 1984 also began the process of redirecting states to improve and expand their programs to train workers in occupations needed by the existing and future work force (Cobb & Neubert, 1998). This Act also required that the outcomes of vocational education for all students be reported to Congress through the National Assessment of Vocational Education (NAVE). The NAVE reports provide data about all students' participation and access to vocational education programs.

The Carl D. Perkins Vocational and Applied Technology Education Act Amendments of 1990, PL 101-392.   While the Carl D. Perkins Vocational and Applied Technology Education Act Amendments of 1990, PL 101-392, continued the themes of improving the quality of vocational education and providing supplemental services to special populations (Boesel & McFarland, 1994), significant changes occurred in the funding patterns. The use of set-aside funding for special populations was eliminated, but strong language remained in the Act that all students were to have access to vocational education programs. Although many feared that the removal of set-aside funding would negatively affect students with disabilities, the NAVE report (Boesel, Hudson, Deich, & Masten, 1994) documented that students with disabilities took more vocational credits than other students. However, they were predominantly enrolled in agriculture, home economics, and trades occupations. Other research also documented that special populations tended to be grouped in certain vocational programs (e.g., Lombard, Hazelkorn, & Neubert, 1992; Adami & Neubert, 1991). Therefore, the mandate for equal access to all programs and services remains a challenge to students with disabilities in secondary vocational education.

Equal Access Assurances.   Although the set-aside funds were eliminated, assurances for equal access and the provision of supplemental services were strengthened throughout the Act. Title II, Section 118, contained provisions similar to the 1984 Perkins Act, calling for assessment activities, supplemental instructional services, career-development activities, and counseling to facilitate the transition from school to postschool employment and career opportunities. Section 118 also mandated that states and locals "assist students who are members of special populations to enter vocational education programs, and with respect to students with disabilities, assist in fulfilling the transition requirement of Section 626 of the IDEA."

The NAVE report (Boesel, Hudson, Deich, & Masten, 1994) also provided documentation that 97 percent of students earned some credits (e.g., a business course or technology education course) in vocational education during high school. However, only 25 percent of students took a sequence of vocational courses for training in a specific area (e.g., cosmetology).

Changes in the Structure of Vocational-Technical Programs.   The 1990 Amendments emphasized educational reform efforts and greater linkages with academic course content, which is evident in many high schools today. An example of these reform efforts is Tech-Prep programs, which are articulated programs between a vocational content area in high school and the community college. (Tech Prep is also known as 2 + 2 or 2 + 4 programs.) Other examples of reform included increased work experience components and the integration of academic and vocational instruction in vocational-technical programs. The 1990 Amendments, in concert with the School-to-Work Opportunities Act of 1994, also provided the impetus for other vocational models currently found in high schools, such as career academies, technical magnet high schools, and youth apprenticeship programs. In addition, PL 101-392 mandated greater local accountability by stating that schools must evaluate the effectiveness of vocational-technical education programs each year according to statewide measures and standards of performance.

The 1990 Perkins Amendments brought about significant changes in terms of the structure and upgrading of many vocational education programs. Special educators must continue to advocate for the inclusion of students with disabilities in a range of vocational education programs. Work force programs provide students with another opportunity to gain work experience and/or vocational training.

The Carl D. Perkins Vocational and Applied Technology Education Act Amendments of 1998, PL 105-332.   The Carl D. Perkins Vocational and Applied Technology Education Act Amendments of 1998, PL 105-332 (Perkins Amendments of 1998), were signed into law on October 31, 1998. Over the past few years, there has been considerable discussion and debate in determining if vocational-technical education should remain separate legislation or if it should be part of the work force investment legislation. Although this legislation is separate from the Workforce Investment Act, the Perkins Amendments of 1998 have been shortened considerably from the 1990 Perkins Amendments. The purpose of PL 105-332 is to develop the academic, vocational, and technical skills of secondary and postsecondary students who elect to enroll in vocational technical education by doing the following:

- Building on the efforts of states and localities to develop challenging academic standards;
- Promoting the development of services and activities that integrate academic, vocational and technical instruction and link secondary and postsecondary education;
- Increasing State and local flexibility to provide services and activities designed to develop, implement, and improve vocational and technical education, including tech-prep education; and
- Disseminating national research and providing professional development and technical assistance that will improve vocational and technical education programs, services, and activities. (American Vocational Association, 1998)

The term *special populations* remains in the definition section of the Perkins Amendments of 1998, and includes individuals with disabilities, individuals from economically disadvantaged families, individuals preparing for nontraditional training and employment, single parents, displaced homemakers, and individuals with other barriers to educational achievement, including individuals with limited

English proficiency. Individuals with academic disadvantages and individuals in correctional facilities are no longer included in this definition (Brustein, 1998). Mention of special populations is also found in the provisions for state and local plans (and uses of funds). To receive federal funding, each state must develop, submit, and implement services outlined in the state plan. In terms of special populations, the contents of the state plan (Section 122) are to include a description of the eligible agency's program strategies for special populations and a description of how individuals who are members of special populations will (1) be provided equal access to activities (2) not be discriminated against on the basis of their status as members of special populations and (3) be provided with programs designed to meet or exceed the state's levels of performance, prepare for further learning, and prepare for high-skill, high-wage careers.

Local recipients of federal funds must also submit a plan that includes a description of (1) how individuals with special needs will not be discriminated against on the basis of their status as members of special populations and (2) how parents, students, teachers, representatives of business and industry, labor organizations, representatives of special populations, and other interested individuals are involved in the development, implementation, and evaluation of vocational and technical education programs and how these individuals are informed about and assisted in understanding these requirements. As with other recently enacted legislation, PL 105-332 requires state and local educators and administrators to be held more accountable for the outcomes of vocational-technical education and establishes a state performance accountability system that is similar to the system in the Workforce Investment Act (Brustein, 1998).

Finally, Tech-Prep Education (Title II) continues to receive emphasis and dollars in the Perkins Amendments of 1998. It will be important for secondary educators to keep abreast of how their states are providing and coordinating (if applicable) vocational-technical education and work force investment programs.

Work Force Training

Work force training programs have a long history in providing training and employment opportunities to individuals with economic disadvantages. Individuals with disabilities are often eligible for these programs. The following legislation is discussed in terms of the services and programs provided under work force training and how secondary students with disabilities might benefit from these programs.

The Comprehensive Employment and Training Act of 1973 and the 1978 Amendments.   In December 1973, PL 93-203, the Comprehensive Employment and Training Act (CETA) was passed to aid people with economic disadvantages to gain access to job training and employment opportunities. This Act was amended with PL 95-524, the 1978 CETA Amendments, and included individuals with disabilities.

CETA programs were required to establish cooperative links with other agencies providing training and employment opportunities. As a result, many special educators referred students to CETA programs for further training after they exited the schools or to gain work experience through the summer youth employment programs during the high school years. CETA programs received intense criticism for their faulty administrative procedures and for training programs that were unresponsive to local employment needs. This, in concert with comprehensive career education practices in the late 1970s, led to improvements in employment training, which were recognized by Congress when the CETA program was replaced in the 1980s.

The Job Training Partnership Act, PL 97-300.   The Job Training Partnership Act (JTPA), PL 97-300, was passed in 1982 to replace CETA and to improve the role of business and industry in training youths and adults with disadvantages. The purpose of the JTPA (Section 2) was to establish programs to prepare youths and unskilled adults for entry into the labor force by providing job training to individuals with economic disadvantages and other individuals facing barriers to employment. Each state was required to identify designated service delivery areas (SDAs) where JTPA programs would be established and administered by local Private Industry Councils (PICs). Representatives on the PICs included employers and education personnel. Training for employment reflected the local job market and funds were used to provide a variety of services including Adult Programs and Summer Youth Employment and Training Programs. Typical services in these programs included job search, remedial and basic education, work experiences, vocational exploration, and literacy training. Part B of this Act also reauthorized the Job Corps, which still operates today. Job Corps programs include residential and nonresidential centers in which individuals participate in programs of education, vocational training, work experience, and counseling. The purpose of Job Corps is to assist young individuals by providing intensive programs in group settings and to contribute to the needs of local and national work forces.

Although JTPA programs were designed to serve individuals with economic disadvantages, individuals with disabilities could qualify for JTPA if their income met either of the following two criteria: (1) received or was a member of a family that received cash welfare payments or (2) was a member of a family that had received a total family income for the six-month period prior to application for the program that was at the poverty level.

The Job Training Partnership Act Amendments of 1986 and Reform Amendments of 1992.   JTPA was amended with the Job Training Partnership Act Amendments of 1986 (PL 99-496) and the Job Training Reform Amendments of 1992 (PL 102-367). The most recent amendments, PL 102-367, modified the previous JTPA acts with a purpose of

> establishing programs to prepare youth and adults facing serious barriers to employment for participating in the labor force by providing job training and other services that will result in increased employment and earnings, increased educational and occupational skills, and decreased welfare dependency, thereby improving the quality of the workforce and enhancing the productivity and competitiveness of the Nation. (Section 2, p. 1023)

The 1992 Amendments continued to fund Adult Programs and Summer Youth Employment Programs while expanding services for students in secondary settings with the addition of Title II-C Year-Round Youth Training Programs. These programs serve in-school youths, 16 to 21 years old (students as young as age 14 or 15 may participate if it is stated on their job training plan), who have economic disadvantages, participate in compensatory education programs under Chapter 1, or are eligible for free meals under the School Lunch Act. This program also targets youths with economic disadvantages who are out of school and in need of remedial education and job training. The final rules for PL 99-496 expanded opportunities for youths and adults with disabilities to participate in JTPA programs by modifying other eligibility requirements. For example, people who received Supplemental Security Income (SSI) no longer could have SSI counted as income when eligibility was determined, and individuals with disabilities could be considered as a "family of one" (the entire family's income is not taken into account) for the purposes of determining eligibility (National Transition Network, 1993).

Under PL 102-367, SDAs must establish links with educational agencies, including formal agreements to identify procedures for referring and serving in-school youths. Many secondary special education students continue to benefit from JTPA through Summer Youth Employment and Training Programs (for students ages 14 to 21), which can include remedial education, work experience, occupational training, and employment counseling. School systems also use JTPA funds to run Year-Round Youth Training Programs for students who are at risk of dropping out and need remedial education and work experience. People who participate in JTPA programs must have an individualized plan, which may include an assessment of basic skills, a list of supportive service needs (e.g., child care), and a review of work experiences, interests, and aptitudes. This provides another opportunity for special educators to share assessment data that they have collected in school and the community with personnel from an outside agency. Finally, JTPA is an appropriate postsecondary option for some students with disadvantages and/or disabilities who need further job training through the Adult Programs or Job Corps.

The Workforce Investment Act of 1998, PL 105-220.   The purpose of PL 105-220 is to consolidate, coordinate, and improve employment, training, literacy, and vocational rehabilitation programs in the United States. This act will consolidate and coordinate many of the employment and training programs (such as the Job Training Partnership Act) through a one-stop delivery system. The intent of this consolidation is to improve employment and training programs for all individuals, including those with disabilities, and to assist the consumer in identifying a range of work force options through a one-stop delivery system. This act contains five titles:

- Title I: Workforce Investment Systems
- Title II: Adult Education and Literacy

- Title III: Workforce Investment-Related Activities
- Title IV: Rehabilitation Act Amendments of 1998
- Title V: General Provisions

Title I contains provisions on how to develop and implement state and local work force investment boards, how one-stop delivery systems are to be established, and how eligible providers of training and youth activities will be identified. Other provisions in Title I include Job Corps (Subtitle C) and national programs (such as Native American, migrant programs, and veterans' work force systems). Although the final regulations have yet to be published for PL 105-220 (as of this writing), it will be important for secondary educators to learn how their states are complying with the mandates in the Workforce Investment Act of 1998. In terms of transition planning, students with disabilities and their families should find it easier to access information on a range of employment and training opportunities through a one-stop delivery system.

Educational Reform Legislation

Recent legislation has targeted the need for state and local school systems to develop high standards for all students and for schools to be held accountable if students cannot meet these standards. Standards identify the content all students need to know to live and work in the twenty-first century. An example of how educational reform focuses on the development of high standards was evident in President Clinton's State of the Union Address on February 4, 1997. He recommended that every student in fourth grade be tested in reading and every eighth-grade student be tested in math. The content for the reading and math tests will be based on the content frameworks developed for the National Assessment of Education Progress. The U.S. Department of Education will make the tests available to state and local education agencies as voluntary tests, and states that "these rigorous tests will provide scores for individual students, measured against widely accepted standards of excellence—national and international standards—that show if students have mastered critical basic skills" (U.S. Department of Education, 1997, p. 1).

A number of federal mandates have had an impact on educational reform. Three legislative acts will be reviewed here highlighting issues for secondary educators: Goals 2000, The School-to-Work Opportunities Act, and Improving America's School Act.

Goals 2000, PL 103-227.   Goals 2000: Educate America Act of 1994, PL 103-227, set eight national goals to improve schools: (1) school readiness; (2) school completion; (3) student achievement and citizenship; (4) teacher education and professional development; (5) mathematics and science; (6) adult literacy and lifelong learning; (7) safe, disciplined, alcohol- and drug-free schools; and (8) parental participation. Specific objectives were included for each goal. Goal 2 called for the high school graduation rate to increase to 90 percent by the year 2000, meaning a significant reduction would be needed in the number of students who drop out of school. Dropout rates for students with disabilities have been estimated to be about 32 percent (Wagner, 1991).

Under Title II of this Act, the National Education Goals Panel was created to report on schools' progress toward achieving national education goals. Title III of this Act established a five-year grant program for the improvement of state and local education systems. Section 306 mandated that state improvement plans include strategies for improving teaching and learning (including standards for content, student performance, and opportunity to learn) and strategies for coordinating school-to-work programs along with the integration of academic and vocational instruction. Finally, Title V of PL 103-227, the National Skill Standards Act of 1994, established a National Skill Standards Board. This board is made up of personnel from business and industry as well as educational institutions. Its task is to identify clusters of major occupations and then develop skill standards, assessment and certification systems, and information dissemination systems. In the future, this may have implications for how secondary students are prepared for the work force.

The School-to-Work Opportunities Act of 1994, PL 103-239.   The School-to-Work Opportunities Act of 1994 (STWOA) was passed by the Clinton administration to establish a national framework for states to create school-to-work systems. The overall purpose of the STWOA "is to prepare students for work and further education, and increase their opportunities to enter first jobs in high-skill, high-wage careers" (Benz & Lindstrom, 1997, p. 5). This Act, in conjunction with Goals 2000, provided the impetus for educational reform, which is based on performance goals for schools and outcome measures for students.

The STWOA is administered by the Departments of Education and Labor at the federal level. The Act provides monies for planning and implementation grants to states to establish school-to-work systems. These school-to-work systems are to build on existing promising practices such as tech-prep education, career academies, school-to-apprenticeship programs, and other work-based learning opportunities (Cobb & Neubert, 1998). It is likely that local school systems in all states have reorganized their vocational programs if they have received STWOA monies. For example, some schools have reorganized their vocational offerings around career themes (e.g., health occupations, communications, technology), with an emphasis on integrating vocational and academic instruction. The STWOA addresses the need for *all* students to have access to school-to-work programs and specifically mentions that individuals with disabilities be included in these reform efforts.

Although states have flexibility in designing their models, the STWOA requires that programs include three components: school-based, work-based, and connecting activities. School-based learning activities target career awareness, exploration, and counseling to assist students in selecting career majors. Students must be evaluated on a regularly scheduled basis to identify their strengths, needs, academic progress, and work place knowledge. Work-based learning activities include job shadowing, on-the-job training, and work experience. Connecting activities include matching students with employers and linking students to community services. It is interesting to note that practices such as job shadowing, career awareness, and work experience have been included in many secondary special education programs for the past 30 years. The STWOA provides secondary special education teachers an opportunity to work with regular and vocational-technical educators regarding school-to-work programs. It also provides students with disabilities a chance to gain academic and vocational skills that will allow them to obtain advanced level jobs. It is important that students with disabilities be offered the opportunity to access and to succeed in these programs with adequate support and reasonable accommodations.

Improving America's Schools Act of 1994, PL 103-382.   A final legislative mandate that deserves consideration is Improving America's Schools Act of 1994, PL 103-382. Title I amends the Elementary and Secondary Education Act of 1965, which focused on educational opportunities for students with disadvantages. This Act continues to emphasize the development of standards and provides funds for school improvement activities. For example, Improving America's Schools Act establishes Title I programs for helping children who are disadvantaged to meet high standards. The Act also authorizes appropriations for prevention and intervention programs for youths who are neglected, delinquent, or at risk of dropping out of school. States who receive monies under this Act must submit state plans that describe how efforts are coordinated with Goals 2000 activities. Sarkees-Wircenski and Scott (1995) detailed how other activities such as vocational-technical education, school-to-work, cooperative education, and apprenticeship programs must also be coordinated with efforts under Improving America's Schools Act of 1994.

Understanding High School Requirements

Legislative mandates and educational reform efforts have resulted in many changes in high school graduation requirements, including the number of academic courses required, the length of school days, minimum gradepoint averages, and high school exit exams. Educational reform has been a topic of continuing discussion, with a primary goal of ensuring that U.S. schools prepare students for the work force of the future. Secondary teachers working with students with disabilities and their families need to understand how educational reform efforts have already had an impact on requirements for graduation in a number of states and how current reform trends affect transition planning.

Minimum Competency Testing and Statewide Assessment Systems

Significant changes occurred in high schools in the 1980s regarding academic requirements and minimum competency testing as a result of educational reform efforts. In 1983, the National Commission on Excellence in Education issued the landmark report *A Nation at Risk,* which recommended an increase in the number of Carnegie units needed for graduation. This included four credits in English, three credits in math, three credits in science, three credits in social science, and half a credit in computers. Although only eight states follow these recommendations exactly (Thurlow, Ysseldyke, & Anderson, 1995), most states have steadily increased the number of credits required for graduation since this time.

During the 1980s, a number of states also began to institute minimum competency testing (MCT) as a requirement for graduation. MCT varies greatly, from a reading test to a set of tests required for graduation. Thurlow and colleagues (1995) reported that 17 states have requirements for minimum competency tests. Under PL 94-142 and Section 504 of the Rehabilitation Act, schools are obligated to provide reasonable accommodations for students with disabilities taking these tests. In certain cases, students are exempted from taking the tests. Some states have instituted alternative or modified diplomas for students who are unable to earn the Carnegie units required for graduation or pass minimum competency tests. This practice has led to some debate regarding whether it is legal to provide students with alternative diplomas or certificates (Kortering, Julnes, & Edgar, 1990).

Many states have also implemented other statewide assessment programs in the 1990s. In the case of statewide assessment systems, both traditional assessments (paper and pencil with a focus on students' achievement) and alternative assessments (performance assessments and portfolios) have been included. Some schools have been reluctant to include students with disabilities in these assessments due to "the existence of high stakes accountability systems that compare the performance of schools and districts, and often make awards or sanctions based on these results" (Erickson, Thurlow, & Ysseldyke, 1996). The National Center on Educational Outcomes has tracked participation rates of students with disabilities in statewide testing since 1991. It reports that participation of students with disabilities varies from state to state and that it is difficult to calculate the actual number of students with disabilities who are included in statewide testing. This situation should change within the next several years, since the IDEA Amendments of 1997 include specific mandates regarding accountability and standards. Students with disabilities must now be included in state- and districtwide assessment programs by 2000 (Mandlawitz, 1997). Under Section 614 of the IDEA Amendments, students' IEPs must include a statement of any accommodations needed to participate in state or district assessment programs. If the IEP team determines that a student will not participate in a particular assessment of student achievement, the team must include a statement that describes why the assessment is not appropriate and how the student will be assessed. State or local education agencies will be responsible for developing guidelines for individuals with disabilities who will participate in alternative assessments by July 2000.

Class Credit Requirements

Thurlow and associates (1995) found that 44 states use Carnegie course unit requirements, ranging from 10.25 credits to 24 credits for graduation requirements.

The average number of credits required for graduation is three to four credits of English, two to three credits of math, two to three credits of social science, and two credits of science. In addition, most states require one to two credits in physical education, art, or health education. Students generally are able to select electives (ranging from two to nine credits) during the high school years. Finally, some states require foreign language or vocational-technical education credits during the secondary years.

Diplomas versus Alternative Exit Documents

As a result of minimum competency testing and increased academic credits required for graduation, some states and local education agencies have developed alternatives to the standard diploma. Thurlow and colleagues (1995) found enormous variation in the exit documents that are awarded to students with disabilities. Through a survey of 50 state departments of education, they reported the following:

- Standard diplomas are awarded in 19 states.
- Standard diplomas or certificates are awarded in 17 states.
- Standard diplomas or modified diplomas are awarded in 10 states.
- Standard diplomas, modified diplomas, or certificates are awarded in 4 states.

Although all states have standard diplomas as an option for students with disabilities, the requirements for obtaining such a diploma vary from the credits a student needs to earn, to completion of the IEP, to passing minimum competency tests. Students with significant disabilities are more likely to be awarded modified diplomas or certificates of attendance because they are often exempt from MCT or other statewide assessments. At this time, it is unclear what the impact of obtaining a modified diploma or certificate of attendance has on employment outcomes or on students' motivation during the secondary years (DeStefano & Metzer, 1991).

Concerns have been raised for some students with mild disabilities that increasing graduation requirements may act as a deterrent to finishing high school. Others have questioned the appropriateness of students spending the majority of time earning academic credits and passing minimum competency tests in lieu of participating in vocational training and functional skill instruction. Therefore, all middle and high school teachers must be familiar with the requirements for a diploma in their states so they can advise students with disabilities and their families on the various diploma options during transition planning, beginning no later than age 14 or the eighth grade, whichever comes first.

Curricula Options

In addition to increased credits required for graduation and differential diplomas, students with disabilities and their families are also faced with choosing curricula options during the secondary years. In the past, secondary students generally had three options: college preparatory, general education, or vocational-technical education. In recent years, many state and local school systems have reorganized their curricula options around a college preparatory option and a vocational-technical education option due to educational reform initiatives. Some have opted to delete the general education track in hopes of preparing non-college-bound youths for better jobs and postsecondary training opportunities through restructured vocational programs. Some states are considering offering a vocational or occupational diploma. Students with more significant disabilities often participate in community-based training programs with an emphasis on functional skills and work experience during the secondary years.

Although there is some degree of overlap among the college preparatory and vocational-technical curricula due to common graduation requirements, some differences in the purpose, course requirements, and anticipated outcomes merit discussion.

College Preparatory Option.   The college preparatory track provides a broad foundation of courses in English, math, science, social studies, and foreign language. The outcome for students in this track is obviously to continue in postsecondary education after graduating from high school. Students may take electives in vocational-technical education, although this is not the focus of their studies. College preparatory programs generally impose more rigorous standards in both content difficulty and level of performance expectations. Some schools also provide advanced placement courses in academic areas, allowing students to earn college credit in some courses. The rigorous academic content classes in concert with state requirements for minimum competency or performance assessments makes this curricula option difficult for some students with disabilities. Careful planning at the IEP meetings is required with the student, family, teachers, and guidance counselors to determine if this option is best suited for the student. In addition, a student's interests, preferences, and needs should be considered in terms of the type of postsecondary institution the student expects to enter after high school (e.g., community college, university) and the type of major the student is interested in pursuing. Not only are these considerations desirable for good planning but they are also necessary to comply with the transition requirements in the IDEA Amendments of 1997. A criticism of the college preparatory option for some students with disabilities is the lack of vocational or work experiences and functional skill instruction.

Vocational-Technical Education Option.   Students who opt for the vocational-technical education curricula option must still meet state and local graduation requirements. Some schools integrate academic requirements such as English and math with the vocational-technical education curriculum. For example, math may emphasize business and consumer economics or skills needed in carpentry. Vocational-technical education programs are often organized around specific occupational areas, including agricultural education, business and office education, health occupations education, home economics or consumer sciences education, marketing and distributive education, trades and industrial education, and technical/communication (Sarkees-Wircenski & Scott, 1995). In addition, out-of-school work experience programs are generally delivered under Cooperative Work Education (CWE). Students in CWE programs are supervised by a work experience teacher in an employment setting for half a day and spend the other time in school earning their academic credits. An obvious strength of this curriculum is the combination of studying about a job and the opportunity to experience an actual job situation under the guidance of school personnel and an employer. CWE has been criticized because many students are placed in entry-level positions with few plans for job advancement or change in their young adult years.

As discussed earlier, vocational-technical programs are changing in structure due to the educational reform efforts mandated in the School-to-Work Opportunities Act of 1994 and the 1990 Perkins Act. Teachers from various states will encounter an array of options in state and local vocational programs, such as Tech-Prep programs, career academies, youth apprenticeships, and school-based enterprises (Cobb & Neubert, 1998). A brief description of these programs follows.

Tech-Prep programs generally require two years of secondary school in a vocational area followed by two (or four) years of higher education. These programs (e.g., nursing, drafting, etc.) often provide competency-based training and bridge the gap between secondary and postsecondary opportunities. Tech-Prep programs have expanded in secondary schools; nearly half of all secondary districts surveyed in the NAVE study had tech-prep programs (Boesel, Hudson, Deich, & Masten, 1994).

A *career academy* is best characterized as "a school within a school," which focuses on a career theme (e.g., communications, medical services, etc.) and integrates technical and academic curricula. Career academies offer students a chance to concentrate in an occupational area while earning academic credits. This option can offer students an avenue to leave school with increased academic and vocational skills and enter jobs that are beyond entry-level positions.

Youth apprenticeships generally prepare students for skilled jobs in areas such as carpentry, plumbing, and other trade areas. Apprenticeship programs are usually operated by union or trade associations, but a number of recent youth apprenticeship programs have been funded by the Department of Labor. Students generally take courses that integrate academic and vocational instruction and spend a certain number of hours in related employment settings. In the past, few students with disabilities have participated in apprenticeship programs (Smith & Rowjeski, 1993). It is hoped that youth apprenticeship programs will offer some students with disabilities a chance to participate in programs that offer advanced skill training.

In *school-based enterprises* programs, students produce goods or services for sale. Examples include school restaurants, construction projects, child-care centers, and auto shops. These programs provide students with work experience in supervised school settings. This may be an appropriate option for students who need more intensive training from school personnel or for students who need exposure to work behaviors and options before entering the job market.

In summary, the vocational-technical education curricula option is changing with an increased emphasis on work-based learning and integration of academic and technical skills. It is important to understand the requirements of these programs, to assess which students with disabilities have the interest and ability to benefit from these vocational opportunities, and to provide appropriate, reasonable accommodations to students with disabilities who enter these programs.

Recommended Practices in Secondary Special Education and Transition Programs

Legislative mandates have clearly laid the foundation for students with disabilities to access diverse career, educational, vocational, and transition programs. During the past 10 or so years, researchers have tried to identify what constitutes effective and validated practices in these programs in secondary settings.

Quality Indicators of Secondary Programs

Halpern (1988, 1990) established and validated a set of indicators of program quality for secondary special education. These indicators were generated from the literature in the field and a systematic statewide evaluation of secondary special education programs in Oregon. The literature in the field of secondary special education and transition programs over the years had identified four basic domains of instruction: academic, vocational, independent living, and social/interpersonal knowledge and skills. These student outcome indicators and related program characteristics indicators were validated in a study in Oregon (Halpern & Benz, 1987) and in an independent external study by Darrow (1990). Halpern and others refined the set of indicators to address six major categories of standards: curriculum and instruction, coordination and mainstreaming, transition, program documentation, administrative support, and adult services. The indicators that are relevant to and the responsibility of schools are shown in Figure 3.2.

Several states (Oregon, Washington, Nevada, Arizona, and Kansas) have endorsed Halpern's indicators and standards for the development of a system for follow-along transition programs in their states' secondary special education programs and transition programs. The set of indicators and standards is accompanied by a system of assessment and data collection that makes the approach highly useful for program planning, program implementation, program evaluation, and, ultimately, program accreditation (particularly outcome-based accreditation).

Recommended Practices in Transition

A number of recommended practices in transition have been identified through other survey research or literature reviews (e.g., Banks & Renzaglia, 1993; Kohler, 1993; Kohler, DeStefano, Wermuth, Grayson, & McGinty, 1994). Examples of these practices include the following:

FIGURE 3.2 Quality Indicators of Secondary Programs

Curriculum and Instruction
- Students with disabilities receive appropriate remedial academic instruction, which prepares them for functioning in their community, including the possibility of post-secondary education.
- Students with disabilities receive appropriate vocational instruction, which prepares them for jobs in their community.
- Students with disabilities receive appropriate instruction in independent living, which prepares them for functioning independently in their community.
- Students with disabilities receive appropriate instruction in social/interpersonal skills, which prepares them for interacting effectively with people in their community.
- Students with disabilities receive appropriate instruction in leisure and recreation skills, which prepares them for leisure opportunities within their community.
- Community-based instruction is available as one option within the special education program offerings.
- Instructional procedures for students with disabilities are designed to ensure that students can perform skills they have learned in new settings (generalization) and that they remember how to use their skills over time (maintenance).
- Appropriate curriculum materials are available for providing instruction to students with disabilities.
- Procedures exist for placing students with disabilities into an instructional program that is tailored to their individual needs.

Coordination and Mainstreaming
- Specific programs exist for facilitating the social integration of all students with disabilities.
- Students with disabilities have opportunities to learn prerequisite skills that are needed to participate in general education academic programs.
- Students with disabilities have opportunities to learn prerequisite skills that are needed to participate in vocational-technical education programs.
- Teachers of general education academic courses are provided with assistance in adapting their instruction in order to meet the needs of students with disabilities.
- Teachers of vocational-technical education courses are provided with assistance in adapting their instruction in order to meet the needs of students with disabilities.
- A process exists for enhancing program planning and administrative collaboration between special education and general education academic programs.
- A process exists for enhancing program planning and administrative collaboration between special education and vocational-technical education programs.

Transition
- Information on community services is available for students with disabilities as they exit the school system.
- Transition goals are addressed as part of the planning process for students with disabilities.
- A process exists for enhancing collaboration between special education and relevant adult agencies in order to facilitate successful transitions of students.
- Procedures exist for securing parents' involvement in the transition process.

- Vocational training
- Parent involvement
- Interagency collaboration
- Social skills training
- Paid work experience
- Follow-up employment services
- Integrated settings
- Community-based instruction
- Vocational assessment
- Community-referenced curricula
- Career education curricula and experience
- Employability skills training
- Academic skills training

Although these practices have been associated with better outcomes for students after they exit school, there has been sharp criticism for the gap between what the literature identifies as "best" or recommended practices and what researchers have actually documented as effective practices (e.g., Greene & Albright, 1995; Kohler, 1993). Hughes and colleagues (1997) extended the knowledge base of recommended practices by validating practices in transition through teachers in Tennessee. They surveyed teachers to determine if they accepted empirically derived strategies that support the transition from school to adult life. The eight secondary transition support strategies that they socially validated are as follows:

- Identify and provide social support.
- Identify environmental support and provide environmental changes.
- Promote acceptance.
- Observe the student's opportunities for choice.
- Provide choice-making opportunities.
- Identify the student's strengths and areas needing support.
- Teach self-management.
- Provide opportunities to learn and practice social skills.

In addition, teachers were asked to list strategies they used under these eight practices, which resulted in a list of 592 identified procedures. These recommended, socially validated practices can assist special educators in forming or improving their secondary programs. A number of other researchers have identified quality indicators of transition practices (Sale, Everson, & Moon, 1991). This research has also contributed to the development of program guidelines for students with disabilities in many secondary settings. Although few exemplary programs exist that use all of the quality indicators or recommended practices that we can affirm as effective, there is no reason for any secondary special education teacher or transition specialist to be working without direction or focus.

Conclusion

Legislation, educational reform efforts, and research on recommended practices will continue to affect secondary education programs for all students. The emphasis on standards, outcomes, and accountability are likely to remain key issues in education as we enter the twenty-first century. Clearly, we need research that documents the effects of educational reform on students with disabilities in terms of graduation rates, exit documents, and employment opportunities.

Educational reform efforts will also continue to spur the debate on how secondary special education programs should be structured along with the required instructional content. This debate is not new in secondary special education, but it is controversial (e.g., Bodner, Clark, & Mellard, 1987; Clark, 1994; Edgar, 1988, 1992; Neubert, 1997). The mandate to include students with disabilities in regular education outlined in the IDEA Amendments of 1997 along with the standards set by state and local education agencies presents challenges for secondary special educators. These challenges include restructuring roles, understanding secondary curricula options to comply with the mandate for earlier transition planning, and understanding postsecondary options to enhance transition planning during the high school years. These challenges are easier if educators are aware of legislative mandates that have an impact on students' access to education and vocational options and endorse practices that enhance effective transition planning.

4

Students and Families

Key Participants in High School Programs for Students with Special Needs

There is no one who cannot find a place for himself in our kind of world. Each of us has some unique capacity waiting for realization. Every person is valuable in his own existence—for himself alone.

—George H. Bender

Although the participants in secondary programming for students with disabilities include student populations and instructors, this chapter focuses on students, the subgroups that comprise them, and their families. No two high school programs are alike, even in the same district, because of the diversity of these subgroups. This chapter describes, defines, and explains some of the diversity that makes planning for educational programs for adolescents who have disabilities so enjoyable, challenging, interesting, and, at times, difficult. This will be done by first presenting a perspective on adolescence, and then describing the various adolescent subgroups with disabilities as well as the family influences on students through their cultural, language, ethnic, and socioeconomic characteristics. Specific roles of students and families as participants in the secondary transition planning and implementation process are presented to conclude the chapter.

Adolescence

Adolescence may be broadly defined as the transition period from dependent childhood to self-sufficient adulthood. It is a time of conflict, redefinition, and pushing for independence. Adolescence may be difficult even for the most intelligent, advantaged, and popular student. For those with disabilities, adolescence may become a Herculean task for which these young people are neither prepared nor capable of dealing. Thus, educators working with adolescents with special needs must be reminded of the characteristics and struggles associated with adolescence in general and the possible effects of this transition period on an adolescent's behavior and personality.

The beginning of adolescence is marked by the genetically and biologically produced onset of puberty. *Puberty* is the time span of physiological development during which the reproductive functions mature. The physiological changes take place over a period of approximately two years. The rate of physical change during this period is greater than at any other time during a person's maturation. The adolescent must deal with a new body and new roles in a very short period of time. New relationships with people of the opposite sex and of the same sex emerge out of both necessity and desire. Masculinity and femininity as well as a new body and self-image are explored. Thus, the adolescent is, in essence, involved in the struggle to develop a new sexual identity. This is apparent in the "nondating game" or the "dating game," in conformity or nonconformity to dress and hairstyles of peers, new relationships with peers and adults, uncommon modesty or immodesty, and experiments in flirtation and sexual relations, all of which are often perceived by adults as being immature, antisocial, or rebellious behaviors.

The biological change is not the only cause of adolescent conflict, however. The adolescent also is being programmed to fit the expectations of his or her culture. Cultural anthropologists have found that in primitive cultures, the period of adolescence is very short (Aries, 1962). Upon reaching puberty, the individual is considered an adult and may be initiated into the adult society through rites and rituals. In Western society, adolescence is an extended period of time during which young people are expected to pattern themselves, over time, after adult standards.

One adult standard of Western culture is for adolescents to begin to demonstrate a work ethic—and the sooner, the better. Because of the change in the family structure, with one or both parents working outside the home, and the formalization of the workplace, the burden is placed on the school to keep students in school and prepare them for adult roles. Keeping students in school and life preparation status extends the adolescent period through secondary and, often, postsecondary years (Starr, 1986). This extension may lead to conflicts concerning independence and self-sufficiency between parents and their adolescent child. Although the adolescent desires to become self-sufficient, he or she may not have the means to accomplish this goal. Parents, still providing financial support, may impose too many restrictions on the adolescent striving for independence.

Theories of adolescence grew with the normal development of a young person as the standard of reference. Havighurst (1953) identified some developmental tasks that adolescents must complete in order to become successful (i.e., "normal") adults. Using some of his tasks and adapting others to more current cultural mores, the following tasks are presented:

1. Achieving new and more mature relations with age-mates of both sexes

   2. Achieving a sexual identity
   3. Accepting one's physique and using the body effectively
   4. Achieving emotional independence from parents and other adults
   5. Achieving economic independence
   6. Selecting and preparing for an occupation
   7. Preparing for marriage, family life, and intimate relationships
   8. Developing intellectual skills and concepts necessary for civic competence
   9. Desiring and achieving socially responsible behavior
   10. Acquiring a set of values and an ethical system as a guide to behavior

Given a set of challenging development tasks such as those listed, adolescence is more than a matter of hormones and physical maturation. It is also a period of psychological and social change (McDowell, 1981). This change involves a great deal of stress for adolescents with disabilities because the pressures of childhood to conform to or achieve intellectual and academic standards expand to include physical, social, and emotional expectations and standards as well. What makes these demands especially stressful for some adolescents with disabilities is that there is an increasing discrepancy between the physical development that is so obvious, and the social and emotional development levels that are not so obvious. Parents, teachers, neighbors, employers, and other significant adults frequently tend to respond primarily to the physical maturation and assume or expect an equal amount of maturational development in the social and emotional areas.

Adolescents with Disabilities

Some of you will be generally familiar with the nature and characteristics of each of the major disability groups. Others may be familiar with only one disability group. There even may be some who are new to the field and need an introduction to the general definitions, characteristics, behaviors, and special needs of the variety of students who might be found in any high school program. Regardless of which group you might fit into, the information on students in high school special education programming reviewed here is important, for it brings into focus the young people who need special services at a critical transition time in their lives.

A number of states are moving away from the process of assigning specific disability labels to students, yet still identifying students who require special education services. Some of these states have adopted the label of *noncategorical*. Other states are using the phrase *students in need of special education services*. Typically, this approach is being used with students with mild disabilities. Although we recognize this trend in classification, we believe it is important for you to be aware of the specific disabilities identified in the Individuals with Disabilities Education Act (IDEA) and the effects these disabilities may have on your work with these students.

The definitions provided in your state plan under the IDEA for each disability condition provide a starting point for any person who may be unfamiliar with certain disability groups. The major conditions that are the review focus of this text are following:

1. Visual impairments
2. Deafness and hearing impairments
3. Orthopedic or other health impairments
4. Speech or language impairments
5. Specific learning disabilities
6. Emotional disturbance
7. Mental retardation (mild and moderate)
8. Traumatic brain injury
9. High-functioning autism

In the early days of special education, segregated programs for each of these groups were the rule rather than the exception. Today, there is less segregation and more heterogeneous, inclusive groupings in most high school programs.

Visual Impairments

Visual impairments under the IDEA refer to both blindness and low vision. Students with visual problems may be placed in a local high school without regard for the severity of the visual impairment. That is, a student who is totally blind or who has a visual acuity of 20/400 with only light perception could be as likely to be in a regular high school program as a student who is partially sighted with a visual acuity of only 20/70 with correction. The major considerations are family goals, independence, mobility skills, available resources, and academic potential rather than degree of loss or severity of impairment.

Legal definitions are of little or no use for educators because they provide no clue as to the instructional requirements of a student. Knowing that a student can see at 20 feet what a person with normal vision can see at 200 feet does not provide much usable information for the teacher in determining an instructional program. As a consequence, functional definitions related to primary reading mode are used more frequently. These definitions differentiate between *partially sighted* and *blind* individuals. Partially sighted persons are those who can use their residual vision for reading print materials with the assistance of eyeglasses, special magnifying equipment, large print, or some combination of these aids. Blind persons must rely on Braille as a primary reading medium and/or other sensory modalities for acquiring information and learning skills.

Individual student characteristics vary greatly, but teachers should be aware that adolescents with visual impairments *may* have one or more of the following characteristics or special needs:

1. Subaverage reading speed and level
2. Limited mobility and orientation skills
3. Restricted range of life experiences
4. Limited spatial orientation
5. Underdeveloped abstract reasoning
6. Peer acceptance and social adjustment problems

The population of students who have visual impairments in public schools is difficult to estimate because of the low incidence of visual impairment generally (7/1,000 school-age children), but the dispersal of students across residential and local community programs and all grade levels makes the probability of working with students who are even partially sighted at the high school level rather low. Even so, a possibility for high schools to have students with visual disabilities exists, and secondary educators should be prepared to accommodate these students' needs and assist them to move through school programs successfully.

High school teachers in general education may or may not have the support of a consulting teacher for students who are visually impaired. If fact, some of these students are not under special education services, but do claim accommodations under Section 504. In either case, the students, themselves, can provide teachers with much of the information to make accommodations in seating, lighting, assignments, alternative modalities for learning and test administration, and social inclusion.

Deafness and Hearing Impairments

Students with auditory impairments range from those who have no hearing ability to those who have difficulty hearing speech, from those who have no speech to those who have near-normal speech, and from those who use manual communication to those who read lips and use speech. There are those who are born deaf and those who become hearing impaired in childhood or adolescence. There are those who choose to identify primarily, or solely, with the deaf community and there are those who want to be accepted as a part of the hearing community. With such diversity, it is difficult to define or characterize students in this population.

As with visual impairment, there is a legal definition of hearing impairment. Educationally, it is more functional to classify the population into those whose hearing deficits are so severe as to preclude learning through audition (deaf) and those whose hearing deficits are such that, with the aid of amplification, they can learn through audition (hard of hearing).

The degree to which the hearing loss results in personal, social, intellectual, and occupational adjustment problems is related partially to the severity of the hearing loss and the age at onset. The key factors in life adjustment for students who are hearing impaired, however, are communication skills and social acceptance variables. Both of these are influenced by the following characteristics, which occur with greater frequency in groups of people with hearing deficits:

1. Language development may be affected markedly in terms of oral and written expression. Vocabulary, verbal comprehension, grammar, syntax, and spelling may be significantly different from those individuals who are not hearing impaired.
2. Reading level is lower than expected for age and grade level.
3. Intelligence scores on verbal tests are lower. This does not suggest a direct cause-and-effect relationship between hearing loss and intellectual ability,

but rather the significant effect verbal reasoning, comprehension, and vocabulary skills have on performance with verbal tests of intelligence.
4. Emotional and behavioral problems interfere with school, peer, and family relationships.

A growing number of students with hearing impairments choose to attend local public schools. Most who do so either have had the benefit of oral instruction or they have enough residual hearing and speech to be able to cope in the regular school environment with support services. A growing number of students who are deaf are being placed in local schools with educational interpreters, thus allowing them to keep manual communication as their primary communication system.

Teachers can ease the educational struggles of youngsters with hearing problems by observing a few important practices. Simply being aware that a student has difficulty hearing may alert the teacher to make special efforts to assure the understanding of instructions, assignments, comments, and class discussions. Such consideration may be about all that is required to compensate for the hearing difficulty of many students, but some additional precautions may be taken. The most obvious is to assign the student a seat as close as possible to the source of sound. The corollary to that is for a lecturing teacher to stand close to the student with the hearing problem when critical information is presented. Students who are engaged in discussion can be encouraged to face in the direction of the student with the hearing impairment so the sound will be directly toward the student, and the verbal communication will be augmented by the visual cues from the speaker's face and body. The visual cues will be easier to see if the primary light source in the room is behind the student with the impairment rather than behind the speaker. For example, if the classroom has a row of windows along one side, the student should have a desk near the windows and toward the front of the room. In addition, during the course of normal instruction, the use of visual aids, notes, sketches, and key words written on the chalkboard or concrete objects to examine will also minimize the possibility of misunderstanding. To accompany instruction, frequent questioning of the student on crucial concepts can reveal problems before they become compounded by additional misinformation.

Orthopedic or Other Health Impairments

This population represents such a range of physical disabilities that no single quantitative, legal, or medical definition can describe it. In general, this classification encompasses all those who have neuromuscular disorders, musculoskeletal disorders, congenital malformations, chronic health problems, or disabilities resulting from disease, accidents, or child abuse. The nature of the disabling condition or health impairment is not as significant to educators as are its effects on cognitive, emotional, and social development. The effects are related to age at onset, the severity of the condition in terms of restricting activity and interaction with others, the extent of visible signs of a disability, and the extent of services and support. In fact, the *Disabilities Statistics Abstract* (1991) has provided statistical data on people with *activity limitation,* rather than a general classification of orthopedic or health impairments.

Only those high school students who have been referred and determined to need an Individualized Educational Program because of their physical disabilities or health problems or who request accommodations under Section 504 will come to the direct attention of high school instructors. Unless a physical disability or health condition interferes with functioning in a regular classroom, there is no reason to identify or attempt to serve this group.

We have no substantial indication that persons with impaired physique or health differ as a group from any other disabled or nondisabled group in their general or overall adjustment. Any blanket generalizations about characteristics would be inappropriate. There is also no clear evidence of an association between types of physical disability and particular personality traits. There is evidence, however, that indicates that physical disability has profound effects on a person's life. These effects come through the process of reaction and adjustment to the disability itself and through the various sources of stress (parental reactions, hospitalization, limitations in activity, dependence on others, sexual development, and limitations in social relationships) on students who have physical disabilities. The case study of Kathy Koons illustrates the individual characteristics that can emerge from type of disability, individual characteristics, and family characteristics.

Kathy Koons

Kathy is a 19-year-old young woman with spina bifida. She has an electric wheelchair that she can control in a very limited way. An instructional assistant works with Kathy to ensure that she is able to get around the school and to assist her with classroom activities. She requires assistance in writing and getting her supplies ready for class, getting her lunch and feeding herself, and controlling her wheelchair.

Kathy is a middle child; she has an older, married sister and a brother who is age 14. Her father is an electrician and her mother does not work outside of the home. The family lives in a very nice house, which has had some modifications made for the wheelchair.

Her school attendance has been very poor. Mrs. Koons has kept Kathy at home for extended periods of time throughout the years, stating that Kathy was not well enough to attend school. The family was told that Kathy would not live to be 5 years old and they have taken care of her every need. The mother does many things that Kathy could do on her own, but it would take her a long time to get it done. When Kathy is at home, she spends the majority of the time in her wheelchair in front of the TV or stretched out on a blanket on the floor. There is nothing that Kathy does at home for herself or the family.

Kathy is in four resource classes (math, language arts, social studies, and vocational exploration), is in two regular education classes (computers and home economics), and spends one hour a day with the instructional assistant working on daily living and functional living skills. Kathy is working on grooming skills, kitchen skills, making change, telling time, and mobility. She has good verbal skills, but has very limited written language skills because of her limited mobility. She is learning to use a computer so that she can increase her written expressive skills. Kathy has indicated an interest in doing a job that would utilize telephone skills, which is something she feels she could learn to do. She has several friends at

Kathy Koons   Continued

school. She says that she would like to have a boyfriend and talks about relationships quite often. She is very concerned about not having someone to marry, being able to leave home, and living on her own.

Kathy's Verbal Scale IQ is 84, Performance Scale IQ is 64, and Full Scale IQ is 75. Curriculum-based assessment results indicate skills functioning at the 7.5 grade level in reading and at the 6.8 grade level in math. She is aware of her academic limitations, but wants to do something with her life. She indicates that she wants to learn to live more independently and to develop job skills. She is older than most of the students in the high school and plans are being made for her to go to a residential independent living center for young adults with physical disabilities, where she can have the opportunity to learn many of the things that will allow her to live in a group home and have a job. Kathy is very excited about these plans, but her parents are somewhat hesitant.

Teachers can make a significant impact on the adjustment problems of students with physical disabilities if they can make a clear distinction between a *disability* and a *handicap* in their own interactions with the students. A teacher must remember that, although the disability persists, a handicap can be eliminated by changing the task, the person, or both. Helping students recognize that disabilities do not always produce handicaps may allow them to develop confidence that they have some control over their roles in life. This may have a critical effect on their personal feelings of worth and sense of destiny. Although there are many sources of information teachers can turn to for suggestions to help them work effectively with students who have orthopedic or health impairments, the writings of Bigge (1991) are an excellent resource.

Speech or Language Impairments

Adolescents with speech or language disorders may or may not be identified with special education programming per se. Generally, they will not require special instructional programs unless their disability is very language oriented, and if so, they may be classified for specific learning disabilities programs. It is not uncommon for students with other primary disabilities to have speech or language problems as secondary disorders. The tendency is to (1) accept the communication problem(s) as a given and pursue no intervention or (2) assign speech therapy intervention a lower priority than the major instructional intervention, with little or no systematic, long-term efforts. Unfortunately, too often communication disorders are not identified as a specific disability amenable to intervention, but rather as a result or manifestation of the primary disability. This is especially the case with individuals who have mental disabilities.

Speech disorders at the high school level, whether they are a primary or secondary disability, are likely to be well-established patterns and affect students' self-concepts significantly. It is surprising to many that this disability category ranks high in comparison to other disability groups in high school dropout rates. Wagner and Shaver (1989) reported a national dropout rate of 32.5 percent. This category ranked fourth behind behavior disorders (54.7 percent), learning disabilities (36.1 percent), and mental retardation (33.6 percent). No significant difference likely exists between rates for students with speech impairments and mental retardation. Wagner and Shaver reported also that secondary students with speech impairments were declassified (deleted from special education classification rosters) at a rate of 18 percent, which is almost three times the rate at which youths in any other category were declassified. The implications for providing more careful attention to this group are clear from these data.

The high school teacher needs to be alert to the existence of communication disorders and must be ready to ensure that the students who have them have the best diagnoses and intervention possible. This begins with an understanding of what constitutes a speech or language problem. Culatta and Culatta (1981) suggested some practical questions to ask in determining whether a person has a speech problem severe enough to warrant referral:

1. Can I understand this person?
2. Does this person sound strange?
3. Does this person have any peculiar physical characteristics when speaking?
4. Is the communication in a style inappropriate to the situation?
5. Do I enjoy listening to this speaker?
6. Is this speaker damaging his or her vocal chords?
7. Does the speaker experience pain or discomfort when attempting to communicate?

Language disorders are much more complex than speech defects, since they involve not only speech but also receptive, integrative, and expressive activities. A student who has difficulty in comprehending questions or directions has a receptive language problem. A student who clearly has greater ability to receive messages than to express them has an expressive language problem. A student who can demonstrate some receptive ability and some expressive ability but has difficulty in coordinating the two is assumed to have some type of integrative deficit in perception, recall, or retrieval of sensory or perceptual input. Language disorders usually affect both oral and written communication, but proper use of facial expressions, gestures, and body language can make oral communication deficits less noticeable.

When dealing with this population, a high school teacher's primary functions include the following:

1. Be alert to students who have speech or language disorders.
2. Encourage and give information to students and their parents about intervention options.
3. Advocate vigorously for adequate intervention.
4. Assist the speech pathologist by encouraging correct use of speech and language and reinforcing generalization of skills learned in therapy
5. Emphasize tolerance and understanding of students with speech or language difficulties and discourage teasing, disparaging remarks, and other negative behaviors from other students.

6. Encourage students to communicate in class by providing nonverbal response options, asking yes-or-no questions, and pairing students with communication difficulties with supportive peers in the class.

Specific Learning Disabilities

Students with specific learning disabilities make up the most heterogeneous of all high school students with disabilities. Abilities range from slow learner to gifted levels, and behavioral characteristics are so diverse as to leave little doubt why this group has practically defied definition. Deficits described and reported as more frequent to populations with learning disabilities include problems in the following:

Discrimination	Memory
Sequencing	Impulse control
Affect	Motor behavior
Auditory activity	Visual-motor functioning
Sensory integration	Conceptual and abstract thinking
Language	Spatial orientation
Self-concept	Body image

These deficit areas are generally considered to be the basic processes or elements of cognitive, social, emotional, and motor behavior in school, at home, or in the community.

High school teachers usually focus on the academic and behavioral problems of students with learning disabilities. The academic failures of these students in reading, writing, math, language, or spelling are major obstacles in school adjustment, and the personal-social problems that accompany them (or emerge as a consequence of them) are the primary targets of school concerns. These academic and social difficulties make it nearly impossible to differentiate students who have learning disabilities from students who are low achieving. Researchers do seem to agree on the following:

1. There is a difference (discrepancy) between what a student should be able to do and what he or she is actually doing.
2. There are some specific tasks that others can do that students with learning disabilities cannot do.
3. Students' difficulties are centered on one or more basic psychological processes involved in using and understanding language.
4. Students are not learning adequately in spite of the basic integrity of their senses, cognitive ability, emotional state, or lack of opportunity to learn.

The case study of Craig Turner is an example of one student with specific learning disabilities. Keep in mind that Craig's characteristics and history are not meant to represent a typical student with specific learning disabilities.

Craig Turner

Craig is 17 years of age and in his third year of high school. His father is an insurance executive and his mother is socially active in Junior League and a local sorority. Craig is an only child and is very verbal and socially adept. He was in classes for dyslexic children at a private school for five years prior to returning to the public high school. During his junior high school years at the private school, he was successful in athletics, earning letter awards in football and track.

Reading has always been difficult for Craig; his current reading achievement level is 1.8. His math performance is 3.6. These grade-level scores are verified through performance on both curriculum-based assessment and commercial achievement measures. He does poorly in spelling and writing and is beginning to refuse to do any assignments that require composition and handwriting. In social studies and science, Craig contributes orally and demonstrates a wealth of information that indicates he acquires information aurally and has good memory skills. He is managing to pass all his subjects and is on schedule to graduate next year.

During the past two years, Craig has frequently been in trouble at school. He has not been eligible to participate in athletics because of poor grades and periodic suspensions due to infractions of school rules. He has been truant on numerous occasions and has been caught at school with liquor and various drugs in his locker. He seeks out friends in regular classes from his affluent neighborhood but is not very successful in his attempts. Those who do choose to be with him are those who are having similar problems with grades and school adjustment.

Craig presents two role identities at school. One is the assertive, outgoing, cooperative but "cool" student who has everything under control, including the teachers, as they respond to this role positively and cater to his mood and wishes. The other role is the restless, impatient, negative student who communicates nonverbally to everyone, "Stay out of my way—don't hassle me." His classmates do not trust him, and some are afraid of him. Teachers have tried to establish a relationship with him that is positive, and have succeeded in preventing any classroom conflicts. Most of his misbehavior occurs outside the classroom in other parts of the school.

Craig's parents are well known to school officials because of their response to the school's disciplinary policies. They do not deny the infractions but believe that the school environment is to blame. They have refused to permit Craig to enter into any vocational or exploratory community-based training experiences during his first two years of high school. They believe he has the ability to work in some occupation that has much higher status than what they associate with the school vocational programs. They insist that the school should remediate his reading problem and provide an academic program that will qualify him for high school graduation and possible admission to a community college. Both parents are college graduates and find it difficult to accept any low-status school or employment alternatives.

Craig does not verbalize any occupational interests and has not wanted to be in any high school vocational or prevocational options. His interests appear to focus on cars, movies, professional football, and his stereo equipment. The only part-time job he has ever had was a summer job as a recreation assistant for a children's soccer league. This was obtained for him by his father. His work was satisfactory, but he did not ask to do it again. His parents provide him with a generous allowance each week of $40, so he has spending money all year long.

Zigmond and Miller (1992) made a convincing case for secondary education in their review of educational program practices for students with learning disabilities. Evidence from data collected since 1975 shows that the traditional models of secondary school services are inadequate. Whether one looks at dropout rates, achievement/performance levels at school, or postsecondary employment or education, the results are not encouraging at all. The researchers proposed two models that dealt more with substance (outcomes and curriculum focus) than form (administrative placement decisions, such as resource room, consulting model, etc.). In both cases, career development and transition outcomes are integral parts of the models. Perhaps this population is at last getting the attention it needs in those areas that are critical after the school years.

Emotional Disturbance

Definitions of emotional disturbances typically revolve around two major issues: (1) the inability to establish appropriate, satisfying relationships with others and (2) demonstration of behavior that either fails to meet or exceeds the expectations of those with whom the person comes in contact (Kauffman, 1997). Since these characteristic behaviors are found to a certain degree in normal adolescents, adolescent emotional disturbances must be viewed differently from those in children or adults. According to societal standards, the fine line between normal adolescent behavior and disordered behavior is drawn among the degree or magnitude of severity, the rate or frequency of occurrence, the duration of the behavior, and the unique form of the behavior.

The definition of *emotional disturbance* used in the IDEA excludes a student with a social maladjustment, unless it is determined that the student has a serious emotional disturbance. Some authors have challenged this exclusion (Kauffman, 1997) on logical grounds, but even on a practical level most states are making no attempt to deal with the nature of the social maladjustment of the problem students labeled as emotionally disturbed.

The kinds of behavior associated with the diagnosis of emotional disturbance are so varied that it is difficult to provide a unified list of characteristics of behaviors. Quay and Peterson (1987) described six dimensions of behavior that are useful in showing some distinct clusters or patterns of emotional disturbances in children and youths. These classifications and associated characteristics or traits are shown in Table 4.1.

Adolescent emotional disturbance ranges from mild to severe, although some would say that, by definition, even mild behaviors are so markedly inappropriate, socially unacceptable, or personally unsatisfying that they are obvious to most observers. In other words, the behaviors must be severe, excessive, and persistent before a teenage student is classified as disturbed or disordered. The relative terms *mild, moderate,* and *severe* are appropriate only when used as a continuum of severity within the population already diagnosed as having an emo-

TABLE 4.1   Quay and Peterson's Dimensions of Behavior

Types of Behavior Disorders	Characteristics
Conduct Disorders	Seeks attention Shows off Is disruptive Annoys others Fights Has temper tantrums
Socialized Aggression	Steals in company with others Is loyal to delinquent friends Is truant from school with others Has "bad" companions Freely admits disrespect for moral values and laws
Attention Problems/ Immaturity	Has short attention span Has poor concentration Is distractible Is easily diverted from task at hand Answers without thinking Is sluggish/lethargic/slow moving
Anxiety/Withdrawal	Is self-conscious Is easily embarrassed Is hypersensitive Feelings are easily hurt Is generally fearful Is anxious Is depressed Is always sad
Psychotic Behavior	Expresses far-fetched ideas Has repetitive speech Shows bizarre behavior
Motor Excess	Is restless Is unable to sit still Is tense Is unable to relax Is overtalkative

Source: Adapted from *Manual for the Revised Behavior Problems Checklist* (Quay & Peterson, 1987).

tional disturbance. Following are some general descriptions distinguishing categories of emotional disturbances:

1. *Mild* emotional disturbance is characteristic of students involved in some type of crisis but who are still able to function within the regular school system with a minimum of support help from a crisis teacher, counselor, or itinerant

resource teacher. Disorders that fall within the mild category tend to be transient and may disappear with time-limited interventions or sometimes even without specific intervention.

2. *Moderate* emotional disturbance requires some type of intensive intervention (e.g., individual or group therapy, medication, special or resource room placement). These tend to be longer lasting and more debilitating, and they interfere more with functioning at home or school.

3. *Severe* emotional disturbance is based on a student's inability to function in a high school environment. The adolescent who has severe emotional disturbance may have difficulty maintaining contact with reality. The behaviors exhibited are more exaggerated and bizarre. The adolescent with a severe disturbance frequently needs a self-contained classroom or possibly placement in a hospital or residential treatment center.

A final note of caution is needed before moving closer to understanding the population with emotional disturbances. Emotional disturbance is now being described as a condition in which significant discrepancy exists between a person's behavior and legal, cultural, moral, or personal expectations (Kauffman, 1997; Gelfand, Jenson, & Drew, 1997; Newcomer, 1993). This description reflects value judgments, which are subjective, change over time, and differ from one environment or culture to another. Given this position, it is possible that the expectations or standards themselves, rather than an individual's behavior, may be inappropriate. The distinction between expected behavior and actual behavior becomes important when making diagnostic or placement decisions and when attempting some type of intervention to change behavior. The case study of Amy Sanders gives an example of a student with unique manifestations of an emotional disturbance.

Amy Sanders

Amy is 16 years old and in the ninth grade in a suburban community. She is the youngest of four children and the only girl. Only one brother lives at home, but he is in and out, depending on his employment. Amy's mother works in a factory and is married to her third husband. Amy's current stepfather works in the same factory but in a supervisory position. He is actively involved in Amy's school and medical problems.

Amy is a low achiever in school, but it has been her emotional and behavioral problems that have dominated school responses. Early on, she was assessed as not needing a

special class, but she was still seen as different from the other children in her classroom. She demonstrated withdrawal, extreme shyness, immaturity, and excessive dependency throughout elementary school. Amy made no academic progress during the elementary and middle school years, but she made significant progress in her personal and social development during eighth grade. Her current reading and math skills are at a first-grade level.

After one semester in the ninth grade, Amy started to withdraw, showed symptoms of depression, and was unable to function or perform as she previously had at home and at

(continued)

Amy Sanders   Continued

school. She was hospitalized twice for depression, hallucinations, and hearing voices. She is currently taking three medications for her emotional state, but these have been changed frequently in attempts to regulate the dosage. Her behavior at school and home is erratic and she is described by her teachers as "deteriorating" and regressing in all areas and skills where she had once shown much positive growth.

It is known that Amy was a victim of sexual abuse by her natural father, second stepfather, and the brother who is still at home occasionally. Amy's mother reports that she is at the end of her rope. Recently, when Amy wandered from home and asked a stranger for a ride, the family found it necessary to seek respite care for Amy after school.

Amy is now demonstrating manipulative and passive-aggressive behaviors at school. She refuses to respond verbally at times, frequently cries over trivial incidents, and wants to call her "mommy" to come get her when school staff attempt to deal with her inappropriate behaviors. She is lacking in any vocational experience outside the school. She has demonstrated some positive work skills in her school-based work experience when she chooses to work.

Recent attention to attention deficit disorders (ADD) and attention deficit hyperactivity disorders (ADHD) by physicians, psychiatrists, mental health professionals, and educators has posed diagnostic and classification problems for schools and even more difficult problems in intervention approaches. Considerable debate continues about the causes of ADD and ADHD, which leads to a variety of placements in special education programs. Some individuals are placed in programs for students with learning disabilities, some in programs for emotional disturbance, and others in programs/services for "other health impairments." At this time, there is not enough research data available to have a great deal of useful information on how to provide these students with appropriate career development and transition programming. Parents and educators have frequently turned to medications for control of inappropriate and exasperating behavior, but there is increasing agreement that this is no cure and that some side effects are more serious than the attention deficits or hyperactivity. In most cases, there will need to be close coordination between career education specialists and medical personnel until such time as research data point to more effective methods of treatment and training. In the meantime, simply recognizing that the behavior or attention disorders are neither willful or controllable by the youngsters can go a long way toward moving teachers and other professionals into meaningful relationships with the youngsters and their families. A student with ADD or ADHD may or may not be eligible for special education and related services. Local schools must follow state and federal regulations in determining eligibility or accommodations under Section 504 and the Americans with Disabilities Act.

Mental Retardation (Mild and Moderate)

In only two characteristics are all adolescents classified as mentally retarded alike: (1) they have intelligence quotients of two or more standard deviations below the mean of 100 and (2) there is evidence of two or more types of adaptive behavior deficit, usually including an inability to succeed in school. Otherwise, they vary considerably in most human characteristics. This introductory statement is important for you to put into perspective; it is the most accepted definition used for identifying this population (American Association on Mental Retardation, 1992). This latest revision of the definition for mental retardation places more emphasis than previous definitions on adaptive behavior. The American Association on Mental Retardation (AAMR; 1992) recommends the following four assumptions as essential to the application of the definition in diagnosis and classification:

1. Valid assessment must consider cultural and linguistic differences in both communication and behavioral response factors.
2. The existence of limitations in adaptive behaviors occurs within the context of specific cultural and community environments typical for an individual's age peers.
3. Specific adaptive limitations often coexist with strengths in other adaptive behaviors or skills, or other personal capabilities.
4. With appropriate supports over a sustained period, the functioning level of a person with mental retardation will generally improve.

Any similarity among those defined as mentally retarded is an artifact of the definition and is very subjective. For example, assume that two persons have significant deficits in intellectual functioning and adaptive behavior. Knowing that one has an IQ of 65 gives one no single clear notion of what the person's capacity to learn, solve problems, acquire knowledge, or think abstractly is, compared to someone with an IQ of 55. Neither does it mean that the person with the higher IQ has a higher level of adapted behavior. Both persons are identified as mentally retarded, but they may be evaluated quite differently—not only on the two factors required for the diagnosis but also in their interests, aptitudes, personalities, physical attributes, and health. The case study of Darrell Cook gives an example of this.

Darrell Cook

Darrell is 17 years of age and is in his first year of high school. His mother does commercial cleaning with a janitorial service in a city high-rise office building. His father is serving a long-term sentence in prison. Prior to incarceration, he had been absent from the home more frequently than he had been in it and had not held a steady job in 10 years. Both of Darrell's parents are uneducated and unskilled, and have not been able to work steadily at the same time to generate two incomes for the family. Both moved to the city from the rural South as teenagers with their parents.

Darrell is the oldest of five children. He has had difficulty in school from the very beginning. His junior high school years were especially difficult. Curriculum-based assessment results for Darrell reveal that he is functioning at about the third-grade level in reading and math (3.1 and 3.2, respectively) but the diagnostician noted that these scores may not reflect his ability, as he did not appear

(continued)

Darrell Cook   Continued

to be showing any sincere effort while taking the tests. His intellectual functioning was assessed as Verbal Scale IQ of 64, Performance Scale IQ of 72, and Full Scale IQ of 68.

Darrell demonstrated some work potential when he began selling newspapers at age 9, and did this for nearly two years. He has worked part time for a neighborhood grocery. He also worked part time for a roller skating rink when he was 15 years old. During that time, he won several cash prizes ($25–$50) in skating contests. He is interested in getting back into the skating contests and winning a lot more money.

The Cook family lives in a slum area in extremely substandard housing. Food is nutritious, but there is not much variety or quantity. Darrell rarely eats more than one meal a day at home. The family lives in a two-bedroom house with his grandmother and an aunt. Privacy is impossible, and tensions from crowding and other factors associated with poverty make family interactions difficult and sometimes volatile. This has encouraged much of the life in the street that Darrell participates in and that his younger brothers and sisters are beginning to experience.

It is fair to generalize, as with the other disability groups discussed, that the severity of mental retardation does lead to differences in performance characteristics. The more severe the mental retardation, the more one can expect to find accompanying physical limitations, problems in language and communication skills, and a wide range of inappropriate social behaviors. The following characteristics are found with greater frequency in populations identified as mildly mentally retarded. They would occur with even greater frequency and severity in persons classified as moderately retarded.

1. Establishing a learning set or frame of reference for novel problems or new learning is difficult.
2. Language deficits are common.
3. Abstract reasoning is limited.
4. Reading skills are at a low level.
5. Reaction time to stimuli is slow.
6. Incidental learning is limited.
7. Short-term memory is inefficient.
8. Transfer of learning and generalization is difficult.
9. Social skills vary widely but are frequently not commensurate with chronological age.
10. Motor development and motor skills are variable but are diminished when retardation is not based on psychosocial factors.
11. Physical impairments or health-related problems are more frequent.

Labels such as *mild* and *moderate* are used frequently by professionals and others to communicate general expectations without specifying behavior deficits. That is, adolescents labeled *mild* (also sometimes referred to as individuals with learning handicaps or learning problems) are meant to be seen as retarded primarily in school. There is also an expectation that they can and will become independent or semi-independent adults. It is assumed that some of them can be educated in regular classrooms with extra help but that others will need special instruction. Adolescents labeled *moderate,* on the other hand, are seen as semidependent and capable of living in the community as participating members with support. In school, they are educated either in self-contained classrooms with emphasis on community-referenced communication, self-help and daily living skills, social skills, vocational skills, and functional academics, or are included part time or full time in general education with curriculum accommodations. Use of these labels, however, poses problems of group stereotyping that can affect individuals and may lead to self-fulfilling prophecies. For that reason, it is best to deal with adolescents—however labeled—as persons first and to help them become who they want to be and can be.

Traumatic Brain Injury

A separate category of eligible disabilities under PL 101-476 (IDEA, Section 300.7 [B] [12]) was established for students with traumatic brain injury (TBI). *Traumatic brain injury* refers to an *acquired brain injury* caused by some external physical force (open- or closed-head injuries), resulting in total or partial impairments in one or more areas, including cognition, language, memory, attention, reasoning, abstract thinking, judgment, problem solving, sensory or motor abilities, perceptual abilities, psychosocial behavior, and communication. Injuries can result in mild, moderate, or severe impairments and frequently involve complex interaction of physical, psychological, and social problems.

Although individuals with some type of acquired brain injury (ABI) have been in schools and public life for decades, it is only recently that schools have begun to address the condition. This is in spite of the fact that brain injuries are a leading cause of death and disability in industrialized Western countries (Kraemer & Blacher, 1997), with one million children each year taken to emergency rooms as a result of accidental or nonaccidental brain injuries (Savage, 1993). Kraus, Fife, Cox, Ramstein, and Conroy (1986) reported a relatively stable rate of incidence of TBI/ABI among adolescents and young adults (the highest incidence group) of 1 out of every 181 persons each year.

Transition from adolescence into adulthood, particularly postsecondary education or training and employment, is difficult for many students with TBI/ABI (Bergland, 1996; Wehman, 1992). Without question, soon after the injury, an adolescent student with TBI/ABI will experience impaired ability in learning new information. This affects continued progress academically in school. In addition, change in student behavior and decision making can affect general performance, self-esteem, and social relationships—usually in a negative direction. These students naturally tend to hold on to their preinjury self-identities and may have real difficulty in recognizing or accepting the need for changes in their lives at school, home, or in the community.

In their comprehensive publication on educational dimensions of acquired brain injury, Savage and Wolcott (1994) related some unique characteristics of this population in contrast to persons born with congenital impairments. First, the sudden intrusion of a loss of functioning significantly changes an individual's life. In many cases, the individual is aware of these changes and what they mean. Although there are usually surviving skills on which to rebuild one's life, the memory of "who I used to be" serves as a continual reminder of the loss that occurred. Savage and Wolcott suggested three other characteristics of ABI that make this disability unique:

1. Severity of injury is not necessarily equal to severity of disability. Because the brain is so complex, what may seem to be a minor head injury involving a small part of the brain can result in an extremely severe disability. On the other hand, massive head injuries resulting in a skull fracture and coma may not necessarily result in any permanent disability following recovery.
2. A wide range of disabilities result from ABI. Students with TBI/ABI defy easy categorization. From an orientation perspective, students with TBI/ABI often experience problems in three major areas, as shown in Figure 4.1.
3. Acquired brain injury is a dynamic condition, especially within the first 12 to 18 months following injury. Students can make rapid progress, plateau, progress again rapidly or slowly, and, of course, perhaps regress. These spurts and pauses can go on for months or even years. Substantial change can occur years after the injury. Teachers need to recognize such changes, be flexible to respond appropriately, and never give up. The case study of Tony Lupino is an example of unpredictable recovery effects.

Tony Lupino

Tony is a 15-year-old student who was struck by a car while in-line skating. He made excellent physical recovery from his head injury and presents himself as an attractive, active teenager. Since the injury, however, he has been more impulsive than he was prior to the injury and often makes poor decisions, taking unnecessary risks to show that he is "cool" and not afraid of getting hurt.

Tony returned to his general education classroom two months after his injury. His school had no specific plan for his reentry and little information on the effects of brain injury. Due to the effects of his injury on his cognitive abilities, Tony is currently unable to understand what is expected of him in class nor can

he work independently on assignments. He has reacted to these changes by refusing to do his work, clowning with his peers, and skipping classes.

Recent curriculum-based assessment and formal testing revealed that Tony has low-average intellectual functioning and performs in the average range, compared with his peers, on measures of academic achievement. The school psychologist recommended special education services and the parents agreed. At the first IEP meeting, Tony's behavior was the focus of concern, and, at the school's recommendation and with the parents' approval, he was placed in a classroom for students with behavior disorders. Tony's behavior quickly

Tony Lupino   Continued

deteriorated further. He viewed the placement as a punishment and was angry that he was separated from his friends.

Tony's continued and accelerated behavior problems caused great concern for the school and Tony's parents. After reviewing the situation, a neuropsychological consultant was invited in to assess the situation. The consultant determined that Tony had returned to school fully expecting to resume his normal school routine. The school expected the same thing. It appeared that no one was prepared for the cognitive or behavioral effects of the injury. Tony was frustrated with his school problems in academics, but either denied his loss of cognitive ability or was unaware of his memory loss and difficulty in learning. His acting out was interpreted by the school and his parents as normal adolescent rebellion.

FIGURE 4.1   Range of Disabilities Resulting from Acquired Brain Injury

Cognitive Problems May Involve
- Communication and language
- Memory, especially for learning new information
- Perception
- Attention and concentration
- Judgment, planning, and decision making
- Ability to adjust to change (flexibility)

Social and Behavioral Problems May Involve
- Self-esteem
- Self-control
- Awareness of self and others
- Awareness of social rules
- Interest and social involvement
- Sexuality
- Appearance and grooming
- Family relationships
- Age-appropriate behavior

Neuromotor-Physical Problems May Involve
- Vision and hearing
- Speed and coordination of movement
- Stamina and endurance
- Balance, strength, and equilibrium
- Motor function
- Speech
- Eye-hand coordination
- Spatial orientation

Source: Adapted from *Educational Dimensions of Acquired Brain Injury* (p. 10) by R. C. Savage and G. F. Wolcott, 1994, Austin, TX: Pro-Ed. Copyright 1994 by Pro-Ed. Adapted by permission.

Very little data are available regarding adult outcomes for students with TBI/ABI. Roessler, Schriner, and Price (1992) reported employment data on a population sample of persons with ABI, indicating employment rates ranging from 52 to 97 percent, depending on the level and length of their postinjury comas. They also reported that of those who were employed, 75 percent were working only part time.

Smith and Tyler (1997) stressed that there can be no single plan used in transition planning for students with TBI/ABI. Of all disability groups, this one requires careful joint planning with the student, family, and any medical rehabilitation personnel associated with the student. The plans need to be flexible, reviewed frequently, and adjusted when necessary to respond to the dynamic nature of this group of individuals.

High-Functioning Autism

Like traumatic brain injury, autism was added to the list of eligible disability groups under the IDEA in 1990. High-functioning autism is highlighted here because of this book's focus on mild to moderate disability populations.

Individuals with autism spend most of their lives as adults, yet most of the literature relating to autism has focused on research, case studies, and practice with young children. The literature has also focused more on low-functioning individuals with autism rather than those whose abilities help them compensate for their autistic behavior. Although a lack of research literature makes our task more difficult, for the purposes of this book, it is important to include this low-incidence group referred to as *high-functioning autism* in our descriptions of high school adolescents with disabilities.

Currently, neither of the two major diagnosis and classification manuals, *International Classification of Diseases,* 9th revision (*ICD-9*; U.S. Department of Health and Human Services, 1989) and the *Diagnostic and Statistical Manual of Mental Disorders,* 4th edition (*DSM-IV*; American Psychiatric Association, 1994), have established any definition or diagnostic criteria for high-functioning autism. Asperger syndrome is sometimes mentioned as a mild type of autism, but research so far has not generated agreement on that view (Tsai, 1992). The difficulties in quantifying severity levels and showing differences between mild, moderate, and severe or low functioning and high functioning have prevented any agreement on a standard system of classification by severity.

In spite of this, the general observation that some individuals with autism or autistic behaviors are clearly able to lead more independent lives than others led some professionals to start studying those with higher-functioning abilities. Tsai (1992) reported on a study of professionals and parents interested in high-functioning individuals with autism regarding descriptive characteristics. Their responses included the following:

- Cognitive development in the normal to near normal range (Full Scale IQ scores of 70 or higher); some academic capabilities

- Communication ability in the normal to near normal range; often excellent vocabularies and grammar, but atypical social and practical language
- Independence in life skills (normal to near normal levels of adaptive behavior)
- Difficulties in social awareness, social relationships, and social interactions
- Sustained interest in unusual, repetitive, and in-depth special-interest topics
- Normal to near normal behavior; behavioral problems are usually mild and restricted to specific events or episodes

Tsai (1992) emphasized that individuals who may be diagnosed or perceived as having high-functioning autism still have many problems in educational achievement, competitive employment, and social life. Of course, there are some dramatic success stories, such as Temple Grandin, the autistic woman who has a successful international career designing livestock equipment and is an assistant professor of animal science at Colorado State University. There are also autistic savant cases, such as the character, Raymond, in the movie *Rain Man;* Jessy Park, the artist; and others. And, finally, there are those who have satisfying, successful lives, with continued encouragement, caring, and support but whose stories are not presented in the media or research literature. The primary point is that autism is highly individual in its manifestations and that every student you have with this diagnosis deserves your best efforts to assist them in their needed transitions as they prepare for adult life. The case study of Simon Huang is not presented as a typical example but accurately reflects one student with high-functioning autism.

Simon Huang

Simon is 20 years old and still in his neighborhood high school. He has average intelligence, with better verbal than performance skills. He does well on rote learning tasks, but his parents and teachers continue to be puzzled by his poor comprehension of abstract ideas and his social naiveté and vulnerability to hazards in everyday life.

Simon has demonstrated some signs of autism since age 1. Very early he became socially aloof and isolated. He spent most of his preschool years gazing at his hands, which he moved in complicated patterns before his face. He passed the major development motor tasks at the appropriate age, but would spend hours running in circles with an object in his hand. Any attempts to stop him resulted in screaming. He performed many stereotyped movements as a young child, including jump-ing, flapping his arms, and moving his hands in circles.

At age 3, Simon recognized the letters of the alphabet and rapidly developed skill in drawing. He did not speak until age 4, and then for a long time used only single words. After age 5, his speech and social contact improved dramatically. Until age 11, he attended a special school, where teachers and the staff tolerated a range of bizarre, repetitive routines. Despite his problems, Simon was able to use his excellent rote memory and absorbed all he was taught. He could recall and reproduce facts verbatim when asked. He was transferred to a public school at age 11.

Simon uses good grammar and has a large vocabulary, but his speech is naive and immature and he is concerned mainly with his own special interests. He has learned not to

(continued)

Simon Huang   Continued

make inappropriate remarks about other people's appearance, but tends to ask repetitive questions. He is socially withdrawn but prefers adults to age peers. He enjoys simple jokes, but cannot understand more subtle humor. Simon is often teased by his classmates and finds it difficult to understand the unwritten rules of teenage social interactions. He says of himself, "I am afraid I suffer from bad sportsmanship."

Simon's main interest is in maps and road signs. He has an exceptional memory for routes and can draw them rapidly and accurately. He is adept at using a citizen's band radio and regularly contacts a wide network of other radio enthusiasts. He also makes large, complicated, abstract shapes out of any material he finds and he shows much ingenuity in getting them to stay together. His finger dexterity is good, but he is clumsy and poorly coordinated in large motor movements.

Progress is beginning to be seen in Simon's ability to verbalize his awareness of his problems, but he is still unable to resist some of his routines and rituals. He is quiet and easy to get along with at home and his parents and sister are very fond of him. He has no friends with whom he associates. Simon is beginning to talk about his dreams for the future, which is to be a cartographer. He has been unable to find work on a part-time basis, and the school has never tried a community-based program because of his unwillingness to participate. Simon's parents are very concerned about what will become of their son in the future.

Variations in Population Characteristics

High school students requiring special education programming vary, then, by definitional factors, physical or mental factors, and educational terminology. The preceding section dealt with these factors, but it is apparent that behavioral characteristics still overlap from one category of exceptionality to another, as well as by degree of severity within categorical areas. Even if each group were homogeneous in disability characteristics, however, there are other ways that populations can vary that affect programming decisions: geographic variables, cultural and ethnic variables, and socioeconomic variables. Each of these will be discussed briefly to highlight the population differences that must be considered in high school programming.

Geographic Variables

People living in the United States have long been aware of geographical factors related to population characteristics. Interests, values, and life-styles are historical phenomena that persist today in spite of the increased mobility of the nation's population. Yankee ingenuity, Southern hospitality, Midwest work ethic, East Coast liberalism, Southwest rugged individualism, and Northwest conservationism are examples of regional stereotypes that are based to some degree on both historical tradition and observed differences. Although these regional values and life-styles may be identifiable, they may or may not be reflected in students' attitudes and behavior during their high school years. These influences tend to be adult culture factors that may be resisted by teenagers, then assumed later as adults. When youths with mental or physical handicaps are more attuned to values and life-styles of their parents than of their peers, then some of these regional influences may be observed during the high school years.

Urban-rural factors probably have more direct and lasting effects than do regional factors. For example, the incidence of handicapping conditions is higher in urban areas than in rural areas. The reason for this may be an artifact of propor-tionately more diagnostic referrals as well as availability of programs for serving people with disabilities. Within each of these geopolitical variables, urban or rural, there are various subcategories. Urban areas, for example, comprise a wide range of urban systems: inner cities of large metropolitan areas, small- to medium-size cities (30,000–150,000), low- to middle-income municipalities adjoining inner cit-ies, and middle- to high-income suburban areas or municipalities (frequently called *bedroom communities*).

Urban Issues.   Urban schools are usually large enough to be able to offer a range of high school special education programs and services. However, some issues or problem areas for urban districts include the following:

1. *Multicultural populations.*   Metropolitan areas particularly have been mag-nets for poor and multicultural populations, especially migrants and immigrants (St. John & Miller, 1995). Hodgkinson (1985) projected that by the year 2000, one of three persons in the United States will be a member of a racial or ethnic minority. His projections are currently on target nationally and have been exceeded in cities such as Los Angeles, San Diego, San Antonio, and Houston. Migrants are of two types—those who move from one part of the country to another to live and those who move around frequently, following crops, or other jobs. Unlike the immi-grants of the past, many today are much like the migrants who are highly mobile and transient. The parents of both groups are frequently ill prepared to cope with the complexities of urban life in a new environment and to provide adequate sup-port for students in special education programs.

2. *Language barriers.*   The street language learned by immigrants to the United States is quite different from school language. The technical vocabulary and preci-sion of school vocational programs may be overwhelming. Students with learning disabilities or mental retardation, who also may have English language deficits, find high school programs in urban areas extremely demanding and beyond their abilities.

3. *Cultural and value differences.*   Youths who have disabilities and who live in urban settings present a wide range of values toward school in general and voca-tional programs in particular. Affluent urban or suburban families, who may not see skilled or semiskilled occupations as being appropriate for their sons or daugh-ters, sometimes insist on an academic emphasis. Families in poverty or lower mid-dle-class working groups may want their children to rise above skilled or semiskilled levels of occupations offered in special education programming and hold higher academic or occupational aspirations. Or, some students feel no family pressures to achieve in school or work and may have learned a negative attitude about work of any kind and do not enroll in any available vocational programs even when they stay in school. Blackorby, Edgar, and Kortering (1991) reported that in their study of students with mild disabilities (learning disabilities, behavior disorders, and mild mental retardation), the ratio of dropouts to graduates was 2:1 among African Americans, Hispanics, and Native Americans, in contrast to a proportion of 1:1 or lower among Caucasian and Asian students.

4. *Size and complexity.*   Another issue of urban education that affects career and vocational planning is the size and complexity of the urban environment, especially in large metropolitan areas. Whether inner city or suburban, the diverse needs of urban students result in highly complex and sometimes almost overwhelming administrative and instructional problems. These include the following:

a. Identification and appropriate placement of students who are educationally disabled
b. Appropriate curriculum offerings that deal with language barriers, cultural pluralism, and retention of dropout-prone youths
c. Transportation resources that permit mobility out of inner city or distant suburban neighborhoods and access to unique community resources
d. Selection and retention of qualified teachers to work with urban students who are educationally handicapped
e. Dropout rates that remain the highest in the nation (Kortering, Haring, & Klockars, 1992)
f. Maintaining safe school environments

5. *Survival behavior.*   The struggle to survive in heavily populated urban areas reaches deep into families of all racial, ethnic, or cultural groups. Economic survival is basic to physical survival, and many students with disabilities are experiencing early the pressures of being an adult in the real world. Having enough money to have a place to live and food to eat is a daily challenge for too many families, and compromises are made in order to have the basics of shelter and food. Just as important, though, is the struggle to survive the social and psychological stresses of poverty, noise, pollution, lack of privacy, and fear. Gangs, child abuse, and both random and directed violence loom as such major problems and concerns that a school may be seen only as a temporary escape, and even then not always as a safe one. Some secondary special education students in a midwest urban city were interviewed informally by their teachers in February of 1992 about their futures. When asked, "What is your greatest fear?" the most frequent responses were a fear of "getting shot" or "being forced to do something bad that I should not do."

Rural Issues.   The factors influencing the nature and characteristics of high school students in rural areas are numerous and varied. Rural communities are characterized as conservative and tend to adhere to traditional values (Flora, Flora, Spears, & Swanson, 1992). These attitudes tend to provide a positive environment in terms of basic morality, ethics, and personal values that rural youths understand and learn very early. Many of these values, attitudes, and personal and social behaviors are taught in the home, in the local churches, and in community youth organizations such as scouting, 4-H clubs, and Future Farmers. Since rural schools are so attuned to the values of the community, they can, at times, reflect conservatism and resistance to change that affects the development of resources and programs. One such example relates to the role of women today. Many rural communities still influence their schools not to encourage and train girls for nontraditional paid occupations except agriculture.

Some isolated rural communities exhibit certain characteristics similar to those of developing countries. Rural areas, just as metropolitan areas, have poverty, alcoholism, inadequate housing, unemployment, and underemployment—but without many resources to remedy or improve the situation. The National Rural Small Schools Task Force ("Rural, Small Schools," 1988) reported more than a decade ago that the biggest problem facing small rural schools is that of educating children of low-income families. As many as 2.2 million children in 2,750 rural school districts across the nation suffer from chronic severe "poorness" across multiple areas: family poverty, low per-pupil expenditures, low student outcomes, and limited curriculum offerings. These circumstances influence students at any age, of course, but in adolescence, these effects become more obvious in attitudes and behaviors. If ever there was a group to be labeled "at risk," adolescents are such a group.

Many rural communities that are economically tied to agriculture have migrant workers. Some of these communities are the rural home bases of the migrant families and some are the seasonal homes. Families may leave south Texas, for example, in March or April, boarding up their doors and windows and removing their children from school. They follow the crops, moving north until the end of the fall harvests of the Northwest and Upper Midwest states, then return to their homes in late September or October and return their children to school. Depending on their ages, the children and youths spend decreasing amounts of time in school (even temporary enrollments) and increasing amounts of time in the fields. Schooling back at the home base may last no longer than four or five months a year. Obviously, this pattern is difficult for all the children, but especially for those who have special learning needs. Consequently, many rural schools find themselves facing the need to offer an increasing number of support services—social work, special education, bilingual education, and guidance. Most of them face these needs without adequate financial resources.

Cultural and Ethnic Variables

Cultural, social, and ethnic influences on values, self-concept, and personality development are well established (Akan & Grilo, 1995; Steward, Giminez, & Jackson, 1995; Thompson, 1995). These influences are at work irrespective of the geographic location or size of a community. That is, cultural, social, or ethnic forces are operating in regional locales and in both urban and rural settings across regions. Urban areas will have many cultural or ethnic groups. Rural areas may have one or two cultural or ethnic groups in relatively small numbers or perhaps a single, predominantly ethnic community. In fact, the United States is the most ethnically diverse nation in the world.

Some urban and rural factors are probably more influential in personality development than are cultural or ethnic variables, so one cannot generalize for any racial, cultural, or ethnic sample without knowing the regional location and size or nature of their community. This is seen in the differences especially between urban and rural African Americans, Native Americans, and Hispanics. The interaction between geographical and cultural or ethnic influences is illustrated in the following brief descriptions.

Urban Ethnic.   Within the inner city of many major cities lives an ethnic group that some call "ghetto dwellers." At least two-thirds of these people are African American, Puerto Rican, Cuban, Mexican American, or members of some of the new minority groups to the United States, such as Southeast Asian refugees and Mexican and Central American aliens. Many are first-generation newcomers to the United States; some are refugees from rural backgrounds and poverty; and some are fleeing political and economic chaos. Many of the children from these families have experienced family disruption, family losses, and despair from failure, stress, and violence. All had hopes of a better way of life when they arrived, but the slums they find as the only affordable neighborhoods quickly diminish their hopes.

The most universal problem shared by those who assume responsibility for individual slum families is an inadequate wage. Inadequate or nonexistent wages result in chronic dependence for many of these families. Others cope through extended families or by working at more than one job. All of these factors affect the children and youths in these families. Many become streetwise and highly enculturated in their neighborhoods and the inner city, but most find school and their environments sources of frustration, failure, and despair.

In contrast to the inner-city ethnic group, there is another urban ethnic group. This group lives between the inner city and the suburbs. These individuals have postage-stamp row houses in or near industrial or commercial areas, and were born and raised in these city neighborhoods and rarely think of moving out. This group lives in the "gray area" fringe of central cities and constitutes the majority of the nation's semiskilled and skilled work force.

Rural Ethnic.   The major ethnic groups that live in rural areas are Hispanics (primarily of Mexican origin), Native Americans, and African Americans. These three minority groups are associated with specific areas of the country—Hispanics in the Southwest (California, Texas, New Mexico, Colorado, and Arizona), Native Americans in the Southwest, West, and Northwest (Oklahoma, Arizona, California, Utah, New Mexico, Washington, and Alaska), and African Americans in the South (Alabama, Georgia, Mississippi, Louisiana, Arkansas, and parts of Texas, Florida, South Carolina, North Carolina, and Tennessee).

Native Americans are the only major minority or ethnic group that is predominately rural. They are tending to become more urban, but this group continues to remain the largest group in rural and isolated locales. They are among the most economically depressed groups in the country. Most rural Native Americans (except in Alaska) live on reservations and are extremely poor. The reservation system tends to hinder social and geographical mobility. It is the ancestral home, the place of tribal activity, a family residence, a buffer against a changing modern world, and a channel for government assistance.

Culturally, Native Americans have maintained many tribal values about family, tradition, and nature. These values provide youths with some sense of security as they mature and face changes in themselves and in the larger culture. Although mostly positive, there are times when such values prevent families from agreeing to certain "unnatural" interventions with their sons or daughters with disabilities at school. Hearing aids, for example, would not be acceptable in some tribes for their adolescents. Thus, it is important for special educators to realize that, in this case, the disability of hearing impairment may not be so much something that exists inside a person, but rather a phenomenon that is defined within an ecological context—a social value judgment.

African American and Hispanic populations are more concentrated in urban areas than in rural areas, but they still constitute a significant number of rural residents. To be African American and rural, or Hispanic and rural, means that the person is likely to be poor. The poverty of many rural African Americans is an example of how the social structure feeds the roots of poverty. Education, health services, and economic opportunity have been systematically denied or restricted over the years, so that domestic service, farm labor, and low-skill, low-paying, nonfarm jobs are the primary occupational opportunities. Rural Hispanic families are found in the same occupational situation, and on every index of socioeconomic status (income, occupation, and education) they are among the lowest. This is especially true of the large proportion who can speak little or no English.

The major effort of rural ethnic minorities to break their poverty cycle and change their social structure is through migrant labor. This is seldom successful, however, as these workers cannot get adequate education; their work is often physically stressful, unhealthful, or hazardous; their housing is often bad; and they are always rootless—strangers in a succession of new environments. There is evidence that African and Hispanic Americans disproportionately encounter barriers to health care (Cornelius & Altman, 1995). Still, not all states regulate labor camps, conditions of travel, working hours of children, and work conditions. Federal law requires registration of crew leaders in at least a minimal gesture toward regulation, but the health and welfare of migratory workers continue to be a problem.

Special education professionals must be responsive to different cultural and ethnic values, styles, and traditions. It is a well-known fact that minority ethnic groups are typically overrepresented in special education programs. Unfortunately, there is very little research on the meaning of disability or its impact on various ethnic groups. The lack of information in this area puts special educators in the position of taking responsibility for finding out the cultural and ethnic perspectives of the parents of their students and how these perspectives affect parent-teacher and student-teacher communication as well as alternatives in educational interventions. Ogbu (1994) argued that neither the core curriculum movement or the multicultural education movement adequately addresses the problem of minority students who do not do well in school. Minorities whose cultural values are oppositional to the American mainstream cultural frame of reference have greater difficulty crossing cultural boundaries to learn.

Walker (1991) and D'Amico and Maxwell (1995) provided a helpful perspective for addressing some important cultural issues that emerge in school and rehabilitation programs preparing individuals for independence and work. The cultural assumptions that educators and adult service agencies bring to their work (e.g., assessment, planning instruction, placement in jobs, etc.) may be quite different from those of their students or clients from other cultural backgrounds. Some of those assumptions and the implications of those assumptions for work include the following:

Cultural Assumptions	*Implications for Education and Employment*
Family boundaries	Life crises and events affect attendance since family is a priority
Quality of life	Independence may be rejected in favor of family interdependence
Importance of social status	Different responses to supervisors
Importance of religion	Generosity and community support may be more important than "profit" or advancement
Meaning of work	May view the purpose and nature of work differently
Decision-making style	May value group decision making or may prefer authoritarian style to avoid individual decision making
Belief in change	May not desire individual control and may see situations as fatalistic
Work routines/expectations	May desire main meal at mid-day with rest period or have preferences for type of clothing that is congruent with their health and safety

Walker (1991) stated that the world view of a member of a minority or multinational group is very important for educational and rehabilitation planning. The more you know about the culture of an individual with disabilities and his or her living environment and value systems, the more effective your intervention and training efforts can be. When you are not familiar with the specific cultural values of a student and his or her family, ask the student directly and get help from someone who does know.

Socioeconomic Variables

It is difficult to categorize or describe the middle-class populations in urban and suburban environments. Popenoe (1985) reviewed some rather familiar descriptors of the middle-class American that set the stage for a brief overview of this group:

1. The middle-class American is not a great reader of books.
2. Television viewing is the most frequent form of entertainment, averaging about 22 hours per week.
3. Most middle-class adults and adolescents do not walk for pleasure or bicycle frequently. Jogging, aerobics, and fitness activities are glamorized and are increasing in frequency but are still engaged in by a minority.
4. Middle-class Americans tend to "neighbor" more than people in other countries. Neighboring may involve giving help, sharing equipment, cooperating in work efforts, and socializing informally.
5. Nearly half of urban and suburban middle-class Americans are actively engaged in church attendance and activities.
6. "Moonlighting" or a second job is common among middle-class families, as are two wage-earners in the family.
7. Mobility is a life-style characteristic of middle-class families with a change of residence at a rate about twice that of Europeans. Most of the moves occur within the same county.
8. Compared with life in Japan and western Europe, the U.S. middle-class life is marked by a relatively high degree of economic security.

The nature of suburban middle-class families has changed considerably from the "Dick and Jane" image of the 1940s and 1950s. The white-collar exodus from the cities to the suburbs led to a stereotyping of suburbia that was characterized by income and life-style. By the 1970s, a broad middle class emerged, making up more than half of the metropolitan population. The primary change of this class expansion was the upward mobility of blue-collar workers. Their incomes increased significantly—enough to enable them to match incomes and status symbols with white-collar workers (suburban homes, numerous household appliances, season tickets to sports events, recreational vans and campers, snowmobiles, boats, designer clothes, etc.).

The life-styles of middle-class families in urban and suburban communities has produced a generation of adolescents with a range of values, aspirations, and life-style dreams. Adolescents with disabilities today are confused by the mixed messages of home, school, and society about what is desirable and what is possible. Societal changes have placed stresses on middle-class families. The force of these changes has greatly weakened parents' authority and diminished their enthusiasm for parenting. As parents have yielded their authority and responsibility—sometimes literally, sometimes symbolically—adolescents with disabilities are seen by many educators as the school's responsibility by default. The adolescents, on the other hand, are increasingly influenced by their peers' values, attitudes, and behavior. Many are more interested in the themes played up by the mass media—glamour, sex, affluence, and entertainment (escape) as solutions to problems—than the themes of the high school, which include academic achievement, responsibility, and occupational goals, interspersed with athletic events, proms, and school-related extracurricular activities.

Families as Participants

Even if the parents' rights and responsibilities for participation in the education planning for their sons or daughters with disabilities were not clearly established in PL 94-142, the emphasis on transition services in the 1997 Amendments to the IDEA make it very clear that a partnership is absolutely critical. It is much easier during the elementary years for parents to yield to the school's considerable authority for educational decisions, particularly on the content of the curriculum. For some teachers and parents, school is more or less an end in itself, rather than a means to an end, and the content and substance of what is taught in school is of secondary importance to being there. When a student with disabilities nears the age of entry into high school, the decisions parents and students make are much more critical in that they are no longer focused on the short-term goal of moving through the educational system reasonably successfully, academically and socially. From age 14 on, the educational meter is ticking and choices that are made regarding courses of study (and even specific courses) should be made with outcomes in mind for postsecondary life.

The provisions of the IDEA state that those decisions should be made based on the students' needs, preferences, and interests. However, families must be active participants in the determination of what those needs, preferences, and interests are and be involved in the guidance and teaching process that the schools cannot do alone. Parent/family roles and responsibilities as participants in a career-development and transition-oriented secondary school program include the following:

1. Encourage student self-determination and independence at home.
2. Encourage and facilitate setting goals.
3. Teach, and assist in teaching, daily living and personal-social skills.
4. Encourage the student to work at home and at a neighborhood or community job.
5. Reinforce work-related and independent living behaviors at home.
6. Explore and promote community resources for transition.
7. Assist in the student assessment process.

8. Assist the student in developing personal and social values, self-confidence, and self-esteem.
9. Work with legal and financial experts, as appropriate, to plan financial, legal, and residential alternatives.

Students as Participants

The regulations for the IDEA (PL 101-476) and the amendments of 1997 (PL 105-17) state that when the purpose of an IEP meeting is to consider transition services for a student, the school shall invite the student to participate in her or his IEP meeting. For any student who is 14 years of age or older, the annual IEP meeting will always have as one of its purposes to consider transition service needs. It is our position that students of 14 years of age (and even younger) should not only be invited but encouraged to attend. Beyond that, the school should provide systematic instruction or guidance for students in how they can participate fully. Without that, the invitation and attendance are only token compliance efforts. For a student younger than age 14, if transition services are initially discussed at an IEP meeting that does not include the student, the school is responsible for ensuring that before a decision about transition services for the student is made, a subsequent IEP meeting shall be conducted for that purpose, the student will be invited to the meeting, and the student will participate in the planning of the IEP. We strongly urge that students be involved in the IEP process, beginning in the elementary school years.

The specific wording of the statute mandating transition services states that the coordinated set of activities described in the definition of transition services "must be based on the individual student's needs, taking into account the student's preferences and interests" [20 U.S.C. 1401(a)(19)]. The student's participation in the determination of needs, preferences, and interests should take place during the assessment process used in establishing present level of functioning for IEP planning as well as during the IEP meeting itself.

Conclusion

The participants in secondary special education programming are an extremely heterogeneous population. The variations of size, location, population characteristics, and local and state laws and policies make for extremely different educational situations. These variations have implications for differences that you can expect as you are introduced to a given program as a newly employed professional or a prospective employee. If educators understand differences in students and use that understanding in providing the best programming possible for identified youths with disabilities, then educators can move closer to being professionals rather than technicians.

5 Transition Assessment

Latent abilities are like clay. It can be mud on shoes, brick in a building, or a statue that will inspire all who see it. The clay is the same. The result is dependent on how it is used.

—James A. Lincoln

As individuals with disabilities make the transition from school to adult life, the process of assessment is critical in all areas and stages of planning. Assessment in career development, vocational decision making, and transition planning is an essential process that is often overlooked, ignored, or misunderstood. The purpose of this chapter is to provide an overview of transition assessment, including history, relationship to current legislation, and assessment areas; methods of gathering assessment information on the individual and his or her future living, working, and educational environments; tying assessment into transition planning; issues to consider when conducting assessments; and people involved in the transition assessment process. The chapter then concludes with a list of resources on assessment and recommendations for transition assessment. As recommended practices in assessment are advanced, it is hoped that individuals with disabilities will experience appropriate, meaningful, and effective assessment activities that will enhance their personal growth and quality of life as they make their transitions to future living, working, and educational environments.

Overview of Transition Assessment

The Division on Career Development and Transition (DCDT; Sitlington, Neubert, & Leconte, 1997) advocated transition assessment for all students moving through the education system to careers and other activities. Transition assessment is especially needed for individuals with disabilities. As planning teams move to identify postsecondary goals, professionals and students with disabilities and their families need to identify effective assessment practices and to understand that assessment is an ongoing process. This does not mean that entirely new methods and approaches of assessment are needed to facilitate transition planning. Considerable information exists on effective methods of assessment that identify vocational, instructional, independent living, community functioning, and personal and social strengths of individuals with disabilities. Transition assessment, however, does require that we determine appropriate methods of assessment at various transition points for individuals with disabilities in order to make appropriate placement and planning decisions.

History of Assessment

The transition assessment process builds on the earlier concepts of vocational evaluation and assessment and career assessment (Sitlington, 1996). Having a history of all of these assessment approaches may help you better understand the concept of transition assessment and how to use this process with your students.

Vocational Evaluation and Assessment.   The vocational evaluation and assessment techniques used in U.S. schools were borrowed from the field of vocational rehabilitation and programs operated in rehabilitation facilities. These techniques first entered the schools through separate work experience and vocational training programs for individuals with disabilities. They also emerged in vocational-technical education programs (Neubert, 1994). The majority of the vocational evaluation and assessment practices in vocational rehabilitation emerged from the parent disciplines of psychology (including industrial psychology), industrial engineering and production management, and medicine (including the related fields of occupational therapy, medical case management, and physical therapy) (Leconte, 1994a, 1994b). Curriculum-based vocational assessment (CBVA; Albright & Cobb, 1988a, 1988b; Cobb & Larkin, 1985; Stodden, Ianacone, Boone, & Bisconer, 1987) was one of the most significant models that emerged out of vocational-technical education programs. This model proposed that assessment data be collected directly on the students while they were enrolled in vocational-technical education programs or in other vocational training programs.

   A number of attempts have been made to take an interdisciplinary approach to the area of vocational evaluation and assessment. In 1981, the Commission on Certification of Work Adjustment and Vocational Evaluation Specialists (CCWAVES) was established as an independent commission. As stated in the CCWAVES *Standards and Procedures Manual for Certification in Vocational Evaluation* (1996), "The primary purpose of this certification process is to provide assurance that those professionals engaged in vocational evaluation meet acceptable standards of quality" (p. 6). In 1991, the Interdisciplinary Council on Vocational Evaluation and Assessment was formed. This council was a national coalition of over 10 organizations that represented the issues and concerns of personnel involved in vocational evaluation and assessment across a variety of settings and disciplines (Schuster & Smith, 1994). The council proposed seven principles to serve as a guide to recommended practices in vocational evaluation and assessment across all settings (Smith, Lombard, Neubert, Leconte, Rothenbacher, & Sitlington, 1994).

A third effort involving collaboration and communication across disciplines in the area of vocational evaluation and assessment was the *Glossary of Terminology for Vocational Assessment, Evaluation and Work Adjustment* (Dowd, 1993). This glossary was a project of the Vocational Evaluation and Work Adjustment Association, which solicited and included input from all the major disciplines involved in the assessment and evaluation process.

Career Assessment.   As the focus shifted from vocational education to the broader concept of career education, the focus of assessment also broadened. A position paper on career and vocational assessment in the public school setting, endorsed by the then Division on Career Development (Sitlington, Brolin, Clark, & Vacanti, 1985), focused on the concept of career assessment and defined it as "a developmental process beginning at the elementary-school level and continuing through adulthood" (p. 3). Career assessment relates to lifelong career development, which affects all life roles. The specific content to be assessed in the career assessment process should be dictated by the components of the career education model being implemented.

In the school years, career assessment provides information on which to make decisions related to all areas of adult life. This process directly parallels the career education stages of awareness, exploration, and preparation as well as provides information upon which to make decisions as soon as the individual enters the educational system. The career assessment process encompasses vocational assessment and the occupationally related information gathered as part of this process. Career assessment also gathers information on the individual's other life roles, such as family member, citizen, and participant in leisure, recreational, and avocational activities (Sitlington, Brolin, Clark, & Vacanti, 1985).

Transition Assessment.   Just as the concept of career assessment was proposed to address the information needs of career education, transition assessment addresses the information needs of transition planning and implementation. Transition services encompass career education, vocational education, and other life skills development. DCDT endorsed the following definition of *transition assessment:*

> Transition assessment is the ongoing process of collecting data on the individual's strengths, needs, preferences, and interests as they relate to the demands of current and future working, educational, living, and personal and social environments. Assessment data serve as the common thread in the transition process and form the basis for defining goals and services to be included in the Individualized Education Program (IEP). (Sitlington, Neubert, & Leconte, 1997, p. 71)

Clark (1998) proposed the following broader working definition of *transitions assessment,* which was meant to address all of the transitions encountered by an individual, from early childhood through adulthood:

Transitions assessment is a planned, continuous process of obtaining, organizing, and using information to assist individuals with disabilities of all ages and their families to make all critical transitions in students' lives both successful and satisfying. (p. 2)

Clark went on to state that good transitions assessment addresses for each individual the goals and expectations that he or she has for a transition period or event. Good transitions assessment also suggests areas of planning, preparation, or decision making that would increase the likelihood of the individual reaching those goals and being satisfied with the outcomes.

Sitlington (1996) attempted to present the relationship among transition assessment, career assessment, and vocational assessment as a beginning point of discussion. As can be seen in Figure 5.1, *transition assessment* is the umbrella term that encompasses both career assessment and vocational assessment. Transition assessment relates to all life roles and to the support needed before, during, and after the transition to adult life. Figure 5.1 also provides information on the relationship among transition, career, and vocational assessment.

Assessment data collected during the transition assessment process should be used to assist individuals with disabilities in making informed choices. Thus, assessment activities serve as the basis for determining an individual's strengths, needs, preferences, and interests related to career development, vocational training, postsecondary education goals, community functioning, health, and personal and social skills. This requires that assessment occur in a variety of environments that are natural to the individual's life. Special and general education personnel must be prepared to work cooperatively with individuals with disabilities, their families, related school personnel, and community service providers to determine what types of assessment data need to be collected and which methods will facili-

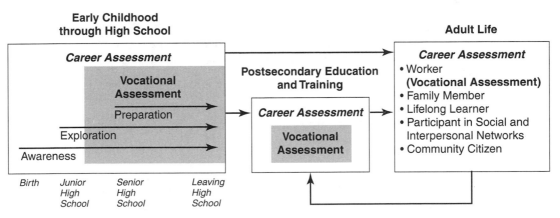

FIGURE 5.1 Transition Assessment

Source: From "Transition Assessment—Where Have We Been and Where Should We Be Going?" by P. L. Sitlington, 1996, *Career Development for Exceptional Individuals, 19,* page 163. Copyright 1996 by the Council for Exceptional Children. Reprinted by permission.

tate the process. In addition, local school district or building policies must be in place to support these activities.

Policies That Facilitate Transition Assessment

For years, special education literature has made a case for assessment as a key part of understanding needs and drawing inferences for curriculum decisions, instruction, and needed support systems. All of these reasons for assessment still hold for transition assessment, with the additional rationale of meeting the spirit and letter of legislation that has specifically targeted transition services as a public school responsibility. Sitlington, Neubert, Begun, Lombard, and Leconte (1996) laid out a compliance rationale for transition assessment for secondary-level students who are of age to be eligible for school transition services, vocational education, vocational rehabilitation services, and employment training under the Job Training Partnership Act (JTPA; PL 97-330) and its amendments. (See Chapter 3 for a description of this legislation.) What is important in using legislation as a rationale for assessment is pointing out the language in the laws or their respective regulations that require or permit certain kinds of assessment activities. Sitlington and associates cited such language in the Individuals with Disabilities Education Act (PL 101-476), the Carl D. Perkins Vocational Education and Applied Technology Act (PL 101-392), the Rehabilitation Act Amendments of 1992 (PL 102-569), and the Job Training Reform Act of 1992 (PL 102-367). All clearly relate to the issue of promoting movement from school to postschool activities. The School-to-Work Opportunities Act of 1994 (PL 103-239) also has direct implications for students with disabilities. Students with disabilities accessing school-to-work program components of school-based learning, work-based learning, and connecting activities will need appropriate assessment.

The IDEA Amendments (1997) lowered the mandate for transition planning as part of the IEP process to students 14 years of age, with some qualitative distinctions between 14 and 15 year olds and those age 16 and older. The Division on Career Development and Transition (DCDT; Clark, Carlson, Fisher, Cook, & D'Alonzo, 1991; Clark, Field, Patton, Brolin, & Sitlington, 1994; Sitlington, Neubert, & Leconte, 1997) had recommended this downward shift in several of its position papers. Both the IDEA Amendments and the DCDT also stressed the involvement of students and family members in the transition assessment process.

The challenge of planning transition services for an exceptionally large number of students who have never before had such planning is enormous. In some school districts, additional assessment procedures are being used or new ones developed to achieve full compliance and adopt recommended practices (Corbey, Miller, Severson, & Enderle, 1993; Clark, 1996; Sitlington, Neubert, Begun, Lombard, & Leconte, 1996; Sitlington, Neubert, & Leconte, 1997). In spite of this, current assessment practices lag behind both the IDEA mandates and recommended practices (Clark, 1998).

As Clark (1998) stated, policy makers, responding to research outcomes and advice from professionals and consumers, recognized that effective assessment is necessary for successful transition, and that both the assessment and transition processes require communication, cooperation, and collaboration among many different players. Recent laws reflect these themes of collaboration among educators, human services professionals, employers in the business sector, community members, parents, family members, and, most importantly, students.

Increasingly, federal and state laws and policy initiatives require interdisciplinary and interagency collaboration. For example, the Rehabilitation Act Amendments of 1992, the Individuals with Disabilities Education Act of 1990, and the Carl D. Perkins Vocational and Applied Technology Education Act of 1990 each cross-referenced the others. The Rehabilitation Act Amendments of 1992 allowed use of vocational and transition assessment data collected by educators for developing Individualized Written Rehabilitation Plans. The Perkins Act mandated that assessment help facilitate placements in integrated settings and serve as the basis for instructional support, accommodations, and transition planning for students with disabilities who receive services under IDEA. IDEA (1990) and the IDEA Amendments (1997) required that transition planning be based on students' interests, preferences, and needs. It is implied that all transition team members (the student, family members, adult service providers, teachers, and others) provide assessment information and assume responsibilities for specific transition goals and objectives.

Student choice is another primary policy theme reflected in these and other laws that assert that individuals with disabilities should be equal partners in planning and decision making for their postsecondary goals. Current legislation, including the Job Training Reform Amendments of 1992 and the School-to-Work Opportunities Act of 1994, emphasizes that students and consumers should direct their own educational, transition, and rehabilitation planning processes. To guide planning processes effectively, students must be sufficiently informed about their strengths, needs, preferences, and interests and how these relate to work and careers, postsecondary education, independent living, community activities, and personal and social relationships. Students acquire this information by participating in assessment; self-discovery leads to self-knowledge, which fosters self-determination. Student choice, consumer self-advocacy, and the need for interdisciplinary planning are policy themes that are likely to continue to be incorporated in future legislation and deserve careful attention in the transition assessment process.

Primary Assessment Areas for Transition Planning

The types of information gathered in the assessment process should relate directly to the areas the teacher and the rest of the IEP team are addressing in the transition planning process. The questions asked in transition planning should translate directly into the information to be gathered. Conversely, the information gathered in the assessment process should be incorporated in the Present Levels of Educational Performance section of the IEP and drive the IEP and transition planning process.

The professional literature related to the outcomes for individuals with disabilities once they leave school (i.e., adult outcomes) has focused on these general areas: independent living (within the home and community living demands), personal-social adjustment, postsecondary education and training, and employment (Clark & Kolstoe, 1995; Halpern, 1985; Kokaska & Brolin, 1985). Dever (1988), Smith and Schloss (1988), Knowles (1990), Brolin (1995b), and Cronin and Patton (1993) expanded these areas into multiple critical life domains of adulthood. The consequence of this refinement is a very specific listing of life skills associated with a variety of transition processes. A descriptive set of outcome areas has particular implications for assessing students' present levels of performance for IEP planning. That listing gives direction to both assessment and intervention for all students with disabilities.

One of the current problems with assessing present levels of performance in areas related to life skills and adult outcomes for the IEP is the narrow range of assessment areas used in schools since 1978. For most teachers working directly with students with mild disabilities, "present level of performance" has been virtually restricted to academic and, in some cases, behavioral assessment data (McBride & Forgnone, 1985; Smith, 1990). Just as existing school instructional program options often drive individual planning and placement, existing school assessment practices emphasizing academic achievement often drive IEP goals and objectives.

The focus areas for transition assessment that we propose are the Knowledge and Skills Domains presented in the Comprehensive Transition Education Model (Figure 2.1) discussed in Chapter 2. Figure 5.2 presents these areas and their relationship to the transition assessment process.

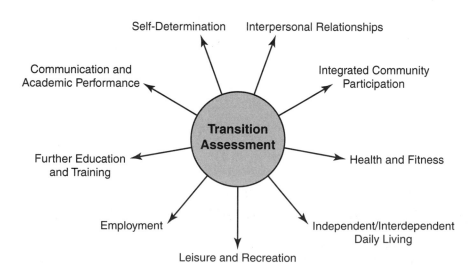

FIGURE 5.2   Knowledge and Skill Domains for Transition Assessment

Methods of Gathering Assessment Information

Transition assessment is an ongoing process that focuses on the individual's current and future roles as a worker, lifelong learner, family member, community citizen, and participant in social and interpersonal networks. We support the position of the Interdisciplinary Council on Vocational Evaluation and Assessment (Smith, Lombard, Neubert, Leconte, Rothenbacher, & Sitlington, 1994), which advocates that the assessment process be student centered and be designed to emphasize individual capabilities rather than disabilities. In addition, working, educational, and living environments should be adapted to accommodate the individual, rather than the individual trying to adjust to fit the environments.

A number of methods have been used in the past two decades to conduct career, vocational, and transition assessment. These methods can be conceptualized in two broad domains. First, assessment methods can be used to assess the *individual* and include techniques such as: (1) analysis of background information, (2) interviews/questionnaires, (3) psychometric instruments, (4) work samples, (5) curriculum-based assessment techniques, and (6) situational assessment. Second, assessment methods can be used to assess or analyze *future working, educational, and living environments*. Although we do not endorse specific methods in the process of transition assessment, we do emphasize the need for personnel to move beyond methods that are isolated from actual life contexts (such as paper and pencil tests) and to move toward methods that are conducted within natural or actual employment, postsecondary, or community settings. For instance, if an individual is participating in transition assessment to identify employment options, assessment activities should take place in a variety of real work settings to determine strengths, needs, preferences, interests, and compatibility with the skill demands and social interactions of each setting. During the assessment process, it would also be necessary to determine the individual's compatibility with the transportation options (e.g., transferring to a subway or riding a bus) required to travel to and from work in the community or to address lack of transportation in rural areas.

Sitlington, Neubert, and Leconte (1997) suggested the following guidelines for selecting methods used in the transition assessment process:

1. Assessment methods must be tailored to the types of information needed and the decisions to be made regarding transition planning and various postsecondary outcomes.
2. Specific methods selected must be appropriate for the learning characteristics of the individual, including cultural and linguistic differences.
3. Assessment methods must incorporate assistive technology or accommodations that will allow an individual to demonstrate his or her abilities and potential.
4. Assessment methods must occur in environments that resemble actual vocational training, employment, independent living, or community environments.
5. Assessment methods must produce outcomes that contribute to ongoing development, planning, and implementation of "next steps" in the individual's transition process.

6. Assessment methods must be varied and include a sequence of activities that sample an individual's behavior and skills over time.
7. Assessment data must be verified by more than one method and by more than one person.
8. Assessment data must be synthesized and interpreted to individuals with disabilities, their families, and transition team members.
9. Assessment data and the results of the assessment process must be documented in a format that can be used to facilitate transition planning. (p. 75)

There is a wealth of information in the general education, special education, rehabilitation, and vocational education literature on methods and models of assessment that identify instructional, vocational, community, independent living, and personal/social strengths and needs of individuals with disabilities. New methods and models of assessment are not needed to identify postsecondary goals and facilitate transition planning. The task is to determine what methods of assessment are needed at various transition points for individuals with disabilities to make appropriate decisions regarding their futures.

This section provides an overview of methods that can be used in transition assessment. Each method is briefly described along with a discussion of the types of information that can be collected through this method. First, methods for assessing individuals are presented. Next, methods of assessing environments are discussed. Much of the information included in the following discussions is taken from *Assess for Success: Handbook on Transition Assessment* (Sitlington, Neubert, Begun, Lombard, & Leconte, 1996). The focus of the handbook is on using the outcomes of assessment for IEP planning. The handbook includes chapters on the role of self-determination in the transition assessment process, roles of key players, and methods of gathering information. The final chapter presents the process of making the match between the individual's strengths, needs, interests, and preferences and the demands of and supports found in future living, working, and educational environments. The text also provides more information on each of the methods presented in the following sections and discusses the strengths and weaknesses of each approach. Examples of each method are also provided in this source.

Methods of Gathering Information on the Individual

Following is an overview of basic methods of gathering information on the individual in need of transition assessment. This will help you in assisting students in planning for the transition from school to all aspects of adult life. The methods covered are (1) analysis of background information, (2) interviews/questionnaires, (3) psychometric instruments, (4) work samples, (5) curriculum-based assessment techniques, and (6) situational assessment.

The IDEA Amendments (1997) mandated that students with disabilities be included in state- and districtwide assessment programs and have any alternate assessments in place beginning in the year 2000. As stated in Section 614 of these Amendments, the student's IEP must include a statement of any accommodations needed to participate in these programs. If the IEP team determines that the student will not participate in a particular state or district assessment of the student's achievement, the team must include a statement of why the assessment is not appropriate and how the student will be assessed. This mandate will require you to review existing alternate assessment instruments as well as all of the methods discussed in this section to determine what is appropriate for your students and the type of information you want to gather on them.

Analysis of Background Information. One of the first sources of information about the student should be existing records, which contain observations of previous teachers, support staff, and staff from other agencies (e.g., mental health, juvenile justice, or youth and family services) who have worked with the individual. In addition to the cumulative folder, there are often other records kept by the teacher or other support staff who have worked with the student. These other records usually have more useful information than the "official" student files. Be sure that you also review past Individual Educational Programs (IEPs), with particular emphasis on transition-related objectives and activities contained in these IEPs. Also ask for any additional formal and informal assessments that have been conducted with the student. Although all of this information should be in the student's official files, this is often not the case. If other youth and adult service agencies have been working with the individual, ask if you may also review their information, after receiving appropriate releases of information from the family or the individual.

Student portfolios provide valuable information that has been selected by the student and staff as representative of his or her interests, goals, and finest work. In fact, a transition portfolio is an excellent means of organizing and summarizing all of the transition assessment and transition planning activities in which the student has participated. These and other existing records often contain a wealth of information on the strengths and interests of the individual, as well as the areas on which the individual needs to focus. This information might be in the form of comments of previous teachers, guidance counselors, and other support staff and adult service providers; formal and informal assessment results; and records of IEP meetings. These records might also contain information on the experiences the individual has had in the community related to living and employment, and the techniques and approaches that have worked (or not worked) with the individual in the past. Information on health-related issues can also be found. If transition planning activities have been conducted with the student in previous years, it is very helpful to review the trends in the student's expressed interests and preferences over these years.

It is important to remember in reviewing records, however, that individuals may react differently to new living or work environments and personnel. They may enter these environments with a changed attitude. Also, in the adolescent years, students often change behavior and attitudes almost overnight. Thus, although previous information should be considered, take some time to form opinions based on your own observations and experiences with the student, as well as his or her self-reports.

Interviews/Questionnaires.   Interviews with the student, family members, former teachers, friends, counselors, other support staff, and former employers may be one of the best sources of information on how the individual functions in the real world and what he or she would like to do as an adult. Frequently, brothers and sisters of students have more realistic and accurate information than their parents about their siblings' long-term goals, their social and personal aspirations, and their abilities. Siblings are major stakeholders in students' transitions, since they may one day assume responsibility for their brothers and sisters who have disabilities. Sitlington, Neubert, Begun, Lombard, and Leconte (1996) is a good resource for specific hints on conducting interviews. If face-to-face or phone interviews are not possible, some of the same information can be gathered through questionnaires that require short, written responses. Care must be taken, though, to make sure those completing the questionnaire can understand the questions and are able to respond clearly in writing.

Psychometric Instruments.   Psychometric instruments (sometimes called *paper-and-pencil instruments*) are often standardized tests and inventories that are available from commercial publishers. Psychometric instruments are farther removed from tasks required in the real world of employment and adult community living than most of the other techniques presented in this section, but they do relate to current academic goals and demands and may relate to choices or decisions for further education and training. Many of these instruments have been formally field tested with sample groups and often include a norm group with which the individual is compared. Some psychometric tests are criterion-referenced and provide information on how the individual has performed related to specific content areas of the test, such as budgeting, health, or job seeking skills. Examples of these instruments include tests of academic achievement, vocational interest, functional living skills, self-concept, learning styles, and vocational aptitude. Although some of these instruments must be administered by individuals formally trained in test administration and interpretation, a number of them can be administered by the classroom teacher. Some standardized instruments are not tests of knowledge, skills, or psychological traits or behaviors, but are self-assessments or rating scales. In these cases, highly trained administrators are rarely required.

At the back of this book, Appendix B offers a listing of selected commercially available assessment instruments for transition planning. This list was developed by Clark (1998) and includes instruments appropriate for students of varying ages. Other sources (Clark, 1996; Corbey, Miller, Severson, & Enderle, 1993) also provide information on the major psychometric tests related to the areas of transition.

Many people think of assessment as these formal instruments. The advantage of this approach is that it provides an "official-looking" score and a standardized method of gathering specific information. Like any of the techniques described in this chapter, however, psychometric tests should not be used as the *only* method of gathering the information you need to assist the student and his or her family in transition planning. These instruments, however, can provide information on the academic functioning level of the student, including the areas of strength and the areas in need of improvement. Many professionals use these instruments as a starting point to plan other assessment activities or to engage in discussion with the student, especially in regard to planning and decision making about college or other postsecondary education expectations.

Psychometric tests can also provide information on the *knowledge* level of the student related to functional living areas (e.g., managing money, maintaining a home, and shopping) and to specific occupations or occupational clusters. These instruments, however, do *not* provide information on how well the individual applies this knowledge in real-life situations. In addition, the ability of the student to perform well on these instruments depends not only on knowledge but also on the amount of experience the student has had with the situations presented in the test.

Work Samples.   *Work sampling* is defined as a "work activity involving tasks, materials, and tools which are identical or similar to those in an actual job or cluster of jobs" (Fry & Botterbusch, 1988, as cited in Dowd, 1993, p. 12). Work samples can be used to assess an individual's interests, abilities, work habits, and personal and social skills. The key to administering work samples is to observe and document information concerning level of interest, attention to task, and requests for assistance or clarification in addition to an individual's actual performance of the task. Work samples often provide a direct link to occupational information, since they simulate specific aspects of vocational training or employment. Daily living activities can also be simulated in a type of community living sample.

Generally, work samples fall into two categories: commercial and locally developed or homemade. Commercial work samples are generally found in vocational evaluation units in school systems or rehabilitation facilities. Information on commercial work samples and the advantages and disadvantages of using them with individuals with disabilities are presented in Brown, McDaniel, and Couch (1994) and Pruitt (1986). Locally developed or homemade work samples are generally developed by a teacher or vocational evaluator and are more often used in the transition assessment process. These work samples can be developed on the basis of local job analyses, tasks in vocational training programs, or as part of the classroom career exploration process.

Work samples generally have a standard set of directions, tasks, materials, and key behaviors to observe. The Rehabilitation Resource (formerly the Materials Development Center) at University of Wisconsin–Stout has developed a manual for practitioners to follow when developing and administering informal work samples. Homemade work samples can also be found within vocational evaluation units and tend to sample tasks found in vocational programs or jobs specific to the local community. These samples tend to have high face validity since individuals can see and think about actual work.

Curriculum-Based Assessment Techniques.   One of the major thrusts in the field of education is toward curriculum-based assessment (CBA). This is assessment based on what a student has been taught within a curriculum. Salvia and Hughes (1990) list eight steps in the curriculum-based assessment approach (CBA):

1. Specify the reasons for the assessment.
2. Analyze the curriculum.
3. Formulate the behavioral objectives.
4. Develop the appropriate assessment procedures.
5. Collect the data.
6. Summarize the data.
7. Display the data.
8. Interpret the data and make decisions.

Curriculum-based assessment is really an *approach* rather than one specific method. This approach is included here, however, because it is often viewed as a specific assessment technique and is being used increasingly in content-area classes, such as math and English, as well as in vocational education programs. Curriculum-based assessment instruments can be developed by the teacher or other staff and should focus specifically on the content being taught. Examples of curriculum-based assessment techniques include criterion-referenced testing, curriculum-based measurement, portfolio assessment, performance-based assessment, and curriculum-based vocational assessment. Each of these approaches will be discussed in the following paragraphs. They can be used to gather information related to planning for future living, working, or educational environments.

Criterion-Referenced Testing.   The criterion-referenced testing approach compares the individual's performance to a preestablished level of performance (e.g., 80 percent) rather than to the performance of others or to a set of norms. In this approach, the emphasis is on the knowledge or skills needed for a specific content area and whether the individual has demonstrated mastery of this knowledge. Results of the assessment would indicate that the student scored 70 percent on two-digit by one-digit multiplication problems and 40 percent on two-digit by two-digit multiplication. The criterion-referenced testing approach is used primarily in academic areas, but can be used in any content area where skills can be broken down into specific subareas.

Curriculum-Based Measurement.   Curriculum-based measurement is an ongoing assessment approach that was developed by individuals at the University of Minnesota. It consists of a specific set of assessment techniques for the areas of reading, written expression, spelling, and math. This approach uses the concept of units per minute to measure the student's performance in the specific content area. Initial probes are taken from the beginning, middle, and end of the instructional content and additional probes of the student's performance are taken at least twice weekly throughout the instructional period. The student's performance is graphed on an ongoing basis and instruction is modified based on his or her progress toward established goals. For more information on curriculum-based measurement, consult Marston and Magnusson (1985) and Shinn (1989).

Portfolio Assessment.   The concept of portfolio assessment has been in use in the fine arts area for a number of years, as well as in vocational programs such as architecture, drafting, and graphic arts. As the emphasis in assessment moves toward the concept of *authentic assessment,* portfolios are being developed in a number of content areas and across content areas. The major steps in portfolio assessment are as follows:

1. Describe the curricular area.
2. Identify the overall goals of the portfolio.
3. Delineate the portfolio format and the type of materials to be included.
4. Describe the procedures for evaluating the work in the portfolio (e.g., student conferences and teacher review of material).
5. Describe how the contents of the portfolio will be summarized.

The following aspects of portfolio assessment are critical:

1. Criteria for selection of materials must be stated.
2. Students must participate in the development of these criteria and in the actual selection of the materials.
3. Criteria for evaluating the materials must be specified.
4. An opportunity for self-reflection on the part of the student must be provided.

The types of materials to be included in the portfolio can range from the results of vocational interest inventories to essays written by the student concerning his or her goals to samples of projects from social studies class or architectural drafting. This approach is an excellent method of compiling and summarizing all of the transition assessment activities of the student. In using this method, it is critical that the student have input into the types of materials to be included in the portfolio and that guidelines be established and followed for including materials in the portfolio. A portfolio with everything the student has completed will be difficult to evaluate and does not truly represent the student's abilities, interests, and preferences. It is also very important that the material in the portfolio be evaluated on an ongoing basis by the student and the teacher.

Performance-Based Assessment.   Performance-based assessment is related to the concept of *authentic assessment.* It lends itself to a variety of academic areas as well as nonacademic areas, such as music, art, dance, theater arts, speech, and physical education. Performance can be an observed performance (song, speech, dramatic monologue, etc.) or a product (musical composition, sculpture, painting, costume design, keyboard printout, etc.). In both types, observed performance or product, assessment is done through preestablished rubrics or criteria for evaluation.

Curriculum-Based Vocational Assessment.   One of the most recognized applications of the curriculum-based assessment approach is curriculum-based vocational assessment (CBVA). This is a process for determining the student's career development, vocational, and transition-related needs based on his or her ongoing performance within existing course content. For the specific application of CBVA, the target is usually performance in vocational education courses or on work experience sites in the school or community, although important information can also be gathered from performance in academic classes. This process not only allows you to collect information on the student's performance in a setting close to real life but it also allows you to determine the support that the student will need to succeed in vocational education classes or on the job. Albright and Cobb (1988b) identified three general phases in the CBVA process:

1. *Assessment during program placement and planning.*   This includes activities prior to and during the first few weeks of student participation in a vocational program. Information gathered during this phase assists in program selection, program placement, and program planning.
2. *Assessment during participation in a vocational program.*   These activities monitor the student's program, determine the appropriateness of the program and service delivery plan, and evaluate the success of the student's program.
3. *Assessment during program exiting.*   Assessment activities in this phase occur near the end of the student's program and immediately following completion of the student's program. Information gathered in this phase assists the team in identifying the special services needed to help the student transition into employment and/or postsecondary education and the best program(s) for the student.

If the student is in vocational education classes or work experiences in the community, information can be gathered on how well the individual actually performs tasks related to specific occupations. The student can also determine whether he or she is interested in the specific vocational area. Additionally, information can be gathered on how well the individual relates to others, including peers and supervisors, and in such areas as working independently, staying on task, and asking for assistance when needed. For more information on CBVA, consult Albright and Cobb (1988a, 1988b) and Stodden, Ianacone, Boone, and Bisconer (1987).

Summary.   Curriculum-based assessment is becoming a major emphasis within content area courses. This presents an ideal opportunity to gather information on the individual across a variety of instructional settings. If data are gathered on the student's performance in academic classes, information can be gathered on basic academic skills and how the student learns best, as well as work habits, preferences and values, and attitudes. The specific academic areas in which the student is interested and in which he or she excels can also be identified. The curriculum-based assessment approach can also provide information on the student's performance and/or knowledge of skills related to daily living, such as managing a checking account, negotiating with authority figures, doing laundry, and preparing meals. Finally, this approach can provide information on the student's interest and skills in leisure-time activities.

Situational Assessment.   *Situational assessment* is the systematic observation process for evaluating behaviors in environments as close as possible to the individual's future living, working, or educational environment. Observing and recording individual behavior in different work and community settings over time provides the foundation for transition assessment. Dowd (1993) defined an *observation procedure* as "an organized method of observing and objectively recording the behavior of an individual for the purpose of documenting this behavior. The emphasis is usually upon productivity, behavior patterns, expressed interest, and interpersonal interaction" (p. 20).

For information to be useful, behavior observation should be systematic and should take place in a variety of settings. It is also helpful to have different team members observe the same individual in various situations to make sure the information gathered is valid and reliable. Many different techniques can be used by practitioners to observe and record behavior, including narrative recording, time sampling, event recording, and rating scales.

The demands of the environment (e.g., work tasks, independent living tasks, and community functioning skills) can be varied while recording behaviors such as interest, actual skill level, use of materials, and social interactions. Situational assessments can be a valid and reliable source of data if the sites are systematically developed (uniform tasks a student will do, amount of time, supervision responsibilities, etc.) and if practitioners systematically record behaviors during the assessment process. The data collected can then be used in planning and placement decisions concerning further situational assessment sites, types of programs to consider for placement, and instructional/social accommodations needed in specific situations. Situational assessments can be conducted in recreation sites, community sites (e.g., a bank facility), and simulated or real sites that require independent living skills (e.g., home economics lab, family home, or supervised apartment).

Situational assessment also can be used to collect data on students' interests, abilities, interpersonal and social skills, and accommodations and needs in school-based work sites, community-based work sites, and vocational training programs.

In arranging situational assessments in work sites, keep in mind that guidelines have been developed by the U.S. Departments of Labor and Education for the purpose of placing students in unpaid job sites while meeting the requirements of the Fair Labor Standards Act. For a complete listing of the guidelines, see Inge, Simon, Halloran, and Moon (1993) or Simon, Cobb, Halloran, Norman, and Bourexis (1994).

Methods of Assessing Potential Environments

The first segment of this section presented information on a number of methods that you can use in gathering information on your students. In order to make a match between each student's needs, preferences, strengths, and interests and his or her future environments, however, you also need to have information on the demands of the living, working, and educational environments in which the individual may be functioning as an adult and the training programs in which the student will enroll on the path to adulthood. Analysis of these environments also involves examining circumstances and situations that occur within these environments.

To determine the training and support your student will need in order to succeed in the future living, working, and educational environments he or she has identified, it is critical that you or someone in your program systematically look at the demands of these environments. In general, the lower functioning the student (or the bigger you feel the gap will be between the student's abilities and the demands of the environment), the more detailed the analysis should be. This will allow you to identify the needed training and supports that the individual will need to succeed. It is important to remember that the environment, situations, and circumstances can be adapted, adjusted, or realigned so that minimal supports will be needed. The following section will present basic information on analyzing community settings, jobs, and postsecondary training programs. Much of this information is taken from *Assess for Success: Handbook on Transition Assessment* (Sitlington, Neubert, Begun, Lombard, & Leconte, 1996). This handbook contains more information on each of these techniques and provides sample forms for conducting the analyses.

Analysis of Community Environments.   The concept of environmental analysis, particularly related to community-based living settings, was first introduced by professionals working with individuals with severe disabilities. In terms of future living environments, it is important to identify the demands of both the home environment in which the individual will be living as well as the current living environment. The structure and demands of the broader community in which the individual will be shopping, banking, and pursuing leisure activities should also be considered.

McDonnell, Wilcox, and Hardman (1991) indicated that you must determine (1) where the individual will perform the activity, (2) what tasks he or she will complete at each site, (3) how the individual will complete difficult steps of the activity, and (4) what level of performance will be expected in order to terminate the training program. If the specific community-based environments are known, the task becomes one of analyzing the demands of these specific environments (e.g., the apartment, the grocery store, the bank, etc.). Often, however, educators do not always know the specific location in which the individual will live. In addition, the individual will want to frequent a number of locations within a given community, such as a number of different restaurants. For this reason, McDonnell, Wilcox, and

Hardman have recommended a "general case procedures" analysis in which the teacher identifies the variations in performance demands across all of the settings in which the individual will be expected to complete each activity. For more information on completing an analysis of community environments, consult McDonnell, Wilcox, and Hardman (1991) or Moon, Inge, Wehman, Brooke, and Barcus (1990).

Job Analysis. The process of analyzing the demands of working environments is called *job analysis.* In essence, it is a task analysis of the job and what it demands. This process involves systematically gathering information on what the worker does, how the work is done, and under what conditions the work is done. This also includes other areas, such as amount of supervision, production requirements, and more. Information should also be gathered on other demands of the workplace, including activities during breaks and transportation to and from work. The job analysis process is time consuming and must be done on site to observe the "essential functions" of the job, as defined in the Americans with Disabilities Act. It is important to directly observe the worker and talk with the worker and direct supervisor. Also check to see if there is an existing job description that has been developed by the employer.

McDonnell, Wilcox, and Hardman (1991) have identified five basic steps in conducting a job analysis. We will use the example of a lab technician.

1. Identify the specific responses that will be required to complete each job assigned. These responses should be both observable and measurable. (Identify the basic tasks that the lab technician must complete. Be very specific. Identify the tasks you have observed and other tasks completed at a time you were not observing.)
2. Identify the environmental cues that will control the completion of the task. These will be cues to tell the individual to perform certain tasks, or certain parts of the task. (Identify the commands of the supervisor or person requesting the test, the written procedures, and the requests of other staff that prompt the specific tasks.)
3. Identify the speed requirements of the job in terms of average time required to complete a response or task or number of analyses to be completed within a given time period. Identify how important this speed requirement is to the employer. (Identify how quickly the lab technician must analyze each sample. Determine the different times allowed for conducting different analyses.)
4. Specify the quality requirements for each job task. The accuracy of the supervisor's expectations should be cross-checked by discussing them with other co-workers who perform the same job. (Identify what criteria will be used to evaluate the quality of the lab technician's performance.)
5. Identify exceptions to the normal routine. These exceptions may include changes in the job routine or unpredictable situations that may arise during the course of the workday. (Identify tasks the lab technician does not perform daily, but that are important to completion of the job, such as quality checks to be conducted on instruments.)

Analysis of Secondary and Postsecondary Training Environments.   The "place and pray" system for putting students in academic environments at both the secondary and postsecondary level is alive and well! Just as teachers should analyze students' current or targeted work environments, they should do the same for current (secondary) and targeted (postsecondary) academic environments. If one of the goals of the student is postsecondary education, the teacher, the student, and/or the family should visit the targeted educational program to determine the demands of specific courses and of the total educational environment. This involves gathering information on the specific courses in which the student will be enrolled and determining the demands of these courses, in terms of daily assignments, amount of reading and writing required, major tests, and the like. Information should also be gathered on the requirements of any field experiences or laboratories related to the class. Support services and available accommodations should also be identified.

Information for postsecondary education environments should be gathered on the following aspects of the training program:

1. Application procedures
2. Admission procedures
3. Support services
4. Willingness of individual faculty members to provide accommodations
5. Career/personal counseling services
6. Training programs, both academically and vocationally related
7. Existing fee structures
8. Availability of financial support

The supports available for all students and specifically for students with disabilities are critical. See Chapter 8 for more information on what to look for in postsecondary education and training programs.

As in the job analysis, it is important for you to identify the types of information you want to gather on postsecondary programs and adopt, adapt, or develop a program analysis form that will provide this information for you. The form should allow you to record information on a specific program and then refer to this information at a later date. The form should also be one that all staff or family members or the individual could use and that would allow the results of a specific program analysis to be shared with others, particularly the individual.

An analysis of the future living, working, and educational environments the individual has chosen will be a major help in determining the training he or she will need to succeed in these programs. This training could involve enrollment in general education courses in high school, participating in work experiences in the community, instruction in learning strategies or study skills, or training in self-determination. If the training involves enrolling in general education classes, such as vocational education classes, math classes, or English courses, it will be helpful to conduct an analysis of the demands of these training environments so that you can determine the support the student will need in order to learn from these programs. The steps involved in this program analysis are identical to those discussed in analyzing postsecondary educational environments.

Summary. The preceding sections have identified a number of methods of gathering information about the individual and about potential living, working, and educational environments. Analysis of each of these environments requires analysis of the personal and social skills required. The best way to determine which methods would be useful to you, the educator, is to determine the questions you need to answer. You—in cooperation with the student, the family, and others on the planning team—can then choose the methods that can provide the information that you need. The portfolio approach presented earlier in this section offers an ideal vehicle for the student, family, and other members of the transition planning team to select and summarize the most relevant transition assessment information that has been collected. This transition assessment portfolio can then be used in making the match between the student's needs, interests, and preferences and the future environments in which the student will function as an adult.

Tying Assessment into Transition Planning

It is very important to have an organized approach for tying the information you gather through the assessment process into transition planning for your students. This involves developing an assessment plan; making the match between each student's strengths, preferences, and interests and the demands of future environments; and using the assessment information properly.

Developing an Assessment Plan

To determine appropriate methods for the transition assessment process, an assessment plan should be developed and periodically updated with the individual and his or her family. The assessment plan should address the following questions (Sitlington, Neubert, Begun, Lombard, & Leconte, 1996):

- What do I already know about this student that would be helpful in developing postsecondary outcomes?
- What information do I need to know about this individual to determine postsecondary goals?
- What methods will provide this information?
- How will the assessment data be collected and used in the IEP process?

Using an assessment plan will ensure that the methods are varied and appropriate for the purposes of the assessment and for the individual's characteristics and stage in the career development and transition process. An existing transition skills assessment (see Appendix B for instruments listed under Transition/Community Adjustment) could be used initially to develop an assessment plan. Most are helpful screening devices to determine what the IEP team can agree they know about a student in a wide range of transition planning areas. Those areas where there is little information or there is disagreement on what is known suggest further assessment needs. The assessment plan can be derived directly from the instrument results.

Making the Match

Figure 5.3 presents the process of making the match between an individual's strengths, needs, preferences, and interests and the demands and culture of current and future environments (Sitlington, Neubert, Begun, Lombard, & Leconte, 1996). A variety of assessment methods in special education, rehabilitation, and vocational education can be used to facilitate this process. The upper left-hand box in this figure presents methods for gathering information about an individual's needs, preferences, and interests. The upper right-hand box lists methods for gathering information on the demands of future working, educational, and community environments. Such assessment requires not only looking at the specific tasks involved in these environments but also observing aspects of the "culture" of these environments with which the individual must interact. This assessment process also uses assistive technology, when appropriate, to enhance an individual's capabilities and adapt the characteristics of the environment prior to, during, and following assessment.

The lower box in Figure 5.3 focuses on the critical process of actually making the match between the individual and the environment. If a match is made, the professional would make the placement and provide the ongoing monitoring and support needed. If a match is possible, but not definite, it is essential that resources,

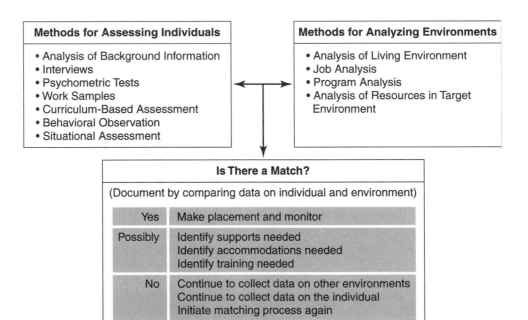

FIGURE 5.3   Making the Match
Source: From *Assess for Success: Handbook on Transition Assessment* (page 99) by P. L. Sitlington, D. A. Neubert, W. Begun, R. C. Lombard, and P. J. Leconte, 1996, Reston, VA: Council for Exceptional Children. Copyright 1996 by the Council for Exceptional Children. Reprinted by permission.

supports, accommodations, and training needs are identified to make the match work. If a match does not seem feasible, based on the available information, then additional data need to be collected on the individual and other target environments, and the matching process must be continued until a viable match is made.

As mentioned previously, a transition profile may be the most useful means of summarizing assessment information and can be incorporated into a portfolio or transition assessment folder. This profile needs to be updated periodically by the student and personnel responsible for the assessment. The outcomes of transition assessment should focus on recommendations for appropriate placements, instructional strategies, accommodations in various environments that support an individual's strengths and abilities, and even recommendations for further needed assessment.

Using Assessment Information

Salvia and Ysseldyke (1995) defined *assessment* as "the process of collecting data for the purposes of making decisions about students" (p. 2). If no decisions are made after collecting assessment information, why collect it? In some cases, the answer to that question depends on whether the information collected is "real" information. In other words, data can be collected but later questioned as to its validity or reliability. Without some sense that the data are real (i.e., valid and reliable), it would be unprofessional and unethical to use the data to make decisions. Thus, the underlying assumption of collecting and then using assessment data is that the data are worthy of using.

The most central and critical use of transition assessment information is as a component of the Present Level of Educational Performance in the student's IEP. Transition goals and objectives, along with official linkages with nonschool agencies, should come directly from transition-referenced assessment and the information in the Present Level of Educational Performance. The data should have direct implications for instructional program decisions, including program design, program placement, curriculum planning, instructional procedures, and additional assessment requirements. If the concept of Present Level of Educational Performance at all age levels is to be broadened to include transition knowledge and skills and any needs for linkages to youth, postsecondary, or adult agency services, it is apparent that assessment practices must extend beyond traditional developmental and psychoeducational assessment. Other authors (Clark, 1996; 1998; Corbey, Miller, Severson, & Enderle, 1993; Sitlington, Neubert, Begun, Lombard, & Leconte, 1996) have also discussed the concept of transition assessment with emphasis on infusion into the IEP process.

It is especially important that everyone using information from the transition assessment process has access to resource persons outside the transition planning team for help with unique or complex concerns that come up with students and their families. It is also important to know when it is critical that a referral be made, rather than wasting time or compounding the problem by attempting to work in isolation or without assistance from referral sources. Confidentiality and appropriate referral procedures must be addressed from the beginning of the referral decision. If a student or family member requests confidentiality, then that must be honored, unless, of course, child abuse, suicidal behavior, or threats involving harm to others are involved. In other cases, general confidentiality and "need to know" criteria should be followed in any referral process or IEP linkages to nonschool agencies.

An important legal use for transition assessment information obtained in developing an IEP is the documentation that it provides. Clearly, documentation of assessment procedures for present level of educational performance for IEP planning, as well as evidence of secondary-level student participation in the IEP planning process, is important. The data may also provide crucial documentation in the event that a student's placement or program service delivery is challenged at a formal hearing or in litigation. Finally, the data may function for high school students as the legal documentation needed for students to be able to access post-secondary education student assistance services or adult services for people with disabilities. This is why the final three-year reevaluation by the school district should be carefully planned and used for successful transition events for students exiting the school system. The types of information being requested by postsecondary education and training programs is discussed in more detail in Chapter 8.

Issues to Consider When Conducting Assessments

A number of issues must be considered when planning and conducting any type of assessment of students, but particularly a transition assessment. These issues are presented in the following sections.

Being Sensitive to Gender and Cultural Diversity

The number-one issue in gender and cultural sensitivity is fairness. The IDEA regulations specify procedures for guaranteeing nondiscriminatory assessment through the requirement that tests and other evaluation material should be administered in the student's native language or other mode of communication, unless it is clearly unfeasible to do so. This effort for fairness is good for non-English-speaking students, but it does not address issues of gender, ethnicity, or cultural variations due to geography or income.

A variety of proposals and efforts have been made to deal with the issue of fairness in testing and assessment practices. Some of these include developing culture/gender-fair tests, culture/gender-free tests, translation of existing tests in English to other languages, and using language interpreters during testing. So far, none of these approaches has been a resounding success. The efforts have probably improved testing practices, but they have not solved all the problems. The Joint Committee on Testing Practices (1988) published the *Code of Fair Testing Practices in Education* as a way of keeping the issues before the field. Code statements are directed toward practices for both test developers and test users in developing and selecting appropriate tests, interpreting scores, striving for fairness, and informing test takers about tests and the rights of test takers.

Commonsense sensitivity to gender and cultural factors in selecting standardized instruments, developing informal procedures, and interpreting and reporting assessment results will ordinarily not only conform to federal mandates for nondiscriminatory evaluation but also go beyond them. Clark (1998) stated some commonsense guidelines that are summarized here (refer to the original source for more detail):

- Be aware of possible past discrimination in the assessment process.
- Be ready to respond positively to identified past discrimination experiences. This may involve assigning a same-gender, same-race, same-language, or same-ethnic group professional to conduct the assessments and provide appropriate interpretations and reports.
- When in doubt about the proper interpretations to be made from a student or family response in the assessment process, use selected members of their cultural community to verify impressions or clarify responses that are difficult to understand.
- When interviewing a student or family of a different cultural group for the first time, be careful about the use of names and titles. Attempting to be friendly too quickly may be insulting and viewed as a violation of social etiquette.
- Talk with the student and family about the best way to communicate, then be sure that comprehension is working both ways in the process by summarizing what has been said or by asking the student or family member to summarize what has been said.
- If translators (for written materials) or interpreters (for oral interactions) are requested and used, spend time with them before their participation to acquaint them with the purpose and context of the assessment activity.

Planning for life transitions is a proactive level of thinking that is associated with middle-class people with education, affluence, and relatively high levels of success in their own life transitions. To many students with disabilities and their families, transition planning is an unfamiliar concept and beyond their current concerns for day-to-day survival. The language used in talking about transitions in assessment activities (e.g., *vision for the future, empowerment, independence/interdependence, self-determination,* etc.) may be difficult for them to understand. Even if they have no difficulty understanding the words, they might have different cultural values associated with the words. Be sensitive to communication barriers and work continuously to establish common understandings when performing student and parent assessments and use those common understandings when drafting IEP goals and objectives.

Making Accommodations for Testing

Any type of assessment procedure, formal or informal, should start with the assumption that the assessment's validity and reliability depend on the individual's ability to respond to items. Each individual may have some unique needs to take into account in determining what accommodations should be considered for the assessment process. Salvia & Ysseldyke (1995) pointed out five factors that can affect accurate assessment with students who have a variety of disabilities:

1. The student's ability to understand assessment stimuli (directions, items, response requirements, etc.)
2. The student's ability to respond to assessment stimuli
3. The nature of the norm group (if the instrument is norm referenced)
4. The appropriateness of the level of the items in the assessment
5. The student's lack of exposure to the curriculum on which the assessment is based

These five factors are critical to think about in terms of a school district's policy for students to participate in both large-scale group assessments (e.g., state competency exams or national assessments) or individual assessments. For assessment to be nondiscriminatory, every reasonable accommodation necessary should be considered. Accommodations involve adapting or modifying assessments or assessment procedures to permit students with disabilities to participate in the assessment process without unfair constraints. Thurlow, Ysseldyke, and Silverstein (1993) reported on a national survey of accommodations used by school districts for both state and national assessments. These included the following major types of accommodations:

1. Accommodations to presentation of format of the assessment (e.g., Braille edition of the test or scale, oral reading of directions)
2. Accommodations in response format of the assessment (e.g., permit student to respond orally, permit student to respond through an interpreter or translator)
3. Accommodations in the testing environment or assessment setting (e.g., permit student to complete the assessment alone or in a semi-isolated area)
4. Accommodations in the timing of the assessment (e.g., permit extended time for completion, extend assessment sessions over several days)

These accommodations are fairly traditional; however, some states use nationally normed standardized tests whose test publishers do not accept extending time limitations or permitting students to respond orally on a writing language sample. Schools can be creative in determining what is a fair and reasonable accommodation for a given student for local tests, but need to follow state guidelines for state and federal assessments. The term *individualized accommodations* should be an oxymoron, but, unfortunately, assessment accommodations are still handled too often as group accommodations.

Organizing and Reporting Information

One of the oldest of criticisms of testing in schools is that the scores get filed somewhere and are never seen again. There is some truth in this criticism. Since most schools are not in the ideal world, a combination of reality and recommended practice suggest that there are alternatives for organizing and making available assessment information. Since the material in assessment files contains a considerable amount of very personal information about students, the issues of organizing and making the materials available must be handled with strict adherence to both ethical and legal standards of confidentiality and rights to access of personal information. The Family Educational Rights and Privacy Act (FERPA) (PL 93-380) states that any educational agency that accepts federal money must give parents the opportunity to inspect, challenge, and correct their children's records. Students of majority age (age 18 and older in most states) also have the same rights in regard to their own records. FERPA also specifies that a school cannot release identifiable data on any student without the parents' or student's (when age 18 and older) written consent. School administrators and school psychologists have specialized training on the responsibilities of the school in maintaining confidentiality in the storage, disposal, and sharing of information of assessment records. If you have questions about confidentiality procedures, consult your building principal or special education administrator.

Whatever organizational format is used with assessment information, it should be designed for a specific purpose. There might be multiple purposes for wanting assessment information organized in a certain way for retrieval and use, including student planning use, school district use, and use by other youth services and adult providers (Clark, 1998). It may be that the traditional cumulative folder is maintained primarily for the school district's need for legal documentation, institutional accountability, and curriculum planning. This does not mean that there cannot be more than one organizational file. Notice should be placed in all files, however, about the existence of information in the other files.

Whatever format or system is used for organizing, maintaining, and making available student assessment information, there are two primary considerations: (1) the protection of students' and parents' rights of privacy and (2) the legitimate need to know of the person or agency who is participating in decision making and service delivery of the student. Maintaining secure files in locked filing cabinets is a basic recommended practice. Further, the FERPA provisions listed previously must be followed to demonstrate commitment to a concern for privacy and legal access.

People Involved in the Transition Assessment Process

As Sitlington, Neubert, and Leconte (1997) stated, the roles and responsibilities of those involved in transition assessment continue to evolve and change as the focus on school to adult transition gains emphasis in the education process. The transition planning process is most effective when (1) assessment data are collected on an ongoing basis through an interdisciplinary team approach and (2) responsibility for using assessment results and coordinating collection of ongoing assessment information is assumed by one person, often called a *service coordinator* or a *case manager*.

Possible roles of key players in the transition assessment process are presented in Table 5.1. Although many people may be involved in assessment activities

TABLE 5.1   Roles of Key Players

Students with Disabilities	Family Members	Special Education Teachers	Secondary and Postsecondary Educators
• Express independent living needs/abilities • Express course-related interests • Express occupational and job-related interests • Express learning style preferences • Identify personal-social skills in need of improvement • Express leisure/recreation preferences • Identify community involvement interests • Express postsecondary education goals • Express post secondary employment goals	• Foster independence by assigning specific responsibilities in the home • Explore community support, training, and employment options • Discuss future goals and adult realities with the student • Develop and support a work ethic common to the family culture • Discuss interests, abilities, and needs • Attend and participate in IEP meetings with the student • Support the student's efforts to direct his or her IEP and transition program • Complete parent and family surveys and needs assessments • Encourage the student's efforts to learn more about work demands and career options • Respond to follow-up surveys sent by local school systems • Jointly plan for financial, living, health, leisure, and transportation needs	• Conduct interviews with family members and the student • Conduct situational assessments by observing student performance in a variety of school and community settings • Implement curriculum-based assessment activities • Administer formal assessments • Interpret assessment results gathered from other professionals • Interpret transition assessment data to students and transform it into functional goals and objectives on IEPs	• Provide information about courses one year before they teach to students with disabilities • Provide information on course options • Provide information on eligibility and entry skill requirements • Provide information on the teaching style preferences of the instructor • Provide information on testing options • Provide information on evaluation and grading options • Provide information on performance standards and learner outcomes associated with a particular course • Observe and record student performance in class in regard to attendance and safety • Observe and record student performance in cooperative group behavior • Observe and record student performance on tests, quizzes, and project completion • Observe and record student performance on general progress toward exit-level skills and learner outcomes

TABLE 5.1   Continued

School Guidance Personnel	Adult Service Providers	Employers, Work Experience Staff, Job Coaches, and Placement Specialists	Support Services Personnel
• Administer formal and informal interest surveys as early as possible • Provide postassessment counseling • Assist in helping students express their individual strengths, limitations, and preferences • Assist students in enrolling in secondary school course consistent with their interests, needs, and learning preferences • Provide information for future planning in postsecondary education, employment, military, and/or community options • Participate in the IEP process	• Participate in transition assessment activities when the student is at least 16 years of age • Communicate information about their agencies' services to individuals with disabilities • Provide a linkage to the school agencies by collaborating with IEP and assessment teams • Attend IEP meetings with the student and family	• Provide information on entry-level job skills • Provide information on possible workplace accommodation options • Provide information on supported employment options • Provide information on possible apprenticeship options • Provide information on technology skills requirements • Observe and record student's workplace readiness • Observe and record student's ability to follow directions and cooperate with coworkers • Observe and record the student's work ethic, behavior, and productivity level • Observe and record the student's ability to work under supervision and accept criticism • Observe and record the student's job-related interest and motivation	• Participate in the transition assessment process • Provide information on the student's special needs: psychological testing, physical and rehabilitation therapies, and community support services

throughout the students' educational, vocational, and transition programming, the secondary special educator is a logical person to assume the major responsibility for coordinating and using assessment information in the decision-making and planning process. Of course, the people who will know students throughout their educational and transition processes are parents or other family members. Parents, guardians, and advocates are needed to provide their perspective on the student's needs, preferences, and interests. It may also be important to know the views of the parents, guardians, or advocates regarding what they prefer for the student. However, because some family members are not in a position to assume the service coordination role immediately, it is incumbent on certified secondary special educators to model that role for family members and the student, who should eventually assume this responsibility. If needed, others who could undertake this responsibility and role modeling include vocational special needs educators, counselors, or transition specialists.

Since transition assessment activities must be tailored to meet the needs of individual students in various placements, it is important that secondary special educators, or service coordinators, understand interdisciplinary roles and learn how service systems operate. Examples of personnel with whom collaboration must occur are general educators, related services personnel, vocational educators, supported employment specialists, vocational evaluators, assistive technology specialists, rehabilitation counselors, employers, employee co-workers, financial aid personnel, social security counselors, residential counselors, and housemates.

Transition assessment may also need to be coordinated with and conducted by assistive technology specialists in employment, educational, and residential settings. IDEA mandates that such assessment be conducted prior to other assessments if accommodations or technology will enhance students' abilities to perform and learn. Assistive technology assessment involves accessing services, identifying financing for these services, coordinating assessment activities, incorporating results into Individualized Education Programs, and determining how students can maintain or upgrade their accommodations or technology.

Most important, service coordinators must become skilled in fostering and facilitating self-advocacy and self-determination skills of students. To begin this process, students must be guided in understanding their strengths, needs, preferences, and interests and then instructed on how to verbalize this information to others in terms that are specific and understandable. Eventually, students should assume responsibility for coordinating their assessment and transition processes.

Competencies for personnel involved in transition assessment should focus on skills related to assessing the individual and assessing the individual's current and potential environments. In addition, skills are needed to establish a match between the culture and demands of these environments and the strengths, needs, preferences, and interests of the individual, and then to use and communicate the assessment data to facilitate transition planning. We support the competencies identified by DCDT (Sitlington, Neubert, & Leconte, 1997), which built on competencies identified by the Interdisciplinary Council on Vocational Evaluation and

Assessment Position Statement (Smith, Lombard, Neubert, Leconte, Rothenbacher, & Sitlington, 1994).

Resources

Following is a list of other resources on assessment that may help you get involved in the transition assessment process with your students:

Albright, L., & Cobb, R. B. (1988). *Assessment of students with handicaps in vocational education: A curriculum-based approach.* Alexandria, VA: American Vocational Association.

Bradley-Johnson, S. (1994). *Psychoeducational assessment of students who are visually impaired or blind* (2nd ed.). Austin, TX: Pro-Ed.

Brown, C. D., McDaniel, R., & Couch, R. (1994). *Vocational evaluation systems and software: A consumer's guide.* Menomonie, WI: Rehabilitation Resource, Stout Vocational Rehabilitation Institute.

Clark, G. M. (1998). *Assessment for transitions planning.* Austin, TX: Pro-Ed.

Corbey, S., Miller, R., Severson, S., & Enderle, J. (1993). *Identifying individual transition needs: A resource guide for special educators working with students in their transition from school to adult life.* St. Paul: Minnesota Department of Education.

Dowd, L. R. (Ed.). (1993). *Glossary of terminology for vocational assessment, evaluation and work adjustment.* Menomonie, WI: Rehabilitation Resource, Stout Vocational Rehabilitation Institute.

Lazear, D. (1994). *Multiple intelligence approaches to assessment: Solving the assessment conundrum.* Tuscon, AZ: Zephyr Press.

Leconte, P. J. (1994). *A perspective on vocational appraisal: Beliefs, practices, and paradigms.* Unpublished dissertation, George Washington University.

Leung, B. P. (1996). Quality assessment practices in a diverse society. *Teaching Exceptional Children, 28* (3), 42–45.

Rothenbacher, C., & Leconte, P. (1990). Vocational assessment: A guide for parents and professionals. *Transition Summary, 6,* 1–15.

Salvia, J., & Ysseldyke, J. E. (1995). *Assessment* (6th ed.). Boston: Houghton Mifflin.

Sitlington, P. L., & Neubert, D. A. (1998). Transition assessment: Methods and processes to determine student needs, preferences, and interests. In M. L. Wehmeyer & D. J. Sands (Eds.), *Making it happen: Student involvment in education planning, decision making, and instruction.* Baltimore: Paul H. Brookes.

Sitlington, P., Neubert, D. A., Begun, W., Lombard, R. C., & Leconte, P. (1996). *Assess for success: Handbook on transition assessment.* Reston, VA: Council for Exceptional Children.

Stodden, R. A., Ianacone, R. N., Boone, R. M., & Bisconer, W. S. (1987). *Curriculum-based vocational assessment: A guide for addressing youth with special needs.* Honolulu: Centre Publications, International Education Corporation.

Recommendations for Transition Assessment

Assessment for planning transition services for students with disabilities need not be overwhelming or take on a life of its own. Assessment must be kept in perspective; it is a means to an end, and never an end in itself. However, because of the state of the field in assessment for transition planning, some initial time and effort in planning and implementation is necessary. Some summarizing suggestions for developing or expanding current transition planning assessment for students with disabilities may be in order. The following suggestions are presented for your thoughtful consideration in your situation. They build on recommendations made in our previous efforts related to transition assessment (Clark, 1998; Sitlington, 1996).

1. Select assessment instruments and procedures on the basis of how to answer key questions in a student's individual transition planning and the assessment plan.

2. Make transition assessment ongoing. Assessment activities should start as early as possible and continue through life. There may be specific times for intensive assessment activity, and there may be key points in a student's educational progress where certain types of assessment should be planned, but much of what is needed for week-to-week instructional planning is ongoing. If at any point a student is seen as "satisfactorily assessed" in any area (educational, vocational, or personal life skills), such that no more questions need to be asked for planning or instruction, then that student essentially has been declared a static, dehumanized object for the school to handle as it chooses. That is an unacceptable position to take.

3. Use multiple types and levels of assessments. No single assessment approach in transition planning is adequate. The variety of life demands on students for adjustment in school, at home, and in the community indicates the need for a variety of assessment approaches for planning how the students can best meet those demands. Standardized, nonstandardized, quantitative, qualitative, group, individual, educational, noneducational, professional, and nonprofessional approaches each have some value at certain points and for certain needs.

4. Make three-year psychoeducational reevaluations count for all students. These will be useful for their next likely placement or self-selected environment. Students moving from middle or junior high schools into high schools who need reevaluations should receive assessments that relate to their preferences and interests for the near future as well as for long-range goals. Any student at risk of dropping out at age 16 should be identified early enough so that the reevaluation is useful for the agency or agencies most likely to need basic data for eligibility determination and program planning. Any student planning to go on to some type of postsecondary education or training may need some official documentation of the disability so that student assistance services are accessible. Careful selection of

assessment instruments in the pregraduation period when a reevaluation is due can facilitate students' access to other agencies.

5. Think of assessment procedures in terms of efficiency as well as effectiveness. A few carefully selected assessment procedures may be more efficient and effective than an extensive array of instruments, forms, and scores based on a hit-or-miss approach. Batteries of tests or assessment procedures routinely administered to all students may be not only inappropriate but also inefficient. Assessments that cover a wide range of outcome areas are excellent for screening purposes, but whenever the results of such procedures are too general or not indicative of present level of performance, more specific choices of assessment must follow.

6. Develop a transition assessment approach that is gender/culture/language fair as well as gender/culture/language enhanced. Transition assessment that meets the challenges of multicultural populations requires careful thought, as evidenced by the cultural bias in traditional cognitive and academic assessment. A great risk of cultural bias also exists in assessing nonacademic knowledge and skills, as well as preferences and interests, when the process is approached from a white, middle-class orientation to life.

7. Organize assessment data for easy access in IEP planning and instructional programming. Good information that goes unrecorded and resides solely in the memory or inaccessible files of school personnel is not usable information. Current recommended practices of portfolio assessment for students and families and well-organized student assessment folders at school are relevant in transition assessment. Some redesign of a school's forms or portfolio formats will be required, in most cases, to accommodate the new sources of transition assessment data.

8. Broaden the focus of transition assessment to add an emphasis on assessing the ecology of future living, working, and educational environments, including the natural supports in these environments.

9. Move from a heavy reliance on formal assessment systems and paper-and-pencil tests to a stronger emphasis on assessment tied to the curriculum and to the individual's performance in the community, particularly for future employment and living areas.

10. Move from dictating how to assess the individual and telling him or her what the results mean, to involving the individual and the family in the design and implementation of the assessment process and deciding together what implications the results have for the individual's future.

11. Move from a set assessment sequence involving the same assessment for all students to one that is individualized based on the future living, working, and educational environments identified by the individual and family.

12. View transition assessment as an integral part of the ongoing assessment effort for all students—not as an add-on or as a process only for certain students.

The techniques advocated as part of transition assessment correspond directly to those advocated in curriculum-based assessment and authentic assessment (Salvia & Hughes, 1990) and in community-based assessment for individuals with developmental disabilities (McDonnell, Wilcox, & Hardman, 1991; Moon, Inge, Wehman, Brooke, & Barcus, 1990).

13. Promote the belief that transition assessment is a responsibility of all special education professionals, not something done solely by the transition specialist or job placement personnel.

14. Integrate competencies related to transition assessment into coursework for all personnel certified to work with secondary special education students. Specific transition assessment coursework must be included in preparation programs for those focusing specifically on the area of transition or vocational preparation. Those individuals preparing to serve as vocational assessment specialists or vocational evaluators should be certified by and meet the Knowledge and Performance Areas required by the Commission on Certification of Work Adjustment and Vocational Evaluation Specialists (CCWAVES).

15. Integrate efforts in transition assessment with those of general education, including the school-to-work and work force development initiatives and the broader school reform initiatives designed for all students.

16. Integrate efforts in transition assessment with those of adult service providers. This must include involving them in the transition assessment process and structuring the assessment conducted in school so that it provides the relevant information needed for adult providers to serve individuals with disabilities more effectively. This must also include summarizing the results of ongoing assessment and, with the individual's and family's permission, transferring these results to the adult providers who will be continuing the transition support.

17. View assessment as a critical component of the transition planning process. The assessment results must provide information on the decisions that need to be made. The assessment questions must flow from the information that is needed to assist the individual and his or her family in making the transition to the living, working, and educational environments they have identified.

Conclusion

The need for workable transition assessment procedures for students with disabilities is urgent. Even as professionals become more sophisticated about assessment, planning, and program and service delivery, new questions arise about how to do each task better and meet federal mandates. Still, the IDEA mandate for IEP planning did not necessarily call for novel kinds of assessment and planning. Common sense and using available assessment procedures and results would be an encouraging start. There is the need, however, to look at educational assessment and the boundaries of "present level of educational performance" more openly. Fortunately, some existing instruments, procedures, and guidelines do exist that can be used immediately while better systems are being developed. The challenge will be to accomplish quality transition-referenced assessment in the context of all the other demands on special educators for better outcomes with students with disabilities across all age levels. The key to this challenge is determining the nature of "better outcomes" for each of those age levels. The way to do that is through sound assessment practices involving a variety of school personnel, with students and their families actively participating.

We firmly believe that transition assessment is not just vocational assessment or career assessment with a new name. It is also not a totally new way of conducting assessment. Transition assessment builds on the concepts of vocational evaluation and assessment as well as career assessment. It broadens the focus of assessment efforts to all aspects of adult life and to the shift from one stage of life to another. The field of career development and transition has not been very effective in implementing the concept of career assessment in the majority of programs that serve students with disabilities. We remain optimistic, however, that the increased emphasis on transition will provide the opportunity to present the case for assessment as an integral part of the transition process. We cannot emphasize enough that educators must coordinate their efforts closely with the overall assessment process; they can no longer function as an island within the educational system. Transition assessment must tie in directly to the school reform efforts occurring nationally and in each state, district, and school building.

The transition assessment process we have described in this chapter provides a framework for you to examine your current or future assessment practices and to focus on methods that will assist students in identifying appropriate employment, postsecondary education, independent living, community functioning, and personal and social outcomes for adult life. In addition, professionals must work with students and their families so that they are actively involved in the transition assessment process. In this way, goals and outcomes can periodically be updated and changed as life roles continue to emerge.

As Sitlington, Neubert, and Leconte (1997) stated, the transition assessment process must allow students, families, and professionals an opportunity to participate in assessment activities that are conducted in a variety of natural environments and that address the multiple outcomes associated with the transition process.

6 Transition to Employment

*We cannot cross a bridge until we come to it; but I always like to lay down a
pontoon ahead of time.*

—Bernard M. Baruch

The transition of youths with disabilities to employment is a key component of all
the transition models presented in Chapters 1 and 2. At times, this transition
occurs directly after high school; other times, it occurs after postsecondary education or training, or after a time as a full-time homemaker. National and statewide
follow-up studies of young adults with disabilities (Frank & Sitlington, 1990; 1993;
Frank, Sitlington, & Carson, 1991; Sitlington, Frank, & Carson, 1992; Wagner,
Blackorby, Cameto, Hebbeler, & Newman, 1993; Wagner, D'Amico, Marder, Newman, & Blackorby, 1992) found that the individuals with disabilities were
employed at rates ranging between 50 and 60 percent. A high percentage of those
employed were employed in part-time, low-status jobs and received few fringe
benefits. The encouraging news is that unemployment rates *do* decrease the longer
the young adults are out of school. In addition, studies have found that transition
education and services *do* decrease the unemployment rate for individuals with
disabilities (Frank & Sitlington, 1997; 1998; Wagner, Blackorby, Cameto, & Newman, 1993; Wagner, D'Amico, Marder, Newman, & Blackorby, 1992).

The transition to employment is closely intertwined with the transition to
postsecondary education and training and life in the community. As you probably
well know, where one lives often determines the boundaries of employment possibilities. Conversely, seeking a certain job often determines where one will live. In
the same way, a certain job determines whether postsecondary education or training is needed. Conversely, the amount of education or training a person has determines the range of jobs open to him or her. Because of this, the knowledge and
skills required for a successful transition to employment involve all nine of the
knowledge and skills domains of the Comprehensive Transition Education Model
presented in Chapter 2. In addition, the process of actual transition to employment

settings involves all of the education and service delivery systems presented in the Comprehensive Transition Services Model, also discussed in Chapter 2.

The focus of this chapter is on the preparation of youths with disabilities with the experiences and skills needed to make the transition to employment, whenever that transition occurs. The content of this chapter is closely coordinated with that of Chapter 7, which focuses specifically on the placement, training, and supervision of adolescents with disabilities on exploration, training, or employment sites. This chapter discusses the instructional content needed to prepare students for the transition to employment, the principles and characteristics of work-based learning, and program models for delivering work-based learning. A list of resources is given to help you in working with students transitioning to employment. This is followed by a discussion of issues in preparing students for the transition to employment and individualized planning for transition to employment.

As you prepare individuals with disabilities to function effectively in the workplace, you will face a number of challenges: (1) the changing nature of the workplace and the increasing demand for employees that possess social, academic, and occupational skills; (2) the growing number of students leaving school without these skills; and (3) the failure of the general education high school curriculum to address these areas (Benz, Yovanoff, & Doren, 1997; National Center on Education and the Economy, 1990; U.S. Department of Labor, 1991).

The nature of occupations has and will change dramatically. Gray and Herr (1996) indicated that approximately 85 percent of the high school seniors they surveyed planned to enroll in a four-year college program. Few had specific occupational goals in mind. In contrast, only 20 percent of those enrolled complete a four-year program. Although, on average, college graduates earn more than high school graduates, many college graduates tend to be underemployed and subsequently return to technical school programs to acquire employable skills (Gray, 1996). Unskilled jobs accounted for approximately 60 percent of the employment in 1950; in the year 2000, unskilled workers will represent only 15 percent of the work force (Brunstein & Mahler, 1994).

Content for Instruction

Preparing any individual for the transition to employment requires instruction and hands-on experiences in all of the knowledge and skill domains of the Comprehensive Transition Education Model presented in Chapter 2. Particular emphasis in instruction will be needed in the following areas: (1) occupational awareness, (2) employment-related knowledge and skills, and (3) specific vocational knowledge and skills. Each of these areas is covered in the following sections.

Occupational Awareness

Brolin (1976, 1978, 1989), Brolin and Kokaska (1979), and Kokaska and Brolin (1985) approached the delineation of critical occupational awareness information through the competency approach. They suggested that the competency domain of occupational guidance and preparation of their career education model contains the primary prevocational information needs of an individual. These competencies include identification of the following:

1. The personal values one can encounter through work
2. The societal values one can encounter through work
3. The remunerative aspects of work
4. Occupational opportunities available locally
5. Sources of occupational information
6. One's own major occupational needs
7. One's own major occupational interests
8. One's own major occupational aptitudes
9. The requirements and demands of appropriate and available jobs

The competencies include understanding of the following:

1. The importance of following directions, working cooperatively with others, accepting supervision, good attendance and punctuality, meeting demands of quality work, and occupational safety
2. The process of searching for a job
3. The process of applying for a job
4. The process of interviewing for a job
5. The behaviors expected in competitive standards on a job
6. The behaviors necessary to maintain postschool occupational adjustment

These kinds of information and knowledge-based competencies represent typical occupational awareness information. Part of the problem in specifying exactly what information should be taught, and when, is the overall issue of scope and sequence in schools' curricula. Established scope and sequence for any instructional content area is rare. The area of occupational information is a good example of this. Clark, Carlson, Fisher, Cook, & D'Alonzo (1991) have detailed the kinds of information that children and youths with disabilities need to learn, beginning in the early childhood years: occupational roles, occupational vocabulary, occupational alternatives, and basic information related to some realities of the world of work. Each of these will be described to show how one can approach the same content suggested by Brolin (1976, 1978, 1989) in a different way.

Occupational Roles.   An occupational information program should provide learning experiences that result in new or expanded awareness of possible roles for students with disabilities. In producer/worker roles, the possibility of productive work, including paid and unpaid work, must be stressed. This includes awareness of roles such as the work of the student as a learner, the work as a volunteer, the work at home as an unpaid family worker, or the work activities or productivity in which one might be involved as a part of daily living (washing clothes, polishing shoes, repairing a leaky faucet, etc). In consumer roles, there needs to be a stress on the variety of roles one can experience as a consumer, such as customer, patient, client, renter, borrower, user, and so on.

Occupational Vocabulary.   Students who are learning about their present and future occupational roles must develop vocabularies to acquire information basic to such learning. This is not unlike a student entering law or medical school. The first few months emphasize the language of the profession. It is said that students in both these professions must acquire up to 20,000 new words during their preparation. Special needs students do not have such a monumental task, but they do have to establish a certain vocabulary base even to begin to understand the world of work. Vocabulary development is not limited to a reading vocabulary; it may also include comprehension in hearing vocabulary and speaking vocabulary. From this perspective, it is obvious that occupational information must include purposefully taught occupational vocabulary. This includes general vocabulary necessary for understanding concepts about employability and employment. Suggested vocabulary words are available through publications by Schilit and Caldwell (1980) Schloss, Schloss, and Misra (1985), and Fisher, Clark, and Patton (in preparation).

Occupational Alternatives.   Before getting too involved in any type of special career-development programming for youths, educators of students with disabilities should have some general perspective on occupational choice theory as it relates to normal growth and development. From a number of theories, only one is mentioned in brief here to serve as an example. Ginzberg and associates (Ginzberg, Ginsburg, Axelrad, & Herma, 1951) studied the occupational choice process and concluded that it is a developmental process. They suggested that the occupational decision-making process occurs in three basic stages or periods: fantasy, tentative choice, and realistic choice. They further suggested that the process involves a series of decisions made over a period of years, and that each step is meaningfully related to what has been decided before. The entire process is characterized by a continuous compromise among many factors—abilities, education, social status, age, physical and mental characteristics, geography, and so on. Some people have to compromise little, others a great deal.

Career education content in the secondary curriculum must include a component of occupational information that relates to occupational choice and awareness of occupational alternatives in a way that provides keen sensitivity to students' needs for self-esteem. In terms of occupational choice development, Ginzberg, Ginsburg, Axelrad, and Herma (1951) stated that the fantasy period in normal development ends around age 11 or 12. It is not unusual for high school youths with mental, educational, or behavioral disabilities to say that they want to be professional basketball players, movie stars, or rock singers. Given that they are functioning cognitively or maturationally at or below the age of 11, their occupational choices may reflect what others perceive as fantasy choices. Rather than be overly concerned with such verbal behaviors, teachers and counselors need to respond with occupational information that encourages any stated desire to want to work or be productive in a legitimate occupation. Teachers and parents should elicit from the students the reasons underlying their stated occupational choices and begin the process of providing information to the students that affirms or challenges their understanding of what they think they want and what the occupation demands. Sometimes the reasons students give for a fantasy choice are very helpful in suggesting other alternatives.

Basic Information on Realities of the World of Work.   There is a point at which providing basic occupational information about the world of work to students with disabilities becomes problematic. On one hand, the goal is to encourage students to want to work; on the other hand, educators have to be forthright in pointing out some of the negative realities of work. This section presents some of the realities—both positive and negative—that are especially important for students with disabilities to know.

Reality 1.   North American society in general, and the United States in particular, is a work-oriented society. It values work and those who are workers. No one can be directly compelled legally to work in U.S. society, except those few who are ordered by the courts to labor as a punishment for some crime. Even so, there are many formal and informal elements of society operating to make people into workers. For many, the system is so effective that unemployment produces high levels of anxiety, personal guilt, or feelings of worthlessness. For persons with disabilities, these feelings may be heightened, even though they may be able to reason that factors beyond their control are responsible for their unemployment.

Some argue that the leisure ethic has replaced the work ethic in U.S. society. Even though the past several years have shown more evidence of worker alienation, an increase in leisure alternatives, and a heavy emphasis on leisure and recreation in the media, the traditional meaning of work is still dictated by the power structure and is still espoused by major societal institutions. Moreover, the fact that most people cannot have any access to leisure or the necessities of life without some means of purchasing them leads people to seek employment. As long as these facts remain, this reality should be communicated to youths in school as part of their occupational information.

Reality 2.   Work, whether paid or unpaid, occurs in a particular locale: the factory, the store, the office, the construction site, the shop, the clinic, or the home. Work can occur in the home for an increasing number of occupations (cottage industries, artist, writer, telephone answering service, etc.), but by and large a person must go outside the home to work. This fact has two important implications for individuals with disabilities. First, one must be mobile in order to get to work. This requires a set of competencies regarding travel that is critical for getting to the work setting. Choices of work alternatives may be influenced by this reality alone. A second implication is that work is most frequently performed in a public place. A place has limitations on privacy; it usually has a set of socially expected behaviors, and there are formal or informal standards for dress and social behaviors.

Whether these realities are positive or negative to an individual depends on whether the individual is attracted to or uninterested by the nature of work that deals with location. One person might want to work alone at home, while another works primarily for the social interaction or the status that might go with a particular locale and its status, behavioral expectations, uniforms, and the like. Choices by one individual may involve no compromises; for another, it might involve significant compromise.

Occupational information about these realities is necessary in preparing youths with disabilities for work. Information on mobility requirements, transportation alternatives, and skills needed for use of transportation options are important curriculum content. Occupational information about the expectations of different kinds of work environments in public places for appearance, dress, speech or language, interpersonal relations, and social etiquette provides additional knowledge for students in entering these new and unfamiliar settings.

Reality 3.   Paid work is largely impersonal work. Work for which there is no pay may or may not be impersonal, depending on its nature; the personalized relationships associated with play, recreation, or love are not expected on a job in most situations. In fact, they may be forbidden. This is one reality that youths may have already been exposed to indirectly at home when they detect a different kind or set of expectations by a parent when the parent tells the child to perform a household chore. The child learns that the parent becomes the "boss" and has expectations about *what* is accomplished, *how well* it is accomplished, and, in some instances, *in what way* it is accomplished. The parent temporarily becomes an impersonal work supervisor and acts out a role that is the norm in the work world.

The reality of working for relative strangers who are "all business" may be discouraging to those adolescents who have strong needs for more personal relationships. Although exposing them to this reality runs the risk of seeing them reject the notion of working, it is even more of an injustice to ignore the reality or, worse, distort reality so that they build up unrealistic expectations about the nature of work. Adult service providers have been critical of special educators who not only do not teach this reality but teach the students that they are special and do not have to measure up in performance. They assert that special education teachers tend to reward their students even when the students do not perform satisfactorily.

If students with disabilities have experienced overprotectiveness from teachers or parents, the impersonality of work may provide them with their first opportunity to produce and be judged honestly on the quality and quantity of their work. Even if the objective opinion of the employer is more negative than feedback from school or home, many young people find the honesty refreshing and motivating. In these cases, the reality of paid work relating to impersonality may prove a positive factor in their work experience. For some, it may be their first experience where the disability is less important than productivity. How many people have you known in your life who might have been voted "least likely to succeed" while they were in school but who blossomed and achieved when given a fair chance to perform in the work world?

Reality 4.   Work has several reward systems. Paid work obviously has the reward of getting money, but unpaid work may provide the reward of saving money— that is, not having to pay someone else to do the work. There are other rewards of work, however, that should be mentioned. Some people see the value of work as offering them the opportunity to be of service, an opportunity to pursue interests and abilities, a means of meeting people, a way of avoiding boredom, or a chance to gain or maintain self-respect or self-esteem.

Youths need to know that people work for money but that they work for other things also. The question What's in it for me? is not inappropriate as students begin to sort out their values and establish a basis for being able to verbalize, "I want to work because. . . . "

Reality 5.   Work is bound by time. Most workers have starting times and ending times. Certain times are set aside for breaks, for eating, or for cleanup. Many jobs are based on payment for certain hours, with extra payment for overtime. Even when pay is based on piecework, the individual is racing against time to produce or complete as many pieces as possible. There are job benefits that relate to time off and there are penalties or sanctions against being late or slow. To waste time at work is always frowned upon, and if it is chronic behavior, it may be grounds for dismissal from the job.

An inability to discipline oneself to meet time demands or constraints is one of the most serious obstacles to adjustment to work. This is frequently an especially difficult area for some individuals who have trouble relating to time concepts. It may also be an obstacle to those youths who believe that those who are slaves to time schedules are irrationally compulsive. Nevertheless, while one might appreciate student resistance to the hectic, time-oriented pace of living in the United States, the reality exists, and their understanding of the system and possible alternatives to it must be taught as a part of occupational information.

Reality 6.   Work is seldom performed in complete isolation or independence. Even with the increasing number of occupations that allow people to work at home, most work involves two or more people who interact in various ways. One of the most important of these interactions is the worker to the supervisor. Others are the interaction with fellow workers, the interaction with customers, and the interaction of the worker with subordinates. Depending on the size and complexity of the work setting, a number of interpersonal reactions are required that may be more critical to staying on that job than is the ability to perform the work tasks.

Expected behaviors in work interactions may not be formally communicated, but they are communicated nevertheless through modeling, the worker grapevine, and events that occur that illustrate the rewards or penalties meted out to workers. People need to learn these basic expectations so they can develop a response system that shows a balance between dependence and independence in job performance (worker-supervisor interactions) and between the intimate and the casual (employee-fellow worker and employee-customer interactions).

Although interpersonal and social interactions are a part of most work environments, the reality of having to work for or with other people is not always a demanding factor that sets up a person with disabilities for adjustment problems or failure. This aspect has the potential also for providing the support and positive reward of working that help an employee with disabilities keep a job. The personal rewards of an identity at least at one place outside the home can be significant. Many people, with and without disabilities, look for any possible social interactions on the job that compensate for the loneliness of nonwork hours.

Reality 7. Work settings, like individual workers, rarely exist in isolation. As societies have moved from agrarian work settings to modern, industrial work settings, there has been an increasing dependence and interdependence among workers and work groups. Producers of goods require the services of workers in raw materials, manufactured goods for tools and equipment, transportation services, marketing and distribution services, and business and office services. Periodically, they may need workers in the building trades, communication and media field, custodial and maintenance services, health services, and public services. Likewise, any one of these work groups will have dependent or interdependent relationships with one or more of the others.

Adolescents should become aware of these relationships in order to understand the importance of all types of work groups and to combat some of the occupational stereotyping and status problems that inevitably arise in a study of the world of work and their own fantasies and plans about being a part of it.

Reality 8. Not everyone who wants to work can obtain work, nor can everyone who obtains work be employed in the work of his or her choice. This reality particularly affects individuals with disabilities. As stated earlier, youths with disabilities should be allowed to have their fantasies about doing various kinds of work, and too much reality too soon can be not only inappropriate but also destructive. Those who work with the student should not set their goals too low. The availability of assistive technology and other supports on the job have opened many doors to occupations that were previously closed to individuals with disabilities. A balance between realism and optimism should be encouraged.

Reality 9. The choice of an occupational area or a specific job is not a permanent or binding action. Choices, whether made with any compromises or not, can be reconsidered. Most people who make choices about job opportunities at the beginning of their careers do so with the view that most jobs will temporarily meet certain needs and preferences now, but movement up or out of the occupational situation is not only probable but also desirable. The emphasis that more or less self-actualized professionals in school and adult service agencies place on making the "right" occupational choice may send the "wrong" message. That is, young people with disabilities may get the message that because the world of work is so tough and that people with disabilities have to prove themselves even more convincingly than people without disabilities, it is absolutely imperative that they choose the right job the first time.

Adolescents with disabilities should be given the facts about the desirability of exploring one's interests and preferences in several occupations and the assurance that most people in the work force have worked at a number of different kinds of jobs. They also should be given some of the disadvantages of job hopping without any pattern of occupational development or responsibility in leaving jobs inappropriately. Educators and adult service providers need to remember that what is myth or reality to an adolescent regarding occupational choices and job selection is difficult to know without probing for beliefs and levels of understanding. Nothing can be assumed for any one student.

In summary, the adolescent with disabilities must begin to come to grips as early as possible with the realities of the world of work so that coping with or challenging those realities will be easier later. These realities must be introduced gradually and must include encouragement as well as cautious, but realistic, optimism.

Employment-Related Knowledge and Skills

There is hardly an end to a description of all the employment-related information that one could use in choosing an occupation, seeking training or employment in that occupation, knowing what is required to maintain employment by performing the work routine adequately, and knowing how, as Dever (1985) put it, "to handle 'glitches'" on the job.

Each school program must decide for itself what should be taught, to whom, and in what way. School personnel tend to approach these decisions in the easiest possible way. It is not uncommon to hear the expression, "We shouldn't reinvent the wheel." There is some truth to that. But if the result of that approach is to select the wheel that is the most fashionable, the least expensive, the most available, or the easiest to use, without consideration for size, durability, or appropriateness, it is better to choose a wheel that has not yet been invented.

There is considerable scope in the content of occupational information. It can be simplified and the tasks analyzed with priorities established for which content elements are the most critical for students who are low functioning, or it can be open ended, reaching for the highest levels of cognitive acquisition for students with physical, behavioral, or sensory impairments. Ideally, secondary schools should lay out a scope and sequence curriculum in this area for all students and ensure that all students have access to it. In many schools, hard decisions must be made about how students with disabilities can acquire this information.

If resource rooms are currently the most typical approach for delivery of selected instruction and support maintenance for regular class instruction, some questions must be asked: Is employment-related content available in one or more elective courses in the regular curriculum? If not, why not? If it is available, is it accessible to *every* student who has been identified as mildly to moderately disabled? If it is not accessible to *every* student, how can the instruction be delivered?"

If self-contained classrooms or a combination of self-contained classrooms and resource rooms are used, the same questions must be asked, with the addition of these: Is the content currently in the self-contained classroom curriculum? If it is not, why not? How can the instruction be delivered within the context of a self-contained classroom model or in conjunction with another program?

Unfortunately, these questions have not been asked as frequently as the basic question, Is occupational awareness and employment-related information so critical to include that one should sacrifice instructional time from basic academics? Many high school programs buy into the need for both academics and either vocational education or community-based work experience options. The assumption is made that all the content just described will be included in the vocational education classes or will be learned in on-the-job training, thus eliminating the need for occupational information being taught purposefully and systematically. We believe that this is a false assumption and that high schools must provide this content as professionally as possible, using all the pedagogy and technology at their disposal.

Specific Vocational Knowledge and Skills

A number of sources of competencies and specific vocational skills are needed for the transition to employment. Perhaps one of the most widespread and organized efforts related to skills needed in the workplace was undertaken by the Secretary's Commission on Achieving Necessary Skills (SCANS). SCANS was established in February 1990 to examine the demands of the workplace and to provide suggestions on how to prepare the current and future work force. Commission members included representatives from the nation's schools, businesses, unions, and government. Specifically, the commission was directed to advise the Secretary of Labor on the type and level of skills required to enter employment.

Figure 6.1 presents the three foundation skills areas and five basic competency areas identified by SCANS. The Resources section near the end of this chapter lists a number of the SCANS documents. Refer to them for a more in-depth explanation of these areas, along with practical ideas on how to prepare your students with these skills. More detailed information on SCANS and SCANS documents is also available on their website (www.ttrc.doleta.gov/SCANS/).

Another source, the Vocational Technical Education Consortium of States (V-TECS), has published over 130 curriculum guides for approximately 250 different job titles. These guides have a standardized format for tasks, tools, performance standards, and support materials. They are organized into an easy-to-read outline format, with diagrams, vocabulary, and step-by-step directions. Each state in the consortium develops new guides and revises old guides as a function of their areas of established expertise. In return, they are then allowed to use guides developed by other members. The Mid-America Vocational Curriculum Consortium and the American Association of Vocational Instructional Materials are other sources of jointly developed curricula (Evers & Elksnin, 1998).

FIGURE 6.1 Foundation Skills and Basic Competency Areas Identified by the Secretary's Commission on Achieving Necessary Skills (SCANS)

A Three-Part Foundation

Basic Skills: Reads, writes, performs arithmetic and mathematical operations, listens and speaks

A. *Reading*—Locates, understands, and interprets information in prose and in documents such as manuals, graphs, and schedules

B. *Writing*—Communicates thoughts, ideas, information, and messages in writing; and creates documents such as letters, directions, manuals, reports, graphs, and flow charts

C. *Arithmetic/Mathematics*—Performs basic computations and approaches practical problems by choosing appropriately from a variety of mathematical techniques

D. *Listening*—Receives, attends to, interprets, and responds to verbal messages and other cues

E. *Speaking*—Organizes ideas and communicates orally

Thinking Skills: Thinks creatively, makes decisions, solves problems, visualizes, knows how to learn, and reasons

A. *Creative Thinking*—Generates new ideas

B. *Decision Making*—Specifies goals and constraints, generates alternatives, considers risks, and evaluates and chooses best alternative

C. *Problem Solving*—Recognizes problems and devises and implements plan of action

D. *Seeing Things in the Mind's Eye*—Organizes, and processes symbols, pictures, graphs, objects, and other information

E. *Knowing How to Learn*—Uses efficient learning techniques to acquire and apply new knowledge and skills

F. *Reasoning*—Discovers a rule or principle underlying the relationship between two or more objects and applies it when solving a problem

Personal Qualities: Displays responsibility, self-esteem, sociability, self-management, and integrity and honesty

A. *Responsibility*—Exerts a high level of effort and perseveres towards goal attainment

B. *Self-Esteem*—Believes in own self-worth and maintains a positive view of self

C. *Sociability*—Demonstrates understanding, friendliness, adaptability, empathy, and politeness in group settings

D. *Self-Management*—Assesses self accurately, sets personal goals, monitors progress, and exhibits self-control

E. *Integrity/Honesty*—Chooses ethical courses of action

FIGURE 6.1 Continued

Five Competencies

Resources: Identifies, organizes, plans, and allocates resources

A. *Time*—Selects goal-relevant activities, ranks them, allocates time, and prepares and follows schedules
B. *Money*—Uses or prepares budgets, makes forecasts, keeps records, and makes adjustments to meet objectives
C. *Material and Facilities*—Acquires, stores, allocates, and uses materials or space efficiently
D. *Human Resources*—Assesses skills and distributes work accordingly, evaluates performance and provides feedback

Interpersonal: Works with others

A. *Participates as Member of a Team*—Contributes to group effort
B. *Teaches Others New Skills*
C. *Serves Clients/Customers*—Works to satisfy customer's expectations
D. *Exercises Leadership*—Communicates ideas to justify position, persuades and convinces others, responsibly challenges existing procedures and policies
E. *Negotiates*—Works toward agreements involving exchange of resources, resolves divergent interests
F. *Works with Diversity*—Works well with men and women from diverse backgrounds

Information: Acquires and uses information

A. *Acquires and Evaluates Information*
B. *Organizes and Maintains Information*

C. *Interprets and Communicates Information*
D. *Uses Computers to Process Information*

Systems: Understands complex interrelationships

A. *Understands Systems*—Knows how social, organizational, and technological systems work and operates effectively with them
B. *Monitors and Corrects Performance*—Distinguishes trends, predicts impacts on system operations, diagnoses systems' performance and corrects malfunctions
C. *Improves or Designs Systems*—Suggests modifications to existing systems and develops new or alternative systems to improve performance

Technology: Works with a variety of technologies

A. *Selects Technology*—Chooses procedures, tools or equipment including computers and related technologies
B. *Applies Technology to Task*—Understands overall intent and proper procedures for setup and operation of equipment
C. *Maintains and Troubleshoots Equipment*—Prevents, identifies, or solves problems with equipment, including computers and other technologies

Source: From *What Work Requires of Schools: A SCANS Report for America 2000* (pages 12 and 16) by Secretary's Commission on Achieving Necessary Skills, 1991, Springfield, VA: National Technical Information Service, Operations Division. NTIS Number: PB92-146711.

Many states have developed lists of competencies associated with vocational areas. These are usually developed by committees of industry representatives and vocational teachers. Consult your state department to see what is available in your state. If you are currently teaching, also contact vocational education or other school-to-work staff in your school.

Principles and Characteristics of Work-Based Learning

Work-based learning experiences are "activities at the high school level that involve actual work experience or connect classroom learning to work" (The National School-to-Work Office, 1996, p. 64). Various principles, characteristics, and approaches should underlie any school program whose goal is to prepare youths to make the transition to employment. These will be presented here first, before discussing some of the approaches to delivering work-based learning.

Benz, Yovanoff, and Doren (1997) explored the extent to which the outcomes experienced by students were actually influenced by the instructional programs and what skill outcomes were identified as important components of school-to-work transition programs. Results indicated that students with and without disabilities who had two or more work experiences during the last two years of high school, exited school with high social skills or high job search skills, or had no continuing vocational instruction needs one year out of school were two to three times more likely to be competitively employed one year out of school. Students with disabilities who possessed high reading, writing, or math skills were also two to three times more likely to be competitively employed than were students with low skills. (*Competitive employment* was defined as working in a paid job over 20 hours per week and earning $4.25 per hour or more at the time of the interview.) The researchers also found that students with high career awareness skills and students who reported having no continuing instructional needs in vocational and personal social content areas were 1.5 times more likely to be productively engaged. (*Productive engagement* was defined as (1) working half time or more only, (2) going to school half time or more only, (3) working and going to school, or (4) participating full time in the military.)

General Principles of Work-Based Learning Programs

Hamilton and Hamilton (1997) identified seven principles that make work a learning experience and provided the following recommendations related to implementing each principle:

1. Youths gain basic and high-level technical competence through work. Recommendations are to (a) identify work tasks that teach technical competence, (b) organize learning activities, and (c) design a multiyear learning plan that is increasingly challenging.

2. Youths gain broad technical competence and understand all aspects of the industry through rotation and projects. Recommendations are to (a) inform youths about all aspects of the industry, (b) rotate youths through several placements within the industry, and (c) design projects and activities that teach multiple skills and broad knowledge.

3. Youths gain personal and social competence in the workplace. Recommendations are to (a) recognize personal and social competencies as key learning objectives, (b) systematically teach personal and social competence in context, and (c) provide extra assistance to individual students as needed.

4. Workplace teachers convey clear expectations to youths and assess progress toward achieving them. Recommendations are to (a) state expectations for behavior and learning at the outset of the work experience; (b) regularly monitor and document the acquisition of competence; (c) provide feedback on progress to youths, school, families, and the business; (d) encourage youths to assemble a portfolio; and (e) use industrywide standards to provide credentials that will go across different employment settings.

5. Youths learn from adults with formally assigned teaching roles. Recommendations are to (a) assign clear teaching roles and responsibilities to personnel involved in the program; (b) specify teaching roles in job descriptions and performance assessments; and (c) orient, train, and support adults who teach.

6. Youths achieve high academic standards. Recommendations are to (a) set high academic standards, (b) specify courses and degrees related to the career area, and (c) open multiple options for postsecondary education.

7. Youths identify and follow career paths. Recommendations are to (a) provide opportunities for career exploration and information on related careers; (b) advise youths about career paths, coordinating planning with high school and college advisors and family members; and (c) pay particular attention to the transition to postsecondary.

Ascher (1994) identified a number of features of good cooperative education programs. Most, if not all, of the following features apply to all work-based learning programs:

- Quality placements in which the student is allowed to perform work that both provides opportunities to develop new competencies and contributes to the productivity of the organization
- Placement coordinators with appropriate occupational experience related to the specific industry, as well as professional preparation for operating a cooperative education program
- Close supervision at the worksite by a training sponsor or supervisor, as well as a mechanism by which the training sponsor can share his or her professional experience with the student
- An accurate and realistic description of the job for the student, as well as accurate expectations by the training sponsor

- Strong links between job training and related instruction, including an individualized, written training plan that is coordinated with the student's in-school curriculum
- Frequent and specific informal and formal evaluations by the placement coordinator, with feedback and follow-up to improve performance
- Involvement of parents or guardians
- Placement of graduates in full-time positions or referrals for additional training, and follow-up of graduates after three and five years
- Strong administrative support

Approaches to Delivering Work-Based Learning

Providing experience at the worksite is the core of all work-based learning programs. Several approaches to this end include (1) cooperative education, (2) student internships, (3) youth apprenticeships, and (4) school-based enterprises (National Center for Research in Vocational Education, 1995). The goal of these learning experiences is to allow learners to observe and perform hands-on work, develop work readiness skills, and learn to draw their own conclusions. Effective work-based learning is integrated with instruction (in school, on the job, or both), follows a training plan, and teaches all aspects of a particular industry or career.

Cooperative Education.   Ascher (1994) defined *cooperative education* as "a program which combines academic study with paid, monitored and credit-bearing work" (p. 1). Cooperative education was established around the turn of the twentieth century as part of a movement to create experience-based education. This approach enhances traditional classroom or academic instruction by providing practical, work-based learning relevant to the learner's educational and career goals. Today, cooperative education is concentrated mainly in the vocational areas of marketing, trade and industry, and business (Ascher, 1994). A cooperative education placement generally lasts a year or less (U.S. General Accounting Office, 1991), with students working half a day and attending both traditional academic and vocational classes the remainder of the day.

Cooperative education typically has a classroom training component that is concurrent with or prerequisite to the off-campus training. In the off-campus component, the student is supervised by the on-site mentor or training sponsor, who is the primary source of instruction and feedback. The school program coordinator typically provides the on-campus instruction and monitors student progress via observations and conferences with the students and their mentors.

Student Internship Programs.   The *School-to-Work Glossary of Terms* (National School-to-Work Office, 1996) defines *student internships* as "situations where students work for an employer for a specific period of time to learn about a particular industry or occupation. Students' workplace activities may include special projects, a sample of tasks from different jobs, or tasks from a single occupation. These may or may not include financial compensation" (p. 31). Internships provide structured work experience for students in a career field that is of interest to them

(National Center for Research in Vocational Education, 1995). Although internships are usually short term, their duration varies along with the complexity of knowledge and skills the student is required to master.

Youth Apprenticeship Programs. The National School-to-Work Office (1996) defined *registered apprenticeships* as

> those programs that meet specific federally approved standards designed to safeguard the welfare of apprentices. The programs are registered with the Bureau of Apprenticeship and Training (BAT), U.S. Department of Labor, or one of 27 State Apprenticeship Agencies or Councils approved by BAT. Apprenticeships are relationships between an employer and employee during which the worker, or apprentice, learns an occupation in a structured program sponsored jointly by employers and labor unions or operated by employers and employee associations. (p. 3)

Apprenticeship completers are perceived by their industry as having the highest level of craft, sometimes more than employees who have been graduated from college.

Currently, there is a movement in some states to develop and implement youth apprenticeship programs in order to meet the School-to-Work reform mandates (McKernan, 1994; Osterman & Iannozzi, 1993; Paris & Mason, 1995; Reisner et al., 1993). Often, however, these programs more closely resemble cooperative education programs than the traditional apprenticeship. *Youth apprenticeship* is defined by the *School-to-Work Glossary of Terms* (National School-to-Work Office, 1996) as "typically a multi-year program that combines school-and work-based learning in a specific occupational area or occupational cluster and is designed to lead directly into either a related postsecondary program, entry-level job, or registered apprenticeship program. Youth apprenticeships may or may not include financial compensation" (p. 65).

School-Based Enterprises. A *school-based enterprise* is a school-sponsored, work-based learning opportunity in which a group of students (1) produce goods or services for sale or use by other people, (2) participate in multiple aspects of the enterprise, and (3) relate service and production activities to classroom learning. School-based enterprises must be student initiated and student run. They give students real practice in entrepreneurship, accounting, budgeting, marketing, inventory control, and business-related skills. They also allow students to develop generic work skills in problem solving, communication, interpersonal relations, and learning how to learn in the context of work. A well-established example of a school-based enterprise program is the Junior Achievement model.

School-Based Approaches and Activities That Bridge across Classrooms and Workplaces

Most work-based learning programs include a special related class in which students are able to reflect on and integrate their job experiences, as well as obtain some of the employment-related and specific vocational skills needed for their vocational area. If the student is on the work site for the entire day, this instruction is provided by the supervisor on the job site. Some programs have a studio, which is a special kind of classroom. It provides students with a specific location in which they may work to complete a project or activity. Students have more space to work, enjoy greater freedom or movement, and bear more responsibility for the internal and external security and maintenance of the space. Teachers empower students through initial training and structuring work schedules and then act as roving floor supervisors, mentors, and technology troubleshooters. They become coaches, mentors, advisors, and supervisors in the learning process. Examples of programs in which students assume these roles are drafting and graphic arts.

In some work-based learning programs, the actual work site is operated by the school. Examples include construction programs that build a house and then sell it to someone in the community, as well as restaurants, automotive mainte-nance centers, and child-care centers operated by the school. Other examples would be school-based enterprises discussed in the previous section.

One major component of school-to-work programs is connecting activities. In addition, the National Center for Research in Vocational Education (1995) identi-fied connecting activities that bridge classrooms and workplaces, including guid-ance and counseling, mentoring, job shadowing, guest speakers, and field trips. In the first type of activity, school counselors, teachers, and business representatives can work together to provide students with experiences early on in high school to determine their focus of study and later to assist with postsecondary decisions.

In most programs, the focus of mentoring is to guide the students who par-ticipate in work-based learning and to help structure their learning and contribu-tion to the workplace. Mentors can provide a safe place for questions to be asked about life outside of school, in particular, work. Observing or "shadowing" a worker in an industry helps students understand the tasks performed in that industry, the knowledge and skills needed, and the work environment. Students have a chance to ask employees questions and reflect on their observations in the classroom. Both guest speakers and field trips tied to classroom learning can pro-vide youths with exposure to a variety of industries, employers, and careers. This helps youths see the connections between what they are studying and the work-place and also helps with future planning.

Program Models for Delivering Work-Based Learning

Numerous program models for the classroom and work-based components of work-based learning exist, along with activities that connect the two. All include the principles of work-based learning discussed in the previous section. These models may have specific names within your state or school district and may be funded by different funding streams. We will outline the basic components of each of the program models, but we encourage you to contact your state department of education and your local school-to-work staff to identify the specific program options available in your area. It is important that you determine the options available for all students, as well as those available solely for students with disabilities.

Vocational Education

Vocational education is a term that traditionally has had very specific meaning. It has been a major part of the public education system since the Smith-Hughes Act of 1917. Evers and Elksnin (1998) provided an excellent history of vocational education in the United States; this history was also traced by Neubert (1997; see also Chapter 3 of this text). The term has been used loosely (and incorrectly) in the past few years by many educators to include all types of vocational training, including that conducted by special educators. It is important to establish a clear distinction between vocational education and other types of work-based learning. The distinction we would like to stress is that vocational education programs are taught by professionals certified in vocational education—not by teachers certified in special education or other areas.

The *Federal Register* (1977) defined *vocational education* as "organized educational programs which are directly related to the preparation of individuals for paid or unpaid employment, or for additional preparation for a career that does not require a baccalaureate or advanced degree." The American Vocational Association (1998) defined *vocational education* as

> part of a program designed to prepare individuals for gainful employment as semi-skilled or skilled workers, technicians, or subprofessionals in recognized occupations and in new and emerging occupations, or to prepare individuals for enrollment in advanced technical education, but excluding any program to prepare individuals for employment in occupations generally considered professional or which require a baccalaureate or higher degree. (p. 73)

Vocational education, then, is an established discipline, just as special education is its own discipline. Traditionally, it does not train in unskilled occupations, such as entry-level service occupations, nor does it train in areas requiring a college degree. Individuals who teach vocational education courses are certified in that area, just as special educators are certified for their specific roles. Special educators can provide work-based learning, such as work experience or vocational training, but they are not providing vocational education. In addition, unless the program is designated as a state-approved vocational education course of study, it is not vocational education. This means that a youth who takes a woodworking class or a foods class may not be receiving vocational education, but rather industrial arts or practical arts training.

Vocational education can be divided into seven occupational concentrations: agriculture, business and office, health occupations, marketing, family and consumer sciences (previously home economics), trade and industry, and technology and technical education (previously industrial arts). The specific course and program offerings per setting are usually a function of the labor training needs of the locality (Hoerner & Wehrley, 1995). Business and office as well as trade and industry programs account for almost 75 percent of secondary vocational education enrollments, with the remaining program enrollments being about equal. Enrollments at the postsecondary level are primarily in technical education, with approximately 75 percent of enrollees in business, health, and technical programs (Scott & Sarkees-Wircenski, 1996).

Vocational Education Program Options and Training Settings.   The three basic administrative arrangements for delivering the content of vocational education are (1) general high schools, (2) comprehensive high schools, and (3) vocational technical centers and career academies (Evers & Elksnin, 1998). General high schools provide programs in four or fewer vocational areas and provide approximately 60 percent of the secondary vocational training programs. Frequently, occupationally specific training is available in only two or three of the vocational training areas, along with some general industrial arts or homemaking. Comprehensive high schools house vocational programs in at least five of the seven vocational areas, along with traditional academic programs, and provide approximately 30 percent of the total vocational instruction. Students typically attend vocational classes on campus for one to three periods (or up to half a day) each day. Classes are traditional lectures with reading assignments, homework, and tests. This training is alternated with actual hands-on instruction, supervised practice of skill development, and completion of projects in the relevant vocational laboratory or job site in the community. Examples of vocational laboratories range from a house built (and then sold on the market) by a construction program, to a restaurant run on or off the school grounds by the quantity foods program, to an auto service center run on campus by the auto mechanics program. If the hands-on experience is provided in community businesses, the program is usually called a *cooperative education program*.

Vocational-technical centers and career academies are stand-alone facilities, usually not located on the high school campus. These centers usually offer only vocational programs and academics associated with these programs. Students typically attend the center for half of each school day and then return to their home schools for traditional classes. Training options are usually limited to occupations that reflect local labor needs (Evers & Elksnin, 1998).

Cluster programs provide a way for vocational programs to deliver training that is not narrowly occupation specific. Cluster programs combine training in similar occupations in order for students to benefit from a broader knowledge and skills base—for example, a construction cluster may include carpentry, construction, plumbing, masonry, electrical technology, and air conditioning, heating, and refrigeration technology. Other clusters would include services, manufacturing, and transportation, or other areas of local need (Evers & Elksnin, 1998). Another program model, such as an all-aspects-of-the-industry approach, would provide instruction in more depth and breadth. For example, the printing industry can be studied from the perspective of commercial printing and newspaper publishing. Specialized skills as well as generalizable skills are reinforced in each application. Thus, a trainee could learn skills that are transferable to other related areas (Bailey, Koppel, & Waldinger, 1994).

Phelps and Wermuth (1992) identified the following eight components that appear to be related to effective vocational education programs for students with special needs:

1. Sufficient financial support
2. Individualized curriculum modifications
3. Ongoing career guidance and counseling
4. Instructional support services
5. Assessment of individual career interests and abilities
6. Family involvement and support
7. Intra- and interagency collaboration
8. Follow-up of graduates and nongraduates

Instruction in regular vocational education programs is the responsibility of vocational education teachers. Support services to the student or the vocational instructor may be provided by the special education teacher, vocational resource teacher, or special needs vocational instructor. These services (sometimes called *vocational special needs services*) are available as a function of meeting the inclusion mandates in the Carl Perkins Vocational Education Act, as well as ongoing requirements of the Vocational Rehabilitation Amendments and the Americans with Disabilities Act. Individuals who staff these programs are usually either special educators who have skills and specialized training in vocational education, or vocational educators who have skills and training in working with students with disabilities. These instructors go by a number of job titles, such as *related vocational instructors, transition coordinators, job coaches,* and *vocational special needs instructors* (Evers & Elksnin, 1998). Special education teachers need to work alongside vocational instructors in integrated settings, just as they do in secondary academic classrooms. With this arrangement, students have the opportunity to be taught by instructors with training and experience in the specific vocational area and to work with peers who have no disabilities. They also have more vocational training options available to them, both in high school and postsecondary vocational training settings.

Support services to the student could include one or more of the following: audiotapes of readings, note-takers, interpreters, modifications of equipment, architectural accommodations, speech or communication assistance, instructional aids or equipment, peer tutoring, individualized contracts, support personnel, or transportation. Some students might also need additional support outside the classroom or shop in reading or math instruction in order to be successful in the regular program (West, Jones, Corbey, Boyer-Stephens, Miller, & Sarkees-Wircenski, 1992).

Characteristics of Vocational Education Programs That Need to Be Considered. The content expertise and connections in the community that vocational educators have developed are invaluable to the transition of individuals with disabilities into adult life. As IDEA and other legislation encourages more cooperative efforts with general education, vocational education is a natural partner for special education. There are, however, a few characteristics of vocational education personnel and programs that require careful consideration as efforts are merged (Evers & Elksnin, 1998). First, vocational instructors are as diverse as the programs they support, especially at the postsecondary level. Business, agriculture, and consumer and home economics instructors are usually trained at the baccalaureate level, where one can major in that academic area. Most trade and industry instructors, however, acquire their expertise by working in their specialty field, and they are often not four-year college graduates. The background of vocational educators usually results in individuals who have broad content-area expertise but who have limited, if any, training in instructional methods (Office of Educational Research and Improvements, U.S. Department of Education, 1994).

Second, the goal of vocational education is to train high-wage, highly skilled, technically oriented individuals. However, vocational teachers continually fight the perception that their programs are easier and of lower status than academic programs, and that they are the default track for students who cannot succeed in academic programs. In addition, the measure of a successful vocational program and its subsequent funding support is the number of students who become employed in their content area within a specific period of time. Because of these factors, some vocational educators are hesitant to accept students with disabilities into their programs.

Although youths with disabilities have learning characteristics that may hinder them in acquiring the more traditional aspects of vocational education, there are also aspects of vocational education that tend to enhance the acquisition of skills and knowledge. Vocational education tends to be tangible as well as goal and outcome oriented, and schooling is made relevant within the context of the world of work. In addition, a portion of the curriculum requires hands-on learning and site-based learning experiences that free students from the confines of the academic environment (Evers & Elksnin, 1998). Finally, vocational education serves as a "holding" function for many adolescents with disabilities. Students who enroll in more than four related vocational courses tend to have higher rates of high school completion and subsequent employment than students in traditional academic programs (Wagner, Blackorby, Cameto, Hebbler, & Newman, 1993).

Vocational Student Organizations. Vocational student organizations are an integral part of the vocational curriculum and should not be confused with social clubs. Vocational student organizations have as their primary focus the development of leadership skills. Many vocational programs have mandatory attendance requirements for these organizations. These groups also emphasize working on community projects, which helps facilitate the development of social and leadership skills and civic responsibility. The 10 vocational student organizations recognized by the United States Department of Education (Evers & Elksnin, 1998) are as follows:

1. National FFA Organization (FFA)—formerly Future Farmers of America
2. National Young Farmers Education Association (NYFEA)
3. National Future Homemakers of America—Home Economics Related Occupations (HERO)
4. Future Business Leaders of America (FBLA)
5. Distributive Education Clubs of America (DECA)
6. Vocational Industrial Clubs of America (VICA)
7. Technology Student Association (TSA)
8. Business Professionals of America (BPA)
9. Health Occupations Students of America (HOSA)
10. National Postsecondary Agriculture Student Organization (NPASO)

School-to-Work Programs

The School-to-Work Opportunities Act of 1994 provided a major thrust for school-to-work programs in general education. The overall purpose of school-to-work transition programs is to prepare *all* students for work and further education and to increase their opportunities to enter first jobs in high-skill, high-wage careers. The federal School-to-Work Opportunities Act of 1994 defined *all students* to include disadvantaged students; students from diverse racial, ethnic, or cultural backgrounds; students with disabilities; school dropouts; and academically talented students (U.S. Department of Education, 1994).

The school-to-work (STW) transition systems in place in local districts offer a great deal of opportunity for individuals with disabilities. These students can be included in ongoing STW programs, although they may need additional support for some of the STW activities. This inclusion of students with disabilities in ongoing programs is in keeping with the local, areawide, and state initiatives to blend the special education and general education systems to serve *all* students.

School-to-work programs should include a variety of school-based and work-based learning opportunities through high school, including (1) career exploration and counseling; (2) academic and occupational instruction that is integrated and focused on high standards of achievement; and (3) a variety of structured work experiences that teach broad, transferable workplace skills (Benz, Yovanoff, & Doren, 1997; Goldberger, Kazis, & O'Flanagan, 1994; Hamilton & Hamilton, 1994).

The purpose of this section is to provide an overview of the STW programs found in many schools and the new components they have added to the concept of work-based learning. We will organize our comments around the three major components of this system: (1) the school-based learning component; (2) the work-based learning component; and (3) connecting activities. Benz and Kochhar (1996) and Benz and Lindstrom (1997) cover these topics in much more detail. The National School-to-Work Learning and Information Center also has an Internet homepage (www.stw.ed.gov). You are encouraged to consult these sources for more information on this topic.

School-Based Learning.   As with all students, the school-based learning component of STW programs is one of the most critical for students with disabilities. Many students will have received some type of background through the classroom instruction that is often associated with experience-based career education programs or work experience programs offered through special education. These programs, however, often do not serve students with disabilities who are receiving most of their education in the general education classroom.

The National Center for Research in Vocational Education (1995) identified four alternative organizational approaches to work-oriented education in the school setting: (1) courses, (2) programs consisting of a number of courses, (3) schools within schools, and (4) commitment (restructuring) of an entire school. Courses are integrated curricula related to education for work. These courses are offered within a single classroom by a single teacher. Teachers within an academic or vocational discipline may work together to implement a program with coordinated or integrated coursework and special activities and services for students. Teachers might be organized within one academic area or across several academic or vocational courses. Schools within a School (SWS) are often called *career majors, clusters, houses,* or *academies.* They are designed as structured programs that are administratively distinct from other school programs. One of the ways in which SWS differs from other school programs is that teachers often have greater autonomy in designing courses, scheduling courses and students, and staffing their teams. The final option, school restructuring, occurs on a much larger scale than the organization of a single program or school within a school. School restructuring might involve setting up multiple programs or SWSs (i.e., forming clusters, pathways, or career majors).

The National Center for Research in Vocational Education (1995) provided information on two approaches to developing curriculum that focuses on learner outcomes, integrates academic and vocational curriculum, and blends the best instructional practices from both disciplines. These two approaches are (1) curriculum focused on specific industry and other work-related themes and (2) projects integrated into the ongoing academic curriculum. A *thematic curriculum* usually involves a single course or teacher and a new team that has usually not worked together before. In this approach, team members want to coordinate their curriculum, but not necessarily participate in joint projects. Often, however, they have the same students. In thematic curriculum units, the process begins with learner outcomes for each course where each course is integrated around the same theme. The team selects an industry theme and then aligns their course material. Team members work on learning activities (in their own courses) that integrate with one common theme. A common project may or may not result.

In the *integrated projects approach,* the instructional team has usually previously worked together on the curriculum. They must have the same students and they want to move toward eliminating discipline boundaries and focus on joint projects and products. In integrated project units, the process begins with learner outcomes for the project or product and aims to incorporate them from each course. Learning activities that support the end project or product are designed for each course. Discipline boundaries may disappear, and a common project results.

The concept of a career major or career pathway is central to the school-based learning component. The career pathways component of STW programs also offers a great opportunity to include students of all ability levels in exploring the same career area. This component allows lower-functioning students as well as higher-functioning students to work in the same career area. Sources of support for students with disabilities in regular STW programs are special education teachers, work experience coordinators, and other special education support staff, such as consultants. These professionals can work closely with general education staff to provide the support needed by students with disabilities to gain the most from regular STW programs.

Work-Based Learning Component. The second component of STW programs, work-based learning, consists of structured learning experiences for students, based in employment settings, that develop broad, transferable skills. This component emphasizes the importance of work and community environments as the context in which students with disabilities can learn and apply the academic and occupational knowledge and skills that they learn in the school-based component. Students with disabilities need real-world experiences in order to be more successful in the transition from school to the world of work. Providing students with these learning experiences will require the participation of students, parents, administrators, teachers, employers, and other school staff.

Connecting Activities. Connecting schools and the world of work does not occur naturally, so connecting activities are the third component in a STW program. Programs must build strong partnerships among secondary schools, postsecondary education institutions, employers, and community agencies. The student can no longer be the only thread to the world of work. All participants must be bound together to enhance outcomes for all students, especially students with disabilities. These connecting activities are focused on individual students, administrative personnel, and those activities that focus on both.

Individual students should be matched with a workplace mentor who will develop a relationship and give the student supports in the workplace to assist with the successful transition into the world of work. Students with disabilities must be matched with work-based learning opportunities that match their interests, abilities, and future goals. School-to-work programs do not end with graduation. Students must be provided with postprogram assistance to secure employment, continue their educational training, and link them with other community services that may be necessary to assure successful transitions.

Benz, Yovanoff, and Doren (1997) stated that special educators should work with their counterparts in the school-to-work movement to ensure the following:

1. Local programs should include (a) options for multiple pathways and time frames, (b) reasonable accommodations and support services, (c) relevant performance indicators, and (d) adequate training and technical assistance for all personnel.
2. Career exploration and planning should provide the foundation and framework for the school-based and work-based activities in which students participate.
3. Emphasis must be on integrating academic and occupational instruction, teaching this content in contextual settings, and holding students accountable for high standards of achievement in these areas.
4. Support services must be available to address the individual needs of students, especially students who are vulnerable to failure in postschool settings, and must be available to students not only during high school but also during the early transition years.

Specially Designed Work-Based Learning Programs

Evers and Elksnin (1998) listed a number of specially designed vocational programs:

1. Career exploration
2. Cooperative work training
3. Student or school-based businesses
4. Job shadowing
5. Volunteer service learning experiences in the community
6. Classroom and school as the workplace

The wider the choice of school-to-work, vocational education, and other work-based learning programs available in general education, the less need there should be for specially designed work-based learning programs. Students with disabilities are often placed in specially designed programs for one of two reasons: (1) no similar programs are available in general education, or (2) even with supports, the student cannot succeed in the general education program.

The focus of programming for students with disabilities should be on including these students in general education programs related to training in occupational awareness, employment-related knowledge and skills, and specific vocational knowledge and skills, as well as providing them the needed supports to succeed in these programs. In establishing a specially designed program, one should incorporate the principles of work-based learning offered in the beginning of this chapter. In addition, it is probable that one would offer a modified or exact version of the approaches and program options discussed earlier. We encourage you to work closely with the school-to-work staff in your school who are offering these programs so that you can build on their expertise and coordinate your efforts with theirs. Use your principal to establish the logic of a single program, rather than segregated programs that duplicate efforts in the general education curriculum.

Supported Employment

Supported employment is a specific example of a specially designed program in which you may be involved if you are working with individuals with more moderate disabilities. It incorporates all of the principles of other work-based learning programs, but it is specific enough in its approach that we believe it should be covered in more detail. In supported empoyment, you will be part of a team of vocational rehabilitation counselors, job coaches, case managers, other school support staff (e.g., occupational therapists, physical therapists, work experience coordinators, assistive technology specialists) and adult service provider staff.

Wehman and associates (1998) outlined nine basic supported employment values (see Figure 6.2). As can be seen from this list, the focus of supported employment is on community integrated jobs with commensurate wages and benefits (Wehman & Moon, 1988). Supported employment's philosophical foundation and implementation strategies challenge the practice of providing services that remove people with disabilities from the mainstream of community activity.

The evolution of supported employment services has required families, educators, adult providers, employers, policy makers, and individuals with disabilities

---

FIGURE 6.2   Supported Employment Values

Commensurate Wages and Benefits—People with disabilities should earn wages and benefits equal to that of coworkers performing the same or similar jobs.

Community—People need to be connected to the formal and informal networks of a community for acceptance, growth, and development.

Everyone Can Work—Everyone, regardless of the level or the type of disability, has the capability to and right to a job.

Focus on Abilities—People with disabilities should be viewed in terms of their abilities, strengths, and interests rather than their disabilities.

Ongoing Supports—Customers of supported employment services will receive assistance in assembling the supports necessary to achieve their ambitions as long as they need supports.

Real Jobs—Employment occurs within the local labor market in regular community businesses.

Right to the Opportunity—Regardless of their disability, everyone has the right to an opportunity to work in the employment of their choice.

Self-Determination—Everyone has the right to make decisions for themselves.

Systems Change—Traditional systems must be changed to ensure customer control, which is vital to the integrity of supported employment.

Source: "Barriers to Competitive Employment for Persons with Disabilities" by P. Wehman, V. Brooke, M. West, P. Targett, H. Green, K. Inge, and J. Kregel, in *Developing Transition Plans* by P. Wehman, 1998, Austin, TX: Pro-Ed. Copyright 1998 by Pro-Ed. Reprinted by permission. Adapted from *Customer-Driven Supported Employment* by Virginia Commonwealth University, Rehabilitation Research and Training Center on Supported Employment, 1997, Richmond, VA: Author.

to examine their values (Wehman et al., 1998). Before the availability of supported employment, sheltered employment programs were valued as an alternative to staying home. The emphasis was on providing a reliable routine and a safe, well-supervised environment. The philosophical foundation for community-based employment services for individuals with cognitive and other developmental disabilities shifted in the 1980s from sanctioning facility-based services to a preferred endorsement of integrated, supported employment (McGaughey, Kiernan, McNally, Gilmore, & Keith, 1995). This shift has been reflected in federal policy, as discussed in Chapter 3. The Rehabilitation Act of 1973 moved away from segregated employment options toward integrated employment. The Rehabilitation Act Amendments of 1992 continued major program changes intended to promote consumer choice, self-determination, and the ability for consumers to pick the jobs and careers they wish (Wehman & Kregel, 1995).

Supported employment has resulted in the provision of integrated employment in regular community settings for thousands of people with severe disabilities (Rehabilitation Services Administration, 1990). Implementation efforts related to supported employment, however, are slowing, and investment in supported employment seems to be dropping off (McGaughey et al., 1995; Wehman et al., 1998). Some adult service providers have experienced a significant drop in the number of referrals for supported employment services. Others have experienced an increase in the numbers of consumers being turned down for authorization of funding for supported employment services. Providers are increasingly hearing that supported employment costs too much.

Use of Natural Supports in Supported Employment. At first, the most critical need faced by providers of supported employment was to find jobs and to provide the support needed by the individuals who were placed. It is becoming clear, however, that the long-term success of persons in supported employment is affected as much by the way in which services are provided as by the presence or absence of such services (Callahan, 1992). Mere placement in a natural setting neither constitutes nor guarantees integration (Hagner, 1992). People with disabilities may be placed in a setting without becoming part of that setting. In particular, the role of the job coach needs to be carefully considered as supports are provided to the individual. As Nisbet and Hagner (1988) warned, the unbridled provision of support from outside the natural setting can result in a number of negative outcomes, including difficulty in fading the support, limited involvement from the natural supports other workers have, limited social interactions, the fostering of a human services perspective within the workplace, and increased costs.

Callahan (1992) defined *natural supports* as "all the assistance typically available from an employer and other employees that can be used to learn job skills and sustain employment" (p. 262). The type and degree of natural supports offered by employers vary greatly, even within the same industry. Just as there is often a discrepancy between the skills required for the job and the skills possessed by the employee, a discrepancy will often exist between the natural supports offered by an employer and the support needs of the individual. Callahan also addressed the relationship between learning the skills required for the job and the support required by the individual. As he stated, the employer/employee relationship has a number of critical conditions. First, every job has a set of skills that are required by the employer and that are necessary for successful performance. Even though the concept of supported employment allows job developers to negotiate job duties, there will always be skills that the employee must perform correctly in order to remain on the job. Because of this, there is almost always an initial skill discrepancy for every employee who begins a new job, whether the employee has a disability or not.

Second, the employee must perform the agreed-upon duties in a manner that satisfies both the quality and productivity needs of the employer. Supported employment conceptually states that assistance in learning and performing job skills will be provided on the job and that the responsibility for acquisition of these skills and productivity can be shared with a support person, traditionally a job coach. Typically, employers insist on acceptable performance as a necessary condition of long-term employment. As Callahan (1992) stated, the problem in supported employment is that people confuse issues concerning acquiring the skills required for the job with those concerning the natural supports available in the work setting.

Butterworth, Hagner, Kiernan, and Schalock (1996) defined *natural supports* as:

> Assistance provided by people, procedures, or equipment in a given workplace or group that:
>
> (a) leads to desired personal and work outcomes,
> (b) is typically available or culturally appropriate in the workplace, and
> (c) is supported by resources from within the workplace, facilitated to the degree necessary by human service consultation. (p. 106)

This definition places primary emphasis on the observed *outcome* of natural supports as experienced by the individual in the workplace. Butterworth and colleagues also proposed a multidimensional model of workplace support, which includes the dimensions of (1) support resources, (2) process, and (3) relationship to culture. *Support resources* are mechanisms though which support is provided; they include people, procedures and routines, and tools and equipment. The *process* dimension addresses how the support will occur. Supports may be spontaneous (developed by resources such as co-workers, supervisors, or family and friends with no input from a service provider), facilitated (provided through natural resources but as a result of intervention by a disability-related service provider), or substituted/imported (provided on site by a job coach, personal assistant, or other external resource). The third dimension, *relationship to culture,* characterizes supports as typical (commonly used within the workplace and considered part of the workplace culture), modified (individually developed or adapted in some way, but a logical extension of a typical practice), or anomalous (provided to only one employee with no roots or counterpart in typical practices of the workplace).

Butterworth and associates (1996) stated that effective supported employment needs to balance the lessons learned over the past with an increased concern for the inclusion of the individual in the social culture of the workplace and the development of relationships for both workplace support and friendship. They also listed three key points to consider relative to the use of natural supports: (1) the major purpose of engaging natural networks and resources is to enhance the community inclusion and quality of life of the individual, (2) the need for support may be of lifelong duration and may fluctuate during different stages of the individual's life, and (3) the goal is to maximize natural supports without any assumption or requirement that they will be fully adequate. External support resources remain an important service function; support is a *both/and* issue, not an *either/or* issue.

Issues in Supported Employment.   Most individuals participating in supported employment programs have found their experience economically and socially rewarding (Wehman & Kregel, 1995). Evidence indicates that participants experience dramatic growth in their earnings (Thompson, Powers, & Houchard, 1992) and enhanced quality of life through increased interaction with other members of their communities (Parent, Kregel, Metzler, & Twardzik, 1992). In addition, individuals generally are satisfied with their jobs and the services they have received through supported employment programs (Schalock & Genung, 1993; Test, Hinson, Solow, & Keul, 1993).

Supported employment today, however, is at a definite crossroads (Wehman & Kregel, 1995). Although much has been accomplished, state and local programs are grappling with an array of challenges that may jeopardize these programs (Albin, 1992). Many of the very individuals for whom the original supported employment model was designed have yet to enter and benefit from the program. Despite recent advances in support technologies (e.g., natural supports, assistive technology, consumer-directed services), low wages, lack of career choices, employment retention, and limited social integration continue to be major concerns for many supported employment participants (Brooke, Barcus, & Inge, 1992; Chadsey-Rusch, Gonzalez, Tines, & Johnson, 1989; Lagomarcino, 1990; Rehabilitation Services Administration, 1993; Shafer, Banks, & Kregel, 1991; West & Parent, 1992). In addition, funding shortages have squeezed program capacity and threatened the ability of local programs to continue to provide high-quality services (Wood & Freeman, 1993).

Hagner, Butterworth, and Keith (1995) found that school and adult service providers had difficulty identifying strategies to facilitate natural supports in the workplace, saying that they "just happened naturally." They also found that despite a large number of strategies addressing family involvement, some respondents evidenced a narrow perspective on the roles that family members may play in job seeking and job support. The majority of strategies they listed focused on providing information to families or reassuring families that everything was okay, rather than involving family members as partners in the support process. A large number of respondents perceived families as barriers to successful employment, stating that they were uninterested, too busy, lacked a work ethic, or were over-protective. A few respondents felt that too much family involvement interfered with an individual's employment. Service providers rarely mentioned strategies involving friends, and no school mentioned enlisting other students or graduates of the school as resources for possible job contacts.

In our view, supported employment is a vital concept that is needed for some students with disabilities. If you feel that your students with mild disabilities need supported employment programs, they should require this support for shorter periods of time than those with moderate levels of disability. In times of decreasing financial support, one must be selective in terms of how many students are included in supported employment programs and how long they remain in these programs. Build into the programs specific strategies for fading out program supports and establishing ongoing natural supports.

Resources

The following resources may be of help to you and your students as you work with them in making the transition to employment:

Benz, M. R., & Lindstrom, L. E. (1997). *Building school-to-work programs: Strategies for youth with special needs.* Austin, TX: Pro-Ed.

Brolin, D. E. (1995). *Career education: A functional life skills approach* (3rd ed.). Englewood Cliffs, NJ: Merrill.

Fadely, D. C. (1987). *Job coaching in supported work programs.* Menomonie: University of Wisconsin–Stout, Materials Development Center, Stout Vocational Rehabilitation Institute.

Ford, L. H. (1995). *Providing employment support for people with long-term mental illness: Choices, resources, and practical strategies.* Baltimore: Paul H. Brookes.

Gajar, A., Goodman, L., & McAfee, J. (1993). *Secondary schools and beyond: Transition of individuals with mild disabilities.* New York: Macmillan.

Hagner, D., & DiLeo, D. (1993). *Working together: Workplace culture, supported employment and persons with disabilities.* Cambridge, MA: Brookline.

National Center for Research in Vocational Education. (1995). *Getting to work: A guide for better schools.* Berkeley, CA: Author.

Nisbet, J. (Ed.). (1992). *Natural supports in school, at work, and in the community for people with severe disabilities.* Baltimore: Paul H. Brookes.

Patton, J. R., & Blalock, G. (1996). *Transition and students with learning disabilities: Facilitating the movement from school to adult life.* Austin, TX: Pro-Ed.

Rusch, F. R. (1990). *Supported employment: Models, methods, and issues.* Sycamore, IL: Sycamore Publishing.

Rusch, F. R., DeStefano, L., Chadsey-Rusch, J., Phelps, L. A., & Szymanski, E. (1992). *Transition from school to adult life: Models, linkages, and policy.* Pacific Grove, CA: Brooks/Cole.

Secretary's Commission on Achieving Necessary Skills. (1992). *Learning a living: A blueprint for high performance. A SCANS report for America 2000.* Washington, DC: U.S. Government Printing Office.

Secretary's Commission on Achieving Necessary Skills. (n.d.). *Skills and tasks for jobs: A SCANS report for America 2000.* Springfield, VA: National Technical Information Service, Operations Division.

Secretary's Commission on Achieving Necessary Skills. (n.d.). *Teaching the SCANS competencies.* Washington, DC: U.S. Government Printing Office.

Secretary's Commission on Achieving Necessary Skills. (1991). *What work requires of schools: A SCANS report for America 2000.* Springfield, VA: National Technical Information Service, Operations Division.

Siegel, S., Robert, M., Greener, K., Meyer, G., Halloran, W., & Gaylord-Ross, R. (1993). *Career ladders for challenged youths in transition from school to adult life.* Austin, TX: Pro-Ed.

Smith, M. D., Belcher, R. G., & Juhrs, P. D. (1995). *A guide to successful employment for individuals with autism.* Baltimore: Paul H. Brookes.

Szymanski, E. M., & Parker, R. M. (1996). *Work and disability: Issues and strategies in career development and job placement.* Austin, TX: Pro-Ed.

Wehman, P. (1992). *Life beyond the classroom: Transition strategies for young people with disabilities.* Baltimore: Paul H. Brookes.

Wehman, P. (Ed.). (1998). *Developing transition plans.* Austin, TX: Pro-Ed.

Witt, M. A. (1992). *Job strategies for people with disabilities.* Princeton, NJ: Peterson's Guide.

Curriculum Materials

American Guidance Service. (1989). *Social skills on the job: A transition to the workplace for students with special needs.* Circle Pines, MN: American Guidance Service.

Aune, E. P., & Ness, J. E. (1991). *Tools for transition: Preparing students with learning disabilities for postsecondary education.* Circle Pines, MN: American Guidance Service.

Brolin, D. E. (1989). *Life centered career education: A competency based approach* (4th ed.). Reston, VA: Council for Exceptional Children.

Loyd, R. J., & Brolin, D. E. (1997). *Life centered career education: Modified curriculum for individuals with moderate disabilities.* Reston, VA: Council for Exceptional Children.

Welsh, J. M., Quinn, L., Benson, D., & LaFollette, M. (1996). *Finding and keeping a job: A course of study* (rev. ed.). Coralville, IA: Grant Wood Area Education Agency.

Issues in Preparing Students for Transition to Employment

Several important factors can affect what vocational programs are offered to students in a given high school. These factors may vary from one community to another, but the following are general issues that persist across most local school districts.

Parental Values

Parents of adolescents with disabilities have a wide range of perspectives on the value of vocational education and vocational training. The traditional view that a high school diploma represents basic academic competence persists, and some parents have a difficult time seeing vocational education or training as a major thrust of a high school course of study. Another variable is the degree to which parents will allow their child to make, or even believe that their child can make, independent occupational choices. Socioeconomic backgrounds, concern for status, and basic views about what a high school education should be about all have an effect on parents' aspirations for their children and the degree to which they can or will accept vocational training in high school, and, if so, what type of training is acceptable.

Postsecondary Vocational Training Opportunities in the Community

Both educators and parents have a tendency to postpone vocational training as long as possible. One way that educators do this is to use the argument that the school need not provide any vocational offerings, or, at best, only a minimum of vocational offerings, because the community has strong postsecondary offerings available. Parents may use these same arguments with their sons and daughters, drawing on their own perceptions of the importance of a regular high school diploma. The lack of postsecondary vocational programs, on the other hand, forces school boards and educators to look at vocational programming as an important alternative to secondary school. The number and kinds of students who might need or want such programs then have an effect on the range of program options in a vocational training continuum.

Labor Market in the Community

All regular vocational education programs must demonstrate a demand for workers in a given area before they can be approved by the state for funding. Community employment levels and the size and nature of the communities enter into the labor market demand. A small town in an isolated area will have few local labor demands, and certain communities—by virtue of their location—will have heavy labor demands in certain kinds of occupational areas and not in others. Program development decisions for youths with disabilities that hinge on the fact that there is a need for general employability skill training for some students may be avoiding the issue of labor demands, but only temporarily. It is a fact that employability skills are vital, but at some point, specific occupational skill training for employment must be addressed in program planning and development.

Philosophical Differences in the Field

The philosophical differences between advocates of academic versus vocational programming are not limited to regular and special educators. Some special educators view vocational education and other vocational training alternatives as having lower status for students and, possibly, for themselves. This is found in all categorical groups of teachers but is more common among special education personnel working with populations in which a proportion of the students have intellectual performance levels above the range associated with students with mental retardation. This includes students with learning disabilities, behavior disorders, orthopedic or other health impairments, and visual or hearing impairments. Philosophical differences over academic versus vocational training are probably the most obstructive factors in getting employability skill and occupational training established in high school special education programs.

Another situation reflects tension among advocates of occupational and vocational training. This tension has developed recently as advocates for community-based employment and supported employment have challenged more traditional vocational training personnel with their placement success data, their zealous articulation of their philosophical view, and their technology. The message to traditionalists, whether intended or not, is: You have been ineffective. You have compromised the rights and dignity of persons with disabilities. You, too, can effect appropriate results if you do it our way. This message has been supported by endorsements through federal initiatives for funding of programs using the supported employment-transition model. This creates some dissonance among traditionalists who resent this message and its implications, even though there is some basis to the message.

Individualized Planning for Transition to Employment

For convenience, this book has dealt with academic goals, employability skills, and occupational goals in separate chapters. The establishment of individual goals and short-term objectives forces the participants in the planning process to ask the question, What do we want this student to know or be able to do at the end of this school year? For the student, as a participant in the planning process, the question is, What do I want to know or be able to do at the end of this school year? This question is directly related, of course, to the long-term issue of what the primary objectives are for the high school experience. Each year's IEP should focus clearly on how it will contribute to the final outcome objectives. The new transition services provision in the IDEA (PL 101-476) should increase the response to appropriate and occupational planning.

An IEP that has the individual student's transition from school to adult living as its focus *must* directly address the part that future employment will play. The planners (including the student as well as the student's family) must analyze the school's resources to provide for preparation for employment and make some definite choices about how to achieve the appropriate preparation for employment. Hasazi, Salembier, and Finck (1983) proposed some excellent objectives to provide a framework for planning and evaluating teaching-learning activities from a student-centered and programmatic perspective. They suggested the following student-centered objectives:

1. Develop and implement assessment procedures that identify functional skills and interests related to current and future employment and training opportunities in the community.
2. Provide necessary support services to ensure access to mainstream vocational classes.
3. Provide at least four work experiences, each six to eight weeks in length, in identified areas of interest and skill for students between the ages of 15 and 18.
4. Assist the student in locating and securing employment before graduation.
5. Provide supervision and follow-up services to students in full-time or part-time employment until graduation (or until the student is 22 years of age).
6. Develop individual plans with appropriate adult service agencies (i.e., vocational rehabilitation, community colleges, state employment service, or mental health services) for students who need continued service following graduation.

Hasazi and colleagues (1983) stated, and correctly so, that in order to plan realistically for these student-centered objectives, certain program-centered objectives must be met. These include the following:

1. Allow for flexible teacher schedules to meet the training and monitoring needs of students placed in community settings.
2. Design and implement a systematic follow-up procedure for contacting students following graduation to determine employment status, utilization of social services, relationship of vocational preparation to present and previous employment, and other relevant information.
3. Develop a "youth find" system for identifying all students with disabilities in need of vocational components in their individual educational plans prior to entering secondary-level programs.

Conclusion

This chapter has discussed the principles and characteristics of work-based learning, as well as the content for instruction and program models for delivering this content. The concept of work-based learning is becoming increasingly popular in the general education curriculum. This offers an excellent opportunity to include students with special needs in general education programs and still provide them with the education and services they need to make the transition to adult life. It is important, however, that the work-based learning activities be built on students' strengths, preferences, and interests and that additional preparation and experiences, with appropriate supports, are provided, if needed.

7 Job Placement, Training, and Supervision

Experience is the best of schoolmasters, only the school fees are heavy.
—Thomas Carlyle

This chapter will deal with the work-based learning component of the training needed to make the most effective transition from school to work. As mentioned in previous chapters, this component must be closely tied to school-based instruction and must be seen as part of the entire instructional process. The work-based learning activities must also be closely tied to the goals and objectives of the IEP and the transition planning process.

Job placement, training, and supervision tasks may be assumed by a professional who does this as a full-time job or by a classroom teacher who teaches for a portion of the day and serves as placement coordinator for the remainder of the day. Professionals who place and supervise students in the workplace are assigned different titles, such as *work-study coordinators, work experience coordinators, vocational adjustment coordinators, vocational special needs coordinators, school-to-work coordinators, cooperative education coordinators, job placement specialists,* and *job coaches.* The term *coordinator* will be used in this chapter to refer to any of these professionals who are involved in the placement, training, and supervision of individuals on job sites.

Four main issues are related to who will conduct placement activities. First, should the coordinator do this as a full-time position or as a teacher and coordinator (called a *teacher-coordinator*)? The advantages of full-time coordinators are (1) they can focus full time on the placement and supervision of students on the job and (2) they can be on call for the training sponsor at all times. The advantages of a position where the coordinator teaches half days and works with students in the workplace the other half are (1) they work daily with students in class, so they know them better; (2) they know the other teachers and staff in the school; and (3) they can more easily infuse the skills needed by each student into the student's other coursework. Full-time coordinators often teach one class, where they relate the in-school work with the demands of the workplace (often called a *related class*). This allows coordinators to become familiar with the students they will be placing and allows them to connect the school-based and work-based learning components.

The second issue concerns whether the placement and supervision activities should be done by a coordinator who is also working with general education students. The argument for this approach centers on the fact that this professional already has ties with work sites in the community and may have stronger preparation and experience in job placement and supervision than someone trained in special education. The argument against this approach centers on the preparation of someone in general education to work with students with disabilities, particularly in terms of placement, training, and supervision demands that may exceed those of students in general education. Whatever decision is made, it is critical that all professionals involved in coordination activities in the school work closely together in obtaining and maintaining training sites.

The third issue relates to the role of paraprofessionals in work-based learning. This is particularly important in working with individuals with more severe disabilities, who often require ongoing supervision on the work site. We recommend that the policies related to the use of paraprofessionals that have been developed for other components of the instructional program, such as community-based experiences, be followed in work placements. It is critical that a certified professional always be responsible for the program of the student. It is also critical that a coordinator be involved in the initial job placement and design of the work-based learning component.

The final issue concerns a philosophical debate as to whether the school should take responsibility for job placement or whether students with disabilities in a school-to-work program should secure their own jobs. Those who believe that the school is responsible have based their arguments on the belief that the school is responsible not only for the student's learning but also for program integrity. They maintain that placement should be based on a match between a student's strengths, preferences, and interests and a specific job situation, and that schools are more able to arrange that match. The advocates of students finding their own jobs believe that the students must learn the skills of job finding while in school and the best way to teach these skills is to provide them with training in job finding and then let them demonstrate their ability to apply these skills. The approach that we will take in this chapter is that the process of making the match between the student and the work-based experience is an intricate one and that the school is more likely to be able to carry out this process.

The district's response to each of these issues depends largely on the structure of the schools, the number of existing work-based learning programs offered by the district for students with and without disabilities, the number of schools and communities served by the coordinator, and the ongoing policies of the school related to students with disabilities and to community-based instruction.

This chapter discusses the resources and strategies needed to place students on work sites in the community, what you need to know related to the legal aspects of work-based learning, and steps in the placement and supervision of students in these work-based learning sites. Information is then given on working with the work-site supervisor to provide the needed training on the work site. The chapter concludes with resources that may help in placing, training, and supervising your students. The purpose of these placements may be to provide students with an opportunity to explore a number of occupations, to gain work experience, or to learn specific vocational skills.

Job Placement

The process of placing students with or without disabilities on work sites that will be the most beneficial for them is a complicated one. Before you begin to place students (or as you refine what you are currently doing), you will need to have knowledge of where to find information on possible occupations and the labor market, knowledge of what to look for in work environments, and an awareness of the legal considerations involved in placing students on the work site. It will also be helpful to know some strategies for finding appropriate work sites for your students and placing them on these work sites.

Sources of Occupational and Labor Market Information

It is important to be aware of the range of occupations that currently exist in the world of work and which of these occupations hold the greatest potential for employment for your students. This information will help in all phases of the transition from school to work—from in-school instruction to experiences on the work site. The information that is gained from the various sources of labor market information should be carefully matched with the information you have gained on each student's strengths, needs, interests, and preferences through the assessment process. Knowing where to go to find this information will be helpful to you and your students and their families in a number of ways. First, you can assist your students and their families in exploring broad groupings of occupations or specific occupations. If you are working with higher-functioning students, they can be taught to use these resources themselves. Regardless of the functioning level of your students, it opens up a whole new world to them to learn the variety of occupations that are available to them. This is particularly important if you are teaching in a small community, where the range of jobs students can directly explore is limited.

The second use of this information is to identify occupational areas that offer the highest potential for employment. Although you should always encourage students to pursue occupations in which they are most interested, it is also important to add the element of reality to their choices. Identification of these occupational areas will also assist you in placing students on work sites with the most potential for future employment. The third use of these sources of information is to secure information on specific jobs. Such information will allow students to refine their career choices and to determine for themselves how much training is needed, what skills are desired, and the basic tasks involved in the job. Again, this information will help in securing specific job placements for your students.

A number of sources of labor market information are available at the national, state, and local levels. It is important to tap all of these sources, particularly if some of your students will seek employment outside their current community or state.

National Sources.   Sources of information at the national level tend to be in written form. Most of these sources are now also on the Internet. The newest source of information is the Occupational Information Network (O*NET; www.doleta.gov/programs/onet/). Other major sources of such information include *Dictionary of Occupational Titles* (*DOT*; 204.245.136.2/libdot.htm); *Occupational Outlook Handbook* (stats.bls.gov/ocohome.htm); and *North American Industry Classification System* (NAICS: www.census.gov/epcd/www/naics.html).

The Occupational Information Network (O*NET) is sponsored by the U.S. Department of Labor, in cooperation with firms from the private sector. O*NET provides a comprehensive database system for collecting, organizing, describing, and disseminating data on job characteristics and worker characteristics. It is designed to replace the *DOT*, but also to go beyond the types of information that the *DOT* provides. One of the goals of O*NET is to link with other sources of information, such as statistical labor market information, from national, state, and local sources. The framework that organizes O*NET is a skills-based structure called the Content Model. This model classifies information into six domains, or categories, that look into all aspects of the workplace, from the characteristics of occupations to the characteristics of the workers who do the job. The six domains and their subdomains of information are as follows:

- Worker Characteristics (abilities, interests, work styles)
- Worker Requirements (basic skills, cross-functional skills, general knowledge, education)
- Experience Requirements (training, experience, and licensing)
- Occupation Requirements (generalized work activities, work context, and organizational context)
- Occupation Specific (occupational knowledge, occupational skills, tasks, and machines, tools, and equipment)
- Occupation Characteristics (labor market information, occupational outlook, and wages)

Before O*NET, the *Dictionary of Occupational Titles* was one of the major sources of organizing the world of work into basic occupational categories and of providing detailed information on occupations within these categories. The information provided on each occupation includes the following: (1) nine-digit occupational code for the occupation, (2) official occupational title, (3) industry designation, (4) alternate occupational titles, (5) basic tasks associated with the occupation,

(6) additional tasks the job may entail, and (7) undefined related occupational titles. In addition, each *DOT* occupational definition includes a *Guide to Occupational Exploration* (GOE) number for the occupation, if one exists, and information on estimated minimum strength and academic functioning requirements for the occupation. (*Note:* We have found through personal experience that the academic functioning requirements often overestimate the academic skills that are needed.)

The occupational classification number from the *DOT* is often used by adult providers in identifying occupational areas or specific occupations that the individual may want to pursue. This number is also often referenced in occupational recommendations from commercial assessment systems. Each occupation in the *DOT* is assigned a nine-digit occupational code or number. The first three digits identify a particular occupational group. All occupations are clustered into one of nine broad categories, such as clerical, sales, and machine trades occupations. This category is the first digit in the code (e.g., 6 is machine trades occupations). These categories are then broken down into 83 divisions. These divisions form the first two digits of the code (e.g., 66 is wood machining occupations). The third digit defines the occupational group (e.g., 660 is cabinetmakers).

The next three digits (after the decimal) represent the Worker Function ratings of the tasks performed in the occupation. The fourth digit represents the worker's relationship with data, the fifth digit represents the relationship with people, and the sixth digit represents the relationship with things. One confusing aspect of this data-people-things classification is that the worker functions involving more complex responsibility and judgment are assigned lower numbers in these three lists, while functions that are less complicated have higher numbers. Thus, an occupation with a Worker Function rating of 084 would require a high level of interaction with data, a low level with people, and a medium level with things. Specifically, according to the *DOT*, this rating would require the worker to synthesize data, take instructions from or help people, and manipulate things. The last three digits of the occupational code number serve to differentiate a particular occupation from all others with the same characteristics; in essence, they are just a way to arrange occupations with the same six first numbers. With the development of O*NET, the Department of Labor will no longer be updating information in the *DOT*. It is expected, however, that the *DOT* will still remain in use as a resource for a number of years.

Another source of information is the *Occupational Outlook Handbook*. This document provides detailed information on the outlook for specific occupations as well as special feature sections on such topics as tomorrow's jobs, sources of career information, and related publications. The handbook is not designed to cover all occupations, but for the occupations it does feature, it provides information on the nature of the work, working conditions, the number of jobs in this area currently held, types of settings in which the workers are employed and trained, other qualifications, advancement, job outlook, earnings, related occupations, and sources of additional information. The handbook is available in hard copy and on the Internet.

The *North American Industry Classification System (NAICS)* provides common industry definitions that cover the economies of the three North American countries of Canada, Mexico, and the United States. NAICS groups establishments with similar production processes and is organized in a hierachical structure with up to five digits of detail for classifying and grouping industries.

State Sources.   One of the major sources of occupational information at the state level is your State Occupational Information Coordinating Committee (SOICC). These groups are linked at the national level by the National Occupational Information Coordinating Committee (www.noicc.gov). This national website has information on each of the state-level committees, as well as information on other sources of occupational information. Each state also has one (or more) professional designated as a labor market information specialist. This individual has a wealth of knowledge about employment trends in your state; these data are often also broken down by regions of the state.

State manufacturers' associations often have listings of companies, including products manufactured, services available, size of work force, and names of key company managers. In addition, state industrial directories and other resources are available, such as *Moody's Industrial Manual, Thomas' Register of American Manufacturers, Encyclopedia of Business Information, Dun & Bradstreet's Middle Market Directory, The Wall Street Journal,* and *Business Week.*

Local Sources.   Some of the best local sources of information regarding occupational and labor market information are the adult providers with whom you work. These include workforce development centers, vocational rehabilitation, Job Training Partnership Act agencies (JTPA), and other state and local agencies. These agencies are now attempting to work even more closely together to form a type of "one-stop-shop," or a *seamless* delivery system. These efforts may include locating their offices in the same building and sharing common databases, with the consumer's permission. This coordination of services and information will make them even more valuable as an information source.

Local advisory committees are an excellent source of information and connections for job placements, as well as a rich resource for input into your program. These committees are used much more frequently in vocational education than special education. An advisory committee is a group composed primarily of individuals outside the education profession who are selected because of their knowledge (and influence) in the community. Major types of people who should be represented on an advisory committee include (1) key employers in the community, (2) a representative from the Chamber of Commerce, (3) a representative from labor, (4) an individual with a disability, (5) a family member, (6) a school administrator, and (7) the teacher. Advisory committee members can provide a perspective for making placements that is difficult for school personnel to acquire. It is important to put time into recruiting the key representatives and organizing regular meetings of this group. Although this will require some effort on your part, the rewards will far outweigh the effort.

Other sources of information and connections for specific job placements include the Chamber of Commerce, service clubs such as Rotary and Kiwanis, and businesses with whom you interact on a daily basis. Because this interaction is so critical to your job placement efforts, we strongly recommend that you live in the community in which you work, or at least frequent the businesses in which you are placing your students. A trip to the dentist may result in a placement for one of your students in the office or lead to a placement elsewhere. A conversation with the person beside you at the ball game or civic club luncheon may lead to a whole new occupational area that you have never considered before. In addition, looking though the yellow pages of the telephone directory or city directory or the newspaper classified ads can open up specific sites or alternative groups of occupations that are just waiting to be explored.

Knowledge of the Work Environment

A placement coordinator is going to have a great deal of difficulty in making effective placements without some firsthand or acquired information about the nature of work environments. Chadsey-Rusch, Gonzalez, Tines, and Johnson (1989) wrote an excellent description of the ecology of the workplace. They approach the ecology of work environments with the basic assumption that to make a match between a student with disabilities and a job, three basic ecological dimensions of the employment context must be considered. All of these dimensions should be systematically observed when the coordinator conducts an analysis of a specific job site.

The first dimension is the physical ecology. *Physical ecology* refers primarily to the architectural and physical designs or layout of environments that may affect behavior, such as enclosed spaces without windows, heights, small work cubicles, presence of loud machines, and so forth. The physical environment can place demands on a worker that may exceed the demands of the work tasks themselves. An important part of the job match, then, is in matching the student with the physical demands. For example, when considering a work setting, the placement coordinator must analyze the location of the primary work area and any mobility barriers for accessibility; the physical layout of the work area for such variables as furniture dimensions, floor coverings, and climatic conditions; as well as the potential hazards. Beyond these factors, however, the analysis must consider how the physical characteristics of the workplace could affect social and emotional behavior. This involves such factors as the number of people in a given workspace, the degree of isolation imposed by a workspace, and the size of a work space.

The second dimension of the ecology of the workplace, according to Chadsey-Rusch and colleagues (1989), is the social ecology. *Social ecology* in a workplace refers to the social interactions and interpersonal relationships that occur between individuals, between individuals and groups, and between groups. Placement in a work environment should consider carefully not only the possible negative effects that the social ecology might have on a given student but also the possible positive effects to meet certain needs. Any social factors that might result in high levels of stress, social discrimination, or social rejection, or that might contribute to problems in job performance, should be noted in a work environment analysis. On the positive side, there might be some highly supportive social factors inherent in a work setting. Examples of these are the employer's attitude toward persons with disabilities, a nurturing, supportive co-worker or supervisor, or a social support system built into the job through an organization like a union, a bowling league, or informal social networks.

The third ecological dimension of the workplace described by Chadsey-Rusch and colleagues (1989) is organizational ecology. *Organizational ecology* refers to the program or policy factors in a work setting that may influence individual and group behavior. Program or policy factors include such things as management style and structure, size of an organization, employee autonomy, worker rules or regulations, safety procedures, or production quotas. Salaries, employee benefits, and opportunities for advancement are very important organizational factors also. Any number of organizational variables may operate within a work environment and affect the work performance or behavior of an individual in the community. The placement coordinator must be extra sensitive to this dimension, since many of the factors reflecting the organizational ecology are not easily observed by an outsider and are not readily identifiable in a slick company brochure.

Strategies in Job Finding

Some placement personnel rely primarily on their experience in the work world, their ability to develop and use resources in the community, their instincts, their history of being at the right place at the right time, or all of these. Many of these persons are extremely effective and develop excellent reputations among their colleagues for their success in finding jobs. Persons in this league may find the challenge of the job hunt so satisfying that they vicariously experience the pleasure of finding someone else a job as if it were their own. In some cases, the jobs found are not necessarily an ideal job match, but a successful job finder is rarely criticized by administrators for that.

At the other extreme, there are placement personnel who rely primarily on their program visibility via high-probability employer contacts, community presentations to organizations to which employers belong, timely and effective media coverage, and, sometimes, the initiative of the students themselves in finding their own jobs. This type of placement person plants the seeds of labor supply and sits back and waits for people to contact the school. Some long-established programs move into this style because the program can begin to proceed on its own momentum in this way after a while. Again, in some cases, the desirability of job match may be sacrificed but is rationalized because of ease of placement or the need to please an employer who has taken the initiative to call.

Both of these placement styles appear to get the job done in terms of number of students placed while in the program. Whether these approaches are more effective in achieving transition outcome goals than a more systematic, technical approach is a researchable question. On the face of it, logic suggests that placement procedures designed to avoid mistakes in placements are more likely to be in the best interests of the individual students, the employers, and the schools. The systematic approach to job placement does not have to deny the effectiveness of personal charisma, persistent contacts and follow-through, "salesmanship," nor the obvious results of good public relations and advertising that attracts employers to the school program. A placement program should incorporate those important features into a systematic approach.

A systematic approach to job placement simply refers to the use of well-established procedures used successfully in employment training programs in the past—job development, job analysis, work-site modification, and job matching. Each of these will be introduced in the sections that follow.

Job Development. The task of *job development* is one of generating a pool of job placement alternatives so that there are real choices to be made when looking for the best possible placement. This pool of job placement alternatives can be developed in several ways. One of the most commonly suggested activities for a placement coordinator who is new to a community or who is establishing a new work-training program is the community survey. A community survey identifies the local job areas that have vacancies, those that anticipate vacancies frequently because of high turnover rates, and those that hire entry-level employees. These three labor market variables reflect the starting point for placement personnel in knowing whether additional activities in job development are needed.

A community survey can involve both formal and informal information-gathering procedures. Mail or telephone surveys to employers or persons responsible for hiring, use of information from a Chamber of Commerce and work force center, and regular and systematic analysis of newspaper classified ads will produce the bulk of the information needed. Some very helpful information on high-turnover occupations comes from job service center representatives and personal contacts with employers. It is helpful to organize this information in files or charts by occupational area (e.g., personal services, health occupations, construction/building trades, manufacturing, agriculture/agribusiness).

A community survey may be only a first step in developing a pool of placement alternatives. For example, assume that a community survey reveals that a given community has no available jobs right now and that the high-turnover jobs are stabilizing because of the competition generated by high unemployment. Another procedure in job development in this situation is to identify areas for job *creation* within the community's labor market. This is a task requiring some skill in analyzing jobs and some creativity in using the analysis data for proposing new jobs. This can occur through the creation of a new job by combining elements of existing jobs or by creating entirely new jobs to fulfill unmet needs of the employer. This was done in the early 1960s within the Federal Civil Service system in response to President Kennedy's executive branch initiative to employ workers with disabilities in the federal government. The Civil Service office issued a directive to all federal office personnel directors and supervisors to review all civil service job descriptions with the purpose of identifying tasks that were required that could be performed by someone else with less training or ability. These task elements were to be deleted and combined with other comparable tasks to develop new positions for persons with disabilities. This job development process resulted in the hiring of thousands of people who had mental or physical disabilities.

Job Analysis.   *Job analysis* has already been mentioned as a necessary element of job development, but it is an important part of the job placement process by itself. A job analysis is no more than a systematic way of determining the specific demands of any job. We have included references on the job analysis procedure in the Resources section at the end of this chapter. We also discussed the job analysis process in more detail in Chapter 5.

Work-Site Modification.   The task of *work-site modification* can be defined as "work-related changes that enable a disabled person to be employed" (Hester & Stone, 1984, p. 1). Work-site modifications, in one form or another, have been made by or for persons with disabilities for as long as people have worked. These accommodations were often made voluntarily by employers in the past when the person with disabilities was already an employee at the time of the modification or had high qualifications and potential for productivity. Since the passage of the Rehabilitation Act of 1973, the federal government has required reasonable accommodations in federal employment or any business or industry under contract with the federal government (Section 504). It has also provided some financial incentives for work-site modification. Now, the Americans with Disabilities Act (ADA) requires any employer with 15 or more employees to make "reasonable accommodations" for a person with a disability if that accommodation will allow the person to perform the essential functions of the job. Appendix C provides a checklist of accessibility and usability of buildings and facilities that serves as a guide for needed work-site modification.

Work-site modifications range from the simplest and least costly ones (changing hours, changing work procedures, changing work locations, or changing task assignments) to the most expensive, most complex ones using high technology or rehabilitation engineering for sophisticated equipment or building adaptations. Placement personnel should be alert to discrepancies in the job analysis and the analysis of individual assessment that could be addressed through work-site modification. The Job Accommodation Network (JAN) is an excellent resource for making work-site modifications (janweb.icdi.wuu.edu).

School-based job developers and job trainers need to use work-site modifications not only to provide better access to employment under the employment provisions of ADA but also to increase the creative aspects of job alternatives. Meers (1992) reported that technological advances in such areas as laser scanners and electronic switches have revolutionized the traditional time and motion studies that defined so many jobs. For example, automated workstations that can be operated by means of a blink of an eye or a sip-and-puff switch are workable in at least 300 different jobs. In the next decade, technology will expand the range of options for employment even more.

Job Matching. The *job-matching process* is the final task in job placement planning. The task of matching job demands with individual interests, strengths, weaknesses, and expectations brings together all the data available for a logical, intelligent placement. It is designed to take the guesswork and chance out of the process and replace them with reason. In the real world, however, it is never so simple. Decision making in any arena assumes that the decision maker can never know with certainty that he or she has made the *right* decision, but in following decision-making rules, the decisions can be judged as the *best possible* decisions, given the data available. This means that compromises may have to be made at times. The job match is rarely perfect, but more often the *best possible* job match. This process was discussed in more detail in Chapter 5.

Strategies in Job Placement

Job placement specialists eventually develop their own strategies for placing students. These strategies fit individual personalities, community values and responses, and changes in a community's occupational outlook. The literature and experienced placement personnel do have some suggestions for placement coordinators. This section presents some of their ideas.

Payne, Mercer, and Epstein (1974) provided some classic practical suggestions as strategies in obtaining job placement opportunities. Among these are the following:

1. Use every means possible in making contacts with employers. Use outside organizations—such as Kiwanis, Rotary, Business Women's Clubs of America, Jaycees, and others—to make many employers or personnel managers aware of the program and who you are as the contact person. Use business cards and other printed material about the program to leave behind.

2. Approach every employer with two goals in mind: (a) making the person aware of the school work-training program and how it fits into the entire school vocational continuum and (b) enlisting their willingness to participate in the program. Participation in the program can be as a training sponsor or as one who will call the program to the attention of his or her friends or others to encourage their participation. Most businesspersons like the idea of working with the public schools, and having the option of promoting the program as one means of participation when they are not able to participate directly gives them a way to do that.

3. An enthusiastic, committed approach, using good sales techniques, works well with employers in initial contacts. The placement specialist should keep the first interview under 10 minutes, unless the employer wishes to discuss the project more fully. Remember that you are asking employers to commit to a program and they have a right to expect something out of it. Be sensitive to what motivates each employer and be prepared to state directly what the program will do for the business and how the school will support their efforts.

The Payne, Mercer, and Epstein (1974) book *Education and Rehabilitation Techniques* contains a section of practical techniques that is impossible to summarize, abstract, or synthesize adequately because of its personal style. For that reason, even though the language is dated, permission has been obtained to use it intact here:

> Counselors who have approached businessmen on a large scale mention the importance of being physically fit, for the majority of this work requires standing, walking, and, on occasion, some running. Appropriate dress is important for initial business contact success, but caution should be exercised not to overly dress the part. Also, a packet of appropriate forms and program brochures, a booklet of matches for offering lights, a roll of nickels for meters, breath mints, extra pencils, and calling cards represent items which enhance the counselor's effectiveness as well as his efficiency.
>
> The decision to "walk in" on a businessman without an appointment should be considered carefully. The general rule of thumb is that, if the proprietor or manager is readily available, then by all means "walk in." If two or three unexpected "drop in" contacts fail to produce results, use the phone to arrange an appointment. Appointments are appropriate for large businesses and corporations, but smaller, local businesses prefer for the counselor just to drop by during slow hours. In a phone conversation the counselor should state his name, organization, who referred him to the business (if applicable), and that he would like to explain the vocational program. The counselor should tell the employer that it will take less than 10 minutes and ask when it would be convenient to meet. He should *not* ask if the employer is interested or if he *can* meet with him. At *no* time should the counselor ask any question which can be answered "Yes" or "No" because the employer might say "No." The key question to ask is, "When would be a good time for me to meet with you?" This question cannot be answered with a simple "Yes" or "No." If the employer does not want to meet with the counselor, he must at least tell him so in sentence form. Surveys indicate that if the individual under question has to respond in sentence form it is more likely that he will respond positively than negatively....
>
> After getting a foot in the door, the counselor needs something to say. It may help for the counselor to bring a couple of pictures of program activities or clients engaged in work so that the businessman has something to look at while the counselor talks. Another introductory device is the business card, but, if a counselor does not wish to go the expense of printing up business cards, a . . . sheet with his name, organization, telephone number, and a description of what he wants to do and why he needs help will suffice....
>
> It is unlikely that the counselor will convince every businessman to participate. However, within a short period of time, he at least should be getting his foot in the door and be having an opportunity to give his presentation to 75 percent of the employers he contacts. If he is falling short of this percentage, he should begin to concentrate on his entry skills because without improving this stage of the business contact he is certain to fail and get discouraged. (pp. 105–108)

Drake University's National Vocational Rehabilitation Job Development/Job Placement Institute supports the notion of the importance of placement personnel strategies in employer contacts. The institute suggests that the following errors are common in contacting employers:

1. Marketing to the wrong staff person
2. Bringing up objections before the employer does
3. Overselling the school, client, services, and oneself
4. Talking too much and talking *at* the employer
5. Listening too little and interrupting the employer
6. Using rehabilitation jargon and terminology
7. Not being organized or well prepared
8. Not establishing an identity or purpose of efforts
9. Failing to leave a business card
10. Overemphasizing placement and deemphasizing service
11. Not being genuine or allowing the employer to be genuine
12. Failing to follow up after making contact with the employer
13. Siding with either management or labor
14. Being impulsive or condescending
15. Not knowing when to "back off"
16. Demonstrating a lack of self-confidence

Culver, Spencer, and Gliner (1990) also suggested some very specific job development and placement strategies that have impact of placement success.

The tone of these descriptions of *dos* and *don'ts* reflects views of those who have experienced the highly personal interactions that occur in job development and job placement. Educators may cringe at this approach and resist having to "sell" to potential employers. Excellent classroom or resource room teachers may balk at pressure to assume a style that they think is contrary to the ones that made them effective teachers. The question often comes up when this apparent conflict is discussed: Is there a personality type for job placement personnel? Our response is that there probably is some common trait or cluster of traits among effective placement specialists, but they are not what typically comes to mind when one thinks of the super-salesperson. We have seen individuals with outstanding placement skills who could be described by others who do not know them as "hyper," "laid-back," "super-organized," "could sell snowshoes at the equator," or "whatever she's selling I'm buying." Obviously, there is no single stereotype here, yet they all were exceptional communicators with people in the work world and had their own strategies and styles that worked for them.

Most of the emphasis thus far in the job placement process has been on the job placement specialist's approach in finding and making the initial contact with an employer. Once the employer indicates a real interest in the program, the placement specialist moves into an instructional role with the employer. Interest alone does not dispel the myths and notions that are widespread in the business community.

Employers do have certain fears and stereotypes related to persons with disabling conditions, and one of the first steps in developing a relationship with the employer is to explore and respond to employer issues, fears, or concerns. Those interested in more specific information on job development and job placement strategies are encouraged to consult the resources at the end of this chapter.

Job Training and the Focus of Employment Placement for Students

The type of job placement that school placement coordinators engage in most often is placement for employment training. Only those last-semester students who have been through a work-training program should be ready for long-term employment. Placement personnel and employers must not lose sight of the fact that the purpose of community on-the-job training placements is *training*. Parrish and Kok (1985) used the term *training stations* rather than *jobs* in their discussion of placement, and pointed out some important differences between the two that involve the employer. These include expectations the school program should have of an employer. Employers and trainers must do the following:

- Alter their method of giving instructions to meet the demands of each student's learning style.
- Maintain a standard of performance.
- Be willing to spend extra time at first.
- Treat students with respect and courtesy.

These are *minimal expectations*, and no placement specialist should hesitate to communicate these early in the discussion of the employer's participation as a trainer.

Although these are minimal expectations of the employer, there are other factors that might not make a given work situation a good training station. Parrish and Kok (1985) cited a number of reasons given by work-study coordinators for deciding against some available jobs. Among them are inconsistent supervision, nonexistent supervision, frequent changes in supervision, inappropriate environment, bad working hours, inappropriate location, pace of work activity, dangers or hazards, and incompatibility of work situation with a student's interests.

Legal Aspects of Work-Based Learning

As you place your students in work-based learning sites either within the school system or the community, it is critical that you are aware of the legal issues that need to be considered. A number of excellent sources are available for in-depth information on these issues (Garfinkle, 1995; Love, 1995; National School-to-Work Office, n.d.; Pumpian, Fisher, Certo, Engel, & Mautz, 1998; Pumpian, Fisher, Certo, & Smalley, 1997; Simon & Halloran, 1994; Simon, Cobb, Halloran, Norman, & Bourexis, 1994). We will highlight the major issues you will need to consider; you are referred to these sources, however, for more in-depth information.

The key legislation in the area of work-based learning is the Fair Labor Standards Act of 1938 and its amendments, which established the guidelines for minimum wage regulations, child labor provisions, and distinguishing nonpaid instructional work experiences from paid employment. Appendix 1 and Appendix 2 at the end of this chapter provide a summary of the child labor requirements in nonagricultural and agricultural occupations, respectively. You should pay particular attention to the issue of age requirements and hazardous occupations.

The other area with which you need to be concerned is the distinction between nonpaid instructional work experiences and paid employment. Pumpian and associates (1998) provided an excellent overview of this issue. As they stated, in the 1980s, large numbers of school programs were rapidly building and expanding job preparation, development, and support programs for individuals with disabilities. Many public school programs had established nonpaid exploration and training opportunities as part of their comprehensive service delivery models. At the same time, interpretation of the Fair Labor Standards Act varied considerably across Department of Labor wage and hour specialists. When the School-to-Work Opportunities Act of 1994 (PL 103-239) was passed, the issue of nonpaid experiences entered the arena of general education, as well. The use of nonpaid work experience seems to be an ongoing component of career development. It has been significant in disability-specific programs and its use will likely accelerate in school-to-work programs (Pumpian et al., 1998).

The Fair Labor Standards Act established the following six criteria that must be met if the trainees or students are not to be considered employees (who must then be paid):

1. The training, even though it includes actual operation of the facilities of the business or industry, is similar to that which would be given in a vocational education program.
2. The training is for the benefit of the students.
3. The students do not displace regular employees, but work under their close observation.
4. The business or industry person who provides training derives no immediate advantage from the activities of the students, and on occasion his or her operations may actually be impeded.
5. The students are not necessarily entitled to a job at the conclusion of the training period.
6. The students understand that they are not entitled to wages for the time spent in training.

In their article, Pumpian and colleagues (1998) interpreted various regulatory guidelines and court decisions related to the use of nonpaid work experience and provided additional information related to U.S. Departments of Labor and Education guidelines for work-training programs. They made three major points in their review: (1) all six criteria delineated in the Fair Labor Standards Act must be met in order to establish a training situation, (2) these criteria are interrelated, and (3) establishing an employee-employer relationship requires examination of the circumstances surrounding the whole activity rather than isolated factors. They also proposed four questions central to every training situation. These questions are critical in determining if no immediate advantage accrues to the business or industry in which the student is placed:

1. Does the business or industry derive first and primary benefit? In other words, does the business or industry benefit more than the student?
2. Does the business or industry derive substantial benefit?
3. Does the trainee replace regular workers?
4. Is the experience educationally valid?

Inherent in all of these questions is the importance of planning work-based learning experiences that are designed specifically around the needs, preferences, and interests of the student and that are closely monitored to determine if the objectives of the experience are being met. The most essential aspect of the placement, training, and supervision process is that it be closely tied to the student's IEP. It is also critical for you to keep accurate records of all aspects of the placement, training, and ongoing supervision, if you are the person responsible for these activities. The next section presents the major steps in the placement and supervision process.

Steps in Placement and Supervision

Nine basics steps are involved in placing and supervising students in the workplace. These steps are taken from the basic coordination techniques used by professionals in vocational education and cooperative education programs. Modifications that are needed in working with students with disabilities and other special needs are addressed under the specific steps.

The steps listed in the following sections are taken from the cooperative education approach initially developed in vocational education. (See Chapter 6 for more information on this approach.) They are also related to the components of the school-to-work initiatives developed as part of the School-to-Work Opportunities Act and other federal- and state-level transition initiatives. In all of these approaches, there are three basic components: school-based learning, work-based learning, and connecting activities that tie the school and work site together. The work site and work-site personnel are seen as important partners in the training process, thus the terms *training station* and *training sponsor* are used throughout. The nine steps are discussed in the following sections. They should be followed, regardless of the purpose of the work placement—exploration, work experience, or training.

- Assessment of the student
- Conference with the student
- Initial contact with the training sponsor
- Analysis of the work site
- Meeting to obtain the training station
- Student interview with the training sponsor

- Meeting to explain the role of the coordinator and training sponsor and the training agreement
- Meeting to develop and discuss the training plan
- Ongoing training of the student
- Continuing evaluation of the student
- Modification of the training program based on ongoing evaluation

Assessment of the Student

Assessment of the student was covered more fully in Chapter 5. The assessment of student needs, preferences, and interests is required by the Individuals with Disabilities Education Act Amendments (IDEA, 1997). In working with students with disabilities, it is crucial to gather this information in cooperation with the student and family and use it to make the best possible match with potential work sites. This assessment is an ongoing process, however, and placement of students at work sites for exploration, for work experience, or for training can provide additional information on the students' needs, preferences, and interests and yield valuable information that can be used in transition planning and future placements for the students. As mentioned in Chapter 5, it is important that the results of current assessment activities be included in the Present Level of Education Performance section of the IEP.

A major part of the assessment may be conducted before the actual placement process is begun. It is still important, however, to review the assessment results carefully and to determine if further assessment needs to be carried out to fill in missing information or update the information previously gathered.

Conference with the Student

As mentioned in Chapter 5, involvement of the student in the assessment and overall placement process is critical. As the placement process begins, you must meet with the student to share the results of the assessments that were conducted and get input from the student regarding work sites that are of most interest to him or her. It is important at this point also to get the student's input on the type of work site at which he or she would like to be placed and the skills he or she would like to gain through this placement. This is an important time to discuss the goal of the placement with the student—whether it be exploration of possible jobs, gaining general work experience, or learning specific job skills through on-the-job training.

Initial Contact with the Training Sponsor

The formality of this step will depend on whether you have used the training station before and how much you know about the actual work site. Even if this training station does not work out for the specific student, you will have this information on file to use in future placements. Before conducting the work-site analysis, of course, you will need to meet with the training sponsor to inform him or her of what you are doing and why. If you have used this training station and this training sponsor before, then the initial contact will be mainly to set up a time to meet and discuss the student and the training process.

Analysis of the Work Site

If you have not used this training station before, or if you are using a different job within this site, it is important to conduct an analysis of the major components of the site. This process was covered in Chapter 5 and in an earlier section of this chapter.

Meeting to Obtain the Training Station

Again, how detailed this meeting is will depend on your previous experience with the training sponsor. In any meeting, however, you will need to cover or review three main types of information: (1) information on the student, (2) information on your program, and (3) overview of the role of the training sponsor.

Four types of information should be shared about the student: his or her interests, strengths and challenges, and previous experiences, as well as the experiences and training you would like the student to gain at this training station. Much of this information can be obtained from the assessment activities you have conducted with the student. A good rule of thumb is to share with the potential training sponsor the information he or she will need in order to work with the student. Another rule of thumb is to share with the training sponsor what *you* would want to know about any new student. In small towns, the training sponsor may already know about the student; in larger settings, this will not be the case. We recommend not focusing on the disability label, but being honest about the challenges as well as the strengths the student will bring to the work site.

You will also want to share information on your program. In particular, you will want to outline the training the student has already received and will receive and the support that your program will provide while the student is at the work site. We have found that ongoing support provided by a program is often the factor most valued by the employers—over such factors as financial incentives and subminimum wage. You will, however, also want to cover any financial incentives that may be available for the training sponsor, such as tax credits and deductions.

Finally, you will want to cover the role of the training sponsor. You will go over this in more depth in a future step, but the businessperson needs to know that he or she will be an integral part of the exploration work experience, or specific skill or training program for the student.

Student Interview with the Training Sponsor

Once the businessperson has agreed to be a training sponsor, the next step is to arrange for an interview between the student and the relevant supervisor(s) at the business. Some programs prefer to have two or more students interview for the position. Others feel that the job match is so important, they would like to hand-pick the student to be placed on a specific job site. Whatever your approach, it is important to get students involved in this stage of the placement process. It allows them to practice the job interview skills they have been taught and also allows the potential training sponsor to see the student firsthand. Depending on the purpose of the job experience, the length, and whether it is paid or unpaid, the training sponsor may ask the student to complete a job application as part of the interview process.

Meeting to Explain the Role of the Coordinator and Training Sponsor and the Training Agreement

If the student interview goes well and the business agrees to serve as a training station, the next step is to meet with the training sponsor to explain his or her role and that of the other players in the training process. A key document to have as part of this process is a training agreement. Consult with your school district to determine if it has an existing format for this agreement that you can adopt or adapt. School-to-work and vocational education programs are the programs most likely to have such agreements.

The training agreement, although not a legally binding document, does outline the roles of the key players in the exploration or training experience. Each training agreement should have the following sections:

- Introductory information, including the student's name, business, training supervisor and title, job title, beginning and end of training period, and overall purpose of the experience
- Information applicable to all parties
- Responsibilities of the student
- Responsibilities of the parent or other family members
- Responsibilities of the training sponsor
- Responsibilities of the coordinator and school

In addition, every training agreement should have a nondiscrimination clause stating that the business and the school do not discriminate against individuals on the basis of race, color, national origin, gender, marital status, or disability. (You may want to consult with your administrator for examples of language used in other documents.) Finally, there should be designated lines for each party (student, parent, training sponsor, and coordinator) to sign and date the document.

It is important that the language of the training agreement be direct and to the point. It is also important that you, as the coordinator, sit down with each of the parties involved and explain his or her role in the exploration or training process. Your program should make needed modifications in training agreements based on whether the experience is paid or nonpaid and whether the goal is exploration, work experience, or specific skill training. Some programs use the term *exploration agreement* when the main goal of the placement is exploration.

Meeting to Develop and Discuss the Training Plan

The next step in the placement process is to meet to develop and discuss the training plan. This plan lists the work habits, attitudes, and specific skills and knowledge that the student will develop on this particular training station. This is the document that is most closely tied to the IEP for students with disabilities. A number of individuals should have input into this plan. First, the student should help identify the general and specific skills he or she would like to develop at this site. Parents and other family members should also be consulted. The student's IEP or other planning documents should be reviewed, as well. As the coordinator, you will also have a set of work habits and attitudes that you want all students to develop. In addition, there may be specific areas on which you want the student to focus.

In terms of specific knowledge and skills related to the job, an array of sources may be of some help. First, vocational education programs often have lists of competencies covered in each program. Second, the job may have a list of specific duties. Third, the work-site analysis you conducted while you were identifying this site will produce definite tasks. Finally, the training sponsor is an excellent source of skills and knowledge (as well as work habits and attitudes) that are expected on the job.

The training plan is one of the most important documents in determining the focus of the work-based learning experience and in monitoring the experiences and progress of the student. It is also the most effective tie to the IEP for students with disabilities. It forces you to identify why this training station was selected for the student. It is also excellent documentation (along with the training agreement) that the placement is, in fact, part of the student's curriculum and an educational experience. This documentation may be needed if there are questions regarding nonpaid placements or claims for unemployment insurance made by the student after the placement ends.

It is most effective for you to enter the meeting with the training sponsor with at least a draft of a proposed training plan. This will have been developed based on input from the student, the family, existing lists of competencies, and you. You can then seek the training sponsor's reaction to the identified skills and knowledge areas and add other competencies as needed. Again, the concept of the training plan can be modified to that of an exploration plan if the purpose of the placement is exploration.

Ongoing Training of the Student

Although the training sponsor will usually provide the actual training in the specific skills required by the job, it is important that you work closely with the training sponsor to ensure that the components of the training plan are carried out, or revised as necessary. This revision may involve adding additional skills or knowledge to be learned, if the student progresses more quickly than planned. It may also involve deleting one or more skills or areas of knowledge from the training plan if the student requires additional time to learn a specific component of the job. It is important, however, that the training plan be referred to often so that the student does not just remain on certain job tasks he or she has already mastered.

You may also need to provide some instruction on the academic tasks related to the job, such as using metric measurements or mastering job-related vocabulary. In addition, you may be required to deal with job-related social skills or work habits and attitudes that you or the training sponsor identify as needing improvement. The areas of needed instruction should clearly emerge from the continuing evaluation of the student, which is described in the following section.

Continuing Evaluation of the Student

It is critical to monitor the student's performance on the work-based learning site. This monitoring should be done more frequently at the beginning of the placement and can be done less frequently as the placement progresses, if it is going well. You will need to make it clear to the training sponsor that he or she should contact you if any questions or concerns arise. Stress that it is important to catch problems as they are developing, rather than waiting until they become major concerns that may lead to the student being asked to leave the site. You should also contact the training sponsor fairly often, either by phone or by stopping by the work site. In either case, these contacts should be made during the least busy time of the day for the training sponsor. You should also stop in to evaluate the student weekly if your schedule allows.

Each time you evaluate the student, there should be a written record of your comments and/or those of the training sponsor. This can be in terms of short notes made on a standard form or a formal rating scale. A formal rating scale should be used *at least* twice during the placement—midterm and at the end. If possible, it is good to use a formal rating scale even more often, particularly at the beginning of the placement.

It is important that the student, you, and the training sponsor each independently rate the student and then compare your ratings. One of the best methods of conducting this comparison is through a three-way meeting, once the ratings have been completed by each party. In addition to providing information to you and the student on how the placement is progressing, this is one of the best sources of ongoing assessment information on the student. These ratings will also be important to you if you need to assign a grade to the student for this placement.

The work habits, attitudes, and specific skills and knowledge identified on the training agreement make an excellent foundation for such a rating scale. You would need to add to this information the following: (1) name of the student, (2) training station, (3) training sponsor, (4) period over which the student is being evaluated, (5) overall job title, and (6) name and position of the person completing the evaluation. You would then need to develop the ratings to which you want the raters to respond, usually on a three- or five-point scale. It is also important to leave a space for comments underneath each item and at the end of the rating scale. (See Chapter 5 for more information on constructing rating scales.)

Modification of the Training Program Based on Ongoing Evaluation

One of the main reasons for continuing evaluation of the student is to determine if the training program is working or if it needs to be modified. The training program in this instance is both the school-based component and the work-based component. If the student is having specific problems on the job, then possibly the problem areas could be addressed in the class session related to the work-based placement. In addition, additional support or instruction could be provided on the job either by the training sponsor, you as the coordinator, or by a co-worker. It is critical that the results of the ongoing evaluations be shared with family members and with the teachers who are working with the student in school.

Job Training

The amount and kind of training that students in special-needs programs need is extremely variable. Certainly, there is a wide range in previous work experience. Work experience, according to Hasazi, Gordon, and Roe (1985), was the primary differentiating factor between employed and unemployed graduates in their follow-up of former special education students. Subjects in a study of characteristics of successfully employed adults with disabilities (Hudson, Schwartz, Sealander, Campbell, & Hensel, 1988) gave verbal support to the finding by Hasazi and others claiming that work experience was an important strategy in successful employment. Work experience, then, may be seen as a type of training that proves beneficial in future employment. Obviously, some work experience for youths with disabilities is not ideal in terms of a totally positive experience and varies considerably in the amount of supervision. Still, previous job experience can make a difference in the amount and kind of job training a person needs.

In addition to work experience backgrounds, there are differences in basic physical and intellectual performance levels. An intelligent, highly motivated, student who is visually impaired may require half the job training time that a student who is moderately learning disabled might require for the same job. A student with mild mental retardation should require less training than one with moderate mental retardation, other things being equal. Job trainers must look at speed of learning all job tasks from an individual basis and plan for job training time on the basis of each student's performance. Furthermore, they must analyze performance errors to determine the kind of training the student needs.

The final factor in training variability is the nature of the job itself. The job analysis described in Chapter 5 gives the job trainer the same basic information he or she needs to anticipate the kind and amount of training that will be required. A job placement on an assembly line requiring the same psychomotor response repeatedly requires much less training than a job in which multiple responses—sensory, motor, and cognitive—are the norm. Payne (1977) provided a good example of this with his description of the complex set of task demands of a fast-food kitchen worker. This is an interesting example because of a general criticism in the past of placement coordinators who use food-service jobs more than any other type. The assumption has been made, and erroneously, according to Payne, that food-service placements were all many students with disabilities could handle. In fact, the food services, and especially fast-food services, were used most frequently because they had more job turnover and offered more opportunities for placement. These placements frequently ended in disaster. Many of the students placed in these settings were placed without job analyses, without any systematic training, and were not able to handle the deceptively difficult task demands of the jobs.

One of the points of tension between professionals who have worked with students with mild disabilities in job training over the years and professionals who are currently engaged in supported employment training with students with severe handicapping conditions is an understanding of what constitutes appropriate job training. The amount and kind of support during training comprise the two major points of debate. Perhaps this is an oversimplification. Perhaps it is a matter of systematic planning and delivery of training. The less-than-spectacular success rate of employment of youths with mild disabilities suggests that a more systematic model is needed.

The concept of supported employment was discussed in Chapter 6; it may be helpful for you to review this information. Like many terms that are made up of familiar component words (in this case, *supported* and *employment*), the concept behind it carries a number of possible interpretations or ways that it might be demonstrated. In fact, a basic principle in understanding supported employment programs is that they will be delivered in a variety of ways, depending on the resources of the community, local economic conditions, available funding, and the type and level of severity of the disabilities of the intended participants in the program.

Steps in Supported Employment

Callahan (1992) stated that the challenge of any instructional approach used in facilitating supported employment is to balance the individual's needs and the natural supports available. *Instructional power* is "the amount of assistance, individualization, efforts, and creativity needed to teach the skills necessary for any given individual to participate successfully in community-based, integrated settings" (p. 264). *Natural validity* refers to "the degree to which a training approach can approximate and accommodate the teaching strategies and other support features available in any given community setting" (p. 164). An effective training system should offer both perspectives. The rule of thumb for effectiveness is to provide instruction that is as naturally valid as possible, but with sufficient instructional power to teach the task successfully (Marc Gold & Associates, 1990).

Callahan (1992) proposed a revised seven-phase sequence, which built on the linear model suggested by Gold (1980):

1. Determine the method in which the task or routine is typically performed in the natural setting.
2. Decide on the content steps into which the job would be divided for the purpose of teaching a typical employee in that setting.
3. Develop training and motivating strategies, taking into account the teaching, support, reinforcement, and interaction approaches identified in the natural work setting.
4. Train the employee in the actual skills in the setting in which they will be used, and collect data as unobtrusively as possible.
5. Redo the training and motivating strategies, based on the individual's needs and learning style.
6. Break problem steps into smaller, more teachable steps.
7. When needed, consider a different way of performing the task than is typical in the setting.

Martin and Mithaug (1990) presented 11 steps in a consumer-directed (student-directed) placement program:

1. Establish a consumer-represented advisory board.
2. Determine job possibilities.
3. Develop a minimum of six community job match assessment sites to help trainees discover what types of work they like, learn what work they can do, and demonstrate their independence.
4. Mail a survey to establish a number of potential sites quickly and inexpensively.
5. Conduct a job analysis of potential entry-level positions to determine required work skills, task demands, and employment conditions.
6. Implement the job match assessment process in which the trainees express what they like, match their preferences to available jobs, and self-evaluate their work and social and personal strengths and weaknesses.
7. Construct a consumer-directed employment plan.
8. Undertake a job tryout in which the consumer "test-drives" his or her first and second job choices for a few hours a day for four weeks on each job.
9. Conduct a self-managed evaluation of performance on each job tryout.
10. Redesign the job to meet the specific needs of the individual, including modifying the job description and adapting the environment.
11. Clarify public support and other financial details, such as the effect of employment on Social Security payments.

Martin and Mithaug provided examples from their consumer-directed supported employment program at the University of Colorado to clarify many of the steps.

Advocacy

Advocacy activities are a major part of any work experience or transition coordinator's job description. Advocating for students at school with administrators, guidance counselors, regular teachers, resource or self-contained classroom teachers, parents, employers, and human services agency personnel is a continuous process. The range of activities in advocacy for students in the program is limitless because any activity that promotes better attitudes, accessibility to the community and school, and the success of the student at school and on the job can be thought of as advocacy. Advocacy relating to the thrust of this chapter—job placement, training, and supervision—is more focused but still is limited only by the imagination and energy of the person or persons responsible for these areas of the program. Moon and colleagues (1986) provided a helpful set of guidelines for advocacy activities, presented in Figure 7.1.

FIGURE 7.1 Guidelines for Advocacy Activities

Job Development
- Explain the capabilities of individuals with disabilities to employers and co-workers during job site visits.
- Meet with civic, business, church, and social groups to change social attitudes and educate them on the advantages of hiring workers with disabilities.
- Develop advertising and educational literature pertaining to your program.

Consumer Assessment
- Counsel parents and guardians on benefits of community-based employment for their son or daughter.
- Work out transportation problems with families.
- Outline specific objectives for school personnel that will improve the employability of future trainees.

Job Placement
- Make sure the job application is filled out correctly.
- Review appropriate dress and behavior with the interviewee and the family.
- Explain the job benefit package (if applicable) to the worker and his or her family.

Job Site Training
- Establish rapport with supervisors and co-workers and adhere to the rules of the job site.
- Never allow job training to interfere with the flow of business or the established work schedule.
- Involve supervisors or co-workers in the training if feasible and briefly explain the systematic training and fading procedure.
- Recognize employers, supervisors, and co-workers who promote the employment of citizens with disabilities (e.g., a plaque, awards banquet).
- Establish rapport with co-workers and involve them in the training of the worker.
- Explain to co-workers the disability, background, and behavioral characteristics of the new employee.
- Encourage co-workers to socialize with the new worker and model appropriate ways to do this.

(continued)

FIGURE 7.1   **Continued**

- Have the supervisor complete written evaluations on the worker's performance and discuss results.
- Work out job modifications with the supervisor when needed.
- Keep the family aware of the individual's job progress and problems that may occur.
- Give family members the "job rules" such as the procedure for calling in sick.
- Explain pay and benefits (if applicable) to family members.
- Do not fade your presence from the job site until you are sure the employee is going to "make it" alone.
- Inform the supervisor and the worker's family of the long-term follow-up services you provide for the employee.

Follow-up
- Mail supervisor evaluations on schedule and respond immediately if any problems are indicated.
- Visit the job site and monitor the worker's performance by talking to supervisors and co-workers and by completing task analytic probes, production rate recordings, and on-task observations.
- Keep up with management and supervisor changes at the job site. Personnel changes can seriously affect job performance.
- Find out about any changes in the worker's home situation through the use of parent surveys, phone calls, and home visits.
- Be prepared to go back on the job site at any time for retraining.

Source: Adapted from *The Supported Work Model of Competitive Employment for Citizens with Severe Handicaps: A Guide for Job Trainers* (p. 81) by S. Moon, P. Goodall, M. Barcus, and V. Brooke, 1986, Richmond VA: Rehabilitation and Training Center, Virginia Commonwealth University. Reprinted with permission.

Resources

The following list includes resources that may help you in all of the major aspects of job placement, training, and supervision. We have referred to many of them throughout this chapter.

Bissonette, D. (1994). *Beyond traditional job development: The art of creating opportunity.* Chatsworth, CA: Milt Wright.

Fabian, E., Luecking, R. G., & Tilson, G. (1994). *A working relationship: The job development specialist's guide to successful partnerships with business.* Baltimore: Paul H. Brookes.

Fine, S., & Getkate, M. (1995). *Benchmark tasks for job analysis: A guide for functional job analysis (FJA) scales.* Mahwah, NJ: Erlbaum.

Garfinkle, L. (1995). *Legal issues in transitioning students.* Horsham, PA: LRP Publications.

Love, L. (1995). *Applying the Fair Labor Standards Act when placing students into community-based vocational education.* Stillwater, OK: National Clearinghouse of Rehabilitation Training Materials.

Moon, M. S., Inge, K. J., Wehman, P., Brooke, V., & Barcus, J. M. (1990). *Helping persons with severe mental retardation get and keep employment: Supported employment issues and strategies.* Baltimore: Paul H. Brookes.

National School-to-Work Office. (n.d.). *School-to-work and employer liability: A resource guide.* Washington, DC: Author.

Pumpian, I., Fisher, D., Certo, N., Engel, T., & Mautz, D. (1998). To pay or not to pay: Differentiating employment and training relationships through regulation and litigation. *Career Development for Exceptional Individuals, 21,* 187–202.

Pumpian, I., Fisher, D., Certo, N., & Smalley, K. (1997). Changing jobs: An essential part of career development. *Mental Retardation, 35,* 39–48.

Simon, M., Cobb, B., Halloran, W., Norman, M., & Bourexis, P. (1994). *Meeting the needs of youth with disabilities: Handbook for implementing community-based vocational education programs according to the Fair Labor Standards Act.* Fort Collins: Colorado State University.

Simon, M., & Halloran, W. (1994). Community-based vocational education: Guidelines for complying with the Fair Labor Standards Act. *Journal of the Association for Severely Handicapped, 19,* 52–60.

U.S. Department of Labor. (1991). *The revised handbook for analyzing jobs.* Indianapolis, IN: JIST Works.

Conclusion

The responsibility for placing, training, and supervising students in community-based work-training programs cannot be taken lightly. The relative ease with which some individuals fulfill such responsibility is very deceiving. For most people, it is an awesome responsibility, especially when they realize all that it involves. It borders on the bizarre that the vast majority of states across the nation do not value this professional role enough to recognize it as a legitimate, highly desirable public school position with appropriate certification requirements. It borders on malpractice that state and local education agencies permit individuals to function in such critical outcome areas with no more than some type of academic teaching endorsement, most frequently with an elementary focus.

Until states and local communities take responsibility for ensuring appropriate training for work experience coordinators, the coordinators will have to be responsible for their own professional development. There is a rapidly growing body of literature that reflects an optimistic philosophy, a demonstrated technology, and a practical agenda for placing, training, and supervising youths with disabilities in community-based employment. Increasing numbers of colleges and universities are offering up-to-date training in vocational training and transition programming for students with disabilities. Individuals in public school roles requiring job placement, job training, and job supervision should seek out these sources of professional development for the sake of the youths they serve, for their own legal protection, and for their own professional pride.

APPENDIX 1   Employment Standards for 14- and 15-Year-Olds

MINIMUM AGE STANDARD FOR NONAGRICULTURAL EMPLOYMENT

Oppressive Child Labor Is Defined as Employment of Children Under the Legal Minimum Ages

14 Minimum age for employment in specified occupations outside school hours.

16 BASIC MINIMUM AGE FOR EMPLOYMENT. At 16 years of age youths may be employed in any occupation, other than a nonagricultural occupation declared hazardous by the Secretary of Labor.

18 Minimum age for employment in nonagricultural occupations declared hazardous by the Secretary of Labor.

- No minimum age for employment which is exempt from the child labor provisions of the Act.
- No minimum age for employment with respect to any employee whose services during the workweek are performed in a workplace within a foreign country or within territory as limited by section 13 (f) of the Act.

Note to Employers

Unless otherwise exempt, a covered minor employee must be paid according to statutory minimum wage and overtime provisions of the Act.

EXEMPTIONS FROM THE CHILD LABOR PROVISIONS OF THE ACT

The Child Labor Provisions Do Not Apply To:

- Children under 16 years of age employed by their parents in occupations other than manufacturing or mining, or occupations declared hazardous by the Secretary of Labor.
- Children employed as actors or performers in motion pictures, theatrical, radio, or television productions.
- Homeworkers engaged in the making of wreaths composed principally of natural holly, pine, cedar, or other evergreens (including the harvesting of the evergreens).

OTHER CHILD LABOR LAWS

Other Federal and State laws may have higher standards. When these apply, the more stringent standard must be observed. All states have child labor laws and all but one have compulsory school attendance laws.

HAZARDOUS OCCUPATIONS ORDERS IN NONAGRICULTURAL OCCUPATIONS

(These Orders are published in Subpart E of Part 570 of Title 29 of the Code of Federal Regulations.)

APPENDIX 1   Continued

Hazardous Occupations Orders

The Fair Labor Standards Act provides a minimum age of 18 years for any nonagricultural occupations which the Secretary of Labor "shall find and by order declare" to be particularly hazardous for 16- and 17-year-old persons, or detrimental to their health and well-being. This minimum age applies even when the minor is employed by the parent or person standing in place of the parent.

The 17 hazardous occupations orders now in effect apply either on an industry basis, specifying the occupations in the industry that are not covered, or on an occupational basis irrespective of the industry in which found.

The Orders in effect deal with:

1. Manufacturing and storing explosives.
2. Motor-vehicle driving and outside helper.
3. Coal mining.
4. Logging and sawmilling.
5. Power-driven woodworking machines.
6. Exposure to radioactive substances.
7. Power-driven hoisting apparatus.
8. Power-driven metal-forming, punching and shearing machines.
9. Mining, other than coal mining.
10. Slaughtering, or meat packing, processing or rendering.
11. Power-driven bakery machines.
12. Power-driven paper-products machines.
13. Manufacturing brick, tile, and kindred products.
14. Power-driven circular saws, band saws, and guillotine shears.
15. Wrecking, demolition, and shipbreaking operations.
16. Roofing operations.
17. Excavation operations.

Additional Information

Inquiries about the Fair Labor Standards Act will be answered by mail, telephone, or personal interview at any office of the Wage and Hour Division of the U.S. Department of Labor. Offices are listed in the telephone directory under U. S. Department of Labor in the U. S. Government listing. (These standards are published in Subpart C of Part 570 of Title 29 of the Code of Federal Regulations, Child Labor Regulation No. 3.) Employment of 14- and 15-year-old minors is limited to certain occupations under conditions which do not interfere with their schooling, health, or well-being.

HOURS-TIME STANDARDS

14- AND 15-YEAR-OLD MINORS MAY NOT BE EMPLOYED:

1. DURING SCHOOL HOURS, except as provided for in Work Experience and Career Exploration Programs.
2. BEFORE 7 A.M. or AFTER 7 P.M. except 9 P.M. from June 1 through Labor Day (time depends on local standards).

(continued)

APPENDIX 1   Continued

3. MORE THAN 3 HOURS A DAY—on school days.
4. MORE THAN 18 HOURS A WEEK—in school weeks.
5. MORE THAN 8 HOURS A DAY—on nonschool days.
6. MORE THAN 40 HOURS A WEEK—in nonschool weeks.

Permitted Occupations for 14- and 15-Year-Old Minors in Retail, Food Service, and Gasoline Service Establishments

14- AND 15-YEAR-OLD MINORS MAY BE
EMPLOYED IN:

1. OFFICE and CLERICAL WORK (including operation of office machines).
2. CASHIERING, SELLING, MODELING, ART WORK, WORK IN ADVERTISING DEPARTMENTS, WINDOW TRIMMING, and COMPARATIVE SHOPPING.
3. PRICE MARKING and TAGGING by hand or by machine, ASSEMBLING ORDERS, PACKING and SHELVING.
4. BAGGING and CARRYING OUT CUSTOMER'S ORDERS.
5. ERRAND and DELIVERY WORK by foot, bicycle, and public transportation.
6. CLEANUP WORK, including the use of vacuum cleaners and floor waxers, and MAINTENANCE of GROUNDS, but not including the use of power driven mowers or cutters.
7. KITCHEN WORK and other work involved in preparing and serving food and beverages, including the operation of machines and devices used in the performance of such work, such as, but not limited to, dishwasher, toasters, dumbwaiters, popcorn poppers, milk shake blenders, and coffee grinders.
8. WORK IN CONNECTION WITH CARS and TRUCKS if confined to the following: dispensing gasoline and oil; courtesy service on premises of gasoline service station; car cleaning, washing, and polishing; other occupations permitted by this section. BUT NOT INCLUDING WORK involving the use of pits, racks, or lifting apparatus, or involving the inflation of any tire mounted on a rim equipped with a removable retaining ring.
9. CLEANING VEGETABLES and FRUITS, and WRAPPING, SEALING, LABELING, WEIGHING, PRICING and STOCKING GOODS when performed in areas physically separate from areas where meat is prepared for sale and outside freezers or meat coolers.

In Any Other Place of Employment

14- and 15-YEAR-OLD MINORS MAY BE EMPLOYED IN any occupation listed above.
14- and 15-year-old minors may not be employed in:

1. Any MANUFACTURING occupation.
2. Any MINING occupation.
3. PROCESSING occupations such as filleting of fish, dressing poultry, cracking nuts, or laundering as performed by commercial laundries and dry cleaning (except in a retail, food service, or gasoline service establishment in those specific occupations expressly permitted there in accordance with the foregoing list).

APPENDIX 1   Continued

4. Occupations requiring the performance of any duties in WORKROOMS or WORK-PLACES WHERE GOODS ARE MANUFACTURED, MINED, or OTHERWISE PROCESSED (except to the extent expressly permitted in retail, food service, or gasoline service establishments in accordance with the foregoing list).
5. PUBLIC SERVICE MESSENGER SERVICE.
6. OPERATION OR TENDING OF HOISTING APPARATUS or of ANY POWER-DRIVEN MACHINERY (other than office machines and machines in retail, food service, and gasoline service, establishments which are specified in the foregoing list as machines which such minors may operate in such establishment.
7. ANY OCCUPATIONS FOUND AND DECLARED TO BE HAZARDOUS.
8. OCCUPATIONS IN CONNECTION WITH:
    a. TRANSPORTATION of persons or property by rail, highway, air, on water, pipeline or other means.
    b. WAREHOUSING and STORAGE.
    c. COMMUNICATIONS and PUBLIC UTILITIES.
    d. CONSTRUCTION (including repair). Except Office or Sales Work in connection with a, b, c, and d when not performed on transportation media or at the transportation media or at the actual construction site.
9. ANY OF THE FOLLOWING OCCUPATIONS IN A RETAIL, FOOD SERVICE, OR GASOLINE SERVICE ESTABLISHMENT:
    a. WORK performed IN or ABOUT BOILER or ENGINE ROOMS.
    b. Work in connection with MAINTENANCE or REPAIR OF THE ESTABLISHMENT MACHINES or EQUIPMENT.
    c. OUTSIDE WINDOW WASHING that involves working from window sills, and all work requiring the use of LADDERS, SCAFFOLDS, or their substitutes.
    d. COOKING (except at soda fountains, lunch counters, snack bars, or cafeteria service counters) and BAKING.
    e. Occupations which involve OPERATING, SETTING UP, ADJUSTING, CLEANING, OILING, or REPAIRING power-driven FOOD SLICERS and GRINDERS, FOOD CHOPPERS and CUTTERS, and BAKERY-TYPE MIXERS.
    f. Work in FREEZERS and MEAT COOLERS and all work in PREPARATION OF MEATS for sale (except wrapping, sealing, labeling, weighing, pricing and stocking when performed in other areas).
    g. LOADING and UNLOADING GOODS to and from trucks, railroad cars, or conveyors.
    h. All occupations in WAREHOUSES except office and clerical work.

Exceptions

WORK EXPERIENCE AND CAREER EXPLORATION PROGRAMS (WECEP) Some of the provisions of Child Labor Regulation No. 3 are varied for 14- and 15-year-olds in approved school-supervised and school administered Work Experience and Career Exploration Programs (WECEP). Enrollees in WECEP may be employed: during school hours; for as many as 3 hours on a school day; for as many as 23 hours in a school week; in occupations otherwise prohibited for which a variation has been granted by the administrator of

(continued)

APPENDIX 1   Continued

the Wage and Hour Division. The State Educational Agency must obtain approval from the administrator of the Wage and Hour Division before operating a WECEP program.

Source: U.S. Department of Labor, Employment Standards Administration, Wage and Hour Division, no date.

APPENDIX 2   Child Labor Requirements in Agriculture under the Fair Labor Standards Act

The Fair Labor Standards Act establishes minimum ages for covered employment in agriculture, unless a specific exemption applies. The Act covers employees whose work involves production of agricultural goods which will leave the state directly or indirectly and become a part of interstate commerce.

Minimum Age Standards for Agricultural Employment

16 years	for employment in any farm job at any time
14–15 years	for employment outside school hours in any farm job that has not been declared hazardous by the Secretary of Labor. No minors under 16 years of age may be employed at any time in hazardous occupations in agriculture, unless exempt.
12–13 years	for employment outside school hours in any nonhazardous farm job, with written parental consent, or on the same farm where their parents are employed.
Under 12 years	for employment outside school hours in any nonhazardous farm job, with written parental consent only on farms where the employees are not subject to the minimum wage provisions of the Act.
10–11 years	local resident children only: for employment outside school hours as hand harvesters of short season crops, for no more than 8 weeks between June 1 and October 15, for employers who receive a waiver from the Secretary of Labor.
Any age	for employment in any farm job at any time on a farm owned or operated by the minor's parents or persons standing in place of parents.

The Fair Labor Standards Act extends minimum wage provisions to farm employees, including minors, whose employer used more than 500 man-days of farm labor during any calendar quarter of the previous calendar year. Unless otherwise exempt, employees covered by the minimum wage provisions must be paid at least $4.25 an hour beginning January 1, 1991.

Certain small farms and hand harvest laborers may be exempt from the minimum wage provisions.

Farmworkers are not subject to the overtime provisions of the Act.

APPENDIX 2 Continued

Other Child Labor Laws
Most states have laws setting standards for child labor laws in agriculture. When both state and federal child labor laws apply, the law setting the more stringent standard must be observed.

Penalties for Violations
Employers who violate the child labor provisions of the Act may be subject to a civil money penalty up to $1,000 for each violation.

The Secretary of Labor has found and declared that the following occupations in agriculture are particularly hazardous for minors under 16 years of age (No minor under 16 years of age may be employed at any time in these occupations, unless exempt*):

1. Operating a tractor of over 20 PTO horsepower, or connecting or disconnecting an implement or any of its parts to or from such a tractor.
2. Operating or assisting to operate (including starting, stopping, adjusting, feeding or any other activity involving physical contact associated with the operating): corn picker, cotton picker, grain combine, hay mower, forage harvester, hay baler, potato digger, or mobile pea viner; feed grinder, crop dryer, forage blower, auger conveyor, or the unloading mechanism of a nongravity-type self-unloading wagon or trailer; or power post-hole digger, power post driver, or non-walking-type rotary tiller.
3. Operating or assisting to operate (including starting, stopping, adjusting, feeding or any other activity involving physical contact associated with the operation): trencher or earthmoving equipment; fork lift; potato combine; or power-driven circular, band, or chain saw.
4. Working on a farm in a yard, pen, or stall occupied by a: bull, boar, or stud horse maintained for breeding purposes; or sow with suckling pigs, or cow with newborn calf (with umbilical cord present).
5. Felling, bucking, skidding, loading, or unloading timber with butt diameter of more than 6 inches.
6. Working from a ladder or scaffold (painting, repairing, or building structures, pruning trees, picking fruit, etc.) at a height of over 20 feet.
7. Driving a bus, truck, or automobile when transporting passengers, or riding on a tractor as a passenger or helper.
8. Working inside: a fruit, forage, or grain storage designed to retain an oxygen deficient or toxic atmosphere; an upright silo within 2 weeks after silage has been added or when a top unloading device is in operating position; a manure pit; or a horizontal silo while operating a tractor for packing purposes.
9. Handling or applying (including cleaning or decontaminating equipment, disposal or return of empty containers, or serving as a flagman for aircraft applying) agriculture chemicals classified under the Federal Insecticide, Fungicide, and Rodenticide Act as Toxicity Category I, identified by the word "Danger" and/or "Poison" with skull and crossbones; or Toxicity Category II, identified by the word "Warning" on the label.
10. Handling or using a blasting agent, including but not limited to, dynamite, black powder, sensitized ammonium nitrate, blasting caps, and primer cord.
11. Transporting, transferring, or applying anhydrous ammonia.

(continued)

APPENDIX 2   Continued

Additional Information
Contact your local Wage and Hour Division office, listed in most telephone books in the
U.S. Government listing, under U.S. Department of Labor, Employment Standards
Administration.

Source: Child Labor Bulletin No. 102 (WH Publication 1295), no date.

*Exemptions:
1. Young workers employed on farms owned or operated by their parents.
2. Student-learners enrolled in a bona fide vocational agriculture program are exempt from Items (1)
    through (6) when certain requirements are met.
3. 4-H Federal Extension Service Training Program and Vocational Agriculture Training Program.
    Minors 14 and 15 years of age who hold certificates of completion of training under either program
    in tractor or machinery operation may work outside school hours on equipment in Items (1) and (2)
    for which they have been trained.

8 Transition to Postsecondary Education

The future is not someplace we are going to
  But one we are creating.
The paths are not to be found,
  But made,
And the activity of making them,
  Changes both the maker
    And the destination.

—John Schaar

Two of the transition outcomes identified by the Individuals with Disabilities Education Act (IDEA) and its amendments are postsecondary education and vocational training. Participation in postsecondary education is perhaps the most common alternative to direct employment, at least within the general population (Halpern, Yovanoff, Doren, & Benz, 1995). This postsecondary education and training can be provided in a number of settings, including four-year colleges and universities; community and junior colleges; private vocational schools that offer certificates in a particular job area, such as hairdressing or truck driving; apprenticeship programs; on-the-job training programs; adult education programs; the military; and others. Community colleges are themselves rather complex, offering a range of programs, including liberal arts preparation for transfer to a four-year college or for an associate's degree, specific vocational training accompanied by an associate's degree or a certificate, and many adult education courses that are not degree oriented. These adult education courses can address either vocational or avocational content. This chapter focuses on formal postsecondary programs offered by educational institutions. The term *postsecondary education* will be used to include programs whose emphasis is further education or institution-based vocational and technical training. Although educational institutions may be involved in some way in apprenticeship and on-the-job training programs, these were covered in Chapter 6.

This chapter focuses on a number of topics: general information on postsecondary education; the skills needed by students in postsecondary education programs; suggested strategies at the secondary level and postsecondary level to assist the student with the transition process; helpful resources; what the law requires of postsecondary education institutions; and the information and documentation required by staff at the postsecondary level in order to determine eligibility and to provide the needed accommodations to your students.

General Information on Postsecondary Education for Individuals with Disabilities

A number of studies of the adult adjustment of individuals with disabilities (Fairweather & Shaver, 1991; Frank & Sitlington, 1997; Sitlington, Frank, & Carson, 1993; Wagner, D'Amico, Marder, Newman, & Blackorby, 1992) have found that young adults with disabilities do not have the same rate of enrollment in postsecondary education as individuals without disabilities.

The National Longitudinal Study (Wagner et al., 1992) reported that 14 percent of all students with disabilities who were out of high school for less than two years attended postsecondary institutions. Graduates had higher participation rates in postsecondary education programs (19 percent) than dropouts (6 percent), and people with physical or sensory disabilities had higher participation rates (28 to 36 percent) than did those with cognitive, emotional, or severe disabilities (4 to 17 percent). Of this group, students with mental retardation had the second lowest rate of participation (6 percent) and students with multiple disabilities had the lowest rate (4 percent).

Fairweather and Shaver (1991) studied a nationally representative sample of youths with disabilities who had recently exited from high school to determine their rate of participation in postsecondary educational programs. They used information on students out of school at least one year from the National Longitudinal Transition Study of Special Education Students and compared it to data from the High School and Beyond surveys (Jones, Sebring, Crawford, Spencer, & Butz, 1986a, 1986b). It should be noted that youths with disabilities were more likely to come from low-income families and from families with lower educational attainment. Postsecondary education settings that were examined included vocational-technical institutions, community or two-year colleges, and four-year colleges.

The researchers (Fairweather & Shaver, 1991) found that high school graduates with disabilities were much less likely to be enrolled in postsecondary education programs than their nondisabled counterparts (21 versus 64 percent). The differences in participation in postsecondary vocational programs were minimal (9 versus 11 percent). Nondisabled high school graduates, however, were approximately 3 times more likely than graduates with disabilities to take some community college courses (20 versus 8 percent) and over 10 times more likely to take some four-year college courses (34 versus 4 percent).

Transition to postsecondary vocational education (in proprietary vocational institutions) was encouraging. On the other hand, the low overall participation rate in two-year institutions was particularly discouraging because of the vocational focus of many of these institutions and because the cost of attending a vocational program in a community college is substantially less than the cost of attending a proprietary vocational institution.

Factors Associated with Enrollment in Postsecondary Education

For the most part, Fairweather and Shaver (1991) found that the factors related to participating in postsecondary education for youths with disabilities were the same as those for nondisabled individuals. Males and females did not differ significantly in their participation rates. Parental level of education and family income, positively related to enrollment in postsecondary programs for the population at large, also appeared related for youths with disabilities. As with nondisabled youths, graduation from high school was significantly related to postsecondary education for youths with disabilities. In contrast to trends for the nondisabled population, however, postsecondary education participation rates between whites and minority youths with disabilities were about the same.

Two studies (Miller, Snider, & Rzonca, 1990; Miller, Rzonca, & Snider, 1991) attempted to determine variables related to the decision of individuals with learning disabilities to participate in postsecondary education, using data from the Iowa Statewide Follow-Up Study for individuals out of school one year (Sitlington & Frank, 1990). Miller, Snider, and Rzonca (1990) found that (1) participants had significantly higher IQ and higher reading and math grade-level scores leaving high school than nonparticipants; (2) participants were significantly more likely to have been involved in extracurricular activities such as athletics, music, speech, drama, and debate than nonparticipants; and (3) participants were significantly more likely than nonparticipants to have talked to representatives of vocational rehabilitation and community colleges as well as high school personnel regarding job information or assistance.

Using the same database, Miller, Rzonca, and Snider (1991) examined the variables related to the type of postsecondary education experience chosen by young adults with learning disabilities. Postsecondary opportunities included were junior college, community college, four-year college or university, and private training programs. (These authors also addressed the military as a postsecondary training option.) Enrollment in junior college was found to have a significantly larger representation of females, as compared to four-year college or community college. The type of resource to which the students were exposed seemed to have affected the type of postsecondary experience selected. For example, exposure to community college resources led to community college participation, and exposure to other agencies led to participation in private training programs. The authors also found that there were considerable similarities among subjects attending the four types of training programs. No statistical significance was found among variables related to IQ score, reading level, math level, or participation in the four types of postsecondary education.

Halpern and colleagues (1995) interviewed carefully constructed samples of students with disabilities from three different states while they were in their last year of high school and again one year after leaving school. They found five predictors to be associated with participation in postsecondary education:

1. High scores on a functional achievement inventory
2. Successful completion of instruction in certain relevant curricular areas (reading, writing, math, problem solving, and getting along with others)
3. Participation in relevant transition planning
4. Parent satisfaction with instruction received by the student in high school
5. Student satisfaction with high school instruction

Variables that were not associated with participation in postsecondary education included:

1. Demographic variables such as gender, ethnicity, family income, and primary disability category
2. Participation in integrated instruction during high school
3. Student dropout status
4. The existence of congruent expectations by both the student and parents that the student would participate in postsecondary education after leaving high school.

Many of these variables have been presumed and sometimes found to be important predictors of various postsecondary outcomes (Wagner, Blackorby, Cameto, & Newman, 1993; Wagner, D'Amico, Marder, Newman, & Blackorby, 1992).

Participation in Postsecondary Education by Specific Disabilities

As you might expect, Fairweather and Shaver (1991) found that participation of both graduates and dropouts (15 percent) in postsecondary education varied greatly by type of disability, from a high of 43 percent for students who had visual impairments, 39 percent who were deaf, 33 percent who were health impaired, 32 percent who were speech impaired, 30 percent who were hard of hearing, 29 percent who were orthopedically disabled, and 17 percent who were learning disabled, to 12 percent who were emotionally disturbed, 8 percent who were deaf-blind, 6 percent who were mentally retarded, and 5 percent who were multiply handicapped. The type of postsecondary setting also varied by type of disability. Youths with mental disabilities were mostly served by vocational programs. Community colleges served youths with speech impairments, youths who were deaf, and youths with other health impairments at rates similar to those for nondisabled youths. Those with visual impairments had the highest level of participation (28 percent) in four-year colleges. This compared with 2 percent and 1 percent of youths with learning and emotional disabilities.

The vast majority of the literature on transition to postsecondary education relates to individuals with learning disabilities. Some exceptions include Aune and Friehe (1996), who addressed issues related to postsecondary education for students with language disorders. In addition, Javorsky and Gussin (1994) addressed college students with attention deficit hyperactivity disorder (ADHD), because, as they pointed out, in September 1991, the Department of Education concluded that ADHD is a "recognized" handicap under Section 504 of the Rehabilitation Act of 1973, and students with ADHD are thereby entitled to appropriate and reasonable accommodations at the elementary, secondary, and postsecondary education levels. Senge and Dote-Kwan (1995) discussed information accessibility in alternative formats in postsecondary education for students who are print disabled. This would include individuals who are blind or visually impaired, those who have physical disabilities and have difficulty manipulating print materials, and those who have learning disabilities that prevent them from gaining access to information in print.

Page and Chadsey-Rusch (1995) addressed the possibility of the community college experience as a viable transition outcome for individuals with mental retardation. They argued that immersion into a university or community college environment can provide a number of outcomes for persons with mental retardation such as lifelong learning, enhanced self-esteem, and friendships. The authors provided a qualitative description of the community college experience for two students with and two students without mental retardation. It was clear that the future career plans of three of the four students were not very firm; the plans of the two students with mental retardation were the most undefined. All of the students, however, were achieving interpersonal benefits from attending a community college. Page and Chadsey-Rusch concluded that the issue of whether students with mental retardation can best meet their transition goals by attending a community college reflects the debate on how students in high school should be educated (Clark, 1994; Edgar, 1992). According to Page and Chadsey-Rusch, if attendance at community colleges would result in higher-paying positions with the possibility of upward mobility on one's career, then community college experiences would seem to be very desirable. They qualified this statement, however, with the statement that the experience should result in some meaningful career objective.

For all individuals, the choice of what path to take after high school should depend on their life goals. In the case of individuals with disabilities, the choice of postsecondary paths should be made more clear through a transition planning process that includes students and families. The discussion of postsecondary education options needs to be framed within the context of admission requirements, performance demands, and expected outcomes of these options. Discussions related to options should also include the availability and quality of support systems for assisting individuals with disabilities in meeting their transition goals. The reality is that some institutions are more "student friendly" than others.

The decision of whether participation in postsecondary education is a desired transition outcome for a specific student is a decision that should be made as early as possible in the transition planning process. In the following sections of this chapter, we discuss the skills that your students will need to pursue postsecondary education and suggest some strategies for making a successful transition to postsecondary education programs. Preparing your students for a successful transition specifically to college and university programs will require that you carefully plan their high school coursework to include the needed college preparatory coursework. When that planning begins under IDEA, the student is age 14, but there are individuals who are intellectually gifted who also have one or more disabilities. Enrichment or acceleration may be appropriate as early as the late elementary or early middle school years. In cases like these, planning that considers advanced placement or acceleration for completing high school courses may need to begin as early as 9 or 10 years of age.

It is critical, however, that training in functional skills be addressed for all students, including those pursuing postsecondary education. Clark (1994) defined a functional curriculum approach as

> a way of delivering instructional content that focuses on the concepts and skills needed by all students with disabilities in the areas of personal-social, daily living, and occupational adjustment. What is considered a functional curriculum of any one student would be the content (concepts and skills) included in that student's curriculum or course of study that targets his or her current and future needs. These needs are based on a nondiscriminatory, functional assessment approach. (p. 37)

The functional curriculum approach described by Clark suggests that functional content be addressed in the IEP, but that it has no restrictions regarding the types or location of instructional delivery.

The concept of quality of life should also be considered in the discussion of postsecondary education options. Halpern (1993) identified three basic domains for classifying quality-of-life outcomes: (1) physical and material well-being, (2) performance of a variety of adult roles, and (3) a sense of personal fulfillment. Primary within the discussion of quality of life is the discrepancy between the individual's point of view and the societal point of view of success.

Further research is needed to determine the outcomes that occur as a consequence of postsecondary education. If students with disabilities are to obtain jobs requiring high-level skills, they will need training beyond what they receive in high school. As Halpern pointed out, however, attainment of employment should not be the sole criterion by which to judge the success of transition efforts. There are other aspects of quality of life to which postsecondary education can contribute. Your view of a student's needs and likelihood of benefiting from postsecondary education should always be based on the broad aspects of quality of life.

Skills Needed in Postsecondary Education Programs

Numerous authors have written on the skills needed by all individuals, but particularly individuals with disabilities, to succeed in postsecondary programs. We have chosen to present information from a number of these authors, even though there is some overlapping of ideas, to provide specific input for preparing your students for the transition to these programs. Much of this information relates to individuals with learning disabilities (LD). The basic concepts and approaches advocated in these articles and textbooks, however, apply to all individuals with disabilities who experience problems with learning or who need special accommodations or learning strategies.

Cowen (1993) pointed out that college-bound students with disabilities must go through the same process as their nondisabled peers, but because of their disabilities, they may face additional challenges that need to be addressed. First, many college-bound students with disabilities do not understand their individual disabilities, how they affect their learning, or how to describe their disabilities to others in plain language. In addition, after years of academic struggle in high school, these students may view themselves as having few learning strengths or abilities, which further lowers their self-concept. Second, many students with disabilities lack the content preparation necessary to succeed in college (McGuire, Norlander, & Shaw, 1990) or have not been provided with learning strategies instruction that will permit them to generalize their skills across settings.

Finally, once students with LD have been admitted into college, they often need further assistance in how to stay in college so that they can graduate (Block, 1993: Brinckerhoff, Shaw, & McGuire, 1992; Vogel & Adelman, 1992). As Cowen (1993) observed, the growing number of services available in colleges and universities requires an extensive knowledge of (1) how to read and evaluate the many guides available, (2) how to locate services in colleges not listed in the guides, and (3) how to evaluate the services that are located.

Scott (1991) highlighted the fact that there is a change in legal status for students with disabilities as they make the transition to postsecondary education. While in high school, the Individuals with Disabilities Act Amendments (1997) and legislation that preceded them ensure individuals with disabilities the right to participate in publicly supported education programs; education in the least restrictive environment; nondiscriminatory testing, evaluation, and placement; procedural due process of law; and appropriate educational services as delineated in a written Individualized Education Program (IEP). In postsecondary programs, Section 504 of the Rehabilitation Act (1973; PL 93-112) and the Americans with Disabilities Act (ADA) are basic civil rights provisions. (We will present information on these laws and the requirements they place on postsecondary education institutions in a later section of this chapter.)

DuChossois and Michaels (1994) commented that for any college-bound student, the process of selecting a college is an emotional as well as an academic decision. They also stated that secondary education must be a process of moving students with disabilities from a state of dependency to independence. They cited the following nonacademic areas that are often problematic for all students making the transition to postsecondary education, but that frequently become overwhelming for the student with learning disabilities: problem solving, organizing, prioritizing multiple task completion, studying, self-monitoring, attacking and following through on tasks, managing time, and interacting socially in a variety of new situations.

In their position paper on transition to postsecondary education, the National Joint Committee on Learning Disabilities (NJCLD, 1994) stated that success in postsecondary educational settings depends on the student's level of motivation, independence, self-direction, self-advocacy, and academic abilities developed in high school. The NJCLD also identified roles and responsibilities for the student, parents, secondary personnel, and postsecondary personnel in the transition process. Although these roles and responsibilities were written specifically for those with learning disabilities, they apply to all individuals with disabilities. The roles and responsibilities proposed for the student are actually skills that the student will need in postsecondary settings. A number of them are listed here:

- Understanding his or her disability, including its effect on work and learning
- Establishing realistic goals
- Stressing strengths, while understanding the influence of the disability
- Knowing how, when, and where to discuss and request needed accommodations
- Developing and using social skills
- Seeking instructors and learning environments that are supportive
- Developing and applying effective studying, test-preparation, test-taking, time-management, and note-taking strategies
- Maintaining an ongoing personal file that includes school and medical records, the IEP, a resumé, and samples of academic work
- Knowing the rights and responsibilities necessary to prepare for and access postsecondary education
- Identifying and accessing resources needed for support
- Selecting courses that meet postsecondary requirements
- Preparing for and actively participating in the postsecondary application process

The NJCLD also identified a number of responsibilities for secondary school personnel. Some of these were the following:

- Include the student and parents in the entire transition planning process.
- Demonstrate sensitivity to the culture and values of the student and family.
- Develop an appropriate packet of materials to document the student's secondary school program and to facilitate service delivery in the postsecondary setting.
- Inform the student about statutes, rules, and regulations that ensure his or her rights.
- Ensure competency in literacy and mathematics.
- Help the student use a range of academic accommodations and technological aids, such as electronic date books, texts on tape, and grammar and spell checkers.
- Provide appropriate course selection, counseling, and academic support services.

- Ensure that the student learns effective studying, time-management, test-preparation, and test-taking strategies.
- Help the student evaluate his or her dependence on external supports and adjust the level of assistance when appropriate.
- Help the student develop self-advocacy skills, including a realistic understanding of the disability.
- Foster independence through increased responsibility and opportunity for self-management.
- Encourage the student to develop extracurricular interests and to participate in community activities.
- Inform the student and parents about admission requirements and demands of diverse postsecondary settings.
- Inform the student and parents about support services that postsecondary settings provide.
- Help the student and parents select and apply to postsecondary institutions that will offer both the competitive curriculum and the necessary level of support services.
- Develop ongoing communication with postsecondary personnel.

Brinckerhoff (1994) has been a strong advocate for the need to teach a variety of academic and self-advocacy skills if students with disabilities are to be successful in postsecondary settings. Building on definitions by Byron (1990) and Goldhammer and Brinckerhoff (1992), he defined *self-advocacy for college students with LD* as "the ability to recognize and meet the needs specific to one's learning disability without compromising the dignity of oneself or others" (p. 229).

In addition, Brinckerhoff (1994) stated that high school teachers need to give students with disabilities a more realistic picture of what to expect in college by describing the different roles assumed by campus support staff and faculty. Many students will anticipate that the support staff on campus will perform the same tasks and provide the same support as the resource room teacher. They may also erroneously expect that all postsecondary institutions will have a specialist on campus who can be a content tutor who can assist with homework, monitor their progress in completing class assignments, and, if necessary, talk to teachers on their behalf. Shaw, Brinckerhoff, Kistler, and McGuire (1990) pointed out that it may be the method of teaching and the content of what is taught in high school special education classes that exacerbate the lack of preparedness experienced by high school students as they approach postsecondary education. Brinckerhoff (1994) also pointed out that students with disabilities need to be forewarned that college classes are typically larger, interactions with faculty are less frequent, and opportunities for extra help are more limited. He identified organization, time management, and communication skills as critical for transition to postsecondary education.

Gartin, Rumrill, and Serebreni (1996) identified four difficulties commonly experienced by students with disabilities when they make the transition from high school to postsecondary education: (1) a decrease in teacher-student contact, (2) an increase in academic competition, (3) a change in personal support networks, and (4) a loss of the protective public school environment. They proposed the Higher Education Transition Model, which utilizes a three-part framework. The first part of this framework is psychosocial adjustment. Instructional objectives related to this area would include self-advocacy skill development, handling frustration, social problem solving, college-level social skills, and mentor relationships. Among the recommendations the authors provided for promoting psychosocial development were including college settings and situations as discussion scenarios to aid in the transfer and generalization of communication and social skills, and using cooperative learning and peer tutoring.

The second component of the Higher Education Transition Model is academic development. Tasks the secondary teacher can perform related to this area include the following:

1. Monitor the students' performance in their college preparatory courses.
2. Teach study strategies and technology skills.
3. Assess the students' academic histories, abilities, and potential for college success.
4. Provide technical assistance to college disability services personnel.
5. Provide information concerning standardized college entrance examinations such as the American College Test (ACT) or the Scholastic Achievement Test (SAT).
6. Provide information on procedures for requesting in-class accommodations.
7. Assist in the evaluation of the appropriateness of career goals by providing opportunities for participation in occupational information groups, vocational assessment, and career exploration programs.
8. Routinely use in-class accommodations similar to those used in postsecondary institutions.
9. Review transcripts yearly to determine if students are enrolled in coursework appropriate for admission to postsecondary programs.

In the area of college and community orientation, Gartin, Rumrill, and Serebreni (1996) suggested the following:

1. Encourage students to link with the postsecondary institution as early as possible through such activities as science fairs, band camps, sports camps, and other special events.
2. Acquaint students with postsecondary campuses by arranging for tours.
3. Prepare students to participate fully in campus life.
4. Teach strategies for accessing community services, such as how to provide for medical needs, banking, shopping.

The family should be included in all of these education components.

Brinckerhoff (1996) categorized the major differences between high school and college requirements under seven basic categories: (1) time in class, (2) class size, (3) time required to prepare for each class, (4) frequency of tests, (5) minimum grades required to remain in school, (6) teaching practices, and (7) amount of freedom allowed the student. The major differences in each of these categories pose significant problems for students with disabilities (and all students) as they make the transition from the secondary to the postsecondary learning environment. He stated that secondary school personnel can help prepare students with disabilities for the challenges of higher education by beginning to replicate some of the demands of postsecondary education while the student is still in high school. Postsecondary providers can help by collaborating with their secondary-level colleagues and by realistically foreshadowing the higher education experience for applicants with disabilities. Parents can assist their sons and daughters by validating their dreams and nurturing their social development and academic growth. The students themselves, however, hold the key to success in higher education and ultimately in their adult lives.

Suggested Instructional Strategies at the Secondary and Postsecondary Levels

A number of strategies or approaches have been suggested to assist youths with disabilities in making the transition from high school to postsecondary education programs. Some of these strategies may be used at the secondary level; others are helpful to teachers, students, and their families as they work with postsecondary institutions.

Secondary Level

Durlak, Rose, and Bursuck (1994) summarized the self-determination skills that a number of researchers had related to students making a successful transition to postsecondary education, including some of the skills described in the preceding section. Those skills included: (1) an awareness of academic and social strength and weaknesses as well as compensatory strategies, (2) the ability to express such an awareness to faculty and staff, (3) an awareness of service needs and appropriate accommodations, and (4) the ability to request information, assistance, and accommodations when appropriate and necessary. They demonstrated that high school students with learning disabilities could be taught these skills by using a training procedure in which the skills were taught systematically. Students received immediate and specific feedback and were given opportunities to practice the skills in both the training setting and the natural environment. Students acquired the skills within two to five instructional trials. Two of the students (out of eight), however, were unable to perform the skills outside the training setting. The authors stressed the importance of intensive practice in describing their disabilities and the enormity and difficulty of generalizing the tasks of telling teachers about their learning disabilities and asking for appropriate accommodations.

Van Reusen, Bos, Schumaker, and Deshler (1994) developed a motivation strategy entitled *The Self-Advocacy Strategy for Education and Transition Planning.* Students may use this strategy when preparing for and participating in any type of education or transition planning conference. The Self-Advocacy Strategy is taught using a modified version of the acquisition and generalization stages that have been developed and expanded as part of the Strategies Intervention Model (Ellis, Deshler, Lenz, Schumaker, & Clark, 1991). The five steps involved in the strategy form the acronym *I PLAN:*

- Inventory—where students identify and list their perceived education and/or transition strengths, areas to improve or learn, goals, needed accommodations, and choices for learning
- Provide your inventory information—which focuses on providing input during the conference
- Listen and respond—which relates to effectively listening to others' statements or questions and responding to them
- Ask questions—which involves asking appropriate questions to gather needed information
- Name your goals—which involves communicating personal goals and ideas on actions to be taken.

VanBiervliet and Parette (1994) advocated for the need for a framework for the development of curriculum for teaching students with and without disabilities about the Americans with Disabilities Act (ADA), and to involve these students as partners in developing their self-determination skills. They described a computer-based interactive program for teaching information access and self-determination skills through a combination of knowledge acquisition and skills development activities. They also recommended careful evaluation of the impact of curriculum materials and the development and evaluation of modules that could be incorporated into the coursework of preservice teachers.

Brinckerhoff (1996) provided a time table for transition planning, beginning with the transition from middle school to high school. The middle school component focuses on preparing for high school success. Although Brinckerhoff's time table focuses on individuals with learning disabilities, we have broadened the focus to include all individuals with disabilities who are planning to transition into postsecondary education:

Freshmen
- Develop an understanding of their overall area of disability.
- Develop an understanding of their own disability.
- Learn about their rights under the law.
- Select courses that will prepare them for college.
- Explore career options.
- Develop greater independence.

Sophomores
- Enroll in college-prep courses, such as Algebra I or Chemistry.
- Work closely with the transition planning team, including the student, family, school, community agencies, employers, and adult service providers.
- Participate in learning strategies instruction.
- Participate in self-determination training.
- Continue to explore career options.

Juniors
- Explore postsecondary education options.
- Evaluate the support services offered by different postsecondary institutions.
- Prepare and register for the PSAT or the PLAN, which are warm-ups for the SAT and ACT, respectively.
- Develop their own personal transition file.
- Begin to narrow postsecondary education options, including visiting campuses and participating in on-campus interviews.

Brinckerhoff's (1996) tasks for seniors include beginning the year with filling out applications and writing college essays. There is a Common Application that is a standard format that can be photocopied and is used by more than 120 colleges nationwide, all of whom have agreed to honor it. In addition, there is a CollegeLink program service that allows applicants to complete a single application on their personal computer that can be forwarded to about 500 institutional subscribers for a fee (Rubenstone & Dalby, 1994). Seniors should also begin to narrow their career exploration process to a preferred area of study for the postsecondary level. This would include becoming involved in internship experiences. The activities would conclude senior year with waiting for the news from colleges, arranging for the important transition planning information to be sent to the selected postsecondary institution, and possibly pursuing other alternatives if the student is not accepted at one of the targeted postsecondary institutions. Refer to Brinckerhoff (1996) for a full version of his time table. Keep in mind that students with disabilities mature at different times and may not become motivated about planning for college or other postsecondary education until late in high school. The time table is ideal and is a guide for you to initiate as many activities as you can, using the suggested time lines and sequence. If students miss planning and preparation activities in the ninth, tenth, and eleventh grades, they should still go through the steps, even if at a more rapid and intensive pace, or be willing to extend their time in school prior to graduation.

Postsecondary Level

Kohler, Rubin, and Rusch (1994) aggregated data on 45 postsecondary education model projects funded by the Office of Special Education Programs and described the outcomes cited by these projects under the following categories: (1) student and family level, such as developing parent support groups and conducting group and individual counseling; (2) program level, including modifying curriculum and developing computer assisted instruction; (3) organizational level, such as developing summer transition programs and developing competencies; and (4) community level, such as conducting community workshops. Barriers mentioned by these programs included lack of student participation, lack of support staff, lack of administrative support, and transportation.

McGuire and Shaw (1987) proposed an extensive list of characteristics that should be considered in examining the services provided for students with disabilities in postsecondary settings. In addition to basic information about the institutional environments and accreditation, the student should gather information on the following areas: specific admission procedures, including characteristics of students with disabilities who have previously been accepted; curricular options, such as reduced course load or course waivers; specific characteristics of the support program, such as program size, extent and availability of services, and number of staff and their expertise; and information about graduation requirements, including minimum number of credits required in different departments.

Brinckerhoff (1996) presented a continuum of postsecondary support services for individuals with learning disabilities (see Table 8.1). This continuum, however, is applicable to all students with disabilities who are accepted into postsecondary institutions. It categorizes support services from institutions meeting minimum requirements under Section 504 to those with data-based services. It can be helpful to the student, family members, and the teacher in helping the student identify the most appropriate postsecondary program.

It is important that individuals with disabilities and their families actually interview postsecondary institutions to identify where each postsecondary institution stands on this continuum. This is best done by carefully reading all of the information sent by the institution and then conducting an on-campus visit and interview of staff, particularly those who will be providing the support services. Richard (1995) suggested a list of questions to ask during college visits. These questions include:

1. What are the regular criteria considered in the application for admission process (ACT/SAT scores, class rank)?
2. Are there special considerations for admission for students who have documented disabilities?
3. Is the student's current diagnosis from high school accepted? Are there guidelines regarding the recency of the test scores used for the current documentation?
4. How many credit hours must be taken to be a full-time student? Are individuals with disabilities permitted to take reduced course loads and still be considered full-time students?

TABLE 8.1   Continuum of Postsecondary LD Support Services

1	2	3	4
Decentralized and Limited Services	*Loosely Coordinated Services*	*Centrally Coordinated Services*	*Data-Based Services*
→ No formal contact person	→ Contact person available	→ Full-time learning disability coordinator	→ Full-time learning disability director
→ Limited services	→ Generic support services available	→ Services often housed in disability student services office	→ Learning disability assistant coordinator
→ Few established policies	→ Peer tutors available to help at-risk students	→ Accommodations provided for testing and coursework	→ Full range of accommodations provided
→ Students dependent on sympathetic faculty	→ Students referred to other on-campus services	→ Established policies on admissions and service delivery	→ Policies and procedures in place
		→ Strong emphasis on student self-advocacy	→ Strong emphasis on student self-advocacy
		→ Peer support groups sometimes available	→ Development of individualized support plans based upon current documentation
		→ Specially trained LD tutors may be available	→ Tutoring in learning strategies available from trained staff and graduate-level interns
		→ Student required to provide current documentation of learning disability	→ Data-based contact records and service use profiles generated for annual report

Source: Resource Guide of Support Services for Students with Learning Disabilities in Connecticut Colleges and Universities by J. M. McGuire and S. F. Shaw (Eds.), 1989 (revised 1996), Storrs, CT: A. J. Pappanikou Center on Special Education and Rehabilitation: A University Affiliated Program, University of Connecticut. Reprinted by permission.

5. Is there an office of student disability services at the school? If so, what are qualifications and size of the staff? What are the student's responsibilities for obtaining services?
6. How willing are faculty members to provide appropriate accommodations?

Resources

Numerous resources on postsecondary education are available for individuals with disabilities, such as the following:

Aune, E., & Ness, J. (1991). *Tools for transition: Preparing students with learning disabilities for postsecondary education.* Circle Pines, MN: American Guidance Service.

Brinckerhoff, L. C., Shaw, S. F., and McGuire, J. M. (1993). *Promoting postsecondary education for students with learning disabilities: A handbook for practitioners.* Austin, TX: Pro-Ed.

Dalke, C. (1991). *Support programs in higher education for students with disabilities: Access for all.* Gaithersburg, MD: Aspen.

DuChossois, G., & Stein, E. (1992). *Choosing the right college: A step-by-step system to aid the student with learning disabilities in selecting the suitable college setting for them.* New York: New York University.

HEATH Resource Center. (1993). *How to choose a college: A guide for the student with a disability.* Washington, DC: American Council on Education.

Kravets, M. & Wax, I. (1991). *The K & W guide to colleges for the learning disabled: A resource book for students, parents, and professionals.* New York: HarperCollins.

Kuperstein, J. S., & Kessler, J. M. (1991). *Building bridges: A guide to making the high school-college transition for students with learning disabilities.* Edison, NJ: Middlesex County College.

Mangrum, C. T., & S. S. Strichart (Eds.). (1995). *Peterson's guide to colleges with programs for students with learning disabilities* (4th ed.). Princeton, NJ: Peterson's Guides.

Michaels, C. A. (Ed.). (1994). *Transition strategies for persons with learning disabilities.* San Diego: Singular.

Rubenstone, S., & Dalby, S. (1994). *College admissions: A crash course for panicked parents.* New York: Macmillan.

Straughn, C. T. (1992). *Lovejoy's college guide for the learning disabled* (3rd ed.). New York: Monarch.

Ticoll, M. (1995). *Inclusion of individuals with disabilities in postsecondary education: A review of the literature.* North York, Ontario, Canada: The Roeher Institute.

University of Kansas Institute for Adult Studies. (1998). *Accommodating adults with disabilities in adult education programs.* Lawrence, KS: Author.

Vogel, S. A. (1993). *Postsecondary decision-making for students with learning disabilities.* Pittsburgh, PA: Learning Disabilities Association of America.

Vogel, S. A., & Adelman, P. B. (Eds.). (1993). *Success for college students with learning disabilities.* New York: Springer-Verlag.

What the Law Requires of Postsecondary Institutions

In 1977, the Department of Health, Education, and Welfare (now the Department of Education) established guidelines for implementing Section 504 of the Rehabilitation Act. Subpart A of the regulations delineated general provisions of the law. It stipulated that an individual with a disability is one who has a "physical or mental impairment which substantially limits one or more major life activities" (Subpart A, 104.3(j)(1)(i)), including learning. The regulations qualify that, in addition to individuals currently manifesting a disability, an individual who has a record of such an impairment or who is regarded as having such a disability is also covered under Section 504. Individuals with disabilities must be afforded "equal opportunity to gain the same result, to gain the same benefit, or to reach the same level of achievement, in the most integrated setting appropriate to the person's needs" (104.4(b)(2)).

Subpart E of the federal regulations for the Rehabilitation Act pertains to postsecondary education. The regulations established that institutions of higher education must modify academic requirements that are discriminatory. Modification may include extending time for completing degree requirements, allowing course substitutions, and adapting the manner in which particular courses are conducted (Section 104.44(a)). Postsecondary institutions are not required to compromise on requirements that are essential to the program or course of instruction or that are directly related to licensing requirements. Institutions of higher education must alter methods of evaluation in order to ensure that test results reflect student achievement rather than areas of disability. Again, institutions are not required to alter content or process that is essential to the evaluation (Section 104.44(c)). Postsecondary institutions must also ensure that students with disabilities do not experience discrimination due to the absence of auxiliary aids. The aids may include taped texts, methods of making orally delivered material available, readers, equipment to aid with manual impairments, or other similar services and actions (Section 104.44(d)). In addition, institutions of higher education may not impose rules that have the effect of limiting the participation of students with disabilities, such as prohibiting tape recording in the classroom (Section 104.44(b)).

Understanding that nonessential methods or criteria may be accommodated without changing the essence of the course is central to understanding the rights to higher education of the student with disabilities. As defined by Section 504 and clarified in the Americans with Disabilities Act, an "otherwise qualified" individual must be able to meet essential program or course requirements when provided reasonable accommodation (*Davis* v. *Southeastern Community College*, 1979). Determination of "otherwise qualified," then, hinges on three considerations: What are program or course requirements? What nonessential methods or criteria can be accommodated without changing the essence of the course or program? and What are the specific abilities and disabilities of the student within this context (Scott, 1991). It should be pointed out, however, that the provision of services is required only if the student informs the institution of a disability and requests services.

Frank and Wade (1993) provided an overview of the responsibilities of post-secondary institutions as a result of current legislation. They stated that the primary goal is that a student with a disability must master the essential education materials or physical skills in question, and not supplant such mastery by academic adjustment or auxiliary aids. The primary decision makers are the student and responsible institutional officials. Students are required to initiate the process through an identification and documentation of the disability and by requesting specific accommodations on a timely basis. Responsible institution officials must then decide on a case-by-case basis whether and how to provide effective accommodations within the context of academic and nonacademic standards, the essential nature of the course of study in question, and the unique abilities of the student.

Information and Documentation Required by Postsecondary Programs

Assisting individuals with disabilities in their transition to postsecondary education has always required organized planning and work with the student and the family. A number of the current innovations in special education that are supported by the IDEA Amendments (1997) offer even more challenges to this transition process. Three innovations, in particular, affect the transition process. First, under the IDEA Amendments of 1997, a district will no longer be obligated to conduct a three-year reevaluation if the IEP team determines that it is unnecessary to do so for eligibility purposes. This may be true for the majority of adolescents in their last years of high school. Second, special educators in many states are moving away from an emphasis on standardized assessments and toward use of curriculum-based assessment. Finally, many states are moving away from specific disability labels and toward the concept of *student in need of special education* or a *noncategorical* label. We are supportive of all of these innovations, but they promise challenges to the smooth transition of adolescents with disabilities into postsecondary education. Just when special education nationally and at the state and local levels is exploring these approaches, we have seen a move toward formal psychological testing for documentation of a given disability on the part of postsecondary institutions. The reason for this documentation is presented in this section.

Kincaid (1997) highlighted the challenges emerging from the divergent directions of special education and postsecondary education in terms of formal testing and labeling. Her recommendation was that the informed family, as part of the student's transition planning, will "know to demand that the district update the youngster's documentation so that it is acceptable in a postsecondary or employment setting" (p. 6).

McGuire, Madaus, Litt, and Ramirez (1996) stated that documentation serves several important purposes. First, it may be used to decide if a student is "otherwise qualified" to meet the technical demands of the institution, in spite of his or her disability, when provided with reasonable accommodations. Second, documentation is essential for determining appropriate academic adjustment and auxiliary aids on a case-by-case basis. Finally, clear and complete documentation is important to help the adult student with a learning disability recognize his or her learning strengths and weaknesses, and to establish clear and realistic goals.

At the conclusion of a comprehensive review of the literature in this area, Scott (1994) made the following recommendations. First, she stated that postsecondary institutions should clearly delineate their essential requirements. This would include institutional policies and procedures, such as those involved with admissions, financial aid, and housing. It would also include determining the essential requirements of academic programs and courses. Second, Scott presented a process for postsecondary institutions for weighing requests for academic adjustments. In this process, she presented four questions: Does the student have a learning disability? Has the student provided adequate documentation? Is the student qualified, in terms of meeting the essential requirements of a task in spite of the disability, when provided reasonable accommodation? and Is the accommodation reasonable?

The Association of Higher Education and Disability (AHEAD) is the main professional group for individuals providing support services for individuals with disabilities at the postsecondary level. They have published guidelines for documentation of a learning disability in adolescents and adults (AHEAD, 1997). The document presents guidelines in four areas: (1) qualifications of the evaluator, (2) recency of documentation, (3) appropriate clinical documentation to substantiate the learning disability, and (4) evidence to establish a rationale supporting the need for accommodations. Although this document relates specifically to those with learning disabilities, it establishes a precedent for evaluating the need for accommodations for students with any disability. This would be particularly helpful for students who received accommodations at the secondary level under Section 504 of the Rehabilitation Act rather than through special education under IDEA. In such cases, adequate documentation of the disability might not exist in the school records.

The AHEAD guidelines indicate that professionals conducting assessments, rendering diagnoses, and making recommendations for appropriate accommodations must be qualified to do so in terms of comprehensive training and direct experience with an adolescent and adult LD population. They consider the following professionals as so qualified, provided they have additional training and experience in the assessment of learning problems in adolescents and adults: clinical or educational psychologists, school psychologists, neuropsychologists, learning disabilities specialists, medical doctors, and other professionals.

According to the guidelines, the provision of all reasonable accommodations and services must be based on assessment of the impact of the student's disabilities on his or her academic performance at a given time in the student's life. AHEAD urges flexibility in accepting documentation, but states that outdated or inadequate documentation may not address the student's current level of functioning or need for accommodations.

The guidelines become much more specific when addressing the substantiation of a learning disability. They state that documentation should validate the need for services based on the individual's current level of functioning in the educational setting. Although an IEP or a 504 Plan can be included as part of a more comprehensive battery, they are not sufficient documentation by themselves. The guidelines state that a comprehensive assessment battery and the resulting diagnostic report should include the following:

1. A diagnostic interview
2. A comprehensive assessment battery that addresses at least the domains of aptitude, academic achievement (in relevant areas such as reading, mathematics, and oral and written language), and information processing
3. A specific diagnosis of LD
4. Standard scores and/or percentiles for all normed measures, including a profile of the student's strengths and weaknesses
5. A diagnostic summary based on the comprehensive evaluation process

It is our interpretation of these guidelines that the emphasis is on standardized assessment instruments. In fact, the document provides a list of commonly used standardized tests in its appendix. The guidelines indicate that other assessment measures such as nonstandard measures and informal assessment procedures or observation may be helpful and may be used in tandem with formal tests.

Finally, in the area of recommendations for accommodations, the AHEAD guidelines state that it is important to recognize that accommodation needs can change over time and are not always identified through the initial diagnostic process. Also, a prior history of accommodation does not, in and of itself, warrant the provision of a similar accommodation. The diagnostic report should include specific recommendations for accommodations as well as an explanation as to when each accommodation is recommended. The evaluator should describe the impact the diagnosed learning disability has on a specific major life activity as well as the degree of significance of this impact. The recommendation should be supported with specific test results or clinical observations.

Clearly, special education and postsecondary institutions are moving in different directions in terms of the documentation needed to provide services to individuals with disabilities. It is imperative that we begin working at the local, state, and national levels to open communication on these issues so that the student is not denied the supports he or she needs, or is required to purchase expensive testing in order to provide new or additional documentation required by a postsecondary institution.

On a positive note, Kincaid (1997) highlighted the assistive technology components of the IDEA Amendments as a possible positive addition. The IEP team is obligated to consider whether the student needs assistive technology services and devices, regardless of the age or disability category, in order to receive an appropriate public education. This may help postsecondary service providers who are often frustrated with the skill level of incoming students with respect to computers and adaptive technology. Other authors (Day & Edwards, 1996; Higgins & Zvi, 1995; Raskind & Higgins, 1998) provided actual examples of the use of assistive technology to support students with disabilities in postsecondary education programs.

Conclusion

This chapter has provided general information on postsecondary education and the participation of individuals with disabilities in this option. It also outlined the skills your students will need in postsecondary programs and some strategies that you can use at the secondary level to assist your students with this important transition. In addition, some strategies were identified for you, the individual, and the family to use in evaluating and accessing postsecondary education options. This chapter also presented information on what Section 504 of the Rehabilitation Act and the Americans with Disabilities Act require of postsecondary education institutions. The final section discussed the information and documentation that many postsecondary institutions are requiring in order to determine eligibility and to provide the needed accommodations to students.

We identified two major issues related to postsecondary education which you and the IEP team need to consider. Key players on this IEP team must be the student and the family. First, Is postsecondary education a transition goal for the student? If so, how will you balance the need for training in individually determined functional skills with preparation in the skills needed to succeed in postsecondary education, particularly at the college or university level? Second, How will you ensure that your student will have the documentation required by the postsecondary institution to determine eligibility and obtain the needed accommodations? There are no quick answers to these questions. We feel that it is imperative, however, that they be asked as part of the transition planning process, which is fully integrated into the IEP process. We also feel that it is critical that you work closely with those individuals and institutions who are providing postsecondary education in your geographic area.

Finally, we would urge that you consider *all* of the postsecondary education options that were presented at the beginning of this chapter. Each of these options provides specific training and experience that can benefit all individuals, including individuals with disabilities. Although much of the literature addresses colleges and universities, junior colleges, and community colleges, private vocational schools and adult education programs also offer a number of programs that may assist your students in meeting their postsecondary education transition goals.

CHAPTER

9 Transition to Adult Independent and Interdependent Living

Be not simply good—be good for something.

—Henry David Thoreau

In Chapter 2, we affirmed the notion that school to adult living transition is not only an outcome-oriented *process* (as stated in the IDEA definition) but also a multidimensional *service delivery system*. Halpern (1994) laid out five outcome goal areas requiring multiple delivery approaches: (1) employment, (2) participation in postsecondary education, (3) maintaining a home (independent living), (4) community involvement, and (5) personal and social relationships. Independent functioning in each of these areas is usually a stated goal, but, realistically, we recognize that none of us is truly independent. Interdependence is necessary and has a positive value in terms of mutually supportive functioning in life. This idea is discussed further in this chapter.

One way of explaining transition from school to adult independent and interdependent living is to describe the major components of independent and interdependent living and then present some of the features of good school and community support systems. The components and features presented in this chapter incorporate Halpern's five areas. They reflect what we believe are current recommended concepts and practices in the transition process and needed service delivery systems. We will focus on all the content areas of transition planning presented in Figure 2.1, with the exception of Employment and Postsecondary Education and Training, since these were covered in other chapters.

Training in Independent and Interdependent Daily Living Skills

The theme of the transition education and services models presented in Chapter 2 is the goal of systematic, quality training in life career and transition skills. It bears repeating here that it is our basic assumption in writing this book that training for community living for every age period and the transition stages between age periods must occur well before transition from school to adult living. This assumption is supported by the Council for Exceptional Children Division on Career Development and Transition (Clark, Carlson, Fisher, Cook, & D'Alonzo, 1991); they concluded that all transition models should contain features that focus on systematic, quality training.

One of the problems with general program models in education is that they typically stop short of describing the instructional procedures that lead to effective implementation of the programs. This frustrating characteristic of models is not solely the failure of their authors, though. Users of a model must adapt the concepts of the general model to their own situations. If a model is too specific, it does not generalize well to other situations. Hence, the development of specific systematic instructional procedures has to occur at the local level. Guidelines from the model's authors or state guidelines can be extremely helpful, but the local ownership is critical.

A systematic approach to training students with disabilities for life demands and life transitions begins with the development of a locally referenced scope and sequence curriculum. This curriculum should address life-centered career competencies and transition skills in community living, social and interpersonal interactions, and employment. The content of the curriculum should stem from the outcomes for education that teachers and parents have determined jointly. This set of outcomes should serve as a basis for developing IEPs. Even with such a set of outcomes, however, unless there is a systematic approach to the generation of annual goals and short-term objectives, a student could end up with a set of objectives that are skewed toward one area, such as academics, vocational outcomes social skills, and leisure.

Most of the existing school transition models call for quality in terms of age-appropriate, integrated, functional, and community-based instruction. The implication here is that instruction should be increasingly functional rather than increasingly academic, but at the same time should be provided in integrated settings. These common features of quality programs come out of the literature on vocational transition programming for students with severe disabilities (McDonnell, Mathot-Buckner, & Ferguson, 1996; Wehman, 1996). There is no intent in this book to deny the value of these features for any student at any level of disability. However, there is a point at which this is a real problem for students classified as having mild disabilities (i.e., learning disabilities, mild behavior disorders, or mild mental retardation). The current instructional options available to this population in high schools are increasingly academic rather than increasingly functional. The one avenue where some functionality exists within general education for some students is in vocational education (Evers & Elksnin, 1998). Where the problem most often occurs is in the areas of daily living skills and personal-social skills. Only so much can be taught through incidental learning in integrated academic classes; the rest must be taught systematically and with direct accountability of outcomes to objectives.

The literature for special education is full of proposals for and support of functional curriculum models (Brolin, 1995a, 1995b; Browning, 1997; Clark, Field, Patton, Brolin, & Sitlington, 1994; Cronin, 1993a, 1993b). What is functional and what is nonfunctional continues to be in the eye of the beholder, however. The student or parent who insists on an academic high school curriculum may view it as highly functional for achieving the goal of participating with peers who are non-disabled or the goal of going on to higher education. It is because of this personal-izing of values, and the goals that emerge from those values, that individual choice in determining what is functional must be honored. The policy implications of this for a high school make it imperative that a high school special education program provide both an option for a regular, integrated course of study with functional content and a functional, life-skills course of study. Each is legitimate for the school to address. Each is worthy of the school's official approval. Persistent attention to outcomes is a feature of any quality program.

Communication Skills and Academic Performance for Independent Living

Reading and writing are communication skills that are essential for success in most academic tasks. Communication and academic skills are both developmental out-comes that are means to an end for goals of further education and training after high school. Attention to academic performance outcome goals is given in Chap-ters 8 and 10. This section presents only the more functional uses in daily living for communication and academic skills.

Communication Skills.   Basic skills of listening and speaking are the founda-tions of people's interactions at home, in the neighborhood, at work, and in the community. For those individuals who have hearing or speech problems, alterna-tive methods of language reception and expression are critical. It is important that transition education includes as much instruction and/or related services as needed for each individual to ensure that he or she can listen and speak satisfacto-rily and independently in as many settings and situations as possible.

If a student is uncomfortable with his or her ability to listen or receive infor-mation in getting and following directions, participating in a social conversation, being a good listener to a friend or family member, or understanding information given by a nurse, attorney, judge, or salesperson, then the student's IEP should include some type of instructional plan to help the student improve. Whether the listening skills are limited because of primary language differences, cultural pat-terns of limited language interaction between adults and children, psychosocial factors, or any other reason, it makes no difference. If a student's present level of performance in listening skills is limited, but he or she has goals and preferences for the future that involves better oral, manual, or augmentative/alternative recep-tive language skills, then there is a transition need for the student to move from one level of communication performance to another.

The same case can be made for speaking, signing, or augmentative/alternative means of expressing information. If you have ever been required to simulate a communication disability by going into a store to purchase an item or trying to get bus or subway information from a stranger in the street, you know that it is not only a frustrating task to communicate, but also a socially stressful situation because of the personal and social reactions to you. One needs to be sensitive to students who stutter, who have limited English proficiency, who have labored and difficult speech due to cerebral palsy, who sign but cannot speak, who use a Speak and Spell device, or those who have any other expressive language problems.

Bashir (1989) stated that language disorders are chronic and can persist across the lifetime of an individual. In addition, the symptoms, manifestations, effects, and severity change over time. Too often, people assume that expressive communication skills are established early or are stabilized by the time a student reaches adolescence. The consequence of that assumption leads students, their families, and professionals to give up on any continuing instruction, therapies, or related services.

Articulation problems in speech are the most common among speech disorders and involve problems with phonology and speech production. It is important to remember that some invisible expressive language problems also exist. Nippold (1993) discussed three important elements of normal language development that may need attention with some adolescents: syntax, semantics, and pragmatics. *Syntax* is the grammatical structure and complexity of language. This element of language can be a problem for students who grew up in a nonstandard English language environment, a non-English speaking environment, or a socioeconomic environment that does not value standard English language structure. *Semantics* involves the meaning of words and sentences as well as the combinations of certain words in special contexts. Examples of semantics are in the various meanings of single words, depending on context and/or inflection of the voice when speaking the word, as well as combinations of words or phrases that have two or more meanings. *Pragmatics* refers to the functional use of both verbal and nonverbal language. This means that using socially appropriate language is important in communication, and sometimes more important than the use of proper syntax and semantics. Pragmatics presents difficulties for many adolescents with learning, behavioral, and communication disorders. These difficulties emerge in job interviews, interacting with salespersons, social interactions with peers, social interactions at work, and in many other life situations.

In planning for communication skill needs for students in the transition planning process, it is important to know as much about these needs as possible. Without knowledge of the difficulties a student has, and how those difficulties contribute to performance in school, interactions with friends and adults, and communication in the community, it is difficult to know whether to write goals that will be delivered via instruction, related services, or both. Assessment of the nature and frequency of communication problems is critical to be able to focus on the real skill problems and determine how best to address them in the IEP.

Academic Skills. Functional academic skills for independent living involve reading, writing, and computation. Just as an inability to read, write, or solve math problems is not an insurmountable handicap for getting and keeping a job, it is not an insurmountable handicap for independent or interdependent living. No one would argue that the more skilled an individual is in functional academics, the more options he or she has in community participation and the more independent he or she can be. Reading street signs, traffic signs, product labels, written instructions, personal notes or letters, public notices, and the like are common adult daily living tasks. Completing forms and writing personal notes or letters are written communication tasks requiring some academic skills in handwriting, spelling, and basic sentence construction. These also are common adult activities, especially in employment and fulfilling the role of a parent. Finally, counting, addition, subtraction, multiplication, division, and use of fractions and decimals are common task demands in managing money, consumer problems, measuring, and job requirements.

One of the most common forms of assistance in an interdependent living relationship is assistance with reading, writing, and math. Parents, siblings, spouses, and sometimes even the children of persons with limited abilities in functional academics provide support for reading, writing, or math tasks. Some individuals can accept this help without loss of self-esteem, but others find accepting help of this kind more difficult. It is important to identify in the IEP transition planning process a student's present level of functioning in functional academics and establish instructional goals for reading, writing, and math on the student's and the family's preferences regarding instructional priorities.

Self-Determination Skills for Independent Living

Self-determination might be defined by high school students as "making our own decisions." Some high school students have developed a mature level of self-determination in making their own choices and acting on those choices, but most students (with or without disabilities) are still at an emerging level of self-determination. Those students are making some choices and decisions, but are still dependent on parents for most major decisions.

Going back to the definition of *self-determination:* Is making one's own decisions all that is involved in self-determination? Although there are a number of formal definitions of self-determination offered by individuals who have a professional interest in self-determination (Field, Martin, Miller, Ward, & Wehmeyer, 1998a), we like the definition and self-determination model of Field and Hoffman (1994). Their definition states that self-determination is "one's ability to define and achieve goals based on a foundation of knowing and valuing oneself" (p. 164). Their model, presented in Figure 9.1, shows how the self-determination process involves affective, cognitive, and behavioral activity by a person, each of which affects the extent of self-determination that that person will achieve. As you can see in the model, there are five major components: (1) know yourself, (2) value yourself, (3) plan, (4) act, and (5) experience outcomes and learn. These involve much more than

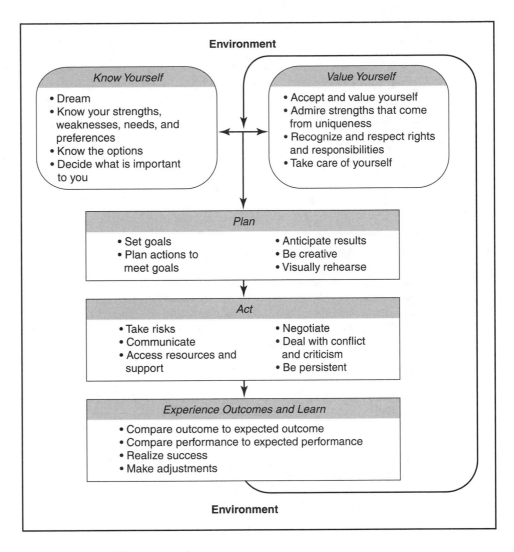

FIGURE 9.1   Self-Determination

Source: From "Development of a Model for Self-Determination" by S. Field and A. Hoffman, 1994, *Career Development for Exceptional Individuals, 17* (2). Copyright 1994 by CDEI. Reprinted by permission.

mere decision making. Field, Hoffman, and Spezia (1998) laid out a set of practical strategies for teachers to use in teaching self-determination skills following this model.

Self-determination skills in an individual are reflected in some of the characteristics of that individual. Using the Field and Hoffman (1994) model of self-determination, one would look for the extent to which a student knows himself or herself, values himself or herself, plans for the future, acts on his or her plans and goals, and experiences the outcomes of the planning and action and learns from that experience. More specifically, Wehmeyer (1997) suggested the following characteristics of self-determined individuals:

- Choice making
- Decision making
- Problem solving
- Goal setting and attainment
- Self-observation skills
- Self-evaluation skills
- Self-reinforcement skills
- Internal locus of control
- Positive attribution of efficacy and outcome expectancy
- Self-awareness
- Self-knowledge

Some individuals inherit an ability to know their own minds and be decisive; many others were taught many of these characteristics. Even someone with a natural ability to solve problems and be internally motivated can improve those abilities with instruction and learn new skills related to self-determination. Learning self-determination skills, then, comes out of learning environments that encourage, nurture, and support self-determination values, thinking, and behavior. Field, Hoffman, and Spezia (1998) stated their belief that schools can and should be encouraging and supportive environments for students in learning self-determination skills. Among these school environmental characteristics, which include both classroom and schoolwide factors, are the following:

- Availability of self-determined role models
- Curriculum variables
- Patterns of response to student behaviors
- Availability of student supports (p. 4)

Self-determination skills are generic, but to be useful, they have to be applied to real problems, interests, preferences, and needs. The transition planning process through the IEP is an ideal way to help students focus their learning of self-determination skills on their own transition planning. Some students may resist planning for the real world after high school because they are very happy with their role as children who do not have to take full responsibility for their food, clothing, or a place to live. Their parents might even provide them with a means of transportation and some spending money. If, at the same time, these same students are enjoying the privileges of adulthood (choosing their friends, choosing life-style activities, determining their own curfews, etc.), it is no surprise to experience some resistance from them to moving out of this phase of life into real independence and personal responsibility. They do not really want to think about that aspect of their futures, especially at ages 15 and 16.

Another type of student who may resist specific planning for life after high school are those who have been sheltered and protected by families and schools. These students have no real information about the possibilities and demands of adulthood nor do they know themselves well enough to know what they want for themselves and whether they have the knowledge and skills to make it in adult life. Some of these students are overly dependent on parents because of parent behavior. Others are dependent because of cultural traditions in the family in regard to ethnic identity and gender roles.

Fortunately, there also are students who are eager to become independent and make choices about vocations, further education and training, type of residence after leaving home, and how they will get involved in the community as citizens, consumers, and participants in leisure and recreation. They find the transition planning process a challenging and enjoyable opportunity. They thrive on assessments of their interests, preferences, and skills that relate to what they see as "real" adult demands as opposed to school or home environment demands.

The perspective of self-determination that we encourage in this book is an understanding that individual students have a variety of backgrounds and influences on them. They are not at the same place as other students in developing self-determination skills simply because they are of a certain age or grade level. Self-determination skills can be taught, but they must be taught with a high degree of individualization, guidance, and support. Students must begin the process of learning and practicing self-determination skills where they are in their own lives. They may or may not be ready for the hard questions that are imposed sometimes in the IEP transition planning process. A careful, thoughtful approach to each student's current and near future goals for himself or herself is necessary.

Interpersonal Relationship Skills for Independent Living

Interpersonal relationship skills as an outcome domain in the Comprehensive Transition Education Model (Figure 2.1) incorporates much of the thinking of the two components of the original School-Based Career Development and Transition Education Model (Clark & Kolstoe, 1990, 1995), which were referred to as *Attitudes, Values, and Habits* and *Human Relationships*. The broader term of *Interpersonal Relationships* necessarily draws on personal values, social attitudes, and interpersonal interactions. We believe the school cannot take full responsibility for these areas because the family's role is critical. Still, for the school to ignore the importance of knowledge and skills in interpersonal relationships seems absurd.

Values, Attitudes, and Habits in Interpersonal Relationships.   People's values are the basis for what they find worthy in other people and in themselves. Values undergird codes of conduct, preferences leading to choices, and ideas leading to decision making. The current calls for reform from both liberal and conservative elements of society send schools different messages. Many school administrators and even some teachers see a problem in the school becoming involved in the process of developing and fostering values, because that raises the question of determining *which* values should be included. Values can be associated with any number of things—money, religious beliefs, race, education, sexuality, length of hair or hemlines, the right to carry a gun, civic responsibility, loyalty to country, work, leisure, and so on. Some of these raise issues that are controversial or sensitive to some students and their families.

In the early days of U.S. education, there was absolutely no problem about teaching moral values in schools. The McGuffey readers explicitly taught reading and moral values in the stories that were included. Over the years, values education became less direct, but schools still persisted in teaching respect for the flag, patriotism and loyalty to country, and, in many areas of the country, certain Christian religious beliefs through school prayer, religious music, and observances of various holidays. The national racial and human rights demonstrations of the 1960s, coupled with the debates over U.S. involvement in the Vietnam war, led the general public and many schools to rethink the school's role in social issues.

Raths, Merrill, and Sidney (1966) offered a workable compromise, though not a solution, to the dilemma of to teach or not to teach values when they suggested in the mid-1960s that educators should not be concerned with the *content* of people's values, but rather with the *process* of valuing. From this viewpoint, the focus changes from thinking about whether to teach students certain value-laden concepts to how to teach students to select, defend, and act on their values. The term *values clarification* became a part of this movement. Advocates of this approach believed that school-age children and youths should be able to know *what* they think or believe, *why* they think or believe in that way, and *how* their actions are related to those beliefs. This approach encourages students to decide for themselves what are positive values and what are not. Obviously, some parents who want their children to adopt specific family values and not make value decisions on their own at school strongly object to this approach.

The values-clarification compromise approach in values education is not completely acceptable to many who believe the school has a responsibility to maintain and preserve historic and traditional moral and social values. We believe that the valuing process is very important in learning self-determination and being able to participate actively in one's own transition planning and education. However, we believe also that the valuing process should not be taught to the exclusion of or apart from certain specific values that are known to be positive and beneficial for individual and group success in life.

Some examples of positive values for all high school students are those suggested by O'Neill and O'Neill (1974) and Popov (1997):

Courage	Conservation	Integrity
Honesty	Health/Fitness	Efficiency
Cooperation	Perseverance	Initiative
Respect	Friendliness	Kindness
Justice	Trust	Loyalty
Hope	Honor	Responsibility

The focus on values thus far has not directly related to attitudes and habits. The reason for this is that values, attitudes, and habits are so interdependent that a rationale for one is a rationale for the other two. Values lead people to assume attitudes or positions that are relatively consistent, which then result in relatively predictable behaviors or habits. For example, if a student values trust and wants others to trust him or her to say or do the right thing, then that student should extend trust to others. Honesty, cooperation, respect, friendliness, kindness (caring), and loyalty are all values that contribute to positive interpersonal relationships in most situations.

Human Relationships.   Historically, schools have not taught human relationships directly. Indirectly, however, they have used classroom discipline, behavior management, and strategies for meeting students' emotional needs through the instructional process. However, these have been taught almost exclusively through rules of behavior and incidental methods rather than through clear-cut, purposeful objectives and procedures. The family has been rightfully viewed as the primary unit responsible for children's basic personal-social development, including interpersonal relationship skills. Carter (1998) presented an eloquent case for better human relationships—what he calls *civility*. In his view, civility is lacking in U.S. society and parents need to respond to the problem. These days of school violence, gang activity, sexual harassment, and sale and use of addictive substances on school property make it imperative for schools to respond in a positive, responsible way with parent and family support.

Aggressive, acting-out behavior is important, whether it is seen among students with disabilities or students without disabilities. The vast majority of students with disabilities do not engage in such extreme, antisocial behavior. However, there are instances of such behavior among students receiving special education services, both as aggressors and victims; thus, the issue cannot be ignored.

Adolescents with disabilities are mostly concerned about peer acceptance, making and keeping a circle of friends, dating, and engaging in the same kinds of social interactions as do most other teenagers. Most all teenagers are concerned about these same things, but there is one major difference between teenagers with and without disabilities that makes interpersonal relationships more difficult. That difference is the social stigma that is attached to being identified or labeled as a person with a disability. Most adolescents with disabilities have far too many memories of emotional pain, social embarrassment, or even anger at the reactions of peers, teachers, counselors, principals, and others toward them. The reactions toward them range from avoidance or outright rejection to poorly concealed curiosity when the disabilities are highly visible. For the more hidden disabilities (deafness, mild mental retardation, learning disabilities, etc.), the reactions may range from disguised rejection to teasing or laughter at situations when their problems in performing various tasks become obvious.

It is commonly accepted that the criteria for acceptance or rejection in social situations are generally classified as pertaining either to personality and social skills or to ability to perform valued skills. Body size, muscular strength, maturational development, and athletic ability also appear to be important to teenagers in sizing someone up for acceptance or rejection into their circle. If this practice is accepted, it is clear that a number of students with disabilities are not going to "make the cut" among their peers without disabilities. If the notion is accepted that instruction, training, and modification of behavior can impact one's manifested personality, social skills, physical appearance, or performance skills, then it is clear that many students need assistance to deal with those aspects of human relationships that affect their acceptance. Such assistance can come from direct instruction (social skills training), modeling (mentors, peer tutors, friendship groups, etc.), skill training (sports, fitness training, recreational skill training, etc.), and related services (school counselor, school social worker, school psychologist, school nurse, physical therapy, occupational therapy, or speech therapy).

Good interpersonal relationship skills affect every area of life. Students in transition from high school to the adult world deserve to have programs and services that will assist them in reaching their potential in this skill area as much as programs and services in academics and vocational training. Quality of life at home, at school, at work, and in neighborhoods and communities is often judged by a general sense of happiness and well-being. These indicators of quality of life are often the result of successful interpersonal relationships. It is no surprise that parents of graduates or dropouts who have been in special education programs frequently rank satisfactory psychosocial adjustment as the number-one problem for their sons or daughters after leaving school.

Some people with disabilities find acceptance in work settings that was missing at school, even though they make no changes in their social behavior. Others, if they continue some of the social behaviors that were typical at school, continue to find social rejection in the workplace. At the extreme, such individuals may even lose their jobs. More people, in fact, lose jobs because of socially related problems than they do for skill deficiencies (Bullis, Nishioka-Evans, Fredericks, & Davis, 1992; Hagner, Rogan, & Murphy, 1992). Elksnin and Elksnin (1998) presented an excellent case for the need to teach occupational social skills for many students, particularly those with disabilities.

Two types of adult service agencies provide various services that can assist individuals with disabilities during the school years or after they leave school: independent living centers and mental health centers. Each is described briefly.

Independent Living Centers.   The whole purpose of independent living centers is to address personal-social adjustment and independent living problems. Counseling, whether peer counseling or professional, is at the heart of the services of agencies like this and continually focuses on learning to take control over one's life—emotionally, socially, occupationally, and functionally at home and in the community. Even the assistance given in transportation, housing, legal problems, interpreting (for the deaf), attendant care, reading, and training in independent living is designed to increase self-confidence and minimize dependence on others. For information on the location of independent living centers,   direct an Internet search through <www.rahul.net/designlink/centers.htm>.

Mental Health Centers.   Two groups that appear to need mental health services more than some other groups classified as having disabilities are those who were classified as students with behavior disorders and students who have mild mental retardation. The latter group is frequently referred to under these circumstances as those with a *dual diagnosis*, because mental health centers generally do not serve persons with mental retardation per se, but rather only those who have some type of severe personal, social, or adjustment difficulty. Community mental health centers or similar agencies offer individual and group counseling to these and other persons in need of assistance in emotional, social, and behavioral problem areas. Some centers use community-based therapeutic activities with the goal of training for functional interpersonal and social skills for home, school, and the community.

Integrated Community Participation Skills for Independent Living

Life skills needed for integrated community participation overlap considerably with communication skills, self-determination skills, independent living skills, employment skills, and leisure and recreation skills. We acknowledge that overlap but separate them for emphasis on certain areas that may be overlooked or ignored otherwise. Inclusive education practices have allowed many students with disabilities to experience integration in the school community in new ways. However, many of the inclusive activities or strategies at school are organized and orchestrated by professionals or peer groups. Preparing students with the skills to integrate themselves without integration programs or advocacy in the adult community is a real challenge.

Just as there are individuals who would prefer not to be integrated with nondisabled peers at school, there are those who will feel the same way about certain settings in the community. Most people, in fact, pick and choose what they want to do in the community based on who they will be doing it with and their abilities. Let us assume, though, that a majority of individuals with disabilities want to be a part of their neighborhoods and community. How can they make that happen? How can you, as an educator, help them make that happen, especially when their choices for certain kinds of participation are very individualized?

One community participation issue is a common one across many different types of disabilities, even though it may play out a little differently for certain types of disabilities. That is the issue of being able to get out into the community. Mobility may be part of the problem for students who are blind or who have physical disabilities affecting movement. It is difficult for these students to have quick and independent access to the community, which may limit their participation in community activities. Training and guidance on obtaining and using mobility strategies for getting around in the community, including assistive technology, is the responsibility of educators or orientation and mobility specialists.

Similarly, students with orientation problems in relation to travel experience limitations in getting where they want to go because of difficulties in knowing where they are and how to reach locations outside their familiar surroundings. This may include students who are blind as well as those who have spatial orientation problems (left-right, north-south, east-west, etc.). Mobility and orientation instruction is not typically taught in general education; therefore, special planning on the IEP may be required for a student to get the specific kinds of instruction and support he or she needs to be able to have the skills and confidence to move out of safe and comfortable surroundings into the community.

Transportation alternatives are related to mobility and accessing the community. Transportation options vary with communities so much that it is difficult to generalize. On the other hand, all students and their parents need to be guided in thinking about the students' future needs in terms of finding, accessing, and using transportation alternatives. Learning to drive, use public transportation, or use carpools may be as important, if not more important, as any employment skill. Having an employment skill without the knowledge or skill to plan for and use transportation options to get to work is meaningless. General issues in available and accessible public transportation and individual issues in having enough money to own a car or use public transportation are common barriers, but one should never fail to give students the opportunity to learn travel and transportation skills so that they are prepared for the future.

Some generic integration opportunities require certain skills, either in accessing the opportunities or in participating in them. Among these are residential alternatives, citizenship alternatives, personal development and fulfillment alternatives, and leisure/recreation alternatives. Since leisure and recreation will be discussed in a later section, we will discuss only the first three of these in this section.

Residential Alternatives.   One of the most discouraging barriers to successful transition for students as they move from school to adult living is the lack of satisfactory or satisfying residential alternatives. Persons with physical disabilities find the inadequacy mostly related to architectural accessibility (see Appendix C for an accessibility checklist). Individuals with mild disabling conditions—such as those with learning disabilities, low vision, or who are hard of hearing—may have more alternatives because of their independent functioning levels. Even so, the high cost of housing makes living away from home prohibitive for many, and so young adults with disabilities often live at home with parents. This is not uncommon even for single young adults who are nondisabled. The practice of living at home or returning home during transition periods among young people decreases some of the negative values attributed by professionals to living at home. Still, the important thing to remember in addressing the issue of residential alternatives is that if there is a need or desire for greater independence in living arrangements, there need to be alternatives.

Residential settings that are most frequently considered as alternatives include the following:

1. Independent living (alone or with a spouse, significant other, or roommates) in a house, mobile home, dormitory, or apartment
2. Supported living (alone or with someone else) in a house, mobile home, or apartment with periodic supervision
3. Living at home with one or both parents or other relatives with minimal to no supervision
4. Group home living with 6 to 10 other residents under minimal but continuous supervision
5. Family care or foster home living with close and continuous supervision

How do young people with disabilities choose their residential settings? Do they really have much choice? Many do not. The vast majority of adults with disabilities can be classified as low-income persons. This poses an immediate barrier to certain kinds of residential alternatives. Because developers are investing in condominiums and other residential options, rental properties are becoming more scarce and expensive. Rental properties that have been especially designed or adapted for architectural accessibility are still more expensive, and many persons with disabilities have to depend on subsidy assistance from the Department of Housing and Urban Development (HUD). Federal rent subsidies, frequently referred to as Section 8 housing subsidies, are available to low-income people whose incomes do not exceed 80 percent of the area average. A tenant typically pays 25 percent of his or her income toward the rent, and the federal government subsidizes the remainder. This has been a major development for adults with disabilities in providing some choice in independent residential living.

In summary, the barriers that exist for providing residential options for adults with disabilities are basically attitudinal, environmental, and socioeconomic. Negative to skeptical attitudes about young persons with disabilities living independently come not only from community neighborhoods, landlords, or apartment managers but also from parents, professionals, and sometimes the individuals with disabilities themselves. Prime concerns usually focus on fears of exploitation, social discrimination, and health and safety. Environmental barriers result from a lack of accessibility to available residential alternatives, lack of accessible transportation, and dangerous or stressful neighborhoods that pose threats to a person's sense of well-being. Socioeconomic barriers include not only exclusive costs for accessing residential options but also the prevention of the development of housing facilities in certain neighborhoods under the fear or expectation of property value loss.

Citizenship Alternatives. Citizenship duties and opportunities stem from three sources: what people must do or must not do under the law, what people are permitted to do under the law, and what people are encouraged to do as good citizens to improve their communities. Adolescents with disabilities probably have some knowledge about what certain laws require citizens to do—such as pay taxes, obey traffic and driving laws, register for marriage licenses, register certain firearms, and the like. They also have some knowledge about certain laws that prohibit citizens from doing certain things—such as assault, murder, robbery, burglary, theft, vandalism, drinking under age, selling or possessing drugs, rape, sexual assault, sexual relations with a minor, driving under the influence of alcohol, breaking curfew, and others. Students are likely to be less informed about what the law permits people to do in terms of their civil rights or how they, as citizens, can contribute to a better community. In all cases, however, students, with and without disabilities, have a greater chance of successful community integration if they are more knowledgeable and skilled in all aspects of community participation. The following knowledge and skill areas should be offered in social studies electives or approved as part of the content of high school graduation requirements for government or civics classes:

- Specific information on laws directly related to good conduct as citizens, including information addressing misconceptions and misinformation the students might have learned from the media, family members, or peers who are not well informed
- Specific information on accessing assistance from law enforcement officers, reporting crimes, what it means to testify in court, and some understanding of penalties that are commonly associated with criminal behavior
- Specific information on civil rights for privacy; freedom of speech; trial by judge versus trial by jury; the right to be represented by counsel; Miranda rights; rights related to nondiscriminatory treatment in relation to race, ethnic background, or disabilities; rights (under the IDEA) upon turning age 18 (or majority age in their state); and the right to vote
- Specific knowledge and skills for obtaining information through accessing public records, public meetings, public services (e.g., libraries, museums, parks and recreation, etc.) and public and private assistance agencies (e.g., legal aid, public health, mental health, Planned Parenthood, and hotlines for suicide, substance abuse, and child abuse)
- Specific information on alternatives for community contributions, including volunteering for organizations and agencies, self-initiated activities for the welfare of the neighborhood and others (e.g., recycling, neighborhood clean-up, etc.), and charitable giving

Personal Development and Fulfillment Alternatives.   Knowledge and skills for personal development and fulfillment are those that relate to being a successful, confident member of the community in those parts of the community where one can engage in personal development and growth activities. Knowing how to access religious group activities, civic organization activities and events, and public agency services as a means of continuing education and personal improvement is important. It is important, first of all, because integrated participation in the community requires some level of knowledge and skill. To be able to join and participate in a community activity, one must have some level of knowledge or skill in order to be accepted. Participation in religious worship, for example, requires some basic knowledge of the nature and purpose of certain rituals, understanding of the personal or social behavior that is expected in a particular synagogue, church, mosque, or meeting place, as well as some expectation of the personal benefits for attending and participating. If a student does not grow up within a family that participates in religious worship, there is no opportunity to learn these things. Or if an individual decides to participate in a different religious group setting, old knowledge or skills might not be sufficient to participate successfully.

Another example of an alternative for personal development in the community is an organization or group that addresses personal problems or concerns. These groups are composed of people who have concerns about their health, weight, addictions (e.g., smoking, alcohol, drugs, gambling, etc.), money management, shyness, fear of public speaking, personal safety, discrimination, or any one of many other problem or concern areas. Will graduates with disabilities be able to access and participate in groups of this type? Will they even know about them? Will they know how to find out when and where they meet and what is expected of them to gain admission? Once admitted to a group, will they have the skills to be able to gain acceptance and maintain themselves in the group?

Integrated community participation is valued by everyone. Where knowledge and skills are the primary keys for young adults to participate in the community independently, educators need to respond by providing appropriate educational experiences. When an individual reaches his or her potential for learning certain participation skills, but still needs supports in the community in order to participate, one needs to respond just as one would for a person who needs support systems for accessing and maintaining employment or residential living. In other words, personal development and fulfillment is no less important as a transition planning and education commitment than employability and life skills.

Health and Fitness for Independent Living

The large amount of information on health and fitness issues today is staggering. It is difficult to pick up any newspaper or magazine or watch television without seeing some article or program on health. Fitness magazines and commercial advertisements for fitness programs, centers, or equipment are numerous also. Concerns for good health (wellness) and fitness are common in adult populations, as are concerns about the cost of healthcare, both preventive care and treatment. Adolescents with or without disabilities typically do not have these concerns. Those students whose disabilities are related to chronic health problems, frequent or extended hospitalizations, persistent pain, or even a terminal illness are exceptions, and undoubtedly think about their current health conditions as well as their futures. We believe it is important that health and fitness be addressed individually in transition planning, and that *all* students have access to physical education and health classes. Knowing how important it may be for many students with disabilities to improve their weight, endurance, flexibility, strength, and stamina, physical education classes are important, both as required and elective credit classes. Health classes are typically offered less frequently, but should be considered as good sources of information on nutrition, common illnesses and how to treat them, preventive measures for diseases, sex education, mental health problems and treatment alternatives, and some of the advantages and disadvantages of medications.

The obvious advantage to more knowledge about good nutrition, rest, and exercise is that individuals can become more self-determined about their physical status. One advantage adolescents do not always recognize in knowing about and following through with health information and fitness is the positive effects on mental health. Exercise has highly beneficial effects in reducing stress, changing self-image, and increasing self-confidence. Consider the example of Paul, who was in a high school self-contained class in Kansas when he started lifting weights and bodybuilding. He was somewhat overweight but not obese. He developed a very muscular body with powerful arms, legs, and broad shoulders and lost his soft, pudgy look. He continued this activity as a young adult in the community at a fitness center and was known as one of the "regulars." He maintained his integrated employment and integrated fitness program in such a way that only a few people knew or remembered that he had ever been in a special education program.

Health and safety concerns naturally overlap with daily living skills in independent living environments (e.g., home security, fire prevention, using toxic chemicals for cleaning in the kitchen or bathrooms, etc.). However, some are health and safety concerns for which some students with disabilities might need instruction, such as the following:

- Preventing colds and other contagious conditions
- Preventing infections
- Preventing sexually transmitted diseases
- Prenatal nutrition and avoidance of tobacco, alcohol, and harmful drugs
- First aid
- Immunizations
- Food handling and storage
- Nutrition
- Healthy sleep patterns
- Personal hygiene
- Substance abuse
- Use of over-the-counter and prescription medications

Independent/Interdependent Daily Living Skills

The need for schools to provide instruction in life skills for students with mild to moderate disabilities is well documented (Brolin, 1993a, 1993b, 1995a, 1995b; Cronin & Patton, 1993a, 1993b; Clark et al., 1994). Still, it is easy to become focused on employment skill training in high school secondary transition programs and forget the importance of direct instruction in daily living or life skills. Keep in mind that the degree to which a person knows about and can perform daily living tasks is directly tied to how independent he or she is. Teachers owe it to their students and their students' families to provide the instruction and learning experiences for students to prepare them to be as independent as possible.

Daily living skills are important as they affect independence, but they also are important for the positive emotional and social supports they provide. There are certain social "penalties" persons with disabilities have to pay if they cannot perform these competencies. Stares, comments by observers, embarrassing interactions, and questions from well-meaning but ignorant persons are typical. Competence in as many skills as possible helps individuals with disabilities present themselves as confident and capable people.

The Life-Centered Career Education curriculum program (Brolin, 1992) specified nine daily living-skill or competency areas:

1. Managing family finances
2. Selecting, managing, and maintaining a home
3. Caring for personal needs
4. Raising children and living as a family
5. Buying and preparing food
6. Buying and caring for clothes
7. Engaging in civic activities
8. Using recreation and leisure
9. Getting around the community (mobility)

This list includes some areas of overlap with several transition competency areas that we have chosen to discuss separately (e.g., engaging in civic activities, using recreation and leisure, and, to some extent, caring for personal needs). The overlap or the different ways of organizing the content of life skills should not be important. What is important is that there is a great deal of agreement on what the basic life skills needed for independence are. The nine broad competency areas, and the numerous subcompetencies that come under each of them, reflect not only a logical, commonsense view of what daily living skills are critical but they also represent validated research results, demonstrating agreement on them.

Most life skills associated with independent living are rarely accomplished solely by an individual. In today's society, no one is truly independent of others and completely self-reliant. It is for that reason that we include the concept of *interdependent living*. Husbands and wives, couples living together, or roommates or housemates typically divide up responsibilities and depend on one another for certain tasks to be completed. People also yield their independence when they employ someone to do what they do not know how to do, do not have time to do, or are unable to do (e.g., repair their cars, prepare their income tax returns, dry clean their clothes, care for their sick pets, etc.). These are examples of interdependence. Interdependence has its own set of skills and subskills, and needs to be considered when looking at the transition planning and instruction needs of students with disabilities.

An example of skills needed for interdependent living is caring for personal needs. One of the most private and independent set of skills that most independent functioning people engage in is personal hygiene. The vast majority of people brush their own teeth, toilet themselves, shampoo their own hair, and perform other personal hygiene tasks. If a person is unable to perform these tasks because of a physical disability, someone else must do them. Individuals who grow up with such disabilities typically had parents or siblings to perform these tasks for them from the beginning, and there was little to learn about how these tasks were done and few or no personal adjustments to make in terms of embarrassment or self-esteem. These same individuals moving into independent living situations, or those who acquire a physical disability later in life, have a lot to learn about how to employ, supervise, and evaluate a personal care attendant. Knowledge and skills are needed in finding resource agencies with approved personal care attendants, interviewing and selecting an attendant, dealing with the psychological aspects of personal identity and vulnerability, and managing the payment, supervision, and evaluation roles as an employer.

Another example of interdependent living skills is child rearing and living as a family. Of all life skills, child rearing and living as a family must be among the most interdependent. Mutual reliance on one another is at the core of having and raising children. Knowledge and skills in making decisions about division of responsibilities, finding and using family resources, supporting and assisting the efforts of others, dealing with conflicts and disagreements, knowing when demands are beyond one's ability, and intimate interpersonal relationships are only a few of the subcompetencies under this general competency area. IEP teams must remember adult-oriented outcomes such as these when considering individual transition service needs of school-age students.

Leisure and Recreation Skills in Independent Living

Barriers to leisure alternatives parallel those of residential options in spite of the recent trends in the United States for leisure and recreational pursuits and the popularization of fitness (Maynard & Chadderdon, n.d.). Leisure alternatives, like residential alternatives, are limited primarily by attitudes. Attitudinal barriers to leisure-time participation, for example, are often reflected in a person's feelings of fear and lack of confidence in skills for participation in community activities. Also, both public and commercial recreational facility managers may have some degree of uneasiness about persons with disabling conditions using the same facilities as their clientele who are nondisabled. Sadly, this even includes church memberships, community social groups, and political action groups. Environmentally, there are still numerous barriers preventing participation because of a lack of accessibility to theaters, public buildings, auditoriums, churches, or natural sites such as parks, plazas, and gardens. This is despite the provisions of Americans with Disabilities Act of 1990 (PL 101-336). Reasonable accommodation, undue hardship, and exemption of historical sites are provisions of this law that maintain some recreation and leisure participation barriers. Socioeconomic factors limit experiences primarily because of the high cost of participation in so many of the more popular leisure-time alternatives. Again, the low-income status of the vast majority of persons with disabilities restricts their choices considerably.

Planning and providing for leisure-time alternatives should focus on normalized settings and nonspecialized leisure activity options for persons with mild to moderately severe disabilities. To accomplish this, however, the emphasis has to be on preparation of individuals with disabilities to be able to use and enjoy the leisure and recreational alternatives that are available. Cain and Taber (1987) suggested that some educational and rehabilitation systems and disability advocacy groups have contributed to the leisure problems of persons with disabilities. Cain and Taber believe they have done this by attempting to duplicate for students with disabilities some of the after-school and after-work activities that are available to those who are nondisabled. Although these programs obviously provide recreational or leisure experiences, they may not be the best preparation for persons with disabilities for participation in leisure activities in a community of people without disabilities.

Transition services in the area of recreation and leisure alternatives are the responsibility of adult service agencies and the community. Training for recreation and leisure skills is the responsibility of parents, public schools, postsecondary education programs, advocacy groups, and adult service agencies. Availability and accessibility to both services and the skills for using them should be planned with the assumption that recreation and leisure activities usually are more an expression of life-style and personality than work, and that one's life-style has consequences for any person's development and well-being.

Systematic Planning

Systematic planning for movement of youths with disabilities from school to adult community alternatives can and should occur at the state, local, and individual levels. Ideally, systematic planning should begin with a state plan. This plan may be based on a legislative mandate for transition services, a legislative mandate for transition planning, or a voluntary planning policy in the form of an interagency agreement or a "memorandum of understanding".

The "Turning 22" Law in Massachusetts was the first and most comprehensive transition legislation to be enacted. It used the basic concepts of PL 94-142 related to free and appropriate education and applied those concepts to free and appropriate services beyond age 22. It mandated an individual transition plan and authorized state funding for services. This legislation became a model for other states, but it has been difficult to enact legislation as far reaching as that in Massachusetts. Most states have chosen to follow federal law.

A multiagency policy or interagency agreement between senders (schools) and receivers (adult service agencies) can also provide a basis for statewide planning. The agencies ordinarily involved in these agreements are the state department of education (including the divisions of special and vocational education), the state division of vocational rehabilitation, and other specific state agencies responsible for services to persons with disabilities, such as the division of vocational rehabilitation for the blind, state mental health and mental retardation services, developmental disabilities services, social welfare, and, sometimes, state corrections services. These policy-planning documents or planning agreements specify who does what, when, and how. Most states have interagency agreements or "memoranda of understanding" on transition in place, but there is little evidence to suggest that the agreements are effective or that they carry through into the provision of cooperative services at the local level (Wehman, Kregel, & Seyfarth, 1985). Overlapping areas from law or regulatory authority have to be addressed, and assurances on "turf" issues have to be included for both the state and local levels before local impact can be felt.

Even if there is no state-level planning, senders and receivers at the local level can join together in planning how to make transition work better for its youth and adult population with disabilities. A written local interagency agreement or plan can be developed. Frequently, this is much less formalized than planning at the state level. These participants know one another, and planning can come out of daily operations of transition skill training, referral for individual planning, and service delivery. Wehman, Moon, Everson, Wood, and Barcus (1988) proposed a model for local interagency planning that is easy to use or adapt. Blalock (1996) and Halpern and Nelson (1990) also suggested very practical procedures for local collaboration teams.

Wehman and Hill (1985) believed that even an excellent secondary program cannot help youth with disabilities unless specific, formalized planning and coordination take place. They warned against focusing exclusively on the transition process while ignoring the quality of transition-skills preparation offered by the schools, and leaving unplanned the development of a range of community adjustment alternatives offered by community agencies. According to Wehman and Hill, a clear plan is vital at the local level and should be based on formal individual transition plans. Wehman (1995, 1998) provided guidelines and numerous examples of individual transition planning.

The transition process of an individual student with disabilities leaving school and entering the community can take place without benefit of a state or local transition plan. The odds against that individual making it these days without an individual transition plan as a component of his or her IEP and a support team are great, however. There is sufficient evidence from experience with Individual Educational Plans to recognize that having transition goals and objectives on the IEP does not guarantee successful outcomes. On the other hand, not having those goals and objectives is not only noncompliance with the law but is flouting the spirit and logic of purposeful intervention.

Communication with Students and Their Families

In contrast to community independent living centers' philosophy, which focuses on direct input from an adult consumer, school transition programs must include parents or guardians in the planning process and, in effect, consider them, as well as the students, to be "consumers" in transition. The informed cooperation and collaboration of parents or guardians in the transition process is considered a very important component. Informed parents and guardians are those who have been provided or have sought and found information that they needed.

Parent and guardian input on IEPs is a starting point for determining their concerns for the future. Sometimes these concerns are justifiable, and the IEPs should reflect goals that speak to these concerns. At other times, the concerns expressed by parents or guardians are viewed as unrealistic or even inappropriate by professionals. When this occurs, it provides a natural opportunity for dialogue. A common example of this is when a parent or guardian insists that his or her child should be placed in regular academic classes so that graduation requirements can be met and college admission requirements met. If the student is a nonreader and functioning in the mild to moderate levels of adaptive behavior, the parent or guardian is clearly uninformed and needs information based on valid assessment data and college admission criteria.

Students are expressly encouraged to be participants in their own transition planning in the regulations for the IDEA (PL 105-17). It makes good instructional sense to include adolescents in their school program planning and long-range goal setting. Students may present different preferences than their parents in joint planning, but even that is preferable as a starting point for effective planning than only a one-sided perspective.

It is highly desirable to train parents and guardians, along with their sons and daughters, to be effective advocates and self-advocates for and consumers of services. Some activities toward this end include the following:

1. Orient students and families to local and regional agencies that provide post-secondary services.
2. Familiarize students and families with the specific responsibilities of the public schools (regular, special, and vocational education), vocational rehabilitation, and adult service programs.
3. Prepare students and families to work with various agencies in the transition process.
4. Train students in self-advocacy, beginning with participating actively in their own IEP meetings.

Much of the literature on transition programming for youths and young adults with disabilities stems from research and demonstration programs for those with severe handicapping conditions. Professionals working with families of students who have mild to moderate disabilities may experience a different kind of response than professionals working with more severe disabilities. Proportionately, it is expected that more parents and guardians of students classified as mildly handicapped will be at a lower educational and socioeconomic level. Families that fit this description frequently bring with them a history of negative experiences with schools and community agencies, a limited amount of information about the alternatives for successful adjustment in the community, and diverse views about middle-class values for work and social acceptance.

Expecting all low socioeconomic, uneducated students and their families to seek out information or to choose to be active participants in the transition process is unrealistic. On the other hand, failure to try to involve and inform them in a positive way is unprofessional and counterproductive. To assume that students and families do not care or are incapable of positive contributions simply because they do not play by the "rules" is unethical for someone in a helping profession. To assume that it is better to leave the student or family out of the process because of those same reasons is counterproductive because they can passively or actively undermine the efforts of professionals when they sense or actually experience that they are being excluded from the process.

It is not defensible in this multicultural, multilingual society for teachers or adult service agency providers to impose only one dominant culture's ideas or values on any group. One must take the initiative in collaboration with parents in planning and executing transition planning and programming, expecting in this process to gain insight into the concerns, fears, and limitations perceived by culturally different or impoverished families. Transition planning must reflect a culturally and economically feasible set of life and work alternatives, and professionals rarely can do this independent of families and individuals involved.

The professional's role in encouraging self-determination and self-advocacy for students and parents might include some of the following:

- Realize that all people have the right to make choices.
- Get to know the students and parents as individuals.
- Ask questions and listen carefully to be sure that you understand not only what the student and family are saying but also what they are feeling.
- Encourage students to set goals for themselves.
- Propose options for decision making rather than giving personal opinions.

Communication between Schools and Service Providers

It may seem that communication that deals with conflicting policy goals between schools and adult service delivery agencies is not the best place to start. This is probably an accurate assessment of the situation for the local level, but it may not be for the state and federal levels. How can there be any hope for consistent, systematic interagency cooperation at the local level, however, without some consistent, systematic policy at the state and federal levels? Many federal and state policies work at cross-purposes and create serious disincentives to appropriate service delivery, employment, and community integration. It is no wonder that one frequently sees at the local level either nothing happening at all in the way of collaborative effort or a service system that is piecemeal, fragmented, and characterized by gaps in or duplication of services.

Still, on the basis of demonstrated working relationships at the local level, even without state or federal support for doing so, communication between transition team participants can happen. When it does, it is usually characterized by a focus on the needs of an individual or individuals and a sharing of information about those needs and the service alternatives available or needed.

Those who work best under informal arrangements find ways to communicate regularly through telephone calls, drop-in visits, sharing information from their respective discipline newsletters or journals, and follow-up contacts to evaluate actions taken. Those who need more of these kinds of activities find regular, planned, goal-oriented staff meetings helpful to keep momentum in the dialogue and collaborative efforts. The more formal, regular schedule approach has the advantages of facilitating more systematic information exchange between transition personnel and being a mechanism for staff development activities, program evaluation, and joint planning for the future.

There is another form of communication between and among service providers at the local level that is much more personal than the local interagency agreement approach and much more systematic than the informal approach. The emergence of the local community transition council as a vehicle for targeting ways and means of improving transition services for a community is an exciting step forward. The interaction a local council provides for school personnel, adult service professionals, parents, and all other stakeholders in the transition process is valuable. The notion of pooling financial resources, energy, and commitment to work together toward mutually determined goals is catching on and the rapid development of local councils across the county is a welcome sign of collaboration and improved communication. School personnel interested in initiating a community transition council should refer to publications by Blalock (1996), Blalock and Benz (1999), Halpern, Lindstrom, Benz, and Nelson (1990), Everson and McNulty (1992), and Johnson, Bruininks, and Thurlow (1987).

Resources

Some of the references cited here will give you much additional information on independent and interdependent living issues and strategies.

Books and Journals

Blalock, G. (1996). Community transition teams as the foundation for transition for youth with learning disabilities. *Journal of Learning Disabilities, 29,* 148–159.

Blalock, G., & Benz, M. R. (1999). *Using community transition teams to improve transition services.* Austin, TX: Pro-Ed.

Cartledge, G. (1996). *Cultural diversity and social skills instruction.* Champaign, IL: Research Press.

Cronin, M. E. (1996). Life skills curricula for students with learning disabilities: A review of the literature. *Journal of Learning Disabilities, 29,* 53–68.

Cronin, M. E., & Patton, J. R. (1993). *Life skills instruction for all students with special needs: A practical guide for integrating real-life content into the curriculum.* Austin, TX: Pro-Ed.

Elksnin, N., & Elksnin, L. K. (1998). *Teaching occupational social skills.* Austin, TX: Pro-Ed.

Field, S., Hoffman, A., & Spezia, S. (1998). *Self-determination strategies for adolescents in transition.* Austin, TX: Pro-Ed.

Field, S., Martin, J., Miller, R., Ward, M., & Wehmeyer, M. (1998). *A practical guide for teaching self-determination.* Reston, VA: Council for Exceptional Children.

Halpern, A. S. (1994). The transition of youth with disabilities to adult life: A position statement of the Division on Career Development and Transition. *Career Development for Exceptional Individuals, 17,* 115–124.

Knapczyk, D., & Rodes, P. G. (1996). *Teaching social competence: A practical approach for improving social skills in students at-risk.* Pacific Grove, CA: Brooks/Cole.

Patton, J. R., Cronin, M. E., & Wood, S. (1999). *Infusing real-life topics into existing curricula: Recommended procedures and instructional examples for the elementary, middle and high school levels.* Austin, TX: Pro-Ed.

Patton, J. R., & Dunn, C. (1998). *Transition from school to adulthood: Basic concepts and recommended practices.* Austin, TX: Pro-Ed.

Powers, L. E., Singer, G. H. S., & Sowers, J. (1996). *On the road to autonomy: Promoting self-competence in children and youth with disabilities.* Baltimore: Paul H. Brookes.

Sands, D. J., & Wehmeyer, M. L. (1996). *Self-determination across the life span: Independence and choice for people with disabilities.* Baltimore: Paul H. Brookes.

Sitlington, P. L. (1996). Transition to living: The neglected component of transition programming for individuals with learning disabilities. *Journal of Learning Disabilities, 29,* 31–39, 52.

Curriculum Materials

Brolin, D. E. (1992). *Life centered career education (LCCE) program.* Reston, VA: Council for Exceptional Children.

Field, S., & Hoffman, A. (1996). *Steps to self-determination: A curriculum to help adolescents learn to achieve their goals.* Austin, TX: Pro-Ed.

Halpern, A. S., Herr, C. M., Wolf, N. K., Doren, B., Johnson, M. D., & Lawson, J. D. (1997). *Next S.T.E.P.: Student transition and education planning.* Austin, TX: Pro-Ed.

Hazel, J. S., Schumaker, J. B., Sherman, J. A., & Sheldon, J. (1995). *ASSET: A social skills program for adolescents.* Champaign, IL: Research Press.

Martin, J. E., Marshall, L., Maxson, L., & Jerman, P. (1996). *Choicemaker self-determination curriculum.* Longmont, CA: Sopris West.

Montague, M., & Lund, K. A. (1991). *Job-related social skills.* Ann Arbor, MI: Exceptional Innovations.

Schumaker, J. B., Hazel, J. S., & Pederson, C. S. (1988). *Social skills for daily living.* Circle Pines, MN: American Guidance Service.

Waksman, S., & Waksman, D. D. (1998). *Waksman social skills curriculum.* Austin, TX: Pro-Ed.

Walker, H. M., Todis, B., Holmes, D., & Horton, G. (1988). *ACCESS Program: Adolescent curriculum for communication and effective social skills.* Austin, TX: Pro-Ed.

Generic Community Services

Thus far, most references to support for independent and interdependent living have been to school services and programs. Generic community support services are also critical in successful transitions from school to adult living. Full access to community resources is absolutely necessary for anyone to approach full citizenship. Housing has already been discussed because it is one of the most basic needs. Other generic services that persons with disabilities need include transportation, legal services, medical services, financial guidance, and mental health services.

Transportation

Transportation systems have had to accommodate the demand for mobility in the United States. Large cities have developed their public transportation systems with taxis, buses, trains, and subways. Many smaller cities and more rural areas have used privately owned vehicles as the primary transportation source. Available and accessible transportation for adults with disabilities becomes, then, both a practical necessity and a symbol of independence. For many persons with disabilities, it is the key to independent living in the sense that without transportation to educational, vocational, cultural, recreational, and commercial opportunities, one might as well live in an institutionalized environment where everything is provided under one roof. Symbolically, transportation sustains the philosophy of independent living and sense of control in life as it makes persons with disabilities feel that they have access to the same resources at the same price at which they are available to everyone else. The reality, however, is that transportation is not available for many persons with physical disabilities, and the complexity or safety factors may inhibit many who have emotional or intellectual disabilities.

Advocacy for better transportation systems by consumers who are disabled, families, advocacy groups, adult service agencies, and schools will eventually result in improvements. Until then, individual arrangements have to be made using creative approaches that provide dependable, affordable transportation, such as car pools, volunteers, bicycles, negotiated discounts with taxi companies, and subsidies from the city or county. School and adult service agency personnel need to elicit the collaboration of community leaders and employers in the transportation field to address local, long-term transportation problems that affect the total population of persons who are disabled, elderly, and low-income families, in addition to their assistance in individual arrangements.

Legal Services

Legal problems are difficult to sort out for most people. Adults with disabilities find themselves needing assistance more than ever now that as a group they are more involved in the process of independent living. They experience rental or lease agreement disputes; civil rights violations; exploitation by high-pressure salespersons, repair and service workers, and personal care attendants; sexual harassment;

divorce proceedings; writing wills; filing small-claims suits; and sometimes felonies and misdemeanors. People with disabilities, like everyone else, sometimes need legal assistance. One man who had epilepsy was evicted from a low-cost housing apartment complex (HUD Section 8 housing) for doing some computer work in his apartment. This computer work at home violated Section 8 regulations that specify that living facilities cannot be used for self-employment activities. Legal assistance over an extended period of time finally resulted in an interpretation in his favor. Without it, he was extremely vulnerable and might have lost his source of income or his residence.

There is a void in the private sector for legal advocacy in cases involving persons with disabilities. The American Bar Association went as far as to create a Commission on the Mentally Disabled in the 1970s. This grew into several separate efforts, including publication of what is now called the *Mental and Physical Disability Law Reporter,* the establishment of a legislative reform section of the American Bar Association to assist in drafting model legislation, and the funding of various demonstration advocacy projects. Still, not enough individual case advocacy and assistance is available for people with disabilities.

Medical Services

Health care and medical services are needed by everyone these days, but adults with disabilities have proportionately more need. Chronic health problems, poor nutrition, weight and stress control, physical fitness needs, susceptibility to respiratory infections, dental problems, vision and hearing problems, and preventive medicine needs occur with greater frequency among persons with disabilities. These needs interfere with daily living routines and affect quality of life by adding to existing problems. The availability and accessibility of a variety of kinds of health services to address these needs cannot be taken for granted. Without medical insurance, a Social and Rehabilitation Services card, or Medicaid, access to hospitalization or medical care is routinely denied. Lack of transportation and little or no information or knowledge about health care needs can contribute to inaccessibility. The difficulties in negotiating complex managed health care programs is an increasingly difficult task for people with disabilities.

In short, the transition from the available and accessible services of school nurses, physical therapists, occupational therapists, and physicians' consultations to the maze of adult medical and health care services can be difficult for young adults with disabilities and their families. Training in self-directed care and information on routine medical services, emergency medical services, physical and other therapies, preventive medicine, nutrition, and weight and stress control needs to be available. For those adults with disabilities who are trying to live independently but who find it difficult to cope with the health care system, a client-management system may need to be instituted to assist them in finding and using community health care resources.

Financial Guidance

Somewhat related to legal questions and concerns is information about consumer issues. Not all financial problems or decisions require an attorney, however; the needs that are highlighted here include the following:

- Assistance in financial planning for a limited, and sometimes fixed, income
- Assistance in obtaining financial guidance for planning major purchases, such as homes, lift vans, adapted automobiles, home or apartment modifications, wheelchairs, electronic devices, and computers
- Guidance in obtaining and retaining entitlements from state and private agencies
- Assistance in money management in general consumer decisions, credit buying, budgeting, and investment of inheritance or trust funds

Mental Health Services

Mental health services should provide an array of options for adults with disabilities to help them in their adjustments to their disabilities, coping with personal and social barriers to daily living and employment, concerns with sexuality, dealing with stress, coping with death or separation from family members, or intensive therapeutic interventions for severe psychological or behavioral disorders. These service options can be provided individually, in groups, or by both means. They can be provided professionally through mental health centers, psychiatric services in hospitals, and individual therapists, or by nonlicensed personnel in postsecondary training programs, independent living centers, religious organizations, vocational rehabilitation services, and various adult service systems.

The availability and accessibility of mental health services to families of persons with disabilities is equally important when their lives are closely involved. Spouses, children, parents, and siblings have many personal and emotional issues to face as they support and advocate for their family members who have disabilities. Many parents of young adults have to adjust to some harsh realities of inadequate adult services after having become accustomed to a wide variety of services from schools. Feelings of anger, frustration, disappointment, confusion, and uncertainty are common, and parents need to have some support for dealing with their concerns.

Conclusion

We hope it is clear to you by now that the transition process for students with disabilities as they prepare at school for adult life and then move into adult roles is complex. The student needs to be involved and self-determined. Families need to be involved and supportive, letting go when appropriate. Schools need to take the transition services mandate seriously and look at adult-oriented outcomes in the transition planning process, making instruction, related services, and transition programs available to students. Communities need to be involved and supportive, with community-based support systems in place for students who leave school.

The outcomes of the transition process from school to adult living for individuals with disabilities depend largely on the effectiveness of all the stakeholders and participants in the process. There is no doubt that good programs and services in schools and in the community can contribute to positive outcomes. On the other hand, programs and services may be available and accessible in school and in the community and the individuals and/or their families do not take advantage of the programs. As a transition educator, you must assume from the beginning that your students and their families want good outcomes. If they appear to be passive or even reluctant to be involved, it could be a lack of trust in schools and community agencies, a lack of information about predictable outcomes without planning and intervention in many areas, or a lack of knowledge and skill in doing what needs to be done. This chapter presented some of the information that all participants in the transition process need to know and some of the implications for how to apply that information to successful transition efforts.

10 Instructional Strategies

MARY E. CRONIN
University of New Orleans

This chapter overviews instructional strategies that will assist you in teaching students the needed skills for transition to their next subsequent environment. The topics covered include integration of the transition goals in the student's IEP, teaching self-determination skills, and teaching in inclusive settings. A resource list is also provided.

Integrating Transition Goals and the IEP

The Individual Educational Plan (IEP) is the guiding force when anticipating the course for a student's future. Wehman (1995) identified a sound school program, a written plan, and realistic options for students and their families to choose as the three essential elements for effective transition. In addition to these elements, much has been written about the necessity of the student's active involvement in planning his or her future (Everson, 1993, 1996; Wehman, 1995, 1998; Wehmeyer & Lawrence, 1995; Wehmeyer & Ward, 1993).

In preparation for the development of an IEP with a focus on the future transitional needs of students, many steps must be taken to ensure the creation of a quality plan. The following concepts are crucial to making certain that every aspect of transition planning is addressed in respect to the student's eventual postschool outcome. These steps are based on the work of Everson (1993, 1996), Mount and Zwernik (1988), O'Brien (1987), Wehman (1995, 1998), Wehmeyer and Lawrence (1995), and Wehmeyer and Ward (1993).

1. *Person-centered planning session(s).* Person-centered planning (PCP) models and approaches were discussed in Chapter 5. Unquestionably, students with moderate to severe disabilities or multiple transition service needs benefit most from PCP. The extended time required for most PCP sessions raises the issue of efficiency planning for the large number of students in the mild to moderate disability group. The concept of PCP, though, can be implemented in a variety of forms. PCP strategies can be used in one-on-one interviews with the student, family members, or other stakeholders. Keep in mind that a PCP session can involve one or more people. These sessions are comprised of individuals who provide a support system and who are significant to the student, such as the student's parents, siblings, extended family, current and past teachers, adult providers, friends, and so on. Topics discussed include the likes, dislikes, and fears of the students, in addition to the student's visions and dreams of his or her future. These discussions could all happen in one formal PCP session or in a number of formal or informal sessions over time. No matter how long it takes, PCP is central to assisting the student in planning his or her future and developing an appropriate IEP.

2. *Responsibilities of the stakeholders.*   By agreeing to assist the person with a disability in planning his or her future, a stakeholder also shares some responsibility in assisting the student in investigating or carrying out steps that bring the student closer to his or her goals. This could take the form of making calls and inquiries regarding services available, writing letters of support or recommendations to work-training sites or postsecondary education training sites, assisting in problem-solving transportation barriers, or any other such assistance.

3. *Student-led meetings.*   One of the most powerful steps toward assisting students in planning their futures is to train them in leading their own IEP meeting. This begins with watching a real or mock student-led IEP meeting, then roleplaying in the classroom. Students need to participate at a more substantive level than presiding over their IEP meetings, however. They need to concentrate by advocating for themselves through a clear presentation of their needs, preferences, and interests; some proposed goals for themselves; and some requests for specific programs and services. Knowledge to be able to do this can come from brainstorming ideas or scenarios of the future; reading materials on various living, working, and postsecondary situations; interviewing adults about their jobs and living situations; talking to former students; observing existing school programs and services; observing individuals in various jobs and work situations; and exploring various postsecondary educational options.

4. *Integrating transition goals into the overall goals of the IEP.*   This is a significant step in the development of an IEP. A link needs to be made from the transition goals to identification of what skills and knowledge the student needs to be successful in achieving these goals and what skills and knowledge he or she currently possesses. The goals and benchmarks on the IEP therefore need to reflect programming to meet those gaps.

Teaching Self-Determination

In our opinion, the best current resource for information on teaching self-determination is *A Practical Guide for Teaching Self-Determination* (Field, Martin, Miller, Ward, & Wehmeyer, 1998a). This publication is one that every middle school and secondary school teacher or transition specialist should own and have available at all times. It is, as the title indicates, a practical guide that shares the ideas of a collection of authors who have had a significant impact on the development of current self-determination models, assessment procedures, and instructional materials for use with students both with and without disabilities.

Self-determination was listed and described as an important component of transition assessment and planning for transition in previous sections of this book. Self-determination, as one aspect of human behavior, is one of many learned behaviors. Parents and significant others in children's lives begin very early in teaching certain aspects of self-determined behavior. Some of the teaching is a result of conscious and unconscious modeling. Some results from natural learning that comes out of both structured and unstructured environmental conditions. Some results from direct instruction. We believe that schools have a role in teaching self-determination knowledge and skills as well as collaborating with families to work toward positive self-determined behavior.

Field and colleagues (1998a, p. 3) described some characteristics of self-determined people. The characteristics they included are as follows:

- Awareness of personal preferences, interests, strengths, and limitations
- Ability to differentiate between wants and needs
- Ability to make choices based on preferences, interests, wants, and needs
- Ability to consider multiple options and to anticipate consequences for decisions
- Ability to initiate and take action when needed
- Ability to evaluate decisions based on the outcomes of previous decisions and to revise future decisions accordingly
- Ability to set and work toward goals
- Problem-solving skills
- A striving for independence while recognizing interdependence with others
- Self-advocacy skills
- Ability to self-regulate behavior
- Self-evaluation skills
- Independent performance and adjustment skills
- Persistence
- Ability to use communication skills such as negotiation, compromise, and persuasion to reach goals
- Ability to assume responsibility for actions and decisions
- Self-confidence
- Pride
- Creativity

This comprehensive list sets a very sophisticated level of self-determination for any person. Nevertheless, the elements are important to keep in mind, remembering that students with disabilities in public schools range cognitively from those who are highly intellectually gifted or creative to those who are at significant levels of intellectual impairment. Your role as an educator is to help each student reach his or her highest level of self-determined behavior. Like families, professionals can also model self-determined behavior, provide environmental structure and opportunities for learning, and provide direct instructional interventions.

Cultural Diversity as an Influence in Teaching Self-Determination

If you are going to commit to teaching self-determination knowledge and skills, you need to consider some issues related to that commitment. The first of these is a consideration of the influence of cultural diversity on self-determination in a person with disabilities. Examples of cultural influence range greatly. One example is the cultural expectation for some families in taking responsibility for "caring for their own" rather than looking to schools or agencies to provide assistance or resources in that care. Another example might be in the traditional values of a cultural group for interdependence rather than independence, or the value of elders making decisions for the entire family rather than each family member assuming responsibility for personal decisions. Still another example is in the cultural view of disability. In the deaf community, for example, deafness is not viewed as a disability, but rather as a communication difference. The approach used by the person who is deaf in determining his or her choices in communication skills (manual communication, oral communication, speech reading, etc.) may be highly influenced by whether the person's parents are deaf or hearing. A final example of cultural influence is in a family's cultural view of planning for the future—the heart of current concepts of self-determination.

Although cultural factors influencing a student's current and future self-determined behavior are numerous, two basic guiding principles should be considered:

1. *Cultural influences in an individual's learning self-determination are important.* Any students coming to class as first- or second-generation immigrants, who represent Native American, Hispanic/Latino, African American, Asian, Middle Eastern, or Eastern European families who value their traditional cultural values, or who are influenced by cultures of poverty, affluence, religious orthodoxy, or sociopolitical extremes may or may not be ready to learn knowledge or skills that reflect American middle-class, success-oriented thinking. Listen and learn from the students and their families as they respond to your efforts to teach self-determination. Try to understand the cultural and family values that are operating and whether there is a conflict between those values and what you are trying to teach. Be especially sensitive to students who are caught in the middle between strong family and cultural values and their desire to learn the self-determined behaviors the school values. Finally, try to keep the concept of self-determination in context for the cultural system of which the student is a part. As Field and colleagues (1998a, p. 144) stated, "Insignificant behavioral changes in one culture may be self-determination milestones in another."

2. *Respect the cultural values of your students and their families, even when they are different from your own.* You may find yourself as the mediator between the school and the student and family with regard to certain values. It may not be easy to reach a solution in which more than one cultural value "wins." If you can be satisfied that the student's and family's needs are met at the same time that cultural values are respected, then you have probably come as close as you can to a win-win solution.

Basic Self-Determination Teaching Content

The specific content for teaching self-determination knowledge and skills varies considerably, depending on a particular self-determination model or curriculum. In some instances, the focus of self-determination is on occupational choice and occupational planning. In others, the focus is on self-advocacy or skills for directing one's own IEP meeting. In others, there is a broader view of self-determination encompassing self-awareness, self-acceptance, knowledge and skill for planning and decision making, self-advocacy, and knowledge and skill in acting purposefully to achieve goals. The teaching concepts and instructional themes presented here were drawn primarily from Field and Hoffman (1994). Teaching self-determination involves the following:

1. How to accept and value themselves, including
   - admiring strengths that come from uniqueness
   - recognizing and respecting their own rights and responsibilities
   - taking care of their physical and emotional well-being
2. How to be a self-advocate for themselves at school or in the community, including
   - how to describe the disability/disabilities they have that require(s) special education or related services in order for them to be able to experience success at school
   - how to communicate needs for accommodations or supports
   - how to solve problems related to barriers they experience in pursuing their goals
   - how to defend a position related to their rights
   - how to handle conflict or disagreements over preferences and interests
3. How to make plans for themselves, including
   - how to set realistic goals
   - how to plan actions to meet goals
   - how to anticipate results
   - how to be creative in planning actions to meet goals
   - how to visually rehearse a plan of action
4. How to participate actively in their own transition planning, including
   - completing individualized assessments and futures planning procedures
   - gathering information on options

- reviewing past goals and performance
- asking feedback from others who know them
- negotiating IEP goals and objectives
- gaining skills in conducting their own IEP meetings

5. How to experience outcomes of planning and learn from the experience, including
   - how to compare actual outcomes to expected outcomes
   - how to compare performance and actions to expected performance and actions
   - how to determine what factors influenced performance and actual outcomes
   - how to accept consequences of decisions and actions
   - how to adjust plans when results are not satisfactory

Instructional concepts and themes like those just presented may seem too sophisticated for many adolescents, some of whom do not seem to have a clue about who they are, that they have choices in life, or that outcomes in life are more influenced by planning and effort than by luck or uncontrollable external factors. Each one of these concepts or themes can be achieved at some level by most students with disabilities. Each one can be made concrete and individual to help them learn. The key to individualization and making the concepts concrete is providing instructional activities and instructional opportunities that make sense to the students. There is nothing magic about instructional activities such as individual projects, individualized assignments, or roleplaying, for example, even though these are frequently recommended instructional techniques. Unless the project, assignment, or roleplay fits into the student's current or near future frame of reference or personal meaningfulness, you can expect limited success. For instructional ideas, see Field and associates (1998a) for many practical teaching suggestions and reviews of numerous self-determination curriculum materials.

Teaching in Inclusive Settings

Over the years, many terms have been used to describe the experiences and time students with disabilities spend in the general education classroom. *Deinstitutionalization, normalization, mainstreaming, integration,* and *inclusion* have all appeared in the literature during the past 30 years (Hallahan & Kauffman, 1991; Friend & Cook, 1992a; Kirk & Gallagher, 1979; Smith & Luckasson, 1995). *Inclusion* is the most current term that has evolved and has probably been the most closely scrutinized concept, especially by general education administrators and teachers.

Various definitions of *inclusive education* have been generated (Bos & Vaughn, 1998; Bradley, King-Sears, & Tessier-Switlick, 1997; Falvey, 1995; Friend & Bursuck, 1996; Friend & Cook, 1996; Salend, 1998; Wehman, 1997) with common themes emerging from them. In this text, inclusive education (learning in inclusive settings) is the "participation by all in a supportive general education environment that includes appropriate educational and social supports and services" (Bradley, King-Sears, & Tessier-Switlick, 1997, p. 6). In the context of this book on transition education and services, we support Wehman's (1997) statement: "The goal of inclusion is to prepare students to participate as fully contributing members of society" (p. 18).

Unfortunately, many variables contribute to the difficult task teachers in the general education classroom face with their students who have disabilities. First, many general education teachers are not familiar with the characteristics of the various disabilities. In addition, general educators are often unfamiliar with methods or strategies used to enhance instruction for students with disabilities. In-service or support programs provided by school systems for general educators cannot happen fast enough. Updating the curriculum of teacher education programs in higher education to reflect changes in how general and special educators should be trained is occurring at a slow pace. Six areas in need of training include (1) collaborative teaching, (2) differentiated instruction, (3) teaching learning strategies and study skills, (4) integration of technology, (5) application of academic content to real-life situations, and (6) teaching community skills.

Inclusive settings are not found only in school buildings. Inclusive settings are as unique and varied as the students who occupy them. Any setting that is a natural learning environment for all students is an inclusive educational setting. As students matriculate in school, their inclusive educational settings increase in number and in scope. This occurs to such an extent that as students prepare to exit their formal school programs, it is logical that more of their instructional time should be spent outside traditional classroom and school buildings and in the numerous inclusive community settings to which they are moving. These types of community settings include work sites, general community sites (e.g., grocery stores, banks, gas stations, parks and gardens, public transportation, etc.), apartments or group homes, and community college or university campuses.

Collaborative Teaching

Friend and Cook (1992b) defined *collaboration* as a style professionals choose to use in order to accomplish a goal they share. Being together as a team does not mean actually working together to accomplish a goal. True collaboration exists when all members of the team feel their contributions are valued, the team goals are clear, each member takes part in the decision-making efforts, and respect is shown for all team members (Cook & Friend, 1993). Friend and Cook (1992a) further clarified collaboration by identifying several key attributes. Those characteristics include voluntary participation, parity in the relationship, shared goals, shared accountability, trust and respect, shared resources, and shared responsibility for decision making.

The day-to-day working of a collaborative team can tackle several different activities that include, but are not limited to, shared problem solving, co-teaching, teaming, and consultation. Each of these tasks are described here.

Shared Problem Solving.   Shared problem solving can occur in several different forms in a school situation. Examples may include brainstorming options for community instruction or assisting a student in a person-centered planning meeting; both may require the problem-solving skills of a team. Friend and Bursuck (1996) offered a model for shared problem solving. Within their model, once a shared need is discovered, the next step is problem identification. Generating or brainstorming a list of solutions for the problem identified is next, keeping in mind that judgment is deferred, and the more ideas generated to select a solution, the better. Generated ideas are then evaluated as to their feasibility and contribution to the resolution of the problem. After one or two ideas are selected, the specific details needed to employ that option should be outlined. The implementation of the solution must happen, followed by an evaluation of its effectiveness by the collaborative team after a predetermined time has passed (a few days to a month or two).

Co-Teaching.   Bauwens and Hourcade (1995) stated that co-teaching occurs when two or more teachers share the instruction for a single group of students. Cook and Friend (1993, 1995) identified five of the more common co-teaching approaches: one teaches, one supports; station teaching; parallel teaching; alternative teaching; and team teaching. In the first delivery example, one teacher leads the lesson while the other supports or assists the educator who is teaching. Curricular content is divided into parts when using station teaching. Part of the content is taught by one teacher, groups then switch teachers, and another part is then taught by the other teacher. When two teachers teach the same information to two different groups in one class, this is considered parallel teaching. This method affords individual teachers the opportunity to teach the same content using different teaching techniques, allowing them to divide the class by students who can benefit the most from one technique or the other (e.g., one teacher might use a hands-on approach while the other would use the discovery method).

Alternative teaching is used when one class is divided into one small group and one large group. This method has been traditionally used to instruct a smaller group of students who need remediation. In recent times, the focus of this subgroup could be enrichment for students interested in a specific topic or preteaching concepts, such as specialized vocabulary, in preparation for a lesson the next day.

Team teaching consists of two teachers who share leadership in the classroom. They can use the team teaching opportunity to roleplay situations or model behaviors such as one teacher outlining on the board as the other teaches the content.

Cook and Friend (1993) offered tips for successful co-teaching experiences. These include advanced planning, discussing differing views on teaching and learning before co-teaching begins, attending to details such as class rules and routines, explaining the co-teaching plan to parents, avoiding one of the teachers becoming the "helping teacher" or taking on tasks of a paraprofessional, talking out disagreements as they happen, and beginning co-teaching slowly.

Teaming.   Teams in secondary special education have long assisted in planning the educational programs of students since the mid-1970s. The purpose of those planning teams has evolved since the 1970s to their current focus of assisting the students in planning their futures, with the student as an active member of the team. The success of teams depends on the commitment of every member of the team to their goals (Wesby & Ford, 1993).

Consultation. Consultation is a more specialized type of problem-solving process in which a professional with specialized expertise assists another professional who requires the knowledge of that expertise (Idol, Nevin, & Paolucci-Whitcomb, 1994). During the transition planning process, teachers frequently seek consultation with adult service providers (e.g., a vocational rehabilitation counselor or a specialist in positive behavioral support) to assist the transition team in planning postsecondary options for the student with disabilities. Once a need or problem has been resolved, the services of the consultant are usually no longer needed.

Differentiated Instruction

The importance of differentiating instruction for students with multiple ability levels cannot be understated when discussing recommended practices or promising practices used in inclusive educational settings. Differentiation has been defined in a number of ways (Reis, Kaplan, Tomlinson, Westberg, Callahan, & Cooper, 1998; Tomlinson, 1995, 1996, 1997; Tomlinson & Kalbfleisch, 1998). It is usually regarded as accommodating learning differences. This is done by identifying students' strengths and using appropriate strategies to meet the needs of students' various ability levels, personal preferences, and learning styles. As these factors are determined, all students can then engage in a variety of educational experiences (Reis et al., 1998). Differentiated curricula and instruction can respond to students' varying readiness levels, interests, and learning profiles.

Reis and colleagues (1998) suggested that after students' various instructional levels, interests, and profiles are identified, whole groups, small groups, and individual students can equally engage in a variety of curriculum enrichment and acceleration experiences. In addition, Reis and colleagues observed that teachers who offer differentiated curricula and instruction view students as individuals with their own skills, interests, styles, and talents.

Tomlinson (1997) offered nine principles of differentiated instruction. These principles offer a framework by which to analyze or identify when differentiated instruction is being used in an educational setting. By analyzing an educational setting for the existence of differentiation of curriculum and instruction, teachers will be more conscious of implementing a differentiated approach. Tomlinson's (1997) nine principles are as follows:

1. Learning experiences are based on student readiness for the task, their individual interests, and learning profiles.
2. Assessment of student needs is ongoing, and all tasks are adapted to meet a student's need based on assessment information.
3. Active and respected participation is required of all students in activities.
4. The role of the teacher is coordinator of instruction and learning variables rather than provider of information.

5. Various and flexible work group configurations are used.
6. Student needs determine the flexibility in time use.
7. Various instructional strategies are used to meet student needs.
8. Specific criteria are determined to ensure student success.
9. Emphasis is on student strengths.

Tomlinson (1995, 1997) suggested differentiating content, activities, and products to increase differentiated instruction in classrooms. Sample strategies for achieving this differentiation for students of varying ability levels include curriculum compacting, independent study, interest centers or interest groups, tiered assignments, flexible grouping, learning centers, adjusting questions, mentorships/apprenticeships, varied rubrics, reading buddies, multiple texts, interest-based minilessons, independent study projects, and learning contracts.

Teaching Learning Strategies and Study Skills

Instruction in learning strategies and study skills has been implemented most extensively at the secondary level with students with learning disabilities. This instruction is being broadened now to include students with all disabilities and even students without disabilities. Deshler, Ellis, and Lenz (1996) identified three approaches to teaching learning strategies: the reductionist approach, the constructivist approach, and the functionalist approach. The *reductionist approach* is based on the idea that to understand or explain something complex, it must be analyzed and divided into simpler, smaller, or more understandable components. Cognitive behavior modification is an example of such an approach. It combines behavior management techniques with self-training methods such as monitoring instruction, evaluation, and verbalization. The reductionist approach focuses on thinking about one's thinking. Much of the research on this strategy and its use with adolescents with disabilities has been conducted at the University of Virginia (Hallahan & Kauffman, 1991). They found the approach useful because it stresses self-initiative and helps the student overcome passivity in learning. This ties directly to the concept of self-determination discussed earlier in this chapter.

The *constructivist approach* argues that learning is too complex to reduce to simple constructs and that learners construct knowledge in their own ways. This construction is based on the student's active involvement with new experiences in the context of previous experiences, values, needs, beliefs, and other factors that remain unknown to observers (Deshler, Ellis, & Lenz, 1996). The *functionalist* approach to understanding learning is based on the idea that learning and the approaches used to promote learning depend on the individual, the place, and the time; it blends the principles of the reductionist and constructive approaches. Probably the most fully developed practices representing the functionalist approach are embodied in the strategies instruction approach, which has served as the basis for the Strategies Intervention Model developed at the University of Kansas. Deshler, Ellis, and Lenz (1996) provided in-depth coverage of the learning strategies approach, with emphasis on the Strategies Intervention Model.

Regardless of the approach used in the teaching of learning strategies, there are basically nine steps that you should follow in systematically teaching any strategy to your students:

1. *Present and obtain a commitment to learn.* Obtain a measure(s) of current student functioning in the area and discuss with the student how the strategy will improve performance. Make the student aware of ineffective or inefficient learning habits.
2. *Describe the strategy.* Give a rationale and situations in which the strategy could be used. Help the student set goals for the strategy's use.
3. *Model the strategy.* Talk out loud and model each of the steps of the strategy using a real-life example.
4. *Verbally rehearse each of the steps of the strategy.* Use rapid-fire verbal rehearsal of all of the steps until the student acquires mastery.
5. *Provide controlled practice.* Provide feedback to the student while supervising practice in easy material. Require mastery.
6. *Provide advanced practice and feedback.* Provide feedback to the student while practice occurs in general education courses or the workplace. Require mastery.
7. *Confirm acquisition of the strategy.* Document the student's mastery of the strategy. Make the student aware of the progress.
8. *Provide opportunities for and monitor generalization.* Obtain the student's commitment to generalize to other classrooms and community situations. Make the student aware of situations in which he or she can apply the strategy, and discuss cues that may signal the need to use the strategy. Discuss adaptations that can be made to the strategy and make periodic checks to be sure the student is using it.
9. *Conduct ongoing evaluation of the strategy instruction process.* Collect ongoing data on the effectiveness of the process used in working with the student.

Many people use the terms *learning strategies* and *basic study skills* synonymously. Deshler, Ellis, and Lenz (1996) distinguished between the two by stating that both are forms of a plan, but that study skills contain little guidance with regard to facilitating effective thinking behaviors, such as decision making, self-motivation, or monitoring. Study skills usually involve just a listing of steps, rather than cues for planning, executing, and evaluating performance. Study skills still need to be systematically taught, and we recommend that you use the steps listed previously in teaching a specific study skill. Hoover and Patton (1995) provided extensive coverage of the concept of study skills, with examples of application of these skills in school and community settings.

Integration of Technology

The use of technological tools to function on a day-to-day basis has become an essential skill for all adults (Lewis, 1993). Lewis suggested using the ABC model of technology when integrating technology into everyday classroom experiences (Male, 1997):

Augment abilities (use a speech synthesizer or magnifier).

Bypass disabilities (use switches, voice command, e-mail, etc.).

Compensate for disabilities (use talking word processors, grammar or spell checker, mapping or networking ideas, etc.).

Integrating technology in inclusive settings has become a priority. In addressing this priority, several variables must be examined (Male, 1997): integrating technology with individual educational programs, assisting in the acquisition of basic skills, improving quality of life and life skills, and utilizing the Internet and World Wide Web.

Integrating Technology into IEPs.   For several years, technology has been used to assist with assessing students' needs and documenting their progress. In addition to using technology in a more traditional sense, such as data collection and record keeping, some unique and creative techniques using technology can equalize a student's participation within a general education setting by presenting projects or reports in a technology format. Using electronic or multimedia portfolios as a means of documenting a student's progress can highlight a student's depth and breath of knowledge and do it in a unique way (Johnson, 1994; Milone, 1995).

Acquiring Basic Skills.   Lewis (1993) suggested six types of software appropriate for increasing a student's skills in content areas: tutorials, drill and practice, educational games, discovery, simulations, and problem solving.

Male (1997) believes a teacher's level of expertise, skill, comfort, and curricular emphasis in the class contributes to his or her use of technology with students. Movement toward more thematic or unit teaching will help increase software use. Male also offers two suggestions to teachers when deciding to use a software program: Try to think of as many ways as possible to use one flexible piece of software, and think of ways of using different pieces of software that approach the same skills from different models or styles of presentation (p. 67).

Establishing criteria when selecting software for classroom use is important. Dollars are limited and versatility and flexibility are essential. The Alliance for Technology Access (1994) has suggested 13 criteria when selecting any software for any population:

1. Easy-to-read screens
2. Consistency
3. Intuitive characteristics
4. Logical labels
5. Instructional choices
6. Friendly documentation
7. On-screen instructions

8. Auditory cues
9. Video cues
10. Built-in access
11. Alternatives to a mouse
12. Optional cursors
13. Creation of custom programs

Improving Quality of Life and Life Skills. Technology can play a significant role in enhancing a student's options beyond school experiences, such as social contacts, business and consumer resources, recreation and leisure, art and music, and career exploration (Male, 1997). Software is available in many core academic content areas, in addition to many of the fine arts. Simulations also offer a game format to learn more about the world. Software is also available to gather information on a variety of topics important to daily life (e.g., plan a vacation, research various car and homeowner policy options with different insurance companies, research new cars, etc.).

Male (1997) suggested five principles when incorporating technology into every-day life:

1. There is no minimum age limit.
2. There is no maximum age limit.
3. Computer skills are not developmental and prerequisites should not apply.
4. Computer skills are expandable.
5. Computer skills can be adapted to any situation and can benefit people of varying ability levels, interests, and ages.

Utilizing the Internet and World Wide Web (WWW). The use of the World Wide Web (WWW) and the Internet provides a valuable tool for all students. The way people communicate, advertise, teach, shop, learn, work, or just have fun has been permanently changed. With this in mind, each student's background and abilities must always be considered when the Internet or the Web is used in classrooms (Leu & Leu, 1997). A variety of resources are listed in the resource section of this chapter to assist you in maneuvering and accessing resources on the Web.

In addition to using the Web as a resource, creating a webpage has become a frequent activity in schools. Cafolla, Kauffman, and Knee (1997), Leu and Leu (1997), and Male (1997) have provided resources for educators who are embarking on the Internet/WWW journey. These resources provide basic information and excellent instructional ideas.

Application of Academic Content to Real-Life Situations. Special educators have been advocating the benefits of relating the application of academics to real life for several decades (Brolin, 1989, 1993, 1995, 1997; Clark, 1979, 1994; Clark, Carlson, Fisher, Cook, & D'Alonzo, 1991; Clark, Field, Patton, Brolin, & Sitlington, 1994; Cronin & Patton, 1993; Kokaska & Brolin, 1985; Sitlington, 1996a, 1996b). The necessity to engage students actively in learning basic life skills needed for success in adulthood has become more important (Sitlington, 1996).

The adult outcome database of the past decade paints a dim picture of unemployment and/or underemployment, low pay, part-time work, frequent job changes, little engagement with the community, limitations in independent functioning, little postsecondary education, and limited social lives for individuals with disabilities. In addition, special educators have been urged for a long time to reexamine the curriculum used with special populations and now, more than ever, are working toward aligning it with the curriculum used in general education programs. The adult outcome research on special populations along with the dropout data nationwide is alarming. This information, coupled with the nationwide mandate that has been handed to all educators is to educate a ready-to-work population in the United States through such federal initiatives as Goals 2000 and the School-to-Work Opportunities Act, created a charge for educators to relate academic knowledge to real life applications. In assisting educators to meet this charge, a discussion addressing how to teach real-life content is warranted.

Although many terms or phrases exist to refer to those skills needed to function successfully in adulthood (Cronin, 1996), the terms *real-life content*, and *life skills* are used interchangeably in this chapter. *Real-life content,* or *life skills,* means "specific competencies (i.e., knowledge and skills) of local and cultural relevance needed to perform everyday activities in a variety of settings typically encountered by most adults" (Patton, Cronin, & Wood, 1999, p. 2).

As noted in the preceding definition, the nature of life skills can vary from one setting to another. For example, a number of life skills are involved in grocery shopping; however, the details of shopping in a grocery store are a function of the city or locale where one lives (Cronin & Patton, 1993). Although the similarities of grocery stores are vast, the uniqueness of each store poses difficulties to many special needs populations.

Sitlington (1996b) outlined a variety of life-skills curricular models currently available (see Table 10.1). The similarities of these models are numerous, such as the suggested materials to use, the content to be taught, suggested classroom and community activities, and the like. The primary differences can be found in the various curriculum designs (Patton, Cronin, & Wood, 1999). Every curriculum format or design establishes a similar yet different set of priorities in response to a set of needs considered important by various professionals and consumers (students, parents, teachers, administrators, community leaders, etc.). Given any one of the curriculum designs outlined in Table 10.1, a discussion of the various options of how to teach life skills can begin. For illustrative purposes, the Cronin and Patton (1993) Domains of Adulthood will be used.

Functionality is an important concept to discuss when talking about life skills or functional curriculum. For many years, the concept of a functional or life-skills curriculum was aligned with students who have mental retardation. This way of thinking must be changed, as everyone needs functional skills. The need for functional skills is as different as each individual. A high school senior who will be attending MIT in the fall has many skills she will need to function independently in that particular environment, just like the student attending the local vocational training institute has many skills he will need to function independently in that sit-

TABLE 10.1   Career Education and Life Skills Education Models

Source	Major components
Life-Centered Career Education (LCCE) (Brolin, 1991)	Three major areas: • Daily living • Personal–social • Occupational guidance and preparation
School-Based Career Development and Transition Education Model (Clark & Kolstoe, 1990)	Four major areas: • Values, attitudes, and habits • Human relationships • Occupational information • Acquisition of job and daily living skills
Hawaii Transition Project (1987)	Four major areas: • Vocational/education • Home and family • Recreation/leisure • Community/citizenship
Community-Referenced Curriculum (Smith & Schloss, 1988)	Five major areas: • Work • Leisure and play • Consumer • Education and rehabilitation • Transportation
Community Living Skills Taxonomy (Dever, 1988)	Five major areas: • Personal maintenance and development • Homemaking and community life • Vocational • Leisure • Travel
Life Problems of Adulthood (Knowles, 1990)	Six major areas: • Vocation and career • Home and family living • Enjoyment of leisure • Community living • Health • Personal development
Domains of Adulthood (Cronin & Patton, 1993)	Six major areas: • Employment/education • Home and family • Leisure pursuits • Community involvement • Physical/emotional health • Personal responsibility and relationships

(continued)

TABLE 10.1   Continued

Source	Major components
Post-School Outcomes Model (National Center on Educational Outcomes, 1993)	Seven major areas: • Presence and participation • Physical health • Responsibility and independence • Contribution and citizenship • Academic and functional literacy • Personal and social adjustment • Satisfaction
Quality of Life Domains (Halpern, 1993)	Three major areas: • Physical and material well-being • Performance of adult roles • Personal fulfillment

Source: From "Transition to Living: The Neglected Component of Transition Programming for Students with Learning Disabilities" by P. Sitlington, 1996, *Journal of Learning Disabilities, 29* (1), page 35. Reprinted by permission.

uation. Your job, as an educator, is to make sure each of these students is prepared to function independently in his or her next subsequent environment, whatever it might be.

A note should be made at his point regarding life-skills instruction for different types of students. The eventual outcome or vision a student has for himself or herself determines the path of life-skills acquisition, whether it is in a formal or informal instructional situation. A student who sees himself or herself pursuing a degree in higher education must have a solid foundation in all the academic subject areas. Yet the student also needs to know learning strategies plus various organizational, research, and study skills, in addition to skills needed to do his or her laundry and balance a checkbook. Some of these students will also need employment-related skills, as part-time employment is often necessary to support themselves during their college years.

Another group of students, on the other hand, sees high school as the termination point of their formal schooling. These students will need more intense life-skills and vocational instruction prior to their high school exit. Both of these scenarios are a challenge for curriculum developers, administrators, and all teachers in the application of course content to real-life situations.

Concern is often voiced by teachers, school administrators, and parents that teaching within a life-skills format ignores teaching basic subjects. Nothing could be farther from the truth. The ability to read, write, compute, problem solve, and converse, as well as social skills, school survival skills, and study skills are all extremely important for every educator to teach, no matter the age of the student or the content of the material taught. Figure 10.1 clearly illustrates through a matrix the interrelationship of scholastic and social skills to life-skills areas. The

FIGURE 10.1   Secondary Matrix: Relationship of Scholastic/Social Skills to Adult Domains

	Employment/ Education	Home and Family	Leisure Pursuits	Community Involvement	Emotional/ Physical Health	Personal Responsibility/ Relationships
Reading	Reading classified ads for jobs	Interpreting bills	Locating and understanding movie information in newspaper	Following directions on tax forms	Comprehending directions on medication	Reading letters from friends
Writing	Writing a letter of application for a job	Writing checks	Writing for information on a city to visit	Filling in a voter registration form	Filling in your medical history on forms	Sending thank-you notes
Listening	Understanding oral directions of a procedure change	Comprehending oral directions about making dinner	Listening for forecast to plan outdoor activity	Understanding campaign ads	Attending lectures for stress	Taking turns in a conversation
Speaking	Asking your boss for a raise	Discussing morning routines with family	Inquiring about tickets for a concert	Stating your opinion at the school board meeting	Describing symptoms to a doctor	Giving feedback to a friend about the purchase of a compact disk
Math Applications	Understanding difference between net and gross pay	Computing the cost of doing laundry in a laundromat versus at home	Calculating the cost of a dinner out versus eating at home	Obtaining information for a building permit	Using a thermometer	Planning the costs of a date
Problem-Solving	Settling a dispute with a co-worker	Deciding how much to budget for rent	Role-playing appropriate behaviors for various places	Knowing what to do if you are the victim of fraud	Selecting a doctor	Deciding how to ask someone for a date
Survival Skills	Using a prepared career planning packet	Listing emergency phone numbers	Using a shopping center directory	Marking a calendar for important dates (e.g., recycling, garbage collection)	Using a system to remember to take vitamins	Developing a system to remember birthdays
Personal/ Social	Applying appropriate interview skills	Helping a child with homework	Knowing the rules of a neighborhood pool	Locating self-improvement classes	Getting a yearly physical exam	Discussing how to negotiate a price at a flea market

Source: From Life Skills Instruction for All Students with Special Needs: A Practical Guide for Integrating Real-Life Content into the Curriculum (page 33) by M. E. Cronin and J. R. Patton, 1993, Austin, TX: Pro-Ed. Reprinted by permission.

sample activities in each of the cells clearly demonstrate that life skills and basic skills can be taught simultaneously.

Figure 10.2 shows a continuum of options for teaching life skills (Cronin & Patton, 1993). The five options for teaching life skills suggested by Cronin and Patton fall into three types: coursework, augmentation, and infusion. All options are dependent on establishing a comprehensive set of competencies identified at the local level.

Coursework. Three options are available for teaching life skills via coursework that can be credit or noncredit courses, elective or required. The first is to develop a comprehensive sequence of life-skills courses that can lead to a diploma (Cronin & Patton, 1993). The purpose is to offer coursework that relates to traditional content courses with a life-skills orientation. Usually, this is done when a specific course of study is essential for those high school students who will not be attending a college or university, but who still need a curriculum that teaches basic skills within a life-skills context (Helmke, Havekost, Patton, & Polloway, 1994). Helmke and colleagues described a comprehensive course approach developed by the Dubuque (Iowa) Community Schools. The Dubuque Schools wanted a set of courses/curriculum that would better prepare their students for successful functioning as adults in the Dubuque community.

The second option is developing one course in a topical content area such as "Math in the Real World," "Health and First Aid," or "Ready to Work." The content of these courses is very focused, yet they are typically thought of in many high schools as electives (as opposed to required courses). An example of how to develop this type of course is described in Helmke and associates (1994).

The third course option, which also has a single-course format, covers introductory life-skills information in a number of areas. "Independent Living Skills," "Living on Your Own," and "Life 101" are examples of the third course option. Again, like the other single-course option, these courses can typically be found in high schools and are usually electives.

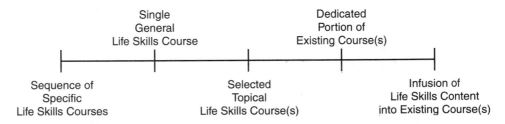

FIGURE 10.2   Options for Organizing Life-Skills Content for Formal Instruction

Source: From *Life Skills Instruction for All Students with Special Needs: A Practical Guide for Integrating Real-Life Content into the Curriculum* (page 25) by M. E. Cronin and J. R. Patton, 1993, Austin, TX: Pro-Ed. Reprinted by permission.

Augmentation. The fourth option, augmentation, involves supplementing existing content courses with additional life-skills information. This option is appropriate in settings where there is no opportunity for the development of separate life-skills coursework. Augmentation is also one of the best methods to use when relating content taught in any of the general education classes to real-life application.

Augmentation can occur in several different formats (Cronin & Patton, in preparation). Some schools have used a schoolwide focus with the entire school devoting every Friday, the last week of every month, or one month of the year (January or May) to applying the content learned in their courses to real-life situations. Still others have focused specific projects, such as service learning projects, to apply what they have learned in the content class to the real world. Individual teachers will use homework assignments or group projects to accomplish this goal.

One of the most popular augmentation techniques is the unit approach. Learning by doing is the basic theory in using the unit approach. Meyen (1981) suggested that the inclusion of a variety of activities lends itself to individualization of instruction. Units are usually motivational because of the individual interests of the students plus their natural curiosity, prior experiences, and cultural backgrounds.

The unit approach relates instruction to a specific topic, problem, theme, or area of interest (Hittleman, 1983). McPhie (1983) described a unit as "smaller bits and pieces of information that are grouped together into a larger, meaningful mass of subject matter" (p. 52). Units can be organized several ways. Within content courses, themes related to content topics can be the organizational structure for a unit. Thematic interest of the class can also provide a direction for the development of a unit; for example, students approaching driving age develop an interest in cars, trucks, sports utility vehicles, and other motor vehicles, which makes a natural match of high interest of students with an area that academic skills can be taught and reinforced. Periodically surveying interests of students will provide a valuable database of information.

Infusion. The structure of the infusion approach is through existing course content. Table 10.2 provides examples of both the augmentation and infusion techniques. The objective of the infusion approach is to capitalize on opportunities presented in the content of the lesson of the day that addresses important material related to life-skills (Patton, Cronin, & Wood, 1999). Figure 10.3 gives an example of the infusion approach using an example from *Most Loved Classics Series, Moby Dick* by Herman Melville. Patton, Cronin, and Wood feel it is important to take advantage of as many opportunities as possible to touch on topics that have life-skills implications.

Patton, Cronin, and Wood (1999) outlined a four-step procedure. The main aspects of each step are crucial to infuse real-life content successfully into courses. The steps are as follows:

1. Familiarity with the comprehensive set of knowledge and skills needed in adulthood (i.e., life skills)

TABLE 10.2   **Augmentation and Infusion Examples**

Source	Topic covered	A/I	Sample activities
Practical math textbook (Secondary level)	"Budgeting for Recreation"	A	Add coverage on the "economics" of dating
		I	Identify best time and cost for going to a movie
	"Credit Card Math"	A	Add coverage of how to get the best deal on a credit card (e.g., low APR, no annual fee)
		I	Present ways to get lower APR or waiver of annual fee
	"Maintaining a Vehicle"	A	Add coverage of the realities of being involved in an accident and what one needs to do
		I	Discuss the importance of keeping tires inflated at the proper levels
Basal math textbook (Elementary level)	"Using Decimals: Adding & Subtracting Money" —buying a sleeping bag	A	Add coverage of costs of purchasing or renting camping gear
		I	Discuss where one can buy or rent a sleeping bag
	"Using Tables to Solve Problems"	A	Add coverage on how to use the weather map from the newspaper
		I	Identify other tables that have numbers

Note: A = augmentation; I = infusion

Source: From "A Life Skills Approach to Mathematics Instruction: Preparing Students with Learning Disabilities for the Real-Life Math Demands of Instruction" by J. R. Patton, M. E. Cronin, D. S. Bassett, and A. E. Koppel, 1997, *Journal of Learning Disabilities, 30,* page 185. Reprinted by permission.

2. Identification of places in the existing [course or] curriculum that can be associated with real-life topics
3. Planning life skills infusion activities
4. Actual instruction of life skills during ongoing lessons (p. 10)

It should be noted that the types of activities for infusion are usually limited due to the short amount of time that can be devoted to the infusion process. The likely selection of activities might include asking a short, to-the-point question that

FIGURE 10.3   Infusion Example

Chapter 2

The Carpetbag

I stuffed a shirt into my old carpetbag and said good-bye to the city of Manhattan. I arrived in New Bedford on a cold, windy, and icy Saturday in December. I was too late for a boat ride to Nantucket, the great sailing port of America. I had to wait until Monday before I could go there. Then, I would go on my great whaling voyage. But for now, I needed some food and a place to sleep. I had little money and knew I had few choices, if any.

I walked for many blocks and looked for shelter from the cold. I saw lots of inns, but they all were too expensive. My steps led me to the waterfront. I found the cheapest places in that part of town. I also found blocks of blackness. A few candles gave the only light. But I had to pass inn after inn because they looked too expensive.

Moving on, I came to a dim light near the docks. The sign over the door said, "The Spouter Inn—Peter Coffin." The place looked quiet. The house was old and *run-down*.

This looked like a good place to stay. If I was lucky, they might even serve coffee. It didn't really matter. I was tired and had ice on my feet. I had run out of choices. So I decided to go into the inn and see it on the inside.

Source: From *Most Loved Classics Series, Moby Dick* (p. 2) by Herman Melville, adapted by Michael Montroy, 1991, Austin, TX: Pro-Ed. Copyright 1991 by Pro-Ed, Inc. Reprinted by permission.

Content Referent	Possible Life Skills Topics	Adult Domain
inn	• Identify employment opportunities in the hotel industry (e.g., desk clerk, manager, bell hop, concierge, room service, food preparation, etc.). • Identify the required education/training for these employment opportunities	Employment/Education
inn	• List different types of lodgings (e.g., hotel, motel, hostel, YMCA, campgrounds, etc.). • Identify the advance preparations or information needed prior to arriving at a hotel (e.g., reservations, room availability, room rates, etc.).	Leisure Pursuits
inn	• List responsibilities you accept once you have checked into a hotel (e.g., notify the hotel if the room condition is not correct, hotel rules, know the check out time).	Personal Responsibilities/ Relationships

(continued)

FIGURE 10.3   Continued

Subject Area:	Literature
Type of Material:	Novel
Grade Level:	Middle School
Title:	*Moby Dick, page 2*
Authors:	Herman Melville (Adapted by M. Montroy)
Publisher:	Pro-Ed
Copyright Date:	1991

Source: From *Infusing Real-Life Topics into Existing Curricula: Recommended Procedures and Instructional Examples for the Elementary, Middle, and High School Levels* (page 49) by J. R. Patton, M. E. Cronin, and S. Wood, 1999, Austin, TX: Pro-Ed. Reprinted by permission.

requires a limited response; listing or brainstorming ideas or examples; describing examples or activities; identifying a sequence of tasks that needs to occur; and citing personal examples from the teacher or students. Teachers who use the infusion approach should keep a systematic inventory of infusion activities. Keeping notes on the effectiveness of the activities tried and ideas that might be helpful for the next year is recommended.

Classroom instruction is important in preparing students to apply basic academic skills to real-life situations in natural environments (Cronin & Patton, 1993). Classroom instruction gives students the opportunity to be introduced to and practice skills prior to encountering them in the natural environment. This might include activities such as filling out forms, roleplaying sales interactions, practicing interview skills, using a laundromat, and the like. The classroom can also be the place where people from the community can visit to meet students and share information on their chosen career prior to the students visiting their place of business.

Teaching Community Skills

Educators have been charged with multiple tasks from the 1997 Amendments of IDEA. Two of those tasks are not in areas most teachers have received training—yet, they are two of the most important sets of activities for *all* students in the transition process. Independent living and community participation are critical for success in adulthood (Sitlington, 1996b). Many of the skills needed for successful day-to-day functioning can be taught within the classroom using any of the options listed in the continuum in Figure 10.2. An important extension of teaching life skills, no matter what option you use, is that the specific life skill is learned or at least practiced often by all students, regardless of the student's exceptionality, in the natural setting (e.g., the community).

Many professionals have been confused with the terminology used to describe community experiences that take place both on and off campus. Figure

10.4 outlines some examples to help discriminate among *community-based instruction (CBI), community-referenced instruction (CRI),* and *community simulations (CS).*

Students must become aware of the constant need in day-to-day living to know a wide range and number of life skills. One activity for students is to do a structured observation in and around the school building, at home, on the bus, or on a community field experience. Students are to complete a form, either with assistance or independently, and count the number and kind of tasks the person they are observing is doing. These tasks could be classified by skill area (reading, writing, listening, speaking, problem solving, mathematics, etc.) and place where the tasks occur (kitchen, office, garage, yard, cafeteria, etc.). The purpose of this

FIGURE 10.4   Differences among *Community-Based Instruction (CBI), Community-Referenced Instruction (CRI),* and *Community Simulations (CS)*

Skill: Dressing
CBI   Putting on a coat to go into the community; taking off a coat when you arrive at the community location (if appropriate); trying on clothes in a department store; changing clothes at the YMCA to participate in swimming or aerobic dance
CRI   Changing clothes for gym; putting on/taking off a coat during school arrival/departure; changing shirts after lunch (if the current one becomes soiled); putting on a painting smock in art class
CS   Five trials of putting on and taking off a shirt in the classroom during a dressing program; tying shoelaces on a dressing board; buttoning clothes on a doll

Skill: Purchasing
CBI   Purchasing items at the drug store; paying for a game of bowling; purchasing a soda at a restaurant; buying stamps at the post office
CRI   Purchasing lunch in the cafeteria; buying a drink from the soda machine; purchasing a ticket to a school basketball game; buying school buttons/ribbons to wear on color day
CS   Counting money in the classroom (e.g., "Show me $6.25"); pretending to shop and pay for items in a classroom grocery store; sorting coins (nickels, dimes, and quarters)

Skill: Communicating/Understanding Pictures
CBI   Locating items in the store from a picture grocery list; ordering in a restaurant using a picture menu; presenting a picture to a store clerk to determine location of a bathroom.
CRI   Reviewing the school lunch choices and selecting pictures of the items desired; choosing a leisure activity from a series of picture choices; using a picture schedule throughout the school day
CS   Matching pictures of various foods with their plastic replicas; identifying a picture by pointing to it when the teacher verbally requests "Show me the _____"

Source: From "Community Living" by S. Dymond in *Functional Curriculum for Elementary, Middle, and Secondary Age Students with Special Needs* (p. 202) by P. Wehman and J. Kregel, 1997, Austin, TX: Pro-Ed. Reprinted by permission.

activity is to bring an awareness to the students of the sheer number of tasks that people perform and where they happen. This will further emphasize and document the need to teach life skills and teach such skills in the natural environment.

Field Experiences.   Teaching students in the natural environment entails, in most cases, leaving the school campus. When teachers plan to leave school campuses for instructional purposes, many issues must be addressed prior to the activity. First, permission from the administration is imperative and guidelines of the school system must be followed. Some teachers have found they must choose their words wisely when trying to arrange off-campus activities. After being denied a request to go off campus, one teacher found that by simply changing her vocabulary from *field trip* to *field experience*, her request was granted (Cronin, Lord, & Wendling, 1991). In addition to changing vocabulary, some teachers have discovered that by submitting a detailed plan of their proposed excursion off campus to their school administrator, emphasis is on the academic purpose of the outing and the individual IEP goals that would be addressed by the activity (Cronin & Patton, in preparation). Figure 10.5 offers an example of a detailed form that can be used for such a purpose.

Figure 10.5 helps the teacher organize the community participation activity prior to going, as well as compiles important information for others in the school (school secretary, principal, paraprofessionals, etc.) and students' parents. Information could include the following: who is going, where and when they are going, what activities will be done, and how they will get to the activity location and return. A form such as this also provides a structure to ensure an evaluation component is addressed, outlines any follow-up activities, and provides ongoing documentation plus a history of places and activities for both individuals and groups of students (Cronin & Patton, in preparation).

In addition to compiling this type of information, several other important components need to be addressed when implementing a community participation instruction program. The following partial list identifies some of the major items (Cronin & Patton, in preparation; Falvey, 1989; Wehman, 1992):

1. Provide a detailed emergency information form with a current photograph of each student containing the following information: name, date of birth, Social Security number, height, weight, hair color, eye color, skin tone, nationality, communication mode(s), student's current schedule, name of school with school contact, school phone, parent/guardian name, home address, home phone, emergency information, and relevant medical information (Falvey, 1989, p. 104).
2. Prepare individual identification cards for each student with pertinent information.
3. Formally contact the manager of the location you are going to visit. Identify yourself, school, purpose of the trip, and when you will be visiting.
4. Establish a realistic adult-student ratio for the size and nature of your group. Discuss this with your school administrators.

FIGURE 10.5   Contacts/Community Sites: Preparation

Adult Domain:
Subdomain:
Major Life Demand:
Life Skill:

Date of Visit: Parent Involvement:
Place/Person: Admin./Staff Involvement:
Phone #/Address:
Transportation:
   A. Goals & Objectives
        1.
        2.
        3.
   B. Discussion Points
        1.
        2.
        3.
        4.
   C. Activities
        1.
        2.
        3.
        4.
   D. Extra Activities
        1.
        2.
        3.
   E. Evaluation Techniques
        1.
        2.
   F. Follow-Up
        1.
        2.
        3.

Source: From *Life Skills Curriculum for Students with Special Needs: A Guide for Developing Real-Life Skills* (2nd ed.) by M. E. Cronin and J. R. Patton, in preparation, Austin, TX: Pro-Ed. Reprinted by permission.

5. Use additional adult volunteers (college students, foster grandparents, service organizations, etc.) for additional supervision.
6. Work with general educators to explore the community cooperatively within the inclusive content class setting or as an augmentation activity.
7. Use support personnel (speech-language pathologists, psychologists, social workers, etc.) to accompany you in the community.
8. Verify with your school system that adequate insurance coverage is in place for this type of activity.

9. Develop an emergency plan for off-campus activities if one does not exist.
10. Train all staff and volunteers in emergency, CPR, and first-aid procedures.
11. Review and practice community safety procedures with all students who go into the community.
12. Identify all the possible transportation options (public transportation, walking, taxi, etc.).
13. Obtain parental permission for every excursion off campus.

Bringing the Community into the Classroom.   In some situations, teachers are unable to take their students into the community for instruction or are restricted as to how often they can go out. In these situations, bring the community into the school or class. Some businesses are mobile, such as auto-related businesses (mobile auto mechanics will change the oil in your car at your place of business or home). Parents of students often will be willing to visit schools or help find specific career-related individuals who will visit. Teachers or staff members at your school are also a willing group to assist in these endeavors.

Service Learning.   Service learning is a method by which young people learn and develop skills through active participation in thoughtfully organized service experiences (Kinsley & McPherson, 1995). Beisser (1996) describes service learning as the integration of the curriculum with a community or school-based need. Many professionals believe that in participating in a service learning project, students experience authentic learning, learn to understand the meaning of community beyond self, and develop a sense of responsibility and respect for others (Beisser, 1996; Boyer, 1987; Kinsley & McPherson, 1995; Lewis, 1995). Service learning is also a way of meeting actual needs in a community that are coordinated with the school and community.

Service learning has become a graduation or exit requirement from high school in many states. It has also been designated as a federal priority with the National Community Service Act of 1990 (PL 101-610) and the National Community Service Trust Act of 1993 (Americorps). Both initiatives provided monies to encourage the young people of this country to serve their communities and schools.

Activities of service learning are integrated into each student's academic curriculum. Service activities provide students with opportunities to use newly acquired academic skills and knowledge in real-life situations in their own communities. Service learning also provides opportunities for students with disabilities to be givers instead of takers (Council for Exceptional Children, 1998). In addition, they learn through hands-on experience skills in problem solving, conflict resolution, self-esteem, as well as academic and social skills that take place in inclusive settings. A student's involvement in service learning also gives him or her the opportunity to think about his or her role in the community as a citizen, to experience volunteerism, and to explore job exploration opportunities for the future.

Resources

The following resources may be helpful to you and your students as you assist them in their transition to adult life.

Bender, M., Valletutti, P. J., & Baglin, C. A. (1996). *Functional curriculum for teaching students with disabilities: Self-care, motor skills, household management, and living skills* (Vol. 1, 3rd ed.). Austin, TX: Pro-Ed.

Bender, M., Valletutti, P. J., & Baglin, C. A. (1998). *Functional curriculum for teaching students with disabilities: Interpersonal, competitive job finding, and leisure-time skills* (Vol. 4). Austin, TX: Pro-Ed.

Benson, P. L., Galbraith, M. A., & Espeland, P. (1998). *What teens need to succeed: Proven, practical ways to shape your own future.* Minneapolis: Free Spirit.

Biehl, B. (1991). *The on my own handbook.* Colorado Springs, CO: Victor Books.

Ciborowski, J. (1992). *Textbooks and the students who can't read them.* Cambridge, MA: Brookline.

Cole, D. J., Ryan, C. W., & Kick, F. (1995). *Portfolios across the curriculum and beyond.* Thousand Oaks, CA: Corwin Press.

Cotton, E. G. (1998). *The online classroom: Teaching with the Internet.* Bloomington, IN: EDINFO Press.

Dede, C. (1998). *Learning with technology.* Alexandria, VA: Association for Supervision and Curriculum Development.

Development Studies Center. (1994). *At home in our schools: A guide to schoolwide activities that build community.* Oakland, CA: Development Studies Center.

Education Research Service. (1996). *The Internet roadmap for educators.* Arlington, VA: Education Research Service.

Ellis, D. B. (1991). *Becoming a master student.* Rapid City, SD: College Survival, Inc.

Fein, J. (1996). *Moving on: How to make the transition from college to the real world.* New York: Plume/Penguin Books.

Giagnocavo, G. (1996). *Educator's World Wide Web tourguide.* Lancaster, PA: Wentworth Worldwide Media.

Glasgow, N. A. (1996). *Taking the classroom into the community: A guidebook.* Thousand Oaks, CA: Corwin Press.

Godin, S. (1996). *The official rules of life.* New York: Seth Godin Production.

Harrington, B., & Christensen, B. (1995). *Unbelievably good deals that you absolutely can't get unless you're a teacher.* Chicago: Contemporary Books.

Harris, J. (1998). *Design tools for the Internet-supported classroom.* Alexandria, VA: Association for Supervision and Curriculum Development.

Heide, A., & Stilborne, L. (1996). *The teacher's complete and easy guide to the Internet.* Toronto, Ontario, Canada: Trifolium Books.

Higgins, K., & Boone, R. (1997). *Technology for students with learning disabilities: Educational applications.* Austin, TX: Pro-Ed.

Hittleman, D. R. (1983). *Developmental reading, K–12.* Boston: Houghton Mifflin.

Hoover, J. J., & Patton, J. R. (1995). *Teaching students with learning problems to use study skills.* Austin, TX: Pro-Ed.

Hoover, J. J., & Patton, J. R. (1997). *Curriculum adaptations for students with learning and behavior problems: Principles and practices.* Austin, TX: Pro-Ed.

Huffman, H. A. (1994). *Developing a character education program.* Alexandria, VA: Association for Supervision and Curriculum Development.

Jist Works. (1996). *The young person's occupational outlook handbook.* Indianapolis, IN: Jist Works.

Jorgensen, C. M. (1998). *Restructuring high schools for all students.* Baltimore: Paul H. Brookes.

Kinsley, C. W., & McPherson, K. (1995). *Enriching the curriculum through service learning.* Alexandria, VA: Association for Supervision and Curriculum Development.

Lake, J. (1997). *Lifelong learning skills: How to teach today's children for tomorrow's challenges.* Markham, Ontario, Canada: Pembrooke Publishers.

Leebow, K. (1998). *300 incredible things to do on the Internet.* Marietta, GA: VIP Publishing.

Lewis, B. A. (1998a). *The kid's guide to service projects.* Minneapolis: Free Spirit.

Lewis, B. A. (1998b). *The kid's guide to social action.* Minneapolis: Free Spirit.

Lewis, B. A. (1998c). *What do you stand for? A kid's guide to building character.* Minneapolis: Free Spirit.

Lieberman, S. A. (1997). *The real high school handbook.* Boston: Houghton Mifflin.

Mannix, D. (1995). *Life skills activities for secondary students with special needs.* West Nyack, NY: Center for Applied Research in Education.

Mannix, D. (1995). *Life skills for special children.* West Nyack, NY: Center for Applied Research in Education.

Mastropieri, M. A., & Scruggs, T. E. (1993). *A practical guide for teaching science to students with special needs in inclusive settings.* Austin, TX: Pro-Ed.

McLain, T. (1997). *Educator's guide to Web Wacker.* Lancaster, PA: Classroom Connect.

Meltzer, L. J., Roditi, B. N., Haynes, D. P., Biddle, K. R., Paster, M., & Taber, S. E. (1996). *Strategies for success: Classroom teaching techniques for students with learning problems.* Austin, TX: Pro-Ed.

Metropolitan Toronto School Board. (1996a). *Homeworking: 101 everyday activities in mathematics.* Markham, Ontario, Canada: Pembrooke Publishers.

Metropolitan Toronto School Board. (1996b). *Homeworking: 101 everyday activities for better reading and writing.* Markham, Ontario, Canada: Pembrooke Publishers.

Metropolitan Toronto School Board. (1996c). *Homeworking: 101 everyday activities in science and technology.* Markham, Ontario, Canada: Pembrooke Publishers.

Metropolitan Toronto School Board. (1996d). *Homeworking: 101 everyday activities in social studies, media, and life skills.* Markham, Ontario, Canada: Pembrooke Publishers.

Otfinoski, S. (1996). *The kid's guide to money: Earning it, saving it, spending it, growing it, sharing it.* New York: Scholastic.

Packer, A. J. (1992). *Bringing up parents: The teenager's handbook.* Minneapolis: Free Spirit.

Pratt, D. (1997). *Terrific teaching: 100 great teachers share their best ideas.* Markham, Ontario, Canada: Pembrooke Publishers.

Radencich, M. C., & Schumm, J. S. (1997). *How to help your child with homework.* Minneapolis: Free Spirit.

Rich, J. (1997). *The everything college survival book.* Holbrook, MA: Adams Media Corp.

Scheiber, B., & Talpers, J. (1987). *Unlocking potential: College and other choices for learning disabled people: A step-by-step guide.* Bethesda, MD: Adler and Adler.

Schrumpf, F., Freiburg, S., & Skadden, D. (1993). *Life lessons for young adolescents: An advisory guide for teachers.* Champaign, IL: Research Press.

Snyder, C. (1984). *Teaching your child about money.* Reading, MA: Addison-Wesley.

Valletutti, P. J., Bender, M., & Hoffnung, A. (1996). *Functional curriculum for teaching students with disabilities: Nonverbal and oral communication* (Vol. 2, 3rd ed.). Austin, TX: Pro-Ed.

Valletutti, P. J., Bender, M., & Sims-Tucker, B. (1996). *Functional curriculum for teaching students with disabilities: Functional academics* (Vol. 3, 2nd ed.). Austin, TX: Pro-Ed.

Weinberg, C. (1996). *The transition guide for college juniors and seniors: How to prepare for the future.* New York: New York University Press.

Windsor, N. (1994). *The safe tourist: Hundreds of proven ways to outsmart trouble.* Los Angeles: CorkScrew Press.

Worthington, J. F., & Farrar, R. (1998). *The ultimate college survival guide.* Princeton, NJ: Peterson's.

Yager, C. O. (1997). *Unbelievably good deals that you absolutely can't get unless you're a parent.* Chicago: Contemporary Books.

Conclusion

This chapter has discussed some instructional strategies to assist you in teaching your students the skills needed to make a successful transition to the next environment. The approaches you choose should be based on the individual needs of each of your students and on the future living, working, and educational environments that each has identified through the IEP process. Once you have identified the approach(es) you want to use with each student, you may need to enlist the support of your building administrator. It is crucial that you have a sound rationale for the approach(es) you have chosen and that you present this rationale to the student, the family, and the staff who are in charge of determining program options and approaches. This task may not be an easy one, but it will result in more satisfying outcomes for your students and higher job satisfaction for you.

11 School-Based and Community Resources

Linkages and Referrals

You cannot hope to build a better world without improving the individuals. To that end, each of us must work for his own improvement, and at the same time, share a general responsibility for all humanity.

—Marie Curie

The well-known anthropologist, Margaret Mead, once said, "Never doubt that a small group of thoughtful, committed citizens can change the world. Indeed, it's the only thing that ever has." One only has to look at any major movement in any society to see some evidence of Mead's view. Governments, religious groups, labor unions, political action/social justice groups (e.g., Green Party, NAACP, Urban League, La Raza, Sierra Club), youth groups (Scouting, F-H, etc.), and international aid agencies such as the Red Cross are examples of the vision of a few, committed people who banded together to solve problems.

The transition movement in the United States is a systems change movement that may never change the world or even have a major impact beyond North America. Still, the broader notion of looking beyond ourselves as individuals or families for ways to support individuals with disabilities is almost universal. Although each of us as individuals or as families can contribute a great deal to the quality of life of persons who have disabilities, there are some things we do not have the training, skills, or experience to do. At these points, it is critical to be able to turn to school and community resources for help. This chapter is designed to help you know some of the ways other people at school or in your community (or nearby community) can be used for referral sources and as collaborators in transition education and services.

The promise of the American Dream—the freedom and opportunity to work and live and lead a satisfying life—is difficult enough to achieve for those who do not have disabilities, let alone those who are disabled in some significant way. Futurists, whose job it is to chart the trends of the world, point to the pressures faced by children growing up in U.S. society. More than half live or will live in single-parent families. Even in two-parent families, both parents may be working. This leads to the phenomenon of latchkey children—children and youths who carry keys to let themselves into their homes or apartments where they stay unsupervised until a parent comes home from work. These children have a burden of self-management that is, for some, simply too much with which to cope (Rowley, 1987). At school, children have the added problem of facing school reforms that emphasize academic curricula with increasingly demanding standards for success. For many students, this additional pressure to succeed results in failure and stress.

When the problems of disability are coupled with the difficulties seen by the futurists, it is apparent that the obstacles to fulfilling the American promise are substantial. Teenagers who have their other problems compounded by disabilities may need all the help they can get to have any chance at all of achieving even a modest measure of success. To a large degree, their chances for adult adjustment may be determined by the referral resources available. Since the difference between dependency and relative independence could be determined by resources support, this chapter examines linkage and referral needs, linkage and referral sources, referral strategies, and the interdisciplinary collaboration that can make more possible the realization of the American Dream.

Referral Needs of High School Students in Special Programs

Although the term *referral* may sound innocuous enough, most high school teachers will have a number of dramatic stories to tell about students who ultimately had to be referred. The reason for the referral may have been a suicide attempt or a student who needed a simple referral initially but somehow slipped through the cracks of the system at every possible juncture until the problem reached crisis proportions. Both types of experiences can prove disheartening and shocking to the teacher who has never encountered such situations.

It is not possible to list and discuss here all the possible needs that students with disabilities might have during their high school years. The examples provided in the following lists will give you an idea of the range and variety of situations that the high school special education teacher, work experience coordinator, or transition specialist might encounter. The kinds of services provided by the various referral sources in the next section, School-Based Linkage and Referral Sources, provide more information about the types of students who require referral.

Physical Needs
- Poor dental health, resulting in problems of appearance, eating difficulties, bad breath, and absenteeism

- Obesity, resulting in social problems, health problems, and practical problems such as fitting into school furniture, using toilets, and finding clothes to fit
- Malnutrition, resulting in frequent illnesses and absenteeism, inability to participate in rigorous activities at school or on job training, and fatigue in classes
- Recurring bruises, scratches, abrasions, or swollen body parts, suggesting physical abuse
- Signs of alcohol or drug abuse, affecting performance at school as well as personal-social relationships

Personal-Social Needs
- Sudden and extreme changes in personal behavior
- Changes in patterns of school attendance
- Signs or direct evidence of illegal conduct
- Complaints from student about being subjected to gang intimidation, "shakedowns," or physical violence, including assault and rape
- Complaints from student about being subjected to sexual harassment at a job site
- Inappropriate sexual behavior
- Evidence of exploitation by real or foster parents, guardians, or welfare agencies

Physical and personal-social needs tend to get the most attention in any discussion of referral needs, but high school teachers and support personnel should remember that referrals can be made for enrichment of students' positive attributes and special interests also. Interest in the positive characteristics that students show at school should receive attention equal to the problem areas, and referrals to appropriate school or community sources can pay dividends in student attitude and performance.

School-Based Linkage and Referral Sources

As simplistic as it may seem, to benefit from the resources furnished by individuals and agencies, a person must first make contact with the resources. Referrals are mainly for services of two kinds: related services within a local education agency and services associated with the community.

General Education Referrals

The school reform movement of the 1980s and 1990s increased pressure on students to achieve academically. For some students with disabilities, academic achievement comes as a precondition for being able to get into more appropriate career or vocational education classes. Thus, the pressure increases for students with learning difficulties to do well in academic programs in which they enjoy few of the intrinsic rewards that students without disabilities enjoy. Furthermore, the usefulness of academics to many of the students who have difficulty with reading and abstract reasoning makes the dilemma even worse. Such an unfortunate situation has been difficult to combat and has caused great frustration and misunderstanding, not just for the students in special programs but for their parents and for school personnel as well.

Brolin (1995a) developed his life-centered career education model around the premise that regular teachers can and should be involved in helping students with learning difficulties acquire various career and transition competencies. He specified how various secondary school staff can contribute in meeting the 22 basic competencies. Table 11.1 is an adaptation of his listing of possible competency instructional responsibilities for both junior and senior high school personnel.

The most common strategy to assure some success in basic academic classes has been to seek out general education teachers who understand the limitations imposed by various disabilities and who adjust their class requirements accordingly. Referral of selected students to these carefully identified teachers is the best way to guarantee any degree of success in placing students with disabilities in high school academic courses.

Guidance and Counseling Services

Any consideration of career or transition programming must speak to the role of guidance and counseling. What are the elements of guidance and counseling that function in a high school program? What are the goals of guidance and counseling activities? Who should provide guidance and counseling services to students with special needs?

The terms *guidance* and *counseling* are frequently used as two independent concepts, but most school personnel in this field view *guidance* as an umbrella term that includes a number of techniques or approaches, with *counseling* being the heart of the guidance program. Guidance, according to Shertzer and Stone (1981, p. 40), is "the process of helping individuals to understand themselves and their world." They presented counseling in school settings as a technique "to assist students to explore and understand themselves so that they can become self-directing individuals" (p. 172). Since these definitions do not clearly differentiate between the two terms, other than one being viewed as a process and the other as a technique, each will be discussed in greater detail.

Guidance Services

Brolin and Gysbers (1989) addressed the challenge for school counselors in responding to the career development and transition needs of students with disabilities with an optimistic note. They have viewed current trends in guidance in the schools as increasingly being conceptualized and implemented as comprehensive competency-based programs. Gysbers and Henderson (1988; see also Gys-

TABLE 11.1   Proposed Competency Instructional Settings for Personnel for Secondary Special Education Students

Competencies	Instructional Setting/Instructional Personnel
Daily Living Skills	
1. Managing personal finances	General business, consumer education, math, home economics
2. Selecting, managing, and maintaining a household	Home economics, home and family living
3. Caring for personal needs	Health, home and family living, home economics
4. Raising children and meeting marriage responsibilities	Home and family living, home economics
5. Buying, preparing, and consuming food	Home economics, home and family living, health, consumer education
6. Buying and caring for clothing	Home economics, consumer education, home and family living
7. Exhibiting responsible citizenship	Social studies (government, history), home room/guidance period, community-based experiences
8. Utilizing recreational facilities and engaging in leisure	Physical education, art, music, theater arts
9. Getting around the community	Driver's education, orientation and mobility (for blind students)
Personal-Social Skills	
10. Achieving self-awareness	All instructional areas; counseling and guidance staff, self-determination/futures planning curricula
11. Acquiring self-confidence	Selected instructional areas of student strengths, selected extracurricular activities, music, speech, theater arts, social and interpersonal skills curricula, counseling and guidance staff
12. Achieving socially responsible behavior	All instructional areas; counseling and guidance staff
13. Maintaining good interpersonal skills	Selected instructional areas of student strengths, selected extracurricular activities, music, speech, theater arts, social and interpersonal skills curricula, counseling and guidance staff
14. Achieving independence	Self-determination curricula, community-based instruction, counseling and guidance staff
15. Making adequate decisions	Self-determination curricula, community-based instruction, counseling and guidance staff
16. Communicating with others	Selected extracurricular activities, English, speech, social and interpersonal skills curricula, foreign languages, English as a second language (ESL)

TABLE 11.1   Continued

Competencies	Instructional Setting/Instructional Personnel
Occupational Skills	
17. Knowing and exploring occupational possibilities	Selected instructional areas, vocational education, home economics, counseling and guidance staff, technology systems for career exploration, community-based experiences (mentoring, job shadowing, job samples, field trips, internships)
18. Selecting and planning occupational choices	Counseling and guidance staff, technology systems for career decision making, mentors
19. Exhibiting appropriate work habits and behaviors	Vocational education, home economics, community-based experiences, community work-based learning programs, art, music, theater arts, computer centers, library, study hall
20. Seeking, securing, and maintaining employment	Counseling and guidance staff, vocational education teachers, community work-based learning staff, job coaches, transition coordinators/specialists
21. Exhibiting sufficient physical-manual skills	Vocational education, home economics, community work-based learning programs, physical education
22. Obtaining specific occupational skills	Vocational education, home economics, community work-based learning programs

bers, 1994) described their proposed model of a comprehensive guidance program as having four program components: (1) guidance curriculum, (2) individual planning, (3) responsive services, and (4) system support. Their program was organized around the need to meet developmental needs and outcomes for students. The guidance curriculum component, for example, was made to incorporate Competencies 10 through 15, 17, 18, and 20 of the Life-Centered Career Education model (Brolin, 1992) described in Chapter 1. These competencies, which focus on personal and social skills and occupational guidance, are particularly appropriate for what one would expect in a guidance curriculum and fit in nicely with current outcomes-based education programs. The individual planning component relates to the counselor's role on the IEP team or as a consultant/collaborator with other school staff in planning for strategies or procedures to help a student. Responsive services would be those assessment, information-giving, referral, or counseling services needed by a student and specified on his or her IEP. The system support component would be the overall support contributions that the counselor makes to the school's operations (testing, scheduling, etc.).

The Gysbers and Henderson (1988; see also Gysbers, 1994) model did not propose that the role of the school guidance counselor be changed dramatically to take on students with disabilities. Rather, it attempted to provide a better focus on the various roles of school counselors and to identify percentages of counselor time that should be devoted to carrying out guidance activities in each of the four components in their model.

The positive implications of this model for students with disabilities are that they are much more likely to receive some needed instruction and programming within the mainstream of a school if that school has a guidance curriculum and if counselors are committed to individual planning for *all* students.

Until comprehensive guidance program models are in place, advocates for students with disabilities must look at any existing guidance and counseling program in terms of the services that are offered and how these services can be accessed. It may be that all of the services that students with disabilities need will never be able to be accessed via the guidance counselor(s) in a school. In those cases, some of the services may have to be provided by others with the support of the guidance counselors. The following sections—Assessment, Informating Giving, and Counseling Services in the Community—describe some of the basic guidance services that students with disabilities need, regardless of who provides them.

Assessment

Counselors and teachers using a comprehensive career guidance approach use assessment as a basic process for getting information to assist students to make decisions and work toward goals. (Assessment techniques were discussed in detail in Chapter 5.) Assessment, as a functional element of a guidance program, is the responsibility of everybody who works with students with disabilities, not just the school psychologist, the vocational evaluator, an educational diagnostician, or the school counselor.

Information Giving

Information services in a guidance program are designed to give students the appropriate educational, personal-social, and occupational data they need to understand themselves and their environments. Counselors and teachers can ensure that a significant amount of this type of information is provided systematically when they work together to schedule students in courses that meet each student's individual needs, preferences, and interests. When available courses are not appropriate for students, information giving may result in course revisions or curriculum development. In a less systematic but a more individualized approach, counselors and teachers should also make available to all students current information on postsecondary education options, occupational information, and information related to adolescent problems and interests.

Information is absolutely critical to the life-career guidance and decision-making process for youths experiencing educational disabilities. Appropriate decisions depend on obtaining complete, timely, and accurate information about all life-career and transition alternatives. How to share this information is the difficult problem. Our position is that it must be transmitted through the curriculum, one-to-one counseling with parents, and through professionals, materials, computer-based information, and guidance systems. No one single approach is adequate

Career Resource Centers.   Information implies a body of knowledge that is of use to someone. Part of that information is in the minds and personal memory systems of counselors, teachers, parents, and other informed sources, but most of it will be in resource documents or systems that can handle large amounts of information—much of which changes rapidly. This suggests a need for an accessible, central location where this information is easily obtained. A career resource center is one common way of providing that. Such a center serves as an identifiable source of information to students and increases the likelihood of use. Even then, many high school students may choose not to use it.

Realistically, the percentage of students with disabilities using a central career resource center in a high school may be lower than for students not identified as having special needs. This raises the issue as to why this would be the case. Some special education teachers say that their students do not feel comfortable going to such a center because they do not identify with the rest of the school. The "ours" and "theirs" problem between regular and special education is at the heart of this. One high school counselor in a study of high school programs for youths with disabilities (Clark, Knowlton, & Dorsey, 1989) spoke openly about special education students, IEP students, and "our" students. An interesting distinction was between special students (in this case, students who are mildly mentally retarded) and IEP students (students who are learning disabled and behavior disordered). However, the more telling attitude was the "ours" and "theirs" referring to identified students with disabilities versus students without such an identification.

Discomfort, whether social or ability related, may be an oversimplification of the problem of low usage of a career resource center by students in special programs. Possibly the problem is compounded by other factors, such as general motivation to seek information, reading difficulties, how encouraging guidance counselors or guidance staff are to students who need more individual attention, the location of the center, a lack of encouragement to students by special class and resource room teachers to use the center, or inadequacy of the center services. The solution to the basic problem—the need for accurate, relevant guidance information—must consider the possibility of all of these factors. At a minimum, a high school should address the issue of adequacy of the center's content. Is the center's material limited to college catalogs? Is it focused on occupations requiring only a college education? Is the material readable and is the information accessible through media other than print? Does the center provide information in career and transition knowledge and skill areas other than education and occupations? Do students identify with any guidance counselor in the career resource center or one specially designed for students who have special needs?

Computer Systems.   Computer-based occupational information systems are rapidly becoming part of the common technology of high school guidance programs. Chapters 6 and 7 suggested references for occupational information, employment trends, legislation, and services available on the Internet.

The microcomputer boom of the 1980s resulted in significant breakthroughs, not only in sophistication but also in affordable costs for schools. Today, the computer literacy of high school students is well beyond the expectations of even the early enthusiasts. Clearly, there are some definite advantages in using computer-based information systems. Among these are the following:

1. Computers reduce the time counselors and career information personnel must spend in repetitive and routine dissemination tasks.
2. Computers provide almost instantaneous information.
3. Computer technology is still novel enough to be motivational and has moved from information storage to interactive decision-making systems.
4. Information can be updated more easily and more quickly than can print information.
5. Information can be made available in rural and remote areas with laptop computers, modems, and other sophisticated equipment.
6. Audio attachments for students with visual impairments or nonreaders open up the systems to new populations.
7. Special switches and voice commands for students with visual or physical disabilities make it possible to use computers more independently.
8. Computers can provide data to teachers and counselors on what information students have obtained and how they have used the system.

Counseling Services in the Community

The degree to which appropriate counseling services can be obtained for individuals in a high school from outside of the school depends largely on the community. Even in the most restricted community, however, there are resources that the school need not duplicate. Certainly, it often requires determined and thoughtful efforts to arrange for the use of these services. But, understanding that, counselors and special education staff can build relationships with community resource persons that lead to referrals and use of an array of guidance assistance services. Because of the broad definition of a comprehensive career guidance program for students with disabilities, the process of counseling referral deserves a full and extensive treatment of its own.

In the context of guidance and counseling services, there are two important issues that relate to referral decisions:

Issue 1:   Counselors or teachers in the school who decide that a student's problems or needs are beyond their guidance or counseling competencies (but the student or parents will not accept referral) must decide whether to continue services to the student.

Issue 2: Who should take the initiative for establishing close, direct, cooperative relationships among school and community resources?

In issue 1, the most common argument against continuation of services is that such continuation may worsen an already serious situation. From a humanitarian perspective, no professional would want to deny services to someone in desperate need, and the question comes down to whether some assistance, however inadequate, is better than none. From a practical perspective, school personnel have to consider their available time, the availability of consultation, and whether there is a reasonable expectation that continuation will make a difference. From a professional ethics perspective, the American Association for Counseling Development (1988) statement of professional ethics for its members is straightforward. Counselors or guidance personnel are expected to terminate any counseling relationships that call for assistance that goes beyond their competencies.

In issue 2, the ideal resolution for initiating cooperative working relationships that make referrals smooth and effective is for schools and community resources to collaborate in planning and service delivery through the transition component of the IEP. It is not uncommon for both school and community agency personnel to be critical of the other's failure to initiate, cooperate, and follow through in their relationships with each other. From our perspective, the school is the most stable, established organization in a community, and it is the school's responsibility to take the initiative to make full use of community agency resources because students and the schools are the ones who benefit most from such efforts.

Counseling in a high school is usually viewed as one part of a guidance program. Any one counselor may approach the counseling relationship from a unique perspective, ranging from an intention to deal primarily with practical information giving for one counselor to working through intense psychological stress with another. The American School Counselor Association (1997) has recently adopted a new definition of *school counseling:* "Counseling is a process of helping people by assisting them in making decisions and changing behavior. School counselors work with all students, school staff, families, and members of the community as an integral part of the education program. School counseling programs promote school success through a focus on academic achievement, prevention and intervention activities, advocacy and social/emotional and career development" (p. 8).

This definition does not limit counseling only to a trained counselor. Jageman and Myers (1986) supported this view in their notion that counseling can take place in a relationship between a counselee and a professional, paraprofessional, or nonprofessional counselor. This opens up the counseling role to transition specialists, teachers, teacher aides, parents, employers, school staff, and even peers.

Although the definition of counseling remains difficult (especially when differentiating it from psychotherapy), the nature of the counseling process can be described. For our purposes in discussing the counseling process with secondary students with mild to moderate levels of disabilities, the following statements reflect the nature of counseling:

- The counseling process, whether successful or not in terms of outcomes, is characterized by a unique, helping relationship between the person performing the counselor role and the student(s).
- The counseling interaction process includes both verbal and nonverbal communication.
- Counseling may be a service used more by students who are well adjusted and whose mental health is stable than those who exhibit extreme modes of behavior or emotional instability,
- Counseling stresses rational planning, problem solving, and support in the face of situational pressures.
- Counseling approaches, whether selected strategically or naturally and spontaneously, are based more on focusing on everyday reality and conscious observations than unconscious motivations, past events, dreams, or symbolic material.
- Counseling tends to rely on the counselee's positive individual strengths for problem solving or decision making rather than stressing the diagnosis and remediation of personality defects.
- Counseling is ordinarily viewed as a short-term process in which specific problems are identified and outcomes are achieved over a relatively short period of time.

Goals of Guidance and Counseling Activities

Professionals responsible for guidance and counseling with high school youths approach their own professional activity goals with a variety of assumptions about career and transition development in the abstract (or ideal) and for career and transition development for youths with disabilities in particular. One way of putting goals into perspective is to challenge the notion that guidance and counseling is highly cerebral and can work only with those who have the intelligence and verbal communication skills to deal with problems, information, and decision making at a self-actualization level. Very few people operate at that level in all areas of their lives. Maslow's (1954) need hierarchy has been related to counseling and guidance goals for persons with severe disabilities by both Lassiter (1981) and Jageman and Myers (1986). These authors have delineated possible goal alternatives in guidance and counseling activities with special-needs students with mild or moderate disabilities. Examples are provided for each of Maslow's need levels in Table 11.2.

Key Providers of Services

Writers in the field of guidance and counseling (Gysbers & Henderson, 1994; Myrick, 1993) generally maintain that, although there are a number of important

TABLE 11.2   Examples of Career Guidance and Counseling Goals and Activities Based on Maslow's Hierarchy of Needs

Need	Prevention Goals	Intervention Goals
Physiological Survival Needs	Assist students in learning effects of good eating and drinking habits.	Assist students in dealing with problems of overeating, alcohol or substance abuse, or eating disorders.
	Assist students in planning exercise and rest schedules.	Provide student support and reinforcement for efforts in accomplishing plans.
	Assist students in understanding sources of pain and pain-reduction alternatives.	Assist students with stress-management techniques or making medication schedules work.
	Assist students in understanding sexual needs and appropriate responses.	Provide students assertiveness training.
	Assist students in acquiring knowledge on health and hygiene requirements of a job.	Confront students with inappropriate sexual behavior and modifying behaviors.
Safety/Security Needs	Assist students in understanding stress in life changes.	Counsel students to assist in coping with stress and adjustment to new settings, new people, new demands.
	Assist students in planning for risk events.	Assist students in coping with risk events.
	Assist students in organizing their behavior and environments to establish order and routine.	Assist students in adjusting to disorganized or chaotic life environments.
Belonging/Love Needs	Assist students in learning about needing to belong.	Provide accepting support system in a counseling relationship.
	Assist students in learning appropriate ways of seeking acceptance and love.	Provide therapeutic environment and assistance in coping with rejection/loneliness.
Esteem Needs	Assist students in learning ways of behaving that are seen as successful and confidence building.	Assist students in coping with low self-esteem or mild depression.
	Assist students in finding places to work, groups to join, or places to live that foster self-esteem.	Assist students in self-evaluation of self-defeating and self-derogatory behavior.
	Assist students in understanding conflicts within themselves relative to their disabilities.	Assist students in coping with continuing adjustment demands to their disabilities.
Self-Actualization Needs	Assist students in learning ways of personal growth and self-improvement.	Provide students with support and encouragement for efforts in personal growth.
	Assist students in learning ways of using their strengths to move beyond their present levels of functioning.	Assist students in coping with routine, boredom, and malaise.

contributors to a guidance and counseling program, the key person is the professionally prepared and personally committed counselor. This position is not a difficult one to defend from a logical and practical point of view, even though some people argue that the teacher is the key person because of day-to-day interactions and knowledge of each student's needs. Lombana (1982) pointed out that the argument that the special education teacher is the best counselor for students with disabilities could logically be extended to conclude that the general education classroom teacher is the best counselor for students who have no disabilities. The main differences between teaching and guidance are inferred from a clear difference between the function of teaching and the various functions of guidance. Since counseling is such an important role in guidance, the differences frequently focus on the dissimilarities between teaching and counseling.

Those who argue in favor of the teacher role being the most important may have an idealized elementary schoolteacher in mind, because it is becoming increasingly clear that high school teachers are being asked to do many more things, few of which are related to guidance and counseling. The typical high school teacher is—by training, by inclination, and by the requirements of a teaching position—a specialist in a single subject. It is as a subject specialist that the teacher expects to make a career and meet the expectations of students and their parents. The counselor, on the other hand, is specifically assigned guidance and counseling responsibilities and has some type of training and credentials supporting competency in those responsibilities.

All of this may seem too obvious for discussion. However, the reality of high schools and their hierarchical bureaucracies (Skrtic, 1991) breaks through the professional logic and presents a disturbing view of the actual achievement of guidance and counseling goals via this system. To emphasize the discouraging persistence of this problem over the years, Arbuckle in 1972 made the following statement:

> Throughout the United States there are tens of thousands of coercive teachers, scores of administrators who are cold and unfeeling, and a school curriculum, a significant proportion of which is dull and deadly, oppressive, and irrelevant. Teachers and administrators should be concerned about these problems, and many of them are very much concerned. But...anyone involved in schools surely would have to be blind to be unaware that tens of thousands of young people are being affected in a negative way by their school experience. (p. 789)

All types of students in today's high schools are falling through the cracks of the guidance system. Our view is that this is especially the case for students receiving special services under IEPs. This is not the fault of school guidance counselors, but rather a symptom of some of the issues confronting high school programs today. Some of the more common issues include the following:

- High school guidance counselors are assigned responsibility for providing guidance services to large numbers of students, making significant individ-

ual contact difficult and forcing students to be aggressive and persistent if
they want to receive assistance.

- High school guidance counselors in small high schools have to be knowledgeable in all areas of guidance; frequently, they have few resources to support their services.

- High school guidance counselors have been assigned administrative support
roles over the years (such as scheduling) that have consumed much of their
time that could be used for less administrative tasks.

- High school guidance counselors have traditionally spent much of their time
helping students to select and apply to colleges. This will continue, if not
increase, in response to educational reform policies being implemented and
will require more planning for academic course of study decisions.

- High school guidance counselors rarely are required to have any preservice
training in even the basic characteristics of exceptional students, much less
training in career development or transition guidance for them.

- High school special education teachers are becoming increasingly involved
in course selection and scheduling for students on IEPs. This requires more
academic planning and guidance in light of new and changing graduation
policies.

- Vocational assessment and career/transitional guidance are not available in
any systematic form in most high schools. High school guidance counselors
claim lack of time or expertise for these services for students in special education services.

- High school special education programs have responded to the guidance and
counseling service void for their students by assigning or reassigning teachers to function in similar roles, either on a part- or full-time basis, such as
vocational counselors, work experience coordinators, vocational-adjustment
coordinators, and so forth. For the most part, these individuals have little or
no preservice training for these roles, and only a few states recognize such a
role with a certificate or endorsement credential.

Some schools are reviewing their guidance and counseling services for students with disabilities in light of the provisions of the Individuals with Disabilities
Education Act of 1990 (IDEA), which authorizes the use of "rehabilitation counseling services" [20 U.S.C. 1401(a)(17)]. Under the final regulations of IDEA, *rehabilitation counseling services* means services provided by qualified personnel in
individual or group sessions that focus specifically on career development,
employment preparation, achieving independence, and integration in the workplace and community of a student with a disability. The regulations also state that
the term *rehabilitation counseling services* includes vocational rehabilitation services
provided to students with disabilities by state vocational rehabilitation programs
funded under the Rehabilitation Act of 1973, as amended. In essence, this means
that students who need the kind of services described under the definition of rehabilitation counseling services should have those related services—as well as who
will be designated as responsible for providing them—specified on their IEPs. This

means that a school may employ someone specifically to provide such services for the school and get reimbursed by the state with special education funds. It also means that a student who needs those services and who is eligible for vocational rehabilitation program services may receive such services while still in school and provided by a nonschool professional from a state vocational rehabilitation agency. It is also possible that a student might receive rehabilitation counseling services from both a school and nonschool qualified person collaboratively.

Hanley-Maxwell and Szymanski (1992) pointed out that rehabilitation counselors' roles in the career-development and transition process depend on a variety of factors. Among these factors are (1) the settings or actual locations of employment of the counselors; (2) the types of disabilities, ages, and needs of the students; and (3) the resources available in the setting, from the family, and in the community. Szymanski and King (1989) proposed the following potential rehabilitation counseling functions for transition:

- Career and psychosocial counseling
- Consultation with school personnel regarding the vocational implications of students' disabilities and possible educational accommodations
- Coordination of career planning and preparation efforts
- Job placement, job analysis, job modification and restructuring, and follow-up
- Work-adjustment counseling
- Coordination of job support services
- Coordination of referrals to and coordination with adult service agencies
- Specialized planning and linkage with postsecondary programs
- Development of individual transition plans

In light of the issues reflecting the reality of school organizations, what should be expected of school guidance counselors? Consider the following as a proposal for what should be exemplary program practice:

- Help with social adjustment problems in general education classes or all-inclusive activities in the school.
- Help with problems that may occur with teachers in general education classes, the resource room, or the special class.
- Provide assistance with questions or decision-making needs about educational goals beyond high school.
- Give help when students find it difficult to establish friendships and communication with peers.
- Provide support when students' interests and goals appear to conflict with those of their parents.
- Help with decision making on appropriate courses in school that are appropriate for students' interests and needs.
- Provide encouragement when students are searching for meaning and values in their lives.

- Give assistance when students need information about their abilities, aptitudes, and interests.
- Help with the development of self-advocacy skills.

The counselor is also expected to be ready to help teachers and other school staff. This list proposes that a high school counselor should take on the following responsibilities:

- View special education teachers and staff as members of the guidance team.
- Serve as an interpreter of the school's pupil personnel policies and guidance program and keep students fully informed on the guidance services and activities that are available to the entire school.
- Share appropriate individual student data with both regular and special education teachers with special regard for confidentiality and assist teachers in incorporating those assessment results in curriculum development and instructional planning.
- Assist regular teachers in making referrals to appropriate school personnel, such as the school nurse, school psychologist, school social worker or visiting teacher, or special education staff specialists.
- Assist special education teachers in making referrals to community agency personnel, such as community mental health staff, city or county health staff, and alcohol and drug-abuse information centers.
- Cooperate with the efforts of middle school or junior high school and high school special education teachers in making the student's transition to the high school a smooth and positive one.
- Assist in the planning of special education curriculum development and serve as a resource person for obtaining age-appropriate, relevant guidance materials and information.
- Make current information about job opportunities for students available to special education staff.
- Involve special education teachers and staff in faculty in-service.
- Serve as a liaison between the special education staff and the principal or administrative staff on guidance issues especially related to students in special programs.

It is unrealistic to believe that secondary school guidance counselors can do all the tasks they know need to be done on an individual basis. Typically, case loads are high and counselors are assigned too many inappropriate noncounseling program tasks. When counselors have a tangible linkage to student planning and instruction for all students, it is easier for them to focus on critical counseling tasks and reach more students. Synatschk (1999) presented a comprehensive developmental counseling model implemented by the Austin (Texas) Independent School District that shows a commitment by the school district to both individual planning and a guidance curriculum. The commitment to individual planning is indicated in the requirement for all students in grades 6 through 12 to have an

Individual Academic-Career Plan (IACP) completed annually. (The state of Utah uses a similar document called the *student educational and occupational plan.*) The commitment to guidance information and teaching self-determination skills is evident in the comprehensive developmental guidance curriculum (Austin Independent School District, 1996). Figure 11.1 shows the strands of the Austin Independent School District Guidance Curriculum and reflects the efforts of a school district to take seriously its role in addressing some of the major adult outcome-oriented goals for all students. When this kind of programming is available and accessible for students with disabilities, the goal of inclusive education as well as guidance and counseling in secondary schools is much more realistic.

School Psychology Services

School psychologists frequently serve primarily in assessment. Assessment for initial identification and placement, periodic reevaluations, and some diagnostic assessment for educational or personal-social adjustment consume much of their time. Training, background, or personal preference may move some school psychologists out of the psychometric role into consultation with teachers on learning or behavior problems, personal adjustment difficulties, interpersonal relationships, and adolescent psychology. Some even seek out opportunities to do some individual or group counseling when their training has included such an emphasis and their school district values that type of service.

For the past two decades, a small but committed group of school psychologists and school psychology educators has gradually moved the field of school psychology to acknowledge the significance of vocational programming as an appropriate role for practitioners (Levinson, 1993). The National Association of School Psychologists provided early support for this group by approving a special-interest group organization for vocational school psychology and included both vocational assessment and intervention into its *Standards for the Provision of School Psychological Services* (Thomas & Grimes, 1995).

Despite these encouraging developments, school psychologists are not significantly involved in vocational assessment or transition planning. Carey (1995) reported that in his national study of school psychologists, less than 1 percent of their time was spent in vocational assessment. Staab (1996) found in her national random sample of 602 school psychologists working with secondary schools that school psychologists were interested in transition planning activities, perceived these activities to be important, but believed generally that they were unprepared to conduct transition activities. Given a list of transition services activity categories (consultation, assessment, direct services, and program planning/evaluation), not one of the categories was described by the respondents as regularly or routinely conducted. Approximately half of the school psychologists responding to the survey indicated that school psychologists' skills were underutilized in the transition process, and about 82 percent saw the transition services activity categories as important to some degree (from a scale of somewhat important, important, or very important).

FIGURE 11.1 Strands of the Guidance Curriculum

A. Self-Knowledge and Acceptance	This domain helps students learn more about their abilities, interests, and personal characteristics. Students learn to identify their strengths and the areas in which they need to improve so that true self-acceptance is possible.
B. Interpersonal and Communication Skills	This domain emphasizes the value of developing positive interpersonal relationships and how communication skills affect the ways in which people interact with each other. They also learn to value differences and uniqueness among people.
C. Responsible Behavior	This domain assists students in developing a sense of personal responsibility for their behavior. It gives attention to how attitudes and perceptions can affect behavior, how feelings and behaviors are related to goals and consequences, and how behavior can be changed, if desired.
D. Conflict Resolution	The focus of this domain is nonviolent solutions to conflict situations. Students will also deal with styles of cooperative behavior, prejudice, and healthy expressions of anger.
E. Decision Making/ Problem Solving	This domain involves learning the steps for making effective decisions and solving problems. It also involves an increased awareness of the factors that influence change and decision making as well as helpful procedures for problem solving. There is an emphasis on responsibility and individual choice.
F. Motivation to Achieve	This area is designed to assist students to achieve success in school and their adult lives. It will help them develop positive attitudes and habits which will enable them to get the most out of schooling. They will also focus on the connections between what they are learning in school and what their future will be like.
G. Goal Setting	This domain is designed to help students understand the importance of setting goals for themselves and monitoring their own progress toward their goals. They will also learn to differentiate between realistic and unrealistic goals.
H. Career Planning	This domain helps students understand more about the world of work, increase their career awareness, and do in-depth career exploration related to personal interests, values, and abilities. It also includes how to make effective educational plans so that students may achieve their career goals.

Source: From "Counseling" by K. O. Synatschk in *Transition and School-Based Services: Interdisciplinary Perspectives for Enhancing the Transition Process* by S. H. deFur and J. R. Patton (Eds.), 1999, Austin, TX: Pro-Ed. Reprinted by permission.

The nature of life-span transitions (discussed in Chapter 2) and the scope of transition planning assessment (discussed in Chapter 5) clearly indicate an overlap between the interests of transition services advocates and school psychologists. These interests converge most obviously in assessment of students' needs, preferences, and interests; the mutual concern for collaborative planning with students and their families; the need for encouraging school sensitivity to cultural, ethnic, experiential, and language backgrounds; and the promotion of self-determined, satisfying involvement at school, in the workplace, and in the community.

Secondary special educators should cultivate good working relationships with school psychologists. On the basis of the Staab (1996) data, school psychologists are more ready now than ever before to shift their roles and use some of the expertise they have in areas other than cognitive testing. Requests for assistance in interpreting tests already given, requests for testing in specialized areas (adaptive behavior, learning styles, emotional/behavioral adjustment, etc.), professional opinions on student or family characteristics, ideas on strategies for teaming and collaboration, support in making school-based services referrals, support in making community-based referrals, and crisis counseling are just a few of the ways school psychologists may be enticed into the transition planning and transition education process.

School Nurse Services

Students having chronic health impairments often seek out the school nurse for assistance on their own, or referrals are made to the school nurse by attending physicians. High school special education staff, however, should be aware of the needs of all students with disabilities and be ready to bring the school nurse into emergency or consultation situations. Students who do not have any chronic health conditions can benefit from the nurse's services in a variety of ways.

School nurses serve all students in public schools, but they have been actively involved with students with chronic conditions since the passage of PL 94-142 in 1975. *Students with chronic conditions* refers to those students with special health needs who may or may not receive special education services. The National Association of School Nurses (NASN) identified the importance of this group by making one of its 10 standards to practice specifically related to students with special health care needs (Proctor, Lordi, & Zaiger, 1993). More recently, the NASN developed an issue brief outlining the specific roles and responsibilities of the school nurse for students with disabilities and called for the inclusion of the professional school nurse as a related services provider under the IDEA (NASN, 1996).

The health care community recognized the need to think about the transition of children and youths from pediatric to adult health care services in 1985 when the National Center for Youth with Disabilities (NCYD) began operating with a goal to improve services for youths through the second decade of life as they transition to adult living, health care, and vocations (Blum, 1995). The NYCD (1996) completed a survey of adolescent health transition programs in the United States. The organization identified 277 programs that support the transition of youths with chronic illness or disabilities from pediatric to adult health care. Responses from 129 of these programs indicated that services are both formal as well as informal and that health education, case management, and individual planning for transition to an independent life-style were the three services offered most often. The vast majority of these programs were direct service health care programs in clinics or community agencies and followed an acute care medical model of health care delivery. Few programs included vocational counselors as part of the team, and even fewer actively engaged in educational transition planning or transition services delivery through collaboration.

In most settings, the school nurse works individually with students and their families. The nurse focuses on training for good health and competence and responsibility for independence in self-management and care of the health condition. The practice of school nursing is accomplished through the development of an individualized health care plan (IHP), which is either incorporated into a student's IEP or is a separate document for health services (Cox & Sawin, 1999). The IHP includes information about the student's needs, nursing interventions designed to meet those needs, and a description of how the care supports the education process of the school.

The National Association of School Nurses (1996) listed the following general roles and responsibilities of students with special health care needs:

- Assists in screening and identifying students who may need health-related services
- Assesses the identified child's sensory and physical health status in collaboration with the student, parent(s), and health care providers
- Develops individualized health and emergency care plans
- Assists the IEP team in developing the IEP when it relates to health needs of the student
- Assists the parent(s) and teachers to find and use community resources
- Provides in-service training for teachers and staff regarding the individual health needs of the student
- Provides and/or supervises assistive personnel to provide specialized health care services in the school setting
- Evaluates the effectiveness of the health-related parts of the IEP with the student, parent(s), and other team members, and makes revisions to the plan as needed

Some specific contributions of nursing to transition programming and service delivery commonly include the following:

- Teaching self-care skills needed to manage specific health conditions
- Coordinating and communicating with school and health providers in implementing IHPs or health-related goals on the IEP
- Providing sexuality education instruction
- Addressing the prevention of secondary conditions

- Focusing counseling on psychological adjustment to special health conditions, long-term treatment, and terminal illnesses
- Providing instruction and guidance in nutrition, weight control, substance abuse, and child abuse
- Providing attendant or personal care provider training (Cox & Sawin, 1999; Igoe, 1994; Johnson, 1996; Magyary & Brandt, 1996; Peterson, Rauen, Brown, & Cole, 1994)

Not all secondary schools have school nurses readily available, and frequently health management caseloads for school nurses are unrealistically high. Still, the obvious relevance of school health and school nurse professionals to transition planning and service delivery for many students with disabilities is clear. We believe that the health component—health decision making and self-management, prevention of secondary disabilities, and health services—must be addressed by school-based transition teams. The school nurse can be an important participant on those transition teams.

School Social Work Services

When influences outside the school setting interfere with the success of the student, school social services workers can become an important transition services partner. Functioning as they do as a bridge between the home and the school, school social workers can evaluate the variables of the home and community setting that could be having an influence on the performance of the young person who has a disability. Although school social workers often can deal directly with a problem, they also broker services, calling on other persons or agencies to supply specific services to the student, the family, or related school personnel.

The actual monitoring of referral sources and services may fall to any of a variety of professionals in the school, such as the guidance counselor, school psychologist, or social worker. Germain (1996) and Bennett, DeLuca, and Allen (1996) have noted the school social worker's role in coordinating and integrating services between school and families, between families and community agencies, and between schools and community agencies. Social work training, in fact, focuses a great deal of attention on social worker skills in understanding and conceptualizing relationships between individuals and multiple services. Networks and linkages outside of school are relatively new to special education teachers, but are routine to school social workers.

Other than the linkage and coordination of services roles of social workers, Markward and Kurtz (1999) cited several additional roles that school social workers can assume in a school's transition services. These include parent involvement, collaboration/teaming, assessment, and organizational work.

Parent Involvement. Parent involvement is seen by many secondary teachers as one of their greatest challenges. For any number of reasons, parents of adolescents with disabilities are less involved with their students' lives at secondary school than they were during the elementary and middle school years. Parent involvement is a primary focus of many school social workers (Chavkin & Brown, 1992; Constable, 1992; Dupper, 1993; Grief, 1993). Constable (1992) stated that school social workers can help remove some of the barriers that keep parents from being involved in their children's school planning and progress. Cultural misunderstandings, current or past communication difficulties, personal histories involving school failure or alienation, intimidation by school personnel, or even adolescents' preferences that their parents not be involved at school are a few of the many barriers that social workers can address through individual or group assistance.

Collaborative Teaming. Collaborative teaming is an attractive alternative for cost effectiveness during times of budget restrictions, but one of the elements of current school reform and restructuring for effective schools is the notion of transdisciplinary teaming and collaborative work. Gibelman (1993) and Buchweitz (1993) both noted that school social work personnel must work closely and collaboratively with other support-service personnel, especially school counselors, school psychologists, and school nurses. School social workers' general knowledge of family systems and mental and public health resources—as well as specialized knowledge of family consumer education, teenage pregnancies, drug and alcohol abuse, domestic violence and child abuse, and dropout prevention—also suggest potential for their collaborative teaming with teachers on curriculum, program development, and actual instruction. Further, in cases where school social workers are intensely involved with students and families related to serious emotional or behavioral problems, they may need to do collaborative planning and coordination with community work-placement supervisors, job coaches, or job supervisors.

Assessment. In Illinois, and possibly other states, school social workers are part of formal diagnostic and assessment teams for the school. The common formal assessments that social workers might provide are social development and adaptive behavior assessments. These two areas change over time and could provide helpful information for transition services planning with students 14 years of age and older, especially the last three-year reevaluation. Informal assessments are also conducted upon request, including social histories, ecological or environmental assessments of the home, observations of parents' understanding of technical or unfamiliar terms related to their children's schooling, and interviews of parents' long-term dreams and fears for their children's futures.

Organizational Work. The interactive, connective nature of school social work gives school social workers a perspective of the school, the community, and families that is unique. They frequently participate on committees and task forces in various organizations to address systems changes in schools or in the community (Bailey, 1992; Raines, 1996). They can be valuable members of local transition teams or councils as well as community interagency councils because of their knowledge and skills in group dynamics, policy development, and advocacy.

Speech and Language Pathology Services

The speech and language pathologist (SLP) is the school-based related services professional primarily responsible for speech and language programs for students with communication disorders. Traditionally, the role of the SLP in schools has been as a service provider who worked independent of, rather than collaboratively with, other school staff. Speech and language services have also been traditionally concentrated on elementary-age schoolchildren. In recent years, however, there has been a growing awareness of the needs of adolescent students with communication disorders as they make transition plans for the future. Communication skills in self-determination, self-advocacy, successful socialization with peers at school and in work settings, and integrated community participation are increasingly seen as critical for successful adjustments and quality of life.

Communication skills assessments are an important beginning point in taking advantage of the school-based services of a speech and language pathologist. From age 14 on, students with communication disorders as a primary or secondary disability should have present level of performance data on their communication skills. It is important to find out how or whether a student's communication problems might interfere with environmental tasks and demands. McCue and colleagues (1994) described assessment of students as useful only to the extent that the assessment results provided information of how an individual functions within his or her natural environments—home, school, work, and in the community. This approach demands functional versus formal or standardized assessments and moves the SLP from traditional clinical practices and techniques to what is referred to as *pragmatics,* a functional approach to communication disorders intervention.

Speech and language intervention that is functional fits in at various points in the transition planning and services delivery process. Helping students articulate their interests, preferences, hopes, dreams, and fears in a safe, accepting communication relationship is a direct transition education intervention. Helping students learn new vocabulary related to adult living in the community is a functional language intervention that may be supplemental to their academic instruction, but, in some cases, it may be the only direct instruction they get in that area. Giving students practical tips on how to control their speech production (voice sounds and fluency) when asking for a date or participating in an interview is much more relevant to an older adolescent than clinical exercises in a small room with a two-way mirror.

Many adolescents with communication disorders are declassified as needing speech or language interventions because they do not choose to be singled out by an SLP in front of their adolescent peers or they feel that the basic techniques or procedures are not suitable for their age and grade. The pressure on SLPs to serve large numbers of students results in a concentration at the elementary school level where the children are more compliant and concentrated in greater numbers. It is important to reevaluate the communication needs of students in secondary schools and provide them with functional, goal-directed interventions to help them get through the difficulties of social relationships and communication problems with adults. Secondary special education personnel should look for those SLPs in the school district who are willing to work with adolescents and who are flexible in their assessment and intervention approaches to allow for a functional approach.

Occupational and Physical Therapy Services

Secondary students with disabilities requiring occupational or physical therapy services are among the low-incidence groups served in special education and related services. Secondary special education teachers and transition services personnel need to know about occupational and physical therapy services, however, so that those services can be accessed quickly and effectively when needed. Transition services personnel particularly need to know the kinds of services that occupational and physical therapists provide, because they will discover a support system group that embraces many of the same values for functional adult outcomes, independence, and self-determination.

Unfortunately, many secondary special education professionals have had little contact with occupational or physical therapists. Infrequent contact results in sparse information about what the therapists' primary professional roles are and how compatible those roles are with transition services goals. For example, current roles and functions for each of these two related services are described here.

Occupational Therapy. Occupational therapy aims to enhance a person's development, increase or restore independence, and prevent disability. Therapy focuses on how individuals spend their time to fulfill life roles within various environments (home, school, work, and community at large). Self-care, work or school, and play or recreational activities are evaluated and used to increase an individual's ability to participate meaningfully (Dunn, Brown, & McGuigan, 1994; Shepherd & Inge, 1999). Specifically, the occupational therapist (OT) may adapt tasks or environments according to an individual's age and social role. In school settings, therapists may address sensory-motor, cognitive, and psychosocial skills and behavior so that students can perform self-care and school work or play tasks in multiple environments (e.g., classrooms, cafeteria, restrooms, gym, school grounds, etc.) (Shepherd & Inge, 1999). In work settings, OTs may assist in vocational exploration, job acquisition, and enhancing job performance (e.g., effective and efficient performance of job tasks, appropriate use of time, self-care skills, social interaction skills, and compensatory techniques needed in the work environment) (American Occupational Therapy Association, 1994).

Physical Therapy. Physical therapy assists individuals of all ages with disabilities resulting from disease or injury in promoting fitness, health, and quality of life (American Physical Therapy Association, 1995). After assessing a person's strength and ability to move and endure physical activities, a physical therapist (PT) plans, designs, and conducts therapeutic interventions to decrease or prevent pain, injury, or further limitations. In school settings, for example, a PT may work with a student's ability to (1) move in organized patterns (e.g., gross motor skills), (2) assume and maintain sitting and standing postures, and (3) perform functional mobility tasks (e.g., getting to and from classes, carrying books, climbing stairs, opening doors, etc.) (Effgen, 1995). In work settings, the PT may address some of these same task demands, with specific attention to specific job environments and job demands.

Occupational therapy and physical therapy are two of the related services that were specified in 1975 under the Education for All Handicapped Children Act (PL 94-142). The use of OTs and PTs in school settings increased significantly after this legislation. According to the American Occupational Therapy Association's (AOTA) 1996 member survey, 18 percent of the occupational therapists employed in the United States work in public schools (AOTA, 1996). The American Physical Therapy Association reports that 8 percent of its members work in schools (Shepherd & Inge, 1998). Still, the numbers remain relatively small and are concentrated on children in the elementary and middle school levels.

Currently, few OTs are participating in transition services planning or service delivery (Inge, 1995), even though their roles and function are highly related to transition services outcomes. It is presumed that participation of PTs is similarly limited. Shepherd and Inge (1999) have laid out some possible roles for the OT and the PT that may inform special educators and transition personnel of possible linkages that can be made and thus increase the future participation of these therapists. Figures 11.1 and 11.2 show some of the possible specific roles Shepherd and Inge (1998) envision for the OT and PT. As is apparent, both OTs and PTs assess and

FIGURE 11.2   Possible Roles for the Occupational Therapist in the Evaluation, Service Planning, or Delivery of Transition Services

1. **Teach functional tasks related to temporal aspects (age, maturation, ability/ disability, and life stage):**
   - Activities of daily living:
     —self-care (e.g., dressing, feeding, hygiene, toileting)
     —communication
     —socialization
     —mobility within home, school and community
   - Home management (e.g., cooking, cleaning, money management)
   - Work and health habits
   - Work skills
   - Leisure

2. **Evaluate environmental supports and barriers and recommend adaptations if needed:**
   - Physical characteristics
     —accessibility (e.g., terrain, furniture, objects)
     —sensory stimulation (e.g., tactile, visual, or auditory cues or distractions)
     —types of objects, tools, equipment
     —temporal cues (e.g., watches with alarms; toothpaste left on sinktop)
   - Social characteristics
     —activities (e.g., individual or group)
     —people
     —role expectations

FIGURE 11.2 Continued

- Cultural characteristics
  —customs, expectations
  —values
  —beliefs

3. **Adapt tasks:**
   - Changing the physical characteristics of the task (e.g., sit instead of stand)
   - Changing the social characteristics of the task (e.g., increase or decrease the number of people involved)
   - Changing the demands (e.g., do part of task; checklists)
   - Work simplification (e.g., get all items together before shower; reorganize kitchen so able to find objects)
   - Use instructional techniques: (e.g., task analysis, forward and backward chaining, partial participation, positive supports, systematic instruction, natural cues)
   - Teach compensatory techniques

4. **Adapt materials and/or recommend assistive technology:**
   - Increase or decrease the size, shape, length, or sensory characteristics of materials/objects being used
   - Adaptive aids (e.g., button hook, reacher, lapboard, talking watch, book holder; memory aids; talking calculators)
   - Switches, computers, appliances, augmentative communication devices, telephones, wheelchairs, environmental control units, positioning devices, alerting systems

5. **Develop interpersonal and social skills to support participation in the school, community, home, or work environment:**
   - Awareness of interests
   - Stress management
   - Time management
   - Self-management/coping techniques
   - Leisure activities to promote socialization and develop friendships
   - Assertiveness training
   - Decision making/problem-solving skills

6. **Educate others and learn from others in the home, classroom, community, or workplace:**
   - Student training
   - Family training
   - Staff training
   - Peer training

7. **Promote self-advocacy, prevention, and health maintenance:**
   - Legal rights and responsibilities
   - Disability and health awareness
   - Talking to others about disability and needs
   - Promote habits to maintain health (e.g., hygiene, medications, pressure reliefs, birth control; equipment maintenance, etc.)

Source: From "Occupational and Physical Therapy" by J. Shepherd and K. J. Inge in *Transition and School-Based Services: Interdisciplinary Perspectives for Enhancing the Transition Process* by S. H. deFur and J. R. Patton (Eds.), 1999, Austin, TX: Pro-Ed. Reprinted by permission.

FIGURE 11.3   **Possible Roles for the Physical Therapist in the Evaluation, Service Planning, or Delivery of Transition Services**

1 **Develop or compensate for skills that support participation in the school, community, or work environment.**
   - Strength
   - Endurance
   - Movement patterns
   - Assume and maintain postures

2. **Improve the student's mobility within the home, school, work, and the community setting.**
   - Ambulation
   - Wheelchair mobility
   - Climbing stairs
   - Opening doors
   - Transfers
   - Carrying items
   - Public and private transportation

3. **Promote self-advocacy, prevention, and health maintenance.**
   - Exercise
   - Nutrition
   - Body mechanics/positioning
   - Disability knowledge and precautions
   - Legal fights

4. **Adapt tasks and environments so the student can participate.**
   - Accessibility
   - Position of student and activity
   - Job site analysis

5. **Recommend or adapt assistive technology.**
   - Mobility aids (e.g., walkers, canes, wheelchairs, standing tables)
   - Computer access and positioning
   - Augmentative communication device
   - Exercise equipment
   - Accessibility.

6. **Educate others and consult in the home, classroom, community, or workplace.**
   - Student training
   - Family training
   - Staff training
   - Peer training

Source: From "Occupational and Physical Therapy" by J. Shepherd and K. J. Inge in *Transition and School-Based Services: Interdisciplinary Perspectives for Enhancing the Transition Process* by S. H. deFur and J. R. Patton (Eds.), 1999, Austin, TX: Pro-Ed. Reprinted by permission.

evaluate students, teach functional tasks, evaluate students' environments, adapt tasks, use assistive technology, and promote self advocacy, prevention of further impairment, and health/fitness maintenance. They also are trained and able to educate others (e.g., school personnel, family members, peers, volunteers, employers, etc.) about how persons outside the field can support and enhance the occupational or physical therapy process.

Assistive Technology Services

The National Council on Disabilities (Morris, 1992) concluded that "with the assistance of technology, almost three-quarters of school-age children were able to remain in a regular classroom...and 45 percent of school-age children were able to reduce school-related services" (p. 5). Connecting these results with a common transition services goal, high school graduation, and spending a greater percentage of the school day in general education (with special education support) is associated with higher graduation rates (United States Department of Education, 1995; Malian & Love, 1998). Thus, it appears that with the assistance of technology, positive outcomes can be achieved.

Educational technology, in the popular sense, brings to mind for most people accessing and using computers. It is much more than that, just as assistive technology is much more than using computers and computer devices for people with disabilities. Assistive technology includes any device or product that helps people with disabilities live, learn, work, and play more independently (Fisher, 1999). Assistive technology can range from products as simple as reaching sticks, Velcro fasteners, or enlarged print to more technical devices such as hearing aids, Opticons, or sophisticated augmentative speech devices. But there is more to assistive technology than products or devices. Under the related services provision of the IDEA, assistive technology services goes beyond devices to those services required to make assistive technology work, such as evaluation of need for assistive technology, training for all involved persons in an assistive technology service, maintenance and repair of assistive technology devices, customization of an assistive technology device, ongoing assessment and monitoring of assessment device use, developing applications of assistive technology to new situations and environments, and coordinating therapies and services with assistive technology. The Technology Related Assistance for Individuals with Disabilities Act of 1988 (PL 100-497), known as the *Tech Act*, laid the groundwork for defining and furnishing guidelines for assistive technology and services in the lives of people with disabilities (Judith Fein National Institute on Disability and Rehabilitation Research, 1996). The Tech Act also provided the legal basis for later provisions of the IDEA and a framework for local and state education agencies to operate in establishing assistive technology services.

The language of the assistive technology requirements of the IDEA came out of the Tech Act, with only minor modifications. It states that the IDEA provides that if a child with a disability requires assistive technology devices or services, or both, in order to receive a free appropriate education, the public agency shall ensure that the assistive technology devices or services are made available to that child, either as special education, related services, or as supplementary aids and services that enable a child with a disability to be educated in regular classes. Determinations of whether a child with a disability requires assistive technology devices or services under this program must be made on an individual basis through applicable individualized education program and placement procedures. (*Federal Register,* 1991, p. 41272)

The 1997 IDEA Amendments emphasized the importance of assistance technology by including a provision requiring the IEP team to consider the specific needs of each child in the general education curriculum, as appropriate, including such needs as assistive technology (*Federal Register,* 1997, p. 55028).

As a related service for local schools to deliver, there is still a great deal of concern about costs and compliance guidelines for delivering assistive technology services. General guidelines are in place in all states, but specific guidelines and policies are in varying stages of development and clarification (Fisher, 1999). Secondary special educators and transition services personnel need to know the person(s) responsible for assisting in accessing assistive technology services. This assistance should be available at the assessment/evaluation stage of planning, the IEP planning stage, and the implementation and evaluation stage. Unfortunately, many school districts have no single qualified individual designated as responsible for providing assistive technology services. It remains the responsibility of the IEP team to know the student's rights in regard to assistive technology and press for assistance or action in implementing an assistive technology provision in the IEP.

According to Chambers (1997), there are four basic questions to ask to determine whether a student really needs assistive technology:

1. Is assistive technology necessary to receive a free appropriate education?
2. Is assistive technology necessary to receive services in the least restrictive environment?
3. Are the devices and services a necessary related service?
4. Will the student have access to school programs and activities with the assistive device or assistive technology services that he/she would not have access to without such devices or services?

From a transition services point of view, these questions might not be explicit enough. Fisher (1999) noted that another reasonable question to ask is: Is assistive technology necessary for a student to achieve employment, independent living, and social and community participation? The school setting is only one of the environments that needs to be considered for assistive technology. Especially for students in one or more types of community-based instruction, employment, transportation, mobility, recreation and leisure, and home living are environments or activity areas that warrant consideration for a student's need for assistive technology.

Community-Based Linkage and Referral Sources

A community services directory usually provides information for four kinds of assistance: emergency, financial, health, and program. *Emergency assistance* should identify sources for food, housing, legal, and any other general kinds of help. *Financial assistance* might include bail bonding, supplementary security income, aid to dependent children, food stamps, mortgages, auto loans, banking and credit unions, tax preparation, and financial planning. *Health problems assistance* would include mental health, dental health, visual assistance, and the subspecialties of physical health, preventive as well as corrective. *Program assistance* lists vocational rehabilitation, the state employment service, state and local advocacy groups, rehabilitation facilities, residential programs, and community agencies such as the chamber of commerce, city commissions, business and industrial councils, trade unions, and associations and human services agencies. In addition, some persons might wish to include sources for recreation and other leisure activities. The preceding is only a partial list of referral agency services and will certainly differ from community to community. (See Appendix A for a listing of national resource agencies.)

Guidelines for Making Referrals

Most school districts have an established policy or procedure for making community referrals. This policy frequently includes a standard referral form. Consequently, the following guidelines are general in nature and are basically reminders for commonsense practice:

1. *Involve the administrator responsible for your program in the decision to make or recommend a referral.* Some administrators want only to be informed on routine cases but insist on involvement for certain kinds of problems or for certain parents.

2. *Involve the parents from the beginning.* Many schools and school personnel have had lawsuits brought against them for providing services without parental permission. By involving the parents in all decisions regarding the referral and obtaining their permission for specific referrals, secondary special education staff will not only protect themselves from lawsuits but also may get helpful information and support from the parents. It is a fact, however, that parental involvement might lead to a refusal to cooperate and a denial of permission to refer. Still, parents are the ones with responsibility for their children, and school personnel must involve them.

3. *Provide all important information to the referral resource.* Referral resource personnel need as much relevant information as possible to be able to respond to the needs of the referred student. The important information should be written down and organized so that it can be used more easily. Whenever possible, discuss the information with the resource person to ensure that nothing is misunderstood and that there are no gaps in the information that the person needs.

4. *Inform key people on all stages of the referral.* Key people include the student who is being referred, his or her parents or guardians, other teachers or school personnel who have a need to know, the immediate supervisor, and the referral resource person. Each of these key participants in the referral process have information or a perspective that might be important as the process moves along. Having access to that information or those perspectives requires that these people be kept informed.

5. *Prompt referral resources into action.* Frequently, referral resource persons are overworked and have many other things to do besides respond immediately to a referral form or even to your personal request. Since one cannot ignore a student's needs, it is important to follow up the initial referral after a courteous time period to inquire as to the status of the referral. A referral situation is not always an emergency situation, so there is no rule of thumb as to how long to wait before prompting. There comes a point, however, in any referral that is based on need—either the need disappears or is heightened as time goes on. Prompting, on behalf of a student in need, is a professional expectation, and the referral resource person will understand a cheerful but persistent follow-up.

6. *Reinforce referral resources.* The referring professionals should not forget to show appreciation personally and to give recognition to all those people who assist with their services. A short letter or memo of thanks with a copy to the person's supervisor or administrator is one simple way to show both appreciation and give recognition at the same time. Over time, one would need to be creative to keep the reinforcement process genuine and spontaneous.

Interagency Cooperation

Interagency and Community Linkages

Interagency and community linkages have developed over the years in some states and local communities. School programs characterized by "recommended practice" or "exemplary programming" have usually included some sort of interagency and community collaboration, usually in the form of an interagency agreement. The definition of *individualized education program* in the IDEA formalizes the concept of interagency and community linkages by making it part of the IEP process for students 16 years of age and older [20 U.S.C., Sec. 1414(d)(1)(A)]: *"beginning at age 16 (or younger, if determined appropriate by the IEP Team), a statement of needed transition services for the child, including, when appropriate, a statement of the interagency responsibilities or any needed linkages."* The law goes on to add the following provision: *"If a participating agency, other than the local education agency fails to provide the transition services described in the IEP in accordance with §300.347(b)(1)(ii), the local educational agency shall reconvene the IEP Team to identify alternative strategies to meet the transition objectives for the child set out in that program."* [20 U.S.C., Sec. 1414(d)(5).

The IDEA clearly establishes the expectation that the delivery of transition services is not solely a school responsibility (Aune & Johnson, 1992). However, the aforementioned sections charge the school with ensuring that linkages with non-school agencies occur, rather than waiting for those agencies to initiate something. Although not exclusively responsible for providing all services, the school is clearly responsible for ensuring that needed educational services are provided and that other needed services are addressed in the planning process. Schools have no authority to compel nonschool agencies to participate in the IEP transition planning process. The only exception would be if the school has a service contract with the agency. In that situation, the state education agency will hold the local school accountable for failing to ensure participation by the nonschool agency under contract. The regulations are clear, however. There is nothing in the provisions of the IDEA that relieves any participating agency, including a state vocational rehabilitation agency, of the responsibility to provide or pay for any transition service that the agency would otherwise provide to students with disabilities who meet the eligibility criteria of that agency.

Elements in Successful Linkages through Transition Councils

Whatever the reasons for initiating interagency linkages, Tindall and colleagues (1986) cautioned that, to be successful, great care must be taken in each step of the process, at both the state and local levels of implementation. The following are suggested steps:

1. In selecting the group or committee that will be at the heart of the process, one person must serve as catalyst and be joined by a core group of equally dedicated persons from other agencies. All the members will work together better if they can subordinate any "turf" problems or local agency rivalries to focus on the goal of improving services for people with disabilities. As difficult as that may be, it is worth considerable effort to try to live up to that ideal.

Often, it is expedient to establish the interagency council by building on an existing committee. This may be a good procedure, provided the existing committee is not currently involved in some major project, the committee's goals are compatible with those of the linkage committee, and the new leader is already a member of the old committee. It is important to recognize that when a new project is introduced to an established advisory group, all the assets of the group are inherited along with all the jealousies, frustrations, inflexibilities, and other liabilities that may have developed during previous work. Obviously, judicious personnel changes can eliminate some of those problems, but sometimes it is prudent to start fresh.

Whatever method is used to establish the linkage council, it should be limited to as few people as possible yet ensure representation from the public schools, consumer groups, government, and business firms.

The effectiveness of the core group is greatly enhanced if each member has the authority to commit his or her group to whatever course of action the committee decides on. The council will be even more effective if each member has some significant measure of personal status to contribute. It is a given that each person would be knowledgeable about the needs and services for persons with disabilities available from the sector he or she represents.

2. As the council begins its work, additional members may need to be added. Suggestions for new members can come from any source, but certainly those persons who represent agencies or services called on frequently should receive high priority for inclusion. Again, a careful balance should be maintained between the effectiveness of services increased by adding new members and the efficiency of operating with the fewest possible council members. Since the goal is to offer optimum services, it is important to add new members only when the effectiveness issue has been carefully considered.

3. As in any cooperative venture, there are barriers that make effective collaborative efforts difficult if not impossible to implement. Tindall and colleagues (1986) pointed out that an issue may become a barrier when (a) the issue generates more concern than the goals, (b) there is reluctance to consider compromises or alternatives, (c) committee members begin to withdraw from the process, and (d) the same issue recurs without being resolved. These barriers generally fall into four categories: those arising from attitudes, those resulting from policies and regulations, those arising from internal agency operations, and those resulting from environmental barriers (e.g., distance, size of agencies, etc.).

Communication problems are the most usual causes for issues developing into barriers. Each issue will probably generate its own problem and therefore call for a unique solution, but a committee that follows the guidelines for group processes facilitation can generally ward off the stalemates that barriers represent. There are some other considerations that may assist the council in its work.

Any cooperative effort exposes the members to some elements of risk. The most prevalent aspect is loss of autonomy over jurisdiction, funding, or service. Just recognizing and acknowledging that the risk is present may go a long way toward reducing the anxiety that may fuel the resistance to giving up some autonomy. Quite often, the risk can become less threatening when the possible gains from collaboration are emphasized. Even when that fails, a spirit of cooperation may still be generated from the recognition that resolving an issue will benefit the person with a disability.

Throughout the council deliberations, a climate of mutual respect should be cultivated. Everyone should be made to feel their presence in their respective agencies is in the best interests of their clients, the committee, the agency, the state, and the nation. If a need for their cooperation did not exist, there would be no need for linkages and no need for the council. It should be continually stressed that disagreements can serve as a positive mechanism for bringing in all the information pertinent to the problem and clarifying the issues. In the absence of disagreement, not all sides of an issue will be fairly represented, so an issue may not be resolved in the best way possible. However, it is absolutely essential that a solution be searched for and reached. No issue should be allowed to fester.

Areas of Responsibility

As the members of the core transition council develop some system of collaboration, a clear statement of the services that can be expected from each agency is basic to their deliberations. Any ambiguity concerning who takes responsibility for various tasks inevitably leads to issues that can become barriers to cooperation.

The most common disciplines involved in school career and transition program linkages are special education, vocational education, and vocational rehabilitation. As each discipline or agency contributes its services to a given student, the effectiveness of the services is multiplied. Although special education and vocational education services have been described elsewhere in a different context, they will be reviewed here in summary form. Vocational rehabilitation services will be described in more detail, because they are the primary nonschool, external participants in the interagency linkage.

Special Education.   Special education provides the usual educational programs and materials as a part of its ongoing responsibilities to high school youth with educational handicaps. However, it also can be expected to provide for physical education, driver education, career awareness and exploration, employment training, and remedial classes when appropriate. Special education also can furnish readers, Braillers, and note-takers for students who have visual impairments, interpreters for students who are hearing impaired, and aids for those students with physical disabilities while they are in school. Occupational, physical, and speech therapy may also be furnished by special education. Motor development, mobility training, assistive technology services, and audiological evaluations are also paid for by special education. In some cases, special psychological, medical, and psychiatric evaluations can be furnished, and special transportation costs can be covered. Finally, special education can provide counseling and provide or arrange for prevocational and vocational evaluations, work-adjustment training, and job placement and follow-up. Comprehensive assessment and evaluation data are especially helpful to vocational education and vocational rehabilitation personnel since they are required to have evaluation data, and duplication of assessment procedures is extremely costly.

Vocational Education.   Vocational educators are responsible for assuring access to all regular vocational education programs whenever possible. However, they must go beyond that to provide adapted programs suitable for students with disabilities, if needed. When called for, vocational education specialists must make modifications to ensure access to the program or adapt or modify the curriculum, materials, instructional methods, sequence, duration, content, and type of instructional units. Vocational educators must ensure that appropriate vocational tools and equipment are available and adapt or modify those tools that are inappropriate. Vocational education must also assure a barrier-free environment for the vocational education programs. Any vocational education goals on the IEP must be based on a vocational assessment, including interests, abilities, and special needs with respect to completing the vocational education program successfully. Special education personnel are to be involved with vocational educators in planning for youths with disabilities or special needs, and their parents must be notified—before the students enter the ninth grade—of the different vocational education programs and services offered.

Vocational educational and school guidance and counseling services are taking the lead in implementing school-to-work or school-to-careers programs in a number of states under the School-to-Work Opportunities Act of 1994 (PL 103-239). States and local school districts that have received funding through the Act are following the required components of school-based programs, work-based programs, and connecting activities. The *school-based component* must use career counseling and assessment to help all students select career majors by the eleventh grade and develop programs of study to pursue their major goals. The *work-based component* is a program designed by the school to complement the students' career major selections and includes instruction in specific occupational competencies as well as competencies related to business or industry gained through paid or unpaid work and on-the-job mentoring. *Connecting activities* are activities and programs designed by the school to ensure active and continuing participation of employers with the school in making the school-based and work-based components successful. Benz and Kochhar (1996) frankly pointed out in their analysis of the School-to-Work Opportunity Act and implementation of state programs thus far, inclusion of students with disabilities is not easily achieved. You will have to be involved in your local program and assertive in helping your students gain access to school-to-work or school-to-career programs.

Vocational Rehabilitation Services.   Although each state has its own organizational structure for its vocational rehabilitation agency, the substantial federal support to states for the program has resulted in a basic sequence of steps that describe the expectations one could have in any state for seeking and obtaining vocational rehabilitation services. Most states do have separate vocational rehabilitation services for persons disabled by visual impairment and those disabled by all other physical, sensory, or mental impairments. The sequence of service delivery of both, however, is parallel. The steps in vocational rehabilitation generally include the following:

Step 1: Referral.   Students in school programs will ordinarily be referred by the school guidance counselor or by someone in secondary special education. The initial contact, however, can be self-referral; students and their parents may contact the local or area vocational rehabilitation counselor on their own. Occasionally, referrals are made by physicians, psychologists, ministers, social workers, or caseworkers in social welfare programs. In any case, contact is made and an initial interview is scheduled or conducted at the point of initial contact.

Step 2: Initial Interview.   In the initial interview, the counselor talks with the student and begins developing case management information. The student's own perceptions of his or her disability and how it relates to employment is an important part of this interview. Because most special education students are still minors at the time of referral, it is also important to obtain one or both parent's views on the disability. Initial probes into short- and long-term goals are usually made, but no decisions are made at this point. The counselor will begin arrangements for obtaining any new assessment and evaluation information that is needed. This will usually include a general medical examination, as well as specialist medical examinations, psychological evaluations, and vocational assessment and evaluations, when necessary. If schools have current psychological or assessment data, the counselor may request such data with the student's or parent's permission.

Step 3: Diagnosis. A vocational rehabilitation counselor must have an authoritative diagnosis of the presence of a physical or mental disability. In addition, there must be some statement or obvious implication relative to the effect of the disability on employability. Thus, examinations and evaluations are scheduled as needed to obtain this type of information and establish official eligibility for services. In this context, it is obvious that vocational rehabilitation insists on current diagnostic data and cannot always use what schools have available. The possibilities are the greatest for sharing of current test data for intellectual functioning, adaptive behavior, and personal-social adjustment.

Step 4: Assessment. Once eligibility is established through medical, psychiatric, or psychological diagnoses, additional assessment and evaluation are conducted to determine feasibility. Vocational rehabilitation has maintained the concept of feasibility as one criterion for acceptance for services for many years. *Feasibility* is a judgment based on all available diagnostic and evaluation data that the services rendered by vocational rehabilitation are likely to result in successful placement and retention in remunerative employment.

The Rehabilitation Act Amendments of 1992 made a major change in the federal regulations in the determination of eligibility and feasibility. The following two amendments are particularly critical:

1. Determinations by other agencies, particularly educational agencies, regarding whether an individual has a disability shall be used to the extent that they are appropriate, available, and consistent with the requirements of the act.
2. It should be presumed that an individual can benefit from vocational rehabilitation services unless the designated state agency can demonstrate, by clear and convincing evidence, that such an individual is incapable of benefiting in terms of an employment outcome. When the issue of "ability to benefit" concerns the severity of the disability, the rehabilitation agency needs to conduct an extended evaluation.

School personnel need to know about this aspect of the process of accepting students for services, so that data that speak to feasibility and eligibility are provided during the assessment and evaluation process.

Many special educators assume that vocational rehabilitation services are automatically available to their students and graduates, simply because of the school's determination that the students have disabilities. It is a shock for many special educators and parents to learn that only about 10 percent of all students who ever received special education services eventually receive services from a state vocational rehabilitation agency. One reason for this low percentage rate is that many students have such mild disabilities that they are able on their own, or with family or school transition services, to move into employment, adult life, and community participation without the assistance of a state vocational rehabilitation agency. Another reason is that other adult service agencies provide assistance through their own service systems, and state vocational rehabilitation agencies are not involved. Two examples of this would be community developmental disabilities organizations (CDDOs) and mental health agencies.

Some individuals, however, need state vocational rehabilitation services and might find it difficult to access those services because of their state's order of selection policy. Under federal regulations, each state vocational rehabilitation agency must develop and follow an order of selection policy. This policy is to be used to ensure fair and consistent eligibility determination practices as well as to provide a basis for acceptance of eligible clients during periods of limited funding.

Step 5: Preparation for Placement.   Once a student is accepted for services by vocational rehabilitation, an Individualized Plan for Employment (IPE) is developed. The plan states what the vocation objective is, what services are required, and how long the service will be needed. Although vocational rehabilitation counselors can provide a variety of services to persons with disabilities, they are required to make use of services offered by other agencies before using their own funds and to stay within the guidelines of the IPE. When a person is eligible for services, vocational rehabilitation can provide or buy a number of services. This may include medical treatment, surgery, therapy, prosthetic fitting, crutches, wheelchairs, glasses, hearing aids, dental work, and cosmetic enhancement. In the area of training, vocational rehabilitation can pay for tuition, on-the-job training fees to employers, books, supplies, transportation, readers for clients who are blind, interpreters for clients who are deaf, and aids for clients who are orthopedically handicapped. At the conclusion of training, it can pay for job development, engineering and redesign, and job-seeking skills. Vocational rehabilitation can also pay for licenses, tools, equipment, and supplies, and handle maintenance and transportation during the rehabilitation process.

Step 6: Placement.   Vocational rehabilitation counselors have a professional stake in the successful culmination of the rehabilitation process, and the placement process is the step in which the counselor may become more active. Large caseloads frequently prevent personal involvement in every placement, however, so placement personnel in public schools, postsecondary training programs, other adult rehabilitation agencies, and the state employment offices are used.

Step 7: Follow-Up. Most state vocational rehabilitation agencies, whether official or unofficial, establish quotas for counselors in achieving successful closures, or *26s*, as the counselors call them (referring to the code number for "successfully closed in rehabilitated status" in their quarterly and annual reports). Counselors are encouraged to follow up on their clients for up to a year before closing the case, but a case could be closed within 90 days. Pressure to meet quotas probably has some influence on the length of time a counselor will spend on follow-up.

Altogether, vocational rehabilitation is an agency that can bring powerful resources to bear on behalf of eligible clients. However, since vocational rehabilitation must use the resources of other agencies first, it will often be unable or unwilling to provide some of its services while the person is a student and therefore the responsibility of the school. (This practice is often referred to as *first dollar*) Since each special education student must have an individual education program, the school can request the attendance of a vocational education representative and a vocational rehabilitation counselor at the IEP meeting. Working together, they can develop the IEP for the school and the (IPE) for vocational rehabilitation. Clearly, such coordinated efforts can do much to focus agency services on common goals. It is no coincidence that this type of joint planning presents such a powerful demonstration of what can be accomplished through linkages.

Multiple Partners in Transition Services. Everson (1993) described a growing list of transition services partners from among the increasing number of adult service programs and agencies that are now becoming more available. In many cases, these are found in larger communities and metropolitan areas. There are not enough these programs and services, but it is encouraging to see the need recognized and efforts being made to address those needs. Figure 11.4 is an updated and adapted version of Everson's list.

FIGURE 11.4   Major Adult Service Programs and Services Used in Transition Services

Employment Services

Job Training Partnership Act (JTPA) Programs	Funds for disadvantaged youths, adult displaced homemakers, Native Americans, migrant workers, and older American employment services. Federally funded by the Department of Labor and locally administered by private sector-organized Private Industry Councils (PICs).
Transitional Employment Services	Time-limited, facility or community-based employment for individuals with a range of disabilities. Provided as individual or group placements and includes the Projects with Industry (PWI) model. Funded by state and federal rehabilitation funds and authorized by the Rehabilitation Act, as amended.

(continued)

FIGURE 11.4   Continued

Work Opportunity Tax Credit	Replaced the previous Targeted Jobs Tax Credit. Available on an elective basis for employers hiring individuals from one or more of several targeted groups, including vocational rehabilitation referrals, qualified summer youth employees, high-risk youth, and qualified food stamp recipients. Credit generally would be equal to 35 percent of qualified wages.

Social Security and Health Care Services

Social Security Disability Insurance (SSDI)	Provides disability insurance in the form of monthly payments to individuals with disabilities who have a work history and thus have paid into the Social Security system. Minors or children with disabilities are also eligible. Does not require a financial needs test. Funded and authorized by the Social Security Act, as amended.
Supplemental Security Income (SSI)	Provides monthly cash assistance to individuals who are needy, elderly, or have disabilities and who have little or no work history. Requires a financial needs test. Funded and authorized by the Social Security Act.
Medicaid	Hospital and health care insurance for eligible poor and persons with disabilities. Federally regulated and state administered under the Social Security Act, as amended. Typically accompanies SSI benefits.
Medicare	Hospital and health care insurance for eligible elderly persons and persons with disabilities. Federally regulated and state administered by the Social Security Act, as amended. Typically accompanies SSDI benefits.

Community Living and Support Services

Housing and Urban Development Programs	Federally administered and state-authorized housing assistance program that provides low-cost loans (Section 202) to finance construction or rehabilitation of residential facilities for persons who are elderly or who have disabilities. This section also provides funding for the development of apartment complexes, known as *independent living complexes (ILCs)*, of up to 24 units per site and for group homes of up to 15 clients. Section 8 provides for rental aid to low-income families and individuals and to persons with disabilities but not elderly.

FIGURE 11.4   Continued

Group Homes/ Supported Apartments	Community-based residences of two or more individuals with disabilities and support staff. May or may not be regulated by Intermediate Care Facility-Mental Retardation (ICF-MR) funds. Also known as *supported homes, community care homes,* and *community living alternatives (CLAS).*
Adult Board and Care Homes	Community-based homes of various sizes that provide room and board for adults with disabilities. Typically, they provide minimal supervision and resident programming.
Food Stamps	Provides stamps that may be exchanged for food at grocery stores. Families, individuals, and groups of individuals (e.g., group home residents) are eligible, depending on income and financial need. Typically, SSI recipients are eligible. Federally funded through the Department of Agriculture and state and locally administered by social service agencies.
Public Health Services	Health care and treatment for persons not covered by health insurance. State funded and locally administered.
Mental Health Services	Outpatient mental health evaluations and treatment for individuals and groups with a range of mental health problems. State and locally funded and locally administered.
Independent Living Centers	Independent living assistance for employment, housing, personal attendant registers, legal assistance, accessibility consultations, personal counseling, and ADA consultations. State and local funding and locally administered.

Conclusion

A host of school and community agencies have been developed to provide various kinds of support efforts to persons with disabilities to enable them to live and work successfully. However, these resources are often fragmented and inadequate by themselves. Agency collaborative efforts, often called *interagency linkages,* have been formed to provide more effective services to people who have disabilities

The linkages may be between school discipline areas, community agencies, or combinations, but they share the common goal of improved support services. The heart of the collaborative effort is a transition council or committee made up of representatives from the various agencies that has full knowledge of all the resources that can be furnished to people with disabilities to help them become successful citizens. Cooperation in furnishing these resources requires a clear understanding of the capabilities and the limitations of each agency, plus a willingness to sacrifice some autonomy, jurisdiction, or ownership for the good of the linkage effort.

12 Issues in the Delivery of Transition Education and Services

It is difficult to say what is impossible, for the dream of yesterday is the hope of today and the reality of tomorrow.

—Robert H. Goddard

As we write this final chapter, we are optimistic about the increase in transition education and services in the nation's high schools. High school teachers working with students with disabilities are becoming more aware of the transition planning mandate of the Individuals with Disabilities Act (IDEA) and the Individuals with Disabilities Act Amendments. State education agencies are increasing their support activities for transition education and services as well as interagency linkages.

In addition, there is new interest in transition education and service options by advocates and professionals not historically interested in postsecondary outcomes (e.g., school social workers, school psychologists, and physical therapists). This interest is supported by the inclusion of related services in the definition of *transition services.* Finally, there is increased awareness and activity among adult service providers relative to their roles in the transition process. Their input is being sought and used through the increasing roles of interagency transition councils at the state and local levels and through their involvement in transition planning components of IEP meetings.

At the same time, the educational reform movements covered in Chapter 3 offer both opportunities and challenges to you and all families and professionals committed to preparing and assisting youths with disabilities to transition to adult life. Schools are under pressure to raise academic standards for all students and are held accountable when they fail to do so. Often, the mandates for transition programs and better postsecondary outcomes have to compete with the mandates to raise academic standards.

We would like to close this book by discussing some of the issues we feel need to be considered in providing transition education and services to youths with disabilities. These issues and our comments on them reflect the perspective we have gained working as secondary special education teachers, a vocational rehabilitation counselor, state department staff members, coordinator of follow-up studies, developers of assessment instruments, members of interagency councils, members of parent advisory groups, providers of in-service training, researchers in the area of transition, and university faculty members preparing future teachers, transition personnel, and other support personnel to provide effective transition education and services. More important, these issues represent the outlook and opinions of the many families, professionals, and individuals with disabilities with whom we have worked. As you read through them, notice that many of these issues are interrelated. Please note that these issues are not listed in any priority order.

Issues

Issue 1:   Life-skills education and the inclusive education movement are often seen as two different approaches.

At present, the relationship between a life-skills education curriculum approach and the traditional academic curriculum is a tenuous one. On the one hand, general education is moving toward a more rigorous academic model, and effective schools and outcomes-based/performance-based education is focusing on fostering higher achievement scores in the traditional subject matter areas, along with increased skills in higher-order thinking and problem solving. On the other hand, some educators are viewing outcomes-based education more broadly than simply increasing academic achievement scores and higher-order thinking. They are advocating functional, generalizable skills for responsible citizenship as the ends and academic skills as the means to those ends. This broader view of outcomes for education provides special educators and families who want a life-skills education approach a window of opportunity to choose to be a part of a single educational system that takes responsibility for *all* students (Furney, Hasazi, & DeStefano, 1997).

A life-skills education perspective on preparing students to leave school and assume adult roles depends on real-life, community-based skills and experiences for learning and generalization. This means that a highly inclusive model can organize and present instruction together with students without disabilities, but it must meet the functional, community-based needs of all students. Functional-skills instruction must be planned deliberately and implemented with families and general education teachers. This becomes increasingly more difficult and complex as students move from elementary to high school settings.

The Division on Career Development and Transition (DCDT; Clark, Field, Patton, Brolin, & Sitlington, 1994) affirmed the notion that every student with a disability has a right to an appropriate education in the least restrictive environment. Inherent in this affirmation is the absolute necessity for appropriate education to be individually determined, documented in the IEP, and delivered through effective instructional practice. We believe that the appropriateness of education must be determined in terms of individual needs for dealing with the demands of adulthood.

The DCDT affirmed that life-skills instruction is important for *all* students. The first consideration for where life skills should be taught is general education settings and the community. It is the responsibility of general educators at the secondary level to ensure the applicability and generalization of subject matter to the demands of employment, postsecondary education, and independent living for all students. As Clark and colleagues (1994) stated, the goals of secondary education are not the same as for elementary and middle school education. Basic skills are assumed for a majority of secondary students, and the goal is to move them to higher levels of performance to prepare them for postsecondary education demands or for advanced levels of skills needed for employment. One appealing alternative is for secondary schools to provide more options among core or required courses that emphasize transferability of academic content to life demands, as well as more elective courses in life-skill areas. These options should be open to all students who choose to take them. Functional assessment of knowledge and performance levels in life skills becomes a critical part of the planning and instructional process. Both general and special educators in collaborative teaching situations should consider the functional application of the general education curriculum content and make accommodations whenever possible.

If it is determined through experience in general education settings, with accommodations and support, that it is not possible to meet a student's life-skills curriculum needs, it is not only appropriate but necessary to consider some other service delivery alternatives. Students who spend part of their instructional day in special education settings should be removed from general education settings only when the nature of the instruction demands a different setting, when every reasonable accommodation has been made, and when the students' needs still have not been met. When a separate setting is determined to be the most appropriate option for specific instructional content, instruction must be delivered at such a level of quality that the students' learning is not compromised. Separate, specialized instructional settings cannot be justified as belonging on the educational continuum of service delivery options if relevant, quality instruction is not ensured and if the educational benefits do not outweigh the disadvantages associated with separation from the general education environment.

We support the position of the Division on Career Development and Transition (Clark et al., 1994) that when the individual life-skills needs of students with disabilities vary significantly from those of other students in general education after accommodations for their needs have been provided, meeting their needs in an alternative fashion becomes a critical responsibility and should not be compromised. In addition, a clear commitment to a life-skills approach in both general and special education is an appropriate long-term goal for achieving both curriculum and inclusive education goals for students with disabilities.

The thrust to include individuals with disabilities more fully in general education has much data to support it (e.g., Hunt, Farron-Davis, Beckstead, Curtis, & Goetz, 1994; Kennedy & Itkenen, 1994). Whether professionals believe in this movement or not, most would agree it is here to stay. Because of this, the focus must be on *changing the system*. Educators must focus on integrating life-skills education into *all* aspects of general education programs. Transition planning is critical for all individuals, with or without disabilities, and this planning should focus on laying the foundation and providing the support for transition to *all* aspects of adult life. The School-to-Work Opportunities Act and the current emphasis on performance-based education are general education initiatives that will assist professionals in changing the system.

Educators must examine more closely what drives the system in secondary education. Once this is determined, professionals need to work within the system for change. Special educators have been notorious for talking among themselves, rather than educating those who can make change happen. Target audiences for these change efforts should include parents, school board members, superintendents, principals, legislators, and state departments of education.

In fact, the Division on Mental Retardation and Developmental Disabilities (MRDD) of the Council for Exceptional Children (Smith & Puccini, 1995) made a number of recommendations regarding secondary curricular and policy issues. Among these recommendations were the following:

a. Local education agencies (LEAs) should offer students with disabilities curricular opportunities that are directly related to their adult needs.
b. Life-skills instruction should be available for all students with disabilities, as well as students in general education who could benefit from a life-skills approach.
c. Students with disabilities should not be included in general education classes and settings and provided curricula that are not germane to their needs in developing independent living skills.
d. All students should receive a regular high school diploma for successfully completing a curriculum that meets the needs of the students.

Issue 2: The assessment of the transition education needs of individuals with disabilities and their involvement in state and districtwide assessment programs is often left to chance.

We see two separate, but related, issues concerning the assessment of individuals with disabilities. The first issue relates to quality assessment of students' transition service needs to ensure good transition planning. In Chapter 5, we presented our approach to transition assessment. Models for assessing the present level of educational performance of individuals with disabilities in the life skills areas discussed in that chapter must be developed. Techniques should include not only formal and informal assessment instruments but also curriculum-based assessment measures. A number of validated instruments and assessment approaches currently exist (Clark, 1998). In spite of this, IEP teams are using very few of these for planning. Further, there is still reluctance to use informal assessments and community-based assessments.

Second, under Section 614 of the IDEA Amendments, students' IEPs must include a statement of any accommodations needed to participate in state or districtwide assessment programs. If the IEP team determines that a student will not participate in a particular assessment, it must include a statement describing why the assessment is not appropriate and how the student will be assessed. State or local education agencies are responsible for developing guidelines for individuals with disabilities who will participate in these alternative assessments. It is critical that these alternative assessments include not only paper-and-pencil tests but also the other approaches presented in Chapter 5. The critical requirement in the development of alternative assessments is that they truly reflect the curriculum content that individual IEP teams determine as appropriate educational content.

Issue 3: Minimum competency testing and standards may adversely affect the graduation and type of exit document of students with disabilities.

We have chosen to combine the issues of minimum competency testing, state and district standards, and type of exit document because we feel they are integrally related. During the 1980s, a number of states began to institute minimum competency testing as a requirement for graduation. Thurlow, Ysseldyke, and Anderson (1995) reported that 17 states have requirements for minimum competency tests. A recent report (Council of Chief State School Officers, 1998) stated that 20 states are requiring some type of competency exam and that by 2003 there will be 23 states making such a requirement. Currently, 6 other states are developing competency exams for future use. Schools are obligated to provide reasonable accommodations for students with disabilities taking these tests under IDEA and Section 504 of the Rehabilitation Act. In certain cases, students are exempted from taking the tests. Some states have instituted alternative or modified diplomas for students who are unable to earn the Carnegie units required for graduation or pass minimum competency tests.

In a study involving four school districts in California, MacMillan, Balow, Widaman, and Hemsley (1990) found that performance on minimum competency tests (MCTs) had a great impact on the types of courses selected, with students passing the MCT enrolling in more elective courses and fewer remedial courses. Students failing the MCT transferred schools up to 10 times more frequently than those passing the MCT. Students failing the minimum competency tests were up to 10 times more likely to drop out of school than passing students; they were also absent more often and had lower self-concepts in the areas of academics in general (particularly math), honesty, and same-sex relations.

For those who have advocated for nearly three decades for the right of the special education student to earn a regular high school diploma, this issue is of great concern. It was easy to argue then, and it is now, where minimum standards are not in place, that a high school diploma really has no common meaning. No one has been able to respond to the challenge that the expectations and outcomes of a college preparatory curriculum, general education curriculum, or vocational education curriculum are equivalent in content or rigor. Nor can anyone refute the differences in expectations and outcomes between school districts with variations in size, cultural, economic, and or geographic factors. Yet, in most cases, it has been basically a matter of completing a prescribed program of some type in any size or type of community and a diploma is awarded. Although this practice may not be educationally defensible, it has met the American public's demand for equality of opportunity to obtain a high school diploma.

Minimum competency standards are dissolving the general tolerance people have for differences in expectations and outcomes. The public's general concern for the low levels of expectations and outcomes is the force behind the minimum competency standards. Now, for the first time in many states, a high school diploma can be operationally defined by "performance level" as well as accumulation of credits or Carnegie units.

In essence, minimum competency standards are in direct conflict with the philosophy of Public Law 94-142, which clearly mandates individual curricula in determining appropriate education. Minimum competency standards based on only one core curriculum take the field of education back to elitism and education for a select population and raise the perennial issue of equity.

Thurlow and associates (1995) found that 19 states use a standard diploma, 17 states use a standard diploma or certificate, 10 states use a standard or modified diploma, and 4 states use a standard or modified diploma or certificate. They also found that similar requirements were associated with different types of exit documents in different states. Freedman (1997) noted that a school district is not required to award a regular diploma to a student with disabilities who does not meet the academic requirements for a regular diploma, regardless of whether the student with disabilities has met the requirement of the IEP. The district must notify the parents in advance if successful completion of an IEP will not result in the award of a regular diploma. It seems reasonable to proceed on the basis that the awarding of a diploma to a special education student is at the discretion of state or local authority. If a decision is made by local school authorities not to award regular diplomas, and instead award a "special" diploma or a certificate of completion to the special education students, the school must notify the student or parent well in advance of any expected graduation. This interpretation reflects the present unwillingness of the Department of Education to take an advocacy position overriding state and local policies on the issue of awarding regular diplomas to students with disabilities who have been in special programs under IEPs that specified different content or different competencies than those required of other students in the school.

Standards-based education can be highly problematic for students with disabilities if the standards reflect solely academic achievement, without regard to alternative performance outcomes or life skills. A number of states are already responding to the flexibility incorporated in Goals 2000 (Bassett & Smith, 1996). In Colorado, for example, opportunities to learn have been crafted for 24 special populations. Alternative curricular requirements for students that could still lead to a regular diploma, appropriate modifications and accommodations in high school graduation exams, and a more comprehensive curriculum for all students must be adopted to ensure that reform efforts do not prove detrimental to students' successful graduations (Bassett & Smith, 1996).

Advocacy for differential programs based on individual differences in these times does not merit serious consideration unless it includes a commitment to two concepts: *legitimacy* (official approval) of each program and *integrity* through adherence to some minimum program performance standards. Legitimacy and official approval are a commitment to the principle of opportunity. And what about the principle of proof? The educational system has allowed students to graduate upon completion of 12 to 14 years of schooling, frequently with nothing more tangible than an attendance record and a collection of Carnegie units or credits as documentation. The United States is the only industrialized nation in the world to grant high school diplomas on the basis of little more than school attendance, acceptable show of effort, and satisfactory conduct. If regular education is questioning its students' final achievement performance in relation to prescribed goals, no less should be done for students with disabilities. In pursuit of excellence, it is neither fair nor appropriate to permit students to graduate without achieving the individual goals set for them through the IEP. That is the principle of proof.

Issue 4:   Transition education and services are still an add-on in many IEPs.

Although the Individuals with Disabilities Act and its Amendments have mandated that a statement of transition service needs be included in the IEP of all students with disabilities beginning at least at age 14, there are still many districts and classrooms where transition education and services are an afterthought—something that is considered after the IEP is completed. One state in particular has taken a major step to make sure that this practice is minimized. One of the six foundations on which the state of Iowa's IEP model is based is that "the IEP reflects the student's and family's vision for the future" (Iowa Department of Education, 1998, p. 5). As part of the IEP meeting, the family, the student, and other members of the student's IEP team are provided with an opportunity to discuss their hopes, dreams, insights, and expectations for the student. This vision is written on the IEP document and is reviewed yearly. The vision statement focuses on the needs of the student and guides the student's plan and the standards used to prioritize needs. It is also used to design a program that meets the student's unique needs and prepares him or her for the future and adult life. It should also guide the development of goals that communicate expectations, which can be monitored periodically. More states and individual districts need to follow this approach and ensure that transition truly does drive the IEP process.

Issue 5: Formal training in self-determination is often not provided.

Ward and Halloran (1993) stated that "the ultimate goal of education must be to increase the responsibility of all students for managing their own affairs" (p. 4). As important and critical as self-determination is, training in self-determination must be infused into the IEP process for all students with disabilities and efforts must align with other reform efforts in general education to open this concept to *all* students.

Field, Martin, Miller, Ward, and Wehmeyer (1998a) summarized the major definitions of *self-determination* as follows:

> Self-determination is a combination of skills, knowledge, and beliefs that enable a person to engage in goal-directed, self-regulated, autonomous behavior. An understanding of one's strengths and limitations together with a belief in oneself as capable and effective are essential to self-determination. When acting on the basis of these skills and attitudes, individuals have greater ability to take control of their lives and assume the role of successful adults. (p. 2)

This view of self-determination emphasizes choice, control, and personally meaningful success.

As the DCDT Position Paper on Self-Determination for Persons with Disabilities (Field, Martin, Miller, Ward, & Wehmeyer, 1998b) stated, the focus on teaching self-determination skills has historical roots in the career-development and transition movement. We support DCDT's position that self-determination instruction during the elementary, middle, and secondary transition years prepares *all* students for a more satisfying and fulfilling adult life. Evidence increasingly shows that encouraging self-determination for *all* youths could help them be more successful in their educational programs as well as in their adult lives (Field, 1997). In addition, several curricula (e.g., Field & Hoffman, 1996a; Halpern, Herr, Wolf, Doren, Lawson, & Johnson, 1997; Huber-Marshall, Martin, Maxson, Miller, McGill, & Hughes, 1998) have been implemented in inclusive environments and have resulted in positive outcomes for students with and without disabilities.

As Field and colleagues (1998b) stated, to teach self-determination skills and attitudes that generalize to real life, educators must realize that self-determination is a function of the interaction between an individual's skills and the opportunities provided by his or her environment. Specific assessments and lessons must be designed to focus on the acquisition of the knowledge, skills, and beliefs associated with self-determination. This includes activities such as student involvement in assessment and IEP transition planning and implementation. Grigal, Test, Beattie, and Wood (1997) found in their study of transition components of the IEP that not one IEP contained a self-determination or self-advocacy goal. Family members are also critical to self-determination. Turnbull and Turnbull (1996) listed a number of familial features: cultural values, beliefs and expectations, and coping styles; family interactions, such as role expectations and relationships; family functions, including economic and daily care needs; and family life-span issues, including developmental stages of family interactions and function over time. We agree with Field and colleagues that the important role that families play in the self-determination process needs to be supported and nurtured.

A closely related issue to self-determination is the transferring of parental rights at the age of majority, which was included in the IDEA Amendments of 1997. When a student reaches the age of majority, schools are to provide a notice to the student and parents, and transfer rights of the parents to the student. If students are determined as not having the ability to provide informed consent with respect to their educational and transition programs, the state has to establish procedures to appoint the parent of the student or another appropriate individual as a legal guardian.

Issue 6: Dropout prevention among students with disabilities remains a low priority activity by public schools.

In the National Longitudinal Transition Study of Special Education Students, Valdés, Williamson, and Wagner (1990) reported that the percentage of out-of-school youths with disabilities who had dropped out was 32.5 percent across all disability categories. The highest dropout percentage was for those with behavior disorders/emotional disturbance (49.5 percent) and the lowest percentage was for those who were deaf (9.4 percent) and deaf/blind (7.8 percent). Of the 32.5 percent who dropped out of school prior to completion of a program, the major reasons given by their parents for the dropouts included "Not doing well in school" (28.1 percent), "Didn't like school/bored" (30.4 percent), and "Had behavior problems" (16.6 percent). Of the dropouts, 36.6 percent were from urban areas, 24.6 percent were suburban, and 31.4 percent were rural. For youths with disabilities who dropped out of school, the employment rates were about 42 percent for youths out of school less than two years and 47 percent for youths out of school for more than three years (Wagner, D'Amico, Marder, Newman, & Blackorby, 1992).

Generally, it is acknowledged that migrant students have higher dropout rates than do nonmigrant students (Kaufman & Frase, 1990: Helge, 1991). Many migrant students cross over federal program areas, such as Chapter 1, Title VII bilingual programs, at-risk populations, and special education. This separation of educational programs and funding sources frequently causes difficulties in programming decisions at the local school level.

The research studies from states confirm that the dropout rates for youths with disabilities are alarmingly higher than for youths who are nondisabled. The data are extremely difficult to compare across state agencies, and cautious interpretations are required. This is especially true when differences across disability groups are studied. What is consistent is that the groups that are most at risk are those with mild disabilities—learning disabilities, behavior disorders, speech and language disorders, and mild mental retardation.

Some students with disabilities do drop out of school to work and help support families or take care of children (younger siblings and/or their own). The vast majority, however, drop out of school because they say they do not like school or it is too hard to pass required courses. If there are no other choices in schools or course of study options, students see dropping out as their only choice. Lange and Ysseldyke (1998) reported some very interesting findings from their study of three school choice options in Minnesota. One of those options was an alternative high school. Some 57 percent of the students with disabilities in alternative high schools reported having dropped out of school at least once before they transferred to the alternative school. The students' reasons for staying in school after enrolling in the alternative school were as follows:

- Treated like individuals
- No suspensions or detentions
- Not being teased or hassled by other students
- Treated equally and with respect by staff

School choice policies are more common in urban areas, including such options as open enrollment (interdistrict choice), intradistrict choice, magnet schools, charter schools, postsecondary enrollment options, second-chance programs for at-risk youths, and vouchers. Over the last 10 years, school choice policies have been passed or proposed in over half of the 50 states (Cookson, 1994; Lange & Ysseldyke, 1998). Could these kinds of programs offer solutions to the dropout problem among students with disabilities?

Lange and Ysseldyke (1998) raised some important questions to consider in regard to alternative programs. They focused on the reality that most of the students with disabilities who enroll in these alternative programs without a special education classification or an IEP. In this context, they asked:

> Do we evaluate these programs on a different set of criteria than we do high schools that are required to service students through the IEP process? Do we allow students who actively choose these options to exit from special education and provide for their educational needs within a setting that does not formally acknowledge special education but often provides similar services? If we can determine that students with disabilities are succeeding in these programs, what does this mean for the special education programs? (p. 268)

Lange and Ysseldyke (1998) followed these questions with these words:

> With the high numbers of students with disabilities who are not completing school, we must look closely at what is not working. While we know that students with disabilities are accessing the options and the reasons for their decisions, we do not know the long-term outcomes of these decisions. More research is needed to determine whether these programs are making an impact on student outcomes and how this relates to secondary special education policy. (p. 268)

We believe that Lange and Ysseldyke have made a significant contribution through their studies and the implications of their findings on the issue of dropouts. We also agree that school choice options must be accountable, as are traditional high schools, for those important outcomes we consider in transition education and services.

Issue 7: The involvement of individuals with disabilities in general education initiatives such as school-to-work programs and vocational education varies greatly across states and districts.

School-to-work and vocational education initiatives offer a tremendous opportunity to include students with disabilities in general education while providing them with the skills and experiences to transition successfully to adult life. Students with disabilities are fully involved in these initiatives in many programs across the country. However, there are also many districts where this involvement is not happening. Research conducted by Lombard, Miller, and Hazelkorn (1998) supported our concerns regarding this issue. They found that the secondary school-to-work and Tech Prep teachers they surveyed did not feel prepared to meet the needs of students with disabilities who were enrolled in their courses. Just over half (53 percent) agreed that, with support from special education staff, the educational needs of students with disabilities could be met in their courses. Over one-half (58 percent), however, reported that no assistance was provided by special education staff to make course modifications. These teachers, who represented 45 states, reported receiving little to no in-service training regarding inclusive practices; the majority (62 percent) also reported that they had never participated in the development of an IEP.

Issue 8: Postsecondary education programs are placing increasing emphasis on standard psychological tests to provide documentation of a disability, whereas programs at the secondary level are moving toward curriculum-based assessments and noncategorical labels.

As we stated in Chapter 8, a number of current innovations in special education that are supported by the IDEA Amendments of 1997 offer even more challenges to the process of transition from secondary to postsecondary education. First, under the IDEA Amendments, a district will no longer be obligated to conduct a three-year reevaluation if the IEP team determines it is unnecessary to do so for eligibility purposes. This may be true for the majority of adolescents in their last years of high school. Second, special educators in many states are moving away from an emphasis on standardized assessments and toward use of curriculum-based assessment. Finally, many states are moving away from specific disability labels and toward the concept of *student in need of special education* or a *noncategorical* label. We are certainly supportive of all of these innovations, but they present challenges to the smooth transition of students with disabilities into postsecondary education. Just when special education at the national, state, and local levels is exploring these approaches, we have seen a move toward formal psychological testing for documentation of a given disability on the part of postsecondary institutions (Kincaid, 1997). This move toward such documentation is supported by the Association of Higher Education and Disability (AHEAD, 1997), the main professional group for individuals providing support services for individuals with disabilities at the postsecondary level.

The party who stands to lose most in this emerging conflict of approaches is the student and the family. We strongly advocate that discussions begin immediately, if they have not already, at the local, state, and national levels to narrow the ever-widening gap between secondary and postsecondary level education systems.

Issue 9: A firm research base is needed for transition in terms of what works and whether transition education and services are making a difference.

Researchers (Bassett, Patton, White, Blalock, & Smith,1997; Rusch, Kohler, & Hughes, 1992) have attempted to categorize past and present research efforts in the area of transition education and services. Others have attempted to categorize the areas of "best practice" in transition education (Hughes, Eisenman, Hwang, Kim, Killian, & Scott, 1997; Hughes, Hwang, Kim, Killian, Harmer, & Alcantara, 1997; Kohler, 1993; Kohler, DeStefano, Wermuth, Grayson, & McGinty, 1994).

As a field, educators need to determine if transition education really makes a difference in the adult adjustment of individuals with disabilities. This task has just begun (Frank & Sitlington, 1997; Sitlington & Frank, 1998). Before one can truly determine the effectiveness of transition education, effective procedures must be developed for determining the quantity and quality of transition planning that occurred in high school. This is a difficult task that has only recently been addressed (e.g., deBettencourt, Vallecorsa, & Strader, 1995; DeFur, Getzel, & Kregel, 1994; Grigal, Test, Beattie, & Wood, 1997; Lawson & Everson, 1993). In addition, educators need to systematically identify what components of transition education appear to have the most impact on the quality of life of young adults with disabilities (Benz, Yovanoff, & Doren, 1997; Wagner, Blackorby, Cameto, & Newman, 1993).

The examination and documentation of the major approaches currently being used in educating adolescents with disabilities and the effectiveness of these approaches must continue. Professionals need to determine the most effective interventions and determine how life-skills programming and transition planning can be integrated into these models or approaches. Educators can no longer take the approach of transition education *or* other options. Transition education needs to be fully integrated into all instructional and curricular approaches used with individuals with disabilities. The emphasis on standards, outcomes, and accountability will remain key issues in education for the years to come. Clearly, research is needed that documents the effects of these educational reform initiatives on students with and without disabilities in terms of graduation rates, exit documents, and independence in all aspects of adult life.

A particular area of research that needs to be continued is follow-up of graduates and dropouts with disabilities as they enter adult life. Variables related to transition to *all* aspects of adult life must be incorporated into these studies. Researchers must also address these variables more consistently, although they are often difficult to quantify. This will allow the field to document the need for laying the foundation and providing the support for transition to all aspects of adult life. Follow-up studies should not focus just on the current adult adjustment status of individuals with disabilities, but on the individual's educational experiences and degree of competency while in school, as well as the degree of transition planning. This information should then be combined to help determine the effectiveness of interventions and transition planning in relationship to adult adjustment.

Halpern (1993) proposed major components of a follow-up model, including specific research questions within each component. Sitlington and Frank (1998) developed a handbook for practitioners who want to develop such studies for their class, district, region, or state. This resource also includes a listing of selected statewide and national follow-up studies. State and federal studies need to share information and data-collection instruments so that data from statewide samples can be aggregated and used to support efforts to infuse transition education and planning into the educational process for all students.

Issue 10: In the area of transition to adult life, there is little formalized preparation of special education personnel.

Transition planning and life-skills content needs to be infused into the college and university programs that prepare teachers to work with individuals with disabilities of all ages. If transition education and services issues are addressed at all in the majority of college and university programs preparing teachers of individuals with disabilities, they are usually addressed in an isolated course (usually only for those preparing to work with adolescents) or in isolated presentations, and account for little of the instructional time in methods or foundations courses. Seldom is the concept of transition education included at all in coursework for those being certified in general secondary education or elementary education.

The Council for Exceptional Children (1998) has published a set of international standards for the preparation and certification of special education teachers. Infused in these standards are a number of knowledge and skill areas related to transition education. Examples of these include (1) life-skills instruction relevant to independent, community, and personal living and employment; (2) social skills needed for educational and functional living and working environments; and (3) creating an environment that encourages self-advocacy and increased independence. The standards also include knowledge and skills for beginning transition specialists.

Clark and associates (1991) made a strong argument for the need for career development for students with disabilities in elementary schools. We would advocate that all trainees being prepared to work with individuals with disabilities (at both the elementary and secondary levels) be exposed to the concept of transition education and services through content infused in their curriculum and methodology coursework. In addition, we would recommend that those preparing to work with adolescents with disabilities have at least three courses related to the provision of transition education and services. These courses should incorporate at least some components of the knowledge and skills proposed by the Council for Exceptional Children (1988) for transition specialists. Finally, those who are preparing to assume the role of transition specialist should have a major concentration of coursework in this area, incorporating all the knowledge and skill areas of the beginning transition specialist. Course requirements for secondary special education teachers should include supervised practical experiences with adolescents with disabilities. Course requirements for those preparing to be transition specialists should include supervised practical experiences involving actual transition planning, interagency collaboration, and community-based placements.

Issue 11: No recognized certification mechanism is in place for personnel whose primary responsibility is the provision of transition education and services.

The Council for Exceptional Children (1998) standards for the preparation and certification of special education teachers include a listing of knowledge and skills for beginning transition specialists. This listing of knowledge and skills was developed by a group of individuals involved in providing transition education and services and in preparing transition personnel, with input from other practitioners in the field. We strongly support the knowledge and skills listed in this standards document. As we examined these knowledge and skills statements, however, we found ourselves thinking that all secondary special educators should have some of this knowledge and skills.

DeFur and Taymans (1995) identified and validated competencies for transition specialist practitioners from the fields of vocational special needs education, special education, and vocational rehabilitation. They identified seven competency domains as central to the role of transition specialist: (1) knowledge of agencies and systems change; (2) development and management of individualized transition plans; (3) working with others in the transition process; (4) vocational assessment and job development; (5) professionalism, advocacy, and legal issues; (6) job training and support; and (7) general assessment. Competencies that were grounded in skills of communication, collaboration, and consultation dominated the highest competency rankings. Competencies to provide direct transition services also were found in this cluster. The highest rated direct service competencies tended to be vocational assessment, placement, and support service provision, rather than direct instructional training. The role of transition specialist as defined by this study suggests a role that provides the coordination among those involved in the transition process, rather than the traditional role of a direct service provider.

The role of transition specialist varies greatly across states, and even within states (Asselin, Todd-Allen, & DeFur, 1998). In some cases, they basically establish policy and procedures, link with adult providers, and provide in-service training to staff, families, and individuals with disabilities. In other cases, they provide direct service to individuals with disabilities, in areas such as job placement and transition assessment. This variety in role and function makes it difficult to formulate a specific recommendation for certification. We also feel it provides an argument against a national certification for transition specialists.

We have two recommendations related to this area. First, we would encourage state departments of education to convene a working group composed of institutions of higher education and transition specialists in their state. The charge to this working group would be to examine the knowledge and skills identified by the Council for Exceptional Children (1998) for beginning transition specialists and to add other content areas typically required of transition specialists in their state. We would then recommend that each state identify an existing certification that would include these knowledge and skill areas or develop a new certification based on these areas. Second, we would recommend that the same or another working group identify the knowledge and skill areas from the beginning transition specialist area that should be incorporated into the certification requirements for all secondary special education teachers.

Conclusion

Many professionals in the field have been advocating for transition education and services for a number of years. Career education and other life-skills initiatives have burst strongly onto the scene and then slowly died. It is easy to become pessimistic and lessen one's efforts. We feel, however, that educators are at a crossroads for change in all education. If efforts are lessened now, the battle could be lost. By working more efficiently in presenting the case, educators will have a better chance than ever of affecting what happens to adolescents and adults with disabilities.

Education has never had a mandate such as that created by the transition component of the Individuals with Disabilities Education Act and its Amendments and other educational reform legislation such as the School-to-Work Opportunities Act. Educators must work now with the federal government, state departments of education, universities, parent groups, individuals with disabilities, local school boards, administrators, and co-workers to ensure that the "spirit" of IDEA and its rules and regulations is implemented. Transition planning must truly *drive* the Individualized Education Program for all students with disabilities. As a student begins to receive special education services, the emphasis must always be on the skills and support needed for successful transition to the next environment and to the ultimate environment of life as an adult. As this planning occurs, the emphasis must remain not only on employment and postsecondary education but also on the roles of maintaining a home, becoming appropriately involved in the community, and experiencing satisfactory personal and social relationships.

Professionals need to become familiar with the reform agenda set forth in general education as well as in state and federal governments. Efforts for transition education must then be fully integrated into the ongoing systems change efforts in the overall educational system. Transition education is critical for adolescents with and without disabilities. It is imperative that this nation's educational systems incorporate this concept into its goals and delivery systems to ensure that *all* students achieve the ultimate outcome of education—preparation for adult life.

APPENDIX A

Resource Agencies

Access to Respite Care and Help (ARCH)
National Resource Center
800 Eastowne Dr., Suite 105
Chapel Hill, NC 27514
(800) 473-1727
www.chtop.com

The Accreditation Council Services for
   Persons with Mental Retardation and
   Other Developmental Disabilities
4435 Wisconsin Ave., NW
Washington, DC 20016
(202) 363-2811

Activities Unlimited, Inc.
760 Market St.
San Francisco, CA 94102
(415) 664-3407

Administration on Developmental
   Disabilities
200 Independence Ave., SW
329d Hubert H. Humphrey Building
Washington, DC 20201
(202) 690-6904
www.acf.dhhs.gov/programs/add/
   index.htm

Adventures in Movement for the
   Handicapped, Inc.
945 Danbury Rd.
Dayton, OH 45420
(800) 332-8210
e-mail: AIMKIDS@aol.com

Alexander Graham Bell Association for the
   Deaf
3417 Volta Pl., NW
Washington, DC 20007
(202) 337-5220
e-mail: agbell@aol.com
www.agbell.org

Allergy Testing Center
118-21 Queens Blvd., Suite 619
Forest Hill, NY 11375
(718) 261-3663

AMC Cancer Research Center: Counseling
   and Info Line
1600 Pierce St.
Lakewood, CO 80214
(800) 525-3777

American Alliance for Health, Physical
   Education, Recreation, and Dance
1900 Association Dr.
Reston, VA 22091
(703) 476-3400
www.aahperd.org

American Association for Adult and
   Continuing Education (AAACE)
1200 19th St., NW, Suite 300
Washington, DC 20036-2401
(202) 429-5131

American Association of Community
   Colleges
One Dupont Circle, NW, Suite 410
Washington, DC 20036-1176
(202) 728-0200
aacc.nche.edu/

American Association for Counseling and
   Development (AACD)
5999 Stevenson Ave.
Alexandria, VA 22304
(703) 823-9800

American Association on Mental
   Retardation
444 N. Capitol St., NW, Suite 846
Washington, DC 20001
(800) 424-3688
e-mail: aamr@access.digex.nex
www.aamr.org

American Association of University
   Affiliated Programs for the
   Developmentally Disabled
8630 Fenton St., Suite 410
Silver Springs, MD 20910

American Association for Vocational
   Instructional Materials (AAVIM)
220 Smithonia Rd.
Winterville, GA 30683
(706) 724-5355
www.aavim.com

American Bar Association: Advocacy Center
1800 M St., NW, Suite 200
Washington, DC 20036
(202) 331-2200
www.abanet.org

American Camping Association
5000 State Rd., 67 North
Martinsville, IN 46151-7902
(800) 428-2267
(765) 342-8456
www.acacamps.org/

American Cleft Palate-Craniofacial
   Association & Cleft Palate Foundation
1829 E. Franklin St., Suite 1022
Chapel Hill, NC 27514
(800) 24-CLEFT
(919) 933-9044
e-mail: cleft@aol.com
www.cleft.com

American Council of the Blind
1155 15th St., NW, Suite 720
Washington, DC 20035
(202) 467-5081
(800) 424-8666
e-mail: ncrabb@acb.org

American Council on Education (ACE)
One Dupont Circle
Washington, DC 20036-1193
(202) 939-9300
www.acenet.edu

American Diabetes Association
1600 Duke St.
Alexandria, VA 22314
(800) 232-3472
www.diabetes.org

American Foundation for the Blind
11 Penn Plaza, Suite 300
New York, NY 10001
(800) 232-5463
e-mail: afbinfo@afb.org

American Kidney Fund
6110 Executive Blvd., Suite 110
Rockville, MD 20852
(800) 638-8299
www.akfinc.org

American Occupational Therapy
    Association, Inc.
4720 Montgomery Ln.
Bethesda, MD 20814-5320
(301) 652-7590

American Orthotic and Prosthetic
    Association (AOPA)
717 Pendleton St.
Alexandria, VA 22314
(703) 836-7116

American Physical Therapy Association
1111 North Fairfax St.
Alexandria, VA 22314
(703) 684-2782
e-mail: apta.org
www.apta.org

American Printing House for the Blind
1839 Frankfurt Ave.
P.O. Box 6085
Louisville, KY 40206
(502) 895-2405

American Society for Deaf Children
1820 Tribute Rd., Suite A
Sacramento, CA 95815
(800) 942-2732 (Voice/TDD)
e-mail: asdcl@aol.com
www.deafchildren.org

American Speech-Language-Hearing
    Association
10801 Rockville Pike
Rockville, MD 20852
(301) 897-5700
www.asha.org/index.htm

American Vocational Association (AVA)
Special Needs Division
1410 King St.
Alexandria, VA 22314
(703) 683-3111
(800) 826-9972

American Wheelchair Bowling
    Association
6264 North Andrews Ave.
Ft. Lauderdale, FL 33309
(954) 491-2886
e-mail: BOWLAWBA@juno.com
www.amwheelchairbowl.qpg.com/

The Arc of the United States
1010 Wayne Ave.
Suite 650
Silver Springs, MD 20910
www.thearc.org

Architectural and Transportation Barriers
    Compliance Board
1331 F St., NW
Washington, DC 20004
(202) 272-5434
(800) USA-ABLE
www.access-board.gov/

Association on Higher Education and
    Disability
P.O. Box 21192
Columbus, OH 43221-0192
(614) 488-4972
fax: (614) 488-1174
e-mail: ahead@postbox.acs.ohio-state.edu
www.ahead.org

Association for Persons with Severe
  Handicaps
29 West Susquehanna Ave., Suite 210
Baltimore, MD 21204
www.tash.org

Association for Persons in Supported
  Employment (APSE)
1627 Monument Ave.
Richmond, VA 23220
(804) 278-9187
fax: (804) 278-9377
www.APSE.org/

Beach Center on Families and Disabilities
Schiefelbusch Institute for Life Span Studies
3150 Haworth Hall
University of Kansas
Lawrence, KS 66045
(913) 864-7600
www.lsi.ukans.edu/beach/beachhp.htm

Better Hearing Institute (BHI)
5021-BS Backlick Rd.
Alexandria, VA 22003
(800) EAR-WELL
betterhearing.org/

Beverly Farm Foundation
3601 Humbert Rd.
Godfrey, IL 62053
(618) 466-0367

Blind Children's Center
4120 Marathon St.
Los Angeles, CA 90029-3584
(213) 664-2153
(800) 222-3566
e-mail: info@blindcntr.org
www.blindcntr.org/bcc

Breckenridge Outdoor Education Center
P.O. Box 697
Breckenridge, CO 80424
(970) 453-6422
www.boec.org/

Canadian Hearing Society
271 Spadina Rd.
Toronto, Ontario
Canada, M5R 2V3
(416) 964-9595
(416) 964-2066
www.chs.ca

Canadian National Institute for the Blind
1929 Bayview Ave.
Toronto, Ontario
Canada M4G 3E8
(416) 486-2500
www.cnib.org

Canadian Rehabilitation Council for the
  Disabled
45 Sheppard Ave. E., Suite 801
New York, Ontario
Canada M2N 5W9

Cancer Information Service National Line
44 Vinney St.
Boston, MA 02215
(800) 4-CANCER

Captioned Films/Videos and Programs
1447 E. Main St.
Spartansburg, SC 29307
(800) 237-6213
e-mail: info@cfv.org
www.cfv.org

CDC (Center for Disease Control) National
   AIDS Clearinghouse
P.O. Box 6003
Rockville, MD 20849-6003
(800) 458-5231
e-mail: aidsinfo@cdcnac.org
www.cdcpin.org

Center on Human Policy
200 Huntington Hall, 2nd Floor
Syracuse, NY 13244-2340
(315) 443-3851

Center for Independence
2829 N Ave., Suite 202
Grand Junction, CO 81501
(800) 613-2270
(970) 241-0315

Children and Adults with Attention Deficit
   Disorder (CHADD)
499 Northwest 70th Ave., Suite 101
Plantation, FL 33317
(954) 587-3700
(800) 233-4050
www.chadd.org

Children's Defense Fund
25 E St., SW
Washington, DC 20001-1591
(202) 628-8787

Coalition on Sexuality and Disability, Inc.
122 E. 23rd St.
New York, NY 10010
(212) 242-3900
(212) 667-6474 (TTY/TDD)

Columbia Lighthouse for the Blind
1421 P St., NW
Washington, DC 20005
(202) 462-2900

Compassionate Friends, Inc.
900 Jorie Blvd.
Oak Brook, IL 60521
(708) 990-0010

Connecticut Post Secondary Disability
   Technical Assistance Center
The University of Connecticut, U-64
249 Glenbrook Rd.
Storrs, CT 06269-2064
(860) 486-0273
vm.uconn.edu/~wwwpcse/pedu.htm

Council for the Education of the Deaf
c/o Gallaudett University
Seventh St. and Florida Ave.
Washington, DC 20002
(800) 451-8834

Council for Exceptional Children
1920 Association Dr.
Reston, VA 22091
(703) 620-3660
www.cec.sped.org/

Cystic Fibrosis Foundation
6931 Arlington Rd.
Bethesda, MD 20814
(800) FIGHT-CF
e-mail: info@cff.org
www.cff.org

Disability Rights Education and Defense
   Fund (DREDF)
2212 6th St.
Berkeley, CA 94710
(800) 466-4232 (Voice/TDD)
e-mail: dredf@dredf.org
www.dredf.org

Disabled and Alone/Life Services for the
  Handicapped, Inc.
352 Park Ave. South, Suite 703
New York, NY 10010
(800) 995-0066
e-mail: disabledandalone.org

Division on Career Development and
  Transition (DCDT)
DCDT-CEC
1920 Association Dr.
Reston, VA 22091-1586
(703) 620-3660
www.ed.uiuc.edu/SPED/dcdt/

Dystonia Medical Research Foundation
1 E. Wacker Dr.
Chicago, IL 60601
(312) 755-0198

Epilepsy Foundation of America
4351 Garden City Dr., Suite 406
Landover, MD 20785
(800) 332-1000
(301) 459-3700
fax: (301) 577-2684

Equal Employment Opportunity
  Commission
1801 L St., NW
Washington, DC 20507
(800) 669-3362

ERIC Clearinghouse on Adult, Career, and
  Vocational Education
Ohio State University
Center on Education and Training for
  Employment
1900 Kenny Rd.
Columbus, OH 43210-1090
(800) 848-4815 ex. 26991
www.ericacve.org

ERIC Clearinghouse on Disabilities and
  Gifted Education
1920 Association Dr.
Reston, VA 22191
(800) 328-0272
(703) 264-9476
(703) 264-9480 (TTY)
e-mail: ncpse@cec.sped.org

Federation of the Handicapped
211 West 14th St.
New York, NY 10011
(212) 727-4200

Fund for Equal Access to Society
1 Thomas Circle, NW, Suite 350
Washington, DC 20005
(202) 223-0570

Gallaudet University
800 Florida Ave., NE
Washington, DC 20002
(202) 651-5000
www.gallaudet.edu

Graphic Futures, Inc.
25 W. 81st St., 16-B
New York, NY 10024
(212) 362-9492

Heath Resource Center
One Dupont Circle, NW, Suite 800
Washington, DC 20036-1193
(202) 939-9320 (Voice/ TTY)
e-mail: health@ace.nche.edu
www.acenet.edu/programs/HEATH

Helen Keller National Center for Deaf-Blind
  Youth and Adults (HKNC)
111 Middle Neck Rd.
Port Washington, NY 11050
(516) 944-8900 (Voice/TDD)
(800) 255-0411 (Parents NPN use only)
fax: (516) 944-7302
www.helenkeller.org/national/index.htm

Independent Living for the Handicapped
1301 Belmont St., NW
Washington, DC 20009
(202) 797-9803

Independent Living Research Utilization
  Program (ILRU)
2323 South Shepherd, Suite 1000
Houston, TX 77019
(713) 520-0232
(713) 520-5136 (TDD)
www.bcm.tmc.edu/ilru

Institute on Community Integration
102 Pattee Hall
150 Pillsbury Dr., SE
Minneapolis, MN 55455
(612) 624-6300
www.ici.coled.umn.edu/ici/

Institute on Disability/UAP
University of New Hampshire
312 Morrill Hall
Durham, NH 03824-3595
(603) 862-4320 (Voice/TDD)

Institute on Health and Disability
University of Minnesota, Box 721
420 Delaware St., SE
Minneapolis, MN 55455-0392
(612) 624-3939 (Voice/TTY)
e-mail: instihd@tc.umn.edu
www.peds.umn.edu/Centers/ihd

International Hearing Aid Society
20361 Middlebelt
Livonia, MI 48152
(313) 478-2610
(800) 521-5247

Job Accommodation Network
918 Chestnut Ridge Rd., Suite 1
Morgantown, WV 26506-6080
(304) 293-7186
(800) 526-7234
fax: (304) 293-5407
e-mail: jan@janweb.icdi.wvu.edu
janweb.icdi.wvu.edu

Job Opportunities for the Blind (JOB)
National Federation of the Blind
1800 Johnson St.
Baltimore, MD 21230
(410) 659-9314
(800) 638-7518
e-mail: nfb@access.digex.net
www.nfb.org

Job Resources for the Disabled
3140 W. Cambridge Ave.
Chicago, IL 60657-4613
(312) 327-4412

John Tracy Clinic (deafness/hearing
  impairments, deaf/blind)
806 West Adams Blvd.
Los Angeles, CA 90007
(213) 748-5481

Juvenile Diabetes Foundation International
120 Wall St.
New York, NY 10005-3904
(212) 889-7575
(800) 223-1138

Laubach Literacy International
P.O. Box 131
Syracuse, NY 13210
(315) 422-9121
www.laubach.org

Lead Line House Ear Institute
2100 W. 3rd St., 5th Floor
Los Angeles, CA 90057
(800) 352-8888
(213) 484-2642 (TDD)
www.hei.org

Learning Disabilities Association of
   America, Inc. (LDA)
4156 Library Rd.
Pittsburgh, PA 15234
(412) 341-1515
fax: (412) 344-0224
e-mail: ldanatl@usaor.net
www.ldanatl.org

Learning Disabilities Network
72 Sharp St.
Hingham, MA 02043
(617) 340-5605

Learning Disabilities Research and Training
   Center
The University of Georgia
534 Aderhold Hall
Athens, GA 30602
(706) 542-1300
fax: (706) 542-4532

Leukemia Society of America, Aid and
   Assistance
5840 Corporate Way
West Palm Beach, FL 33407
(561) 478-8550

Life Services for the Handicapped
352 Park Ave., South
New York, NY 10010
(212) 532-6740

Little City Foundation
1760 W. Algonquin Rd.
Palatine, IL 60067-4799
(847) 358-5510

Little People of America, Inc.
P.O. Box 47324
Aurora, CO 80047
(303) 368-9080

Mainstream, Inc.
3 Bethesda Metro Center
Bethesda, MD 20814
(301) 654-2400

Manpower Demonstration Research
   Corporation (MDRC)
3 Park Ave.
New York, NY 10016-5936
(212) 532-3200
(800) 833-MDRC

March of Dimes Defect Foundation
1275 Manaroneck Ave.
White Plains, NY 10605
(914) 428-7100
www.modimes.org

Montreal Association for the Intellectually
   Handicapped
633 Cremazie East Blvd., Suite 100
Montreal, Quebec
Canada, H2P 2G5
(514) 381-2307

Muscular Dystrophy Association
10 E. 40th St.
New York, NY 10016-0202
(212) 679-6215
www.mda.org

National Adult Literacy and Learning
   Disabilities Center (The Center)
Academy for Education Development
1875 Connecticut Ave., NW, Suite 800
Washington, DC 20009-1202
(800) 953-2553
fax: (202) 884-8422

National Amputation Foundation
75 Church St.
Malverne, NY 11565-1746
(516) 887-3600

National Arthritis Foundation
1330 Peachtree St.
Atlanta, GA 30309
(404) 872-7100
www.arthritis.org

National Association on Alcohol Drugs and
   Disability
2165 Bunker Hill Drive
San Mateo, CA 94402
(415) 578-8047
e-mail: jdem@aimnet.com

National Association of the Deaf
814 Thayer Ave.
Silver Springs, MD 20910-4500
(301) 587-1788
(301) 587-1789 (TTY)
fax: (301) 587-1791
e-mail: NADHQ@juno.com
www.nad.org

National Association for Industry-Education
   Cooperation (NAIEC)
235 Hendricks Blvd.
Buffalo, NY 14226-3304
(716) 834-7047

National Association of Private Residential
   Resources
6400 H Steven Corners Pl.
Falls Church, VA 22044
(703) 536-3311

National Association of Private Schools for
   Exceptional Children (NAPSEC)
1625 Eye St., NW
Washington, DC 20006
(202) 223-2192

National Association of Protection and
   Advocacy Systems, Inc. (NAPAS)
900 Second St., NE, Suite 211
Washington, DC 20002
(202) 408-9514
www.protectionandadvocacy.com/

National Association for the Visually
   Handicapped
22 W 21st St., 6th Floor
New York, NY 10010
(212) 889-3141
e-mail: staffnavh
www.navh.org

National Ataxia Foundation
2600 Fernbrooklyn, Suite 119
Plymouth, MN 55447
(612) 553-0020
e-mail: naf@mr.net
www.ataxia.org

National Career Development Association
   (NCDA)
5999 Stevenson Ave.
Alexandria, VA 22304
(301) 461-5574
129.219.88.111/

National Center on Accessibility
5020 State Rd. 67 North
Martinsville, IN 46151
(800) 424-1877
e-mail: nca@indiana.edu
www.indiana.edu/~nca/

National Center for Disability Services
201 I.U. Willets Rd.
Albertson, NY 11507-1599
(516) 747-5400

National Center for Research
Career Development Program
University of Illinois
345 Education Building
1310 South 6th St.
Champaign, IL 61820
(217) 333-0807

National Center for Stuttering
200 E. 33rd St.
New York, NY 10016
(800) 221 2483
e-mail: executivedirector@stuttering.com
www.stuttering.com

National Clearinghouse on Postsecondary
   Education for Individuals with
   Disabilities (HEATH Resource Center)
One Dupont Circle NW, Suite 800
Washington, DC 20036-1193
(202) 939-9320
e-mail: heath@ace.nche.edu
www.acenet.edu

National Clearinghouse for Professions in
   Special Education
1920 Association Dr.
Reston, VA 22191
(800) 641-7824
(703) 264-9476
(703) 264-9480 (TTY)
e-mail: ncpse@cec.sped.org

National Clearinghouse on Women and
   Girls with Disabilities
Educational Equity Concepts, Inc.
114 East 32nd St., Suite 701
New York, NY 10016
(212) 725-1803

National Council on Disability
1331 F St., Suite 1050
Washington, DC 20004-1107
(202) 272-2004
e-mail: mquigley@ncd.gov
www.ncd.gov

National Council of Independent Living
   Programs
Access Living
310 S. Peoria, Suite 201
Chicago, IL 60607
(312) 226-5900
(312) 226-1687 (TTY)

National Down Syndrome Society
666 Broadway
New York, NY 10012
(800) 221-4602
e-mail: jszerlip@ndss.org
www.ndss.org

National Down's Syndrome Congress
1605 Chantilly Dr., Suite 250
Atlanta, GA 30324
(800) 232-6372
(404) 633-1555
e-mail: ndsc@charitiesusa.com
members.carol.net/ndsc/

National Easter Seal Society
138 Riddle Rd.
Chambersburg, PA 17201
(717) 263-4300
www.seals.com

National Education Association of Disabled
   Students
4th Level Unicenter
1125 Colonel By Drive
Carlton University
Ottawa, ON K1S 5B6
indie.ca/neads/

National Federation of the Blind
1800 Johnson St.
Baltimore, MD 21230
(410) 659-9314
(800) 638-7518
e-mail: nfb@access.digex.net
www.nfb.org

National Foundation of Dentistry for the
   Handicapped
1800 Glenarm Pl.
Denver, CO 80202-3862
(303) 298-9650

National Foundation for Teaching
   Entrepreneurship to Handicapped and
   Disadvantaged Youth, Inc. (NFTE)
64 Fulton St., Suite 700
New York, NY 10038-1854
(212) 233-1777

National Foundation of Wheelchair Tennis
940 Calle Amanecer
San Clemente, CA 92673-6218
(714) 361-6811

National Handicapped Sports
4405 East-West Highway #603
Bethesda, MD 20814
(301) 652-7505

National Head Injury Foundation
1776 Massachusetts Ave., NW
Washington, DC 20036
(202) 296-6443
(800) 444-6443

National Health Information Center
P.O. Box 1133
Washington, DC 20013-1133
(800) 336-4797
e-mail: nhicinfo@health.org
www.nhic-nt.health.org

National Hemophilia Foundation
110 Green St.
New York, NY 10012-3813
(212) 219-8180

National Information Center for Children
   and Youth with Disabilities (NICHCY)
P.O. Box 1492
Washington, DC 20013-1492
(800) 695-0285
(202) 884-8200 (Voice/TTY)
e-mail: nichcy@aed.org
nichcy.org/

National Information Center on Deafness
Gallaudet University
800 Florida Ave., NE
Washington, DC 20002
(202) 651-5051
www.gallaudet.edu/~nicd

National Institute of Child Health and
   Human Development
31 Center Dr., NIH
Bethesda, MD 20892
(301) 496-3454

National Institute on Deafness and Other
   Communication Disorders Information
   Clearinghouse
1 Communication Ave.
Bethesda, MD 20892-3456
(800) 241-1044
(800) 241-1055 (TTY)
fax: (301) 907-8830
e-mail: nidcd@aerie.com
www.nih.gov/nidcd

National Institute for Mental Health (NIMH)
5600 Fishers Ln, Rm 77-99
Rockville, MD 20857
(301) 443-3673
e-mail: nimhinfo@nih.gov
www.nimh.nih.gov

National Institute for Rehabilitation
 Engineering
Upper Greenwood Lake, NJ 07421
(201) 853-6585

National Institute for Work and Learning
 (NIWL)
1255 23rd St., NW
Washington, DC 20037
(202) 862-8845

National Library Service for the Blind and
 Physically Handicapped
1291 Taylor Street, NW
Library of Congress
Washington, DC 20542-0001
(202) 707-5100

National Mental Health Association
 (NMHA)
1 Gateway Center
Pittsburgh, PA 15222
(412) 392-6604

National Mental Health Consumers
Self-Help Clearinghouse
1211 Chestnut St., Suite 1000
Philadelphia, PA 19107
(800) 553-4539
e-mail: THE KEY@delphi.com
www.mhselfhelp.org/

National Multiple Sclerosis Society
733 3rd Ave.
New York, NY 10017-3204
(212) 986-3240

National Network of Parent Centers
TAPP Network
Technical Assistance for Parent Programs
312 Stuart St., 2nd Floor
Boston, MA 02116
(617) 482-2915

National Neurofibromatosis Foundation,
 Inc.
120 Wall St.
New York, NY 10005-3904
(212) 334-6633

National Occupation Information
 Coordinating Committee (NOICC)
2100 M Street NW, Suite 156
Washington, DC 20037
(202) 653-2123
e-mail noicc@digex.gov
www.noicc.gov

National Organization on Disability (NOD)
910 16th St., NW, Suite 600
Washington, DC 20006
(202) 293-5960
(202) 293-5968 (TDD)
e-mail: ability@nod.org
www.nod.org

National Organization for Rare Disorders
P.O. Box 8923
New Fairfield, CT 06812-8923
(800) 999-6673
e-mail: orphan@nord-rbd.com
www.rarediseases.org/

National Parent Network on Disabilities
   (NPND)
1727 King St., Suite 305
Alexandria, VA 22314
(703) 836-0850
(703) 684-6763 (TDD)
e-mail: npnd@cs.com
www.npnd.org

National Rehabilitation Information Center
8455 Colesville Rd., Suite 935
Silver Springs, MD 20910-3319
(800) 346-2742
(301) 588-9284 (Voice/ TTY)
e-mail: naric@capaccess.org

National Resource Center
Syracuse University, School of Education
805 South Crouse Ave.
Syracuse, NY 13244-2280
(800) 894-0826
(315) 443-4355 (TTY)
e-mail: thechp@sued.sry.edu
soeweb.syr.edu/thechp

National Retinitis Pigmentosa Foundation
1401 Mount Royal Ave.
Baltimore, MD 21217
(410) 225-9400

National School-to-Work Learning and
   Information Center
400 Virginia Ave., SW, Room 210
Washington, DC 20024
(800) 251-7236
fax: (202) 401-6211
e-mail: stw-lc@ed.gov
www.stw.ed.gov

National Spinal Cord Injury Association
545 Concord Ave.
Cambridge, MA 02138-1122
(617) 441-8500

National Tay-Sachs and Allied Diseases
   Association
101 Greenwood Ave.
Jenkinstown, PA 19046
(214) 887-0877

National Tech Prep Network
Center for Occupational Research and
   Development
P.O. Box 21689
Waco, TX 76702-1689
(800) 972-2766
www.cord.org

National Therapeutic Recreation Society
22377 Belmont Ridge Rd.
Ashburn, VA 20148
(703) 858-2151
e-mail: NTRSNRPA@aol.com
www.nrpa.org

National Transition Network
Institute on Community Integration
University of Minnesota
Patee Hall
150 Pillsbury Dr., SE
Minneapolis, MN 55455
(612) 624-1062

National Tuberous Sclerosis Association,
   Inc.
8000 Corporate Dr., Suite 120
Landover, MD 20785

North American Riding for the
   Handicapped Association, Inc.
P.O. Box 33150
Denver, CO 80233
(800) 369-RIDE
(303) 452-1212
e-mail: narha@frii.com
narha.org

Office of Special Education and
Rehabilitative Services (OSERS)
Department of Education
Switzer Building
330 C St., SW
Washington, DC 20202
(202) 732-1245

Orton Dyslexia Society
8600 Lasalle Rd.
Baltimore, MD 21286
(410) 296-0232

Outward Bound
Route 9D 122, Box 280
Garrison, NY 10524
(800) 243-8520
(914) 424-4000
www.outwardbound.org/index.html

PACER Center, Inc.
4826 Chicago Ave., South
Minneapolis, MN 55417-1098
(800) 53-PACER (7-2237)
e-mail: pacer@pacer.org
www.pacer.org

Parent Educational Advocacy Training
(PEAT)
10340 Democracy Ln.
Fairfax, VA 22030
(703) 691-7826

Parents Are Vital in Education (PAVE)
6316 South 12th St.
Tacoma, WA 98465
(800) 572-7368 (Voice/TTY)
e-mail: wapave9@washingtonpave.com
www.washingtonpave.org

Parents Helping Parents (PHP)
3041 Olcott St.
Santa Clara, CA 95054-3222
(408) 727-5775
www.php.com/

Parents of John Tracy Clinic
806 West Adams Blvd.
Los Angeles, CA 90007
(213) 748-5481
(800) 522-4582
e-mail: jtclinic@aol.com
www.johntracyclinic.org

Physically Challenged Resource Center
Automobility Program Headquarters
P.O. Box 3124
Bloomfield Hills, MI 48302-3124
(800) 255-9877

Prader-Willi Syndrome Association
2510 S. Brentwood Blvd.
St. Louis, MO 63144-2328
(314) 962-7644

President's Committee on Employment of
People with Disabilities
1331 F St. NW, Suite 300
Washington, DC 20004
(202) 376-6200
fax: (202) 376-8422

Promote Real Independence for the Disabled
and Elderly (PRIDE)
391 Long Hill Rd.
Groton, CT 06340-1293
(800) 332-9122
(203) 445-1448

Recording for the Blind and Dyslexic
20 Roszel Rd.
Princeton, NJ 08540
(800) 221-4792
www.rfbd.org

Rehabilitation International
25 E. 21st St.
New York, 10010
(212) 420-1500

Rehabilitation Resource
University of Wisconsin–Stout
Stout Rehabilitation Institute
Menomonee, WI 54751
(715) 232-1342
www.chd.uwstout.edu/svri.pwi/trr/
   trr.html

Research and Training Center on
   Independent Living
University of Kansas
4089 Dole Building
Lawrence, KS 66045
(913) 864-4095 (Voice/TTY)
www.lsi.ukans.edu/rtcil/rtcil.htm

Retinitis Pigmentosa Foundation, Inc.
1401 W. Mount Royal Ave.
Baltimore, MD 21217
(410) 225-9400

Rural Institute on Disabilities
52 Corbin Hall
University of Montana
Missoula, MT 59812
(800) 732-0323 (Voice/TDD)
e-mail: muarid@selway.umt.edu
ruralinstitute.umt.edu/

Secondary Commission on Achieving
   Necessary Skills (SCANS)
200 Constitution Ave., NW
Washington, DC 20210
(202) 523-4840
(800) 788-7545

Sex Information and Education Council of
   the U.S.
130 W. 42nd St., Suite 350
New York, NY 10036-7802
(212) 819-9770
e-mail: siecus@siecus.org
www.siecus.org/

Sibling Information Network
A. J. Pappaniken Center
249 Glenbrook Rd., U-64
University of Connecticut
Storrs, CT 06269-2064
(806) 486-4985
e-mail: SPEADM01@uconnvm.uconn.edu

Sibling Support Project
Children's Hospital and Medical Center
P.O. Box 5371, CC-09
Seattle, WA 98105-0371
(206) 368-4911
e-mail: dmeycn@chmc.org
www.chmc.org/departmt/sibsupp/

Social Security Administration
U.S. Department of Health and Human
   Services
1801 L St., NW
Washington, DC 20507
(800) 772-1213

Special Olympics, Inc.
1325 G St., NW, Suite 500
Washington, DC 20005
(202) 628-3630
e-mail: specialolympics@msn.com

Spina Bifida Association of America
343 S. Dearborn, Suite 317
Chicago, IL 60604
(800) 621-3141

Technical Assistance for Special Population
   Program (TASPP)
National Center for Research in Vocational
   Education (NCRVE)
University of Illinois Site
345 Education Building
1310 S. 6th St.
Champaign, IL 61820

Tourette Syndrome Association
42-40 Bell Blvd., Suite 205
Bayside, NY 11361-2820
(718) 224-2999
(800) 888-4TOURET
e-mail: tourette@ix.net.com
tsa.mgh.harvard.edu/

TransCen, Inc.
451 Hungerford Dr., Suite 700
Rockville, MD 20850
(301) 424-2002
fax: (301) 251-3762
e-mail: gtilson@transcen.org

Transition Research Institute
University of Illinois
113 Children's Research Center
51 Gerty Dr.
Champaign, IL 61820
(217) 333-2325

United Cerebral Palsy Association
66 East 34th St.
New York, NY 10016
(607) 432-6404

United Leukodystrophy Foundation
2304 Highland Dr.
Sycamore, IL 60178
(800) 728-5483
e-mail: ulf@ceet.niu.edu
www.ulf.org

United Ostomy Association, Inc.
36 Executive Park
Irvine, CA 92714-6744
(714) 660-8624

U.S. Department of Education
Secondary Education and Transition
   Programs Branch
400 Maryland Ave., SW
Washington, DC 20202
(202) 732-1163

U.S. Department of Education
Office of Vocational and Adult Education
Washington, DC 20202
www.ed.gov/offices/OVAE

Very Special Arts
1331 F St., NW
Washington, DC 20004-1121
(202) 628-2800

Virginia Commonwealth University
Rehabilitation Research and Training Center
   on Supported Employment
P.O. Box 842011
Richmond, VA 23284-2011
(804) 828-1851
(804) 828-2494 (TDD)

Vocational Evaluation and Work
   Adjustment Association (VEWAA)
801 W. 10th St., Suite 200
Juneau, AK 99801
(907) 465-2814
(800) 478-4467

Wilderness Inquiry
1313 5th St., SE
P.O. Box 84
Minneapolis, MN 55414
(612) 379-3858

Williams Syndrome Association
1312 N. Campbell Rd.
Royal Oak, MI 48067-1555
(810) 541-3630

Work, Achievement, Values and Education,
    Inc. (WAVE)
501 School St., SW, Suite 600
Washington, DC 20024
(202) 484-0103
(800) 274-2005
e-mail: wave4kids@aol.com

APPENDIX B

Selected Commercially Available Assessment Instruments for Transitions Planning

Test	Publisher or Distributor	Ages for Assessment
Academic Achievement and Learning Styles		
Adult Basic Learning Examination— Second Edition	Psychological Corporation 555 Academic Ct. San Antonio, TX 78204	Adults
Basic Academic Skills Individual Screener	Psychological Corporation 555 Academic Ct. San Antonio, TX 78204	Students in Grades 1–12
BRIGANCE® Diagnostic Inventories (Three batteries)	Curriculum Associates North Billerica, MA 01862	Children below age 7; students in Grades K–6; students in secondary schools
BRIGANCE® Diagnostic Inventory of Essential Skills	Curriculum Associates, Inc. P.O. Box 2001 North Billerica, MA 01862	Elementary-age students through adulthood
California Achievement Tests—Fifth Edition	CTB/McGraw-Hill 20 Ryan Ranch Rd. Monterey, CA 93940	Kindergarten; students aged 10–22
Canfield Learning Styles Inventory, Form S–A	Western Psychological Services 12031 Wilshire Blvd. Los Angeles, CA 90025	Individuals aged 13–64
Diagnostic Achievement Battery— Second Edition	PRO-ED, Inc. 8700 Shoal Creek Blvd. Austin, TX 78757	Students in elementary and middle schools
Diagnostic Mathematics Inventory/Mathematics Systems	CTB/McGraw-Hill 20 Ryan Ranch Rd. Monterey, CA 93940	Students in Grades K–9

Note: The authors recognize Ms. Laura Alexander, doctoral student at the University of Kansas, for her significant contribution to the development of the content for Appendix B.

Source: From *Assessment for Transitions Planning* (pages 80–91) by Gary M. Clark, 1998, Austin, TX: Pro-Ed. Copyright 1998 by Pro-Ed. Reprinted by permission.

Test	Publisher or Distributor	Ages for Assessment
Durrell Analysis of Reading Difficulty—Third Edition	Psychological Corporation 555 Academic Ct. San Antonio, TX 78204	Students in Grades K–6
Gates-MacGinitie Reading Tests—Third Edition	Riverside Publishing Company 8420 Bryn Mawr Blvd. Chicago, IL 60631	Students in Grades 1–12
Gates-McKillop-Horowitz Reading Diagnostic Tests	Teachers College Press P.O. Box 2032 Colchester, VT 05449	Students in Grades 1–6
Hammill Multiability Achievement Test	PRO-ED, Inc. 8700 Shoal Creek Blvd. Austin, TX 78757–6897	Children and adolescents aged 7–0 through 17–11
Individual Reading Placement Inventory	Follett Press 2233 West St. River Grove, IL 60171	Students in elementary and secondary schools
Iowa Tests of Basic Skills, Form M	Riverside Publishing Company 8420 Bryn Mawr Blvd. Chicago, IL 60631	Elementary through secondary school students
Kaufman Assessment Battery for Children	American Guidance Service P.O. Box 99 Circle Pines, MN 55014	Students aged 2–5 to 12–5
Kaufman Test of Educational Achievement	American Guidance Service P.O. Box 99 Circle Pines, MN 55014	Students in Grades K–12
Key Math—Revised: A Diagnostic Inventory of Essential Mathematics	American Guidance Service P.O. Box 99 Circle Pines, MN 55014	Students in Grades K–8
Learning Styles Inventory	Piney Mountain Press, Inc. P.O. Box 333 Cleveland, GA 30528	Individuals aged 7–adult
Learning Styles Inventory	Price Systems, Inc. Box 3067 Lawrence, KS 66044	Students in Grades 3–12
McCarthy Individualized Diagnostic Reading Inventory—Revised	Educators Publishing Service, Inc. 31 Smith Place Cambridge, MA 02138	Students in Grades 2–12
Metropolitan Achievement Test, Survey Battery—Seventh Edition	Psychological Corporation 555 Academic Ct. San Antonio, TX 78204	Students in Grades K–12

Test	Publisher or Distributor	Ages for Assessment
Metropolitan Readiness Tests—Sixth Edition	Psychological Corporation 555 Academic Ct. San Antonio, TX 78204	Level I, children in preschool through middle of kindergarten; Level II, children in middle of kindergarten through middle of first grade
Peabody Individual Achievement Test— Revised	American Guidance Service P.O. Box 99 Circle Pines, MN 55014	Students aged 5–18 and Grades K–12
Prescriptive Reading Inventory/ Reading System	CTB/McGraw-Hill 20 Ryan Ranch Rd. Monterey, CA 93940	Students in Grades K–9
Stanford Achievement Test Series— Ninth Edition	Psychological Corporation 555 Academic Ct. San Antonio, TX 78204	Students in kindergarten through community college
Stanford Diagnostic Mathematics Test—Third Edition	Psychological Corporation 555 Academic Ct. San Antonio, TX 78204	Students in Grades 2–12
Stanford Diagnostic Reading Test	Psychological Corporation 555 Academic Ct. San Antonio, TX 78204	Students in Grades 1–8; students in Grades 8 through community college
Test of Adolescent and Adult Language—Third Edition	PRO-ED, Inc. 8700 Shoal Creek Blvd. Austin, TX 78757	Students in middle school through high school; adults
Test of Language Development —Primary: Third Edition —Intermediate: Third Edition	PRO-ED, Inc. 8700 Shoal Creek Blvd. Austin, TX 78757	Students aged 4–0 to 8–11; students aged 8–6 to 12–11
Test of Mathematical Abilities—Second Edition	PRO-ED, Inc. 8700 Shoal Creek Blvd. Austin, TX 78757	Students in Grades 3–12
Test of Reading Comprehension— Third Edition	PRO-ED, Inc. 8700 Shoal Creek Blvd. Austin, TX 78757	Students aged 7–0 to 17–11
Test of Written Language—Third Edition	PRO-ED, Inc. 8700 Shoal Creek Blvd. Austin, TX 78757	Students ages 6 and older; adults
Test of Written Spelling—Third Edition	PRO-ED, Inc. 8700 Shoal Creek Blvd. Austin, TX 78757	Students aged 6–6 to 18–5
Wechsler Individual Achievement Test	Psychological Corporation 555 Academic Court San Antonio, TX 78204	Students in Grades K–12 (aged 5–19)
Woodcock-Johnson Psycho-Educational Battery—Revised	Riverside Publishing Company 8420 Bryn Mawr Blvd. Chicago, IL 60631	Individuals aged 3–99

(continued)

Test	Publisher or Distributor	Ages for Assessment
Intelligence/Cognitive Performance/Aptitudes or Abilities		
American College Evaluation / Survey (ACT)	American College Testing P.O. Box 168 Iowa City, IA 52243	Students in high school and adults
American College Testing Asset Program	American College Testing P.O. Box 168 Iowa City, IA 52243	Students in high school and adults considering community college or postsecondary education
American College Testing–Proficiency Examination Program (ACT–PEP)	American College Testing P.O. Box 168 Iowa City, IA 52243	Students in high school and college; adults
APTICOM Program	Vocational Research Institute 1528 Walnut St. Suite 1502 Philadelphia, PA 19102	Adolescents and adults; reading level is at the 4th grade
Armed Services Vocational Aptitude Battery	Department of Defense Defense Manpower Data Center Personnel Testing Division 99 Pacific St., Suite 155A Monterey, CA 93940	Students in Grades 10–12 and post-secondary school
Battelle Developmental Inventory	Riverside Publishing Company 8420 Bryn Mawr Blvd. Chicago, IL 60631	Children aged 0–8
Bayley Scales of Infant Development— Second Edition	Psychological Corporation 555 Academic Court San Antonio, TX 78204	Children aged 0–42 months
Career Ability Placement Survey	EdITS/Educational and Industrial Testing Service P.O. Box 7234 San Diego, CA 92107	Students in Grades 7–12; college students
College Board Scholastic Aptitude Test (SAT)	College Board Educational Testing Service P.O. Box 6736 Princeton, NJ 08541	High school students and adults
Comprehensive Test of Nonverbal Intelligence	PRO-ED, Inc. 8700 Shoal Creek Blvd. Austin, TX 78757	Individuals aged 6–0 through 90–11
Detroit Tests of Learning Aptitude— Fourth Edition; Detroit Tests of Learning Aptitude–Primary: Second Edition	PRO-ED, Inc. 8700 Shoal Creek Blvd. Austin, TX 78757	Children aged 3–0 through 8–11; students aged 6–0 through 17–11
Differential Aptitude Test—Fifth Edition	Psychological Corporation 555 Academic Ct. San Antonio, TX 78204	Students in Grades 7–12

Test	Publisher or Distributor	Ages for Assessment
General Aptitude Test Battery	United States Employment Service Western Assessment Research and Development Center 140 East 300 South Salt Lake City, UT 84111	Individuals 18 and older
Hammill Multiability Intelligence Test	PRO-ED, Inc. 8700 Shoal Creek Blvd. Austin, TX 78757	Children and adolescents aged 6–0 through 17–0
Hiskey-Nebraska Test of Learning Aptitude	PRO-ED, Inc. 8700 Shoal Creek Blvd. Austin, TX 78757	Subtests designed for varying age groups, ranging from 3–16; designed for deaf and hearing persons
Infant Mullen Scales of Early Learning	American Guidance Service P.O. Box 99 Circle Pines, MN 55014	Children aged 0–36 months
JEVS Work Sample System	Vocational Research Institute 1528 Walnut St., Suite 1052 Philadelphia, PA 19102	Individuals aged 18–64
Kaufman Assessment Battery for Children	American Guidance Service P.O. Box 99 Circle Pines, MN 55014	Children aged 2–6 through 12–6
McCarron-Dial System	McCarron-Dial Systems P.O. Box 45628 Dallas, TX 75245	High school students and adults
MESA Microcomputer Screening and Assessment	Southern Illinois University Rehabilitation Institute Carbondale, IL 62901	High school students and adults
Micro-TOWER System	International Center for the Disabled Micro-Tower Research 340 E. 24th St. New York, NY 10010	Individuals aged 15–64
Mullen Scales of Early Learning	American Guidance Service P.O. Box 99 Circle Pines, MN 55014	Children aged 21–63 months
Occupational Aptitude and Interest Scale—Second Edition	PRO-ED, Inc. 8700 Shoal Creek Blvd. Austin, TX 78757	Students in Grades 8–12
Practical Assessment Exploration System	Talent Assessment, Inc. P.O. Box 5087 Jacksonville, FL 32247	Students in Grades 8–12
Scholastic Abilities Test for Adults	PRO-ED, Inc. 8700 Shoal Creek Blvd. Austin, TX 78757	Individuals aged 16 and older

(continued)

Test	Publisher or Distributor	Ages for Assessment
Stanford-Binet Intelligence Scale— Fourth Edition	Riverside Publishing Company 8420 Bryn Mawr Blvd. Chicago, IL 60631	Individuals aged 2–23
Talent Assessment Program	Talent Assessment, Inc. P.O. Box 5087 Jacksonville, FL 32247	High school students and adults
Test of Nonverbal Intelligence— Third Edition	PRO-ED, Inc. 8700 Shoal Creek Blvd. Austin, TX 78757	Individuals aged 5–85
Wechsler Scales of Intelligence: Wechsler Preschool and Primary Scale of Intelligence—Revised; Wechsler Intelligence Scale for Children—Third Edition; Wechsler Adult Intelligence Scale—Third Edition	Psychological Corporation 555 Academic Ct. San Antonio, TX 78204	Children aged 3–7; children aged 9–16; individuals aged 16 and older
Testing, Orientation, and Work Evaluation in Rehabilitation System (TOWER System)	International Center for the Disabled Micro-Tower Research 340 E. 24th Street New York, NY 10010	Adults

Adaptive Behavior/Functional Capacity

Test	Publisher or Distributor	Ages for Assessment
AAMR Adaptive Behavior Scales– Residential and Community: Second Edition; AAMR Adaptive Behavior Scale–School: Second Edition	PRO-ED, Inc. 8700 Shoal Creek Blvd. Austin, TX 78757	Individuals aged 6 and older; separate school edition for students aged 6–14
Adaptive Behavior Inventory	Harcourt Brace Educational Measurement 555 Academic Ct. San Antonio, TX 78204	Children aged 5–11
Assessment of Adaptive Areas	PRO-ED, Inc. 8700 Shoal Creek Blvd. Austin, TX 78757	Individuals aged 6–79; students aged 6–21
Basic Living Skills Scale	Dallas Educational Services P.O. Box 831254 Richardson, TX 75083	Students in Grades 3–6
Checklist of Adaptive Living Skills	Riverside Publishing Company 8420 Bryn Mawr Blvd. Chicago, IL 60631	Individuals in all age ranges
Communicative Abilities in Daily Living—Second Edition	PRO-ED, Inc. 8700 Shoal Creek Blvd. Austin, TX 78757	Students in Grades K–12; adults

Test	Publisher or Distributor	Ages for Assessment
Denver Developmental Screening Test	Denver Developmental Materials, Inc. P.O. Box 6919 Denver, CO 80206	Children aged 0–6
Independent Living Behavior Checklist	West Virginia Research and Training Center One Dunbar Plaza, Suite E Dunbar, WV 25064	Adults
Normative Adaptive Behavior Checklist	Psychological Corporation 555 Academic Ct. San Antonio, TX 78204	Children aged 0–21
Personal Capacities Questionnaire	Materials Development Center Stout Vocational Rehabilitation Institute University of Wisconsin–Stout Menomonie, WI 54751	High school students and adults
Responsibility and Independence Scale for Adolescents	Riverside Publishing Company 8420 Bryn Mawr Blvd. Chicago, IL 60631	Students aged 12–19
Scales of Independent Behavior— Revised	Riverside Publishing Company 8420 Bryn Mawr Blvd. Chicago, IL 60631	Individuals aged 0–65
Street Survival Skills Questionnaire	McCarron-Dial Systems P.O. Box 45628 Dallas, TX 75245	Middle school students through adults
Test of Pragmatic Language	PRO-ED, Inc. 8700 Shoal Creek Blvd. Austin, TX 78757	Students in Grades K–12
Vineland Adaptive Behavior Scales Survey Edition Expanded Edition Classroom Edition	American Guidance Service P.O. Box 99 Circle Pines, MN 55014-1796	Ages 3–12

Personality/Social Skills/Personal-Social Adjustment

Adult Personality Inventory	Institute for Personality and Ability Testing 1801 Woodfield Dr. Savoy, IL 61874	For employee selection and placement; only computerized scoring
Analysis of Coping Style	Psychological Corporation 555 Academic Ct. San Antonio, TX 78204	Students in Grades K–12
Attention-Deficit/Hyperactivity Disorder Test	PRO-ED, Inc. 8700 Shoal Creek Blvd. Austin, TX 78757	Students in Grades K–8
Autism Screening Instrument for Educational Planning—Second Edition	PRO-ED, Inc. 8700 Shoal Creek Blvd. Austin, TX 78757	Age appropriateness varies with subtest

(continued)

Test	Publisher or Distributor	Ages for Assessment
Basic Personality Inventory	Sigma Assessment Systems, Inc. Research Psychologists Press Division P.O. Box 610984 Port Huron, MI 48061	Individuals aged 13–65
Behavior Assessment System for Children	American Guidance Service P.O. Box 99 Circle Pines, MN 55014	Individuals aged 4–18
Behavior Rating Profile—Second Edition	PRO-ED, Inc. 8700 Shoal Creek Blvd. Austin, TX 78757	Students aged 6–6 to 18–6
Child Behavior Checklists 1991 Profile 1992 Profile	Department of Psychiatry University of Vermont Burlington, VT 05405	Children aged 2–3; children aged 4–18
Childhood Autism Rating Scale	Western Psychological Services 12031 Wilshire Blvd. Los Angeles, CA 90025	Children aged 2–12
Children's Attention and Adjustment Survey	American Guidance Service P.O. Box 99 Circle Pines, MN 55014	Children aged 5–13
California Personality Inventory	Consulting Psychologists Press, Inc. 3803 East Bayshore Rd. Palo Alto, CA 94303	Individuals aged 12–70
Clinical Analysis Questionnaire	Institute for Personality and Ability Testing, Inc. P.O. Box 188 Champaign, IL 61820	Individuals aged 16–64
Coping Responses Inventory	Psychological Assessment Resources, Inc. P.O. Box 998 Odessa, FL 33556	Children 12–18 years of age; adults 18 years of age and older
Devereux Behavior Rating Scale– School Form	Psychological Corporation 555 Academic Ct. San Antonio, TX 78204	Children aged 5–12; individuals aged 12–18
Dial Behavior Rating Scale	McCarron-Dial Systems P.O. Box 45628 Dallas, TX 75245	Individuals aged 16–64
Katz Adjustment Scale	*Psychological Reports* (1963) vol. 13, pp. 503–535	Adults
Life Stressors and Social Resources Inventory	Psychological Assessment Resources, Inc. P.O. Box 998 Odessa, FL 33556	Children 12–18 years of age; adults 18 years of age and older

Test	Publisher or Distributor	Ages for Assessment
Parent-Adolescent Communication Inventory	Northwest Publications 710 Watson Drive Natchitoches, LA 71457	Individuals aged 13 and older
Psychological Screening Inventory	Research Psychologists Press, Inc. P.O. Box 984 Port Huron, MI 48040	Students in Grades 9–12
Self-Esteem Index	PRO-ED, Inc. 8700 Shoal Creek Blvd. Austin, TX 78757	Students aged 8–18
Self-Esteem Scale	Society and the Adolescent Self Image Princeton University Press Princeton, NJ 08541	Students in Grades 9–12
Sixteen Personality Factor Questionnaire—Fifth Edition	Institute for Personality and Ability Testing, Inc. P.O. Box 1188 Champaign, IL 61824-1188	Individuals aged 16 and over
Social Skills Rating System	American Guidance Service P.O. Box 99 Circle Pines, MN 55014	Preschool children; children in Grades K–6; students in Grades 7–12
Student Self-Concept Scale	American Guidance Service P.O. Box 99 Circle Pines, MN 55014	Students in Grades 3–12
Survey of Personal Values	Science Research Associates 155 North Wacker Dr. Chicago, IL 60606	High school students and adults
Teacher's Report Form and 1991 Profile for Ages 5–18	Department of Psychiatry University of Vermont Burlington, VT 05405	Students aged 5–18
Tennessee Self-Concept Scale	Western Psychological Services 12031 Wilshire Blvd. Los Angeles, CA 90025	Individuals aged 12–64
Walker-McConnell Scale of Social Competence and School Adjustment	Singular 401 West A Street Suite 325 San Diego, CA 92101	Elementary and secondary school students (separate forms)
Work Personality Profile	Arkansas Research and Training Center in Vocational Rehabilitation 346 N. West Blvd. Fayetteville, AR 72701	Adolescents and adults
Work Values Inventory	Riverside Publishing Company 8420 Bryn Mawr Ave. Chicago, IL 60631	Individuals aged 12–64
Youth Self-Report and 1991 Profile for Ages 11–18	Department of Psychiatry University of Vermont Burlington, VT 05404	Students aged 11–18; minimum 5th grade reading level

(continued)

Test	Publisher or Distributor	Ages for Assessment

General and Occupational Interests

Test	Publisher or Distributor	Ages for Assessment
Career Assessment Inventory— Enhanced Version	NCS Assessments 5605 Green Circle Dr. Minneapolis, MN 55343	High schools, 2- and 4-year colleges, human resources and vocational rehabilitation
Career Exploration Inventory	JIST Works, Inc. 720 N. Park Avenue Indianapolis, IN 46202	Students in Grades 9–12
Career Occupational Preference Survey for Professional Level Occupations (Form P)	EdITS/Educational and Industrial Testing Service P.O. Box 7234 San Diego, CA 92167	Grades 7–12, college students, and adults
Career Decision Making System— Revised	American Guidance Service, Inc. P.O. Box 99 Circle Pines, MN 55014	Secondary students and adults
Career Decision Scale	Psychological Assessment Resources, Inc. P.O. Box 998 Odessa, FL 33556	High school and college students
Edwards Personal Preference Schedule	Psychological Corporation 555 Academic Ct. San Antonio, TX 78204	Individuals aged 18 and older
Kuder General Interest Survey, Form E—Revised	CTB/McGraw-Hill 20 Ryan Ranch Rd. Monterey, CA 93940	Grades 6–12; 6th grade reading level
Minnesota Importance Questionnaire	Vocational Psychology Research N620 Eliot Hall University of Minnesota 75 East River Rd. Minneapolis, MN 55455	Students aged 16 and older; 5th grade reading level
Occupational Aptitude Survey and Interest Schedule—Second Edition	PRO-ED, Inc. 8700 Shoal Creek Blvd. Austin, TX 78757	Students in Grades 8–12
Pictorial California Occupational Preference Survey	EdITS/Educational and Industrial Testing Service P.O. Box 7234 San Diego, CA 92167	Students in Grades 7–12, college students, and adults
Pictorial Inventory of Careers	Talent Assessment, Inc. P.O. Box 5087 Jacksonville, FL 32247	Middle school students through adults
Quality of Life Questionnaire	IDS Publishing P.O. Box 389 Worthington, OH 43085	Individuals aged 18 and over

Test	Publisher or Distributor	Ages for Assessment
Quality of Student Life Questionnaire	IDS Publishing P.O. Box 389 Worthington, OH 43085	Students aged 14–25
Reading Free Vocational Interest Inventory—Revised	Elbern Publications P.O. Box 09497 Columbus, OH 43209	Students aged 13 and older; developed for individuals with special needs
Self-Directed Search, Form E	Psychological Assessment Resources, Inc. P.O. Box 998 Odessa, FL 33556	Junior high school students through adults; specific forms for age groups
Strong-Campbell Interest Inventory	Consulting Psychologists Press, Inc. 3083 E. Bayshore Dr. Palo Alto, CA 94303	High school students through adults; 6th grade reading level
United States Employment Service Interest Checklist	U.S. Department of Labor Western Assessment Research and Development Center 140 East 300 South Salt Lake City, UT 84111	High school students through adults
United States Employment Service Interest Inventory	U.S. Department of Labor Western Assessment Research and Development Center 140 East 300 South Salt Lake City, UT 84111	High school students through adults
Vocational Preference Inventory	Psychological Assessment Resources, Inc. P.O. Box 998 Odessa, FL 33556	Older adolescents and adults
Wisconsin Career Education Needs Assessment	Wisconsin Department of Public Instruction Supervisor of Career Education 126 Langdon St. Madison, WI 53702	Individuals aged 8–65

Transition/Community Adjustment

Arc's Self-Determination Scale	The Arc of the United States 1010 Wayne Ave., Suite 650 Silver Springs, MD 20910	Students in high school
BRIGANCE® Life Skills Inventory	Curriculum Associates, Inc. P.O. Box 2001 North Billerica, MA 01862	Students in junior high school and up
Enderle–Severson Transition Scales	Practical Press P.O. Box 455 Moorhead, MN 56561	Students aged 14–21

(continued)

Test	Publisher or Distributor	Ages for Assessment
Functional Skills Assessment and Programming Catalog	Milligan Catalogs 11212 So. Hawk Hwy. Sandy, UT 84094	Students in middle or junior high school; students in high school (separate forms)
Independent Living Behavior Checklist	West Virginia Research and Training Center One Dunbar Plaza, Suite E Dunbar, WV 25064	Adults
Life-Centered Career Education (LCCE) *Knowledge and Performance Batteries*	Council for Exceptional Children 1920 Association Dr. Reston, VA 22070	Students in middle and high school
Self-Determination Knowledge Scale	Wayne State University Office of the Dean 441 Education Bldg. Detroit, MI 48202	Students in secondary schools
Social and Prevocational Information Battery—Revised	CTB McGraw-Hill 20 Ryan Ranch Rd. Monterey, CA 93940	Students in Grades 7–12
Tests for Everyday Living	CTB/McGraw-Hill 20 Ryan Ranch Rd. Monterey, CA 93940	Individuals aged 12–64
Transition Behavior Scale—Revised	Hawthorne Educational Services, Inc. P.O. Box 7570 Columbia, MO 65205	Students in Grades 11–12
Transition Planning Inventory	PRO-ED, Inc. 8700 Shoal Creek Blvd. Austin, TX 78757	Students aged 14–25
Transition Skills Inventory	PRO-ED, Inc. 8700 Shoal Creek Blvd. Austin, TX 78757	High school students
Work Adjustment Rating Form	Educational Testing Service Princeton, NJ 08541	Students in middle school through adults
Work Adjustment Scale	Hawthorne Educational Services, Inc. P.O. Box 7570 Columbia, MO 65205	Students in Grades 11–12

Vocational/Employability

Test	Publisher or Distributor	Ages for Assessment
BRIGANCE® *Employability Skills Inventory*	Curriculum Associates, Inc. P.O. Box 2001 North Billerica, MA 01862	Students in middle and high school
Crawford Small Parts Dexterity Test	Psychological Corporation 555 Academic Ct. San Antonio, TX 78204	Adults

Test	Publisher or Distributor	Ages for Assessment
Minnesota Rate of Manipulation Tests	American Guidance Service P.O. Box 99 Circle Pines, MN 55014	Adults
Pennsylvania Bi-Manual Worksample	American Guidance Service P.O. Box 99 Circle Pines, MN 55014	Adults
Preliminary Diagnostic Questionnaire	West Virginia Research and Training Center One Dunbar Plaza, Suite E Dunbar, WV 25064	High school students and adults
Prevocational Assessment Screen	Piney Mountain Press P.O. Box 333 Cleveland, GA 30528	Middle school students, secondary students, and adults
Purdue Pegboard	McGraw-Hill/London House 9701 W. Higgins Rd. Rosemont, IL 60018	Adults
Social and Prevocational Information Battery—Revised	CTB/McGraw-Hill 20 Ryan Ranch Rd. Monterey, CA 93940	Students in Grade 6 and up; adults
Valpar	Valpar International Corporation P.O. Box 5767 Tucson, AZ 85705	High school students through adults
Vocational Behavior Checklist	West Virginia Research and Training Center One Dunbar Plaza, Suite E Dunbar, WV 25064	Adults

Speech/Language Communication

Test	Publisher or Distributor	Ages for Assessment
Carrow Elicited Language Inventory	PRO-ED, Inc. 8700 Shoal Creek Blvd. Austin, TX 78757	Children aged 3–0 to 7–11
Communicative Abilities in Daily Living—Second Edition	PRO-ED, Inc. 8700 Shoal Creek Blvd. Austin, TX 78757	Adults with aphasia or traumatic brain injury
Comprehensive Receptive and Expressive Vocabulary Test	PRO-ED, Inc. 8700 Shoal Creek Blvd. Austin, TX 78757	Children 4–0 to 17–11 (receptive); 5–0 to 17–11 (expressive)
Goldman-Fristoe Test of Articulation	American Guidance Service, Inc. P.O. Box 99 Circle Pines, MN 55014	Children aged 6–6 through 16–0
Test of Auditory Comprehension of Language—Revised	PRO-ED, Inc. 8700 Shoal Creek Blvd. Austin, TX 78757	Children aged 3–9 to 11–0

(continued)

Test	Publisher or Distributor	Ages for Assessment
Motor Skills/Manual Dexterity		
Bayley Scales of Infant Development— Second Edition	Psychological Corporation 555 Academic Ct. San Antonio, TX 78204	Children 0–8
Crawford Small Parts Dexterity Test	Psychological Corporation 555 Academic Ct. San Antonio, TX 78204	Adults
Developmental Test of Visual-Motor Integration—Fourth Edition	Modern Curriculum Press, Inc. 13900 Prospect Road Cleveland, OH 44136	Students aged 2–19
Developmental Test of Visual Perception—Second Edition	PRO-ED, Inc. 8700 Shoal Creek Blvd. Austin, TX 78757	Children aged 4–10
Mullen Scales of Early Learning	American Guidance Service P.O. Box 99 Circle Pines, MN 55014	Children aged 0–36 months
Minnesota Rate of Manipulation Tests	American Guidance Service P.O. Box 99 Circle Pines, MN 55014	Adults
Peabody Developmental Motor Skills Activity Cards	PRO-ED, Inc. 8700 Shoal Creek Blvd. Austin, TX 78757	Early childhood
Pennsylvania Bi-Manual Worksample	American Guidance Service P.O. Box 99 Circle Pines, MN 55014	Adults

APPENDIX C

Checklist for Accessibility and Usability of Buildings and Facilities

Yes *No* *Passenger Arriving-Leaving Space*

___ ___ Is there an adequate number of accessible parking spaces available (8 feet wide for car and 5 feet accessible space to car)?

___ ___ Are the accessible spaces closest to the accessible entrance to the facility?

___ ___ Are the access aisles part of the accessible route to the accessible entrance?

___ ___ Are 8-feet wide spaces with minimum 8-feet wide access aisles and 98 inches of vertical clearance available for lift-equipped vans? (1:8 access spaces *must* be van accessible.)

___ ___ Are accessible spaces marked with the international symbol of accessibility?

___ ___ Are there signs reading "van accessible" at van spaces?

___ ___ Is there an enforcement procedure to ensure that accessible parking is used only by those who need it?

___ ___ Is there a safe place designated for passengers to get into and out of cars (on the street or off the street)?

___ ___ Is that space zoned to prohibit parking?

___ ___ If space is at curbside, is the curb ramped up to the sidewalk?

___ ___ Do curbs on the route have curb cuts at drives, parking, and drop-offs?

Walks

___ ___ Are public walks at least 48 inches wide (60 inches needed to facilitate passing where wheelchair traffic is heavy)?

___ ___ If a walk is sloped, is the grade not greater than 5 percent (1 foot of rise for 20 feet of length)?

___ ___ If there are steps in the walks, are there also ramps to bypass the steps?

___ ___ If doors open onto walks, is there a level platform at least 5 feet by 5 feet?

Parking

___ ___ Is parking available for persons with mobility impairment either at end of rows or in diagonal or head-in (perpendicular) stalls 12 feet wide?

___ ___ Are pedestrian (wheelchair) inclines or sloped walks provided in place of, or in addition to, curbs and steps from parking area?

Yes No *Entrances*

___ ___ Is there at least one ground level or ramped primary entrance usable by persons in wheelchairs?

___ ___ Is there at least 18 inches of clear wall space on the pull side of the door, next to the handle?

___ ___ Is there a route of travel that does not require the use of stairs?

___ ___ Is the route of travel stable, firm, and slip-resistant?

___ ___ If there are stairs at the main entrance, is there also a ramp or lift, or is there an alternate accessible entrance?

___ ___ Do all inaccessible entrances have signs indicating the location of the nearest accessible entrance?

___ ___ Can the alternate accessible entrance be used independently?

Horizontal Circulation

___ ___ Does the accessible entrance provide direct access to the main floor, lobby, or elevator?

___ ___ Are all public spaces on an accessible route of travel?

___ ___ Is there a 5-foot circle or a T-shaped space for a person using a wheelchair to reverse direction?

___ ___ Is carpeting low-pile, tightly woven, and securely attached along the edges?

___ ___ Are all aisles and pathways to materials and services at least 36 inches wide?

___ ___ Are there ramps, lifts, or elevators to all public levels?

___ ___ If emergency systems are provided, do they have both flashing lights and audible signals?

___ ___ On each level of the facility, is there an accessible alternate route?

Signage for Goods and Services

___ ___ If provided, do signs and room numbers designating permanent rooms and spaces where goods and services are provided comply with the appropriate requirements for such signage?

Seats, Tables, and Counters

___ ___ Are the aisles between fixed seating at least 36 inches wide?

___ ___ Are the spaces for wheelchair seating distributed throughout?

___ ___ Are the tops of tables or counters between 28 and 34 inches high?

___ ___ Are knee spaces at accessible tables at least 27 inches high, 30 inches wide, and 19 inches deep?

___ ___ At each type of cashier counter, is there a portion of the main counter that is no more than 36 inches high?

___ ___ Is there a portion of food-ordering counters that is no more than 36 inches high, or is there space at the side for passing items to customers who have difficulty reaching over a high counter?

Yes No   Doorways

__ __ Do doorways have a clear, unobstructed opening of at least 32 inches? (Revolving doors are unacceptable unless accompanied by a side leaf door with a 32-inch minimum opening.)

__ __ If there are two leaf doors side by side, does one leaf provide at least 32 inches of clear opening?

__ __ Do doors in series (vestibule doors) have at least 84 inches between sets?

__ __ If a door has a closer, does it take at least 3 seconds to close?

__ __ Can doors be opened without too much force?

__ __ Are door handles no higher than 48 inches and operable with a closed fist?

__ __ Are thresholds flush with the floor? If not, are they less than 1/4-inch, or if beveled, no more than 3/4-inch high?

Ramps

__ __ Do ramps rise no more than 1 foot for every 12 feet of length?

__ __ Do ramps rise no more than 30 inches between landings?

__ __ Do ramps have handrails between 34 and 38 inches?

__ __ Do handrails extend 1 foot beyond the top and bottom of the ramp?

__ __ Is the width between railings or curbs at least 36 inches?

__ __ For rest and safety, do long ramps and sloped walks have level platforms 5 feet long at least every 30 feet?

__ __ Are ramps non-slip at the top and bottom of ramps and at switchbacks?

Elevators

__ __ Are elevators accessible on the same level as entrance?

__ __ If this facility is more than one level (including basement, balcony, etc.), are *all* levels served by an elevator?

__ __ Does the elevator doorway provide at least 32 inches of clear, unobstructed opening?

__ __ Is the elevator cab at least 4 feet wide by 6 feet deep?

__ __ Is the space between the building floor and the elevator floor 1/2-inch or less?

__ __ Are the controls (including emergency switches and light) no more than 42 inches from the floor?

__ __ Do the controls inside the cab have raised and Braille lettering?

__ __ Are there both visible and verbal or audible door opening/closing and floor indicators?

__ __ Is there a sign on both door jambs at every floor identifying the floor in raised and Braille letters?

__ __ If an emergency intercom is provided, is it usable without voice communication?

__ __ Is the emergency intercom identified by raised and Braille letters?

Yes   No   Lifts

___ ___ Can the lift be used without assistance? If not, is a call button provided?

___ ___ Is there at least 30 by 48 inches of clear space for a person in a wheelchair to approach and reach the controls and use the lift?

___ ___ Are controls between 15 and 48 inches high?

Stairs

___ ___ Do steps have rounded nosings with sloping risers?

___ ___ Are there handrails on both sides of all stairways?

___ ___ Are stairway handrails mounted 32 inches above front edge of stair tread?

___ ___ Do handrails extend 1 foot beyond top and bottom step?

___ ___ Are step risers no greater than 7 inches in height?

___ ___ Do treads have a nonslip surface?

Toilet Room

___ ___ Do doors to toilet room (men *and* women) have at least 32 inches of clear opening?

___ ___ Is there at least one toilet stall that is a minimum of 3 feet wide by 5 feet deep?

___ ___ Does that toilet stall have a doorway with 32 inches of clear opening?

___ ___ Does the toilet stall door swing out?

___ ___ Is that toilet stall also equipped with handrails on both sides, 33 inches from the floor?

___ ___ Is the toilet seat 20 inches from the floor?

___ ___ Will the area from the toilet room entrance to the stall allow a wheelchair to pass (32 inches of unobstructed space)?

___ ___ Is the bottom edge of at least one mirror no higher than 40 inches above the floor?

___ ___ Are lavatories (sinks) mounted so that persons in wheelchairs can use them (29 inches from floor to top of wheelchair armrest)?

___ ___ Are soap, towel, and other dispensers mounted no higher than 40 inches above the floor and operable with one closed fist?

___ ___ Does one lavatory have a 30-inch wide by 48-inch deep clear space in front?

___ ___ Is the lavatory rim no higher than 34 inches?

___ ___ Can the faucet be operated with one closed fist?

___ ___ Is there a 36-inch wide path to all fixtures?

___ ___ Can doors be opened easily (5 lbf. maximum force)?

___ ___ Are doorways equipped with accessible handles (operable with closed fists) 48 inches high or less?

___ ___ Are pictograms or symbols used to identify restrooms, and, if used, are raised letters or Braille characters included below them?

___ ___ Are there signs at inaccessible restrooms that give directions to accessible ones?

Yes   No   *Tub*

___   ___   Is a handrail (grab bar) securely mounted at either the foot or head end of the tub that can easily and safely be reached for getting in and out?

___   ___   Is a handrail mounted parallel to the length of the tub to safely facilitate sitting or rising?

___   ___   Does the bottom of the tub have an abrasive, antislip surface?

Shower

___   ___   Does shower stall doorway have at least 32 inches of clear opening?

___   ___   Is shower stall floor level with room floor without an obstructing riser or curb between?

___   ___   Does shower stall have an antislip surface?

___   ___   Is there a handrail on at least one side of the shower stall when facing the shower head and also near the stall entrance to facilitate going in and out?

___   ___   Is there a seat in the shower stall? (*Note:* A fold-down, permanent, or portable seat may be used, but it must have a smooth, easy-to-clean surface. A solid mold toilet seat is recommended.)

___   ___   Is the shower equipped with mixing faucet with nonscalding temperature control valve? (*Note:* A hose-type, detachable shower head is preferable.)

Drinking Fountains

___   ___   Are water fountains both hand and foot operated?

___   ___   On wall-mounted fountains, is the spout not higher than 36 inches from the floor?

___   ___   On floor-mounted models, is there a side fountain 30 inches from the floor?

___   ___   Is there one fountain with its spout no higher than 36 inches from the ground, and another with a standard height spout (or a single "hi-lo" fountain)?

___   ___   Is there at least one fountain with clear floor space of at least 30 by 48 inches in front?

___   ___   Are controls mounted on the front or on the side near the front edge, and operable with one closed fist?

___   ___   Is each water fountain cane-detectable by being located within 27 inches of the floor or protruding into the circulation space less than 4 inches from the wall?

Phones

___   ___   Do telephone booth doorways have 32 inches of clear opening?

___   ___   Are coin drops not higher than 48 inches from the floor?

___   ___   Are some phones equipped with receiver volume control for the hard of hearing?

___   ___   Are phones for the hard of hearing readily identifiable?

Yes   No

____ ____ Is there clear floor space of at least 30 by 48 inches in front of the telephone?

____ ____ Does the phone protrude no more than 4 inches into the circulation space?

____ ____ Does the phone have push-button controls?

Controls

____ ____ Are switches and controls within reach from wheelchair position (not higher than 48 inches from the floor)?

____ ____ Are all controls that are available for use by the public (including electrical, mechanical, cabinet, game, and self-service controls) accessible (9 to 54 inches for side reach, 15 to 48 inches for front or forward reach)?

____ ____ Are controls operable with a closed fist?

Warnings for Persons Who Are Deaf and Blind

____ ____ Are there raised letters or numbers for identifying rooms?

____ ____ Are the numbers at the side of the door 5 feet above the floor?

____ ____ Are potentially dangerous areas identified by a knurled door handle or knob?

____ ____ Are warning signals both audible and visible?

____ ____ Are signs, lights, and hazardous hanging objects at least 7 feet above the floor?

____ ____ Do directional and informational signs comply with legibility requirements?

____ ____ Can all objects protruding into the circulation paths be detected by a person with a visual disability using a cane?

____ ____ Are signs mounted with the centerline 60 inches from floor?

____ ____ Are signs mounted on a wall adjacent to the latch side of the door or as close as possible?

____ ____ Are raised characters sized between 5/8 and 2 inches high with high contrast?

____ ____ If a pictogram or graphic is used, is it accompanied by raised characters or Braille?

____ ____ Is the phone hearing-aid compatible?

____ ____ Is the phone with volume control identified with appropriate signage?

____ ____ If there are 4 or more public phones in the building, is one of the phones equipped with a text telephone (TT or TDD)?

____ ____ Is the location of the text telephone identified by accessible signage bearing the international TDD symbol?

Note: Each state and community has its own regulations and/or codes regarding accessibility. Many states and communities use federal standards. To ensure compliance with all codes, you need to know your own state and local codes and use the more stringent technical requirements for evaluating or recommending modifications. The checklist here is a composite of several accessibility guideline checklists following federal requirements under the Americans with Disabilities Act Standards for Accessible Design. The Standards are part of the Department of Justice Title III Regulations, 28 CFR Part 36. The checklist is not inclusive of all standards that must be met for any new construction. It is designed for use in evaluating existing facilities for accessibility barriers and can be used with students with disabilities in terms of accessibility concerns for them in their own school as well as possible placements in the community for training. For a more elaborated checklist of accessibility and possible solutions for accessibility problems, contact your regional Disability and Business Technical Assistance Center (1-800-949-4232). Ask for "The Americans with Disabilities Act Checklist for Readily Achievable Barrier Removal: Checklist for Existing Facilities (Version 2.1)." To obtain a copy of the Title III Regulations and the Standards or other technical information, call the U.S. Department of Justice ADA Information Line at 1-800-514-0301 Voice, (202) 514-0381 TDD, or (800) 514-0383 TDD.

GLOSSARY OF TERMS IN TRANSITION PROGRAMS AND SERVICES

adult services: Adult services include support services and programs provided by both public and private agencies for persons with disabilities. Usually, these services are provided to individuals after they have exited the school system, but there are times when adult services and schools both provide needed services simultaneously. Most public adult service programs have eligibility requirements that vary across agencies.

advocacy/legal service needs: Advocacy needs could be as simple as a student's need to learn how to advocate for self more effectively. Students may need specific planning for transition that relates to legal advocacy for themselves or specific legal services they will need. The Individualized Education Program (IEP) team members and families may need to anticipate needs of current students as adults in the areas of guardianship and conservatorship, estate planning (wills and trusts), or parent surrogates. Planning decisions made for a student with disabilities in relation to certain legal issues may affect eligibility for programs and services.

alternative assessment: This assessment approach, developed in the 1990s, moves away from standardized assessment. Alternative assessment usually takes the form of performance-based assessment, authentic assessment, or portfolio assessment.

alternative curriculum: This alternative curriculum varies from the general education curriculum. Such a curriculum may serve students with high cognitive abilities or lower functional levels. Alternative curricula may also address such areas as vocational and life skills.

assistive technology devices and services: The Office of Special Education Programs (OSEP) has issued a policy ruling that "consideration of a child's need for assistive technology must occur on a case-by-case basis in connection with the development of a child's individualized education program (IEP)." An assistive technology device is any item, piece of equipment, or product system that is used to increase, maintain, or improve functional capabilities of individuals with disabilities. Assistive technology services include any service that directly assists an individual with a disability in the selection, acquisition, or use of an assistive technology device.

audiology: Audiology services are generally provided by audiologists who screen, assess, and identify students with hearing loss. Audiological services also include referrals for medical or other professional attention for the habilitation of hearing, auditory training, speech reading, speech conservation, determining the need for group or individual amplification, and selecting and fitting a student for an appropriate hearing aid.

career education: An educational emphasis stressing the teaching of life career roles (e.g., family member, citizen, community participant, worker, etc.) early in life, to be followed up throughout the student's education, in preparing him or her for those roles.

career planning options: Students are provided with options for making tentative and, ultimately, realistic life-career decisions. Systematic provision of career information in coursework at school, occupational exploration opportunities through field experiences and job shadowing experiences, community experiences, and summer camps (art, music, computer, etc.) are examples of career planning options.

collaborative consulting model: Collaborative consultation is one of the administrative models used in inclusive education. It emphasizes consulting teachers working with general education teachers who have special education students in their classes. Both teachers collaborate in different ways to benefit all students.

community-based instruction: Community-based instruction is a method of instruction in which a student is taught to perform skills in actual community environments, rather than teaching students skills in a classroom and expecting them to generalize to the community.

community participation options: Students are provided with opportunities to learn and develop age-appropriate life skills in real-life settings. Community-based experiences could include job training, job or work sample tryouts, living skills instruction, community survival skills, job search and application skills, leisure or recreational skills, and so forth. Instruction and experiences are acquired outside of the school environment (also referred to as *community-based instruction* and *community-based education*).

continuing education: This optional education service is offered to youths and adults who have completed or withdrawn from regular education programs. The programs offer training and knowledge in specific fields. Examples include adult education programs, institutes, colleges or other postsecondary education, community workshops, seminars, or correspondence courses.

counseling services: Counseling services are typically provided by counselors who work with students to develop and improve students' understanding of themselves, their awareness of occupational alternatives, and their social and behavioral skills. Guidance and counseling techniques are used with students to assist them and their families in decision making about school and postschool options.

Dictionary of Occupational Titles: A Department of Labor publication providing extensive listing and classification of jobs in the United States.

Fair Labor Standards Act: The Fair Labor Standards Act is commonly known as the Federal Wage and Hour Law. The act establishes minimum wage, child labor control, overtime, and equal pay standards for employment. The act applies to people with and without disabilities.

financial assistance/support: Eligibility for certain programs is based on the individual characteristics and needs of each student. Some of the procedures for obtaining financial support are cumbersome and involve lengthy application periods. Planning may focus on need for Social Security Income, Social Security Disability benefits, Survivor's Benefits, home- and community-based waivers, food stamps, HUD Section 8 low-income housing eligibility, Medicaid, public health services, and so forth.

functional curriculum: A functional curriculum is a purposefully designed program of instruction that focuses on teaching specific skills in daily living, personal and social interactions, and employability. Each individual student will have unique preferences and needs, which require individualization of functional curriculum and instruction. Functional curriculum instruction will occur both within and outside of the school setting.

functional evaluation: A functional evaluation or assessment process is one that is an organized approach to determining the interests, needs, preferences, and abilities that an individual student has in the domains of daily living skills, personal-social skills, and occupational/employability skills. It is a continuous process, using both formal and informal assessment procedures, that provides a basis for planning and instruction.

independent living: An expanded view of independent living is that it comprises all the demands of living on one's own. This includes residential choices and skills, economic decisions and money management, time management, maintenance of equipment or technological devices, community mobility, involvement in community activities and citizenship responsibilities, and so forth. Some agencies limit their meaning of this term to residential living, but that is not the case in IDEA.

independent living skills: Independent living skills are those needed by persons so they can function in a home or community environment, with as few supports as necessary.

Individualized Education Program (IEP): The IEP is a written document required of all individuals in school who have been classified as needing special education programs or related services because of some disabling condition. The document should include the student's present level of functioning in each identified needs area, a statement of annual goals for the student, a statement of appropriate short-term objectives with the evaluation approach and evaluation criteria for determining progress toward achievement of annual goals, a statement of any required related services and who will provide them, a statement of transition service needs (beginning at least by age 14), and a statement that relates to the issue of least restrictive environment for the student relative to each of the programs and services to be provided.

Individualized Education Program planning meeting: The IEP planning meeting is one that occurs at least once annually. The student's present level of functioning is discussed, progress made since the last meeting (for continuing students) is reviewed, and goals and objectives are established for the next year. Every third year, the IEP planning group will conduct a review of the student's status based on appropriate reevaluation data.

Individualized Education Program team: The IEP team is a support and planning group made up of the student, his or her parents or guardians, the student's teacher(s), the person responsible for implementing or supervising the implementation of transition services, a school administrator, relevant school support services personnel, and other relevant agency representatives. The team is charged with the responsibility of developing and implementing an individualized education program for the student, based on his or her needs, interests, and preferences.

informal assessment: A procedure in which non-standardized assessment tools are used to gather data on specific characteristics. Typical examples of informal assessments are teacher-made tests, rating scales, checklists, survey or interview forms, and observation forms.

insurance needs: Insurance coverage should be active during school years while students are engaged in school programs. Community job training, transportation on field trips, and vocational education shops are examples of school-related insurance planning needs. Insurance needs for postschool life planning frequently include health and accident insurance and automobile liability insurance.

integrated employment: Integrated employment is viewed in most cases as employment where a person with disabilities has real work opportunities in settings where the interactions are primarily with people who are nondisabled.

job coach: A person designated as a work supervisor for a person in employment training or competitive employment. The job coach serves as an instructor and work model alongside the individual at work.

job sample: A sample of a standard work activity that involves all or part of the total operations required of a particular job. Job samples are often used as an evaluation of a person's ability to perform certain tasks or to predict task performance in a real work environment.

job shadowing: The process of following an employee performing his or her daily tasks. The goal is to gain an understanding of what the employee's job entails, and whether a person would be interested in or qualified to perform such duties.

leisure life skills: Those life skills an individual uses in his/her time while not working or attending classes.

leisure/recreation needs: Leisure and recreation are critical factors in the long-term success of persons with disabilities. Planning ahead for the skills needed to access and engage in leisure and recreation opportunities is a responsibility of the IEP team. There should be ongoing assessment of interests and encouragement of participation in a variety of activities. Accessing leisure and recreational activities through school clubs, parks and recreation programs, sport leagues, church groups, school and public libraries, and community facilities (movie theaters, bowling alleys, skating rinks, parks, etc.) should be planning and programming goals.

lifelong career development: A lifelong approach for persons to acquire the skills and resources they need to acquire, maintain, or improve independent living and quality of life throughout their lives.

living arrangement options: Planning for living options after leaving school depends on a variety of factors, beginning with the abilities and preferences of the student. In addition, the living alternatives vary from community to community. Planning should address the need to provide instruction in the basic skills necessary to take full advantage of the living options that are available. This might include the areas of consumer skills, home management skills (cleaning, cooking, laundry, use of appliances, etc.), safety, and dealing with emergencies. Planning for accessing living arrangement options would address the issues of living at home with parents, supervised apartment living, group home life, adult foster care, independent apartment with assistance services, and independent apartment options.

medical/mental health needs: Planning for the current and future medical or mental health needs of an individual student must involve the student's family. In cases where parents are not well informed regarding the importance of continuing medical or mental health treatment or support, or of the resources in the community for their son or daughter, the IEP team should consider planning for accessing such resources as Arc-USA health insurance, Medicaid, sliding fee scale services (community mental health centers, public health centers, Easter Seal, March of Dimes, and some drug and alcohol centers), and state rehabilitation services.

medical services: Medical services are considered a related service only under specific conditions. They are provided by a licensed physician, and at the present time, services are restricted to diagnostic and evaluation purposes. Services do not include direct, ongoing medical treatment. (See *School health services.*)

occupational therapy: Occupational therapy services are provided by therapists who focus on assessing and training students whose disabilities impair their daily life functioning. Emphasis on motor functioning in everyday living demands helps individual students to be more prepared for functioning at home, school, and in the community.

outcome-based education: Outcome-based education programs are based on predetermined outcome goals for students in a class. Instructional activities, materials, and assessments are designed with these outcomes in mind.

parent counseling and training: Parent counseling and training is an increasingly important related service. Counseling and training may be provided when necessary to help the student with a disability benefit from the school's educational program. Specific areas of counseling and training include assisting parents in understanding the special needs of their child, providing parents with information about child/adolescent development, and providing parents with referrals to parent support groups, financial assistance and resources, and professionals outside the school system.

personal management needs: Personal management needs overlap several other planning areas for IEP teams. Personal management of money, personal belongings, health care needs, personal hygiene needs, dental hygiene needs, and management and use of time are examples of needs in this area. Desirable personal habits—such as self-control of emotions and behaviors, responsibility, and honesty—are also examples of personal management needs to consider in planning for curriculum and instruction.

physical therapy: Physical therapy services are provided by a therapist following a referral by a physician or other school or health-related professional. Emphasis is placed on increasing muscle strength, mobility, and endurance, and improving gross motor skills, posture, gait, and body awareness. Therapists may also monitor the function, fit, and proper use of mobility aids and devices.

postsecondary education or training: Any education program beyond high school that has an academic, vocational, professional, or preprofessional focus is considered postsecondary education.

postsecondary education or training options: Postsecondary education options include adult education, community college, or college or university programs. Any vocational or technical program beyond high school that does not lead to an associate of arts or baccalaureate degree is considered postsecondary training. Postsecondary training may be obtained in public vocational and technical schools, community college vocational or technical programs, private vocational or technical schools, labor union trades/skills training, military vocational or technical skills training, apprenticeship programs, or state/federal employment training programs. Some of these programs require a license or certificate for an individual before being permitted to practice his or her occupational skills.

psychological services: Psychological services are usually provided by a school psychologist. In addition to psychological testing and interpretation, school psychologists may obtain and interpret information about a student's behavior and conditions for learning or functioning in school environments. Psychologists consult with school staff, assist in planning individual educational programs, and provide counseling for students and parents or lawful custodians.

quality of life: Quality of life is a subjective concept that should drive all outcome goals, programs, and services for adults and students with disabilities. It emphasizes personal choice and personal satisfaction with life experiences.

recreation therapy: Recreation therapy is included as a related service because all children with disabilities need to learn how to use their leisure time and recreation time constructively and with enjoyment. For those students who need recreation therapy in order to benefit from their educational experience, the therapy usually focuses on improvement of socialization skills, as well as eye-hand coordination and physical, cognitive, or language skills. Recreation therapists assess students' leisure capacities and functions, give therapy to remediate functional difficulties, provide leisure education, and assist students in accessing leisure/recreation options.

rehabilitation counseling services: Rehabilitation counseling services is a related service under IDEA. The services are defined in the regulations as "services provided by qualified personnel in individual or group sessions, that focus specifically on career development, employment preparation, achieving independence, and integration in the work-place and community of a student with a disability." The term also includes "vocational rehabilitation services provided to students with disabilities by vocational rehabilitation programs funded under the Rehabilitation Act of 1973, as amended" [IDEA, Sec. 602(A)(1)].

related services: Those services, other than special education services, that are necessary for a student to benefit from special education. Examples of related services include speech therapy, physical therapy, and occupational therapy. Other related services include auxiliary services, computers, wheelchairs, summer schooling, and many others. PL 94-142 describes related services as those that are supportive of and may or may not be part of classroom instruction, including transportation, counseling, assistive technology, and so forth.

residential facility or institution: A living arrangement in which individuals are housed most of the day in a protective environment. Examples include state schools/hospitals, intermediate care facilities for persons with mental disabilities/developmental disabilities, nursing homes, and so on.

school health services: School health services are typically provided by a qualified school nurse or a specifically trained nonmedical person who is supervised by a qualified nurse. These services are available to those students who would be unable to attend school without such supportive health care and monitoring. Services may include clean intermittent catheterization, special feedings, suctioning, administering of medications, and planning for the safety and well-being of a student while at school.

self-advocacy needs: IEP planning for self-advocacy needs refers to instruction or related services that will help develop an individual student's skills in assuming responsibility for himself or herself at school and in the community. Skill training for self-advocacy in the IEP meeting is a starting goal that is recommended. Skill training should also include awareness of one's own needs and assertiveness training in other settings (also referred to as *self-determination*).

sheltered employment: A structured program of activities involving work evaluation, work adjustment, occupational skill training, and remunerative employment designed to prepare individuals either for competitive employment or for continued work in a protective environment (e.g., workshop).

social work services in schools: Social work services are provided when the whole welfare of the student with a disability must be addressed. Home, school, and community interactions result in complex problems, and educators may not be able to work effectively alone. Social work services in schools are performed by qualified personnel and are focused on mobilizing school and community resources to enable students to learn as effectively as possible in their school programs.

socialization opportunities: Successful transitions begin while students are still in school. IEP teams should look at each individual student's social skills with peers with disabilities, peers without disabilities, family members, adults at school and in the community, and children. Socialization opportunities can be made a part of the instructional program for a student at first as social skills training, but later as a maintenance activity through program and school activities.

speech-language pathology: Speech and language pathology services are provided by qualified professionals trained to deal with communication disorders in students. Speech-language pathologists screen, identify, assess, and diagnose communication problems, provide speech and language corrective services, consult on use of augmentative and alternative communication systems, and refer students for medical or other professional attention necessary for the habilitation of speech and language disorders. It is not necessary for students to be manifesting academic problems in addition to speech or language problems for them to be considered eligible for speech-language pathology services under the IDEA.

task analysis: The process of breaking down learning tasks into the smallest elements in the proper sequence. The resulting instruction involves systematically teaching specific elements in sequence.

transition councils: Transition councils or teams are representative groups of persons at the local level who organize to promote, develop, maintain, and improve secondary special education, transition planning, transition services, and adult services for individuals with disabilities who move from school settings to adult living. The councils or teams are comprised of persons with disabilities, their families, school personnel, adult service agency personnel, and members of the community who can contribute to the mission of the council.

transportation options: Since transportation is key to mobility in a community, transportation options must be considered and planned for in the IEP. Instructional goals and objectives may be appropriate for skill training in accessing available transportation options. Related services goals and objectives may be needed to provide a transportation option that does not exist. Long-term planning should be initiated to try to ensure that appropriate transportation options will be available after the student leaves school. Transportation options include the following examples: driving one's own vehicle, taxi service, public transit service, and elderly/disabled transportation services.

transportation services: Transportation services may be a related service provided to those students who need special assistance because of their disabilities or the location of the school relative to their homes. Not all identified special education students are eligible to receive special transportation services. For those who are, the school must provide travel to and from school and between schools, provide travel in and around school buildings, and provide specialized equipment, if required, to meet the special transportation needs of students.

vocational/applied technology training: Training that may be offered at the secondary or postsecondary level to provide students with specific vocational or technical skills. These programs vary from semiskilled to skilled levels, and include such areas as building trades, industrial trades, printing and graphics production, commercial art, health occupations, cosmetology and barbering, food preparation, office machines, computer programming, marketing and distribution occupations, agriculture and agribusiness, automotive mechanics, and automotive body repair.

vocational and technical education: Organized educational activities that (1) offer a sequence of courses that provides individuals with the academic and technical knowledge and skills he or she needs to prepare for further education and careers (other than careers requiring a baccalaureate, master's, or doctoral degree) in current or emerging employment sectors and (2) includes competency-based applied learning that contributes to the academic knowledge, higher order reasoning and problem-solving skills, work attitudes, general employability skills, technical skills, and occupation-specific skills of an individual.

work adjustment theory: Work adjustment theory provides a conceptual framework that can be used in transition planning. It takes into account (1) work personality, (2) work samples, and (3) work goals.

work experience: A program that helps a student acquire desirable job skills, attitudes, and habits and is provided through supervised part-time or full-time employment.

work-study program: A method of teaching secondary-level students specific work skills by assigning them to employment in competitive jobs for partial days or sometimes full days. If they are assigned to partial days, the remainder of the day is spent in school (also referred to as *on-the-job training* and *community-based work experience*).

REFERENCES

Adami, H., & Neubert, D. A. (1991). A follow-up of vocational assessment recommendations and placement in secondary vocational education programs for students with disabilities. *Vocational Evaluation and Work Adjustment Bulletin, 24,* 101–107.

Affleck, J. Q., Edgar, E., Levine, P., & Kortering, L. (1990). Postschool status of students classified as mildly mentally retarded, learning disabled, or nonhandicapped: Does it get better with time? *Education and Training in Mental Retardation, 25,* 315–324.

Akan, G. E., & Grilo, C. M. (1995). Sociocultural influences on eating attitudes and behaviors, body image and psychological functioning: A comparison of African-American, Asian-American, and Caucasian college women. *International Journal of Eating Disorders, 18,* 181–187.

Albin, J. (1992). *Quality improvement in employment and other human services: Managing for quality through change.* Baltimore: Paul H. Brookes.

Albright, L., & Cobb, R. B. (1988a). *Assessment of students with handicaps in vocational education: A curriculum-based approach.* Alexandria, VA: American Vocational Association.

Albright, L., & Cobb, R. B. (1988b). Curriculum-based vocational assessment: A concept whose time has come. *The Journal of Vocational Special Needs Education, 10,* 13–16.

Alliance for Technology Access. (1994). *Computer resources for people with disabilities.* Alameda, CA: Hunter House.

American Association for Counseling Development. (1988). *Ethical standards.* Alexandria, VA: Author.

American Association on Mental Retardation. (1992). *Mental retardation: Definition, classification, and systems of support* (9th ed.). Washington, DC: Author.

American Guidance Service. (1989). *Social skills on the job: A transition to the workplace for students with special needs.* Circle Pines, MN: American Guidance Service, Inc.

American Occupational Therapy Association. (1994). Uniform terminology for occupational therapy. *American Journal of Occupational Therapy, 48,* 1047–1054.

American Occupational Therapy Association. (1996). *Member data survey.* Bethesda, MD: Author.

American Physical Therapy Association. (1995). A guide to physical therapist practice. Volume I: A description of patient management. *Physical Therapy, 75,* 709–719.

American Psychiatric Association. (1994). *Diagnostic and statistical manual of mental disorders* (9th ed.). Washington, DC: Author.

American School Counselor Association. (1997). *The national standards for school counseling programs.* Alexandria, VA: ASCA Press.

American Vocational Association. (1998). *The official guide to the Perkins Act of 1998.* Alexandria, VA: Author.

Americans with Disabilities Act of 1990. 42 U.S.C., 12101. (PL101-336).

Anastasi, A. (1976). *Psychological testing* (4th ed.). New York: Macmillan.

Arbuckle, D. S. (1972, June). The counselor: Who? What? *Personnel and Guidance Journal, 50,* 785–790.

Aries, P. (1962). *Centuries of childhood: A social history of family life.* (R. Baltic, Trans.). New York: Vintage.

Arkansas Rehabilitation Research and Training Center. (1978). *The role of vocational rehabilitation in independent living.* Proceedings of the Fifth Institute on Rehabilitation Issues, Omaha, NE: May 23–25.

Ascher, C. (1994, January). Cooperative education as a strategy for school-to-work transition. *Centerfocus, 3,* 1–4. (ED 365 798)

Asselin, S., Todd-Allen, M., & DeFur, S. (1998). Transition coordinators define yourselves. *Teaching Exceptional Children, 30*(3), 11–15.

Association of Higher Education and Disability (AHEAD). (1997, July). *Guidelines for documentation of a learning disability in adolescents and adults.* Columbus, OH: Author.

Aune, B., & Friehe, M. (1996). Transition to postsecondary education: Institutional and individual issues. *Topics in Language Disorders, 16*(3), 1–22.

Aune, E., & Ness, J. (1991). *Tools for transition: Preparing students with learning disabilities for postsecondary education.* Circle Pines, MN: American Guidance Service.

Aune, E. P., & Johnson, J. M. (1992). Transition takes teamwork! A collaborative model for college-bound students with LD. *Intervention in School and Clinic, 27,* 222–227.

Austin Independent School District. (1996). *Curriculum design and management manual for guidance curriculum.* Austin, TX: Author.

Bailey, D. (1992). Organizational change in a public school system: The synergism of two approaches. *Social Work in Education, 14*(2), 94–105.

Bailey, T., Koppel, R., & Waldinger, R. (1994). *Education for all aspects of the industry: Overcoming barriers to broad-based training.* Berkeley, CA: National Center for Research in Vocational Education.

Banks, R., & Renzaglia, A. (1993). Longitudinal vocational programs: A review of current recommended practices for individuals with moderate to severe disabilities. *Journal of Vocational Rehabilitation, 3*(3), 5–16.

Bashir, A. S. (1989). Language intervention and the curriculum. *Seminars in Speech and Language, 10*(3), 181–190.

Bassett, D., Patton, J., White, W., Blalock, G., & Smith, T. (1997). Research issues in career development and transition: An exploratory survey of professionals in the field. *Career Development for Exceptional Individuals, 20,* 81–100.

Bassett, D., & Smith, T. (1996). Transition in an era of reform. *Journal of Learning Disabilities, 29,* 161–166.

Baumgart, D., Filler, J., & Askvig, B. (1991). Perceived importance of social skills: A survey of teachers, parents, and other professionals. *The Journal of Special Education, 25*(2), 236–251.

Bauwens, J., & Hourcade, J. J. (1995). *Cooperative teaching: Rebuilding the schoolhouse for all children.* Austin, TX: Pro-Ed.

Beisser, S. (1996). Service learning: Developing a curriculum for caring. *Delta Kappa Gamma Bulletin, 62*(2), 15–19.

Bellamy, G. T., Peterson, L., & Close, D. (1975). Habilitation of the severely and profoundly retarded: Illustrations of competence. *Education and Training of the Mentally Retarded, 10,* 174–186.

Bender, M., Valletutti, P. J., & Baglin, C. A. (1996). *Functional curriculum for teaching students with disabilities: Self-care, motor skills, household management, and living skills* (Vol. 1, 3rd ed.). Austin, TX: Pro-Ed.

Bender, M., Valletutti, P. J., & Baglin, C. A. (1998). *Functional curriculum for teaching students with disabilities: Interpersonal, competitive job finding, and leisure-time skills* (Vol. 4). Austin, TX: Pro-Ed.

Bennett, T., DeLuca, D., & Allen, R. (1996). Families of children with disabilities: Positive adaptation across the life cycle. *Social Work in Education, 18*(1), 31–41.

Benson, P. L., Galbraith, M. A., & Espeland, P. (1998). *What teens need to succeed: Proven, practical ways to shape your own future.* Minneapolis: Free Spirit.

Benz, M., & Kochhar, C. A. (1996). School-to-work opportunities for all students: A position statement of the Division on Career Development and Transition. *Career Development for Exceptional Individuals, 19,* 31–48.

Benz, M., & Lindstrom, L. (1997). *Building school-to-work programs: Strategies for youth with special needs.* Austin, TX: Pro-Ed.

Benz, M., Yovanoff, P., & Doren, B. (1997). School-to-work components that predict postschool success for students with and without disabilities. *Exceptional Children, 63,* 151–165.

Bergland, M. M. (1996). Transition from school to adult life: Key to the future. In A. L. Goldberg (Ed.), *Acquired brain injury in childhood and adolescence* (pp. 171–194). Springfield, IL: Charles C. Thomas.

Biehl, B. (1991). *The on my own handbook.* Colorado Springs, CO: Victor Books.

Bigge, J. L. (1991). *Teaching individuals with physical and multiple disabilities* (3rd ed.). New York: Merrill.

Bissonette, D. (1994). *Beyond traditional job development: The art of creating opportunity.* Chatsworth, CA: Milt Wright.

Blackorby, J., Edgar, E., & Kortering, L. (1991). A third of our youth: A look at the problem of school dropout. *Journal of Special Education, 25*(1), 102–113.

Blalock, G. (1996). Community transition teams as the foundation for transition services for youth with learning disabilities. *Journal of Learning Disabilities, 29,* 148–159.

Blalock, G., & Benz, M. R. (1999). *Using community transition to improve transition services.* Austin, TX: Pro-Ed.

Block, L. (1993). Students with learning disabilities. In S. Kroeger & J. Schuck (Eds.), *Responding to disability issues in student affairs* (pp. 69–78). San Francisco: Jossey-Bass.

Blum, R. W. (1995). Transition to adult health care: Setting the stage. *Journal of Adolescent Health, 17,* 3–5.

Bodner, J., Clark, G. M., & Mellard, D. F. (1987, November). *State graduation policies and program practices related to high school special education pro-*

grams: *A national study*. A report from the National Study of High School Programs for Handicapped Youth in Transition. Lawrence: University of Kansas, Department of Special Education.

Boesel, D., Hudson, L., Deich, S., & Masten, C. (1994). *National Assessment of Vocational Education Final Report to Congress. Volume II: Participation and quality of vocational education.* Washington, DC: U.S. Department of Education, Office of Educational Research and Improvement.

Boesel, D., & McFarland, L. (1994). *National Assessment of Vocational Education Final Report to Congress. Volume I: Summary and recommendations.* Washington, DC: U.S. Department of Education, Office of Educational Research and Improvement.

Bos, C. S., & Vaughn, S. (1998). *Strategies for teaching students with learning and behavior problems.* Boston: Allyn and Bacon.

Boyer, E. (1987). Service linking school to life. *Community Education Journal, 8*(1), 7.

Bradley, D. F., King-Sears, M. E., & Tessier-Switlick, D. M. (1997). *Teaching students in inclusive settings: From theory to practice.* Boston: Allyn and Bacon.

Bradley-Johnson, S. (1994). *Psychoeducational assessment of students who are visually impaired or blind* (2nd ed.). Austin, TX: Pro-Ed.

Brannan, S. A. (1999). Leisure and recreation. In S. H. DeFur & J. R. Patton (Eds.), *Transition and school-based services: Interdisciplinary perspectives for enhancing the transition process* (pp. 273–308). Austin, TX: Pro-Ed.

Brendtro, L. K., Brokenleg, M., & Van Bockern, S. (1990). *Reclaiming youth at risk: Our hope for the future.* Bloomington, IN: National Educational Service.

Brinckerhoff, L. C. (1994). Developing effective self-advocacy skills in college-bound students with learning disabilities. *Intervention in School and Clinic, 29,* 229–237.

Brinckerhoff, L. C. (1996). Making the transition to higher education: Opportunities for student empowerment. *Journal of Learning Disabilities, 29,* 118–136.

Brinckerhoff, L. C., Shaw, S. F., & McGuire, J. M. (1992). Promoting access, accommodations, and independence for college students with learning disabilities. *Journal of Learning Disabilities, 25,* 417–429.

Brinckerhoff, L. C., Shaw, S. F., & McGuire, J. M. (1993). *Promoting postsecondary education for stu-*

dents with learning disabilities: A handbook for practitioners. Austin, TX: Pro-Ed.

Brolin, D. E. (1974). Programming retarded in career education (Project PRICE), Working Paper No. 1. The University of Missouri-Columbia.

Brolin, D. E. (1976). *Vocational preparation of retarded citizens.* Columbus, OH: Charles E. Merrill.

Brolin, D. E. (1978). *Life centered career education: A competency based approach.* Reston, VA: The Council for Exceptional Children.

Brolin, D. E. (1982). *Vocational preparation of persons with handicaps* (2nd ed.). Columbus, OH: Charles E. Merrill.

Brolin, D. E. (1983). *Life centered career education: A competency based approach* (rev. ed.). Reston, VA: The Council for Exceptional Children.

Brolin, D. E. (1988, March). Personal communication.

Brolin, D. E. (1989). *Life-centered career education: A competency based approach* (3rd ed.). Reston, VA: The Council for Exceptional Children.

Brolin, D. E. (1992). *Life-centered career education (LCCE) curriculum program.* Reston, VA: The Council for Exceptional Children.

Brolin, D. E. (1993). *Life-centered career education: A competency based approach* (4th ed.). Reston, VA: The Council for Exceptional Children.

Brolin, D. E. (1995). *Career education: A functional life skills approach* (3rd ed.). Englewood Cliffs, NJ: Prentice-Hall.

Brolin, D. E. (1997). *Life-centered career education: A competency-based approach* (5th ed.). Reston, VA: The Council for Exceptional Children.

Brolin, D. E., & D'Alonzo, B. J. (1979). Critical issues in career education for handicapped students. *Exceptional Children, 45,* 246–253.

Brolin, D. E., & Gysbers, N. C. (1989). Career education for students with disabilities. *Journal of Counseling and Development, 68,* 155–159.

Brolin, D. E., & Kokaska, C. J. (1979). *Career education for handicapped children and youth.* Columbus, OH: Charles E. Merrill.

Brolin, D. E., & Kolstoe, O. P. (1978). *The career and vocational development of handicapped learners.* The ERIC Clearinghouse on Adult, Career and Vocational Education, Ohio State University.

Brolin, D. E., & Thomas, B. (Eds.). (1971). *Preparing teachers for secondary level educable mentally retarded: A new model.* Final report. University of Wisconsin–Stout, Menomonie.

Brooke, V., Barcus, M., & Inge, K. (Eds.). (1992). *Consumer advocacy and supported employment: A vision for the future.* Richmond: Virginia Commonwealth University.

Brown, C. D., McDaniel, R., & Couch, R. (1994). *Vocational evaluation systems and software: A consumer's guide.* Menomonie, WI: Rehabilitation Resource, Stout Vocational Rehabilitation Institute.

Browning, P. (1997). *Transition in action for youth and young adults with disabilities.* Montgomery, AL: Wells Printing.

Bruininks, R. H., Hill, B. K., Lakin, K. C., & White, C. C. (1985). *Residential services for adults with developmental disabilities.* Logan: Utah State University Developmental Center for Handicapped Persons.

Brunstein, M. (1998). *Analysis of 1998 Perkins Act.* October 20, 1998. <www.vocserve.berkeley.edu/VOCNET.html>

Brunstein, M., & Mahler, M. (1994). *AVA guide to the School-to-Work Opportunities Act.* Alexandria, VA: American Vocational Association.

Buchweitz, S. (1993). Birchwood: An exemplary educational program for students with emotional disabilities. *Social Work in Education, 15*(4), 241–246.

Bullis, M., Nishioka-Evans, V., Fredericks, H. D., & Davis, C. (1992). *Assessing job-related social skills of adolescent and young adults with behavioral disorders: Development and preliminary psychometric characteristics of two measures.* Monmouth: Western Oregon State College. (ERIC Document Reproduction Service No. ED 395 965)

Butler, A. J., & Browning, P. L. (1974). Predictive studies on rehabilitation outcomes with the retarded. In P. L. Browning (Ed.), *Mental retardation: Rehabilitation and counseling* (pp. 198–227). Springfield, IL: Charles C. Thomas.

Butterworth, J., Hagner, D., Kiernan, W., & Schalock, R. (1996). Natural supports in the workplace: Defining an agenda for research and practice. *Journal of the Association for Persons with Severe Handicaps, 21*(3), 103–113.

Byron, J. (1990). *Self-advocacy for college students with learning disabilities.* Presentation at Postsecondary Training Institute, Training College Students with Learning Disabilities, Conference of University of Connecticut, Hartford.

Cain, E. J., Jr., & Taber, F. M. (1987). *Educating disabled people for the 21st century.* Boston: Little, Brown.

Cafolla, R., Kauffman, D., & Knee, R. (1997). *World Wide Web for teachers: An interactive guide.* Boston: Allyn and Bacon.

Callahan, M. (1992). Job site training and natural supports. In J. Nisbet (Ed.), *Natural supports in school, at work, and in the community for people with severe disabilities.* Baltimore: Paul H. Brookes.

Carey, K. (1995). *A national study of the role and function of the school psychologist.* Paper presented at the annual meeting of the National Association of School Psychologists, Chicago, IL.

Carl D. Perkins Vocational and Applied Technology Education Act of 1990, Public Law 101-392, 20 U.S.C., 2301.

Carl D. Perkins Vocational Education Act of 1984, Public Law 98-524, 98 STAT., 24345-2491.

Carnegie Foundation for the Advancement of Teaching. (1909, October). *Fourth annual report of the president and of the treasurer.* New York: Author.

Carter, S. L. (1998). *Civility: Manners, morals, and the etiquette of democracy.* New York: Basic Books.

Cartledge, G. (1996). *Cultural diversity and social skills instruction.* Champaign, IL: Research Press.

Cartledge, G., & Milburn, J. F. (1986). *Teaching social skills to children.* Elmsford, NY: Pergamon.

Chadsey-Rusch, J., Gonzalez, P., Tines, J., & Johnson, J. R. (1989). Social ecology of the workplace: Contextual variables affecting social interactions of employees with and without mental retardation. *American Journal on Mental Retardation, 94*(2), 141–151.

Chaffin, J. D. (1968). *A community transition program for the mentally retarded.* Final Report RII NHO 1731, Parsons State Hospital and Training Center, Parsons, Kansas (supported in part by Social Rehabilitation Services, U.S. Department of Health, Education, and Welfare).

Chaffin, J. D., Spellman, C. R., Regan, C. E., & Davison, R. (1971). Two follow-up studies of former educable mentally retarded students from the Kansas work study project. *Exceptional Children, 37*, 733–738.

Chambers, A. C. (1997). *Has technology been considered? A guide for IEP teams.* Albuquerque, NM: Council of Administrators of Special Education and the Technology and Media Divisions of the Council for Exceptional Children, CASE/TAMS Assistive Technology and Practice Group.

Chavkin, N., & Brown, K. (1992). School social workers building a multiethnic family-school-community partnership. *Social Work in Education, 14*(3), 160–164.

Ciborowski, J. (1992). *Textbooks and the students who can't read them: A guide to teaching content.* Cambridge, MA: Brookline Books.

Clarendon Press. (1961). *The Oxford English dictionary* (Vol. 11). Oxford, England: Author.

Clark, G. M. (1974). Career education for the mildly handicapped. *Focus on Exceptional Children, 5*(9), 1–10.

Clark, G. M. (1979). *Career education for the handicapped child in the elementary classroom.* Denver: Love Publishing.

Clark, G. M. (1980). Career preparation for handicapped adolescents: A matter of appropriate education. *Exceptional Education Quarterly, 1*(2), 11–17.

Clark, G. M. (1981). Career and vocational education. In G. Brown, R. L. McDowell, & J. Smith (Eds.), *Educating adolescents with behavior disorders* (pp. 326–346). Columbus, OH: Charles E. Merrill.

Clark, G. M. (1994). Is a functional curriculum approach compatible with an inclusive education model? *Teaching Exceptional Children, 26,* 36–39.

Clark, G. M. (1996). Transition planning assessment for secondary-level students with learning disabilities. *Journal of Learning Disabilities, 29,* 79–92.

Clark, G. M. (1998). *Assessment for transitions planning.* Austin, TX: Pro-Ed.

Clark, G. M., Carlson, B. C., Fisher, S., Cook, I. D., & D'Alonzo, B. J. (1991). Career development for students with disabilities in elementary schools: A position statement of the Division on Career Development. *Career Development for Exceptional Individuals, 14,* 109–120.

Clark, G. M., Field, S., Patton, J. R., Brolin, D. E., & Sitlington, P. L. (1994). Life skills instruction: A necessary component for all students with disabilities. A position statement of the Division on Career Development and Transition. *Career Development for Exceptional Individuals, 17,* 125–134.

Clark, G. M., & Knowlton, H. E. (1988). A closer look at transition for the 1990s: A response to Rusch and Menchetti. *Exceptional Children, 54,* 365–367.

Clark, G. M., Knowlton, H. E., & Dorsey, D. (1989). Special education for high school students with educational handicaps in a rural setting: A Vermont case study. In H. E. Knowlton & G. M. Clark (Eds.), *National study of high school special education programs for handicapped youth in transition: Volume 1, Qualitative component.* Lawrence: University of Kansas, Department of Special Education.

Clark, G. M., & Kolstoe, O. P. (1990). *Career development and transition education for adolescents with disabilities.* Boston: Allyn and Bacon.

Clark, G. M., & Kolstoe, O. P. (1995). *Career development and transition education for adolescents with disabilities* (2nd ed.). Boston: Allyn and Bacon.

Clark, G. M., & Oliverson, B. S. (1973). Education of secondary personnel: Assumptions and preliminary data. *Exceptional Children, 39,* 541–546.

Cobb, R. B., & Larkin, D. (1985, March). Assessment and placement of handicapped pupils into secondary vocational education programs. *Focus on Exceptional Children, 17*(7), 1–14.

Cobb, R. B., & Neubert, D. A. (1998). Vocational education: Emerging vocationalism. In F. Rusch & J. Chadsey (Eds.), *Beyond high school: Transition from school to work* (pp. 101–126). Boston: Wadsworth.

Cole, D. J., Ryan, C. W., & Kick, F. (1995). *Portfolios across the curriculum and beyond.* Thousand Oaks, CA: Corwin Press.

Commission on Certification of Work Adjustment and Vocational Evaluation Specialists. (1996). *Standards and procedures manual for certification in vocational evaluation.* Washington, DC: Author.

Comprehensive Employment and Training Act of 1973, Public Law 93-203, U.S.C. 29 874, 918, 919 (1976).

Comprehensive Employment and Training Act Amendments of 1978, Public Law 95-524, U.S.C. 29 893, 899, 906, 942, 991: Supplement V (1981).

Constable, R. (1992). The new reform and the school social worker. *Social Work in Education, 14*(2), 106–113.

Conway, C. (1984). Vocational education and handicapped students. *Programs for the handicapped: Clearinghouse on the handicapped.* Washington, DC: Office of Special Education and Rehabilitation Services.

Cook, L., & Friend, M. (1993). Educational leadership for teacher collaboration. In B. Billingsley (Ed.), *Program leadership for serving students with disabilities* (pp. 421–444). Richmond: Virginia Department of Education.

Cook, L., & Friend, M. (1995). Co-teaching guidelines for creating effective practices. *Focus on Exceptional Children, 20*(3), 1–12.

Cookson, P. W., Jr. (1994). *School choice: The struggle for the soul of American education.* New Haven, CT: Yale University Press.

Corbey, S., Miller, R., Severson, S., & Enderle, J. (1993). *Identifying individual transition needs: A resource guide for special educators working with students in their transition from school to adult life.* St. Paul: Minnesota Department of Education.

Cornelius, L. J., & Altman, B. M. (1995). Have we succeeded in reducing barriers to medical care for African and Hispanic Americans with disabilities? *Social Work in Health Care, 22*(2), 1–18.

Cotton, E. G. (1998). *The online classroom: Teaching with the Internet.* Bloomington, IN: EDINFO Press.

Council of Chief State School Officers. (1998). *Key state education policies on K–12 education.* Washington, DC: Author.

Council for Exceptional Children. (1998). *What every special educator must know: The international standards for the preparation and certification of special education teachers* (3rd ed.). Reston, VA: Author.

Council for Exceptional Children. (1998, January). Service learning yields real benefits for students with disabilities. *CEC Today, 4*(6), 1, 9.

Cowen, S. (1993). Transition planing for LD college-bound students. In S. A. Vogel & P. B. Adelman (Eds.), *Success for college students with learning disabilities* (pp. 39–56). New York: Springer-Verlag.

Cox, A. W., & Sawin, K. J. (1999). School nursing. In S. H. DeFur & J. R. Patton (Eds.), *Transition and school-based services: Interdisciplinary perspectives for enhancing the transition process* (pp. 167–205). Austin, TX: Pro-Ed.

Cronin, M. E. (1996). Life skills curricula for students with learning disabilities: A review of the literature. *Journal of Learning Disabilities, 29,* 53–68.

Cronin, M. E., Lord, D. C., & Wendling, K. (1991). Learning for life: The life skills curriculum. *Intervention in School and Clinic, 26,* 306–311.

Cronin, M. E., & Patton, J. R. (in preparation). *Life skills curriculum for students with special needs: A guide for developing real-life skills* (2nd ed.). Austin, TX: Pro-Ed.

Cronin, M. E., & Patton, J. R. (1993). *Life skills instruction for all students with special needs: A practical guide for integrating real-life content into the curriculum.* Austin, TX: Pro-Ed.

Culatta, R., & Culatta, B. K. (1981). Communication disorders. In A. E. Blackhurst & W. H. Berdine (Eds.), *An introduction to special education* (pp. 145–181). Boston: Little, Brown.

Culver, J. B., Spencer, K. C., & Gliner, J. A. (1990). Prediction of supported employment placements by job developers. *Education and Training in Mental Retardation, 25*(3), 237–242.

D'Amico, R., & Maxwell, N. L. (1995). The continuing significance of race in minority male joblessness. *Social Forces, 73,* 969–991.

Dalke, C. (1991). *Support programs in higher education for students with disabilities: Access for all.* Gaithersburg, MD: Aspen.

Darrow, M. A. (1990). *A Delphi approach to cross-validation of Halpern's general transition follow-along model for persons with disabilities.* Doctoral dissertation, University of Kansas, Lawrence, KS.

Davis v. Southeastern Community College, 442 U.S. 397 (1979).

Day, S. L., & Edwards, B. J. (1996). Assistive technology for postsecondary students with learning disabilities. *Journal of Learning Disabilities, 29,* 486–492, 503.

Deaton, A. V., & Waaland, P. (1994). Psychosocial effects of acquired brain injury. In R. C. Savage & G. F. Wolcott (Eds.), *Educational dimensions of acquired brain injury* (pp. 239–255). Austin, TX: Pro-Ed.

deBettencourt, L., Vallecorsa, A., & Strader, J. (1995). The transition process: What's happening in practice. *LD Forum, 20*(3), 18–22.

deBettencourt, L. U., Bonaro, D. A., & Sabornie, E. J. (1995). Career development services offered to postsecondary students with learning disabilities. *Learning Disabilities Research and Practice, 10,* 102–107.

Dede, C. (1998). *Learning with technology.* Alexandria, VA: Association for Supervision and Curriculum Development.

DeFur, S., Genzel, E., & Kregel, J. (1994). Individual transition plans: A work in progress. *Journal of Vocational Rehabilitation, 4,* 139–145.

DeFur, S., & Taymans, J. (1995). Competencies needed for transition specialists in vocational rehabilitation, vocational education, and special education. *Exceptional Children, 62,* 38–51.

DeJong, G. (1980). The historical and current reality of independent living: Implications for administrative planning. In S. J. Sigman (Ed.), *Policy planning and development in independent living* (pp. 2–6). Proceedings of a Region V Workshop presented by the University Center for International Rehabilitation/ USA, Michigan State University, East Lansing.

DeJong, G. (1983). Defining and implementing the independent living concept. In N. M. Crewe, I. K. Zola, & Associates (Eds.), *Independent living for physically disabled people* (pp. 4–27). San Francisco: Jossey-Bass.

Department of Education. (1992). *Federal Register 34 CFR Parts 300 & 301: Assistance to States for the Education of the Children with Disabilities Program* and Preschool Grants for Children with Disabilities; Final Rule, 57(189), 44804–44815.

Department of Education. (1997). *Federal Register 34 CFR Part 361 et al., The State Vocational Rehabilitation Services Program; Final Rule, 62*(28), 6308–6363.

Department of Education. (1999). *Federal Register 34 CFR Parts 300 and 303 et al.: Assistance to States for the Education of Children with Disabilities and the Early Intervention Program for Infants and Toddlers with Disabilities; Final Regulations, 64*(48), 12420–12670.

DeProspo, C. J., & Hungerford, R. H. (1946). A complete social program for the mentally retarded. *American Journal of Mental Deficiency, 51,* 115–122.

Descoeudres, A. (1928). *The education of mentally defective children* (E. F. Row, Trans.). Boston: D. C. Heath.

Deshler, D. D., Ellis, E. S., & Lenz, B. K. (1996). *Teaching adolescents with learning disabilities: Strategies and methods.* Denver: Love Publishing.

DeStefano, L., & Metzer, D. (1991). High stakes testing and students with handicaps: An analysis of issues and practices. In R. E. Stake (Ed.), *Advances in programs evaluation: Volume 1A* (pp. 281–302). Greenwich, CT: JAI Press.

DeStefano, L., & Wermuth, T. R. (1992). IDEA, PL 101-476: Defining a second generation of transition services. In F. Rusch, L. DeStefano, J. Chadsey-Rusch, L. A. Phelps, & E. Szymanski (Eds.), *Transition from school to adult life: Models, linkages, and policy* (pp. 537–550). Sycamore, IL: Sycamore.

Development Studies Center. (1994). *At home in our schools: A guide to schoolwide activities that builds community.* Oakland, CA: Development Studies Center.

Dever, R. B. (1985). *Taxonomy of instructional goals and objectives for developmentally disabled learners.* (Field Test Version). Bloomington: Indiana University Center for Innovation in Teaching the Handicapped.

Dever, R. B. (1988). *Community living skills: A taxonomy.* Washington, DC: American Association on Mental Retardation.

Dinger, J. C. (1961). Post school adjustment of former educable retarded pupils. *Exceptional Children, 27,* 353–360.

Disability Statistics Abstract. (1991, December). Disability Statistics Program, School of Nursing, University of California, San Francisco, CA.

Dowd, L. R. (Ed.). (1993). *Glossary of terminology for vocational assessment, evaluation and work adjust-ment.* Menomonie, WI: Rehabilitation Resource, Stout Vocational Rehabilitation Institute.

DuChossois, G., & Michaels, C. (1994). Postsecondary education. In C. A. Michaels (Ed.), *Transition strategies for persons with learning disabilities* (pp. 79–117). San Diego: Singular.

DuChossois, G., & Stein, E. (1992). *Choosing the right college: A step-by-step system to aid the student with learning disabilities in selecting the suitable college setting for them.* New York: New York University.

Dugdale, R. L. (1910). *The Jukes: A study of crime, pauperism, disease, and heredity.* New York: Putnam.

Duncan, J. (1943). *The education of the ordinary child.* New York: Ronald Press.

Dunn, L. M. (1968). Special education for the mildly retarded: Is much of it justifiable? *Exceptional Children, 35,* 5–22.

Dunn, W., Brown, C., & McGuigan, A. (1994). The ecology of human performance: A framework for considering the effect of context. *American Journal of Occupational Therapy, 48,* 595–607.

Dupper, D. (1993). Preventing school dropouts: Guidelines for school social work practice. *Social Work in Education, 15*(3), 141–150.

Durlak, C. M., Rose, E., & Bursuck, W. D. (1994). Preparing high school students with learning disabilities for the transition to postsecondary education: Teaching the skills of self-determination. *Journal of Learning Disabilities, 27,* 51–59.

Edgar, E. (1987). Secondary programs in special education: Are many of them justifiable? *Exceptional Children, 53,* 555–561.

Edgar, E. (1988, September). Employment as an outcome for mildly handicapped students: Current status and future directions. *Focus on Exceptional Children, 2*(1), 1–8.

Edgar, E. (1992). Secondary options for students with mild intellectual disabilities: Facing the issue of tracking. *Education and Training in Mental Retardation, 27,* 101–111.

Education for All Handicapped Children Act of 1975, Public Law 94-142, 20 U.S.C. 1410(i), 1412(2),(A), 1414(a)(i)(C), (1982).

Education for the Handicapped Act Amendments of 1983, Public Law 98-199, 97 STAT., 1357–1377.

Education Research Service. (1996). *The Internet roadmap for educators.* Arlington, VA: Education Research Service.

Effgen, S. K. (1995). The educational environment. In S. Campbell (Ed.), *Pediatric neurologic physical therapy* (3rd ed.). New York: Churchill Livington.

Elksnin, N., & Elksnin, L. K. (1998). *Teaching occupational social skills.* Austin, TX: Pro-Ed.

Ellis, D. B. (1991). *Becoming a master student.* Rapid City, SD: College Survival, Inc.

Ellis, E., Deshler, D., Lenz, K., Schumaker, J., & Clark, F. (1991). An instructional model for teaching learning strategies. *Focus on Exceptional Children, 23,* 1–23.

Encyclopedia of Education. (1971). Public high school, United States. *Encyclopedia of Education* (Vol. 7). New York: Macmillan.

Erickson, R., Thurlow, M., & Ysseldyke, J. (1996). *Neglected numerators, drifting denominators, and fractured fractions: Determining participation rates for students with disabilities in statewide assessment programs.* Minneapolis, MN: National Center on Educational Outcomes.

Evers, R. B., & Elksnin, N. (1998). *Working with students with disabilities in vocational-technical settings.* Austin, TX: Pro-Ed.

Everson, J. M. (1993). *Youth with disabilities: Strategies for interagency transition programs.* Austin, TX: Pro-Ed.

Everson, J. M. (1996). Using person-centered planning concepts to enhance school-to-adult life transition planning. *Journal of Vocational Rehabilitation, 6*(1), 7–15.

Everson, J. M., & McNulty, K. (1992). Interagency teams: Building local transition programs through parental and professional partnerships. In F. R. Rusch, L. DeStefano, J. Chadsey-Rusch, L. A. Phelps, & E. Szymanski (Eds.), *Transition from school to adult life: Models, linkages, and policy* (pp. 341–351). Sycamore, IL: Sycamore.

Fabian, E., Luecking, R. G., & Tilson, G. (1994). *A working relationship: The job development specialist's guide to successful partnerships with business.* Baltimore: Paul H. Brookes.

Fadely, D. C. (1987). *Job coaching in supported work programs.* Menomonie, WI: University of Wisconsin–Stout, Materials Development Center, Stout Vocational Rehabilitation Institute.

Fairweather, J. S., & Shaver, D. M. (1991). Making the transition to postsecondary education and training. *Exceptional Children, 57,* 264–270.

Falvey, M. A. (1989). *Community-based curriculum: Instructional strategies for students with severe handicaps* (2nd ed.). Baltimore: Paul H. Brookes.

Falvey, M. A. (1995). *Inclusive and heterogeneous schooling: Assessment, curriculum, and instruction.* Baltimore: Paul H. Brookes.

Federal Register. (August 14, 1987). 34 CFR, Part 363, pp. 30546–30552.

Federal Register. (August 19, 1991). p. 41272.

Federal Register. (October 22, 1997). p. 55028.

Fein, J. (1996). *Moving on: How to make the transition from college to the real world.* New York: Plume/Penguin Books.

Field, S. (1997). A historical perspective on student involvement in the transition process: Toward a vision of self-determination for all students. *Career Development for Exceptional Individuals, 19,* 169–176.

Field, S., & Hoffman, A. (1994). Development of a model for self-determination. *Career Development for Exceptional Individuals, 17,* 159–169.

Field, S., & Hoffman, A. (1996a). Increasing the ability of educators to support youth self-determination. In L. E. Powers, G. H. S. Singer, & J. Sowers (Eds.), *Promoting self-competence in children and youth with disabilities: On the road to autonomy* (pp. 171–187). Baltimore: Paul H. Brookes.

Field, S., & Hoffman, A. (1996b). *Steps to self-determination: A curriculum to help adolescents learn to achieve their goals.* Austin, TX: Pro-Ed.

Field, S., Hoffman, A., & Spezia, S. (1998). *Self-determination strategies for adolescents in transition.* Austin, TX: Pro-Ed.

Field, S., Martin, J., Miller, R., Ward, M., & Wehmeyer, M. (1997). *A practical guide for teaching self-determination.* Reston, VA: The Council for Exceptional Children.

Field, S., Martin, J., Miller, R., Ward, M., & Wehmeyer, M. (1998). Self-determination for persons with disabilities: A position statement of the Division on Career Development and Transition. *Career Development for Exceptional Individuals, 21,* 113–128.

Findley, W. (1967). *A follow-up of the financial assets and liabilities of mentally retarded youth as related to the cost of vocational training in the public schools.* Unpublished doctoral dissertation, University of Northern Colorado.

Fine, S., & Getkate, M. (1995). *Benchmark tasks for job analysis: A guide for functional job analysis (FJA) scales.* Mahwah, NJ: Erlbaum.

Fisher, S. K. (1999). Assistive technology. In S. H. DeFur & J. R. Patton (Eds.), *Transition and school-based services: Interdisciplinary perspectives for enhancing the transition process* (pp. 309–385). Austin, TX: Pro-Ed

Fisher, S. K., Clark, G. M., & Patton, J. R. (in preparation). *Understanding occupational vocabulary.* Austin, TX: Pro-Ed.

Flora, C. B., Flora, J. L., Spears, J. D., & Swanson, L. E. (1992). *Rural communities: Legacy and change.* Boulder, CO: Westview Press.

Ford, L. H. (1995). *Providing employment support for people with long-term mental illness: Choices, resources, and practical strategies.* Baltimore, MD: Paul H. Brookes.

Frank, A., & Sitlington, P. (1990). Adult adjustment of recent graduates of Iowa mental disabilities programs. *Education and Training in Mental Retardation, 25*(1), 62–75.

Frank, A., & Sitlington, P. (1993). Graduates with mental disabilities—The story three years later. *Education and Training in Mental Retardation, 27,* 75–80.

Frank, A., & Sitlington, P. (1997). Young adults with behavioral disorders—Before and after IDEA. *Behavioral Disorders, 23,* 40–56.

Frank, A., & Sitlington, P. (1998). *Young adults with mental disabilities—Does transition planning make a difference?* Manuscript submitted for publication.

Frank, A., Sitlington, P., & Carson, R. (1991). Transition of adolescents with behavioral disorders—Is it successful? *Behavioral Disorders, 16,* 180–191.

Frank, K., & Wade, P. (1993). Disabled student services in postsecondary education: Who's responsible for what? *Journal of College Student Development, 34,* 26–30.

Freedman, M. (1997). *Individuals with Disabilities Education Law Report: Special Report No. 18: Testing, grading and granting diplomas to special education students.* Horsham, PA: LRP Publications.

Friend, M., & Bursuck, W. (1996). *Including students with special needs: A practical guide for classroom teachers.* Boston: Allyn and Bacon.

Friend, M., & Cook, L. (1992a). The new mainstreaming: How it really works. *Instructor, 10*(7), 30–32, 34, 36.

Friend, M., & Cook, L. (1992b). *Interactions: Collaboration skills for school professionals.* White Plains, NY: Longman.

Friend, M., & Cook, L. (1996). *Interactions: Collaboration skills for school professionals* (2nd ed.). White Plains, NY: Longman.

Furney, K., Hasazi, S., & DeStefano, L. (1997). Transition policies, practices, and promises: Lessons from three states. *Exceptional Children, 63,* 343–355.

Gajar, A., Goodman, L., & McAfee, J. (1993). *Secondary schools and beyond: Transition of individuals with mild disabilities.* New York: Macmillan.

Garfinkle, L. (1995). *Legal issues in transitioning students.* Horsham, PA: LRP Publications.

Gartin, B. C., Rumrill, P., & Serebreni, R. (1996). The higher education transition model: Guidelines for facilitating college transition among college-bound students with disabilities. *Teaching Exceptional Children, 29*(1), 30–33.

Gelfand, D. M., Jenson, W. R., & Drew, C. J. (1997). *Understanding child behavior disorders* (3rd ed.). Fort Worth, TX: Harcourt Brace College Publishers.

Germain, C. (1996). An ecological perspective on social work in the schools. In R. Constable, J. Flynn, & S. McDonald (Eds.), *School social work: Practice and research perspectives* (3rd ed.). Chicago: Lyceum.

Giagnocavo, G. (1996). *Educator's World Wide Web tourguide.* Lancaster, PA: Wentworth Worldwide Media.

Gibelman, M. (1993). School social workers, counselors, and psychologists in collaboration: A shared agenda. *Social Work in Education, 15*(1), 47.

Gillet, P. (1981). Career education for exceptional children and youth. *Of work and worth: Career education for the handicapped.* Salt Lake City: Olympus Publishing.

Ginzberg, E., Ginsburg, S. W., Axelrad, S., & Herma, J. L. (1951). *Occupational choice.* New York: Columbia University Press.

Glasgow, N. A. (1996). *Taking the classroom into the community: A guidebook.* Thousand Oaks, CA: Corwin Press.

Goals 2000: Educate America Act, 20 U.S.C. § 5801 (1994).

Goddard, H. H. (1912). *The Kallikak family.* New York: Macmillan.

Godin, S. (1996). *The official rules of life.* New York: Seth Godin Production.

Gold, M. (1972). Stimulus factors in skill training of the retarded on a complex assembly task: Acquisition, transfer, and retention. *American Journal of Mental Deficiency, 76,* 517–526.

Gold, M. (1973). Research on the vocational habilitation of the retarded: The present, the future. In N. R. Ellis (Ed.), *International review of research in mental retardation* (Vol. 6, pp. 97–147). New York: Academic Press.

Gold, M. (1980). *Try another way: Training manual.* Champaign, IL: Research Press.

Goldberger, S., Kazis, R., & O'Flanagan, M. K. (1994). *Learning through work: Designing and implement-*

ing quality worksite learning for high school students. New York: Manpower Demonstration Research Corporation. (ERIC Document Reproduction Service No. ED 369 940)

Goldhammer, K. A. (1972). A careers curriculum. In K. A. Goldhammer & R. E. Taylor (Eds.), *Career education: Perspective and promise* (pp. 121–167). Columbus, OH: Charles E. Merrill.

Goldhammer, K. A., & Taylor, R. E. (1972). Career education perspectives. In K. A. Goldhammer & R. E. Taylor (Eds.), *Career education: Perspective and promise* (pp. 1–12). Columbus, OH: Charles E. Merrill.

Goldhammer, R., & Brinckerhoff, L. C. (1992). Self-advocacy for college students. *Their World,* 94–97.

Gordon, E. W. (1973). Broadening the concept of career education. In L. McClure and C. Buan (Eds.), *Essays on career education.* Portland, OR: Northwest Regional Educational Laboratory.

Gray, K. (1996). The baccalaureate game: Is it for all teens? *Phi Delta Kappan, 77,* 528–534.

Gray, K., & Herr, E. (1996, May 10). B.A. degrees should not be "the only way." *The Chronicle of Higher Education,* pp. B1–B2.

Greene, G., & Albright, L. (1995). "Best practices" in transition services: Do they exist? *Career Development for Exceptional Individuals, 16,* 1–18.

Grief, F. (1993). A school-based support group for urban African American parents. *Social Work in Education, 15*(3), 133–139.

Grigal, M., Test, D., Beattie, J., & Wood, W. (1997). An evaluation of transition components of individualized education programs. *Exceptional Children, 63,* 357–372.

Grosenick, J. K., & Huntze, S. L. (1980). *National needs analysis in behavior disorders: Severe behavior disorders.* University of Missouri-Columbia.

Gysbers, N. C. (1994). *Developing and managing your school guidance program* (2nd ed.). Alexandria, VA: American Counseling Association.

Gysbers, N. C., & Henderson, P. (1988). *Developing and managing your school guidance program* (2nd ed.). Alexandria, VA: American Association for Counseling and Development.

Gysbers, N. C., & Moore, E. J. (1974). *Career guidance, counseling and placement: Elements of an illustrative program guide.* Columbia: Career Guidance, Counseling and Placement Project. University of Missouri-Columbia.

Hagerty, G., Halloran, W., & Taymans, J. (1981). Federal perspectives on the preparation of voca-tional personnel to serve handicapped students. In C. A. MacArthur & C. Allen (Eds.), *Vocational education for the handicapped: Models for preparing personnel* (pp. 5–22). Urbana-Champaign, IL: Leadership Training.

Hagner, D., Butterworth, J., & Keith, G. (1995). Strategies and barriers in facilitating natural supports for employment of adults with severe disabilities. *Journal of the Association for Persons with Severe Handicaps, 20,* 110–120.

Hagner, D., & DiLeo, D. (1993). *Working together: Workplace culture, supported employment and persons with disabilities.* Cambridge, MA; Brookline.

Hagner, D., Rogan, P., & Murphy, S. T. (1992). Facilitating natural supports in the workplace: Strategies for support consultants. *Journal of Rehabilitation, 58,* 29–34.

Hagner, D. C. (1992). The social interactions and job supports of supported employees. In J. Nisbet (Ed.), *Natural supports in school, at work, and in the community for people with severe disabilities.* Baltimore: Paul H. Brookes.

Hallahan, D., & Kauffman, J. (1991). *Exceptional children: Introduction to exceptional children.* Englewood Cliffs, NJ: Prentice-Hall.

Halpern, A. S. (1985). Transition: A look at the foundations. *Exceptional Children, 51,* 479–486.

Halpern, A. S. (1988). Characteristics of a quality program. In C. Warger & B. Weiner (Eds.), *Secondary special education: A guide to promising public school programs.* Reston, VA: The Council on Exceptional Children.

Halpern, A. S. (1990). A methodological review of follow-up and follow-along studies tracking school leavers from special education. *Career Development for Exceptional Individuals, 13,* 13–28.

Halpern, A. S. (1993). Quality of life as a conceptual framework for evaluating transition outcomes. *Exceptional Children, 59,* 486–498.

Halpern, A. S. (1994). The transition of youth with disabilities to adult life: A position statement of the Division on Career Development and Transition, the Council for Exceptional Children. *Career Development for Exceptional Individuals, 17,* 115–124.

Halpern, A. S., & Benz, M. (1987). A statewide examination of secondary special education students with mild disabilities: Implications for the high school curriculum. *Exceptional Children, 54,* 122–129.

Halpern, A., Herr, C. M., Wolf, N., Doren, B., Johnson, M., & Lawson, J. (1997). *Next S.T.E.P.:*

Student transition and educational planning. Austin, TX: Pro-Ed.

Halpern, A. S., Lindstrom, L. E., Benz, M. R., & Nelson, D. (1990). *Community transition team model: Team leader's manual.* Eugene, OR: University of Oregon.

Halpern, A. S., & Nelson, D. J. (1990). *Secondary special education and transition teams: Procedures manual.* Eugene: University of Oregon.

Halpern, A. S., Yovanoff, P., Doren, B., & Benz, M. R. (1995). Predicting participation in postsecondary education for school leavers with disabilities. *Exceptional Children, 62,* 151–164.

Hamilton, M., & Hamilton, S. (1997). When is work a learning experience? *Phi Delta Kappan, 78*(9), 682–689.

Hamilton, S., & Hamilton, M. (1994). *Opening career paths for youth: What needs to be done? Who can do it?* Washington, DC: American Youth Policy Forum. (ERIC Document Reproduction Service No. ED 374 265)

Hanley-Maxwell, C., & Szymanski, E. M. (1992). Transition and supported employment. In R. M. Parker & E. M. Szymanski (Eds.), *Rehabilitation counseling: Basics and beyond* (2nd ed.). Austin, TX: Pro-Ed.

Harrington, B., & Christensen, B. (1995). *Unbelievably good deals that you absolutely can't get unless you're a teacher.* Chicago: Contemporary Books.

Harris, J. (1998). *Design tools for the Internet-supported classroom.* Alexandria, VA: Association for Supervision and Curriculum Development.

Hasazi, S., Gordon, L., & Roe, C. (1985). Factors associated with the employment status of handicapped youth exiting high school from 1979 to 1983. *Exceptional Children, 51,* 455–469.

Hasazi, S. B., Salembier, G., & Finck, K. (1983). Directions for the 80's: Vocational preparation for secondary mildly handicapped students. *Teaching Exceptional Children, 15,* 206–209.

Havighurst, R. J. (1953). *Human development and education.* New York: Longman's, Green.

Hazel, J. S., Schumaker, J. B., Sherman, J. A., & Sheldon, J. (1995). *ASSET: A social skills program for adolescents.* Champaign, IL: Research Press.

HEATH Resource Center. (1993). *How to choose a college: A guide for the student with a disability.* Washington, DC: American Council on Education.

Heide, A., & Stilborne, L. (1996). *The teacher's complete and easy guide to the Internet.* Toronto, ON: Trifolium Books.

Helge, D. (1991). *Rural, exceptional, at-risk.* Reston, VA: The Council for Exceptional Children.

Helmke, L. M., Havekost, D. M., Patton, J. R., & Polloway, E. A. (1994). Life skill programming: Development of a life skill science course. *Teaching Exceptional Children, 26*(2), 49–53.

Hester, E. J., & Stone, E. (1984). *Utilization of worksite modification.* Topeka, KS: The Menninger Foundation.

Higgins, E. L., & Zvi, J. C. (1995). Assistive technology for postsecondary students with learning disabilities: From research to practice. *Tools for Remediation, 45,* 123–142.

Higgins, K., & Boone, R. (1997). *Technology for students with learning disabilities: Educational applications.* Austin, TX: Pro-Ed.

Hittleman, D. R. (1983). *Developmental reading, K–12.* Boston: Houghton Mifflin.

Hodgkinson, H. L. (1985, June). *All one system: Demographics of education—Kindergarten through graduate school.* Washington, DC: Institute for Educational Leadership, Inc.

Hoerner, J., & Wehrley, J. (1995). *Work-based learning: The key to school-to-work transition.* New York: Glencoe, McGraw-Hill.

Hoover, J. J., & Patton, J. R. (1995). *Teaching students with learning problems to use study skills.* Austin, TX: Pro-Ed.

Hoover, J. J., & Patton, J. R. (1997). *Curriculum adaptations for students with learning and behavior problems: Principles and practices.* Austin, TX: Pro-Ed.

Hoyt, K. B. (1975). *An introduction to career education.* Policy Paper of the United States Office of Education, DHEW Publications No. (OE) 75–00504. Washington, DC: U.S. Government Printing Office.

Hoyt, K. B. (1977). *A primer for career education.* Washington, DC: U.S. Government Printing Office.

Hoyt, K. B. (1979). Career education for exceptional individuals: Challenges for the future. In C. J. Kokaska (Ed.), *Career futures for exceptional individuals.* Reston, VA: The Council for Exceptional Children.

Huber-Marshall, L., Martin, J., Maxson, L., Miller, T., McGill, T., & Hughes, W. (1998). *Take action: A goal attainment strategy.* Longmont, CO: Sopris West.

Hudson, P. J., Schwartz, S. E., Sealander, K. A., Campbell, P., & Hensel, J. W. (1988). Successfully employed adults with handicaps. *Career Development for Exceptional Individuals, 11*(1), 7–14.

Huffman, H. A. (1994). *Developing a character education program.* Alexandria, VA: Association for Supervision and Curriculum Development.

Hughes, C., Eisenman, L., Hwang, B., Kim, J., Killian, D., & Scott, S. (1997a). Transition from secondary special education to adult life: A review and analysis of empirical measures. *Education and Training in Mental Retardation and Developmental Disabilities, 32,* 85–104.

Hughes, C., Hwang, B., Kim, J., Killian, D., Harmer, M., & Alcantara, P. (1997b). A preliminary validation of strategies that support the transition from school to adult life. *Career Development for Exceptional Individuals, 20,* 1–14.

Hughes, C., Kim, H., Hwang, B., Killian, D. J., Fischer, G. M., Brock, M. L., Godshall, J. C., & Houser, B. (1997). Practitioner-validated secondary transition support strategies. *Education and Training in Mental Retardation and Developmental Disabilities, 32,* 201–212.

Hungerford, R. H. (1941). The Detroit plan for the occupational education of the mentally retarded. *American Journal of Mental Deficiency, 46,* 102–108.

Hungerford, R. H. (1943). *Occupational education.* New York: Association for New York City Teachers of Special Education.

Hunt, P., Farron-Davis, F., Beckstead, S., Curtis, D., & Goetz, L. (1994). Evaluating the effects of placement of students with severe disabilities in general education versus special classes. *The Journal of the Association for Persons with Severe Handicaps, 19,* 200–214.

Idol, L., Nevin, A., & Paolucci-Whitcomb, P. (1994). *Collaborative consultation.* Austin, TX: Pro-Ed.

Igoe, J. B. (1994). School nursing. *Nursing Clinics of North America, 29*(3), 443–458.

Independent Living Research Utilization Project. (1978, May). *Final draft.* Houston: Texas Institute for Rehabilitation and Research.

Individuals with Disabilities Education Act of 1990 (IDEA), PL 101-476, § 602a, 20 U.S.C., 1401.

Individuals with Disabilities Education Act Amendments of 1997, 20 U.S.C. § 1400 (1997).

Inge, K. J. (1995). *A national survey of occupational therapists in the public schools: An assessment of current practice, attitudes, and training needs regarding the transition process for students with disabilities.* Unpublished doctoral dissertation, Virginia Commonwealth University, Richmond.

Inge, K. J., Simon, M., Halloran, W., & Moon, M. S. (1993). Community-based vocational instruction and the labor laws: A 1993 update. In K. J. Inge & P. Wehman (Eds.), *Designing community-based vocational programs for students with severe disabilities.* Richmond, VA: Rehabilitation

Research and Training Center on Supported Employment, Virginia Commonwealth University.

Ingram, C. P. (1960). *Education of the slow-learning child* (3rd ed.). New York: Ronald Press.

Iowa Department of Education. (1998). *Their future— Our guidance: Iowa IEP guidebook.* Des Moines, IA: Author.

Jageman, L. W., & Myers, J. E. (1986). *Counseling mentally retarded adults: A procedures and training manual.* Menomonie: University of Wisconsin–Stout Materials Development Center.

Javorsky, J., & Gussin, B. (1994). College students with attention deficit hyperactivity disorder: An overview and description of services. *Journal of College Student Development, 35,* 170–177.

Jist Works. (1996). *The young person's occupational outlook handbook.* Indianapolis, IN: Author.

Job Training Partnership Act of 1982, Public Law 97-300, 29 U.S.C. 1512(a)(b), 1604, 1605, 1632 (1982).

Job Training Reform Amendments of 1992, 29 U.S.C. § 1501 (1992).

Johnson, C. P. (1996). Transition in adolescents with disabilities. In A. Capute & P. Accardo (Eds.), *Developmental disabilities in infancy and childhood* (2nd ed., pp. 549–570). Baltimore: Paul H. Brookes.

Johnson, D. R., Bruininks, R. H., & Thurlow, M. L. (1987). Meeting the challenge of transition service planning through improved interagency cooperation. *Exceptional Children, 53,* 522–530.

Johnson, G. O. (1962). Special education for the mentally handicapped: A paradox. *Exceptional Children, 29,* 62–69.

Johnson, J. (1994). Portfolio assessment in mathematics: Lessons from the field. *The Computing Teacher, 21*(6), 22–23.

Joint Committee on Testing Practices. (1988). *Code of fair testing practices in education.* Washington, DC: Author.

Jones, C., Sebring, P., Crawford, I., Spencer, B., & Butz, M. (1986a). *High school and beyond: 1980 senior cohort second follow-up (1984).* Washington, DC: U.S. Department of Education.

Jones, C., Sebring, P., Crawford, I., Spencer, B., & Butz, M. (1986b). *High school and beyond: 1980 sophomore cohort second follow-up (1984).* Washington, DC: U.S. Department of Education.

Jordan, T. E. (1973). *America's children: An introduction to education.* Rand McNally.

Jorgensen, C. M. (1998). *Restructuring high schools for all students.* Baltimore: Paul H. Brookes.

Judith Fein National Institute on Disability and Rehabilitation Research. (1996). A history of legislative support for assistive technology. *Journal of Special Education Technology, 13,* 1–3.

Kauffman, J. M. (1997). *Characteristics of emotional and behavior disorders of children and youth* (6th ed.). New York: Merrill.

Kaufman, P., & Frase, M. (1990). *Dropout rates in the United States: 1989.* Washington, DC: National Center for Education Statistics.

Kennedy, C., & Itkenen, T. (1994). Some effects of regular class participation on the social contacts and social networks of high school students with severe disabilities. *The Journal of the Association for Persons with Severe Handicaps, 19,* 1–10.

Kincaid, J. M. (1997). IDEA revisions may have "ripple effect" on college transition. *Disability Compliance for Higher Education, 3*(4), 1, 6–7.

Kinsley, C. W., & McPherson, K. (1995). *Enriching curriculum through service learning.* Alexandria, VA: Association for Supervision and Curriculum Development.

Kirk, S., & Gallagher, J. (1979). *Educating exceptional children* (3rd ed.). Boston: Houghton Mifflin.

Kirk, S. A., & Johnson, G. O. (1951). *Educating the retarded child.* Cambridge, MA: Riverside Press.

Klein, J. (1992). Get me the hell out of here: Supporting people with disabilities to live in their own homes. In J. Nisbet (Ed.), *Natural supports in school, at work, and in the community for people with severe disabilities* (pp. 277–339). Baltimore: Paul H. Brookes.

Knapczyk, D., & Rodes, P. G. (1996). *Teaching social competence: A practical approach for improving social skills in students at-risk.* Pacific Grove, CA: Brooks/Cole.

Knowles, M. (1990). *The adult learner: The neglected species.* Houston: Gulf.

Kohler, P. (1993). Best practices in transition: Substantiated or implied? *Career Development for Exceptional Individuals, 17,* 187–202.

Kohler, P., DeStefano, L., Wermuth, T., Grayson, T., & McGinty, S. (1994). An analysis of exemplary transition programs: How and why are they selected? *Career Development for Exceptional Individuals, 17,* 187–202.

Kohler, P., Rubin, S., & Rusch, F. (1994). Descriptive analysis of OSERS-sponsored post-secondary education model programs. *Career Development for Exceptional Individuals, 17,* 53–63.

Kokaska, C. J., & Brolin, D. E. (1985). *Career education for handicapped individuals* (2nd ed.). Columbus, OH: Merrill.

Kolstoe, O. P. (1961). An examination of some characteristics which discriminate between employed and not-employed mentally retarded males. *American Journal of Mental Deficiency, 66,* 472–482.

Kolstoe, O. P. (1970). *Teaching educable mentally retarded children.* New York: Holt, Rinehart and Winston.

Kolstoe, O. P. (1972). Special education for the mildly retarded: A response to critics. *Exceptional Children, 35,* 51–55.

Kolstoe, O. P., & Frey, R. M. (1965). *A high school work study program for mentally subnormal students.* Carbondale, IL: Southern Illinois University Press.

Kortering, L., & Elrod, G. F. (1991). Programs for mildly handicapped adolescents: Evaluating where we are and contemplating change. *Career Development for Exceptional Individuals, 14,* 145–157.

Kortering, L., Haring, N., & Klockars, A. (1992). The identification of highschool dropouts identified as learning disabled: Evaluating the utility of a discriminant analysis function. *Exceptional Children, 58,* 422–435.

Kortering, L., Julnes, R., & Edgar, E. (1990). An instructive review of the law pertaining to the graduation of special education students. *Remedial and Special Education, 11*(4), 7–13.

Kraemer, B. R., & Blacher, J. (1997). An overview of educationally relevant effects, assessment, and reentry. In A. Glang, G. H. S. Singer, & B. Todis (Eds.), *Students with acquired brain injury: The school's response* (pp. 3–31). Baltimore: Paul H. Brookes.

Kranstover, L., Thurlow, M., & Bruininks, R. (1989). Special education graduates versus non-graduates: A longitudinal study of outcomes. *Career Development for Exceptional Individuals, 12,* 153–166.

Kraus, J. F., Fife, D., Cox, P., Ramstein, K., & Conroy, C. (1986). Incidence, severity, and external causes of pediatric brain injury. *American Journal of Public Health, 140,* 687–694.

Kravets, M., & Wax, I. (1991). *The K & W guide to colleges for the learning disabled: A resource book for students, parents, and professionals.* New York: HarperCollins.

Kregel, J., & Wehman, P. (1989). Supported employment: Promises deferred for persons with severe disabilities. *Journal of the Association for Persons with Severe Handicaps, 14*(4), 293–303.

Kuperstein, J. S., & Kessler, J. M. (1991). *Building bridges: A guide to making the high school-college transition for students with learning disabilities.* Edison, NJ: Middlesex County College.

Lagomarcino, T. (1990). Job separation issues in supported employment. In F. Rusch (Ed.), *Supported employment: Models, methods, and issues* (pp. 301–316). Sycamore, IL: Sycamore.

Lake, J. (1997). *Lifelong learning skills: How to teach today's children for tomorrow's challenges.* Markham, Ontario: Pembrooke Publishers.

Lange, C., & Ysseldyke, J. (1998). School choice policies and practices for students with disabilities. *Exceptional Children, 64,* 255–270.

Lassiter, R. A. (1981, December). *Work evaluation and work adjustment for severely handicapped people: A counseling approach* (pp. 13–18). Paper presented at the International Roundtable for the Advancement of Counseling Consultation on Career Guidance and Higher Education, Cambridge, England.

Lawson, S., & Everson, J. (1993). *A national review of statements of transition services for students who are deaf-blind.* New Orleans: Helen Keller National Technical Assistance Center.

Lazear, D. (1994). *Multiple intelligence approaches to assessment: Solving the assessment conundrum.* Tucson, AZ: Zephyr Press.

Leconte, P. J. (1994a). *A perspective on vocational appraisal: Beliefs, practices, and paradigms.* Unpublished dissertation, George Washington University.

Leconte, P. J. (1994b). Vocational appraisal services: Evolution from multidisciplinary origins and applications to interdisciplinary practices. *Vocational Evaluation and Work Adjustment Bulletin, 27,* 119–127.

Leebow, K. (1998). *300 incredible things to do on the Internet.* Marietta, GA: VIP Publishing.

Leu, D. J., Jr., & Leu, D. D. (1997). *Teaching with the Internet: Lessons from the classroom.* Norwood, MA: Christopher-Gordon.

Leung, B. P. (1996). Quality assessment practices in a diverse society. *Teaching Exceptional Children, 28*(3), 42–45.

Levinson, E. M. (1993). *Transdisciplinary vocational assessment: Issues in school-based programs.* Brandon, VT: Clinical Psychology Publishing.

Lewis, B. A. (1995). *The kid's guide to service learning.* Minneapolis: Free Spirit.

Lewis, B. A. (1998a). *The kid's guide to service projects.* Minneapolis: Free Spirit.

Lewis, B. A. (1998b). *The kid's guide to social action.* Minneapolis: Free Spirit.

Lewis, B. A. (1998c). *What do you stand for? The kid's guide to building character.* Minneapolis: Free Spirit.

Lewis, R. B. (1993). *Special education technology: Classroom applications.* Pacific Grove, CA: Brooks/Cole.

Lieberman, S. A. (1997). *The real high school handbook.* Boston: Houghton Mifflin.

Lilly, M. S. (1970). Improving social acceptance of low sociometric status, low achieving students. *Exceptional Children, 37,* 341–347.

Linthicum, E., Cole, J. T., & D'Alonzo, B. J. (1991). Employment and the Americans with Disabilities Act of 1990. *Career Development for Exceptional Individuals, 14*(1), 1–13.

Lombana, J. H. (1982). *Guidance for handicapped students.* Springfield, IL: Charles C. Thomas.

Lombard, R., Miller, R., & Hazelkorn, M. (1998). School-to-work and technical preparation: Teacher attitudes and practices regarding the inclusion of students with disabilities. *Career Development for Exceptional Individuals, 21,* 161–172.

Lombard, R. C., Hazelkorn, M. N., & Neubert, D. A. (1992). A survey of accessibility to secondary vocational education programs and transition services for students with disabilities in Wisconsin. *Career Development for Exceptional Individuals, 15,* 179–188.

Love, L. (1995). *Applying the Fair Labor Standards Act when placing students into community-based vocational education.* Stillwater, OK: National Clearinghouse of Rehabilitation Training Materials.

Loyd, R. J., & Brolin, D. E. (1997). *Life centered career education: Modified curriculum for individuals with moderate disabilities.* Reston, VA: The Council for Exceptional Children.

MacMillan, D., Balow, I., Widaman, K., & Hemsley, R. (1990). *A study of minimum competency tests and their impact: Final report.* Riverside, CA: University of California, Riverside. (ERIC Document Reproduction Service No. ED 360 803)

MacMillan, D. L. (1977). *Mental retardation in school and society.* Boston: Little, Brown.

Magyary, D., & Brandt, P. (1996). A school-based self-management program for youth with chronic health conditions and their parents. *Canadian Journal of Nursing Research, 28*(4).

Male, M. (1997). *Technology for inclusion: Meeting the special needs of all students.* Boston: Allyn and Bacon.

Malian, I. D., & Love, L. (1998). Leaving high school: An ongoing transition study. *Teaching Exceptional Children, 30*(3), 11–15.

Managan, T. (1992, Spring/Summer). Promoting integration on the job: Building natural support in the workplace. *What's Working, 1,* 5. Institute on Community Integration, University of Minnesota.

Mandlawitz, M. R. (1997). *Washington Update: 1997 Amendments to IDEA.* October 13, 1997. <www.dssc.org/nta/transcrp/myrna.htm>

Mangrum, C. T., & Strichart, S. S. (Eds.). (1995). *Peterson's guide to colleges with programs for students with learning disabilities* (4th ed.). Princeton, NJ: Peterson's Guides.

Mannix, D. (1995). *Life skills for special children.* West Nyack, NY: Center for Applied Research in Education.

Marc Gold & Associates. (1990). *Systematic instruction training materials.* Gautier, MS: Author.

Marder, C., & D'Amico, R. (1992, March). *How well are youth with disabilities really doing? A comparison of youth with disabilities and youth in general.* A Report from the National Longitudinal Transition Study of Special Education Students. Menlo Park, CA: SRI International.

Markward, M., & Kurtz, D. (1999). School social work. In S. H. DeFur & J. R. Patton (Eds.), *Transition and school-based services: Interdisciplinary perspectives for enhancing the transition process.* Austin, TX: Pro-Ed.

Marland, S. P. (1971). *Career education now.* Speech presented to the Convention of the National Association of Secondary School Principals in Houston, TX, January 23.

Marland, S. P., Jr. (1974). *Career education: A proposal for reform.* New York: McGraw-Hill.

Marston, E., & Magnusson, D. (1985). Implementing curriculum-based measurement in special and regular education settings. *Exceptional Children, 52,* 266–276.

Martens, E. H. (1937). Occupational preparation for mentally handicapped children. *Proceedings and Addresses for the Sixty-First Annual Session of the American Association on Mental Deficiency, 42,* 157–165.

Martin, J. E., Marshall, L., Maxson, L., & Jerman, P. (1996). *Choicemaker self-determination curriculum.* Longmont, CA: Sopris West.

Martin, J. E., & Mithaug, D. E. (1990). Consumer-directed placement. In F. R. Rusch (Ed.), *Supported employment: Models, methods, and issues* (pp. 87–110). Sycamore, IL: Sycamore.

Maslow, A. H. (1954). *Motivation and personality.* New York: Harper and Row.

Mastropieri, M. A., & Scruggs, T. E. (1993). *A practical guide for teaching science to students with special needs in inclusive settings.* Austin, TX: Pro-Ed.

Maynard, M., & Chadderdon, L. (n.d.). *Leisure and life-style: A cross national report on issues and models for people with disabilities.* East Lansing, MI: Michigan State University Center for International Rehabilitation.

McBride, J. W., & Forgnone, C. (1985). Emphasis of instruction provided LD, EH, and EMR students in categorical and cross-categorical programming. *Journal of Research and Development in Education, 18*(4), 50–54.

McCue, M., Chase, S. L., Dowdy, C., Pramuka, M., Petrick, J., Aitken, S., & Fabry, P. (1994). *Functional assessment of individuals with cognitive disabilities: A desk reference for rehabilitation.* Pittsburgh, PA: Center for Applied Neuropsychology.

McDonnell, J., Mathot-Buckner, C., & Ferguson, B. (1996). *Transition program for students with moderate and severe disabilities.* Pacific Grove, CA: Brooks/Cole.

McDonnell, J., Wilcox, B., & Hardman, M. (1991). *Secondary programs for students with developmental disabilities.* Boston: Allyn and Bacon.

McDowell, R. L. (1981). Adolescence. In G. Brown, R. L. McDowell, & J. Smith (Eds.), *Educating adolescents with behavior disorders* (pp. 10–29). Columbus, OH: Charles E. Merrill.

McGaughey, M. J., Kiernan, W. E., McNally, L. C., Gilmore, D. S., & Keith, G. R. (1995). Beyond the workshop: National trends in integrated and segregated day and employment services. *Journal of the Association for Persons with Severe Handicaps, 20,* 270–285.

McGuire, J. M., Madaus, J. W., Litt, A. V., & Ramirez, M. O. (1996). An investigation of documentation submitted by university students to verify their learning disabilities. *Journal of Learning Disabilities, 29,* 297–304.

McGuire, J. M., Norlander, K. A., & Shaw, S. F. (1990). Postsecondary education for students with learning disabilities: Forecasting challenges for the future. *Learning Disabilities Focus, 5,* 69–74.

McGuire, J. M., & Shaw, S. (1987). A decision-making process for the college-bound student: Matching learner, institution, and support program. *Learning Disability Quarterly, 10,* 106–111.

McKernan, J. R. (1994). *Making the grade: How a new youth apprenticeship system can change our schools and save American jobs.* Boston: Little, Brown.

McLain, T. (1997). *Educator's guide to Web Wacker.* Lancaster, PA: Classroom Connect.

McPhie, W. E. (1983). The teaching unit: What makes it tick? In W. J. Stewart (Ed.), *Unit teaching: Perspectives and prospects* (pp. 51–57). Saratoga, CA: R & E.

Meers, G. D. (1992). Getting ready for the next century: Vocational preparation of students with disabilities. *Teaching Exceptional Children, 24*(4), 36–39.

Meltzer, L. J., Roditi, B. N., Haynes, D. P., Biddle, K. R., Paster, M., & Taber, S. E. (1996). *Strategies for success: Classroom teaching techniques for students with learning problems.* Austin, TX: Pro-Ed.

Metropolitan Toronto School Board. (1996a). *Home working: 101 everyday activities in mathematics.* Markham, Ontario, CN: Pembrooke Publishers.

Metropolitan Toronto School Board. (1996b). *Home working: 101 everyday activities for better reading and writing.* Markham, Ontario, CN: Pembrooke Publishers.

Metropolitan Toronto School Board. (1996c). *Home working: 101 everyday activities in science and technology.* Markham, Ontario, CN: Pembrooke Publishers.

Metropolitan Toronto School Board. (1996d). *Home working: 101 everyday activities in social studies, media, and life skills.* Markham, Ontario, CN: Pembrooke Publishers.

Meyen, E. (1981). *Developing instructional units for the regular and special educator* (3rd ed.). Dubuque, IA: William C. Brown.

Michaels, C. A. (1994). *Transition strategies for persons with learning disabilities* (pp. 79–117). San Diego: Singular.

Miller, R. J., Rzonca, C., & Snider, B. (1991). Variables related to the type of postsecondary education experience chosen by young adults with learning disabilities. *Journal of Learning Disabilities, 24,* 188–191.

Miller, R. J., Snider, B., & Rzonca, C. (1990). Variables related to the decision of young adults with learning disabilities to participate in postsecondary education. *Journal of Learning Disabilities, 23,* 349–354.

Milone, M. (1995). Electronic portfolios: Who's doing them and how? *Technology and Learning, 16*(2), 28–36.

Mithaug, D., Horiuchi, C., & Fanning, P. (1985). A report on the Colorado statewide follow-up survey of special education students. *Exceptional Children, 51,* 397–404.

Montague, M., & Lund, K. A. (1991). *Job-related social skills.* Ann Arbor, MI: Exceptional Innovations.

Moon, M. S., Inge, K. J., Wehman, P., Brooke, V., & Barcus, J. M. (1990). *Helping persons with severe mental retardation get and keep employment: Supported employment issues and strategies.* Baltimore: Paul H. Brookes.

Moon, S., Goodall, P., Barcus, M., & Brooke, V. (1986). *The supported work model of competitive employment for citizens with severe handicaps: A guide for job trainers* (rev.). Richmond, VA: Rehabilitation Research and Training Center, Virginia Commonwealth University.

Morris, M. (1992). Policy in the making: The right to take assistive technology home from school. *AT Quarterly: RESNA Technical Assistance Project, 3*(2), 5.

Mount, B., & Zwernik, K. (1988). *It's never too early. It's never too late: A booklet about personal futures planning* (Publication # 42-88-109). St. Paul, MN: Governor's Planning Council on Developmental Disabilities.

Myrick, R. D. (1993). *Developmental guidance and counseling: A practical approach* (2nd ed.). Minneapolis: Educational Media Corporation.

National Association of School Nurses. (1996). *Issue brief: School nurses and the Individuals with Disabilities Education Act (IDEA).* Scarborough, ME: Author.

National Center on Education and the Economy. (1990). *America's choice: High skills or low wages.* Rochester, NY: Author. (ERIC Document Reproduction Service No. ED 323 297)

National Center for Research in Vocational Education. (1995). *Getting to work: A guide for better schools.* Berkeley: Author.

National Center for Youth with Disabilities. (1996). *Transitions from child to adult health care services: A national survey.* Minneapolis: Author.

National Joint Committee on Learning Disabilities. (1994). Secondary to postsecondary education transition planning for students with learning disabilities. *Collective perspectives on issues affecting learning disabilities: Position papers and statements* (pp. 97–104). Austin, TX: Pro-Ed.

National School-to-Work Office. (n.d.). *School-to-work and employer liability: A resource guide.* Washington, DC: Author.

National School-to-Work Office. (July, 1996). *School-to-work glossary of terms.* Washington, DC: Author.

National Transition Network. (1993, Spring). Job Training Reform Amendments of 1992: Expanded opportunities for youth and adults with disabilities. *Policy Update,* 1–8.

Neubert, D. A. (1994). Vocational evaluation and assessment in vocational-technical education: Barriers and facilitators to interdisciplinary services. *Vocational Evaluation and Work Adjustment Bulletin, 27,* 149–153.

Neubert, D. A. (1997). Time to grow: The history and future of preparing youth for adult roles in society. *Teaching Exceptional Children, 29*(5), 5–17.

Newcomer, P. L. (1993). *Understanding and teaching emotionally disturbed children and adolescents* (2nd ed.). Austin, TX: Pro-Ed.

Nippold, M. (1993). Developmental markers in adolescent language: Syntax, semantics, and pragmatics. *Language, Speech, and Hearing Services in Schools, 24,* 21–28.

Nisbet, J. (Ed.). (1992). *Natural supports in school, at work, and in the community for people with severe disabilities.* Baltimore: Paul H. Brookes.

Nisbet, J., & Hagner, D. (1988). Natural supports in the workplace: A reexamination of supported employment. *Journal of the Association for Persons with Severe Handicaps, 13,* 260–267.

NISH. (1996). Rehabilitation Act Amendments of 1992. *The Workplace, 22*(10), 4–8.

Noddings, N. (1992). *The challenge to care in schools: An alternative approach to education.* New York: Teachers College Press.

Nosek, M. A. (1992). Independent living. In R. M. Parker & E. M. Szymanski (Eds.), *Rehabilitation counseling* (2nd ed., pp. 103–133). Austin, TX: Pro-Ed.

Nystrom, D. C., & Bayne, G. K. (1979). *Occupational and career education legislation* (2nd ed.). Indianapolis, IN: Bobbs-Merrill.

O'Brien, J. (1987). A guide to lifestyle planning. In B. Wilcox & G. T. Bellamy (Eds.), *A comprehensive guide to the activities catalog: An alternative curriculum for youth with and adults with severe disabilities* (pp. 175–189). Baltimore, MD: Paul H. Brookes.

Office of Educational Research and Improvements, U.S. Department of Education. (1994). *National assessment of vocational education final report to Congress: Volume I: Summary and recommendations.* Washington, DC: U.S. Government Printing Office.

Ogbu, J. U. (1994). Understanding cultural diversity and learning. *Journal for the Education of the Gifted, 17,* 355–383.

O'Neill, N., & O'Neill, G. (1974). *Shifting gears.* New York: M. Evans and Co.

Osterman, P., & Iannozzi, M. (1993). *Youth apprenticeships and school-to-work transition: Current knowledge and legislative strategy.* Philadelphia: National Center on the Educational Quality of the Workforce.

Otfinoski, S. (1996). *The kid's guide to money: Earning it, saving it, spending it, growing it, sharing it.* New York: Scholastic.

Packer, A. J. (1992). *Bringing up parents: The teenager's handbook.* Minneapolis: Free Spirit.

Page, B., & Chadsey-Rusch, J. (1995). The community college experience for students with and without disabilities: A viable transition outcome? *Career Development for Exceptional Individuals, 18,* 85–96.

Parent, W., Kregel, J., Metzler, H., & Twardzik, G. (1992). Social integration in the workplace: An analysis of the interaction activities of workers with mental retardation and their co-workers. *Education and Training in Mental Retardation, 27*(1), 28–37.

Paris, K., & Mason, S. (1995). *Planning and implementing youth apprenticeship & work-based learning.* Madison, WI: Center on Education and Work.

Parrish, L. H., & Kok, M. R. (1985). *Procedures handbook for special needs work-study coordinators.* Rockville, MD: Aspen.

Patton, J. R., & Blalock, G. (1996). *Transition and students with learning disabilities: Facilitating the movement from school to adult life.* Austin, TX: Pro-Ed.

Patton, J. R., Cronin, M. E., Bassett, D. S., & Koppel, A. E. (1997). A life skills approach to mathematics instruction: Preparing students with learning disabilities for the real-life math demands of instruction. *Journal of Learning Disabilities, 30,* 178–187.

Patton, J. R., Cronin, M. E., & Wood, S. (1999). *Infusing real-life topics into existing curricula. Recommended procedures and instructional examples for the elementary, middle and high school levels.* Austin, TX: Pro-Ed.

Patton, J. R., & Dunn, C. (1998). *Transition from school to adulthood: Basic concepts and recommended practices.* Austin, TX: Pro-Ed.

Payne, J. S. (1977). Job placement: How to approach employers. In R. L. Carpenter (Ed.), *Colloquium series on career education for handicapped adolescents.* West Lafayette, IN: Special Education Section, Department of Education, Purdue University.

Payne, J. S., Mercer, C. D., & Epstein, M. H. (1974). *Education and rehabilitation techniques.* New York: Behavioral Publications.

Peterson, P. M., Rauen, K. K., Brown, J., & Cole, J. (1994). Spina bifida: The transition into adulthood begins in infancy. *Rehabilitation Nursing, 19*(4), 229–238.

Phelps, L. A., & Frasier, J. R. (1988). Legislative and policy aspects of vocational special education. In R. Gaylord-Ross (Ed.), *Vocational education for persons with special needs* (pp. 3–29). Palo Alto, CA: Mayfield.

Phelps, L. A., & Wermuth, T. R. (1992, November). *Effective vocational education for students with special needs: A framework.* Berkeley, CA: National Center for Research in Vocational Education.

Popenoe, D. (1985). *Private pleasure, public plight: American metropolitan community life in comparative perspective.* New Brunswick, NJ: Transaction Books.

Popov, L. K. (1997). *The family virtues guide.* New York: Penguin Books.

Powell, T. H., Pancsofar, E. L., Steere, D. E., Butterworth, J., Itzkowitz, J. S., & Rainforth, B. (1991). *Supported employment: Providing integrated employment opportunities for persons with disabilities.* New York: Longman.

Powers, L. E., Singer, G. H. S., & Sowers, J. (1996). *On the road to autonomy: Promoting self-competence in children and youth with disabilities.* Baltimore: Paul H. Brookes.

Pratt, D. (1997). *Terrific teaching: 100 great teachers share their best ideas.* Markham, Ontario, CN: Pembrooke Publishers.

Proctor, S. T., Lordi, S. L., & Zaiger, D. S. (1993). *School nursing practice: Roles and standards.* Scarborough, ME: National Association of School Nurses.

Pruitt, W. (1986). *Vocational (work) evaluation* (2nd ed.). Menomonie, WI: Walt Pruitt Associates.

Pumpian, I., Fisher, D., Certo, N., Engel, T., & Mautz, D. (1998). To pay or not to pay: Differentiating employment and training relationships through regulation and litigation. *Career Development for Exceptional Individuals, 21,* 187–202.

Pumpian, I., Fisher, D., Certo, N., & Smalley, K. (1997). Changing jobs: An essential part of career development. *Mental Retardation, 35,* 39–48.

Quay, H. C., & Peterson, D. P. (1987). *Manual for the revised behavior problems checklist.* Coral Gables, FL: Authors.

Radencich, M. C., & Schumm, J. S. (1997). *How to help your child with homework.* Minneapolis: Free Spirit.

Raines, J. (1996). Appropriate versus least restrictive: Educational policies and students with disabilities. *Social Work in Education, 18*(2), 113–127.

Raskind, M. H., & Higgins, E. L. (1998). Assistive technology for postsecondary students with learning disabilities: An overview. *Journal of Learning Disabilities, 31,* 27–40.

Raths, L., Merrill, H., & Sidney, S. (1966). *Values and teaching.* Columbus, OH: Charles E. Merrill.

Rehabilitation Act of 1973, PL 93-112, 29 U.S.C. 723(a), 721(a)(9), 793, 794, 795(a), 795(g) (1982).

Rehabilitation Act Amendments of 1984, PL 98-211.

Rehabilitation Act Amendments of 1986, 29 U.S.C., 701, PL 99-506.

Rehabilitation Act Amendments of 1992, 29 U.S.C. § 701 (1992).

Rehabilitation Services Administration. (1990). *Annual report to Congress, 1989,* Supported Employment Activities, Secondary. 311(d) of the Rehabilitation Act of 1973. Washington, DC: Department of Education: Author.

Rehabilitation Services Administration. (1993). *Series AI Preliminary Tabs Fiscal Year 1991.* Unpublished report. Washington, DC: Author.

Reichard, C. L. (1979). *Project RETOOL Report.* Reston, VA: The Council for Exceptional Children, Teacher Education Division.

Reis, S. M., Kaplan, S. N., Tomlinson, C. A., Westberg, K. L., Callahan, C. M., & Cooper, C. R. (1998). Equal does not mean identical. *Educational Leadership, 56*(3), 74–77.

Reisner, E., McNeil, P., Adelman, N., Kulick, C., Hallock, R., & Leighton, M. (1993). *Using youth apprenticeship to improve the transition to work: An evaluation of system development in eight states.* Washington, DC: Council of Chief State School Officers.

Repetto, J. B., & Correa, V. I. (1996). Expanding views on transition. *Exceptional Children, 62,* 551–563.

Rich, J. (1997). *The everything college survival book.* Holbrook, MA: Adams Media Corp.

Richard, M. M. (1995). Pathways to success for the college student with ADD: Accommodations and preferred practices. *Journal of Postsecondary Education and Disability, 11,* 16–29.

Roessler, R. T., Schriner, K. F., & Price, P. (1992). Employment concerns of people with head injury. *Journal of Rehabilitation, 58*(1), 17–22.

Roos, P. (1970). Normalization, de-humanization, and conditioning—Conflict or harmony? *Mental Retardation, 8*(4), 12–14.

Rothenbacher, C., & Leconte, P. (1990). Vocational assessment: A guide for parents and professionals. *Transition Summary, 6,* 1–15.

Rowley, J. (1987). From your president. *Phi Delta Kappa Newsletter, 32,* 1.

Rubenstone, S., & Dalby, S. (1994). *College admissions: A crash course for panicked parents.* New York: Macmillan.

Rural, small schools: Miles to go, promises to keep. (1998, Summer). *SEDLETTER, 1*(2), 1–2. (Newsletter published by Southwest Educational Development Laboratory News, Austin, Texas.)

Rusch, F. R. (Ed.). (1986). *Competitive employment: Issues and strategies.* Baltimore: Paul H. Brookes.

Rusch, F. R. (1990). *Supported employment: Models, methods, and issues.* Sycamore, IL: Sycamore Publishing.

Rusch, F. R., DeStefano, L., Chadsey-Rusch, J., Phelps, L. A., & Szymanski, E. (1992). *Transition from school to adult life: Models, linkages, and policy.* Pacific Grove, CA: Brooks/Cole.

Rusch, F. R., Kohler, P., & Hughes, C. (1992). An analysis of OSER-sponsored secondary special education and transitional services research. *Career Development for Exceptional Individuals, 15,* 121–143.

Rusch, F. R., & Menchetti, B. M. (1988). Transition in the 1990s: A reply to Knowlton and Clark. *Exceptional Children, 54,* 363–365.

Rusch, F. R., & Phelps, L. A. (1987). Secondary special education and transition from school to work: A national priority. *Exceptional Children, 53,* 487–492.

Sacks, S. Z., Tierney-Russell, D., Hirsch, M., & Braden, J. (1992). Social skills training: What professionals say they do. In S. Z. Sacks, M. Hirsch, & R. Gaylord-Ross (Eds.), *The status of social skills training in special education and rehabilitation: Present and future trends* (Chapter 1). Monograph supported by the National Institute on Disability Research, Grant No. H133G0096, Special Education Department, Peabody Teachers College of Vanderbilt University.

Sale, P., Everson, J. M., & Moon, M. S. (1991). Quality indicators of successful vocational transition programs. *Journal of Vocational Rehabilitation, 1*(4), 47–63.

Salend, S. J. (1998). *Effective mainstreaming: Creating inclusive classrooms.* Columbus, OH: Merrill.

Savage, H. J. (1953). *Fruit of an impulse: Forty-five years of the Carnegie Foundation, 1905–1950.* New York: Harcourt, Brace and Company.

Savage, R. (1993). *Children with traumatic brain injuries.* Unpublished report developed for the National Head Injury Pediatric Task Force.

Savage, R. C., & Wolcott, G. F. (1994). *Educational dimensions of acquired brain injury.* Austin, TX: Pro-Ed.

Salvia, J., & Hughes, C. (1990). *Curriculum-based assessment: Testing what is taught.* New York: Macmillan.

Salvia, J., & Ysseldyke, J. E. (1995). *Assessment* (6th ed.). Boston: Houghton Mifflin.

Sands, D. J., & Wehmeyer, M. L. (1996). *Self-determination across the life span: Independence and choice for people with disabilities.* Baltimore: Paul H. Brookes.

Sarkees-Wircenski, M., & Scott, J. L. (1995). *Vocational special needs.* Homewood, IL: American Technical Publishers.

Schalock, R., & Genung, L. (1993). Placement from a community-based mental retardation program: A 15-year follow-up. *American Journal on Mental Retardation, 98,* 400–407.

Scheiber, B., & Talpers, J. (1987). *Unlocking potential: College and other choices for learning disabled people: A step-by-step guide.* Bethesda, MD: Adler and Adler.

Schilit, J., & Caldwell, M. L. (1980). A word list of essential career/vocational words for mentally retarded students. *Education and Training of the Mentally Retarded, 35,* 113–116.

Schloss, P. J., Schloss, C. N., & Misra, A. (1985). Analysis of application forms used by special needs youths applying for entry-level jobs. *Career Development for Exceptional Individuals, 8,* 80–89.

School to Work Opportunities Act, 20 U.S.C. § 6101 (1994).

Schrumpf, F., Freiburg, S., & Skadden, D. (1993). *Life lessons for young adolescents: An advisory guide for teachers.* Champaign, IL: Research Press.

Schumaker, J. B., Hazel, J. S., & Pederson, C. S. (1988). *Social skills for daily living.* Circle Pines, MN: American Guidance Service.

Schuster, D. L., & Smith, F. G. (1994). The Interdisciplinary Council on Vocational Evaluation and Assessment: Building consensus through communication, advocacy and common goals. *Vocational Evaluation and Work Adjustment Bulletin, 27,* 111–114.

Scott, J. L., & Sarkees-Wircenski, M. (1996). *Overview of vocational and applied technology education.* Homewood, IL: American Technical Publishers.

Scott, S. (1990). Coming to terms with the "otherwise qualified" student with a learning disability. *Journal of Learning Disabilities, 23,* 398–405.

Scott, S. (1991). A change in legal status: An overlooked dimension in the transition to higher education. *Journal of Learning Disabilities, 24,* 459–466.

Scott, S. (1994). Determining reasonable academic adjustments for college students with learning disabilities. *Journal of Learning Disabilities, 27,* 403–412.

Secretary's Commission on Achieving Necessary Skills. (n.d.). *Skills and tasks for jobs: A SCANS report for America 2000.* Springfield, VA: National Technical Information Service, Operations Division. (NTIS Number: PB92-181379)

Secretary's Commission on Achieving Necessary Skills. (n.d.). *Teaching the SCANS competencies.* Washington, DC: U.S. Government Printing Office. (029-000-00438-2)

Secretary's Commission on Achieving Necessary Skills. (1991). *What work requires of schools: A SCANS report for America 2000.* Springfield, VA: National Technical Information Service, Operations Division. (NTIS Number: PB92-146711)

Secretary's Commission on Achieving Necessary Skills. (1992). *Learning a living: A blueprint for high performance. A SCANS report for America 2000.* Washington, DC: U.S. Government Printing Office. (029-000-00439-1)

Senge, J. C., & Dote-Kwan, J. (1995). Information accessibility in alternative formats in postsecondary education. *Journal of Visual Impairment and Blindness, 89,* 120–128.

Shafer, M. (1988). Supported employment in perspective: Traditions in the Federal-State Vocational Rehabilitation System. In P. Wehman & M. S. Moon (Eds.), *Vocational rehabilitation and supported employment* (pp. 55–66). Baltimore: Paul H. Brookes.

Shafer, M., Banks, P., & Kregel, J. (1991). Employment retention and career movement among individuals with mental retardation working in supported employment. *Mental Retardation, 29,* 103–110.

Shaw, S., Brinckerhoff, L., Kistler, J., & McGuire, J. M. (1990). Preparing students with learning disabilities for postsecondary education: Issues and future needs. *Learning Disabilities: A Multidisciplinary Journal, 2*(1), 21–26.

Shepherd, J., & Inge, K. J. (1999). Occupational and physical therapy. In S. H. DeFur & J. R. Patton (Eds.), *Transition and school-based services: Interdisciplinary perspectives for enhancing the transition process* (pp. 117–165). Austin, TX: Pro-Ed.

Shertzer, B., & Stone, S. C. (1981). *Fundamentals of guidance* (4th ed.). Boston: Houghton Mifflin.

Shinn, M. R. (Ed.). (1989). *Curriculum-based measurement: Assessing special children.* New York: Guilford.

Siegel, S., Robert, M., Greener, K., Meyer, G., Hallo-ran, W., & Gaylord-Ross, R. (1993). *Career ladders for challenged youths in transition from school to adult life.* Austin, TX: Pro-Ed.

Simon, M., Cobb, B., Halloran, W., Norman, M., & Bourexis, P. (1994). *Meeting the needs of youth with disabilities: Handbook for implementing community-based vocational education programs according to the Fair Labor Standards Act.* Fort Collins: Colorado State University.

Simon, M., & Halloran, W. (1994). Community-based vocational education: Guidelines for complying with the Fair Labor Standards Act. *Journal of the Association for Severely Handicapped, 19,* 52–60.

Sitlington, P., & Frank, A. (1993). Success as an adult—Does gender make a difference for graduates with mental disabilities? *Career Development for Exceptional Individuals, 16,* 171–182.

Sitlington, P., & Frank, A. (1994). Rural vs. urban: Does it affect the transition of individuals with disabilities? *Rural Special Education Quarterly, 13*(1), 9–15.

Sitlington, P., & Frank, A. (1998). *Follow-up studies: A practitioner's handbook.* Austin, TX: Pro-Ed.

Sitlington, P., Frank, A., & Carson, R. (1992). Adult adjustment among graduates with mild disabilities. *Exceptional Children, 59,* 221–233.

Sitlington, P. L. (1996a). Transition assessment—Where have we been and where should we be going? *Career Development for Exceptional Individuals, 19,* 159–168.

Sitlington, P. L. (1996b). Transition to living: The neglected component of transition programming for individuals with learning disabilities. *Journal of Learning Disabilities, 29,* 31–39, 52.

Sitlington, P. L., Brolin, D. E., Clark, G. M., & Vacanti, J. M. (1985). Career/vocational assessment in the public school setting: The position of the Division on Career Development. *Career Development for Exceptional Individuals, 8,* 3–6.

Sitlington, P. L., & Frank, A. R. (1990). Are adolescents with learning disabilities successfully crossing the bridge into adult life? *Learning Disabilities Quarterly, 13,* 97–111.

Sitlington, P. L., Frank, A. R., & Carson, R. (1991, October). *Iowa statewide follow-up study: Changes in the adult adjustment of graduates with mental disabilities one vs. three years out of school.* Iowa Department of Education, Des Moines, IA.

Sitlington, P. L., & Neubert, D. A. (1998). Transition assessment: Methods and processes to determine student needs, preferences, and interests. In M. L. Wehmeyer & D. J. Sands (Eds.), *Making it happen: Student involvement in education plan-*

ning, decision making, and instruction. Baltimore: Paul H. Brookes.

Sitlington, P. L., Neubert, D. A., Begun, W., Lombard, R. C., & Leconte, P. J. (1996). *Assess for success: Handbook on transition assessment.* Reston, VA: The Council for Exceptional Children.

Sitlington, P. L., Neubert, D. A., & Leconte, P. J. (1997). Transition assessment: The position of the Division on Career Development and Transition. *Career Development for Exceptional Individuals, 20*(1), 69–79.

Skrtic, T. M. (1991). *Behind special education: A critical analysis of professional culture and school organization.* Denver: Love Publishing.

Smith, C. L., & Rowjeski, J. W. (1993). School-to-work transition: Alternatives for educational reform. *Youth and Society, 25,* 222–250.

Smith, D. D., & Luckaasson, R. (1995). *Introduction to special education: Teaching in an age of challenge.* Boston: Allyn and Bacon.

Smith, F., Lombard, R., Neubert, D., Leconte, P., Rothenbacher, C., & Sitlington, P. (1994). The position statement of the Interdisciplinary Council on Vocational Evaluation and Assessment. *The Journal for Vocational Special Needs Education, 17,* 41–42.

Smith, M. A., & Schloss, P. J. (1988). Teaching to transition. In P. J. Schloss, C. A. Hughes, & M. A. Smith (Eds.), *Community integration for persons with mental retardation* (pp. 1–16). Austin, TX: Pro-Ed.

Smith, M. D., Belcher, R. G., & Juhrs, P. D. (1995). *A guide to successful employment for individuals with autism.* Baltimore: Paul H. Brookes.

Smith, S. (1990). Comparison of IEPs of students with behavioral disorders and learning disabilities. *The Journal of Special Education, 24,* 85–99.

Smith, S. M., & Tyler, J. S. (1997). Successful transition planning and services for students with ABI. In A. Glang, G. H. S. Singer, & B. Todis (Eds.), *Students with acquired brain injury: The school's response* (pp. 185–200). Baltimore: Paul H. Brookes.

Smith, T., & Puccini, I. (1995). Position statement: Secondary curricula and policy issues for students with mental retardation. *Education and Training in Mental Retardation and Developmental Disabilities, 30,* 275–282.

Snyder, C. (1984). *Teaching your child about money.* Reading, MA: Addison-Wesley.

Staab, M. J. (1996). *The role of the school psychologist in transition planning.* Unpublished doctoral dissertation, University of Kansas, Lawrence.

Starr, J. M. (1986). American youth in the 1980's. *Youth and Society, 17,* 323–345.

St. John, C., & Miller, S. M. B. (1995). The exposure of black and Hispanic children to urban ghettos: Evidence from Chicago and the southwest. *Social Science Quarterly, 76,* 562–576.

Stainback, S., & Stainback, W. (1996). *Inclusion: A guide for educators.* Baltimore: Paul H. Brookes.

Steward, R. J., Gimenez, M. M., & Jackson, J. D. (1995). A study of personal preferences of successful university students as related to race/ethnicity and sex: Implications and recommendations for training, practice and future research. *Journal of College Student Development, 36*(2) 123–131.

Stodden, R., Ianacone, R. N., Boone, M. R., & Bisconer, W. S. (1987). *Curriculum-based vocational assessment: A guide for addressing youth with special needs.* Honolulu, HI: Centre Publications, International Education Corporation.

Straughn, C. T. (1992). *Lovejoy's college guide for the learning disabled* (3rd ed.). New York: Monarch.

Synatschk, K. O. (1999). Counseling. In S. H. DeFur & J. R. Patton (Eds.), *Transition and school-based services: Interdisciplinary perspectives for enhancing the transition process* (pp. 231–271). Austin, TX: Pro-Ed.

Szymanski, E. M., & King, J. (1989). Rehabilitation counseling in transitional planning and preparation. *Career Development for Exceptional Individuals, 12,* 3–10.

Szymanski, E. M., & Parker, R. M. (1996). *Work and disability: Issues and strategies in career development and job placement.* Austin, TX: Pro-Ed.

Technology Related Assistance for Individuals with Disabilities Act of 1988. PL 100-497.

Test, D., Hinson, K., Solow, J., & Keul, P. (1993). Job satisfaction of persons in supported employment. *Education and Training in Mental Retardation, 28*(1), 38–46.

Thomas, A., & Grimes, J. (1995). *Best practices in school psychology III.* Washington, DC: National Association of School Psychologists.

Thompson, L., Powers, G., & Houchard, B. (1992). The wage effects of supported employment. *Journal of the Association for Persons with Severe Handicaps, 17,* 87–94.

Thompson, V. L. S. (1995). Sociocultural influences on African-American racial identification. *Journal of Applied Social Psychology, 25,* 1411–1429.

Throne, J. M. (1975). Normalization through the normalization principle. Right ends, wrong means. *Mental Retardation, 13*(5), 23–25.

Thurlow, M. L., Ysseldyke, J. E., & Anderson, C. L. (1995). *High school graduation requirements: What's happening for students with disabilities?* Minneapolis, MN: National Center on Education Outcomes, University of Minnesota. (ERIC Document Reproduction Service No. ED 385 056)

Thurlow, M. L., Ysseldyke, J. E., & Silverstein, B. (1993). *Testing accommodations for students with disabilities: A review of the literature* (Synthesis Report #4). Minneapolis: National Center on Educational Outcomes, University of Minnesota.

Ticoll, M. (1995). *Inclusion of individuals with disabilities in post-secondary education: A review of the literature*. North York, Ontario, Canada: The Roeher Institute.

Tindall, L. W., Gugerty, J. J., Getzel, E. E., Salin, J. A., Wacker, G. B., & Crowley, C. B. (1986). In L. W. Tindall (Ed.), *Handbook on developing effective linking strategies*. Madison, WI: University of Wisconsin–Madison Vocational Studies Center.

Tomlinson, C. A. (1995). *How to differentiate instruction in mixed-ability classrooms*. Alexandria, VA: Association for Supervision and Curriculum Development.

Tomlinson, C. A. (1996). *How to differentiate instruction in mixed-ability classrooms*. [Professional Inquiry Kit]. Alexandria, VA: Association for Supervision and Curriculum Development.

Tomlinson, C. A. (Developer). (1997). *Differentiating instruction*. [Facilitator's Guide and Video]. Alexandria, VA: Association for Supervision and Curriculum Development.

Tomlinson, C. A., & Kalbfleisch, M. L. (1998). Teach me, teach my brain: A call for differentiated classrooms. *Educational Leadership, 56*(3), 52–55.

Tsai, L. Y. (1992). Diagnostic issues in high-functioning autism. In E. Schopler & G. B. Mesibov (Eds.), *High-functioning individuals with autism* (pp. 11–40). New York: Plenum Press.

Turnbull, A., & Turnbull, H. (1996). Self-determination within a culturally responsive family systems perspective: Balancing the family mobile. In L. E. Powers, G. H. Singer, & J. Sowers (Eds.), *Promoting self-competence in children and youth with disabilities: On the road to autonomy* (pp. 195–220). Baltimore: Paul H. Brookes.

U.S. Department of Education. (1983). *Report of services to adolescent handicapped, 1968–1982*. Washington, DC: U.S. Government Printing Office.

U.S. Department of Education. (1994). *School-to-Work Opportunities Act of 1994, PL No. 103-239*. (Online). Available: <www.stw.ed.gov/factsht/act.htm>

U.S. Department of Education. (1995). *To assure the free appropriate public education of all children with disabilities: Seventeenth annual report to Congress on the implementation of the Individuals with Disabilities Education Act*. Washington, DC: Author.

U.S. Department of Education. (1997, Summer). Voluntary national tests development under way. *Office of Educational Research and Improvement Bulletin*, 1–12.

U.S. Department of Labor. (1991, June). *What work requires of schools: A SCANS report for America 2000*.

U.S. Department of Labor. (1991). *The revised handbook for analyzing jobs*. Indianapolis, IN: JIST Works, Inc.

U.S. General Accounting Office. (1991). *Transition from school to work: Linking education and worksite training*. Washington, DC: Government Printing Office.

University of Kansas Institute for Adult Studies. (1998). *Accommodating adults with disabilities in adult education programs*. Lawrence, KS: Author.

Valdés, K. A., Williamson, C. L., & Wagner, M. M. (1990). *The national transition study of special education students*. Menlo Park, CA: SRI International.

Valdés, K. A., Williamson, C. L., & Wagner, M. (1990, July). *Statistical almanac, Vol. 2: Youth categorized as learning disabled*. The National Longitudinal Transition Study of Special Education Students (Contract 300-87-0054), SRI International, Menlo Park, CA.

Valletutti, P. J., Bender, M., & Hoffnung, A. (1996). *Functional curriculum for teaching students with disabilities: Nonverbal and oral communication* (Vol. 2, 3rd ed.). Austin, TX: Pro-Ed.

Valletutti, P. J., Bender, M., & Sims-Tucker, B. (1996). *Functional curriculum for teaching students with disabilities: Functional academics* (Vol. 3, 2nd ed.). Austin, TX: Pro-Ed.

VanBiervliet, A., & Parette, H. P. (1994). Teaching Americans with Disabilities Act (ADA) self-advocacy skills to college students. *College Student Journal, 28*, 267–272.

Van Reusen, A., Bos, C., Schumaker, J., & Deshler, D. (1994). *The self-advocacy strategy for education and transition planning*. Lawrence, KS: Edge Enterprises.

Vocational Education Act of 1963, PL 88-210, 26 U.S.C. 5 (1964).

Vocational Education Act Amendments of 1968, PL 90-576, U.S.C. 1262(c), 1263(b), (F), (1970).

Vocational Education Act Amendments of 1976, PL 94-482, U.S.C. 2310(a), (b) (1982).

Vogel, S. A. (1993). *Postsecondary decision-making for students with learning disabilities*. Pittsburgh, PA: Learning Disabilities Association of America.

Vogel, S. A., & Adelman, P. B. (1992). The success of college students with learning disabilities: Factors related to educational attainment. *Journal of Learning Disabilities, 25,* 430–441.

Vogel, S. A., & Adelman, P. B. (Eds.). (1993). *Success for college students with learning disabilities.* New York: Springer-Verlag.

Wagner, M. (1991). *Dropouts with disabilities: What do we know? What can we do?* A report from the National Longitudinal Transition Study of Special Education Students. Menlo Park, CA: SRI International.

Wagner, M., Blackorby, J., Cameto, R., Hebbeler, K., & Newman, L. (1993). *The transition experiences of young people with disabilities: A summary of findings from the National Longitudinal Transition Study of Special Education Students.* Menlo Park, CA: SRI International.

Wagner, M., Blackorby, J., Cameto, R., & Newman, L. (1993). *What makes a difference? Influences on postschool outcomes of youth with disabilities: The third comprehensive report from the National Longitudinal Transition Study of Special Education Students.* Menlo Park, CA: SRI International. (ERIC Document Reproduction Service No. ED 365 085)

Wagner, M., D'Amico, R., Marder, C., Newman, L., & Blackorby, J. (1992). *What happens next? Trends in post-school outcomes of youth with disabilities: The second comprehensive report from the National Longitudinal Transition Study of Special Education Students.* Menlo Park, CA: SRI International. (ERIC Document Reproduction Service No. ED 356 603)

Wagner, M., & Shaver, D. M. (1989). *Educational programs and achievements of secondary special education students: Findings from the National Longitudinal Transition Study.* Presentation to the Special Education Interest Group at the meetings of the American Educational Research Association, San Francisco.

Waksman, S., & Waksman, D. D. (1998). *Waksman Social Skills Curriculum.* Austin, TX: Pro-Ed.

Walker, H. M., Todis, B., Holmes, D., & Horton, G. (1988). *ACCESS Program: Adolescent curriculum for communication and effective social skills.* Austin, TX: Pro-Ed.

Walker, M. L. (1991, Fall). Rehabilitation service delivery to individuals with disabilities: A question of culture competence. *OSERS News in Print, 4*(2), 7–11.

Ward, M. J. (1992). OSERS initiative on self-determination. *Interchange, 12*(1), 1–7. Champaign, IL: Transition Research Institute, University of Illinois.

Ward, M. J., & Halloran, W. (1993, Fall). Transition issues for the 1990s. *OSERS News in Print, 6*(1), 4–5. (ERIC Document Reproduction Service No. ED 364 035)

Warren, F. G. (1976). *Report of the Kent County Educational Training Center.* Grand Rapids, MI.

Wehman, P. (1981). *Competitive employment: New horizons for severely disabled individuals.* Baltimore: Paul H. Brookes.

Wehman, P. (1992). *Life beyond the classroom: Transition strategies for young people with disabilities.* Baltimore: Paul H. Brookes.

Wehman, P. (1995). *Individual transition plans: The teacher's curriculum guide for helping youth with special needs.* Austin, TX: Pro-Ed.

Wehman, P. (1996). *Life beyond the classroom: Transition strategies for young people with disabilities* (2nd ed.). Baltimore: Paul H. Brookes.

Wehman, P. (1997). *Exceptional individuals in school, community, and work.* Austin, TX: Pro-Ed.

Wehman, P. (Ed.). (1998). *Developing transition plans.* Austin, TX: Pro-Ed.

Wehman, P., Brooke, V., West, M., Targett, P., Green, H., Inge, K., & Kregel, J. (1998). Barriers to competitive employment for persons with disabilities. In P. Wehman (Ed.), *Developing transition plans.* Austin, TX: Pro-Ed.

Wehman, P., & Hill, J. W. (Eds.). (1985). *Competitive employment for persons with mental retardation: From research to practice, Vol. 1.* Richmond, VA: Rehabilitation Research and Training Center, Virginia Commonwealth University.

Wehman, P., & Kregel, J. (1995). At the crossroads: Supported employment a decade later. *The Journal of the Association for Persons with Severe Handicaps, 20,* 286–299.

Wehman, P., Kregel, J., & Seyfarth, J. (1985). Transition from school to work for individuals with severe handicaps: A follow-up study. *Journal of the Association for the Severely Handicapped, 10,* 132–139.

Wehman, P., & Moon, M. S. (Eds.). (1988). *Vocational rehabilitation and supported employment.* Baltimore: Paul H. Brookes.

Wehman, P., Moon, M. S., Everson, J. M., Wood, W., & Barcus, J. M. (1988). *Transition from school to work: New challenges for youth with severe disabilities.* Baltimore: Paul H. Brookes.

Wehman, P., Moon, M. S., & McCarthy, P. (1986, January). Transition from school to adulthood for youth with severe handicaps. *Focus on Exceptional Children, 18*(5), 1–12.

Wehmeyer, M. (1997). Self-directed learning and self-determination. In M. Agran (Ed.), *Student-*

directed learning: A handbook of self-management. Pacific Grove, CA: Brooks/Cole.

Wehmeyer, M., & Lawrence, M. (1995). Whose future is it anyway? Promoting student involvement in transition planning. *Career Development for Exceptional Individuals, 18*(2), 69–83.

Wehmeyer, M., & Ward, M. (1993). The spirit of the IDEA mandate: Student involvement in transition planning. *The Journal for Vocational Special Needs Education, 3,* 108–111.

Weinberg, C. (1996). *The transition guide for college juniors and seniors: How to prepare for the future.* New York: New York University Press.

Welsh, J. M., Quinn, L., Benson, D., & LaFollette, M. (1996). *Finding and keeping a job: A course of study* (rev. ed.). Coralville, IA: Grant Wood Area Education Agency.

Wesby, C. E., & Ford, V. (1993). The role of team culture in assessment and intervention. *Journal of Educational and Psychological Consultation, 4,* 319–334.

West, L., Jones, B. L., Corbey, S., Boyer-Stephens, A., Miller, R. J., & Sarkees-Wircenski, M. (1992). *Integrating transition planning into the IEP process.* Reston, VA: The Council for Exceptional Children.

West, M. D., & Parent, W. S. (1992). Consumer choice and empowerment in supported employment services: Issues and strategies. *Journal of the Association for Persons with Severe Handicaps, 17,* 47–52.

Will, M. (1984). *OSERS programming for the transition of youth with disabilities: Bridges from school to working life.* Washington, DC: Office of Special Education and Rehabilitative Services.

Windsor, N. (1994). *The safe tourist: Hundreds of proven ways to outsmart trouble.* Los Angeles: Cork-Screw Press.

Witt, M. A. (1992). *Job strategies for people with disabilities.* Princeton, NJ: Peterson's Guide.

Wood, W., & Freeman, T. (1993). Supported employment services based on actual cost: A necessity for quality service delivery over time. *The Advance, 4* (4), 1–3.

Worthington, J. F., & Farrar, R. (1998). *The ultimate college survival guide.* Princeton, NJ: Peterson's Guide.

Yager, C. O. (1997). *Unbelievably good deals that you absolutely can't get unless you're a parent.* Chicago: Contemporary Books

Younie, W. J. (1966). *Guidelines for establishing school work-study programs for educable mentally retarded youth.* Vol. 48 (10). Richmond, VA: Special Education Service, State Department of Education.

Zigmond, N., & Miller, S. E. (1992). Improving high school programs for students with learning disabilities: A matter of substance as well as form. In F. Rusch, L. Destefano, J. Chadsey-Rusch, L. A. Phelps, & E. Szymanski (Eds.), *Transition from school to adult life: Models, linkages, and policy* (pp. 17–32). Sycamore, IL: Sycamore.

AUTHOR INDEX

SUBJECT INDEX